Letters of H. P. Lovecraft

LETTERS TO WOODBURN HARRIS AND OTHERS

Woodburn Prescott Harris

H. P. Lovecraft

Letters to Woodburn Harris and Others

Edited by S. T. Joshi and David E. Schultz

Hippocampus Press

New York

Published by Hippocampus Press
P.O. Box 641, New York, NY 10156.
www.hippocampuspress.com

First Edition
3 5 7 9 8 6 4 2

ISBN 978-1-61498-374-3

Contents

Introduction

H. P. Lovecraft stood astride two quite different publishing worlds. On the one hand, he was an avid amateur journalist, ever since boyhood when he published his chemistry and astronomy journals. He remained active in amateur journalism all his days. On the other hand, he was a professional writer—or rather, an amateur writer at heart who sometimes had success placing his stories in professional magazines. Beyond this, he was a freelance editor and ghostwriter. And aside from all this, he was an enthusiastic correspondent who enjoyed chatting about his antiquarian travels, his reading program, and other topics, but who also enjoyed stimulating debates. This collection contains colorful examples of all these elements in letters to a broad array of recipients.

Jacob Clark Henneberger (1890–1969) was a magazine publisher who, with J. M. Lansinger, founded Rural Publications, Inc., in 1922, to publish a variety of popular magazines. Henneberger achieved great success with the magazine *College Humor* (begun in 1922) and envisioned founding a line of varied periodicals in the detective and horror fields. Having received assurances from such established writers as Hamlin Garland and Ben Hecht that they would be willing to contribute stories of an "unconventional" sort to a new magazine, Henneberger started *Weird Tales* in March 1923. In the end these and other well-known authors did not submit to the magazine, leaving its early issues open to tyros and amateurs. Henneberger installed Edwin Baird as his first editor, and the latter ultimately accepted all five of the stories Lovecraft submitted to him in May 1923. Henneberger commissioned Lovecraft to ghostwrite "Under the Pyramids" for Harry Houdini, paying him $100 in advance and another $100 upon receipt of the manuscript in early March 1924. By then, however, the magazine was in serious financial trouble; it and its companion, *Detective Tales*, were $40,000 in debt. For this and other reasons, Lovecraft turned down Henneberger's offer to be the new editor of the magazine; specifically, Lovecraft, newly married and settled in Brooklyn, did not wish to move to Chicago to edit the magazine, as would have been required.

Henneberger sold his share of *Detective Tales* to Lansinger, appointed Farnsworth Wright as editor of *Weird Tales*, and came to an agreement with B. Cornelius, the printer of the magazine, whereby Cornelius would be the chief stockholder with an agreement that if the $40,000 owed him was ever repaid by profits from the magazine, the stock would be returned to Henneberger. This never happened. In the fall of 1924 Henneberger provisionally hired Lovecraft to edit a new humor magazine that he was planning (the *Magazine of Fun*) at $40 per week; Lovecraft spent the next several weeks preparing jokes for the magazine, but it never got off the ground. Henneberger gave Lovecraft a credit of $60 at the Scribner Book Shop. Lovecraft attempted to have the credit converted to cash, but was unable to do so, and so he and Frank Belknap Long selected a large number of books (see *SL* 1.355–56). Henneberger sporadically communicated with Lovecraft over the next few years, but to no particular effect. Late in life Henneberger wrote "Out of Space, Out of Time,"[1] a memoir discussing Lovecraft.

Edwin C. Baird (1886–1957) was the first editor of *Weird Tales* (March 1923–April 1924). He was a prolific writer for the popular magazines during the early decades of the century. (Lovecraft presumably read some of his stories in the Munsey magazines.) He also published several novels. J. C. Henneberger picked Baird to edit *Weird Tales,* even though he seemed to have no particular expertise in weird fiction, his own fiction being primarily mystery and adventure tales. Baird provisionally accepted five of Lovecraft's stories when he submitted them in May 1923—"Dagon," "Facts concerning the Late Arthur Jermyn and His Family," "The Cats of Ulthar," "The Hound," and "The Statement of Randolph Carter"—if Lovecraft were to retype them double-spaced. Lovecraft blandly suggested that he might not bother, but it is doubtful he was in the least serious. These were not his earliest appearances in professional magazines, though they were among the first professional appearances of his fiction. And Lovecraft briefly enjoyed what seemed to be easy success. When *Argosy* rejected "The Rats in the Walls," Baird snatched it up. He also accepted "The Picture in the House" and "Hypnos." The acceptance of eight stories in the first year of the editor's tenure must have been a heady experience for the hitherto insulated Lovecraft. His letters to Baird exhibit a certain cockiness—indeed, when he was presented with a transcript of his letter of 3 February 1924 by a young fan, he was distressed at how he must have come across a dozen years previous.

> I gape with mortification at its egotistical smugness, florid purple passages, ostentatious exhibitionism, ponderous jauntiness, & general callowness. It wouldn't be so bad if I had written it at 13 or 23—but at 33! What a complacent, self-assured, egocentric jackass I was in those days! All that gabble about the shaping & development of—the world's most perfect cipher! Well—the excuse, if any, is this: that the invalidism & seclusion of my earlier years had left me, at 33, as naive & inexperienced & unused to dealings with the world as most are at 17 or 18. As you see by the letter, I had only just burst out of a shell of retirement, & was finding the external world as novel & fascinating as a kid finds it. I was drunk with a sense of expansion, as it were—fascinated by new scenes (I'd just been to New Hampshire, Salem, Marblehead, New York, & Cleveland for the first time) & allured by the will o' the wisp of literary success (first WT placements the year before—& the future easily imagined)—so

---

1. *Deeper Than You Think* 1, No. 2 (July 1968): 3–5.

that my whole psychology was that of a belated adolescence, with the usual egotism, pompous writing, jauntiness, & show-off tendencies of the callow. It is hard for me to recapture the mood of that far-off age—but very obviously, I thought I was quite a guy. Probably—in fact, certainly—I had a better time then than I have now . . . but only because I didn't realise what a vacuous, snobbish, & complacent ass I was.[2]

He also was embarrassed when Baird printed in *Weird Tales* his rash insulting comments about George Sterling and Vincent Starrett not meant for publication.

Lovecraft had little luck persuading Baird to seek fiction comparable to that of M. P. Shiel, Lord Dunsany, Algernon Blackwood, and others. However, he did persuade Baird to consider publishing verse by Clark Ashton Smith and thus to relax his no-poetry policy. The magazine regularly published poetry thereafter, with Lovecraft's and Smith's work being the most abundant.

When the Arthur Jermyn story was published as "The White Ape," Lovecraft was very displeased. It was the *last* title he would have used to replace his somewhat ungainly title. And Baird probably found "Under the Pyramids" too tame a title for an adventure ostensibly involving Harry Houdini, and he tantalizingly renamed it "Imprisoned with the Pharaohs."

Weird Tales lost considerable money under Baird, and so he was fired. Henneberger thought highly of Lovecraft and offered editorship of the magazine to him. The previously cocksure Lovecraft demurred, and another editor was found. Baird continued to work for Henneberger, editing his *Detective Tales*, but in that capacity he rejected, in July 1925, Lovecraft's "The Shunned House," as did Farnsworth Wright, the current editor of *Weird Tales*. It is uncertain how Lovecraft would have fared with *Weird Tales* had Baird remained in his position. When Lovecraft started to write fiction in what he would call a "cosmic" vein, would Baird have received "The Call of Cthulhu" as readily as he accepted "The Rats in the Walls"?

Farnsworth Wright (1888–1940), second and longest-serving editor of *Weird Tales,* is well recognized as a nettlesome figure in Lovecraft's life. And yet, he and Lovecraft had a very similar background in their early writing careers. As Wright has written,

> [. . .] I once belonged to both the National Amateur Press Association and the United during my last year in grammar school and for three years when I was a student in Lowell High School, San Francisco. I published a little paper (tritely enough) THE LAUREL. I wrote it all myself, set the type, and printed it on the

---

2. Letter to Willis Conover, 31 January 1937; *Letters to Robert Bloch and Others* 416.

hand press of a friend of mine. All my copies of it, and the magazines with which I exchanged, were lost in the earthquake and fire, I am sorry to say.[3]

Wright graduated with a B.A. in Journalism from the University of Washington in 1914. His first job was as a reporter with the *Seattle Sun*. In 1917, he was drafted into the U.S. Army, in which he served in the infantry during World War I. He also served as an interpreter. After the war, he seems not to have returned to journalism, and began writing fiction. His work appeared in *Munsey's Magazine*, the *New Magazine*, the *Open Road*, and *Overland Monthly*, and he also published some pieces in Baird's *Weird Tales*. He even translated "Les Trois Messes Basses" by Alphonse Daudet for publication in *Weird Tales*. He also published verse in *Weird Tales* under the pseudonym "Francis Hard." Wright was music critic for the *Chicago Herald and Examiner*, continuing in this capacity for a time even while editing *Weird Tales*.

By early 1921 he had contracted Parkinson's disease, and by around 1930 he was incapable of signing his letters; the disease ultimately would prove fatal. Wright was given editorship of *Weird Tales* in early 1924, when Edwin Baird was fired. Whereas Baird enthusiastically published all that Lovecraft submitted, Wright's aim was to balance the interests of the magazine's readers (many of whom were relatively unsophisticated and ill-educated) with the search for quality work to publish in "The Unique Magazine." Lovecraft tended to feel Wright was unduly influenced by the readers who wrote to the magazine's letter column, "The Eyrie." Wright published a vast amount of rubbish in *Weird Tales*, often rejecting work that was imaginative and well-written but challenging for some readers; sometimes he accepted stories he had rejected more than once. He managed to keep *Weird Tales* afloat through the Depression, when many other pulp magazines (notably the rival *Strange Tales* [1931–33]) failed. He was not so successful with the short-lived *Oriental Stories* (later *The Magic Carpet Magazine*).

Initially Lovecraft had no difficulty landing stories with the new editor. Wright took "The Festival," "The Unnamable," and "The Temple." But then he rejected "The Shunned House" when it was submitted in 1925, Lovecraft's first ever rejection by *Weird Tales*. Thereafter Wright tended to accept Lovecraft's more conventional tales and to reject those that were more out of the ordinary. Wright was also greatly concerned about censorship: the May–June–July 1924 issue had been temporarily banned in Indiana because of the gruesomeness of the Lovecraft–Eddy story "The Loved Dead," and Wright (according to Lovecraft) was in terror of a repeat of such an incident; accordingly, he rejected Lovecraft's "In the Vault" and "Cool Air" on the grounds

---

3. Quoted in Donald A. Wollheim, "Phantagraphy," *Phantagraph* (September 1937). Note that Wright is not mentioned in Stan Oliner's "NAPA Official Roster: 1876–1959."

that they were too grisly. Wright also rejected several of Lovecraft's Dunsanian fantasies. Wright somewhat capriciously reconsidered some stories, accepting some, rerejecting others. He seemed to wish Lovecraft to be more explicit as to the causes of his supernatural phenomena; Lovecraft felt that this repeated plea had a deleterious effect on his later work by making it too obvious and explanatory.

In late 1926 Wright proposed a collection of Lovecraft's stories, to be part of a series of books issued by *Weird Tales*. In a long letter to Wright (22 December 1927), Lovecraft outlined a proposed table of contents for the book (which he wished to call *The Outsider and Other Stories* because "I consider the touch of cosmic *outsideness*—of dim, shadowy *non-terrestrial* hints—to be the characteristic feature of my writing"). But the Popular Fiction Publishing Company's first book, *The Moon Terror* by A. G. Birch and others, sold so poorly that plans to issue further volumes were dropped.

In 1931 Wright gravely offended Lovecraft by rejecting *At the Mountains of Madness*, which the author considered his most ambitious work. Although Lovecraft felt the short novel was suited for serialization by simply dividing it after Chapter 6, Wright felt that it was "'too long,' 'not easily divisible into parts,' 'not convincing'—& so on."[4] For the next five and a half years Lovecraft submitted only one story to *Weird Tales*, even though Wright repeatedly urged him to submit work, and he reprinted several earlier tales in the absence of new work. (August Derleth submitted "The Shadow over Innsmouth" in 1933 and "The Dreams in the Witch House" in 1934 without Lovecraft's knowledge or permission; the former was rejected, the latter accepted.) In 1932 Wright further angered Lovecraft by urging him not to deal with Carl Swanson, who was attempting to form a magazine, *Galaxy*, that Wright regarded as a potential rival to *Weird Tales*. Lovecraft grudgingly submitted "The Thing on the Doorstep" and "The Haunter of the Dark" to Wright in the autumn of 1936; they were promptly accepted. After Lovecraft's death Wright published many previously rejected Lovecraft stories when they were submitted by August Derleth to earn money for Lovecraft's surviving aunt. He edited *Weird Tales* until his failing health forced him to resign, when Dorothy McIlwraith took the helm. McIlwraith was editor until the magazine folded in 1954, serving almost as long as Wright. But the heyday of *Weird Tales* was attained under Wright's editorship.

It is not certain how Lovecraft came to know Walter John Coates, but it was probably through the intercession of their common friend W. Paul Cook. Coates is never mentioned in any of Lovecraft's critical articles in the amateur press, and it does not appear that Coates issued any paper to be distributed in the bundles of journals sent to members of the amateur press associations.

---

4. *Letters to J. Vernon Shea and Others* 29.

Coates had written poetry since 1917, and Lovecraft may have read some of it thanks to Cook. But how did they reach each other? In 1926, both Lovecraft and Coates were researching and writing material for Cook's *Recluse*, which would appear the following year. In April 1926, Coates published the first issue of *Driftwind: A Tramp Magazine*, "issued for the love of literature." (Not long thereafter, the magazine was called *Driftwind: From the North Hills*.) Lovecraft received a copy and praised it. Upon Lovecraft's death, Coates recalled:

> Lovecraft was one of the earliest and most valued friends of *Driftwind*. He encouraged us at the start, and did not withdraw his support, as many do, at the last. He was no "fair weather friend," merely. It was always a pleasure to publish his work; a pleasure to get, every issue, his cordial and appreciative comments; a pleasure to receive innumerable post-cards from him—post-cards that were as unique and exceptional in character as were the thoughts in his own mind.[5]

It is not known if the congratulatory letter was Lovecraft's first to Coates. But as Coates acknowledges, they remained correspondents and friends until Lovecraft's death.

Coates was born in Montague (near Lowville), N.Y., in 1880 and educated at the St. Lawrence University divinity school in Canton. He served as student pastor in Marshfield and East Calais, Vt., and was also postmaster and a merchant. While at university, Coates married Florence Webster Gray (b. 1884) in December 1902.[6] Their son John Webster Coates was born in April 1904. Coates was ordained a Universalist minister in 1904. Florence died of tuberculosis in 1906, and her distraught husband took to woodcutting for a time as a distraction. In 1908, Coates married Florence's cousin Nettie Allan Gove (1882–1967), with whom he had two daughters: Frances Eugenia (1909–2006) and Flora Whitford (1914–2002). Coates called himself "a peace advocate, but a scion of warlike stock [. . .] a Liberal in religion and a Progressive in politics."[7]

Coates did not stay in the ministry. Instead, he partnered with his father-in-law to run a store in East Calais, where Coates served as postmaster for ten years. In 1922 he and his wife purchased George Pray's store in North Montpelier which they ran with their son. He combined store-keeping with the publication of writing by himself and other Vermont poets, printing on an antique foot-powered Golding press that came with the store. In the summer of 1925, he met with W. Paul Cook and Vrest Orton, Vermont natives who had read Coates's *Mood Songs*, to discuss how to stimulate literary activity and to encourage aspiring writers. The fateful meeting was the stimulus for Coates to launch *Driftwind* the following year and to commence work on his essay

---

5. "Howard P. Lovecraft," in Joshi and Schultz, *Ave atque Vale* 443.

6. Findagrave.com incorrectly states they married in 1900.

7. *Hubbardton Battle: A Ballad* [17].

"Early Vermont Minstrelsy" for Cook's *Recluse*. If Coates and Lovecraft did not know each other at the time, Cook may have suggested Lovecraft to Coates as an appreciative audience for his new publication. *Driftwind*, a monthly magazine, was distributed free at first and in small quantities, but grew over time. Coates set the type himself and operated the press. The printed covers—on wallpaper and even birch bark—were a distinctive trademark.

When John Coates died of tuberculosis in November 1926, Coates almost abandoned *Driftwind*. But he, Nettie, and their daughter Flora persevered, and Coates continued to publish it until his untimely death at sixty in 1941. By 1932, they were printing 400 copies monthly. Nettie, Flora, and W. Paul Cook continued to issue *Driftwind* until 1948, when Cook died. Cook also published his memoir *In Memoriam Howard Phillips Lovecraft: Recollections, Appreciations, Estimates* (1941) and the *Ghost* through Driftwind Press. Following Cook's death, Mrs. Coates closed the printing operation, and Arthur Murphy bought the rights to the magazine, moving it to Winchendon, Mass., where he produced it for a few years.

Coates was so taken with a letter Lovecraft had written around May 1926 that he abstracted a few paragraphs from it and published them as an "essay" titled "The Materialist Today." He also issued an offprint of the piece in an edition of fifteen copies for private distribution. On the occasion of his first visit to Vermont, Lovecraft wrote "Vermont: A First Impression" for *Driftwind*. *Driftwind* also published ten sonnets from Lovecraft's *Fungi from Yuggoth* and included one of them in a booklet of poems that had appeared in the magazine—the first appearance of Lovecraft's poetry in a book (save for the birthday tributes in *The Poetical Works of Jonathan E. Hoag*). Coates himself was the author and editor of many volumes of poetry. Besides publishing and printing, Coates offered criticism on verse—for a fee.

Lovecraft and Coates finally met in 1928. Coates had learned that Lovecraft would be visiting Vrest Orton in Brattleboro, Vt., so he and his wife drove more than 120 miles to meet Lovecraft. As Lovecraft reports to his aunt: "We discussed literature all the afternoon, & after dinner settled down to a fireside argument on philosophy which lasted till 3 a.m."[8] Always promoting the work of local authors, Coates helped found the League of Vermont Writers in 1929, of which he long served as president. Coates published numerous books of his verse, five volumes of *Favorite Vermont Poems, Vermont Verse: An Anthology* (with Frederick Tupper), and two anthologies with J. Howard Flower.

Coates later found himself in the middle of a somewhat awkward situation involving Cook and Lovecraft. In 1928, Cook set type for and printed

---

8. HPL to Lillian D. Clark (19 June 1928); *Letters to Family* 695. The occasion of HPL's visit was written up as "Literary Persons Meet in Guilford," *Brattleboro Daily Reformer* (18 June 1928): 1. Coates is not mentioned.

Lovecraft's story "The Shunned House," to be issued as a slim book. But Cook was unable to bind the book, as he was dealing with both financial and health difficulties, as well as the failing health of his wife, Adeline, who died in January 1930. Cook was unable to endure the loss, and subsequent financial failure caused him to leave Athol behind. *The Shunned House* sat in storage at his sister's home. Cook found himself drifting about, staying with friends. In August 1931 he turned to Coates, who took him in as a printer at the Driftwind Press. It must have been not long after that Cook broached to Coates the subject of the unbound sheets of *The Shunned House*, completely unknown to Lovecraft. As Coates's fellow printer, he could oversee the job to completion. Coates agreed to the arrangement, but it appears they were simply too busy to do the work, for they issued *Driftwind* monthly and also various other books through the Driftwind Press, including two by Cook.[9] Furthermore, the sheets were still in storage in Sunapee, N.H. Inability to access the sheets readily may have furthered the delay. When Lovecraft's intrepid young correspondent R. H. Barlow learned in February 1933 that the printed sheets still existed, he approached Cook about obtaining them so that he himself (a lad of fifteen with no experience in bookbinding) might finish the job. Cook agreed, but forgot that he had previously asked Coates to do it. Coates was irked that Cook had made such an arrangement with Barlow, for he surely intended to do the job himself, following the acquisition of a new linotype equipment in 1931 and increasing work, and so the offer to Barlow was retracted. In the end, "it became clear that he [Coates] could do nothing in his desperate financial state,"[10] and the sheets were turned over to Barlow, who himself bound only a few copies—including one in leather for Lovecraft.

Driftwind for April 1937 sadly reported the death of Coates's good friend from Providence, R.I. In 1938, Coates received an honorary LL.D. from the University of Vermont–Montpelier. Some of East Montpelier's town reports were published by the Driftwind Press. With his extensive collection of Vermontiana at hand, Coates long worked at a bibliography of Vermont poetry but died of a heart attack before he could complete it. The Vermont Historical Society published *A Bibliography of Vermont Poetry and Gazetteer of Vermont Poets* posthumously, but the book covered only the letters A through K.

Woodburn Prescott Harris (1888–1988) may have the distinction of having received the longest known letter from Lovecraft's pen—a behemoth of 70 leaves.[11] As with many of Lovecraft's correspondents, very little is known of

---

9. *Told in Vermont* (1938) and *Heard in Vermont* (1939). Ironically, the latter was not bound until nearly a decade after printing, and well after Cook's death.

10. *O Fortunate Floridian* 103.

11. There is a surviving ms. letter to Frank Belknap Long of 60 leaves, but the concluding leaf or leaves are missing, so the total length cannot be verified.

Harris. Harris graduated in 1911 from Middlebury College in Vermont and had a five-year career as a high school teacher of English and drama before he served in World War I. With his hearing impaired by service in the war, he could no longer be an instructor, and so he took to farming, a strenuous job far different from the intellectual pursuits to which he previously had been devoted. He lived in Vergennes, Vt., with his wife Ethel Pauline (Jenkins) Harris (1896–1972), whom he married in November 1919. He characterized his situation at the farm as starving him to death mentally. He called his correspondence with Lovecraft, instigated by Walter J. Coates, fellow Vermonter to Harris, life-saving. They began writing each other in 1927.

Lovecraft called Harris "my controversial Vermont correspondent," but there is little mention of Harris in other letters to indicate why this was so. At first Lovecraft observed that "Harris is a political conservative of the traditional Yankee mould—a solid Coolidge man."[12] Coates also knew Henry George Weiss ("Francis Flagg") and introduced him to Lovecraft. Lovecraft delighted in stirring controversy between the two: "As for our young communist [Weiss]—I have just set Farmer Woodburn Harris of Vermont on to him, and expect some brilliant fireworks. [. . . H]is keen wit and horse-sense will form a delightful foil to young Weiss's bolshevism."[13] It was not long before Harris began voicing sympathy for communism, which may be the reason that Lovecraft characterized him as a "controversial" correspondent. Lovecraft mentions Harris only twice, and only slightly, in letters to R. H. Barlow, and yet when Barlow listed for August Derleth the names and addresses of Lovecraft's correspondents following his death, he knew enough of Harris to comment next to his name that his letters from Lovecraft "should have many pink discussions," implying heated argument about leftist political opinions.[14]

Harris met Lovecraft's friends Coates, Vrest Orton (also from Vermont), and W. Paul Cook, but he and Lovecraft never met in person. Lovecraft revised some of Harris's tracts against Prohibition, although these do not appear to have been published. He wrote to Frank Belknap Long, "Our intelligent rustick friend Woodburn Harris has suddenly blossom'd into a prolifick professional client—being intent on saving the country by devising and publishing ways and means to repeal the 18th Amendment . . . . (O why did I bring this up! It reminds me that I must type about 12 pages of the damn stuff before nightfall!)."[15]

Lovecraft recommended many books to Harris to read, and Harris did so

---

12. HPL to Frank Belknap Long, 17 October 1930, *SL* 3.187.

13. Ibid.

14. See Kenneth W. Faig, Jr. "Lovecraft's 1937 Diary," *Lovecraft Annual* No. 6 (2012): 167–68.

15. HPL to Frank Belknap Long, 14 March 1930, *SL* 3.130.

dutifully. He was profoundly disappointed when he lent John Strachey's *The Nature of Capitalist Crisis* (1935) to Lovecraft at Lovecraft's request. Lovecraft told Harris, "It looks pretty damned stiff" at 400 pages, but he professed a wish to read it. He had been holding it since at least September 1936, and only began to read it in late November but found himself

> too much interrupted to do it justice as yet. It demands close attention & analysis. So far it has merely confirmed me in *socialism*—i.e., the fact that any large-scale capitalism produces unbearable tension, & that non-profit operation of industry as a whole is the only way out—without making me any the less critical of the far-reaching claims & dogmatisms of orthodox communism. I must know more of the foundations of general economics before I can deal readily with these matters.[16]

In fact, Lovecraft wished to read Strachey's *The Theory and Practice of Socialism* (1936). But he appeared less enthusiastic about the book in writing to James F. Morton: "Not much energy for reading these days, but some of my political-minded colleagues are bullying me into digesting Strachey's 'Nature of Capitalist Crisis.'"[17] At the time, Lovecraft was desperately ill, and was unable to finish the book. It was returned to Harris without comment and Lovecraft went silent. Harris was deeply hurt by the perceived snub—he did not see fit to continue corresponding with Lovecraft, but perhaps Harris might have felt otherwise had he known Lovecraft was dying. Indeed, he did not learn of Lovecraft's death until he read numerous letters of encomium on Lovecraft in the June 1937 *Weird Tales,* to which Harris was a subscriber. Annie Gamwell had found Harris's address in her nephew's "Instructions in Case of Decease" and herself had returned the Strachey volume.

All we have of Lovecraft's letters to Harris, from a period covering nearly ten years, are three preserved (in truncated form) in the Arkham House transcripts. It is difficult to conceive what has been lost, in light of Lovecraft's comment that "He & I are slinging reams of paper in a complete settlement of all the problems of the cosmos!"[18]

Zealia Brown Reed Bishop (1897–1968) was one of Lovecraft's revision clients. She was born Zealia Margaret Caroline Brown on 4 June 1897 in Asheville, N.C. On 2 March 1914 she married James Reed; they had a son, James Reed, Jr. (b. 20 December 1914). At some point in the 1920s she divorced Reed; she married Dauthard W. Bishop on 22 July 1930. Her own memoir of her association with Lovecraft, "H. P. Lovecraft: A Pupil's View" (1953), is notoriously

---

16. *O Fortunate Floridian* 369.

17. *Letters to James F. Morton* 402.

18. WJC 28.

unreliable. She states that she learned of Lovecraft's work as a reviser when she met Samuel Loveman in a bookstore he managed in Cleveland in 1928. But, as is obvious from the text of the letters, she was already writing to Lovecraft in the spring of 1927; moreover, Loveman had moved from Cleveland to New York no later than the fall of 1924. The first mention of Loveman in the letters occurs on 25 January 1928, when Lovecraft writes of "Samuel Loveman, once of Cleveland, to whom you wrote last spring." Possibly Bishop, although apparently living in Cleveland in 1927, did not in fact meet Loveman face to face at that time; she may have gone to the bookstore where Loveman had once worked, been given his address, and written to him. He in turn presumably suggested that she get in touch with Lovecraft, as someone who could assist her with her budding career as a writer.

Bishop further confuses matters by stating that "I was already qualified as a court reporter and selling short stories and articles as a means of supporting myself and young son while furthering my education in journalism at Columbia University."[19] This suggests that Bishop was living in New York at the time, but she was not: Lovecraft's letter of 18 May 1927 makes it clear that Bishop was still in Cleveland, although about to move; and that she was only planning a visit to New York in the near future.

The question of Bishop's one face-to-face meeting with Lovecraft is also a bit puzzling. She herself states that he was "only thirty-five"[20] when the meeting took place in the apartment occupied by Frank Belknap Long and his parents; but this would place the meeting in 1925, which is of course impossible. In a letter to his aunt, Lillian D. Clark, Lovecraft notes that the meeting took place on 29 May 1928, when he was on an extended stay in Brooklyn while assisting his wife, Sonia, in setting up a hat shop. He records the encounter with Bishop laconically: "Today—Monday—I rose at noon & went to Sonny's [i.e., Frank Belknap Long] to meet our client Mrs. Reed, who was in town Sun. & Mon. She seems quite prepossessing & intelligent."[21]

In any event, Bishop became one of Lovecraft's most persistent revision clients during the later 1920s and early 1930s, sending him story after story for analysis and touching up. And while it is of substantial interest to see how exhaustive Lovecraft's knowledge of current magazine markets was (see his letter of 23 May 1927), it is also plain that Lovecraft and Bishop had quite different views on the type of work she was writing and wished to write. Almost from the beginning Lovecraft encouraged Bishop to banish "superficial modern fiction" (letter of 5 June 1927) from her course of reading, even though it is evident that this is exactly the kind of fiction she wanted to read and write.

---

19. "H. P. Lovecraft: A Pupil's View," *Ave atque Vale* 253.
20. "H. P. Lovecraft: A Pupil's View" 260.
21. H. P. Lovecraft to Lillian D. Clark, [29 May 1928]; *Letters to Family* 676.

Bishop herself betrays considerable resentment against Lovecraft for attempting to steer her in a direction she did not wish to go:

> Being young and romantic, I wanted to follow my own impulse for fresh, youthful stories. Lovecraft was not convinced that this course was best. I was his protégé and he meant to bend my career to his direction. [. . .]
>
> Lovecraft's tutorial attitude was that of the master toward his protégé. Perhaps it could not have been otherwise. He either had no conception of a pupil's own direction and aims or he was not sympathetic to them, for he tried to direct his pupils into lines of development similar to his own. He lacked the catholicity of taste that the best teachers of writing must have. There is, for example, nothing wrong in writing confession or love stories if one knows what one is about and does his best.[22]

There is a good deal of truth in Bishop's statement; but Lovecraft was also correct in believing that even "confession or love stories" have to be well written and avoid trite and hackneyed tropes if they are to sell even to popular markets. In a later letter Lovecraft does admit that "I cannot enter into the spirit of commercial writing" (letter of 24 February 1928), and another letter (undated, but probably written in April 1928) at last correctly identifies Bishop's chosen form of expression as "light, domestic fiction in the popular vein"; but it was precisely this kind of work that Lovecraft was least able to help her with. Lovecraft apparently did assist Bishop in the revision of one such story, "One-Man Girl" (*Cupid's Diary*, 26 December 1928), which is discussed in the letters under the title "Red Blood." It is printed here in the Appendix.

The Lovecraft–Bishop relationship takes an interesting turn in early 1928. A letter that apparently dates to late February provides a plot synopsis of "The Curse of Yig." Bishop's own account of the genesis of the story is, once again, quite different from what can be inferred from Lovecraft's letters. She states:

> The stories I sent him always came back so revised from their basic idea that I felt I was a complete failure as a writer. Disappointed and confused, I put aside everything that looked like a writer's tool and, with my son, set out for my sister's ranch in Oklahoma, a barren lonely place near the Texas border [. . .]
>
> There in Oklahoma, doubting more and more that I would ever become a writer, let alone a successful one, I sat one evening with a group of old Oklahoma settlers who had driven out to my sister's ranch. We sat around the kitchen fire and talked. Finally the conversation rambled on to folklore. Grandma Compton, my sister's mother-in-law, told a horror story about a couple who pioneered in Oklahoma not far from where we were. This story was a spark to me. I wrote a tale called "The Curse of Yig," in which snakes figured, wove it around some of my Aztec knowledge instilled in me by

---

22. "H. P. Lovecraft: A Pupil's View," 255–56, 262–63.

Lovecraft, and sent it off to him. He was delighted with this trend toward realism and horror, and fairly showered me with letters and instructions.[23]

There is reason to doubt numerous details of this account. There is no question that Bishop provided some kind of plot germ or outline for "The Curse of Yig"; but Lovecraft's undated letter (only leaf VI of which survives) makes it clear that the detailed synopsis of the story (appearing on the now-lost leaves IV and V of the letter) were of his own devising, and all that he asks of Bishop is for her to send these leaves back to him and supply "some more notes on points of local colour." In his letter of 9 March Lovecraft sends Bishop the completed story, which manifestly is largely of his own composition. Lovecraft confirms this supposition in a letter to August Derleth:

> By the way—if you want to see a new story which is practically mine, read "The Curse of Yig" in the current W.T. Mrs. Reed is a client for whom Long & I have done oceans of work, & this story is about 75% mine. All I had to work on was a synopsis describing a couple of pioneers in a cabin with a nest of rattlesnakes beneath, the killing of the husband by snakes, the bursting of the corpse, & the madness of the wife, who was an eye-witness to the horror. There was no plot or motivation—no prologue or aftermath to the incident—so that one might say the story, as a story, is wholly my own. I invented the snake-god & the curse, the tragic wielding of the axe by the wife, the matter of the snake-victim's identity, & the asylum epilogue. Also, I worked up the geographic & other incidental colour—getting some data from the alleged authoress, who knows Oklahoma, but more from books.[24]

There are other problems with Bishop's account. She states that, after the story was written, it was sent out "not once, but many times" to various magazines but rejected, forcing her to shelve the story. Lovecraft then submitted the story to *Weird Tales*. It was, she claims, only when she personally visited editor Farnsworth Wright in Chicago at some unspecified date that he accepted the story—"four months later."[25] But this cannot be right. The story was written in early March and, by Lovecraft's account, already accepted by Wright by mid-May.[26] Bishop may be thinking of the long delay in the story's actual appearance in print (it was published only in the November 1929 issue).

It was around this time that Frank Belknap Long entered into Bishop's life. He and Lovecraft were beginning to work together on a revision service, as a now well-known advertisement in the August 1928 issue of *Weird Tales* attests. Long appears to have worked on both weird and non-weird speci-

---

23. "H. P. Lovecraft: A Pupil's View" 257–58.

24. H. P. Lovecraft to August Derleth, 6 October [1929]; *Essential Solitude* 1.222.

25. "H. P. Lovecraft: A Pupil's View" 262.

26. H. P. Lovecraft to August Derleth, [19 or 26 May 1928]; *Essential Solitude* 1.146.

mens by Bishop; indeed, at one point Lovecraft speaks of Long revising an entire novel she had written (letter of 25 August 1929). This appears to be a work that Bishop cites in her memoir as "a novel which dealt with a Catholic upbringing,"[27] since both Bishop and Lovecraft refer to its central character, Deon, in their discussions of the work. (In his letter of 31 March 1936, Lovecraft speaks of a novel by Bishop entitled *The Adopted Son;* whether this is the same novel is uncertain, but probably it is.) This novel clearly did not sell, nor did a rewriting of a mainstream story, "The Unchaining," as a weird tale (under the new title of "On the High Places"), which *Weird Tales* rejected.

In his letter of 25 August 1928, Lovecraft discusses a "weird tale of the Indian" that he is working on; there are further mentions of this in his letters of 28 October 1928 and 22 January 1929. One suspects that this is "The Mound"; but if so, it took Lovecraft quite some time to undertake the actual writing of the work, for it was only written in December 1929–January 1930. The story was completed by no later than 14 January, and Bishop probably had no more input in it than in "The Curse of Yig." Indeed, in a note on one of the two surviving typescripts of the story, R. H. Barlow suggests as much as he records Bishop's synopsis: "There is an Indian mound near here, which is haunted by a headless ghost. Sometimes it is a woman."[28] Bishop introduces further confusion by stating that, at Lovecraft's suggestion, Long became involved in the writing of the tale ("At Lovecraft's gentle insistence, I left 'The Mound' with Frank Belknap Long, and it was Long who advised me and worked with me on that short novel").[29] In his memoir, *Howard Phillips Lovecraft: Dreamer on the Nightside* (1975), Long flatly denied that he had anything to do with the story;[30] and it is safe to say that both the conception and composition of the tale are entirely Lovecraft's. As a curious postscript, Lovecraft urged Bishop to hire his Providence friend C. M. Eddy, Jr., to type the handwritten manuscript. Eddy was suffering extreme poverty at the time, and Lovecraft's accounts of how he tried to assist Eddy financially and in other ways make for poignant reading. Bishop did indeed hire Eddy to type the story.

But the tale was far longer than it needed to be—at least, it was so long (more than 25,000 words) that Farnsworth Wright rejected the story in short order. In an undated letter to Bishop, Lovecraft expressed outrage, believing that Wright could have run the story as a two-part serial, and he encouraged her to submit it to other pulp magazines. Whether she did so is unclear; if she did, it was again rejected, and only appeared in abridged form in *Weird Tales* for November 1940.

---

27. "H. P. Lovecraft: A Pupil's View" 258.
28. Cited in Joshi, *I Am Providence* 2.745.
29. "H. P. Lovecraft: A Pupil's View" 260.
30. See Joshi, "Who Wrote 'The Mound?," in *Lovecraft and a World in Transition: Collected Essays on H. P. Lovecraft* (New York: Hippocampus Press, 2014), 343–46.

It is unfortunate that letters discussing the composition of "Medusa's Coil" are apparently not extant. Lovecraft wrote the tale in the spring and summer of 1930. A synopsis of the story has recently come to light,[31] and it is clearly the work of Lovecraft. It features a general plot outline along with a five-part "Manner of Narration." One point in this document—"woman revealed as vampire, lamia, &c. &c.—& unmistakably (surprise to reader as in original text) a negress"—is highly intriguing. Does that mention of an "original text" suggest that there was an existing draft by Bishop that Lovecraft overhauled? If so, then there would be some reason to believe that the racist conclusion of the story—the revelation that the witch-woman Marceline Bedard is a negress, and that such a revelation is a horror far surpassing the horror of her supernatural powers—should be attributed to Bishop and not Lovecraft. In her memoir, Bishop makes note of "'Medusa's Coil,' which I had picked up as an idea from a Negress who did some housecleaning for me and expanded into a story similar in treatment to my earlier horror tale."[32] This remark is itself a little confusing, especially since "Medusa's Coil" is set in eastern Missouri and not Oklahoma; but we may infer that Bishop did provide a synopsis, and perhaps simply an actual draft, of the story to Lovecraft. But the story as written is without doubt entirely of his composition, at least as far as the prose is concerned. It too was rejected by *Weird Tales,* probably on account of length (or perhaps because it is just not a very good story). There was some talk between Lovecraft and Long of submitting it to *Ghost Stories,* an inferior pulp magazine that featured stories of the "true confession" type; but if it was sent there, it was also rejected. It finally appeared in *Weird Tales* for January 1939, only because August Derleth submitted the story to an editor now hungry for work by Lovecraft.

Zealia Bishop stayed in touch with Lovecraft almost to the end of his life, and she was at least contemplating giving him some additional revisory work as late as 1936 (to say nothing of paying off, in small increments, the debt she owed for past work).[33] And although she states in her memoir that "I have carefully filed all his letters, postcards, and instructions,"[34] it is evident that a fair number of letters have now been lost. Nevertheless, what remains sheds a wealth of light on Lovecraft as a professional revisionist as well as a genial and considerate correspondent—one who seemed genuinely interested in his colleague and her family (one letter is charmingly written to her son, James) and happy to share with her his own evolving thoughts and beliefs.

---

31. First published in *CE* 5.243–44.

32. "H. P. Lovecraft: A Pupil's View" 259–60.

33. HPL's "Instructions in Case of Decease" included the note "Mrs. D. W. Bishop, 5001 Sunset Drive, Kansas City, Mo. owed H. P. Lovecraft $26 for revision work."

34. "H. P. Lovecraft: A Pupil's View" 256.

Barring the unexpected discovery of caches of letters to Adolphe de Castro, Hazel Heald, or other of his major revision clients, these letters may provide the best window we will ever have into the occupation that, for better or worse, Lovecraft made his own.

William Sylvester Lumley (1880–1960) must surely be one of Lovecraft's obscurest correspondents. And yet, Lovecraft mentions him to numerous correspondents and urged Lumley to write to them. Soon Lumley was reading their circulating manuscripts. It has been learned that Lumley was a watchman at a chemical plant. But virtually all that is known of him comes from Lovecraft's own pen. He wrote that Lumley had "an occasionally rich imagination, but tends to be crude technically. He is an oldish man—quite a quaint & interesting character who has been at sea & seen odd parts of the earth—now living in Buffalo, N.Y. Some of his occult beliefs are rather naive & amusing."[35] To Clark Ashton Smith, Lovecraft waxed on at length:

> He is surely an unique survival from the earth's mystical childhood—a combination of priceless credulity & gorgeous Munchausenism. I think I've told you about his claims of extensive travel in China, Nepal, & all sorts of mysterious & forbidden places, & his air of familiarity with such works as the arcana of Paracelsus, Hermes Trismegistus, Albertus Magnus, Apollonius of Tyana, Eibon, von Junzt, & Abdul Alhazred. He says he has witnessed monstrous rites in deserted cities, has slept in pre-human ruins & awaked 20 years older, has seen strange elemental spirits in all lands (including Buffalo, N.Y.—where he frequently visits a haunted valley & sees a white, misty Presence), has written & collaborated on powerful dramas, has conversed with incredibly wise & monstrously ancient wizards in remote Asiatic fortresses (one of them, referred to as The Oriental Ancient, was in Buffalo last year & had several solemn conclaves with Bill, but has now returned to his own far-off demesne at the edge of the world!), & not long ago had sent him from India for perusal a palaeogean & terrible book in an unknown tongue (unknown & primordial tongues are as easy to Bill as high-school Latin to you & me!) which he could not open without certain ceremonies of purification, including the donning of a white robe! He has, of course, suffered persecution & ridicule, but nothing can swerve him from his devotion to the secret & soul-shattering lore of the nether cosmic gulfs! His own sorceries, I judge, are of a somewhat modest kind; though he has had very strange & marvellous results from clay images & from certain cryptical incantations. He is firmly convinced that all our gang [. . .] are genuine agents of unseen Powers in distributing hints too dark & profound for human conception or comprehension. We may think we're writing fiction, & may even (absurd thought!) disbelieve what we write, but at bottom we are telling the truth in spite of ourselves—serving unwittingly as mouthpieces of Tsathoggua,

---

35. *Letters to F. Lee Baldwin* 153.

Crom, Cthulhu, & other pleasant Outside gentry. Indeed—Bill tells me that he has fully identified my Cthulhu & Nyarlathotep . . . . so that he can tell me more about 'em than I know myself! With a little encouragement, good old Bill would unfold limitless chronicles from beyond the border—but I like the old boy so well that I never make fun of him. He is really tremendously likeable—& with a spontaneous gratitude & generosity that are almost pathetic. Whenever I can do him a favour I like to—such as revising his occasional bits of verse. In turn, he has given me two highly welcome books—a Vathek with Mahlon Blaine's illustrations, & Edward Lucas White's "Lukundoo." His reading has really—apart from all romanticised claims—been unusually wide, & his taste in weird literature is emphatically & unmistakably good. Old Bill may be a character, but he's no fool—not by a long shot![36]

Lumley had reached Lovecraft through *Weird Tales,* and in time sent Lovecraft some of his own writing. Lovecraft observed that "His poems have a certain elusive, cryptic charm even before revision."[37] Lovecraft revised some of Lumley's verse, which was published in fan magazines. *The City of Dim Faces* was to be his magnum opus, but either it was never written or it has been lost. The depth of their correspondence is unknown, since all that survives are brief extracts of Lovecraft's letters found in the Arkham House transcripts. But it must have been quite extensive and persisted until Lovecraft's death. Lumley generously gave Lovecraft copies of *Vathek* illustrated by Mahlon Blaine and Edward Lucas White's *Lukundoo,* books he knew Lovecraft would appreciate deeply. When Lovecraft visited R. H. Barlow in De Land, Fla., in 1934, Barlow fashioned a bas-relief of Cthulhu using a sketch Lovecraft had made for him. Because of Lumley's fondness for elephant images, Barlow made him a clay model of an elephant-god that he greatly admired.

After a few years of attempting to determine how to write salable fiction that *Weird Tales* would accept (by injecting his pseudomythological tropes into work he was revising or writing for clients), Lovecraft swore off such collaborations, only to relent in the case of his struggling correspondent:

> [. . .] my sympathy for old Bill Lumley has caused me to break my new anti-collaboration rule & fix up a tale of his . . . so that he can get the satisfaction of seeing it printed somewhere . . . . by Hill-Billy or somebody. I had meant to ask somebody else—perhaps yourself—to share the philanthropic enterprise to the extent of typing the 23-page finished product; but when I looked at the MS. I realised to my horror that no eye but my own could ever decipher it! [. . .] So all I could do was to groan & tackle the thing—which I did at the cost of a night's sleep & a prostrating headache. But now, gawddam it, it's

36. *DS* 448–49.
37. *Letters to C. L. Moore* 56.

done! In view of my task, the title of this immortal work has a peculiarly ironic significance—"The Diary of Alonzo Typer"!!!!![38]

When Lumley sent Lovecraft the sixteen-page handwritten story, Lovecraft not only reworked the crude draft (the impecunious Lumley had not approached Lovecraft as a would-be client), he also typed the story—all at no cost. Lovecraft strove to preserve Lumley's conceptions, and even some of his prose. Lumley gave Lovecraft a copy of E. A. Wallis Budge's *Egyptian Book of the Dead* as recompense. Although Lovecraft assumed the story suitable only for fan publications, Lumley immediately and successfully placed the story with *Weird Tales* in November 1935 (see WL 5) for $70, but as Lovecraft observed in February 1937, the story had not yet been published—in fact, it did not appear until a year later.[39] Farnsworth Wright was curious about getting yet another story from someone whose style was uncannily like Lovecraft's, but happily took the story since Lovecraft was no longer submitting tales for publication. Lumley "let the cat out of the bag" when he mentioned that Lovecraft not only had helped him but also other writers whose work Wright had accepted.

Although Lumley was long-lived, his publishing career was not, for he published nothing after "The Diary of Alonzo Typer" and only a scant handful of poems, perhaps because he no longer had the impetus of Lovecraft's unstinting encouragement.

—S. T. JOSHI AND DAVID E. SCHULTZ

A Note on the Text

The text of the letters in this volume derives from an olio of sources, and it is highly likely that Lovecraft wrote many more to the individuals represented herein than we were able to obtain. The typed letter to J. C. Henneberger, held at the Harry Ransom Center, came to light fairly recently. Extracts of the letters to Edwin Baird were published in *Weird Tales,* with the exception of the letter dated 3 February 1924. Willis Conover had obtained the letter (partially visible in *Lovecraft at Last* 198) and presented Lovecraft with a transcription of it, much to Lovecraft's mortification. (The transcript is at JHL.) No manuscripts have come to light. Nor are there originals of the letters to Farnsworth Wright. The letters to Wright, Woodburn Harris, and William Lumley are contained only partially in the Arkham House transcripts. The letters to Zealia Brown Reed Bishop derive from two sources. Manuscripts of

---

38. *O Fortunate Floridian* 299.

39. In his report (c. February 1939) on the progress of getting a volume of HPL's stories published, August Derleth indicates that Annie Gamwell had been compensated by co-authors Kenneth Sterling and Zealia Brown Reed, but says nothing about Lumley, who presumably kept the entire amount he was paid because *Weird Tales* accepted the story before HPL's death.

some of Lovecraft's letters to her came to light only recently. However, the Arkham House transcripts contain text not found in the available manuscripts.

The letters and postcards to Walter John Coates are, unfortunately, poorly represented herein. Five letters to Coates constitute the opening letters contained in Vol. 2 of the Arkham House transcripts, meaning the letters were very early received. (Vol. 1 comprises selections from Derleth's own letters from Lovecraft.) Inexplicably, a single letter to Coates along with letters to Paul J. Campbell is found in Vol. 38, the penultimate and very late volume of the Arkham House transcripts. Coates's missives from Lovecraft have been offered by different book dealers over the years and so we know the dates of those items, but only a very few have been found.

Acknowledgments

The editors would like to thank the following for their assistance in preparation of this volume: Bobby Derie, Kenneth W. Faig, Jr., Donovan K. Loucks, Sean Branney and Andrew Leman of the H. P. Lovecraft Historical Society, James Machin, Sean and Jackie McCall, J.-M. Rajala, and Dan Sauer. Special thanks go to Martin Andersson for his careful and meticulous proofreading.

Abbreviations

EB	Edwin Baird
FW	Farnsworth Wright
HPL	H. P. Lovecraft
WJC	Walter John Coates
WL	William Lumley
ZB	Zealia Brown Reed Bishop
CE	HPL, *Collected Essays*
CF	HPL, *Collected Fiction*
CY	ZB, *The Curse of Yig*
DS	HPL and Clark Ashton Smith, *Dawnward Spire, Lonely Hill*
WT	*Weird Tales*
AHT	Arkham House transcripts
ALS	autograph letter, signed
ANS	autograph note, signed
JHL	John Hay Library, Brown University (Providence, RI)
TLS	typed letter, signed

J. C. Henneberger, owner and founder of Weird Tales

Letter to J. C. Henneberger

[1]   [TLS, Harry Ransom Center]
[HOTELL KENDALL . . .
Springfield, Mass.]

598 Angell St., Providence, R.I.,
February 2, 1924

My dear Mr. Henneberger:—

I was very glad to hear from you, and to receive so many sidelights on WEIRD TALES, whose chosen field makes me very eager for its success. I know the financial end of magazine publishing must be a tremendous and often discouraging responsibility, and I have a sincere respect for the pluck and determination of anybody who undertakes such a venture. Most certainly do I hope that some favourable turn will gradually transform your burdensome debt on the two magazines[1] into an increasingly gratifying profit—and it seems to me that many facts warrant such optimism, for in the weird field you are practically alone and with a good start, whilst in the detective field there see[m]s to be an insatiable demand for new material. Still, I know that marketing is a venturesome and uncertain process—especially with dealers in the unscrupulous state of mind you describe!

I assure you that I was not at all disconcerted by the presence of "The Transparent Ghost" beside my "Hound".[2] In the first place, I don't take myself too seriously; and in the second place, I can appreciate the sort of humour involved in such touches of "comic relief"—like the gravedigger in "Hamlet" or the porter in "Macbeth". When a magazine covers a popular clientele and appeals to one particular interest, it is peculiarly apt to elicit literary—or more or less literary—contributions from its readers; so that I suppose a very large proportion of those who have seen WEIRD TALES have flooded the office with unacceptable manuscripts. To them the whole subject of impossible contributions has become a live issue, so that the exploitation of some comically illiterate attempt carries a piquancy which they can feel and smile at even though others may find it somewhat tedious and inapropos. "The Transparent Ghost" may not be an austerely literary asset, yet I cannot doubt but that it will make many friends for the magazine, and perhaps assuage more than one subtle sting left behind by rejected MSS.

I hope, anyway, that this matter won't be instrumental in deposing Mr. Baird from the editorship[3] until he is himself ready to relinquish it; for I feel that he must have done very well on the whole, considering the adverse conditions encountered in the quest for really weird stories. That he could get hold of as many as five perfectly satisfactory yarns is an almost remarkable phenomenon in view of the lack of truly artistic and individual expression among professional fiction-writers. When I see a magazine tending toward the commonplace, the last people I blame are the editors and publishers; for even a cursory survey of the professional writing field shows that the trouble is something infinitely deeper and wider—something concerning no one publication, but the whole atmosphere and temperament of the American fiction business. And even when I get to such large units as this, I can't be any too savage about the blaming—because I realise that much of the trouble is absolutely inevitable—as incapable of human remedy as the fate of any protagonist in the Greek drama. Here in America we have a very conventional and half-educated public—a public trained under one phase or another of the Puritan tradition, and almost dulled to aesthetic sensitiveness because of the monotonous and omnipresent overstressing of the ethical element. We have millions who lack the intellectual independence, courage, and flexibility to get an artistic thrill out of a bizarre situation, and who enter sympathetically into a story only when it ignores the colour and vividness of actual human emotions and conventionally presents a simple plot based on artificial, ethically sugar-coated values and leading to a flat denouement which shall vindicate every current platitude and leave no mystery unexplained by the shallow comprehension of the most mediocre reader. That is the kind of a public publishers confront, and only a fool or a rejection-venomed author could blame the publishers for a condition caused not by them but by the whole essence and historic tradition of our civilisation. If publishers of general magazines sought and used artistically original types of fiction, they would lose their readers almost to a man. Half of the people wouldn't understand what the tales were about, and the other half would find the characters unsympathetic—because they would think and act like real people instead of like the dummies which the American middle classes have been taught and persuaded to consider and accept as people. Such, I repeat, is the inevitable condition regarding *general* fiction; the enormous bulk of fiction which sets the national standard and determines the type of technical training given all fictional students. But even this is not all! Added to this, as if by the perversity of a malign fate, is the demand of an overspeeding public for excessive *quantity production*. Baldly put, the American people demand more stories per year than the really artistic authors of America could possibly write. A real artist never works fast, and never turns out large quantities. He can't contract to deliver so many words in such and such a time, but must work slowly, gradually, and by mood; utilising favourable states of mind and refraining from putting down the stuff his brain turns out when it is tired or disinclined to such work. Now this, of course, won't do when there are hundreds of magazines to fill at regular intervals. So many pages per month or week have got to be filled, and if the artistic writers can't do it, the publishers must find the next-best thing—persons of mere talent, who can learn certain mechanical rules and technical twists, and put forth stuff of external smoothness, whose sole merit is conforming to patterns and rehashing the situations and reactions which have been found interesting to the people by previous experience. In many cases these writers achieve popularity—because the public recognise the elements that pleased them before, and are satisfied to receive them again in transposed form. Actually, the typical reader has very little true taste; and judges by absurd freaks, sentimentalities, and analogies. So it has come to be an accepted tradition that American fiction is not an art but a trade—a thing to be learnt by rule by almost anybody, and demanding above all else a complete submergence of one's own personality and thought in the general stream of conventional patterns which correspond to the bleakly uniform view of life forced on us by mediocre leadership. Success therefore comes not to the man of genius, but to the clever fellow who knows how to catch the public point of view and play up to it. Glittering tinsel reputations are built up, and dumb driven hundreds of otherwise honest plumbers take correspondence courses and try to be like these scintillant "great ones" whose achievements are really no more than mere charlatanry. Such is our fictional situation—indiscriminate hordes of writers, mostly without genius, striving by erroneous methods toward a goal which is erroneous to start with! You see the thing at its zenith in papers like THE SATURDAY EVENING POST— where men of more or less real talent are weighted down with the freely-flung gold which forms the price of their originality and artistic conscience. A fearful incubus—which only a few adroit or daring souls ever shake off.[4]

Now weird fiction, even in America, is not subject to the limitations of general fiction. When a person—the sort of person forming the readers of macabre fiction—wants an outré narrative at all, he is willing and anxious to take something removed from the beaten track of the national tradition; the tradition of conventional insipidity. Here is our real exception—the man who wants something original—but in the face of a general tradition which usurps all the education of our story-tellers, we can only ask in tragic accents, who is going to give it to him? Popular custom dins it into every young author that he must conform to patterns and reflect a smug artificial world and psychology. How can he beat this game of loaded dice in the one matter of the weird, which as a minority branch can hardly be expected to develop a school all its own in defiance of general fictional custom? I've yet to see the person who can answer that question. I've tried to take in hand a bright young chap in this town—a fellow with a conventional start, but who is now anxious to succeed with the weird.[5] Time and again I alter his work, deleting commonplace situations, images, and reactions, and introducing touches which he never thought of, but which I consider dramatically effective in that kind of work. Time and again I do this, yet with the most discouraging results. I succeed for a time—then in some knotty tangle his old training asserts itself and he surmounts a situation in the stereotyped, unimaginative popular way. And all the time I am trying to help him I have a curiously contrary sensation of *guilt,* in that I may be spoiling him for salable work in the non-weird field by shaking his faith in flashy conventions!

So when I read WEIRD TALES, and note here and there a story full of hackneyed stuff—the laboratory, the club-room with well-groomed men around the fire, the beautiful queen of remote planets, the ghost that is a human villain trying to scare somebody out of a house . . . etc. etc. . . . I never think of blaming Mr. Baird; for out of a somewhat wide knowledge of non-eminent writers, gained through various club affiliations, I am perfectly well aware that he had to take the stuff because no man living could get enough of anything else to fill the required number of pages at the required intervals. I don't believe there is enough first-rate weird fiction written in America to fill a monthly magazine the size of WEIRD TALES—and it could be developed only by catching the author young and making it possible for him to abstain from doing conventional fiction. The best you'll ever get is from men of liberal culture who do that sort of thing as an avocation—for the sheer thrill of it, and not with a professional frame of mind. I should say Paul Suter is like that— or Burton Peter Thom,[6] or Seabury Quinn, or M. Humphreys, or Anthony M. Rud (though he's had a book published),[7] or several others I don't recall plainly by name. These people have all been represented by excellent work, and I believe it would almost be better to have more than one tale by each in a single issue than to use less vivid material merely for the sake of non-repeating on the same table of contents. "Beyond the Door" was a finely effective piece—as were "The Floor Above", "Ooze", and "The Phantom Farmhouse".[8] Another thing I noted—some of the best ideas—the ideas which showed the most original power and understanding of the essence of the terrible and grotesque— were handled by obvious novices or at least writers with no command of technique or sense of literary balance. I'm quite enthusiastic about "The Weaving Shadows", by W. H. Holmes in your very first issue.[9] That thing is bungling and halting so far as form goes—but I'll be hanged if it hasn't got a thrill which no commonplace person, however highly trained, could ever duplicate. "The Open Window" by Frank Owen (January) is not dissimilar as a case of first-rate idea and third-rate development; though here the poignancy of the idea and the crudeness of the narration are both less marked. I honestly believe that one way to get good weird material is to tell the editor to sharpen his scent for the genuinely bizarre irrespective of technique, accept any powerful plot or atmospheric triumph irrespective of technique or even literacy— paying half the usual market price and telling the author why—and then have the raw material completely re-written by some staff writer of competent training, who could add his name as collaborator or not, according to the amount of work he puts into it. In this way, I am confident, you could get many better things than you could by excluding all MSS. below a certain technical standard. It isn't always the college man, or even the reasonably proficient writer, who has the mental slant that makes vivid ideas. Of course, there would hardly be an abundance of these notable but inadequate MSS., yet I think there would be enough to warrant their acceptance and re-writing. I know I've many a time doctored up something for another fellow which seemed very crude at first, but which after completion made me wish I were its full author. But at best it's hard work getting convincing horror material. Among even the most eminent the true touch of sublime and delirious fear is deucedly hard to find. Arthur Machen is the only living master—in the full sense of the word—I could possibly name in this field . . . . . a point which I think anyone can appreciate by comparing his episode of "The White Powder" in "The Three Impostors" with every other tale of terror known to this generation. I think, though, that with the requisite capital, a magazine could train up a group of effective weird writers by offering them a free and lucrative field, and letting some expert give them recommendations as to reading—what authors to avoid, and what ones to emulate. I know a kid—a junior at Columbia named Frank B. Long, Jr.,—who could give you some creepy stuff if he could be persuaded to write out half the ideas he has. I'm inducing him to send in a poem—"An Old Wife Speaketh It"—to WEIRD TALES, and if he receives encouragement he may furnish more.[10] There must be more like him—if one has the time to look them up. A youth in your own city—Alfred Galpin Jr., now holding a post-graduate fellowship at the University of Chicago—wrote something at sixteen which would chill any average blood;[11] but circumstance—and the general scholastic genius which is going to make an eminent professor of him some day—sidetracked this phase of his genius.

What you say about writing up and amplifying real horrors and ghastly tragedies is interesting and probably sensible from the standpoint of popular interest. It ought to attract readers because of its appeal to the strings of memory—nearly everyone will have heard each theme mentioned in Associated Press items, hence will feel an added sense of shuddering reality. Yet from the art standpoint—from the standpoint of the effective evocation of nameless ecstacies [*sic*] of keen-edged and titillating fear—I don't think anything can equal *good* weird fiction. There is only a passing horror in sordid, sanguinary gruesomeness—in bloody axe murders and sadistic morbidities. What really moves the profoundest springs of human fear and unholy fascination is something which suggests black infinite vistas of cryptic, brooding, half-inscrutable monstrosities for ever lurking behind Nature and as capable of being manifested again as in the case treated. The supreme principle of this sort of horror is any suggestion of the major violation of some basic law of Nature—the breaking down of the line betwixt life and death, man and the other animals, etc.—or the annihilation of the principle of time and space, bringing vastly remote ages or localities into juxtaposition. A true artist in the terrible can always invent ideas and plots a thousandfold more effective than any real tragedy or fright which ever darkened the earth, gilding them—or ebonising them—with a subtlety of atmosphere which is after all the most potent single factor in any imaginative tale. Come to think of it, I guess atmosphere and colour mean more any day than idea or plot—this being the reason we have so few effective phantasies in these days when plot and action are played up at the expense of the more leisurely attributes of writing. Of course, atmosphere is the one thing which a skilful developer *can* give a real-life tragedy. He can colour it to his heart's content, and inject suspicions of more than mortal motives and agencies which bring it close to the effective fictional state. I certainly think your idea is worth trying, though as a lover of fictional art for its own sake I should hate to see the monthly quota of stories descend to the minimum record of two or three, exclusive of the novel. I don't think I really enjoy anything so much as a really good weird story. I would give a thousand dollars not to have read Poe's "House of Usher" or "Ligeia", just for the thrill of following them breathlessly with pristine suspense over what was coming! I have never seen a copy of "The Terrific Register", and must confess to a perfect ignorance of what it is.[12] If you can connect me with a copy, at my expense, I shall consider myself ever afterward your debtor! By the way, though—just before I forget it—let me say that I think the weakest thing about the present WEIRD TALES is the prevalence of news "fillers", some of which have a very remote connection with actual weirdness. Bald news certainly needs a skilful retouching before it assorts well with the fictional atmosphere. I'd suggest that the new policy of using poetry is very good . . . . and don't think I say this because Mr. Baird has just accepted some verse from me![13] I wish you could use more verse by my California friend Clark Ashton Smith, who has perpetrated some terrific flights such as "The Hashish-Eater; or, The Apocalypse of Evil." Smith also draws splendidly, and with more encouragement than he received from Houtain, could turn out some sketches much better than his illustrations to my "Lurking Fear". But all this is mere random suggestion, made whilst I think of it.

I am interested in the idea you originally formed from my stuff in HOME BREW—especially interested because I consider that stuff among my poorest. Ordinarily I refuse altogether to write to order, or to give my tales any mechanical limitations to suit other people. But Houtain is a personal friend of mine—he'd have to be, to get me to read his ribald rag—and when he started HOME BREW he was desperately anxious to get me to give him some of my stuff. I offered him his pick of all my MSS., but they didn't look quite flashy and lowbrow enough to suit him; so he began to entreat that I prepare him a series of six tales, each of 2000 words and complete in itself, which should go the limit for sensational morbidity. I might add that my taste does not run especially to the morbid as such. What I love is the unreal and the fantastic in every form; though of course only such of my work as is terrible could ever please a popular audience. Finally I agreed, for friendship's sake, to give Houtain what he wanted, running over a list of possible plots until he took a fancy to the notion of a grave-robbing physician who restored life to bodies and was finally snatched himself by the bodies he had resuscitated, together with certain nameless companions of theirs. This I developed into the series "Herbert West—Reanimator", and I can assure you I was sick of the job before I was half done. The necessity for the completeness of each instalment spoiled the artistry of the whole thing—involving as it did the wearisome recapitulation of former matter in each instalment, and the eternal repetition of the description of Dr. Herbert West and his unamiable pursuits. When I had that out of the way, I vowed I would never again write a tale to order; and succumbed in the case of "The Lurking Fear" only because Houtain permitted me to forego the series form and make it a regular serial. The prospect of Smith's illustrations was another bait—though in the end they proved much below his usual pictorial batting average. But "The Lurking Fear" never satisfied me, because I unwisely tried to follow Houtain's wish for perfectly equal instalments—irrespective of dramatic values—and for a smashing sub-climax at the end of each instalment. The result of all this was a certain artificiality and straining, and a redundancy of incident in many of the instalments. I still feel that I have half-wasted a good plot idea, and often believe I would like to rewrite the thing for my own artistic satisfaction and let some magazine publish the new version free after securing the necessary permission from Houtain! I don't think it ought to be a serial at all—it's short enough to be complete without a break or chapter-division, especially with the redundant matter cut out. But it taught me one thing—never to try to suit the other fellow or let my original instincts of form get overridden! Now I'm fully resolved to let all my work stay unpublished unless somebody will print it without a comma or semicolon changed! The old-fashioned touch in my work is the result of my natural temperament and reading. I grew up with a large family library in a big house, and browsed at random because I was too ill to attend school or even follow a tutor's course with any regularity. Somehow I acquired a fondness for the past as compared with the present—a fondness which had plenty of chance to reign because my semi-invalidism continued and kept me from college and business despite the most extravagant ambitions of boyhood. Nothing modern had any permanent power to fascinate me—and until my WEIRD TALES venture my only acquaintance with modern magazines was a spell of ALL-STORY and ARGOSY reading ten or fifteen years ago, undertaken for the purpose of capturing the occasional weird yarns in these periodicals—especially the former. The classics were my diet, and I have never found anything else half so good! My style, of course, is fundamentally and immutably antique—complacently antique, I might add—and most of my tastes correspond. A new interest which has grown as my health has grown during the past three years, is that of Colonial architecture—the visual re-creation of the 18th century by study of its surviving landmarks—and most of my new-born strength has been utilised in the exploration of the antique towns which abound in my native New-England. So really, I don't think you could have paid me a handsomer unconscious compliment than when you suspected my "Lurking Fear" of being a re-written antique. I hope you didn't think it was very extensively re-written! Only a charge of verbatim plagiarism from an 18th century master could have pleased me more!

I shall watch the modified future of WEIRD TALES with keen interest, looking with especial avidity for your own work, since you so emphatically share my aversion for the insipid rubber-stamp popular magazine atmosphere. The acquisition of Houdini ought to be a great selling asset, for his fame and ability in his spectacular line are vast and indisputable. I am not much of a vau-deville follower, but it happens that I saw him at the old Keith's Theatre here nearly a quarter of a century ago—it must have been at the very outset of his career, for he was not then especially well known. Since then it interested me to hear that he comes from Appleton, Wisconsin,[14] the home town of my learned young friend Alfred Galpin, whom I mentioned earlier in this epistle. I did not know that he writes, or that he possessed such a notable library as you describe. Certainly, it will afford me unmeasured delight to meet this li-brary and its versatile owner—a thing the more probable because, although not much given to long trips, it is very likely that I shall live in New York af-ter the coming spring. I suppose his articles naturally would have the imper-fect background you mention, because he has been mainly accustomed to expressing his personality in different ways. I can tell better after seeing the one in the March issue.[15] Perhaps Houdini furnishes an instance of the condi-tion I mentioned before—the creator of genius who needs a re-writer to give his recorded work the form which may perfectly express its spirit.

Your compliment anent "The Rats in the Walls" delights me mightily—the more so because Robert H. Davis of the Munsey firm rejected it after some deliberation as too horrible for his readers[16] . . . . . another illustration of the essential insipidity and conventionality inculcated into our writing pub-lic by some of its leaders. When the manuscript was read among the circle of my friends in New York, Arthur Leeds—the man who conducts the "Thinks and Things" department in THE WRITER'S MONTHLY—was gratifyingly enthusiastic about it, but declared pretty dogmatically, I am told, that no American magazine would ever accept it. Such are the tacitly acknowledged and submissively accepted conventions of the timid majority!

I feel flattered that you should wish to see a long manuscript of mine—25,000 words or more—and will probably have something of the sort to show you in the near future. Formerly I wrote only short stories, believing that this was the ideal form for weird fiction; but perusal of certain weird novels gradually changed my point of view, until after my Houtain experiments in greater length I began to map out certain of my more involved ideas as possible novels. I keep plot ideas and skeletonic synopses recorded in a blank-book—the sort one would call a "commonplace-book" if the term did not carry a certain irony as applied to the contents of this particular one! My main novel idea is that of a long phantasy to be called (subject to change) "Azathoth", dealing with bizarre scenes somewhat in the exotic spirit of the Arabian Nights.[17] I don't know when I shall tackle the actual writing of this, but I'm sure you wouldn't care for it for WEIRD TALES, since it will be horrible only in parts, and contain also much prose-poetic matter and descriptions of cities and landscapes which are marvellous and weird, but not gruesome or terrible. It will belong to the category of "Vathek",[18] or some of Dunsany's longer, more ethereal, and less sophisticated things. In the horrible parts, though, I don't intend to be in the least insipid or commonplace! The scene will probably be in a distant planet, and there may be no human characters in the accepted sense of the word. Other things than humans, you know, may go through very vivid adventures and embark on very picturesque quests. But I think I shall send you, unless it pans out too long, a second tale which is about ready for the actual composition. This (also provisionally) will be known as "The House of the Worm",[19] and deal with the frantic message sent by a dying and prematurely aged father to the boy who ran away twenty years before because of a nameless dread of his new stepmother . . . . the heiress who lived in the dark house in the swamp. The young man comes, and finds his father alone in the house (or castle—I'm not sure whether I'll put it in New England or Old England or the German Black Forest) . . . . . alone, yet not alone . . . . . for he looks furtively about him . . . . and other forms flit through remote corridors, strangely attracting swarms of flies after them . . . . and vultures hover over the whole swamp . . . . . . and the young man sees things when he goes out on one occasion . . . . . . but I needn't say more. You can see what sort of a yarn it is, and I shall certainly send it when it is done; unless, as I say, it comes to an odd and peculiarly unacceptable length. Perhaps I'll send it anyway.

But I see that I've rattled this letter out to unconscionable lengths—for which I trust you'll duly forgive me. I hope my various remarks may have buried in them some grains of sense which will answer for intelligent suggestions, though as a practical planner I never was very notable. I certainly wish you the very best of luck with WEIRD TALES, and hope every modification may develop in the right direction; though I realise very fully all the difficulties besetting any experiment of the sort. Is it ethical and possible to get in touch with writers in other magazines? In thinking over my old ALL-STORY reading, and newer specimens brought to my attention, I recall several people who did very fair work—and one case of actual excellence. This last is a writer signing himself A. Merritt, who some five years ago had a novelette in the ALL-

STORY called "The Moon Pool". The power of dark and titanic suggestion in this unexplained mystery was enormous; and I was not surprised when the thing came out in book form, with two errors of astronomical nature removed. Later Merritt had two more things in the All-Story, both inferior, and showing the devitalising pressure of the cheap popular-magazine ideal. Given a free hand, I feel that this writer could snap back into his old mood and beat any other weird author in the current magazine field; and I wish there were a way of getting in touch with him. Another man with promise is Philip M. Fisher, Jr., who had a fine thing in a recent ALL-STORY, spoiled only by a tame ending obviously designed to suit the gentle Bob Davis. Told to let the human race go to hell, Fisher could accomplish wonders. His tale was called "Fungus Island".[20] Then there were some old-timers whom I recall only dimly. Victor Rousseau was an ALL-STORY star of the first magnitude, who wrote at least one noxiously powerful thing called "The Sea-Demons".[21] Street and Smith in 1919 published a magazine called THE THRILL BOOK, which although I unfortunately never saw it, is spoken of very highly by those who did see it. Some of its writers must be useful hands to have around WEIRD TALES, and I think they would be worth looking up unless my informant greatly exaggerates. This same informant, by the way, is quite certain that the best story in the November WEIRD TALES is pilfered word for word from a story in that magazine—"The Crawling Death", by P. A. Connolly.[22] I think he wrote Mr. Baird about it, and he is still uncertain whether it was an out-and-out steal, or a case of the same writer selling his work twice on the chance that THE THRILL BOOK was too short-lived to be remembered.

But I certainly have rambled enough! I shall be very glad to see the cheque when it comes, though well knowing that my own straits are shared more or less by everybody else all along the line! I hope the difficulty of payment doesn't deter any first-rate writers from contributing . . . . I suggested to Mr. Baird that it might have exactly the opposite effect, scaring off the mercenaries, and leaving those artistic writers who draw horror for horror's sake!

With all good wishes and appreciations, believe me,

most sincerely yours,

H P Lovecraft

P.S. A new pictorial artist will work wonders for W.T. There is a special technique to weird drawing—a sort of sinister, mocking approach to conventional design & a subtle grotesquerie & distortion. The best example I know of is S. H. Sime, who illustrates the standard editions of Dunsany's books.

Notes

1. I.e., *WT* and *Detective Tales*.
2. Isa-Belle Manzer's "The Transparent Ghost" (*WT,* February, March, and April

1924) was either a parody or a poorly written story that Edwin Baird published in order to make fun of the author and of bad writing in general. The first installment appeared along with HPL's "The Hound."

3. Henneberger fired Baird after the April issue appeared and offered the position to HPL, largely based on HPL's comments on magazine editorship in this letter. He replaced Baird with Farnsworth Wright.

4. Many of HPL's comments as expressed here were repeated in the essay "The Professional Incubus" (*National Amateur*, March 1924; *CE* 2).

5. I.e., C. M. Eddy, Jr. At least four stories that HPL revised for him appeared in *WT*.

6. Burton Peter Thom (1874–1933), author of the treatises *Syphilis* (1922), *Hygeia; or, Disease and Evolution* (1926), and *Dust to Life: The Scientific Story of Creation* (1929). He published three stories in *WT* in 1923–24.

7. Rud (1893–1942) had published a novel, *The Second Generation* (1923).

8. Paul Suter, "Beyond the Door" (*WT*, April 1923); M. L. Humphreys, "The Floor Above" (*WT*, May 1923); Anthony M. Rud, "Ooze" (*WT*, March 1923); Seabury Quinn, "The Phantom Farmhouse" (*WT*, October 1923).

9. March 1923. It was the only story Holmes published in *WT*, although he previously appeared in *Black Cat* and *Black Mask*.

10. The poem did not appear in *WT*. It was first published in Long's poetry collection *The Goblin Tower* (1935).

11. HPL may be referring to the sketch "Marsh-Mad: A Nightmare" (*Philosopher*, December 1920; rpt. in *Letters to Alfred Galpin and Others* 404–6), written in 1918, when Galpin was 17.

12. *The Terrific Register* (1823–25), a weekly magazine published in London that purported to be a "Record of Crimes, Judgments, Providencies, and Calamities."

13. "Nemesis."

14. The family of Harry Houdini (Ehrich Weiss) had settled in Appleton in 1878 after emigrating from Budapest.

15. The article "The Spirit Fakers of Hermannstadt" appeared as a two-part serial in the March and April 1924 issues of *WT*. Presumably it was ghostwritten. The column "Ask Houdini" appeared in the issues of March, April, and May/June/July 1924.

16. Robert H. Davis (1869–1942) was managing editor of the *Argosy All-Story Weekly* when HPL submitted "The Rats in the Walls" to him in the fall of 1923. Davis's superior, Matthew White, Jr. (1847–1940), editor of *Argosy* 1886–1928), was even more dead set against it.

17. HPL wrote fewer than 500 words of this "novel."

18. By William Beckford.

19. It does not appear as if HPL ever began this work.

20. Philip M. Fisher, Jr. (1891–1973), "Fungus Isle" (*Argosy All-Story Weekly*, 27 October 1923).

21. Victor Rousseau (pseud. of Avigdor Rousseau Emanuel, 1879–1960), "The Sea Demons" (*All-Story Weekly*, 1–22 January 1916); published as a book in 1924.

22. P. A. Connolly, "The Crawling Death" (*WT*, November 1923). The "plagiarized" (actually revised) story is Connolly's own "Crawling Hands" (*Thrill Book* 1, No. 6 [1 May 1919] and 1, No. 7 [1 June 1919]).

Edwin Baird, Weird Tales' *first editor*

Letters to Edwin Baird

[1]   [*WT*]¹

[c. May 1923]

My Dear Sir:

Having a habit of writing weird, macabre, and fantastic stories for my own amusement, I have lately been simultaneously hounded by nearly a dozen well-meaning friends into deciding to submit a few of these Gothic horrors to your newly-founded periodical. The decision is herewith carried out. Enclosed are five tales written between 1917 and 1923.²

Of these the first two are probably the best. If they be unsatisfactory, the rest need not be read.... "The Statement of Randolph Carter" is, in the main, an actual dream experienced on the night of December 21–22, 1919;³ the characters being myself (Randolph Carter) and my friend, Samuel Loveman, the poet and editor of *Twenty-One Letters of Ambrose Bierce.*

I have no idea that these things will be found suitable, for I pay no attention to the demands of commercial writing. My object is such pleasure as I can obtain from the creation of certain bizarre pictures, situations, or atmospheric effects; and the only reader I hold in mind is myself.

My models are invariably the older writers, especially Poe, who has been my favourite literary figure since early childhood. Should any miracle impel you to consider the publication of my tales, I have but one condition to offer; and that is that no excisions be made. If the tale cannot be printed as written, down to the very last semicolon and comma, it must gracefully accept rejection. Excision by editors is probably one reason why no living American author has a real prose style.... But I am probably safe, for my MSS. are not likely to win your consideration. "Dagon" has been rejected by [*The Black Cat*], to which I sent it under external impulsion⁴—much as I am sending you the enclosed. This magazine sent me a beautifully tinted and commendably impersonal rejection slip....

I like *Weird Tales* very much, though I have seen only the April number. Most of the stories, of course, are more or less commercial—or should I say conventional?—in technique, but they all have an enjoyable angle. "Beyond the Door" by Paul Suter, seems to me the most truly touched with the elusive quality of original genius—though "A Square of Canvas", by Anthony M. Rud, would be a close second if not so reminiscent in denouement of Balzac's "Le Chef d'Oeuvre Inconnu"⁵—as I recall it across a lapse of years, without a copy at hand. However, one doesn't expect a very deep thrill in this sophisticated and tradesman-minded age. Arthur Machen is the only living man I know of who can stir truly profound and spiritual horror.

Notes

1. Text taken from *WT* 2, No. 2 (September 1923): 80, 82.

2. See HPL to James F. Morton (3 May 1923): "Once again I've followed a Mortonian tip . . . and have slipped *Weird Tales* five of my hell-beaters" (*Letters to James F. Morton* 40). The stories were "Dagon" (1917), "The Statement of Randolph Carter" (1919), "Facts concerning the Late Arthur Jermyn and His Family" (1920), "The Cats of Ulthar" (1920), and "The Hound" (1922).

3. See HPL to the Gallomo, 11 December 1919 (*Miscellaneous Letters* 77–79).

4. That is, at the urging of James F. Morton; see letter referred to above.

5. Anthony M. Rud, "A Square of Canvas" (*WT*, April 1923). Honoré de Balzac, "Le Chef d'oeuvre inconnu" (*Artiste*, August 1831; in Balzac's *Etudes philosophiques* [1837]); usually translated into English under the title "The Unknown Masterpiece." The story hints at a painting whose central figure (a beautiful woman) comes to life. In Rud's story an elderly painter in a sanitarium tells a young woman about the dire effects that his work as a painter has had on his psyche.

[2] 　　[*WT*][1]

[c. June 1923]

Dear Mr. Baird:

　　　　　I should apologise if my former letter seemed to tax *Weird Tales* with seeking conventional material. Such was not my intention in any way. I only meant that I presumed you would not wish too subtle or cryptical material for presentation to the general public. There is a difference between mere originality and delicate symbolism, or hideously nebulous adumbration. How many American readers outside the frankly "high-brow" class, for example, would find any pleasure or coherent impression in Arthur Machen's "The White People", or in the fantastic passage of the author's *Hill of Dreams*? In a word, I take it that *Weird Tales* wants definite stories, with a maximum of plot, tension of situation, explosive climax, and statement rather than too elusive suggestion—this rather than the Baudelairian prose-poem of spiritual Satanism, where chiselled phrase, lyrical tone, colour, and an opiate luxuriance of exotic imagery form the chief sources of macabre impression. . . .

　　I lately read the May *Weird Tales,* and congratulate you on Mr. Humphreys' "The Floor Above" (for a moment I had a shiver which the author didn't intend—I thought he was going to use an idea which I am planning to use myself! But it wasn't so, after all), which is a close second to my favourite, "Beyond the Door". Evidently my tastes run to the architectural! "Penelope" is clever—but Holy Pete! If the illustrious Starrett's ignorance of astronomy is an artfully conceived attribute of his character's whimsical narrative, I'll say he's right there with the verisimilitude![2] I wrote monthly astronomical articles for the daily press between 1906 and 1918, and have a vast affection for the celestial spheres.[3]

Some day I may send you a possible filler, beginning:

> "Through the ghoul-guarded gateways of slumber,
>   Past the wan-moon'd abysses of night,
> I have liv'd o'er my lives without number,
>   I have sounded all things with my sight—
> And I struggle and shriek ere the daybreak, being driven to madness with fright."[4]

. . . . .

I shall venture "Dagon" as a sort of test of my stuff in general. If you don't care for this, you won't care for anything else of mine. . . . It is not that "Dagon" is the best of my tales, but that it is perhaps the most direct and least subtle in its "punch"; so that for popular publication it is most likely to please most. In copying it I have touched up one or two crude spots—it having been written in 1917, directly after a lull of nine years in my fiction-writing.[5] Naturally I was a bit rusty in the management of the prose. A friend of mine—Clark Ashton Smith, the California poet of horror, madness, and morbid beauty—shewed this yarn to George Sterling, who declared he liked it very much, though suggesting (absurdly enough, as I view it!) that I have the monolith topple over and kill the "thing" . . . a piece of advice which makes me feel that poets should stick to their sonneteering. . . .[6]

My love of the weird makes me eager to do anything I can to put good material in the path of a magazine which so gratifyingly cultivates that favourite element. I shall await with interest the next issues, with the tales you mention, and am meanwhile trying to get the opening number through a newsdealer. I am sure the venture will elicit some notable contributions as its fame spreads—and the extent of that fame may be judged from the fact that people in Massachusetts, New York, Ohio, and California have been equally prompt in calling my attention to it and urging me to try my luck![7]

Notes

1. Text taken from *WT* 2, No. 3 (October 1923): 82.

2. Vincent Starrett, "Penelope" (*WT*, May 1923).

3. These included articles for the *Pawtuxet Valley Gleaner* (July 1906–08?), the [Providence] *Tribune* (August 1906–June 1908), the [Providence] *Evening News* (January 1914–May 1918), and the *Asheville* [NC] *Gazette-News* (February–May? 1915).

4. "Nemesis." *WT* later published the entire poem.

5. The story was first published in the *Vagrant* (November 1919). Some divergences between that appearance and that in *WT* include the substitution of "the Hun" for "the Kaiser" in paragraph 2 and "continuous" for "unbroken" in paragraph 4.

6. In a letter to Smith, George Sterling (1869–1926), Smith's poetic mentor, had said of "Dagon": "I've a suggestion to make—a valuable one, I think. The tale is disappointing at its climax, because there's not enough detail, enough suspense, enough action. It's all over in ten seconds, like a rabbit's amour. My advice is that he have the monster appear, approach the monolith with horrible sounds of worship, and prostrate itself. Then have the mire quake and Dagon fall upon the monster, slaying it, just as other heads of its kind rise from the slime" (*DS* 52n3). HPL makes reference to his comments in a letter to Frank Belknap Long (7 October 1923), saying he made "some very . . . unflattering allusions to Messrs. Vincent Starrett & George Sterling. Grandpa'll have to be careful what he writes to this Baird person, for the latter seems to have the repeating habit to a very alarming degree. If Starrett & Sterling don't start out after their Grandpa Theobald with stilettos & automatics, it'll be merely because they don't believe in bothering to swat small skeeters" (*SL* 1.253–54).

7. The colleagues are Charles W. Smith of Massachusetts, James F. Morton of New York, Samuel Loveman of Ohio, and Clark Ashton Smith of California.

[3]   [*WT*]¹

[c. October 1923]

My dear Baird:

I was exceedingly pleased with the appearance of "Dagon", which seems virtually free from misprints, and which has a particularly excellent illustration. You can't imagine how relieved I was to see that drawing, for there is always such danger of a hasty sketch which either literally or subtly belies the text, or perhaps cheapens the whole thing by poor style or technique. The "Dagon" illustration delighted me; for not only is it very good, but it carries out the conception of the story as though projected out of my own imagination.² Thanks, too, for the favourable send-off in "The Eyrie". I hope, though, that Messrs. Starrett and Sterling won't start gunning for me because of the allusions I made in those letters! It so happens that I have a particular respect for both of these gentlemen in their respective provinces! Starrett is practically the American introducer of my revered idol Machen, whilst Sterling upholds almost single-handed the sane tradition in American poetry.

Assuming that your readers won't hand me a "razz" which discourages future contributions, I am sending along a third story to follow "The P. in the H." This is one of those you had before in single-spaced form, now neatly retyped by a gifted young man whose acquaintance I have lately made, and who tells me he has had considerable correspondence with you.³

I haven't fully read the October *Weird Tales,* but I think it is going to prove a very attractive issue, judging from "The Phantom Farmhouse", by Seabury Quinn, which I liked exceedingly. There is a maturity to this tale which seems annoyingly absent from much popular magazine fiction.⁴ I like the idea of reprinting old weird classics—it is surprising to discover how many persons have failed to read certain noted standbys. I have many such lacunae—for example, I have never read F. Marion Crawford's "Upper Berth", which you are about to use, much to my gratification.[5]

Every once in a while I discover some weird masterpiece by an author either wholly unknown or unknown in America, which I wish could be popularised. Just now I am enthusiastic about a tale called "The House of Sounds", by M. P. Shiel, which occurs in a book of short stories named after the first one, "The Pale Ape", and published by T. Werner Laurie, Clifford's Inn, London. This is the most haunting thing I have read in a decade—a creeping horror and menace trickling down the centuries on a sub-Arctic island off the coast of Norway, where, amidst he sweep of daemon winds and the ceaseless din of hellish waves and cataracts, a vengeful dead man built a brazen tower of terror. It is vaguely like—yet infinitely unlike—"The Fall of the House of Usher". I wish there were a way of getting republication rights from the publisher—for it would surely be a sensation in *Weird Tales*.

Notes

1. Text taken from *WT* 3, No. 1 (January 1924): 86, 88.
2. The illustration by William F[red] Heitman (1878–1945) depicts a man in a rowboat drifting over a vast expanse of sea.
3. Probably C. M. Eddy, Jr.
4. HPL's opinion of Quinn's work became less favorable in time as Quinn's tales (especially those featuring the detective Jules de Grandin) became more and more formulaic.
5. The story did not appear until the June 1926 issue.

[4]   [*WT*][1]

[c. late October 1923]

My dear Baird:

I was indeed glad to receive yours of the 14th, and to learn that your readers are taking kindly to my tenebrous effusions, as represented by "Dagon". I hope they'll like its successors as well—for I can certainly give them all you think they'll take! That "The Hound" merits you favour is pleasing news to me. I wrote it a year ago in New York, when I had been exploring an old Dutch cemetery in Flatbush, where the ancient gravestones are in the Dutch language, with such beginnings as "Hier Lydt" or "Hier leght begraaven". My companion was Rheinhart Kleiner (whose verse you may have seen in some of the popular magazines)[2] and when we picked some scaling red slate from one of the slabs as souvenirs, I wondered what *thing* might come to us some midnight to punish us for the wanton desecration.

And here is another horror for your approval or rejection. This thing—whose long title you can shorten to "The Late Arthur Jermyn" if the original presents typographical problems—was written about two years ago. Its origin is rather curious—and far removed from the atmosphere it suggests. Somebody had been harassing me into reading some work of the iconoclastic moderns—those young chaps who pry behind exteriors and unveil nasty hidden motives and secret stigmata—and I had nearly fallen asleep over the tame backstairs gossip of Anderson's "Winesburg, Ohio." The sainted Sherwood, as you know, laid bare the dark arcana which many whited village lives concealed; and it occurred to me that I, in my weirder medium, could probably devise some secret behind a man's ancestry which would make the worst of Anderson's disclosures sound like the annual report of a Sabbath school. Hence Arthur Jermyn. Most of those who have seen the MS. profess themselves properly horrified—all, in fact, except one chap who has travelled in Rhodesia,[3] and declares himself bound by ties of the purest and most undaunted affection to all the denizens, negro and simian alike, of the Dark Continent.

Popular authors do not and apparently cannot appreciate the fact that true art is obtainable only by rejecting normality and conventionality in toto, and approaching a theme purged utterly of any usual or preconceived point of view. Wild and "different" as they may consider their quasi-weird products, it remains a fact that the bizarrerie is on the surface alone; and that basically they reiterate the same old conventional values and motives and perspectives. Good and evil, teleological illusion, sugary sentiment, anthropocentric psychology—the usual superficial stock in trade, and all shot through with the eternal and inescapable commonplace. Take a werewolf story, for instance—who ever wrote a story from the point of view of the wolf, and sympathising strongly with the devil to whom he has sold himself? Who ever wrote one from the point of view that man is a blemish on the cosmos, which ought to be eradicated?[4] As an example—a young man I know[5] lately told me that he means to write a story about a scientist who wishes to dominate the earth, and who to accomplish his ends trains and overdevelops germs (à la Anthony Rud's "Ooze"), and leads on armies of them in the manner of the Egyptian plagues. I told him that although this theme has promise, it is made utterly commonplace by assigning the scientist a normal motive. There is nothing outré about wanting to conquer the earth; Alexander, Caesar, Napoleon, and Wilhelm II wanted to do that. Instead, I told my friend, he should conceive a man with a morbid, frantic, shuddering hatred of the life-principle itself, who wishes to extirpate from the planet every trace of biological organism, animal and vegetable alike, including himself. That would be tolerably original. But after all, originality lies within the author. One can't write a weird story of real power without perfect psychological detachment from the human scene, and a magic prism of imagination which suffuses theme and style alike with that grotesquerie and disquieting distortion characteristic of morbid vision. Only a cynic can create a horror—for behind every masterpiece of the sort must reside a driving, daemonic force that despises the human race and [its] illusions, and longs to pull them to pieces and mock them. This is true in even greater degree of pictorial artists—I wish you could get a staff of Clark Ashton Smiths to illustrate *Weird Tales!* The normal artist has conventional conceptions of line and detail, light and shade; but the macabre genius has the magic prism, and sees the world in that leeringly twisted, mockingly decorative light which gives rise to the achievements of an Aubrey Beardsley, Sidney Sime, John Martin, Gustave Doré, or—immortal of immortals—Francisco Goya y Lucientes. I wish you could get some illustrations and cover designs from Clark Ashton Smith himself—even though he isn't doing so much in that line lately as he used to do. He lacks technical assurance, but has the lurid vision to an abnormal degree.

I find Eddy rather a delight—I wish I had known him before. Next Sunday we are going on a trip which may bring you echoes in the form of horror-tales from both participants. In the northwestern part of Rhode Island there is a remote village called Chepachet, reached by a single car line with only a few cars a day. Last week Eddy was there for the first time, and at the post office overheard a conversation between two ancient rustic farmers which inspired our coming expedition. They were discussing hunting prospects, and spoke of the migration of all the rabbits and squirrels across the line into Connecticut; when one told the other that there were plenty left in the *Dark Swamp*. Then ensued a description to which Eddy listened with the utmost avidity, and which brought out the fact that in this, the smallest and most densely populated state of the Union, there exists a tract of 160 acres which has never been fully penetrated by any living man. It lies two miles from Chepachet—in a direction we do not now know, but which we will ascertain Sunday—and is reputed to be the home of very strange animals—strange at least to this part of the world, and including the dreaded "bobcat", whose half-human cries in the night are often heard by neighbouring farmers. The reason it has never been fully penetrated is that there are many treacherous potholes, and that the archaic trees grow so thickly together that passage is well-nigh impossible. The undergrowth is very thick, and even at midday the darkness is very deep because of the intertwined branches overhead. The description so impressed Eddy that he began writing a story about it—provisionally entitled "Black Noon"—on the trolley ride home. And now we are both to see it . . . we are both to go into that swamp . . . and *perhaps* to come out of it. Probably the thing'll turn out to be a clump of ill-nourished bushes, a few rain-puddles, and a couple of sparrows—but until our disillusion we are at liberty to think of the place as the immemorial lair of nightmare and unknown evil ruled by that subterranean horror that sometimes cranes its neck out of the deepest pot-holes . . . It.[6]

[. . .]

Notes

1. Text taken from *WT* 3, No. 3 (March 1924): 89–92.

2. Kleiner published largely in amateur journals, but he had a few poems in *High Life* and *Top-Notch Magazine* around this time.

3. I.e., Edward Lloyd Sechrist.

4. H. Warner Munn read this letter and then wrote "The Werewolf of Ponkert" (*WT,* July 1925), but he fundamentally misunderstood the purport of HPL's letter, depicting the werewolf as regretting his condition. A few years later he came into contact with HPL.

5. Probably Frank Belknap Long.

6. The trip was made in August 1923, but HPL and Eddy did not find the swamp. Cf. *SL* 1.250f. and Eddy's "Walks with H. P. Lovecraft" (*The Dark Brotherhood and Other Pieces* [1966], 245). Eddy's "Black Noon" was never completed, and the fragment was published in Eddy's collection *Exit into Eternity* (Providence: Oxford Press, 1973), 97–121.

[5]   [*Lovecraft at Last*]

[Hotel Kimball
Springfield, Massachusetts]
598 Angell St., Providence, R.I.
February 3, 1924.

My dear Baird:—

I was delighted to receive your two communications, and to hear that you like "Nemesis". This delight atones fairly well for the sensation of gastric depression caused by the implication that "Arthur Jermyn" is going to press as "The White Ape"! I wish I could convert you to my point of view regarding the annoying literalness and flaccidity of that latter title . . . . but all I can do is [to] say that it is the one title which I could never possibly have applied to that particular tale; that it is at war with the spirit and internal harmonies of the narrative, and clashes fearsomely with the effect of the opening paragraph. One thing—you may be sure that if I ever entitled a story "The White Ape", *there would be no ape in it.* There would be something at first taken for an ape, which would not be an ape. But how can one ever get those subtleties across? . . . . At any rate, I know I am partly to blame for this, since I voluntarily offered to shorten the original title to "Arthur Jermyn". Now, however, after seeing just what a feeling of melancholy that un-Lovecraftian caption has given me, I am returning to my original resolve that my titles must be considered as integral with the tales, and the whole rejected unless the titles also are preserved. The weakening in this case was my own, but it wasn't worth while! Thanks prodigiously for the proofreading offer, of which I shall avail myself with the utmost avidity despite the laboriousness of the process. Ambrose Bierce hated proofreading, and used to complain of the bother in letters to Samuel Loveman. He read proof for the Neale edition of his collected works.[1] Glad that "Hypnos" is coming. Are you giving me a vacation for March, or are the "Rats" to gnaw their uncanny course through that issue?

Yes indeed, I have heard from Mr. Henneberger! Cheque? Bless me, no! Such details are so vulgar! But I am told that the twin ventures DETECTIVE and WEIRD TALES have reduced the Hennebergian capital from plus eleven thousand to minus forty thousand; hence presume that I ought to be very meek and inaudible about my lesser minus . . . if minus there be in a matter of aesthetics. Henneberger seems determined to hang on to his venture till the last ditch, and shows a rugged pluck I can't but admire. He spoke of a coming reorganisation to include work from the magician Houdini and the elaboration of gruesome crime material at the expense of fiction, reducing the latter to a novel and two or three short stories per issue. I can't say that this strikes me as following the Machen or Poe tradition in art (unless Marie Roget is a keynote in Poe), but if it increases circulation and saves the magazine from annihilation, who shall quarrel too arbitrarily? At any rate, Henneberger has the right idea in savage unrestraint and departure from the conventional point of view . . . . I'll bet he'd snap up that Eddy yarn, "The Loved Dead", which is presenting such a doubtful case! But I should hardly say that H. made me any "proposition", as he intimated to you he might. The only part of his letter that brought me in was a request for a novel of 25,000 words or over, which I shall be happy to send when I finish it. I've nothing of that length complete, but after trying serial stuff for HOME BREW I experimented a bit with the novel form, and have an idea partly shaped which will probably suit Mr. H.'s requirements. It is a hideous thing whose provisional title (subject to change) is "The House of the Worm". All this apart from my big novel idea—"Azathoth"—which will be exotic and high-brow, and wholly unsuited to WEIRD TALES. By the way, I felt complimented when Henneberger expressed his opinion that my "Rats" is the best tale W.T. ever received! I wish he'd tell sister Bob Davis that!

H's curiosity about my age, habits, and personality is quite interesting . . . . a taste, I suppose, of what I should encounter if I were a celebrity! Have you read Dunsany's "Fame and the Poet"?[2] I vastly admire Dunsany. I must write my autobiography some day . . . . every mediocre, uninteresting person of late seems absolutely determined to write his autobiography, especially if he has done nothing whatsoever to warrant it. I must be pompous and colourful, and supply the element of dramatic interest where life has failed to supply it . . . . . helas! Lifelong indolence and nearly lifelong ill-health have made my annals as short and simple as those of the class who subsist on W.T. cheques! Une vie cerebrale—nothing more, if even that!

Howard Phillips Lovecraft was born on August 20, 1890, in a large Victorian house in Providence, set on a terrace amidst expansive shady grounds, and close to the fields of what was then the edge of the settled district. His ancestry was that of unmixed English gentry; quite directly on the paternal side, where his own grandfather had left Devonshire as a poorish younger son and sought fortune in the state of New York, and in a Yankeefied way maternally, his emigrant ancestor being the Reverend George Phillips, who came from Norfolk in 1630 with Mr. Winthrop's colony, buried his first wife in Salem in the same year, and finally settled in Watertown, rearing a numerous posterity and earning from Cotton Mather the not unfulsome epitaph: "Hic Jacet GEORGIUS PHILLIPPI, Vir Incomparabilis, nisi SAMUELUM genuisset".[3] It is the cankering sorrow of my life, that I am descended through another son than the more than incomparable Samuel! At an early age—an age of very few months, in fact—the future master of literature emigrated to the Province of the Massachusetts-Bay, taking his parents with him on account of a desire of his father's to transact business—commonplace thought—in the village of Boston. It was here that first contacts with literary people were established; for as a provisional residence the young philosopher chose that of a friend of his mother whose name is not unknown to fame, but whose finances made co-operative living a very useful expedient at that period—I refer to the late poetess Louise Imogen Guiney.[4] Oliver Wendell Holmes came not infrequently to this menage, and on one occasion (unremembered by the passenger) is said to have ridden the future WEIRD TALES disciple on his venerable knee. But such a career of promise was not for long. At the time, indeed, young Lovecraft shewed signs of considerable literary progress. Ever a nervous child, he began linguistic experiments at shortly after 1, knew his Anglo-Roman alphabet at 2, and at 2.5 was wont to astonish the suburban throng (for the Guiney castle was at Auburndale, 11 miles from Mr. Bulfinch's aureate dome whereon the cosmos rotates)[5] with poetic recitations from the dizzy eminence of a table's top. In 1893, however, his father's health passed into the decline from which it never emerged; so that Lovecraft and his mother returned to Providence, to that materno-grandpaternal roof at 454 Angell St. under which he originally beheld the solar illumination. But what was tragedy for the elder generation was nothing of the sort to the younger. The future dictator of literature was intensely attached to his grandfather, whose travels in Europe and taste for Italian art made him a varied and piquant converser, and to the whole place with its trees and terraces, fountains and stables, walks and gardens—and best of all, its proximity to the dreaming fields and mystic groves of antique New-England (now solid blocks of homes and apartment-houses) which the young sage's vibrant imagination peopled with every conceivable sort of unreal presence. Within the house was a vast array of books—the fusion of two hereditary libraries—and to this the rising aesthete turned when, at four, the ars legendi became his. By a curious

twist of taste, only old-fashion'd things and fantastic things attracted the infant marvel. Save for vivid tales of faery, and dark whisperings of the nether
world, he would read nothing without the "long ſ", ſo that his Taſte became
compleatly that of the 18th Century, and his firſt Writing (or rather hand
printing), perform'd at the Age of five, (Script came at the age of seven) hath
this ſelfſame long ſ as its moſt ſalient Characteriſtick. The child was weak,
nervous, and inclined to keep his own company after he found his voluble
conversation disrelish'd by those gentlemen of his grandfather's circle who
form'd the only persons he ever car'd to talk to. Children he dislik'd on account
of their freakishness, and their disinclination to cast their playing into coherent
narrative and dramatick channels. Further adding to his unpopularity was his
utter aloofness of opinion and independence of utterance. Born amongst orthodox Christians, he was at first a pagan and later (and still) a scientifick
sceptick. Born amongst patriotick Yankees and Sons of the Revolution and
Cincinnati, he was a dyed-in-the-wool Tory who curs'd the Fourth of July
from the age of three, and sang "God Save the King" when other folk sang
"America".* A queer duck, altogether—and so frail that formal school[ing] was
out of the question. Snatches of school appear here and there, but only
snatches. After all, a cultivated family is the best school, and I am singularly
complacent about the training this young man did not get. He did stick out
four years at high school,[6] but at the cost of a breakdown which kept him
from college and put him practically out of the world till three years ago. In
those middle years the poor devil was such a nervous wreck that he hated to
speak to any human being, or even to see or be seen by one; and every trip
down town was an ordeal. Not that he ever liked people as well as cats—it is
among the felidae that he has had his most valued friends . . . . I can assure
you that Nigger-Man is (or was, alas!) a glorious and purring reality![7] But this
whole history is one of slow impoverishment and decay. Lovecraft was born
to a household of four servants and three horses—and he has seen them all
go . . . . all of these, and the old home as well, for the death of his grandfather
with a burdened estate forced a removal to a small flat three blocks east on
the same street . . . . the flat wherein this machine is now clicking, but which
will probably go in turn during the coming spring, when finances will decree a
final disintegration landing me in all probability in New York. Events? Nothing ever happens! That is why, perhaps, my fancy goes off to explore strange
and terrible worlds. My mother was stricken in 1919, and one aunt or another
has subsequently reigned here. Around 1920–1921 my health began of itself
to effect that mending which legions of specialists had for the past thirty
years sought in vain to bring about; and I have done more travelling since
than I ever thought I should do in my lifetime. In 1920 I went for a visit to

---

*I am also a Confederate as regards the Civil War.

Boston, and slept under another roof than my own for the first time in nineteen years. The last time had been in 1901, when nervous nostalgia had forced a speedy return. My daily life is a sort of contemptuous lethargy, devoid alike of virtues or vices. I am not of the world, but an amused and sometimes disgusted spectator to it. I detest the human race and its pretences and swinishnesses—to me life is a fine art, and although I believe the universe is an automatic, meaningless chaos devoid of ultimate values or distinctions of right and wrong, I consider it most artistic to take into account the emotional heritage of our civilisation and follow the patterns which produce the least pain to delicate sensibilities. Thus, although holding the pompous and theocratic philosophy of the Puritans in the most abysmal contempt, I believe in an honour and fastidiousness of conduct which makes me act like a Puritan and earn the name of Puritan from all who are not of that dull breed of cattle themselves. I am myself—alone—as the Bard makes crook-back'd Richard say.[8] All schools of thought I hold in equal contempt.

Ah, yes—that is my history—the history of intellectual and aesthetic experience. It is damned odd that I, a nearly six-foot chalk-white Nordic type—the type of the master-conqueror and man of action—should be as much of a brooding analyst and dabbler in impressions as any ox-eyed, sawed-off Mediterranean brunet. My hair and eyes are dark, though—I suppose there is something of the Cymric elder Briton in me . . . . at times I have liked to think that I am part Roman, as if some provincial governor or general had left his blood in the Blessed Isle, to be later mixed with that of the Saxon and the Norman as they in their turn came. And yet it is the Nordic I most admire—I am sure I would rather be a general than a poet . . . safe preference, since I shall never be either. Futility and ineffectiveness are my keynote. I shall never amount to anything, because I don't care enough about life and the world to try. Heigho![9] I am a sceptic and an analyst by nature, and early settled into my present attitude of cynical materialism. I was instructed in the legends of Santa Claus and the bible at the age of about two, and gave to both a passive acceptance not especially distinguished either for its critical keenness or its enthusiastic comprehension. Within the next few years I added to my supernatural lore the fairy tales of Grimm and the Arabian Nights; and by the time I was five had small choice amongst these speculations so far as truth was concerned, though for attractiveness I favoured the Arabian Nights. At one time I formed a juvenile collection of Oriental pottery and objets d'art, announcing myself as a devout Mohammedan and assuming the pseudonym of "Abdul Alhazred"—which you will recognise as the author of that mythical "Necronomicon" which I drag into various of my tales. When I was six my philosophical evolution received its most aesthetically significant impulse—the dawn of Graeco-Roman thought. Always avid for faery lore, I had chanced on Hawthorne's "Wonder Book" and "Tanglewood Tales", and was enraptured by the Hellenic myths even in their Teutonised form. Then a tiny book in the private library of my elder aunt—the story of the Odyssey in "Harper's Half-Hour Series"—caught my attention. From the opening chapter I was electrified, and by the time I reached the end I was for evermore a Graeco-Roman. My Bagdad name and affiliations disappeared at once, for the magic of silks and colours faded before that of fragrant templed groves, faun-peopled meadows in the twilight, and the blue, beckoning Mediterranean that billowed mysteriously out from Hellas into the reaches of haunting wonder where dwelt Lotophagi and Laestrygonians, where Aeolus kept his winds and Circe her swine, and where in Thrinacian pastures roamed the oxen of radiant Helios. As soon as possible I procured an illustrated edition of Bulfinch's "Age of Fable", and gave all my time to the reading of the text, in which the true spirit of Hellenism is delightfully preserved, and to the contemplation of the pictures—splendid designs and half-tones of the standard classical statues and paintings of classical subjects. Before long I was fairly familiar with the principal Grecian myths, and had become a constant visitor at the classical art museums of Providence and Boston. I commenced a collection of small plaster casts of the Greek sculptural masterpieces, and learned the Greek alphabet and rudiments of the Latin tongue. I adopted the pseudonym of "Lucius Valerius Messala"—Roman and not Greek, since Rome had a charm all its own for me. My grandfather had travelled observingly through Italy, and delighted me with long first-hand accounts of its beauties and memorials of ancient grandeur. This aesthetic trend had its result in a philosophical way, and prompted my last flickering of religious belief. When about seven or eight I was a genuine pagan, so intoxicated with the beauty of Greece that I acquired a half-sincere belief in the old gods and nature-spirits. I have in literal truth built altars to Pan, Apollo, Diana, and Athena, and have watched for dryads and satyrs in the woods and fields at dusk. Once I firmly thought I beheld some of these sylvan creatures dancing under autumnal oaks; a kind of "religious experience"[10] as true in its way as the subjective ecstasies of any Christian .. [.] whose unimaginative emotionalism and my unemotional imaginativeness are of equal valuelessness from an intellectual point of view. If such a Christian tell me he has *felt* the reality of his Jesus or Jahveh, I can reply that I have *seen* the hoofèd Pan and the sisters of the Hesperian Phaëthusa.

But in my ninth year, as I was reading the Grecian myths in their standard poetical translations and thus acquiring unconsciously my taste for Queen-Anne English, the real foundations of my scepticism were laid. Impelled by the crude but fascinating pictures of scientific instruments in the back of Webster's Unabridged, I began to take an interest in natural philosophy and chemistry; and soon had a promising laboratory in my cellar, and a new stock of simple scientific text-books in my budding library. The books will never leave me, but the laboratory, after being transferred to this house, I

am now giving to my "Alma Mater", Hope Street high School, as final domestic dispersal becomes imminent. Ere long I was more of a scientific student than pagan dreamer. In 1897 my leading literary work was a "poem"
entitled "The Poem of Ulysses; or, The New Odyssey." In 1899 it was a
compendious treatise on chemistry in several pencil-scribbled volumes.[11] But
mythology was by no means neglected. In this period I read much in Egyptian, Hindoo, and Teutonic mythology, and tried experiments in pretending
to believe each one, to see which might contain the greatest amount of truth.
I had, it will be noted, immediately adopted the method and manner of science! Naturally, having an open and unemotional mind, I was soon a complete sceptic and materialist. My scientific studies had enlarged to include
geographical, biological, and astronomical rudiments, and I had acquired the
habit of relentless analysis in all matters. My pompous "book" called "Poemata Minora", written when I was eleven, was dedicated "To the Gods, Heroes, and Ideals of the Ancients", and harped in disillusioned, world-weary
tones on the sorrow of the pagan robbed of his antique pantheon. One of the
stanzas from my "Ode to Selene or Diana" runs as follows:

> Take heed, Diana, of my humble plea;
>   Convey me where my happiness shall last—
> Draw me against the tide of time's rough sea,
>   And let my spirit rest amidst the past.

Hitherto my philosophy had been distinctly juvenile and empirical. It was
a revolt from obvious falsities and ugliness, but involved no particular cosmic
or ethical theory. In ethical questions I had no analytical interest because I did
not realise that they were questions. I accepted Victorianism, with consciousness of many prevailing hypocrisies and aside from Sabbatarianism and supernatural matters, without dispute; never having heard of inquiries which
reached "beyond good and evil".[12] Though at times interested in reforms, notably prohibition, I was inclined to be bored by ethical casuistry; since I believed conduct to be a matter of taste and breeding, with virtue, delicacy, and
truthfulness as symbols of gentility. Of my word and honour I was inordinately proud, and would permit no reflections to be cast upon them. I
thought ethics too obvious and commonplace to be scientifically discussed,
and considered philosophy solely in its relation to truth and beauty. I was,
and still am, pagan to the core. Regarding man's place in Nature, and the
structure of the universe, I was as yet unawakened. This awakening was to
come in the winter of 1902–3, when astronomy asserted its supremacy
amongst my studies.

The most poignant sensations of my existence are those of 1896, when I
discovered the Hellenic world, and of 1902, when I discovered the myriad
suns and worlds of infinite space. Sometimes I think the latter event the

greater, for the grandeur of that growing conception of the universe still excites a thrill hardly to be duplicated. I made of astronomy my principal scientific study, obtaining larger and larger telescopes, collecting astronomical books to the number of 61, and writing copiously on the subject in the form of special and monthly articles in the local daily press. As I mentioned in the preceding letter, my intention was to become a professor of astronomy. By my thirteenth birthday I was thoroughly impressed with man's impermanence and insignificance, and by my seventeenth, about which time I did some particularly detailed writing on the subject, I had formed in all essential particulars my present pessimistic cosmic views. The futility of all existence began to impress and oppress me; and my references to human progress, formerly hopeful, began to decline in enthusiasm. Always partial to antiquity, I allowed myself to originate a sort of one-man cult of retrospective suspiration. Realistic analysis, favoured by history and by diffusive scientific leanings which now embraced Darwin, Haeckel, Huxley, and various other pioneers, was checked by my aversion for realistic literature. In fiction I was devoted to the phantasy of Poe and his congeners; in poetry and essays to the elegant formalism and conventionality of the eighteenth century. I was not at all wedded to what illusions I retained. My attitude has always been cosmic, and I looked on man as if from another planet. He was merely an interesting species presented for study and classification. I had strong prejudices and partialities in many fields, but could not help seeing the race in its cosmic futility as well as in its terrestrial importance. By the time I was of age, I had scant faith in the world's betterment, and felt a decreasing interest in its cherished pomps and prides. By the age of 25 I was well on the road to my present cynicism—a cynicism marked by a contemptuous indifference toward mankind in the aggregate, but tempered with an ironic pity for his eternal tragedy of aspirations beyond the possibility of fulfilment.

As I now approach thirty-four I have no particular wishes, save to perceive facts and to receive refined and agreeable aesthetic impressions.* My objectivity, always marked, is now paramount and unopposed; so that there is nothing I am not *willing* to believe. I no longer really desire anything but oblivion, and am thus ready to discard any gilded illusion or accept any unpalatable fact with perfect equanimity. I can at last concede willingly that the wishes, hopes, and values of humanity are matters of total indifference to the bland, blind cosmic mechanism. Happiness I recognise as an ethereal phantom whose simulacrum comes fully to none and even partly to but few, and

---

*Just now my chief interest is 18th century decoration & Colonial architecture. Providence is full of it, & I wander appreciatively among buildings dating from 1750, 1762, 1770, 1773, 1775, 1783, & so on. I am planning an essay on Old Providence which may distend to the proportions of a book before I am through with it. It will strive to recall visually the 18th century scene.

whose position as the goal of all human striving is a grotesque mixture of farce and tragedy. That is the essence of H. P. Lovecraft. A very queer old gentleman, as all dashing and arrogant moderns will agree!

Pray don't hurry to read those other verses I sent. None are as good as "Nemesis", and could scarcely hope to rise above the filler class at best. Here are a few more of their little brothers . . . . also to be read only at leisure. In my last epistle I said you might throw them away if of no use, but upon mature reflection I'll modify that. Since I've bothered to make fresh copies, I guess I'll hang on to the latter; wherefore I will ask you to return the discarded jingles both of this shipment and the last—in an envelope herewith provided. I'm no poet—as I copy these I see that I am generally harping on one idea, wholly subservient to the Poe influence, and not infrequently repeating myself to all intents and purposes—as if somebody's praise of one piece prompted me to try to duplicate the feat. Heigho, 's' a grea' life!

As to this Reading Lamp business[13]—my word! I'm half inclined to believe you've started something! Shortly after your former letter came, I mentioned your recommendation to a friend in New York—the Mrs. Sonia H. Greene whose "Horror at St. Martin's Beach" you re-named "The Invisible Monster" after I had very carefully removed Mrs. G's original title "The Nameless Monster"!—and she, knowing of my indolent habit of never getting around to anything, took it upon herself to visit the office and carry a lot of my stuff (both manuscripts and discursive letters) for the editor or editors to look over. She found the enterprise in the hands of a courteous, obliging, and literary palaeoparthenoid lady yclept Miss Tucker, whose amiability extended to the length of inviting Mrs. G. to a dinner to meet the actress Mme. Petrova[14] and some Russian princess whose name would be too much for this 1906 rebuilt Remington. But to return to the main thread—this dictatress or virgin of the lamp was very favourably impressed with my junk—so much so, Mrs. G. writes, that her reaction might almost be termed enthusiasm. And as a result she told Mrs. G. that she intended to write me about some reviewing proposition . . . . which I shall certainly welcome if it means a more than theoretical augmentation of my fiscal balance. Thus your kind suggestion may possibly result in my gathering a few berries in a new pasture—though advance optimism is never judicious. At all events I thank you . . . . and thank you also for the reading-lamp bracket enclosed in yours of the 28th. If I ever nail that 25-fish bevy of biblia (it's only $25.00 worth—the 50 was the combined sum of three separate prizes!)[15] I shall begin my pickings (if so permitted) with the complete works (as far as published) of Arthur Machen. Slave as I am to his daemoniac spell, I don't own a bally line he ever wrote—for the Knopf reprints are all affairs of too recent date to coincide with my bygone days of financial solvency. Certe, nullas bananas hodie habemus.[16]

By the way, I hope you can pardon my garrulousness today. What moves me to such extremes must be the influence of the recrudescent Muse—for though I told you my verses were all incidents of a buried past, I neglected to mention the one corner of the grave I am forced to keep open. Long years ago I formed the habit of writing annual birthday verses to a very old gentleman of my acquaintance, a poet named Jonathan E. Hoag. He, as a co-worker in the domain of doggerel, relished my fraternal tributes very much; so that I came to feel that I could not stop without offending him. Then Parnassian disillusion came—and I put the Babylonish rebeck behind me for ever . . . . for ever, I say, save for this one annual misdemeanour, which I could not forego lest I hurt a gentle spirit now turning ninety-three. Feby. 10 is the day, so I have just been smitin' the bloomin' lyre in ancient fashion . . . with the following disastrous result, which you, by the way, will be the first to behold:

TO MR. HOAG, UPON HIS 93D BIRTHDAY

Warm eastern winds, with Grecian perfumes fragrant,
　　Play soft about thee tho' the plain be cold,
And music trembles from each airy vagrant
　　That hails thee: "Ninety-three but never old!"

Breezes from green Cithaeron call thee brother,
　　Bearing the glow of many an ancient sun;
Arcadian airs to thee and one another
　　Whisper the lore that makes ye all as one.

From Naxian shores a purple breath diurnal
　　Brings dreams of vineyards basking sweet at noon.
Whilst Latmos sends a gift of youth supernal,
　　Filch'd from the dower of an enamour'd moon.

And ev'ry gentle wanderer aërial
　　Is vocal with the chant of elder choirs;
With songs of love divine and immaterial,
　　Bright with the fervour of forgotten fires.

The Delian string for thee again is sounded,
　　And Faunus wakes once more the oaten reed;
Old haunting tunes, of faery spells compounded,
　　Distil thee flow'rs from a nymphaean mead.

Crystal and roseal, azure, gold, and argent,
　　Flow'rs of a ripen'd wizardry of sight;
Flow'rs that adorn the visionary margent
　　Of some celestial stream or lake of light.

These dost thou ever, dreamer Apollonian,
　　Weave in gay wreaths to deck our drear abode;
As on thy brow the nobler crown Aonian
　　Sits to reward thee for each joy bestow'd.

Year upon year comes laden to thy portal,
　　Swelling thy store with riches rare and pure;
Riches of mem'ry and of grace immortal,
　　Hoarded for thee in antique vaults obscure.

So now as three and ninety years exalt thee
　　To heights that winds ethereal touch and charm,
No pow'r of grosser earth may chain or halt thee,
　　Or any fate thy singing spirit harm.

Kin of the aeons, rapt with visions olden,
　　Flaming with sight of loveliness sublime,
'Tis thine to make all things about thee golden—
　　Inspir'd, unfading, and unbow'd with Time!

I edited Mr. Hoag's one volume of verses, and wrote the critical and biographical preface—without pay, for friendship's sake. He's a delightful old chap, and will probably have some verses of his own about the birthday in his local paper. But gawd, how I ramble! Believe me, Sir, I am cover'd with confuſion and conſum'd with contrition!

　　Ever yr moſt obt Servt

HPL

Notes

1. Bierce's *Collected Works* (1909–12) were published in 12 volumes by the Neale Publishing Co., run by Walter Neale.

2. Lord Dunsany's play *Fame and the Poet* (*Atlantic Monthly*, August 1911; in *Plays of Near and Far*, 1922) tells of how Fame comes to a poet but is only interested in mundane aspects of his life.

3. "Here lies George Phillips, an incomparable man if he had not begat Samuel."

4. It appears that HPL and his parents stayed in the home of poet Louise Imogen Guiney (1861–1920) in the winter of 1892–93. She was a friend of the noted literary figure Oliver Wendell Holmes (1809–1894).

5. HPL refers to the Massachusetts State House (1798) in Boston, designed by Charles Bulfinch. Boston is known as "The Hub" (hence the name of the local amateur journalism group, "The Hub Club"), short for "The Hub of the Universe" (or "of the Solar System"). See Oliver Wendell Holmes, "The Autocrat of the Breakfast-Table," *Atlantic Monthly* (April 1854): "[The] Boston State-House is the hub of the so-

lar system. You couldn't pry that out of a Boston man, if you had the tire of all creation straightened out for a crowbar."

6. In fact, HPL attended only three years of high school, sitting out nearly the entirety of the 1905–06 term.

7. HPL refers to the fact that he owned a cat named Nigger-Man, a name he then used for a cat in "The Rats in the Walls."

8. "I am myself alone." Spoken by Richard III in Shakespeare's *3 Henry VI* 5.6.83.

9. Beginning with the following sentence, HPL copies much of the text of his essay "A Confession of Unfaith."

10. HPL perhaps alludes to William James's *Varieties of Religious Experience* (1902), a covert defense of Christian orthodoxy under the guise of a sociological study of religious belief.

11. These unpublished treatises still exist at JHL under the titles *Chemistry; Chemistry, Magic, & Electricity; Chemistry III;* and *Chemistry IV*.

12. An allusion to Friedrich Nietzsche's *Beyond Good and Evil (Jenseits von Gut und Böse,* 1886).

13. HPL refers to The Reading Lamp, an agency (and apparently also a magazine, for which HPL wrote at least one review [not located]) run by Gertrude Tucker (evidently an unmarried elderly woman, hence HPL's reference to her as a "palaeoparthenoid" [= old maid]). Tucker had attempted to find literary work for HPL, but was unsuccessful.

14. Olga Petrova (stage name of Muriel Harding, 1884–1975), a British-American stage and film actress and playwright.

15. In a letter to his aunt Lillian D. Clark (4–6 November 1924), HPL says that he had received $60 in credit from Henneberger at Scribner's bookstore. With it he bought 19 books, one for Frank Belknap Long (*Letters to Family and Family Friends* 184–85).

16. Latin for the title of the recent novelty song "Yes! We Have No Bananas" by Frank Silver and Irving Cohn from the Broadway revue *Make It Snappy* (1922).

In the editorial offices of Weird Tales *in Chicago.*
William R. Sprenger, secretary-treasurer; Farnsworth Wright, editor;
Henry Kuttner, writer and agent, Robert Bloch, writer.

Letters to Farnsworth Wright

[1]   [*WT*][1]

[c. December 1925]

I have lately read your December issue, and believe the general qualitative level is kept commendably high—we don't find any of the frank crudities that marked the earlier issues. Long's "The Sea Thing" strikes me as the best tale, with Owen's "The Fan" as a good second.[2]

Notes

1. Text taken from *WT* 7, No. 2 (February 1926): 273.
2. HPL is commenting on stories by Frank Belknap Long and Frank Owen in the December 1925 issue of *WT*.

[2]   [AHT]

10 Barnes St.,
Providence, R.I.,
July 5, 1927

My dear Mr. Wright:—

Yours of the 1st. arrived this morning. Wandrei has written me of his long and pleasant call at the *Weird Tales* headquarters, and was very complimentary in his description of those whom he met there. He is now in New York, and I expect to see him here on or about the tenth. I shall try to induce him to stay in New England long enough to imbibe some of our fascinating scenery and antiquities—including the prototypes of "Kingsport" and "Arkham", and the hellish North End district in Boston which forms the locale of "Pickman's Model".[1]

In accordance with your suggestion I am re-submitting "The Call of Cthulhu",[2] though possibly you will still think it a trifle too bizarre for a clientele who demand their weirdness in name only, and who like to keep both feet pretty solidly on the ground of the known and the familiar. As I said some time ago, I doubt if my work—and especially my later products—would "go" very well with the sort of readers whose reactions are represented in the "Eyrie". The general trend of the yarns which seem to suit the public is that of essential normality of outlook and simplicity of point of view—with thoroughly conventional human values and motives predominating, and with brisk action of the best-seller type as an indispensable attribute. The weird element in such material does not extend far into the fabric—it is the artificial weirdness of the fireside tale and the Victorian ghost story, and remains external camouflage even in the seemingly wildest of the "interplanetary" con-

59

coctions. You can see this sort of thing at its best in Seabury Quinn, and at its worst in the general run of contributors. It is exactly what the majority want—for if they were to see a *really* weird tale they wouldn't know what it's all about. This is quite obvious from the way they object to the *reprints,* which in many cases have brought them the genuine article.

Now all my tales are based on the fundamental premise that common human laws and interests and emotions have no validity or significance in the vast cosmos-at-large. To me there is nothing but puerility in a tale in which the human form—and the local human passions and conditions and stand-ards—are depicted as native to other worlds or other universes. To achieve the essence of real externality, whether of time or space or dimension, one must forget that such things as organic life, good and evil, love and hate, and all such local attributes of a negligible and temporary race called mankind, have any existence at all. Only the human scenes and characters must have human qualities. *These* must be handled with unsparing *realism,* (*not* catch-penny *romanticism*) but when we cross the line to the boundless and hideous unknown—the shadow-haunted *Outside*—we must remember to leave our humanity and terrestrialism at the threshold.

So much for theory. In practice, I presume that few commonplace readers would have any use for a story written on these psychological principles. They want their conventional best-seller values and motives kept paramount throughout the abysses of apocalyptic vision and extra-Einsteinian chaos, and would not deem an "interplanetary" tale in the least interesting if it did not have its Martian (or Jovian or Venerian or Saturnian) heroine fall in love with the young voyager from Earth, and thereby incur the jealousy of the inevitable Prince Kongros (or Zeelar or Hoshgosh or Norkog) who at once proceeds to usurp the throne etc.; or if it did not have its Martian (or etc.) nomenclature fol-low a closely terrestrial pattern, with an Indo-Germanic '-a' name for the Prin-cess, and something disagreeable and Semitic for the villain. Now I couldn't grind out that sort of junk if my life depended on it. If I were writing an "inter-planetary" tale it would deal with beings organised very differently from mun-dane mammalia, and obeying motives wholly alien to anything we know upon Earth—the exact degree of alienage depending, of course, on the scene of the tale; whether laid in the solar system, the visible galactic universe outside the solar system, or the *utterly unplumbed* gulfs still father out—the nameless vorti-ces of never-dreamed-of strangeness, where form and symmetry, light and heat, even matter and energy themselves, may be unthinkably metamor-phosed or totally wanting. I have merely got at the edge of this in "Cthulhu", where I have been careful to avoid terrestrialism in the few linguistic and no-menclatural specimens from Outside which I present. All very well—but will the readers stand for it? That's all they're likely to get from me in the future—except when I deal with definitely terrestrial scenes—and I am the last one to urge the acceptance of material of doubtful value to the magazine's particular purpose. Even when I deal with the mundanely weird, moreover, I shan't be likely to stress the popular artificial values and emotions of cheap fiction.

However—you can best judge this matter from some recent samples of my scribbling; wherefore I'll enclose, purely for your personal perusal, (although gawd knows you can print 'em if you like, since nobody else is likely to do so!) two characteristic neo-Lovecraftian outbursts—"The Silver Key" and "The Strange High House in the Mist".[3] I fancy you won't find much of professional interest in 'em—so that you may be sure your readers aren't missing much! When I do write any more things with a fairly earthly "slant", I'll certainly send them along, but my winter fiction crop consisted only of two novelettes too long for any but serial use, (and I haven't had the energy to type them yet, either!) whilst this spring and summer I've been too busy with revisory and kindred activities to write more than one tale—which, oddly enough, was accepted at once by *Amazing Stories* despite its full possession of the nonterrestrial qualities so characteristic of my recent work.[4] Toward autumn I hope to arrange for some writing leisure, and shall then 'get off my chest' several plots which have been insistently clamouring for expression lately. Among these are at least two which I shall try on you—though they won't seem much like the recent *Weird Tales* type. Which reminds me that in the latest (July) issue I found Hugh Irish's "Mystery of Sylmare" closest to my notion of a weird tale, with R. Ernest Dupay's "Edge of the Shadow" as a not very close second.[5] Munn's tale was good, but he seems to be getting the popular fiction 'bug'. Has he shown you his ninety-two page sequel to the story—"The Werewolf's Daughter"?[6] And by the way let me congratulate you on your new illustrator Rankin. He's the best yet!

Glad to hear of the improving rates—they ought to attract new cohorts of able authors. I feel sure that scores of 'top-notchers' would be glad to write weird stories if they could find any place to market them on their own terms.

With every good wish, and hoping the enclosed won't bore you too badly,

I remain—most sincerely yrs—

H. P. Lovecraft.

P.S. My history of weird fiction[7] is all in type, and I have told Cook (whose private publication will contain it) to be sure to send you a copy. He is later going to issue my "Shunned House" as a little book uniform with Long's poems.[8]

[P.]P.S. Besides my visit from Wandrei, I'm expecting a visit from young Long and his parents on the 21st. If Wandrei can stay over until then, we'll have quite a weird conclave beneath my lowly rooftree! Wandrei is a great boy—he has had some poignant imaginative glimpses *Outside* which few living writers have shared, and will undoubtedly develop remarkably. In sheer, daemonic extramundaneness he excels anybody I know except Clark Ashton Smith.

Notes

1. Wandrei, in the course of hitchhiking from St. Paul, MN, to Providence, stopped at the *WT* offices in Chicago around June 20. He visited HPL in Providence on 12–29 July 1927. When they visited Boston, they were dismayed to see that the ancient houses and warehouses of the city's North End (which HPL described the previous year in "Pickman's Model") had recently been demolished.

2. HPL surely had never heard the following testimony from Wandrei: "I casually worked in a reference to a story, 'The Call of Cthulhu,' that Lovecraft was revising and finishing and which I thought was a wonderful tale. But I added that for some reason or other, Lovecraft had talked about submitting it to other magazines. I said I just couldn't understand why he was apparently planning to by-pass *Weird Tales* unless he was seeking to broaden his markets or widen his reading public. None of this was true, but I could see that my fanciful account took effect, in the way Wright began to fidget and show signs of agitation." Donald Wandrei, "Lovecraft in Providence" (1959), in Joshi and Schultz, *Ave atque Vale* 276. Wandrei came to read "The Call of Cthulhu" because Clark Ashton Smith had sub-lent the ms. to him. Wandrei writes as though HPL had not previously submitted the story to *WT*, but HPL had told him *WT* rejected the story. See also *DS* 134.

3. FW initially rejected both stories, but later accepted them.

4. "The Colour out of Space." HPL's comment suggests that he had not previously mentioned or submitted the story to *WT*, as some scholars have maintained.

5. *WT* characterized the stories as "the story of a conspiracy of plant life against humanity" and "a tale of the terror that hides in the night—a story of an evil entity, and the howling of dogs in the darkness."

6. H. Warner Munn's tale in the July 1927 issue was "The Return of the Master." "The Werewolf's Daughter," a sequel to "The Werewolf of Ponkert," appeared as a three-part serial (*WT*, October–December 1928).

7. "Supernatural Horror in Literature."

8. HPL refers to Frank Belknap Long's *The Man from Genoa and Other Poems*. Cook's edition of *The Shunned House* (1928) was printed but not bound or distributed. *WT* rejected the story "most emphatically" when it was submitted in 1925, as did *Detective Tales*. *WT* accepted it in 1937 only after HPL had died.

[3]　　[AHT]

10 Barnes St.,

Providence, R.I.,

July 16, 1927

My dear Wright:—

　　　　　I am very glad to hear that you have found "Cthulhu" available for use, and assure you that $165.00 is entirely adequate remuneration. I hope that Price will like "The Strange High House",[1] and would certainly be surprised and pleased if it found its way to ultimate publication! A third pleasure is given me by the news of "Red Hook's" anthological reprinting; and I'd like to see the book if you can get me a copy later on. I can most emphatically and advantageously use any royalties, be they ever so humble, which may chance to trickle in from Mr. Lovell.[2] I've been meaning to ask Belknap whether he obtained anything for the two stories reprinted in previous issues.[3]

What you say of Price interests me very much—he must be a delightful companion, with his many unique accomplishments. Indeed, you seem to be building up a "gang" eclipsing even our famous aggregation of a couple of years ago—Long, Leeds, Morton, Loveman, Talman, Kirk, etc.[4] I recall Kline's work, but can't say I was ever exactly bowled over with it. His Semitic phiz must be quite a cross—but I know a man of mixed Irish and French Huguenot ancestry who is in the same boat. I imagine that in the Middle Ages many Jews mixed into the Aryan population of all European nations, so that strains may crop out in unexpected places. Then, too, the Phoenicians may have left a bit of their hook-nosed blood in sundry parts of the ancient world. I once wrote a couple of replies to that famous pair of monometer couplets during a discussion of their authorship. They were:

> *"De gus-*
> *tibus—*   In haste
>   and   His taste,
> Why scan   Perhaps,
> His plan?   Might lapse!"

This Carr certainly appears to be a phenomenal being, and I congratulate him upon a spectacular success which I—with my elderly and antiquarian indifference to the sensational—am never likely to achieve.[5] I fancy that for the next few years "flaming youth" will occupy the same place in the vulgar eye that Greenwich Village did ten years ago, studio life twenty years ago, and stage life thirty or forty years ago. Those who are informed and glib can cash in—and I trust that the Carr of today may be the Robert W. Chambers of yesterday. Chambers, by the way, used to write weird tales. Do you know his "King in Yellow"? I hope that Carr will always gratefully remember the start which you and the group have given him.

Thanks for the "Pickman's Model" sketch—which isn't at all bad. Rankin certainly has the stuff in him and cannot even be considered in the same breath with Olinick. I am anxious to see the heading for Wandrei's tale.[6] Wandrei is still with me—after Tuesday's Newport trip we spent two days in the haunted woods north of Providence, and are in Boston today—taking in the art museum and waiting for a thundershower to blow over. He's a great kid—watch his stuff grow in the years ahead! Tomorrow we hope to "do" Salem (Arkham) and Marblehead, (Kingsport) and next Thursday we shall be on hand in Providence to welcome Long. I was glad to see Long's and Talman's tales in the current issue. That "Symphony Hall" tale was very fair—we're about to pass the building now, and I'm all a-tremble![7]

With all good wishes,
Sincerely yrs—
H. P. L.

P.S. I shall be interested in the book proposition when—or if—it develops.[8]

[*Addition by Wandrei:*]
Dear W.—I'm very glad you found "Cthulhu" acceptable—I'll look for it. Am enjoying myself with H. P. L., and trying to convince him he never should have sent "The Colour Out of Space" to *Am. St.* Will drop in again on my return in two or three weeks, with perhaps a brief case full of manuscripts.—Donald Wandrei.

Notes

1. E. Hoffmann Price (with whom HPL was not then acquainted) was apparently an informal editorial adviser to FW.

2. Charles Lovell was *WT*'s London agent.

3. "Death Waters" in *Not at Night* and "The Sea Thing" in *More Not at Night,* both ed. Christine Campbell Thomson.

4. I.e., the Kalem Club.

5. HPL refers to Robert Spencer Carr (1909–1994), who sold his first story to *WT* at the age of 15 and had a best-selling novel, *The Rampant Age* (1928), published when he was 19.

6. "The Red Brain" (*WT,* October 1927). It was illustrated by Hugh Doak Rankin (1878–1956). HPL also mentions another *WT* artist, George O. Olinick (1888–1957).

7. Stories in *WT,* August 1927: Frank Belknap Long, "The Man with a Thousand Legs"; Wilfred B. Talman, "Two Black Bottles" (revised by HPL); George Malcolm-Smith, "Satan's Fiddle," which mentioned "Symphony Hall" as the venue where the story's events take place.

8. It did not in fact bear fruit. HPL regarded this as the first of several rejections of his work by book publishers.

[4]   [AHT]

10 Barnes St.,
Providence, R.I.,
Dec. 22, 1927

Dear Mr. Wright:—
I'm glad *The Recluse* came through safely. Cook was so uneven about mailing the copies that some haven't received it yet; and I've been quite besieged with inquiries. I hope my article won't bore you. It is

abominably written, some whole sections having been thrust in at the eleventh hour when most of the type was set up; and if it were ever to be reprinted as a brochure, (as your fellow-townsman Mr. Starrett and Cook himself both suggest for the future) I would want to change whole chapters. Chamisso's stuff, for example, which I could not unearth in either Providence or New York, and which I rashly wrote up from hearsay, is not really part of the authentic horror-tradition. I got hold of "The Man Without a Shadow" this autumn, and was bored to death. So out it goes from any future edition![1] Note also the misprint of *Clarence* for *Clemence* Housman. That was a final insert on which I couldn't read proof.

I may have some more tales to send you before spring—but just now revision has me in a daemon clutch. An old fellow once associated with Ambrose Bierce is having me do over a whole book full of execrable short stories[2]—published and forgotten twenty-five years ago—for a second edition which he wants to float on the strength of some publicity gained in connexion with a new Bierce death report. And if this thing goes through, he may want me to help him on a book of Bierce reminiscences. Poor old Ambrosius—how the ghouls feed! This especial old bird, according to an anecdote recorded by George Sterling, parted from Bierce under the dramatic circumstance of having a cane broken over his head![3] When I saw his fiction I wondered why Ambrosius didn't use a crowbar.

As to that problematical volume of my tales—I'm really not very particular about the contents, since of course it would have to be formulated with the *Weird Tales* clientele in view and couldn't represent any real choice of mine. However, it appears to me that a certain group of tales can be considered as definitely better than the rest from *both* popular and artistic points of view; and I will here record their names as I conceive them—together with my rough estimates of their length in words:

"Outsider"	2500
"Arthur Jermyn"	3500

("White Ape")—that title concocted by Baird, gives me acute cervical agony. The original title is "Facts Concerning the Late Arthur Jermyn and His Family"—but I think plain "Arthur Jermyn" is the best.

"Rats in Walls"	7500
"Picture in House"	3000
"Pickman's Model"	5500
"Erich Zann"	4000
"Dagon"	2000
"Randolph Carter"	3000
"Cats of Ulthar"	<u>1400</u>
	32400

Here, then, is what I call the *indispensable* nucleus of any book purporting to represent the *popular* side of my fiction. I omit all things of any length—"Cthulhu", "Red Hook", &c.—because only one long tale can be included in a volume of this length. As for a *title*—my choice is "The Outsider and Other Stories". This is because I consider the touch of cosmic *outsideness*—of dim, shadowy *non-terrestrial* hints—to be the characteristic feature of my writing.

Thus we have 32,400 words accounted for. I would advise piecing out with one of the longish (10,000-word) tales and as many more shorter ones as are needed to fill the space you have in mind. Of my longer tales—exclusive of the two novelettes never typed or seen by anyone but Wandrei[4]—I think the following classification in order of merit is possible:

1. "The Colour Out of Space"
2. "Cthulhu"
3. "Red Hook"

"The Shunned House" won't be available, since Cook wants to print that as a thin book uniform with Belknap's poems. Incidentally—I have my doubts about the *popular* appeal of "The Colour". I advise choice of "Cthulhu", for in spite of what Belknap says and what the British anthologist chose, I think "Red Hook" is comparatively poor. Another alternative, though, is that thunderously melodramatic thing which I let Houtain publish in his nauseous *Home Brew** (ugh!) five years ago—"The Lurking Fear"—which of course I have the right to use again in a *book*. It is poor art, because it was written to order with certain limitations, but it ought to please the followers of Nictzin Dyalhis and his congeners. I'll enclose a manuscript of it—which please return if you don't care for it.[5]

Now as to shorter "fillers" to round out your 45 or 6 thousand words—(32400 plus 10000 = 42400; 46000 − 42400 = 3600)—here are my suggestions:

"Festival"	3000
"Unnamable"	2500
"Terrible Old Man"	1400

These can be juggled around as you like, since the *exact* size of the volume is not a fixed quantity. Incidentally, by the way—that 32400-word essential nucleus is only my own estimate. I'm perfectly agreeable to any changes in that which you may choose to make. Cut out anything you fancy would decrease

---

*Don't give this damn thing credit if you use the tale. The magazine failed amidst many debts and dubieties in 1924, and Houtain can't afford to raise objections anent lack of recognition!

the book's profit, and insert anything you think would increase it. If you want a touch of my other and more fantastic style, try "The White Ship".*

But of course the thing may never take form, so just file away this letter as a possible source of suggestion in case it does. If I were more affluent I'd order a copy of the "Moon Terror"[6]—though I have the story in my complete *Weird Tales* file. I trust the volume may prove successful, and the first of a long series. A really fine book could be made of certain selections from different authors covering the entire history of the magazine.

By the way—I was flattered last Monday by receiving a letter from the anthologist Edward J. O'Brien, asking for an autobiographical note for "The Best Short Stories of 1927". It was addressed to *Amazing Stories* and forwarded, so I suppose his mention of me will be based on "The Colour Out of Space". I don't fancy he'll go so far as to reprint it—but even a favourable allusion from so Olympian a source will be encouraging. I note from his letter that he is residing in Switzerland.

With best wishes for a Merry Christmas and Happy New Year,

I remain

most cordially and sincerely yrs—

H. P. L.

P.S. I duly received the Selwyn and Blount anthology which you forwarded. Not half bad! My first appearance between cloth covers, save for prefaces to two books of other people's poetry which I've edited.[7] I note that their illiterate proofreader copied the misprinted punctuation of the Latin quotation—the comma after *tali* which so lacerated my heart in *Weird Tales*.[8] *O tempora, O mores!*

Notes

1. HPL refers to Adalbert von Chamisso (1781–1838), a German author. In the first publication of "Supernatural Horror in Literature" HPL had written: "Adalbert von Chamisso, in his famous *Peter Schlemihl*, (1814) tells of a man who lost his own shadow as the consequence of a misdeed, and of the strange developments that resulted." He removed the sentence in the revised edition of the essay. "The Man without a Shadow" is the subtitle of *Peter Schlemihl*.

2. Adolphe de Castro.

3. Sterling's anecdote appears in his introduction to Bierce's *In the Midst of Life* (New York: Modern Library, 1927; *LL* 99).

4. *The Dream-Quest of Unknown Kadath* and *The Case of Charles Dexter Ward*, neither of which were published in HPL's lifetime.

5. FW reprinted the story in *WT* the following June.

---

*Although of course "The Strange High House", "Doom that Came to Sarnath", etc. are vastly better.

6. By A. G. Birch et al., consisting of three stories from *WT*. The book sold so poorly that plans for volumes by HPL and others were indefinitely postponed.

7. HPL refers to *The Poetical Works of Jonathan E. Hoag* and John Ravenor Bullen's *White Fire*.

8. HPL refers to the Latin quotation from Antoine Delrio ("An sint unquam dae-mones incubi et succubae, et an ex tali congressu proles nasci queat?") in "The Hor-ror at Red Hook."

[5]   [*WT*][1]

[November 1927]

There's one fine story in your current issue[2]—"The Shadows", by Henry S. Whitehead. Wish you could get more of his material—it has the marks of a real brain and fancy behind it.

Notes

1. Text taken from *WT* 11, No. 1 (January 1928): 136.

2. *WT*, November 1927.

[6]   [*WT*][1]

[c. January 1928]

That[2] was what I call a *genuine weird tale,* with all the subtle atmospheric condi-tions adequately realised. Why in heaven's name can't the bulk of the writers catch at least some faint echo of the black, brooding whispers from unholy abysses and blasphemous dimensions which give a narrative like this its im-ponderable element of competence and mastery? Next best thing in the issue was Burks' "Bells of Oceana". That had the genuine thrill of Outsideness, too.

Notes

1. Text taken from *WT* 11, No. 3 (March 1928): 427.

2. "The Canal" by Everil Worrell (*WT*, December 1927).

[7]   [AHT]

10 Barnes St., Providence, R.I.,
Sept. 24, 1928

My dear Wright:—

        Pardon my bothering you with the enclosed manuscript by Mrs. Z. B. Reed,[1] (joint revision client of Belknap and myself) but she insists that she wants you to see it despite its thoroughly non-weird nature and its consequent ineligibility for *Weird Tales*. Why she wants to send it is beyond me—unless perhaps she has read in the "Eyrie" how you helped young Robert S. Carr to fame, and imagines you can do likewise with her. I pass it up—I personally would consider it a damned imposition to load you with irrelevant manuscripts—but in this case I can only carry out orders! The tale itself I don't consider at all bad for a novice.

Another thing—Mrs. Reed would be prodigiously grateful if you could tell her the approximate date when her "Curse of Yig" will appear. You might drop a card to her address—4125 Walnut St., Kansas City, Mo.—if the time of publication is decided upon. Within a month—if other work lets me get at it—I may send you a new Reed weird story; a thing with an Oklahoma locale like "Yig", but at present in such poor shape that it will require careful retouching. If I can't get at it soon, I'll let my bright little partner Belknap tackle it with his fresh young wits.[2]

Incidentally—here's a new thing of my own,[3] which I cooked up last month by ruthlessly neglecting all the piled-up work before me. It embodies some of the rural atmosphere which I picked up during my summer wanderings,[4] and the two people who have seen it (Belknap and Bernard Dwyer) speak so favourably of it that I've decided to let you have a look at it. I can't resist enclosing Sonny's card of criticism—though I must not be thought of as endorsing the child's ecstatic opinion. I hope the *length* won't repel you. Lately my ideal of fiction has shifted toward the longish short tale, in which there is opportunity for cumulative incident and gradually thickening atmospheric clouds. I suppose you'd call this a "novelette" in modern magazine language. Don't feel any undue hurry about reading it, and don't hesitate to shoot it back if it doesn't look right for *Weird Tales*.

Trusting that the submission of this Reed tale does not form a wholly unwarranted encroachment, (you can return it to the author unread if you like, of course)

I remain

      Yr most oblig'd obt Servt

        H. P. L.

Notes

1. The ms. HPL submitted was presumably one ZB wrote on her own without HPL's assistance. See ZB 36.

2. It is unclear what story HPL is referring to. The next story HPL revised for Bishop, "The Mound," was not begun until December 1929.

3. "The Dunwich Horror."

4. HPL had spent a week in North Wilbraham, MA.

[8]   [AHT]

10 Barnes St.,
Providence, R.I.,
Nov. 8, 1928

My dear Wright:—

I hate to bother you, but I thought I'd ask what you think of the enclosed—which came in the envelope you have just forwarded to me.[1] I don't believe I would ever be likely to achieve a more profitable re-sale of "Cthulhu", so would be inclined to accept Mr. Harré's offer but for the fact that I recall your mentioning "Cthulhu" as one of the things you might like to reprint yourself some time in a collection of my stuff. Of course, that plan may have long been abandoned—but I thought I ought to ask you nevertheless before disposing of "Cthulhu" otherwise. If you *do* want it eventually, I think I'll suggest to Harré that he use my "Colour out of Space"—which, by the way, got a three-star or Roll of Honour classification in O'Brien's annual *Transcript* article last month.

I'm rather interested in the idea of a new anthology, and hope that some of my popularly unknown favourites will be included. In answering Mr. Harré I am suggesting that he use Shiel's "House of Sounds", and Robert W. Chambers' "Yellow Sign" and "Harbour-Master".[2]

Haven't had time to read the last two *Weird Tales,* but am glad to note a respite from Senf covers. In the Nov. issue I did read Hamilton's "Polar Doom" and thought it splendid in conception.[3]

With best wishes, and hoping to hear soon about "Cthulhu", I remain
Yr most oblig'd and obt
H. P. L.

Notes

1. HPL refers to T. Everett Harré's request to reprint "The Call of Cthulhu" in his anthology *Beware After Dark!* (1929).
2. Harré reprinted Shiel's "Huguenin's Wife" but not "The House of Sounds." No story by Chambers was included in the book.
3. HPL refers to the *WT* artist C. C. Senf and to Edmond Hamilton's "The Polar Doom" (*WT,* November 1928).

[9]   [AHT]

Feby. 15, 1929

My dear Wright:—

I am indeed interested to hear of the proposed action regarding "Not at Night", and certainly hope the matter can be properly straightened out.[1] It seems rather a tangle—I never heard of this Jeffries before; but was told last September by the agent Lovell that a certain Hutchinson and Co. had bought the edition of the book containing "Red Hook", and that I would receive from them such royalties as would have been due me from the late lamented Selwyn and Blount. At that time nothing was said of any other sale of rights, British or American. I fancied that Macy-Masius might have later bought the rights from Hutchinson—and bought the rights to the earlier books from the receiver of the deceased corporation—but in any case it seemed to me that something was due the various authors represented.

As to including me on the list of plaintiffs—I suppose it's all right so long as there is positively no obligation for expense on my part in case of defeat. My financial stress is such that I am absolutely unable to incur any possible outgo or assessment beyond the barest necessities; so that, unsportsmanlike though it may seem, I cannot afford to gamble on any but a "sure thing"—sure, that is, not to involve loss. If, however, the guarantee of non-assessment on your part is to be taken literally as covering all possible expenses both principal and incidental, I suppose it would be foolish not to stand behind the action and reap whatever royalties might be due me in case of victory. I certainly need all such things that human ingenuity can collect!

Therefore—it being understood that I am in no position to share in the burthens of defeat—you may act for me if you wish; though I doubt if my profits will amount to very much in case of victory. I will pass on your letter to Little Belknap, and fancy he will extend similar authorisation.

I read the March *Weird Tales* the other day, and think it is the best issue in several months.[2] Of the new material Belknap's "Tindalos" and your British cousin's "Rat" seem to me to divide first honours, with second honours shared by "The Immortal Hand" (good idea, but with mediocre development) and "The Sea Horror" (splendid atmosphere and promise until it falls into the familiar Hamilton formula). Third I would place Whitehead's "People of Pan"—pretty fair, but not up to its author's usual standard. The popular-magazine formula is apparently threatening to "get" Whitehead as it "got" Quinn long ago. Speaking of Quinn—"The Phantom Farmhouse", which I well recall from 1923, is really the *lucida* of the issue. It almost makes one weep to see this fine tale and realise what the author *can* do, and then to turn and behold that endless stream of artificial rabble-catering hokum featuring the trick mechanical dolls De Grandin and "Friend Trowbridge"! *Sic transit gloria Quinni!*

With best wishes both literary and litigational, I am, Sir,

Ever yr most oblig'd obt Servt

H. P. L.

Notes

1. Herbert Asbury edited an anthology, *Not at Night!* (New York: Macy-Macius/The Vanguard Press, November 1928), that included "The Horror at Red Hook." The book was assembled from various anthologies edited by Christine Campbell Thomson and was later withdrawn by the publisher.

2. HPL refers to the following stories in *WT,* March 1929: Frank Belknap Long, "The Hounds of Tindalos"; S. Fowler Wright, "The Rat"; Arlton Eadie, "The Immortal Hand"; Edmond Hamilton, "The Sea Horror"; Henry S. Whitehead, "The People of Pan"; Seabury Quinn, "The Phantom Farmhouse" (rpt. from the October 1923 issue).

[10]   [AHT]

> Saturday
> [January? 1930]

My dear Wright:—

Well—here are your 10 hand-picked Fungi—and may they adorn with appropriate morbidity the unhallowed gardens which bloom betwixt your covers! Trust I've copied them correctly, and hope the typothetae Corneliarum will do likewise.[1]

Shall be interested to know what you think of "The Mound" when you get around to it. You will learn therein—back to a certain point—where Klarkash-Ton's nighted *Tsathoggua* came from.[2] Possibly later documents will trace Its history still farther back into the hellish mists of elder entity, and across the unthinkable voids whence It first came. It is incredibly palaeo-ouranian—even Cthulhu and Yog-Sothoth are parvenus in comparison. In the *Necronomicon* Abdul Alhazred could do little more than hint of it under another name— ‫العزيف‬ in the original Arabic, (Al Azif) and Θασσογος[3] in the Greek translation (A.D. 950) (TO NEKRONOMIKON) of the Byzantine monk Theodorus Philetas of Constantinople.

Last week I went over my whole file of *Weird Tales* in an effort to check up a list of best stories prepared by young Derleth, and came to the conclusion that, of everything published since the first number, the following items have the greatest amount of truly cosmic horror and macabre convincingness. I don't know whether Derleth will agree with me or not, but these are all on his vastly longer list of superior tales. They are:

"Beyond the Door"	—	Paul Suter
"The Floor Above"	—	M. Humphreys
"The Night Wire"	—	H. F. Arnold
"The Canal"	—	Everil Worrell
"Bells of Oceana"	—	Arthur J. Burks
"In Amundsen's Tent"	—	John Martin Leahy.

I'd include Belknap's "Black Druid" if it were published—the Child has improved steadily since the "Death Waters" period when the impress of the artificial Kipling convention was on him.[4] The authors producing the best and most consistent average of high-grade material (not necessarily the most poignant in sheer horror) are Henry S. Whitehead, Arthur J. Burks, E. Hoffmann Price, Belknap, Munn, Frank Owen, and Clark Ashton Smith. Quinn probably *could* make the grade if he (a) wouldn't try to write so much, and (b) would write seriously for persons of adult mental age (as in "The Phantom Farmhouse") instead of frankly catering to the microcephalic rabble. Hamilton has great stuff in him, but like Quinn has become the slave of the herd and of his one recurrent plot formula. Robert E. Howard is on the up-grade. If he will avoid popular catering, he will turn out important stuff in future. Little Derleth, too, is growing—though his most marked improvement is in his non-weird work . . . . reminiscent stuff in the Proust vein. Klarkash-Ton's future prose work will be worth watching, and Wandrei is always splendid when he writes at all.

But pardon the rambling.

     Best wishes—

          Yr most obt Servt

          H. P. L.

Notes

1. B. Cornelius was the creditor and printer of *WT*. The 10 poems published in *WT* were numbered 1 through 10 to show they were part of a series, but the numbering and sequence are not that of the overall sonnet cycle.

2. FW rejected "The Mound" (ghostwritten for ZB) but published it in abridged form after HPL's death. HPL used Clark Ashton Smith's Tsathoggua, from "The Tale of Satampra Zeiros" (which he had recently read in ms.), before Smith's own story appeared.

3. HPL is attempting to render "Tsathoggua" in a putative Greek version (Thassogos).

4. J. Paul Suter, "Beyond the Door" (April 1923; rpt. September 1930); M. L. Humphreys, "The Floor Above" (May 1923; rpt. June 1933); H. F. Arnold, "The Night Wire" (September 1926; rpt. January 1933); Everil Worrell, "The Canal" (December 1927; rpt. April 1935); Arthur J. Burks, "Bells of Oceana" (December 1927; rpt. April 1934); John Martin Leahy, "In Amundsen's Tent" (January 1928; rpt. August 1935); Frank Belknap Long, "The Black Druid" (July 1930) and "Death Waters" (December 1924; rpt. September 1933). It is likely that HPL's list contributed to the eventual reprinting of some of these stories.

[11]   [AHT]

                                    Feby. 18, 1932

Dear Mr. Wright:—

          I'll tell Swanson that tales prior to "The Moon-Bog" are unavailable for magazine publication.[1] The commercial tangles connected with literature, near-literature, and not-so-near literature are certainly annoy-ing enough—but I hope that the new magazine will not prove an injurious competitor to *Weird Tales*. If reprints prove to be really in demand, you could buy up the best items yourself and get ahead of other media—though per-haps, after all, only the newer readers would forego fresh material in favour of something which had appeared before. It is very possible that the new ven-ture will not survive in a field so overcrowded. If it does, it will probably be due less to its reprints than to its admission of material which the established magazines reject because of purely conventional standards of length, style, mood, and subject-matter*. The feeble newcomer unable to pay much to au-thors *has* to "take a chance"—and in so doing often prints not only some no-tably bad things, but many notably original and unhackneyed things of which the vested interests are rather afraid.

Sorry to say I haven't anything new which you would be likely to care for. Latterly my tastes have run to studies in geographical atmosphere requir-ing greater length than the popular editorial fancy relishes—my new "Shadow over Innsmouth" is three typed pages longer than "Whisperer in Darkness", and conventional magazine standards would undoubtedly rate it "intolerably slow", "not conveniently divisible", or something of that sort.[2] For the pre-sent I don't think I'll submit any new material anywhere, for the constant pressure of arbitrary requirements—plus the psychological effect of repeated rejections—leaves me absolutely tongue-tied so far as creation goes. I think I shall write with only my own tastes—and those of disinterested critics—in mind for a considerable period in the future; once more accumulating a stack of unpublished material as I did before 1923. Later, perhaps, there will be some opportunity for placing the accumulation. But of course—if by chance I turn out anything short and apparently conventional I may try my luck with it now and then; and if I do, I shall certainly send it to *Weird Tales* first of all.

With best wishes—

　　　　Yrs most sincerely—

　　　　　　H. P. L.

Notes

1. Carl Swanson was attempting to establish a magazine, *Galaxy,* consisting in part of reprints from *WT*.

2. HPL is making a sarcastic reference to the reasons given by FW for his rejection of HPL's *At the Mountains of Madness* in the summer of 1931. HPL never submitted "The

---

*The new *Strange Tales* illustrates the recent trend. Nothing but flat, juvenile non-sense aside from the Whitehead, deRezske, and Barker tales. The Clayton policy absolutely excludes anything original or sincere in the way of mood, atmosphere, or development.[3]

Shadow over Innsmouth" to FW, but August Derleth did so on two occasions without HPL's knowledge; the story was rejected both times, and, as HPL predicted, because it was "not conveniently divisible."

3. HPL refers to stories in the March 1932 issue of *Strange Tales of Mystery and Terror*, published by Clayton Magazines: Henry S. Whitehead, "The Trap" (revised by HPL); Eugene de Rezske, "The Veil of Tanit"; S. Omar Barker, "Back Before the Moon."

[12] [AHT]

> 10 Barnes St.,
> Providence, R.I.,
> Jan. 6, 1933

Dear Mr. Wright:—

Yours of 28th ult. awaited me when I returned from a holiday visit to young Belknap in N.Y. I also saw Wandrei, who is making good progress on a non-weird psychological novel.[1] Derleth wrote of his pleasant dinner with you in Chicago—too bad your cold prevented more frequent contacts.

Whitehead's passing has caused more universal regret among the group than any other event of recent years. He was almost undoubtedly the most well-rounded character contributing to the pulp magazines, and it will be long before work of the Canevin calibre can be found again. I am glad that he furnished you with biographical data by which later notices can be checked. In my own rambling account I forgot to mention that H.S.W. was a *liturgiologist* of note—performing valuable services in many churches through artistic arrangements of the rituals and sacerdotal pageantry. No doubt his own notes mentioned this point. I read "The Chadbourne Episode"[2] with extreme interest, and wish you could get hold of the other two Chadbourne stories which are in existence. One was accepted by the Clayton outfit and returned when *Strange* and *Astounding* collapsed, while the other seems not to have been submitted anywhere. Whitehead also had another story under way—his old tale "The Bruise", with a new ending (suggested and mapped out by myself) involving the fabulous lost continent of Mu 20,000 years ago; but whether this was ever put in final publishable shape I don't know. Another unpublished Whitehead manuscript—"White Wool of Lambs"—is in the possession of Bernard Austin Dwyer, Box 43, West Shokan, N.Y. This is not really a weird tale, but a delicate phantasy of rather religious cast about a Chicago gangster in a castle in his hereditary Italy.[3] I suppose Whitehead's father will appoint some sort of literary executor to go over his papers and do what is possible toward placing unpublished manuscripts—at least, he ought to. Many tales like "Henri Menjou", hitherto rejected, certainly deserve printing.[4]

Glad to hear that a memorial notice will appear in the March "Eyrie". Readers tell me that the current issue is above the average. I've been buying the magazine right along, but have been so driven to the wall with work that

I've not had time to look at any pulp magazine since September.
    With every good wish for 1933—
        Yrs most cordially and sincerely,
                            H. P. L.

Notes

1. *Invisible Sun.*
2. *WT,* February 1933.
3. The story title alludes to the *pallium,* a white woollen vestment conferred by the Pope on an archbishop.
4. "The Bruise" was posthumously published in *West India Lights* (1946) as "Bothon." "White Wool of Lambs" and "Henri Menjou" are unpublished and may not survive.

[13]   [AHT]

                            Tenbarnes—
                            Feby. 8, 1933
Dear Wright:—
        I have just had a letter from Harry Bates—late editor of the defunct *Strange* and *Astounding,* and now in Clearwater, Fla., writing a play—which sheds much light on the details of good old Canevin's passing. Clearwater lies between Dunedin and St. Petersburg, and Bates has been in touch with Whitehead's father and friends. On account of your interest in H.S., and your long connexion with him, I fancy you will be eager to hear the melancholy particulars.
    It seems that during the autumn of 1932 H.S.'s cousin from the north was replaced by the bright little "cracker" boy C. J. Fletcher (whom he had had before—in 1930) as secretary and general factotum. On the Sunday before his death—Nov. 20—he complained of what he termed a "general malaise"—*not* connected with his long-afflicted stomach. His friend Miss M. I. Starr (a middle-aged lady who, during my 1931 visit, lent him the use of her car) was rather worried, and told young Fletcher to watch him carefully and telephone her if anything alarming developed. Late that night the boy heard a thud—as of someone falling—in Whitehead's room, and found H.S. in a queer and disturbing condition—partly deprived of speech. He telephoned Miss Starr, and she went over—finding H. S. semi-conscious. She then telephoned Dr. Mease (prop. of the Dunedin Sanitorium, and H.S.'s regular physician),[1] who came at once and sent for two other doctors. They diagnosed the case as concussion of the brain caused by a fall. Before morning old Mr. Whitehead was notified and rushed up from St. Petersburg. H.S. was still semi-conscious, recognised his father, raised an arm, smiled, and said "My daddy." Those were his last words. From then until the end the doctors kept him under opiates. Fletcher, Dr. Mease, Miss Starr, Mr. Whitehead, and others

were on hand and awake most of the time. Death came early and imperceptibly on the morning of Wednesday the 23d. It is clear that H.S. never had a chance to read my reply to his last letter.

H. S. was feeling *unusually well* until Sunday, Nov. 20, hence I doubt if the old gastric trouble was really the *direct* cause of death. To me it looks like a malignly tragic *accident*—the fall in the night; which, though doubtless caused by the general weakness resulting from the old trouble, might easily have not occurred. It seems that shortly before his death H.S. had had all his books and household effects shipped down from the north, where for years they had been in storage. He had also just finished a new sun porch on the roof of his new home in Pasadena Drive. It is tragic that he could not have lived to enjoy these things.

Old Mr. Whitehead (now eighty-five), Bates says, is visibly failing under the shock—although he carries on with outward cheerfulness—the hereditary Canevin stamina. He is quite deaf, and of late his eyes have been developing cataracts. H.S.'s body has been placed temporarily in a St. Petersburg mausoleum, and Mr. Whitehead plans later to unite all the family dust by having Mrs. Whitehead's remains brought south and arranging for three graves (including his own) side by side in St. Petersburg cemetery—father, mother, and only child.[2] Thus good old Canevin will rest under the semi-tropical sky he loved so well, and beside the parents to whom he was so warmly and undeviatingly devoted.

With best wishes—
Yrs most sincerely,
H. P. L.

Notes

1. Dr. Jack Mease opened a 10-bed sanatorium in Dunedin in 1929.
2. Whitehead and his parents Henry Hedden Whitehead (1846–1937) and Mary B. Whitehead (1857–1919) are interred at the Royal Palm South Cemetery.

[14] [AHT]

10 Barnes St.,
Providence, R.I.,
Feby. 16, 1933

Dear Wright:—
Yours of the 13th arrived just after I had dropped you a card in reply to your earlier note. So little Augie has been shewing Grandpa's stories, eh? Quite a boy![1]

Yes—if you want to use the "Witch House", go ahead. Surely $140 is as much as can be expected in these times. As for radio dramatisation rights—I really think an author ought to be able to have at least a censorship of anything which goes out under his name—for what a popular dialogue-arranger could do to the atmosphere and artistic integrity of a seriously written story is appalling to contemplate! Indeed, it is not likely that *any* really finely wrought weird story—where so much depends on mood, and on nuances of description—could be changed to a drama without irreparable cheapening and the loss of all that gave it power. Of course, weird drama *can* be written—when the author starts out *from the first* to utilise the dramatic form. Dunsany's "Gods of the Mountain" and "Night at an Inn" are typical specimens. But when a thing is written *as a story,* it will fare best by staying that way. What the public consider "weirdness" in drama is rather pitiful or absurd—according to one's perspective. As a thorough soporific I recommend the average popularly "horrible" play or cinema or radio dialogue. They are all the same—flat, hackneyed, synthetic, essentially atmosphereless jumbles of conventional shrieks and mutterings and superficial, mechanical situations. "The Bat" made me drowse back in the early 1920's—and last year an alleged "Frankenstein" on the screen *would* have made me drowse had not a posthumous sympathy for poor Mrs. Shelley made me see red instead. Ugh! And the screen "Dracula" in 1931—I saw the beginning of that in Miami, Fla.—but couldn't bear to watch it drag to its full term of dreariness, hence walked out into the fragrant tropic moonlight![2]

Of course, as you say, the dramatisation of my "Witch House" is very unlikely; but on the whole, if it's all the same to you, I wouldn't mind seeing it protected against the dialoguer's unconscious caricaturing. You may recall that I wouldn't contribute to *Strange Tales* because Bates couldn't guarantee me immunity from the copy-slasher's shears and blue pencil.

So I fancy that, on general principles, it would be simplest to sell First N.A. serial rights only. I hope that doesn't sound too fussy—but when I reflect on how much the force of any carefully written story depends on atmospheric effects peculiar to the *original wording,* I really feel that demands for integrity of form are justified . . . even in instances of second presentation.

Price is getting me to attempt collaboration on a sequel to "The Silver Key", involving some of his dimensional theories. If I can't work up the proper synthesis, I may turn the job over to Klarkash-Ton.

Best wishes—

Yrs most cordially,

H. P. L.

Notes

1. August Derleth had submitted "The Dreams in the Witch House" to FW without HPL's knowledge.

2. *The Bat* (United Artists, 1926) directed by Roland West; starring George Beranger, Charles Herzinger, and Louise Fazenda; based on the play by Mary Roberts Rinehart. *Frankenstein* (Universal, 1931), directed by James Whale; starring Colin Clive, Mae Clarke, and Boris Karloff; based on the novel by Mary Shelley. *Dracula* (Universal, 1931), directed by Tod Browning and Karl Freund; starring Bela Lugosi, Edward Van Sloan, and Helen Chandler; based on the novel by Bram Stoker.

[15]   [AHT]

66 College St.,
Providence, R.I.,
June 18, 1933.

Dear Mr. Wright:—

Thanks for the sheets—I wish I had asked for proofs, since there are at least six slips in the text; three occurring in the manuscript (which I ought to have gone over more thoroughly) and the balance made by the printer.[1]

ERRATA

(a)—p. 92, co. 1.—l. 11:—for *love* read *lore* (printer's error)

(b)—p. 93, co. 1.—l. 11:—for *the doctor's* read *a doctor's* (error in manuscript)

(c)—p. 93, co. 2.—l. 39:—for *his* read *its* (error in manuscript)

(d)—p. 100, co. 2.—l. 41:—for *Desrocher's* read *Desrochers'* (printer's error)

(e)—p. 101, co. 2.—l. 25:—for *human element* read *known element* (printer's error)

(f)—p. 102, co. 2.—l. 35:—for *hearty-sleeping* read *heavily-sleeping* (error in manuscript)

The worst two are (a) and (e), which make the text sound like vapid nonsense. The most damnable kind of a misprint is that which does not *look* like an error, but which gives a false appearance of sense—though really misrepresenting the author's intention and sometimes making him appear responsible for unutterable vapidities. A slip like that in Klarkash-Ton's "Ubbo-Sathla"[2] (*palaegean* for *palaeogean*) hurts nobody, for it is *obviously* a mistake of the printer. But where an allusion to *magical lore* becomes, seemingly a coherent yet inanely meaningless allusion to *magical "love"*—or where the expression *known (chemical) element* seems to be the coherent but out-of-place phrase *"human" element*—the author is unjustly laid open to the suspicion of rambling feebleness and semi-illiteracy. I wish there were a way of getting these two errata indicated on the cards to be sent friends.

As for a list of names—I recall your similar experiment in 1925, when my "Erich Zann" was thus heralded. Enclosed is a list based upon the principle then followed—a membership roll of the amateur press association, with likely names marked, plus a number of additional names. I hope that this measure may prove effective in increasing the sale of the magazine—it ought to work in the case of some authors, even if not in this one.

I shall certainly send along any tales of mine which may seem to suit your ideas of length and content. Recently I have had no time for original composition, though I did perform one piece of collaboration with our brilliant friend Malik Taus, the Peacock Sultan—the results of which he will probably forward for your editorial attention before many weeks have flown. Incidentally, I hope you will take Little Belknap's latest venture—which he calls "The Dark Beasts", but for which I'd prefer a subtler title such as "When They Came".[3] This thing has a brooding atmosphere of ineffable potency, and seems to me to mark a "comeback" on Sonny's part to his very best form. My own opinion is that seriously written stories are not as badly resented by the illiterate contingent as is commonly supposed, and I wish that more of them could appear in magazines like *Weird Tales*. These specialised magazines—since there are no publications of a parallel nature on a more fastidious literary level—undoubtedly have a larger percentage of cultivated readers than most observers suspect; though because of the dislike of such readers for cheap publicity, they do not write in to the "Eyrie" as the more mediocre and inferior readers do. Thus, I maintain, readers' letters are not always a perfect guide to a magazine's reception. If a larger proportion of seriously written material were presented, it would probably attract a very fair-sized fringe of readers who would not otherwise buy the magazine—yet would not be likely to alienate the cheap and vociferous element which thrives on conventional Hamiltonian formulae and Klinesque mechanical puppet-tableaux. Whilst a high-grade reader can *never* stand this latter junk, the converse is by no means true—as witness the obviously ignorant multitudes who do manage to appreciate Poe somehow, and who like good writers of Klarkash-Ton's type even though they don't know why. If I were editing *Weird Tales,* I'd accept virtually all of the Klarkash-Ton items which meet disfavour because of their allegedly too-poetic quality . . . . which reminds me, I suppose C.A.S. has sent you a copy of the brochure printed for him by the *Auburn Journal.* To my mind this is a collection of extraordinary merit—and I have an idea that its sale may belie many popular notions about the unmarketability of poetic phantasy.[4] I have offered to enclose circulars of it to all my correspondents. It is certainly a marvellous value for a quarter—despite the crowded format and the typically careless typography of the *Journal's* job press. I think C.A.S. means to advertise it in *Weird Tales.*[5]

I have been glad to see in *Weird Tales* lately a good many items with real atmospheric value. Howard's tales of elder worlds are growing rapidly in stature, and now and then—as in "The Scarlet Citadel" and "The Tower of the Elephant"—reach a level of really tremendous power. Jacobi's "Revelations in Black" is another high spot, and Hugh B. Cave (despite a professedly hard-boiled hack attitude) did marvellously well in "Dead Man's Belt". "The Ice-Demon" and "Genius Loci" are among Klarkash-Ton's most distinctive work. And of course I was glad to see my old favourite, "The Floor Above", again.[6]

Before I forget it—Walter J. Coates, North Montpelier, Vt., wants to know how much a small advertisement in *Weird Tales* would be. He has taken over the loose sheets of my "Shunned House" booklet—printed by W. Paul Cook five years ago—and proposes to bind and attempt to market the edition, aided in part by his editorship of *Driftwind* and his proprietorship of the semi-amateur *Driftwind Press.*[7] If not too expensive, he would like to reach your readers.

I see you have my new address—the result of a financial pressure which made it necessary for my surviving aunt and myself to combine households in as cheap a haven as possible.[8] Oddly—and indeed quite ironically—the move has the *externals* of a rise rather than a fall in the world; since an extraordinary opportunity put us in touch with a flat in the university district which, though having a minimum rent, involves no sacrifice of either comfort or quality of neighbourhood. For me in particular there is an added advantage which outweighs all the rest—namely, the fact that the house is one of those archaic reliques of other days which have fascinated me all my life, but which I have never till now inhabited. Not that it quite parallels the "Witch-House"—but it is a Georgian edifice built about 1800, of a type abundant on Providence's ancient and fascinating central precipice. Yellow and wooden, it lies on the crest of the great hill in a quaint grassy court just off College St.—behind and next to the marble John Hay Library of Brown University, and about half a mile south of 10 Barnes St. The fine colonial doorway is like my bookplate (done by Talman—I think I sent you a copy in 1929) come to life, though of course of a slightly later period. On the western side, and at a higher level behind, is a picturesque, village-like garden; while in front is a hedge, a row of old-fashioned posts, and a flower-bed or two. We plan to train up the facade a slip of ivy from the Washington plantation at Mt. Vernon. The upper flat we have taken has five rooms besides kitchenette nook and bath on the main (2nd) floor, plus two attic storerooms—one of which is so attractive that I wish I could have it for an extra den! My quarters—a large study and small bedroom—are on the south side, with my working desk under a west window affording a splendid view of the lower town's outspread roofs and of the mystical sunsets that flame behind them. The interior is as fascinating as the exterior—with colonial fireplaces, mantels, and chimney-cupboards, curving Georgian staircase, wide floor-boards, old-fashioned latches, small-paned windows, six-panel doors, rear wing with floor at a different level (three steps down), quaint attic stairs, etc.—just like the old houses open as museums. After admiring such all my life, I find something magical and dreamlike in the experience of actually *living in one*—in coming *home* through a carved Georgian doorway and sitting beside a white colonial mantel gazing out through small-paned windows over a sea of ancient roofs and sun-golden foliage. The old family furniture fits the place well—and many things unseen for decades (through lack of space) have emerged from storage to give it an odd air of similarity (in miniature) to the original home broken up in 1904. Enhancing the atmosphere of quaintness is the veritable symphony of chimes which proceeds every hour from the numerous old belfries that surround the place—a retinue including the famous First Baptist (1775) and Unitarian (1816) steeples,[9] as well as the vast clock tower on the college campus. Yet the practical side is not neglected—for steam heat and hot water are piped in from the adjacent John Hay Library; the house being owned by the university. Rent is no more than what I've been paying for my one room and alcove alone—but now the problem is how to meet even this halved obligation! But I hope I can hang on here as long as possible. Just now all is chaos because of my aunt's departure for the hospital with a broken ankle—the result of a hasty step on the stairs while answering the doorbell. Clearly, it will be a long time before the new household can boast of complete and tranquil settledness! Still—under any old conditions it is an inspiration to be in an ancient house of the sort around which my dreams have always revolved.

With every good wish, and thanking you again for the advance sheets, I remain

Yr most oblig'd, most obt Servt
H. P. L.

Notes

1. The corrections are to "The Dreams in the Witch House." None were made.

2. *WT,* July 1933.

3. The story was evidently rejected by *WT.* It appeared in *Marvel Tales* (July–August 1934) under Long's title.

4. *The Double Shadow and Other Fantasies.* HPL not-so-subtly twits FW, who had rejected all the stories in the book.

5. Smith advertised *The Double Shadow* in the July, November, and December 1933, and January 1934 issues of *WT.*

6. Robert E. Howard, "The Scarlet Citadel" (January 1933) and "The Tower of the Elephant" (March 1933); Carl Jacobi, "Revelations in Black" (April 1933); Hugh B. Cave, "Dead Man's Belt" (May 1933); Clark Ashton Smith, "The Ice-Demon" (April 1933) and "Genius Loci" (June 1933); M. L. Humphreys, "The Floor Above" (May 1923; rpt. June 1933).

7. Coates's plans came to naught.

8. HPL and his aunt Annie E. P. Gamwell moved into 66 College St. on 15 May 1933.

9. The First Baptist Meeting House, 75 North Main Street, and the First Unitarian Church at 301 Benefit Street.

[16]   [*SL* 668; AHT 13.13]

66 College St.,
Providence, R.I.,
Nov. 14, 1933.

Dear Wright:—

Yrs duly received—and I sent the "Silver Key" sequel back under separate cover yesterday.[1] Sultan Malik possibly overstates the matter in assigning me almost full authorship of the thing. The *language* is mine, but the whole system of mathematical concepts in the central portion is his. That kind of background is quite alien to me—indeed, while the Peacock Sultan is primarily *intellectual* in his methods and appeal, I am basically non-intellectual or even anti-intellectual. *My* attempts represent a striving for emotional emancipation from rigidities and certainties—a reaching toward vague suggestions of liberation and adventurous expectancy on far horizons, and a struggle to crystallise certain moods too ethereal and indefinite for description. The original "Silver Key" is characteristically mine (although it has naive aspects which I would not duplicate today), but the present sequel is something I would never have thought of creating alone. Therefore don't be misled by M. de Marigny's modesty into fancying that the dual authorship is merely nominal!

You have certainly been fortunate in obtaining first-hand views of contributors this year. The Peacock Sultan dropped me a card during his Chicago sojourn, and seemed to be enjoying the conference most acutely. I enjoyed his visit here—last July—tremendously, and hope that Old Juggernaut[2] will hold together long enough to bring him this way again in 1934.

My own programme was paralysed by the accident to my aunt—which kept me very closely chained around home. My one real vacation was a trip to Quebec in early September—a glorious affair which gave me four hot, sunny days in the ancient fortalice of the north. No other town in North America can rival Quebec in sheer beauty—and only Charleston can match its atmospheric glamour and sense of accumulated ages. My aunt is now much better—all around and out with a cane—though my liberation comes too late in the season to permit of much travelling. I did, though, improve the mild days of October by taking many long walks in ancient and unfrequented parts of the countryside, where the autumnal scenery appeared to fullest advantage. Hibernating time is near now, but in my present venerable abode an indoor regime has its compensations. My desk faces a sunset vista of the utmost charm and imaginative appeal—ancient roofs and boughs in the foreground, old church towers and a Georgian belfry in the middle distance, and beyond them all a strip of far-off violet horizon with a mystical hilltop steeple silhouetted faintly against the west. It's really almost enough to keep one's mind off one's work!

Well—the fate of the S. K. is in your hands.

Best wishes—

Yrs most cordially and sincerely—

H. P. L.

P.S. In recent *Weird Tales* I note some elements of promise in at least two new authors—Mearle Prout, with "The House of the Worm", and C. L. Moore, with "Shambleau".[3] Both tales have immaturities and inadequacies, but they seem to indicate an originality with great possibilities unless the respective authors get sidetracked amongst commercial formulae.

Notes

1. HPL had submitted the story c. July 1933 and it was rejected. See Farnsworth Wright to HPL, 17 August 1933 (ms., JHL):

> I have carefully read THROUGH THE GATES OF THE SILVER KEY and am almost overwhelmed by the colossal scope of the story. It is cyclopean in its daring and titanic in its execution. . . .
>
> But I am afraid to offer it to our readers. Many there would be . . . who would go into raptures of esthetic delight while reading the story; but just as certainly there would be a great many—probably a clear majority—of our readers who would be unable to wade through it. These would find the descriptions and discussions of polydimensional space poison to their enjoyment of the tale. The story is so much more than a piece of fiction, and so far transcends not only the experiences of the readers, but even their wildest dreams, that they would have no point of contact with the ideas and thoughts presented in this opus. [. . .]
>
> It may seem strange that I reject a story which arouses my admiration as much as THROUGH THE GATES OF THE SILVER KEY; but with business as poor as it is now, I feel that we cannot risk discouraging so many readers from buying the magazine, merely by printing a story that is so utterly alien to even their wildest dreams and reveries that they are incapable of comprehending it—let alone appreciating it.
>
> [. . .] I assure you that never have I turned down a story with more regret than in this case.

2. The name HPL gave Price's 1928 Ford Model A. A *juggernaut* is a force regarded as mercilessly destructive and unstoppable; an allegorical reference to the Hindu temple cars of Jagannath Temple in Puri, reputed to crush devotees under their wheels.

3. Mearle Prout, "The House of the Worm" (October 1933); C. L. Moore, "Shambleau" (November 1933). The Prout story, influenced by HPL's work, uses phrases from HPL's stories.

[17] [AHT]

66 College St.,

Providence, R.I.,

Nov. 21, 1933.

My dear Wright:—

I am indeed glad that the collaboration has finally proved acceptable, and hope that no epistolary alarms of outraged illiterati may cause you to regret the decision. For my part, as I have often said, I think that a restriction of contributions to the sort of thing the densest clods like would alienate nearly as many readers as an all-literate policy would. I know surely a dozen or more followers of the magazine who would certainly not continue to follow it if its contents uniformly represented the lifeless, mechanical, stock-figure, diagrammed type of hack-work so dearly beloved by the "Eyrie"-bombarding proletariat—and that dozen can scarcely be altogether unrepresentative. The trouble is, that the readers who do the most letter-writing—in an eagerness to publicise themselves—tend to reflect a stratum of taste distinctly lower than that of the best (and by no means negligible) part of the magazine's clientele. There seems to me little doubt but that *Weird Tales* is bought and read by large numbers of persons infinitely above the pulp-hound level—persons who relish Machen and Blackwood and M. R. James, and who would welcome a periodical of the Machen–Blackwood–James degree of maturity and fastidiousness if such were published. Naturally, they tolerate the hack stuff merely for the sake of the occasional real stories—Clericashtoniana, Howardiana, Caneviniana, etc.—which accompany it, and would certainly drop off if not assured of at least a fair supply.

I can well imagine the regret caused by the southward clattering of Old Jug, for Sultan Malik is surely a rare tonic and banisher of ennui and lassitude. Of him it may well be said, in paraphrase of the famous Johnsonese tribute to another refreshing spirit, that *Nullum quod tangit non laetificat!*[1] I don't believe you'd find any other of the living writers as interesting, though good old Canevin was in the same piquant, inexhaustibly brilliant, and intensely vital class. I am, by the way, keenly interested in your description of young Williamson—who seems to me one of the most notably promising of the new writers. His "Wand of Doom" impressed me strongly a year ago as having a certain real originality and atmospheric richness never found in hack work; and on the strength of that I tackled "Golden Blood", though I seldom spend time on serials nowadays.[2] I was not disappointed—for despite a certain quota of conventional accessories the tale reflected the same vitality, freshness, colour, and unaffectedness as its predecessor. It had crude spots—abrupt transitions, scanted emotional values, patently melodramatic combats and tableaux—but the vitality, imagery, and inexhaustible fertility of the whole thing made full atonement. If Williamson will keep on in the same vein, and refuse to make increased concessions to mass taste, he will certainly be a consistent top-notcher. It is curious that he has such a misleading shyness in person, but this may wear off with the years. Judging from his stories, his inarticulateness cannot be the result of any lack of ideas or imaginative moods! Anent his dream-world one may only echo the tribute of the Peacock Sultan. The various social events of the late season seem to have been quite notable and pleasing. I had pictured Single-Plot Hamilton as decidedly brilliant, for his earlier tales (especially "Mamurth")[3] had a remarkably original flavour. It was a distinct loss to literature when he discovered his facile sales-making formula!

It is odd that "The House of the Worm" did not get an ample response from the readers—though this only goes to show the superficiality of their judgments. That thing had the malign, brooding tension and gathering menace which make a real story. Picture succeeded picture, each suggesting just a *little* more of the festering evil that lurked at the heart of the evil wood; and some of the images were magnificently powerful and to the point. After the first visit there was a slight letdown or trace of cumbrousness, but the tension was soon recovered. The climactic tableau was splendid—even though the existence of the cult was sprung a little abruptly—but the conclusion would have been more effective without the explanatory epilogue. Altogether, it was a great story; and I'd like to see more by the same author. It was not finished in technique, but it had the *substance*. It would have captured my vote in spite of parallel material by Klarkash-Ton, Sonny Belknap, and Two-Gun Bob. "Shambleau" is great stuff, too. It begins *magnificently*, on just the right note of terror, and with black intimations of the unknown. The subtle evil of the Entity, as suggested by the unexplained horror of the people, is extremely powerful—and the description of the Thing itself when unmasked is no letdown. Like "The House of the Worm", it has real atmosphere and tension—rare things amidst the pulp tradition of brisk, cheerful, staccato prose and lifeless stock characters and images. The one major fault is the conventional interplanetary setting. That weakens and dilutes the effect both by introducing a parallel or rival wonder and by removing the episode from reality. Of course a very remote setting had to be chosen for so unknown a marvel—but some place like India, Africa, or the Amazon jungle might have been used . . . with the horror made more local. I trust your revisions may make Mrs. Moore's second story[4] as striking and interesting as this one. Malik's "Fourth Axis", in the same issue, has a magnificent incantation scene; and "The Accursed Isle" embodies a gnawing terror close to the real thing.[5]

I am surely sorry to hear of your sister's accident, and hope it will not result in any such long siege as my aunt went through. Fortunately an arm is not quite so crucial and pivotal as an ankle.

With every good wish—

Yrs most cordially and sincerely—

H. P. L.

P.S. I am intensely glad to hear that you are letting Klarkash-Ton illustrate his "Weaver in the Vault". For ten years I have wanted to see some of his monstrous pictorial conceptions in the magazine and now comes realisation! I hope his designs may become frequent features. Couldn't you let him try his hand at the "Silver Key" sequel?[6] He could make Yaddith—or the abyss beyond the ultimate gate—stand out with malign and marvellous vividness.

Notes

1. "He cheers everything he touches." An adaptation of a line from Samuel Johnson's Latin epitaph on Oliver Goldsmith at his monument in Westminster Abbey (*Nullum quod tetigit non ornavit* ["He adorned everything he touched"]).
2. Jack Williamson, "The Wand of Doom" (October 1932); "Golden Blood" (6-part serial, April–September 1933).
3. Edmond Hamilton, "The Monster-God of Mamurth" (*WT,* August 1926; rpt. September 1935).
4. "Black Thirst" (*WT,* April 1934).
5. E. Hoffmann Price, "Lord of the Fourth Axis"; Mary Elizabeth Counselman, "The Accursed Isle" (*WT,* November 1933).
6. Clark Ashton Smith, "The Weaver in the Vault" (January 1934). "Through the Gates of the Silver Key" was illustrated by H. R. Hammond.

[18]   [AHT]

% Barlow,

Box 88,

De Land, Fla.,

May 21, 1934.

My dear Wright:—

I am interested to hear of your plan to reprint the "Arthur Jermyn" tale—which was always one of my favourites. So far as I can recall, Baird made no inexcusable excisions or conspicuous blunders in the text, although he did stick on the outrageously naive and give-away title. The original title of this story was "Facts Concerning the Late Arthur Jermyn and His Family", although I have always had plain "Arthur Jermyn" in reserve as a possible alternative title. In view of the possible awkwardness of the full title in the table of contents, it might be best for you to call the story just "Arthur Jermyn". But certainly, I'd like to avoid the inept Baird-given title if it can possibly be managed.

I have a tattered carbon of this tale somewhere; but it is either going the rounds among various correspondents, or else lost among the piled-up non-letter mail on my desk at home, where my aunt could not possibly pick it out. Accordingly I'd be vastly obliged if you could let me have a copy of some sort to look over. I'll keep you in touch with my various temporary addresses of the near future—Barlow's will be the one until further notice.

I am certainly having a great time down here—with twice the energy I have in the north, and with a complete freedom (as in Dunedin in '31) from my usual sinus trouble. I ought to live here—but with my attachment to New England's antiquities the process of transition would be a hard one. Sorry I couldn't have met Hamilton and Williamson while they were in Florida. I understand that Ray Cummings, also a practitioner of certain forms of the weird, is or was in Ft. Lauderdale—but it's some time since Barlow has been in touch with him.[1] Barlow is a great kid—incipient writer, printer, sculptor, painter, landscape gardener, book and relique collector, and what not! You ought to see the bas-relief of "Cthulhu" which he finished some time ago! He is, however, gravely handicapped by poor eyesight. In the course of time I think he'll be importantly heard from in one way or another. Which reminds me—I hope you can find it convenient to accomodate him in the matter of *Weird Tales* manuscripts and drawings, as mentioned in a recent letter of his.

Have seen some interesting antiquities recently—including the picturesque, vine-clad ruins of a Franciscan mission built in 1696. Hopes of Havana are very dim indeed, but I shall spend a week in St. Augustine and return north by slow stages. I hate to think of facing northern weather again—but what you report of the thermometer is encouraging! I'm staying here longer than I intended, but Barlow and his family are so hospitable that all suggestions for an immediate moving-on have been vetoed.

Hope you haven't been affected by the recent fire—radio reports of which were quite alarming Saturday night.[2] I am completely ignorant of Chicago topography, hence descriptions of the burned area went quite over my head.

With every good wish, and trusting that the correction of "Arthur Jermyn" may be accomplished with a minimum of inconvenience, I remain

> Yrs most sincerely,
> H. P. L.

Notes

1. Ray Cummings (1887–1957), American author recognized as one of the "founding fathers" of the science fiction pulp genre. HPL never met him.
2. The Union Stock Yards Fire of 19 May 1934 was the most destructive blaze since the great Chicago fire of 1871.

[19]   [*WT*][1]

[December? 1935]

"The Way Home" is one of the most atmospherically satisfying things I have seen lately, and I was interested to note that the author is Paul Ernst under an anagrammatic alias.[2] I live in hope that the purely weird element may regain its ascendancy, as tales like that would imply. . . . Other good yarns in recent issues of WT are "The Cold Gray God", "The Mystery of the Last Guest", "Shadows in Zamboula", "The Hand of Wrath", and "The Chain of Aforgomon".[3]

Notes

1. Text taken from *WT* 27, No. 2 (February 1936): 250.
2. HPL refers to a story by Paul Frederick Stern (November 1935).
3. Stories by C. L. Moore (October 1935), John Flanders (October 1935), Robert E. Howard (November 1935), E. Hoffmann Price (November 1935), and Clark Ashton Smith (December 1935).

[20]   [AHT]

66 College St.,
Providence, R.I.,
July 1, 1936.

Dear Wright:—

Young Schwartz[1] has persuaded me to send him a lot of manuscripts for possible placement in Great Britain, and it occurs to me that I'd better exhaust their cisatlantic possibilities before turning them over to him. Accordingly I am going through the formality of obtaining your official rejection of the enclosed—so that I won't feel I've overlooked any theoretical source of badly-needed revenue.[2] In the absence of other American markets for purely weird material, I won't need to try them elsewhere—hence, if you don't mind, you might send them on after rejection to *Julius Schwartz, 255 East 188th St., New York, N.Y.,* instead of returning them to me.

I was greatly shocked about a fortnight ago to receive a card from Miss Moore with the dire news (without details, and allegedly obtained directly from Texas) of the death of Robert E. Howard by his own hand. It sounds incredible to me—for I had a long normal letter from good old Two-Gun Bob written as recently as May 13. He was worried about his mother's health, but otherwise seemed perfectly all right. I am wondering whether there can be any hope of a mistake—either a ghastly hoax, or some strange confusion of names springing from the suicide of another southwestern writer (the young science-fictionist David R. Daniels)[3] slightly earlier in the year? If the news is indeed true, it forms weird fiction's worst blow since the passing of good old Canevin in '32. Scarcely anybody else in the pulp field had quite the driving zest and spontaneity of R.E.H. He put himself into everything he wrote—and even when he made outward concessions to pulp standards he had a wholly unique inner force and sincerity which broke through the surface and placed the stamp of his personality on the ultimate product. How he could surround primal megalithic cities with an aura of aeon-old fear and necromancy! And his recent "Black Canaan" (*Weird Tales'* best story in the last three issues)[4] is likewise magnificent in a more realistic way—reflecting a genuine regional background and giving a clutchingly powerful picture of the horror that stalks through the moss-hung, shadow-cursed, serpent-ridden swamps of the farther south. Others' efforts seem pallid by contrast. I can't understand the tragedy, for although R.E.H. had a moody side expressed in his resentment against civilisation (the basis of our perennial and voluminous epistolary debate), I always thought that this was a more or less *impersonal* sentiment—like Sonny Belknap's rage against the injustices of a capitalistic civilisation. He himself seemed to me pretty well adjusted to his beloved southwestern environment. Well—weird fiction certainly has occasion to mourn, unless the melancholy report turns out to be false. I'm telling Price (the only one of the group who ever met R.E.H. in person) that he ought to prepare an obituary for *Weird Tales*[5]—just as I did of H.S.W. four years ago.[6] (I've written a paragraph or two for the fan magazines.) But alas that there should be occasion for such!

I've had a hell of a year—rotten health, and aunt seriously ill and at hospital—though now recovering well. Programme in chaos.

Apologising for the enclosed perfunctory inflictions—

Yrs most sincerely—

H. P. L.

Notes

1. Julius Schwartz (1915–2004), editor of *Fantasy Magazine*, who acted as HPL's agent in marketing *At the Mountains of Madness* to *Astounding Stories*.

2. HPL was submitting "The Thing on the Doorstep" and "The Haunter of the Dark." Both were accepted.

3. David R. Daniels (1915–1936), author of several science fiction tales in *Astounding Stories* and *Wonder Stories*. He died on 17 April.

4. *WT*, June 1936.

5. Price's "In Memoriam: Robert E. Howard" appeared in *Fantasy Magazine*.

6. "In Memoriam: Henry S. Whitehead."

[21]   [AHT]

66 College St.,
Providence, R.I.,
July 4, 1936

Dear Wright:—

Sorry to bother you again, but a letter from Schwarz makes it necessary for me to do so.

(1). He asked me to get your permission for the British reprinting (book form) of those stories (prior, I believe, to some time in 1926) to which I didn't reserve residual rights. I presume you will have no objection.

(2). He has so large an assortment of my stuff that he will not need more. Hence I'll change my former request and ask that rejected manuscripts be sent back to *me* instead of to *him*.

Incidentally—he claims that material once used in a British anthology is not available for book reprinting in England. Do you think this is so? In all the American book fiascos the publishers have never objected to tales previously appearing in American anthologies, although I have been careful to state the full history of each one.

Another matter—I've been meaning for some time to get another copy of the *March 1934 Weird Tales* if such is still obtainable. I like to keep the file complete, and this issue seems to have been lost by an irresponsible borrower.[1] Enclosed are stamps covering the presumable price. Hope you can supply the magazine—*MARCH, 1934.*

Reports of R.E.H.'s suicide all too conclusively confirmed. I have just had a letter from his father, together with some Cross Plains papers. The act was impelled by grief at his mother's approaching death—indicating that his moody, neurotic side went deeper than we ever suspected. What a blow for poor old Dr. Howard—losing at once his wife and a tremendously gifted only child!

Renewed regrets at bothering you—

Yrs most sincerely
H. P. L.

Notes

1. The issue contained "Winged Death," a story that HPL ghostwrote for Hazel Heald. He must have obtained the copy, for his set of *WT* is complete (now at JHL).

Farnsworth Wright, Weird Tales *second editor,*
1924–1940

[22]   [AHT]

66 College St.,
Providence, R.I.,
Dec. 26, 1936

Dear Wright:—

Thanks endlessly in advance for the two Finlay originals, which will have a place of honour in my files. That second specimen—for "Doorstep"—is a memorable imaginative achievement.[1]

Regarding spelling—to my mind would-be reformers overlook two all-important principles (which in a way are connected) and thereby lead themselves needlessly into traceless labyrinths of confusion and instability:

(1) *Logic* in orthography is not to be expected save in the vaguest and most fragmentary degree. Spelling is primarily an arbitrary matter depending upon the association of massed eye-images with given words. It can be fairly logical only in a very homogeneous language of unified tradition, and even there exceptions are multitudinous. In a strongly heterogeneous language drawing on three main culture-streams or verbal sources—Anglo-Saxon, Norman-French, and the Latin and Greek of classical scholarship (as distinguished from the Latin transmitted through Norman-French)—even approximate logic is impossible. Every attempt to give a unified orthographical symbol to similar verbal sounds of different derivation is likely to violate the etymological traditions of one or more of the verbal elements involved; and such violations do more to cut off the vitality of a word—to induce a forgetfulness of its history and overtones, and to introduce a touch of uncertainty and deficient authority regarding its visual rendering—than could any amount of bad logic or inconsistency in the spelling. In view of the varied history of the words in any living and naturally evolved language—especially such a heterogeneous one as ours—no real logic in orthography could ever be obtained except through the adoption of a sort of radical symbolism or shorthand so grotesquely unlike anything we know as "spelling" that even the most traditionless radicals would refuse to stand for it. As things really work out, a good part of the well-meant attempts to increase logic and consistency in various isolated instances merely create fresh breaches of logic and consistency in sundry *other* phases of the given problems—and in addition help to undermine the foundations of orthographical stability and associative word-values. These attempts could form only a meaningless drop in the bucket if successful—and in cold fact they are not only largely unsuccessful (for no two reformers reform the same way), but are hurtful in other ways even when fairly successful in their primary objective. They all lead away from unity and stability, and toward chaos and a permanent state of irresponsible flux. One may add that *the use of similar-sounding words and roots to express different meanings* would always constitute a barrier to perfect linguistic logic even if a bizarre system

of absolutely perfect and consistent phonetics were devised. In such a system, the few remaining necessary illogicalities would doubtless be resented even more hotly than are the countless normal illogicalities of our present system—in which no broad student expects or demands logic. Therefore—this alphabet and orthography having been already reduced to a traditionless scheme of unfamiliar symbols looking something like Pitman's shorthand[2]— the faddists would next begin to agitate for a series of changes in the *sound* of certain words . . . . . or more probably, for prefixes, and the substitution of new and synthetic terms in their place. Thus with *missed* and *mist* . . . . perhaps spelled *mĭst* in each case . . . the reformers would insist that the latter term be dropped in favour of a new word such as gak, zib, or thop (spelled ℉ᶜ ,ℨ⌐ᴕ, or ℺"ℙ,or some similar way), or that its place be supplied through synonyms or circumlocution. To such absurd extremes does the quest for phonetic and linguistic logic lead. And the joke is that such logic is *not important enough* to warrant the frightful concomitant destruction. Of course, most reformers do not seek to attain the uttermost limits of logic—and destruction. They merely meddle around the edges of the matter—creating occasional monstrosities in an effort to remedy two or three surface inconsistencies, and wreaking only enough damage to produce a generation of increasingly bad spellers and associationless linguistic drifters.[3] The ancestral speech still lives in spite of their ministrations. But why must they nibble as they do when the whole fabric would be better off if left alone as it naturally crystallised between (say roughly) 1730 and 1830? To recapitulate Principle I—orthographical logic in our language is (a) impossible anyhow, and (b) not worth bothering about even if it *were* possible at a high cultural cost.

(2) The most important thing about spelling is *not* its appeal to the analytical abstract reason, but its appeal to the *eye* as a familiar and association-wreathed pattern or set of natural symbols. The vital thing to be demanded of spelling is that it *satisfy the expectations we have formed* from our normal reading of books printed in all periods, and from our knowledge of the sources—in our own and other languages—which lie behind the words we use. To assume that the daily reading of a generation consists only of the editions published within its own lifetime is to adopt a curiously rootless and parvenu perspective. Actually, *the usage of the immediate past* cannot be ignored. For all truly literate persons, it exists as a constant, vital, and insistent reality— moulding habits and expectations, and standing out as a norm by which present usages must necessarily be measured. Gradual departures from it will of course occur; but unless they are to cause trouble and disgust they must be *evolutionary and spontaneous* departures—departures in which all the most cultivated users of the language quietly concur without external propaganda— rather than freakish theoretical changes cooked up for change's sake by abstract visionaries. This element of *familiar and traditional eye-appeal* is of course

the more important of the two elements under discussion. Historical and etymological associations, while tremendously valuable and worthy of preservation whenever they *can* be preserved, are often lost through *natural* change, and cannot be expected to be omnipresent. What we *can* ask of modern writers is simply that they refrain from meddling artificially with any historical or etymological vestigia which *have* naturally survived. Thus, we for example, must accept the loss of the normal dip[h]thongs in *Ægypt* (although Harpers retained this form in the 1850 edition of "Anthon's Ancient Geography"), *aera, oeconomy,* but there is no sense in forcibly ejecting them from *aeon, mediaeval, aesthetic,* and other words where they naturally survive in the usage of the most cultivated persons and most solid books and periodicals. Let us— without trying to stifle any natural mutation which may seem justified and non-decadent—simply refrain from endorsing propaganda for the artificial disturbance of naturally settled usage. To recapitulate Principle II—the two most important things about spelling are (a) first and foremost, easy familiarity to the eye accustomed to the varied books normally encountered in study and reading in home and public libraries (including imprints from all over the Anglo-Saxon world, and of dates largely involving the nineteenth century), and (b) less vitally but nevertheless far from negligibly, preservation of as many associative elements—historical and etymological—as can naturally be preserved.

These two principles appear to me extremely sound—and indeed almost irrefutable. With their basic essence a clear majority of all with whom I have discussed them (including many who follow the more standardised and natural American provincialisms of Webster et al.) seem to agree. Naturally, different individuals interpret them differently—but those who recognise their general validity are usually as one in spurning the *thrus, esthetics, advertizes,* and *ilands* of the rootless (or else Elizabethanly flexible) extremists. I myself simply follow the majority of the books—printed on both sides of the Atlantic— which shaped my education and which form the bulk of my library today. I can't follow the local flag-waving of the *meter* (for *metre* . . . shades of the gas man!) and *theater* enthusiasts who demand something radically different from the normal usage of our ancestors and relatives in the Mother Land. As well demand that California have a different spelling from Maryland, or that Ohio studiously depart from Massachusetts usage. (In all truth, this *is* the case to some extent, since the better grade of Eastern papers and magazines—to say nothing of books—adhere as always to normal forms like *theatre, centre, programme, traveller, mediaeval,* etc., although they usually drop the u in *labour* etc., and give certain *-ise* terminations the neo-American *-ize*.) Those 250% American critics forget that most of the local departures from the general norm are of relatively recent growth—within the last century at most. That is, their rise to local predominance is as recent as that. American books from the middle eighteenth century to around 1840 are divided in their handling of words like *honour* and *labour*, with the normal *u* forms probably predominating in the better grade of books until after 1830. As one with a fair percentage of pre-1830 books in his library, I can assert this from solid evidence. However—I have no quarrel with *hono'r, favo'r*, and *civilize*. These form a truly spontaneous variant sanctioned by general usage over an enormous area. There is a distinct uniformity in the mutation producing them. I can even endure *travel'er* (ugh!) with only minor nausea. It is the *sulfur, iland, brot, criticize, thru, eon, fetor*, etc. kind of stuff that completely empties my stomach. But even here, of course, I scarcely contemplate starting a crusade. After all, I recognise that the whole subject of spelling is a comparatively minor matter, and that in the greatest age of our literature—that of Elizabeth—it was in as bad a state of chaos and multiple usage as it is now in theory-ridden America. I can take it—or most of it! And I realise also that correct spelling is no sign of *intelligence*—being perhaps even the reverse, since the supernormally alert mind holds abstract concepts which run ahead of forms. I have never held up spelling as a matter of the foremost cultural significance, or tended to regard it as in any way an art or science. To my mind, it is simply a *very useful accessory* of literature—an accomplishment to be cultivated by the high-grade printer and publisher rather than by the creative author. *As a writer* I have no views whatever on orthography. Such views as I do entertain, I entertain as an amateur critic—or as one interested in neatness in the externals of expression. A bad or commercially servile story, or a trite and inane "pome", can get me seeing much redder than even a whole page full of "eons" and "esthetes", or a whole archipelago of "ilands"!

My statement of the two general principles which I follow will undoubtedly serve as an inclusive answer to many of the specific usage-points you cite. About the render of φ-derivatives—you will perceive that I am governed wholly by considerations of historic precedent and etymological usage—or rather, by a standard of *familiar and acceptable eye-appeal* as conditioned by these things. True, in Spain and Italy the spontaneous evolution of many centuries (though in Spain's case accelerated by the quasi-official dictionary of the Academy in 1803) gradually changed to *f* the *ph* transliteration of φ which had universally existed in Latin. But the fact remains that we do not inherit the linguistic stream of Spain or of Italy. On the contrary, the classical element in our language came either through the Norman-French, where the *ph* form remained intact, or directly through Latin scholarship. For us, the natural evolutionary tendency which gave the Mediterranean nations their spontaneous f-substitution has never existed. *Ph* as a φ-equivalent is the only normal and familiar form with us except in a few special cases. But I'm no stickling purist. When *natural drift* causes a φ-derivative to acquire an f-rendering in English (generally because the transition had previously occurred in French), I accept that rendering as readily as I accept the *ph* rendering of the bulk of such derivatives. Thus I say *fantastic* and *fantasy* (as did Dr. Johnson and Walker,[4] and most after them), though I reject "fantasm" for *phantasm*. Curiously enough, Dr. Johnson *did* accept "fantasm"—although Walker balked at it, and the nineteenth century generally refused to endorse it. *Usage,* not *abstract logic,* is the criterion. The only possible orthographical norm is that remarkable *settling-down*—a novel and unprecedented development in English spelling—which began about the Restoration period, became very manifest by 1750, and a *striking and spontaneous uniformity* (not yet disturbed in Great Britain and many of the Dominions, and only fragmentarily shaken (as in *hono'r, wag'on,* etc.) in cultivated circles in the Eastern U.S.) during the first half of the nineteenth century. To break up this valuable natural growth and deliberately re-create the irresponsible chaos of Tudor times seems to me little short of a crime.

For the American modernistic chaos in spelling is by no means universal. Great Britain and most Dominions feel only feeble echoes (in Eastern Canada the less offensive American variants predominate, but not the delirium tremens fringe. I can't answer for the prairie provinces), and the eastern U.S. (despite some wild vagaries in *N.Y. Times* and *Tribune* style sheets) as a whole has not wandered far from its spontaneous "Websterian"* variant. Few freaks can be discerned in the columns of the *Boston Transcript, Providence Journal, Atlantic Monthly, Harper's Magazine,* etc. There is still left in the world enough of the solid fabric of naturally crystallised English spelling to form a practical and sensible anchorage for friends of the language. And on the other hand, the principles and possible rewards of chaotic agitation and propaganda are so involved in fallacy and misconception that such roiling of the waters seems pitifully futile and wantonly destructive. Logic and consistency there can never be. Uniformity and traditional acceptability there can be, have been, and to some extent continues to be. And I'm for preserving the reality instead of chasing the shadow. Lord Falkland once said "where it is not necessary to change, it is necessary not to change,"[5] and I can see what he meant. If we lose all landmarks, we lose all reasons for living, and find ourselves floating directionlessly in a meaningless chaos. I believe in changing what has to be changed, but in keeping what can be kept. We can't cling to old beliefs and values and economic systems which the progress of knowledge, technology, and social consciousness has rendered obsolete and injurious—but we *can* cling to accustomed ways of doing things when there is no reason whatever for doing them any differently. I don't believe in the Ptolemaic universe of the Middle Ages, the Laplacian nebular hypothesis of the nineteenth century, or the capitalism of Herbie Hoover and the cobweb-brained constitution-savers of contemporary reactiondom. But on the other hand I don't see why the hell I

---

*I use "quotes" because N. W. himself endorsed certain forms more radical than the solid norm which worked itself out in America.

should spell *sulphur* with an "f" or clutter up my study with futuristic chairs which look like emergency 'bus seats or bear-traps or henroost spring guns!

I can appreciate all that you say about popular carelessness with spelling. Even Klarkash-Ton spells "cemet*a*ry" that way—or has done so until recently! And I lugubriously echo your observations anent *pronunciation*. One of the phases of my big autumn job (the English text book)[6] was to compile a list of "100 words often mispronounced"—and by the time I had given the matter a little open-eared attention I began to despair for the orthoëpical future of the race. Some of the juiciest bits came from lecturers at the college . . . "son'-o-rous", "har-ass'", etc. etc. etc.

Well—pardon the ex cathedra bull[7] of a sour, wretchedly old geezer!

My aunt and I had a Christmas tree, as in '34 and '35. Hope your Yule was pleasant, and that your New Year will be.

Yr obt Servt H. P. L.

P.S. Had an interesting and appropriate Christmas gift from young Conover—one of the *Science-Fantasy Correspondent* boys. A mouldering human skull exhumed from an ancient and mysterious necropolis! It came from an Indian mound near Conover's home—a scene of previous ghoulish and archaeological exploits of his.

Notes

1. The other illustration was for "The Haunter of the Dark."

2. Pitman shorthand is a phonetic system of shorthand for the English language developed by Englishman Sir Isaac Pitman (1813–1897), first presented in 1837.

3. See Dolton Edwards, "Meihem in ce Klasrum" [i.e., "Mayhem in the Classroom"], *Astounding Science Fiction*, 38, No. 1 (September 1946): 94–95. The story proposes, and embodies, the gradual reform of spelling, and at the conclusion is virtually unrecognizable as English. See also HPL's also "The Simple Spelling Mania" (1918).

4. HPL refers to Samuel Johnson's *Dictionary of the English Language* (1755; HPL owned an 1802 ed.) and John Walker's *A Critical Pronouncing Dictionary and Expositor of the English Language* (1804; HPL owned an 1807 ed.).

5. Lucius Cary, 2nd Viscount Falkland (1610?–1643), English politician and Secretary of State (1642–43). The statement was made in the context of debates in Parliament preceding the English Civil War (Falkland was a Royalist).

6. HPL refers to his revision of Anne Tillery Renshaw's *Well Bred Speech*.

7. A papal bull is a type of decree or charter issued by a pope of the Catholic Church, named after the leaden seal (*bulla*) traditionally used to authenticate it. When the Pope speaks *ex cathedra* (from the chair) on issues of faith or morals, he is infallible.

Walter John Coates of Driftwin

Letters to Walter John Coates

[1]   [*Drift-Wind*][1]

[11 March 1926]

The Drift-Wind, which [*sic*] came today and is certainly of unusual interest and merit. Though a conservative myself, I admire the grace of your arguments.[2]

H. L.

Notes

1. An extract from a letter to Coates regarding the first number of *Drift-Wind*, printed with comments by others under the heading "Baptizing the Baby": "The new-born Drift-Wind was christened in part as follows:—"
2. Probably referring to "Our Sleeping Liberals" by WJC.

[2]   [AHT]

169 Clinton Street
Brooklyn, New York
March 30, 1926

My dear Mr. Coates:—

[. . .]

Your sonnet from the *Republican* is very interesting, & reflects a mood which most contemplative persons come at last to experience. In my younger days I was fond of these philosophical speculations, but finally reached so complete a degree of scepticism that the very process of philosophising ceased to interest me. I am an absolute sceptic & materialist, & regard the universe as a wholly purposeless & essentially temporary incident in the ceaseless & boundless rearrangements of electrons, atoms, & molecules which constitute the blind but regular mechanical patterns of cosmic activity. Nothing really matters, & the only thing for a person to do is to take the artificial & traditional values he finds around him & pretend they are real; in order to retain that illusion of significance in life which gives to human events their apparent motivation & semblance of interest. I'm through with intellectualism now—my tastes are wholly those of an antiquarian, & of one who is amused by certain special trifles in literature & the arts. An epicurean & dilettante, in short.

H. P. Lovecraft

[3]   [AHT]

> 10 Barnes Street,
> Providence, R.I.
> May 6, 1926[1]

My dear Coates:—

[. . .]

I'd like some day to do for Rhode Island literature what you are doing for Vermont literature,[2] but fear I am too constitutionally lazy. We have had at least two golden ages—yea, four, counting the early activity in the middle of the 18th century (when Stephen Hopkins founded the Providence Library & Joseph Brown distinguished himself alike in architecture & science) & the still earlier Newport period when Bishop Berkeley's visit (he wrote his "Alciphron" in R.I.) stimulated the growth of a very learned & lettered circle—the one culminating in the foundation of the Redwood Library in 1750.[3] The two ages first thought of are those of the 1840's, when Poe used to lecture in Providence & the Athenaeum in Benefit St. was a meeting-place of the artistic, & of the '60's & '70's, when Mrs. Sarah Helen Whitman was in her mellow later years, & Nora Perry & Augustus Hoppin were rising figures.[4] In some respects, these two later periods may be considered as merging into each other. We have not in this generation produced much literature, tho' our artistic & musical life is very healthy. Right upstairs in this house lives one of the finest miniature-painters—an old lady named Miss Talfourd[5]—that I have ever observed. Yes—I wish some soul more energetic than I would compile an ample & authentic history of the fine arts in R.I. *Art* is our strong point. We produced Gilbert Stuart & J. S. Lincoln (the latter a relative of mine by marriage)[6] & have today one of the foremost art institutions in the country—the R.I. School of Design, whose magnificent new museum opened only two weeks ago next Sunday. [. . .]

Notes

1. WJC to HPL (30 May 1926; ALS, JHL) mentions receiving a letter dated 5 May 1926.

2. WJC was a champion of Vermont writers. It is not known what HPL was addressing, but WJC may have informed him of articles he was writing for W. Paul Cook's forthcoming *Recluse*.

3. The Redwood Library and Athenaeum at 50 Bellevue Avenue, Newport, RI, was founded in 1747 and completed in 1750. It is the oldest community library still occupying its original building in the US.

4. Sarah Helen Whitman (1803–1873), poet and friend of Edgar Allan Poe; Nora Perry (1831–1896), poet, journalist, and author of children's books; Augustus Hoppin (1828–1896), book illustrator.

5. Florence L. Talfourd (1870?–?), identified as an "artist" in various Providence city directories from 1901 onward.

6. James Sullivan Lincoln (1811–1888), painter who was called the "father of Rhode Island art." Lincoln's wife, Rosina Child Chase, was the sister of Mary Ann (Chase) Clark, the mother of Franklin Chase Clark, HPL's uncle.

[4]　　["The Materialist Today"][1]

[c. May 1926]

Today a fresh wave of interest in philosophical speculation has arisen. The dissolution of old doctrines under the influence of science in the nineteenth century gave rise for a time to a rational materialism of which Huxley and Haeckel were conspicuous exemplars; but the later crumbling of moral standards, amidst the dizziness of mental liberation, has brought about a sense of restlessness and cerebral panic, and for the moment we witness the amusing spectacle of a reactionary scrambling for shelter beneath the wing of a supernatural belief either blindly conceived without intelligent reflection, or tenuously modified to accommodate as many angles of scientific truth as can be accommodated by a system of extra-rational origin.

Hence spring Fundamentalism and Modernism:[2] both defensive emotional reactions against the ethical chaos of the present; and, as such, entitled to the sincere respect of all who realise that the sole beauty of life resides in its traditional patterns. It would not be the wish of any responsible materialist to destroy or combat the major social conditions at which these fervid believers are aiming; and the utmost attack of logic on faith serves only to replace an irrational with a rational reason for orderly life and thought.

The materialist denies that any standard is divine or absolute, and would free our conceptions of conduct from those supernatural fetters which impart a false perspective and cause the former believer to lose his moral sense as soon as he loses his faith. Conduct, of course, is only a side issue in the search for truth. But, so far as the modern materialist is interested in it at all, he merely recommends with gentle cynicism the adherence of each person to the ethical system in which he was reared, as constituting the only authentic source, in a purposeless cosmos without absolute standards, of those relative standards necessary to the orderly life and mental comfort of mankind.

Many specious arguments continue to be advanced by those labouring for a survival of religion. Fundamentalists, of course, do not argue; but the Modernists are very ingenious in adapting the language and conceptions of their ancient enemy, science, to their own uses, thus hoping to effect a reconciliation with that powerful adversary. Foremost among their contentions is that which affirms the existence of a "soul" and the truth of immortality by proclaiming mind a *thing* and thereupon invoking the scientific principle of the conservation of matter and energy to prove that it can never be destroyed—an argument, of course, which not only confuses the general mental principle with individual personality, but forgets that the law of conservation denies the fresh creation as well as the destruction of matter and energy, a point which would not allow for the birth of new souls! To the materialist, *mind* seems very clearly not a *thing*, but a *mode of motion* or *form of energy*.

Now, although the sum of energy in the universe is (speaking without reference to the very recent discoveries in intra-atomic physics and chemistry) virtually indestructible, we see very clearly that it is most eminently subject to transformations from one form to another. Mechanical energy becomes electricity under the appropriate conditions, and, under other conditions, that electricity becomes light and heat. Nothing is *lost,* but all is *changed.*

Now I regard the vital principle as just such a form of energy—and *mind* is only one of the many complex manifestations of that principle. It is a product and attribute of certain forms and processes of matter; and when that matter is disintegrated, it ceases to exist—just as molecular heat ceases to exist upon the dispersal or disintegration of the material molecules which make it possible. Nothing is *lost,* any more than when electrical energy is transformed to luminous energy; but a complete metamorphosis occurs, and the identity of mind and life becomes effaced as the units of energy pass away in other forms— mostly radiant heat and other waves in the ether. Mind is no more immortal than a candle flame. The flame is just as *immortal,* if we wish to take a poetic view and reflect that the units of energy therein are never lost to the universe, but merely dissipated and incorporated into other forms and phenomena.

> "Imperious Caesar, dead and turn'd to clay,
> Might stop a hole to keep the wind away."[3]

One might add, as noted above, that ultra-modern discovery, as based upon the phenomena of radio-activity, has opened wide and strange vistas, and perhaps defeated *in the last analysis* the idea of the indestructibility of matter and energy. Whilst matter and energy are clearly indestructible so far as any hitherto understood principles are concerned, it seems increasingly clear that cosmic force and substance have other and deeper relations and limitations— whose kinship to the phenomena we know is like that of an hour-hand to a minute- or second-hand on a clock.

It seems, in the light of recent discoveries, that all matter is in a state of balance betwixt formation and disintegration—evolution and devolution— and that the infinite cosmos is like a vast patch of summer sky out of which little cirrus clouds gather here and there, presently to be dissolved into blankness again. The universes we know correspond to the little cirrus clouds of that summer sky, being merely transient aggregations of electrons condensed from that field of ungrouped electrons which we call space, and soon to be dissolved into that space again. This process of formation and destruction is the fundamental attribute of all entity—it is infinite Nature, and it always has been and always will be. The world, life, and universe we know, are only a passing cloud—yesterday in eternity it did not exist, and tomorrow its existence will be forgotten. Nothing matters—all that happens happens through the automatic and inflexible interacting of the electrons, atoms, and molecules of infinity according to patterns which are co-existent with basic entity itself. The general idea is that of a kaleidoscope with its endless rearrangements—there is no object or purpose in ultimate creation, since all is a ceaseless repetitive cycle of transitions from nothing back to nothing again.

However, all this need give worry to none. The aspirations of the human spirit, so movingly cited by theists, are pretty enough in themselves; and one need neither go to the trouble of breaking them up and finding their physiological components (although that is relatively easy to do) nor impute to them a cosmic significance which, though poetic to imagine, is certainly not logically deducible from their existence and characteristics. It is most sensible just to accept the universe as it is, and be done with it. All is illusion, hollowness, and nothingness—but what does that matter? Illusions are all we have, so let us pretend to cling to them; they lend dramatic values and comforting sensations of purpose to things which are really valueless and purposeless. All one can logically do is to jog placidly and cynically on, according to the artificial standards and traditions with which heredity and environment have endowed him. He will get most satisfaction in the end by keeping faithful to these things.

Notes

1. See letter 5. The original letter is lost, and the text presented here is a revised version of what he wrote WJC.
2. By Modernism HPL refers to a tendency among some contemporary religious thinkers to reject such notions as the total inerrancy of the Bible and to urge an updating or modernizing of some of the metaphysical and ethical teachings of Christianity.
3. Shakespeare, *Hamlet* 5.1.235–36.

[5]   [ALS, JHL]

May 11[, 1926]

My dear Coates:—

I am flattered by your wish to print my humble epistle, & am herewith returning it with such hasty emendations as occur to me. Of course, being a reply to another letter, it begins somewhat abruptly & requires the addition of some prefatory raison d'etre—& this I have endeavoured to supply. If the full text is too long, you might cut out page 1 altogether—but the brief text on p. 2 is really essential to give the reader a clear idea of what the row is all about! So far as titles are concerned, I think "The Materialist Today" is as good as any; & the signature can be my own, since there is nothing in the least private about my opinions—tho' I don't try to force them on others.

Pardon brevity, but I'm in a vortex of work today. Here's hoping my maunderings won't bore your readers to death!

Cordially & sincerely—

H P L

[6]

[1 June 1926?]

[Text unavailable.]

[7]　[AHT]

10 Barnes Street,
Providence, R.I.
June 3, 1926

My dear Coates:—

[. . .]

I am interested to hear that you are unearthing copies of "The Rhode-Island Book."[1] . . . Providence certainly had a delightful literary circle in that period—I love to look at the old Athenaeum (still unchanged in every detail) which formed their unofficial headquarters & rallying-point. In the corridors of that good old building Poe used to walk with Mrs. Whitman, & on one occasion she shewed him a copy of "Ulalume" anonymously printed in one of the magazines on the tables, expressing her admiration and wondering who the author was.[2] When Poe modestly admitted his authorship, the local poetess chid him for hiding his light under a bushel; whereupon he proceeded to sign the nameless verses with a lead-pencil, casting the magazine back on the table whence his companion had taken it. Such was the anecdote informally told around Providence for sixty years, during which time no record of it had appeared in print. Captivated by this bit of folklore, the librarian of Brown University, Prof. Harry Lyman Koopman,[3] determined in 1909—the season of the Poe centenary—to investigate it more closely; & accordingly examined the bound magazine files of the Athenaeum with the utmost care. At last, surely enough, he found the number in question—& there, traced in delicate pencil-strokes, was the signature "Edgar A. Poe" beneath the Ulalume verses! Perfect verification! Now the volume is usually kept on exhibition under glass, open at the proper place. It may be remarked that this copy contains the extra stanza about 'the limbo of planetary souls' which Poe afterward deleted on Mrs. Whitman's recommendation—& which one will also find in the earlier edition of Griswold's "Poets & Poetry of America". . . . . . . As for my letter on materialism—I'll welcome any reply you care to make either in or out of print. Heaven knows that amateur journalism needs some good controversy to arouse it from the present lethal torpor! Your line of argument is one which I have encountered before, but which I cannot honestly say appeals to me enough to cause any alteration in my present conclusions. The motto of Descartes,[4] true or false, proves very little concerning the *reality* of the material world—whilst your argument about the mental and subjective origin of the visible world (a form of argument adopted by Bishop Berkeley, who did his writing in Rhode Island in 1729–31, just outside Newport!) has many vulnerable spots—unless, indeed, you bring to it many points not hit upon by earlier users of it. I might say here that although of course our image of an object is infinitely different from the actual object itself (the *sich an ding*,[5] I think Kant called it, tho' my knowledge of German is a hazy memory) there must certainly be a very fixed relation betwixt object & image; so that we can scarcely believe in the absolute *unreality* of the matter as such. Very few contemporaries, I may add—even among the believers in spirit & immortality—still adhere to this pure Berkelian idealism. [. . .]

Notes

1. By Anne C. Lynch.

2. The magazine in question was the *American Review* (December 1847), the first appearance of the poem.

3. Harry Lyman Koopman (1860–1937), Librarian of Brown University (1893–1930).

4. Presumably a reference to the celebrated statement *Cogito, ergo sum* (I think, therefore I am), indicating that in Descartes' view everything about external reality can be the subject of doubt, but the reality of an individual's thought (and, therefore, his/her existence) cannot be doubted. The doctrine is fallacious in that in writing *Cogito* Descartes has already assumed his own existence.

5. Actually *Ding an sich*, a thing as it is in itself independent of observation.

[8]   [ANS][1]

[Postmarked Providence, R.I.,
19 July 1926]

Thanks exceedingly for latest Drift Wind, which I have just received & read appreciatively. ¶ A local bookshop has just issued a catalogue of books by R.I. authors, & I see that there are an astonishing number! To treat of these all would constitute a life work. Here's wishing you luck with the Vermont contingent!
Sincerely yrs—H P Lovecraft

Notes

1. *Front:* Middle Campus, Brown University, Providence, R.I.

[9]

[9 August 1926]

[Text unavailable.]

[10]

[9 September 1926]

[Text unavailable.]

[11] [ANS][1]

[Postmarked Providence, R.I.,
16 October 1926]

Thanks exceedingly for the [distin]ctive November *Driftwind*, [which] I have perused throughout with keen interest. When your contributor Flower[2] has finished his article on poetic ideals, I may have a word or two of reply to give; for I think he underestimates the principle of classic restraint & [force] through limitation of [ornament] in art. But I welcome anything [tending?] to start a really intelligent discussion in amateurdom.—HPL

Notes

1. *Front:* Trinity Church, Built 1726, Newport, R. I.
2. James Howard Flower (1883–1967), a Vermont poet, author of *Flower of the Road* (1919) and *Bobolinks at Dawn and Whippoorwills at Dusk* (1923). HPL refers to "Poetic Ideals: Part 1," *Driftwind* [1], No. 8 (November 1926): 7, and "Poetic Ideals: Part 2," *Driftwind* [1], No. 9 (December 1926): 2–3.

[12]

[4 November 1926]

[Text unavailable.]

[13]

[28 December 1926]

[Text unavailable.]

[14]   [ALS, JHL]

10 Barnes St.,
Providence, R.I.,
Jany. 4, 1927

My dear Coates:—

I must hasten to express my sympathy regarding the bereavement you have sustained—a bereavement which this household can well
understand, since it was exactly ten years ago that I lost a brilliant young
cousin from the same cause.[1] He was taken by his mother to Colorado
Springs as soon as the presence of consumption was discovered, but died on
the last day of 1916. The shock to you must indeed be great—though it is just
as true as it is trite to point out that time works certain comforting readjustments; abating the acuteness of the emotion even while never diminishing the
affectionate remembrance & the sense of loss. You had mentioned your son's
illness, & I had hoped to hear of his improvement & recovery—but there is
little foreseeing in such matters, & one must learn to practice a philosophic
resignation. Activity, I think, is the best immediate counteractive of such a
blow. It deadens pain, even when it cannot cure it.

I am sorry to hear that you are having to consider a departure from Vermont, since your services in preserving Vermont poetry have so closely identified you with the Green Mountain State. Necessity, however, is a stern
leader; & one may only hope that some later circumstance may lead you back
in triumph. What part of N.Y. state do you think you can manage to land in?
If it is anywhere near Greenwich or Schuylerville or Saratoga you must call on
amateur journalism's Grand Old Man, the poet Jonathan E. Hoag, who cele-
brates his 96th birthday on the 10th of the coming February.[2] He is so near
Vermont (he was born at Hoosick Falls N.Y., not far from the border) that it
seems as though he ought to be semi-eligible for *Driftwind*—which impels me
to send you his latest poem for possible publication;[3] he having entrusted me
with the placing of it. Not many men of 96 are so active & tuneful—but he
comes of a long-lived stock, & used to hear eye-witness anecdotes of the Fort
Edward massacre of 1757 from a great-aunt who lived to be 103.

I shall be glad to see the February & March *Driftwinds,* & do not blame
you for the cessation of a regular monthly programme whose regularity is
sadly ill-rewarded by your amateur contemporaries. I wish your energy & as-
siduity were contagious, for amateurdom certainly has fallen into a woefully
anaemic state! However—one may only plug along as best one can. Bacon
will issue another *United Amateur* shortly,[4] & there is talk of organising a local
branch in a mid-Western high-school—a form of auxiliary activity found very
helpful in the past. Your aspirations for Vermont literature are surely those of
a true patriot & native son—but revivals seem to come only by accident.
Rhode Island has been literarily unproductive for years, though music &

painting flourish very healthily.

Orton & Flower certainly succeed in striking the keynote of what one might call a sort of faecal sprightliness! Your woodcuts are exceedingly clever, the bookplate in particular having a very poignant charm. I always envy pictorial or decorative ability because my own skill in design is so utterly a nullity, despite an ardent wish to fix many an image in line & perspective, or light & shade, rather than in words.

I am writing, slowly & leisurely, a fantastic novel of adventures in dreamland, being now on page 87.[5] It will probably never see the light, but it diverts me none the less.

With renewed expressions of sympathy, & every good wish for every day of 1927, I remain

Most cordially & sincerely yrs

H P L

Notes

1. John Webster Coates, WJC's first child, died of tuberculosis at the age of 22 on 30 November. *Land of Allen* contains WJC's elegy to him, "The Son That Was: John: 1904–1926" (73). Phillips Gamwell (23 April 1898–31 December 1916), son of HPL's aunt Annie E. Phillips Gamwell and Edward F. Gamwell, also died of tuberculosis.

2. For that occasion, HPL wrote "To Jonathan E. Hoag, Esq., upon His Ninety-sixth Birthday, February 10, 1927." His final tribute to Hoag, who would die in October, was "Ave atque Vale."

3. "Home: [Hoosick Falls, N.Y.]," *Driftwind* [1], No. 12 (March 1927): 7.

4. In fact, Victor E. Bacon, Official Editor of the United Amateur Press Association, published no issue of the *United Amateur* after the September 1926 issue.

5. *The Dream-Quest of Unknown Kadath.*

[15]   [AHT]

[A Thursday in early 1927]

My dear Coates:—

[. . .]

As to Poe in Providence—I've made no original discoveries. The incident of the Ulalume signature was unearthed by Prof. Koopman, Librarian of Brown Univ., whilst Poe's other local manoeuvres are now pretty well incorporated into recent biographies. The only personal touch for me is the amusing dislike of Poe current in my family, & based on surviving memories of his alcoholic proclivities as observed & discussed in the 'forties. The mother & aunts of my elder aunt's husband[1] knew Mrs. Whitman quite well—admiring her in the main, though smiling at her occasional harmless affectations in attire—such as white shoes out of season, & so on. [. . .]

Notes

1. Dr. Franklin C. Clark (1847–1915), M.D. had married Lillian D. Phillips (1856–1932) in 1902. His mother was Mary Ann (Chase) Clark (1814–1906).

[16]

[4 August 1927]

[Text unavailable.]

[17]

[21 August 1927]

[Text unavailable.]

[18]   [dealer catalogue]

Thursday [29 September 1927]

[. . .] a rather impressionistic account of my one delectable & memorable glimpse of Vermont[1] . . . . I couldn't seem to boil it down to the desiderate 850 words, but herewith accord you full permission to delete ad libitum—slash it all you like.[2] [. . .]

Notes

1. "Vermont: A First Impression" (written 29 September 1927).
2. On 2 October 1927, WJC replied: "I will not delete it an atom."

[19]   [ANS][1]

[Postmarked Providence, R.I., 3 October 1927]

Thanks exceedingly for November *Driftwind*, whose size & excellence make it impressive indeed. I surely hope it may achieve, in time, a satisfactory professional foothold.

I think you might find an appreciative contributor—& an artist, in case you wish any illustrations—in the person of Bernard Dwyer, Box 43, West Shokan, N.Y., who lives on a farm & has much in common with the Vermont spirit. I'd send him a copy if I were you. Regards—H P Lovecraft

Notes

1. *Front:* College St. to Market Sq. Showing Hospital Trust and Chamber of Commerce, Providence, R.I.

[20]   [AHT]

October 13, 1927

My dear Coates:—

[. . .]

You may be interested to know that I own a copy of Fessenden's New England Farmer's Almanack for 1830—No. 3. The format is much like that of Robert B. Thomas's old standby,[1] but it lacks the vignettes at the head of the Farmers' Calendar. I infer from your article[2] that this venture was not continued after the founder's death—a less happy fate than that of another early rival of the immortal Robert; Dudley Leavitt's Farmer's Almanack (founded 1796) which I have just discovered is *still published* in full splendour, & embellished by the same early-19th-century woodcuts.[3] Leavitt's Almanack apparently serves New Hampshire, or perhaps Northern New England generally, as the Old Farmer's serves Southern New England. I am collecting all the ancient New England almanacks I can find—having started with my own family file of the Old Farmer's, which we have always had, generation after generation. This file had become rather fragmentary with the passing of the years, so that when it came into my possession it was *continuous* only back to 1877, with anterior scattered numbers going back to 1815. I have, by purchase, filled up many of the gaps, so that my present file goes back continuously to 1839, & has scattering numbers back to 1805. I want eventually to complete it absolutely, from 1773 to the present moment—but I fear that will be a long & costly task. These old almanacks have a quaint flavour of archaism very alluring to me—they are symbols of New England's Arcadian past, as Prof. Kittredge realised when he wrote his delightfully retrospective "Old Farmer & His Almanack".

[. . .]

H. P. L.

Notes

1. Robert B. Thomas (1766–1846) produced *The (Old) Farmer's Almanac* from 1792 until his death.

2. Possibly "The Future for a Literary Magazine in Vermont," *Driftwind* 2, No. 1 (June 1927).

3. *Leavitt's Farmer's Almanack,* produced by Dudley Leavitt (1772–1851), ran from 1797 until his death, whereupon it was taken over by his nephew, William B. Leavitt.

[21]

[26 January 1928]

[*Text unavailable.*]

[22]

Tuesday [early 1928?]

[Text unavailable.]

[23]　[ANS][1]

[Postmarked Springfield, Mass.,
7? June1928]

Still on the move! Visited a week in North Wilbraham,[2] & am now bound for the Mohawk Trail. I mean to see something of the country before I die! Yr obt Servt
　H P L

Notes

1. *[Card description at back:]* The Eastern States Exhibition occupies a tract of 172 acres, and is the largest institution of its kind in the East. Buildings are of brick, steel and concrete. Plant is valued at $1,250,000. Attendance each year, 250,000. Accommodations for 1200 cattle, 600 horses, 1000 sheep and swine. More than 100,000 ft. of general exhibition space under roof. Special buildings for agricultural, state, home and boys and girls exhibits. Coliseum buildings, 200 × 300 ft., seats 5600, with arena 100 × 206. Grand stand seats 10,000. Half mile race track, record 2.03½.

2. HPL's hosts at the time were Edith Miniter (1867–1934) and Evanore O. Beebe (1858–1935). He wrote about the region (as "Dunwich") in "The Dunwich Horror" (1928).

*At Arthur Goodenough's place in West Brattleboro, Vermont, Sunday, 16 June 1928.
Left to right: Walter John Coates, Goodenough, Helen Miller,
Vrest Orton, Paul P. Jones, Nettie (Mrs.) Coates, H. P. Lovecraft*

[24]

[13 June 1928]

[Text unavailable.]

[25]

[27 June 1928]

[Text unavailable.]

[26]

[7 July 1928]

[Text unavailable.]

[27]　[Sotheby's]

10 October [1928?]

Thanks for Driftwind [. . .] The present issue is splendid [. . .] I was particularly interested in your account of Ethan Allen's philosophic beliefs.[1] Our friend Woodburn Harris is much perturbed by what he considers the attempt of modern Vermonters to conceal the fact that Allen was Deist & that he wrote the "Oracle"[2] [. . .]

Notes

1. WJC, "Ethan Allen's Religion."
2. Allen (1737–1789), American Revolutionary War patriot, published *Reason: The Only Oracle of Man* (1785) and other works of freethought.

[28]　[ANS][1]

[Postmarked Providence, R.I.,
22 October 1928]

Thanks for the intermediate *Driftwinds*—I had had a peek at the July issue at Orton's, but the Sept. was wholly new to me. It is, like all the issues, extremely interesting; & I was especially taken with the material pertaining to the mysterious Dr. Wilson.[2] One might invent a new explanation of his reticence & watchfulness, & write a weird tale about him! I must see that round schoolhouse some time. ¶ Hope you had an interesting argument with Woodburn Harris. He & I are slinging reams of paper in a complete settlement of all the problems of the cosmos! ¶ Again thanking you, & promising a real subscription before long—
Yr most obt servt
H P L

Notes

1. *Front:* The Arcade, Westminster St. Front, Providence, R.I.
2. WJC, "Dr. Wilson," a poem; prefaced by "The Round Schoolhouse in Brookline."

[29]   [ALS, JHL]

[H. P. LOVECRAFT
10 BARNES STREET
PROVIDENCE, R. I.]

Jany. 27, 1929

My dear Coates:—

The Declaration arrived yesterday, & after a few changes of text (though not of sense) I am sending it on to Orton for his approval or emendation. I have given the syntax & word-selection a slightly smoother cast, & have supplied something of the late 18th century atmosphere proper to such a declaration, by eliminating such expressions as are incongruous with the spirit of Ethan Allen's aera. The genius of this production much impresses me, & I have no fears for the future of a Republic based upon so firm & spirited a foundation. As Ambassador to the Rhode-Island Free State, I hereby accord the document my imprimatur; & trust that its publication may produce that salutary effect for which it was intended.[1]

Yes—I secure *Weird Tales* each month, but have not so far noticed the work of your friend. I will keep a sharp watch for it hereafter, & will look over my files for older specimens when I get a spare moment. I shall have a long story, "The Dunwich Horror", in the April issue—out March 1st.

I am eagerly looking forward to the time when circumstances will again let me visit your captivating Commonwealth, & hope strongly that it may be the coming summer. You may count upon me for the promotion of all plans for Vermont's secession from the Machine Age—though you must watch closely lest I return the province to His Majesty's dominions, of which I have never ceased to be a loyal subject!

Early this year I was in Boston, Salem, & Marblehead, absorbing my favourite antiquities. There is a magnificent new wing of colonial architecture & its sources in the Museum of Fine Arts, & I absorbed it with the most poignant pleasure. It quite outclasses the famed American Wing at N.Y.'s Metropolitan Museum.

Well—I trust I haven't delayed the Declaration so long as to cause you inconvenience, & hope that Orton will be equally prompt. The text really ought to have another typing at this stage, & I hope Orton will provide such after he has made all his final alterations. I feel sure that I haven't appreciably added to the document's length.

With all good wishes for you & the Republic,
    I remain, Sir,
        Yr most oblig'd, most ob[dt] Servt,

                                    H P L

Ambaſsador Extraordinary & Minister Plenipotentiary from the Republic of
Vermont to the Empire of Rhode-Island

Notes

1. "A Declaration of Independence for Vermont," *Driftwind* 3, No. 5 (March 1929):
197–201. It concludes: "Given, in the year of our Lord nineteen hundred and twenty-
nine, and in the first year of the Republic of Vermont at Montpelier, Vermont, by /
VREST ORTON, Secretary of the Committee of Safety / H. P. L., President of the
Committee." The byline suggests a collaboration between Orton and HPL, but probably HPL simply edited Orton's draft. About the declaration, Orton has written: "in
Windham County that summer [1928] Lovecraft, Cook and myself concocted and
issued a formal *Declaration of Independence of The Republic of Vermont* couched in the idiom of the 18th century and sent out to an incredulous world. It was not taken seriously, as we intended, by that world. Many years later (in 1977) my book was
published on the *History of the Republic of Vermont,* inspired by those talks Lovecraft,
Cook and I had in Windham County that summer." "Recollections of H. P. Lovecraft," in Joshi and Schultz 244.

[30]   [ALS]

                        [H. P. LOVECRAFT
                        10 BARNES STREET
                        PROVIDENCE, R. I.]
                                    Idibus Februarii,
                            Anno Reipublicae Viridimontanae
                                        I[1]
                                    [13 February 1929]

To His Worship, the Chief Consul, the lowly President of the Committee
sends greeting:
            Glad to get your note, & am on the lookout for the book.[2]
Pleased to hear that the latter is enthroned in the John Hay Library of Brown
University. I'll send you a postcard of the building to shew you what a fine
marble house on the hill-crest your cerebral progeny has won! Hope the review idea goes through all right.
    As for my comments on the new *Driftwind*—they really represent merely
the spontaneous preferences dictated by my personal bias rather than any objective estimate of relative intrinsic merit. "River in Spring" seems to win the

straw vote—but why didn't somebody back me up on "Winter Tragedy"? I *almost* mentioned "Blind Cat", but on second thought fancied that my extreme fondness for cats might have led me to overestimate it. I can see poor old Sophia this minute! Your "Youth Ego" is delightful, too, & I would certainly have voted for it were I not a cynic & anti-didacticist! "Night" is very good, though it would be better if a regular form matched the excellent imagery. "Winter Dusk" & "Vermont Pastoral" both have the pictorial, atmospheric note I like. "Haunted Hogan" is good, but "Laboratorically [*sic*] Speaking" seems to me too much of a philosophical concoction to be a *poem*. It's clever stuff, whatever it is, but it hasn't the singing beauty & ecstasy that make *poetry*. So far as clever stuff goes, you can't beat Orton's dry little comment on settled habits & domestic bliss![3]

[I liked the season of _____] but I can name one reader of yours who won't. Do you know who I mean . . . . or must I explain that our noble friend W. Paul Recluse has an undying hatred of blueberries & everything connected with them, dating from a juvenile time when their garnering was amongst his most abhorred of compulsory tasks?

I shiver at the thought of your present temperatures. Our warm spell broke a couple of days ago, & we are having what is subarctic weather for us—though thank heaven, the ground is snowless. But as Percy B. said—"If winter comes," & all that![4] So by June I hope I can be availing myself of your household's kindly hospitality, & helping to further Vermont's withdrawal from the hated Federal yoke![5]

By the way—I heard yesterday from your friend & contrib "Francis Flagg", whose pseudonym clears up his W.T. position for me. He is the author of a truly excellent story, "The Chemical Brain", in the January issue.[6]

Feby. 14

"Land of Allen" came yesterday afternoon, & I spent a pleasant evening digesting it from cover to cover. It is surely a major contribution to Vermontiana, & carries the sturdy spirit of the undefeated republic to gratifying lyric heights. Some of the poems I recognise from various issues of *Driftwind;* others are wholly new to me. How sincerely can I subscribe to the spirit of "Winter" on page 56! That's just what I would have written myself if I were a poet! As for my other preferences in the volume—of course they aren't likely to coincide with your own tastes; because as you know, I believe very profoundly that ethics & philosophy have no place in art, & that they merely *dilute* poetry instead of *constituting* it. The true function of aesthetics is simply to describe & symbolise the actual scenes, objects, & phenomena of the universe in poignant & ecstatic fashion, without any infusion of personal opinion or philosophic theory. It was the fault of Victorianism to read a pack of non-existent "laws" & values & trends into the impersonal cosmos, & then to get excited about them, as if they represented realities of Nature in the same way that the tangible &

genuine beauties of objective existence do. The Victorian forgot that art is not an affair of the speculative intellect, but of the senses, emotions, & imagination alone. Literature with an ethical bias—or with any purpose other than self-expression with Nature & stark sincerity as a basis—is not, per se, art or even real literature at all; because it is encroaching on the province of philosophy, a speculative science antipodal to aesthetics. Of course, any given piece of literature may have the *externals* of didacticism; but if it is the real thing, its inner motive will not be didactic at all. Real poetry has no relation to intellectual or moral purpose, or to anything else except the poet's ecstasy at the sight of beauty, & his unconquerable will to sing of what moves him—purely for the joy of the singing & for nothing else. Poe, Swinburne, & Oscar Wilde had the right idea about this. As a matter of fact, the only use of opinions & convictions, or ideas of good & evil, in poetry, is to get the poet emotionally excited enough to sing at the required pitch of ecstasy. If he can sing thus without the added stimuli—as Keats did—so much the better. All the poet ought to do is to sing whatever is in him, & the excellence of the result can properly be judged on only two counts aside from technique: (a) Truth to human experience, (*real* experience, & not conventional myths about what experience ought to be) & (b) Intensity of the emotion or lyrical impulse. The strength of the modern aesthete lies in the fact that he understands these principles. His weakness lies in his occasional misapplication of them, as when he isolates fragments of uncorrelated experience & imagines that they have the same significance as when they are scaled against the totality of life.

Thus you see that my standard of judging poetry *as poetry* is likely to be widely different from yours, since it prevents one from assigning *poetic* credit for clever turns of *thought* (not fancy or imagery) or brilliant presentations of *intellectual & moral* conviction (not ecstasy in the presence of beauty).

All told, I think I extracted a maximum of personal enjoyment from "Pardon Janes"[7]—which you'll recall my praising when it appeared in *Driftwind*. That has genuine colour & vitality, & is redolent of the Vermont scene & of the anfractuosities of human nature in general. A close rival, though, is "Night in Vermont", which has all the visual vividness & concrete colour that mean poetry to me. "Earth Pangs" is a very powerful piece in another way. The sonnets are all a rich mine of valuable material—so notably so that I'd be inclined to call the sonnet form a natural medium of expression for you. It is here that your spontaneous eloquence—the sheer artistry of winged words—shows to best advantage. Pieces like "Life & I" represent what is almost your technical high-water mark—marking your closest adherence to the essential structure & vocabulary of poetry, & your maximum avoidance of phrases, words, & types of expression belonging essentially to the language of the prose intellect. I hope to see more specimens in future volumes. But in truth, I greatly enjoyed everything in the book, & congratulate you strongly on its excellence. Cook did well by

you, too—the volume is a credit to the Recluse Press! ¶ With all best wishes—
> Yr most obt
>> Viceroy of Rhode-Island

Notes

1. The ides of February, in the first year of the Republic of the Green Mountains.
2. *Land of Allen and Other Verse.*
3. *Driftwind* 3, No. 5 (March 1929) contained the following: Jean Burrows, "River in Spring" (216–17); Arthur Truman Merrill, "Winter Tragedy" (211); Nellie S. Richardson, "The Blind Cat" (194–95); WJC, "The Youth-Ego" (210); Jeannette Slocomb Edwards, "Night" (190); Bertha Oppenheim, "Winter Dusk" (214b–15); Elisabeth Kent, "Vermont Pastoral" (219–20); Norman Macleod, "Haunted Hogan" (204); Lillian Pauline Haeussler, "Laboratorially Speaking" (214); and Vrest Orton, "Translation from the American—No. 5:—Bliss" (225).
4. "If winter comes, can spring be far behind?" The last line of Shelley's "Ode to the West Wind."
5. Around this time Vrest Orton had embarked on a campaign in *Driftwind* against the exploitation of the Vermont state. The January 1929 issue contained a jocular proclamation ("How to Set Vermont Free") from a "Vigilance Committee" suggesting that "the State of Vermont secede from the Federal Union! To be explicit, we advocate that Vermont set itself up as a Republic, independent and free from all other governing and social influences." The March 1929 *Driftwind* further carried a "Declaration of Independence for Vermont," by a "Committee of Public Safety."
6. "The Chemical Brain" (*WT,* January 1929). Flagg was a pseudonym of Henry George Weiss.
7. The poems in *Land of Allen* are "Pardon Janes: The Mystery May of Calais" (17–22); "Night in Vermont" (31); and "Earth Pangs" (54). The section "Sonnets" (75–93) contains 17 poems, including "Life and I" (84). WJC had once lived in Calais, VT.

[31]   [AL] [dealer catalogue]

[29 February 1929]

[Contains HPL's written copy of his "Revelation" and states, regarding poems in a recent *Driftwind*] all the freshness, colour, expectancy, interest, happiness, & sense of dignity, values, & direction which make ordinary life endurable [. . .] Years ago I wrote some verses on the same theme myself—though with only a fraction of the grace & assurance of these poignant lines. Smith printed them in The Tryout.[1]

The one thing that reconciles me to the passing of time is the fact that I do manage to shed a little more nonsense & mawkishness each year.

Notes

1. HPL, "Revelation," *Tryout* (March 1919).

[32]

[1 May 1929]

[*Text unavailable.*]

[33]

[17 May 1929]

[*Text unavailable.*]

[34]   [dealer catalogue]

[4 October 1929]

[. . .]

There is no question that Melville is great & that Longfellow is mediocre. I'm not sure about Dickinson [. . .] Vast gulfs between 1880 & 1929 are apparent there [England], as here; & thence shows us about how our own race & tradition responds [*sic*] to the intellectual readjustments of the period. It is our job to repudiate the Jewish admixture if we can, & to follow the curve of purely Anglo-Saxon thought without becoming arbitrarily reactionary or ostrich-headed. Another thing—Hawthorne at his best cannot be said to be seriously challenged today. [. . .]

P.P.S. If I were you, I'd discriminate more about changing values. Milton is not seriously challenged today, & Wilkie Collins never was accepted as a major figure. Moreover, Fielding & Smollett have always been in the first rank.

[35]   [ALS]

Tuesday
[mid-October? 1929]

My dear Coates:—

I wasn't especially defending Emily Dickinson, but was merely pointing out the multiplicity of the causes—& the soundness of a few of them—which impel occasional revaluations of literature from age to age. The present case is not unique, as you may easily see by following the reputation of any varied assortment of authors through a space of several centuries. It is a mistake, too, to single out Victorian opinion as a basis of comparison. In many ways the middle 19th century formed a naive & curious Dark Age of taste in all the arts—I hardly need point out its architectural barbarities. If we want to formulate a norm for the Anglo-Saxon main stream, we must consider the average massed opinion all the way down from Chaucer's time. The Elizabethan age represented a far truer flowering of our racial impulses than did the Victorian.

However—as I said on my card, your main thesis seems to me perfectly sound & well taken. Undeniably—all apart from the effects of natural change & altered philosophic-scientific-psychological perspective—the world of American taste & opinion is distinctly & lamentably Jew-ridden as a result of the control of publicity media by New York Semitic groups. Some of this influence certainly seeps into Anglo-Saxon critical & creative writing to an unfortunate extent; so that we have a real problem of literary & aesthetic fumigation on our hands. The causes are many—but I think the worst factor is a sheer callous indifference which holds the native mind down to mere commercialism & size & speed worship, allowing the restless & ambitious alien to claim the centre of the intellectual stage by default. In a commercialised civilisation, publicity & fame are determined by economic causes alone—& there is where the special talents of Messrs. Cohen & Levi count. Before we can put them in their place, we must de-commercialise the culture—& that, alas, is a full-sized man's job! Some progress could be made, though, if all the universities could get together & insist on strictly Aryan standards of taste. They could do much, in a quiet & subtle way, by cutting down the Semitic percentage in faculty & student body alike. It is really amusing how we simple Western Europeans have allowed Orientals to trample over our brains for 1500 years & more—ever since we let them saddle us with the sickly Jew slave-religion of Christus instead of our own virile, healthy, Aryan polytheistic paganism. In this matter of religion, though, we are coming back—for the Jew-Christian tradition will be extinct in the Western world in two or three more generations, save for the nominal Catholic ritualism of the eternal rabble. We are getting back to the same Aryan philosophy & paganism which are naturally ours by right of blood & instinct.

However—that isn't what we were discussing. As for literature—you'll find that the causes for contemporary change are many & complex, & that Semitisation is only one contributing influence. Let Great Britain, still largely unSemitised, be your index of comparison. Scientific thought in England is pretty straight Anglo-Saxon stuff—Bertrand Russell, Aldous & Julian Huxley, H. G. Wells, Sir J. Jeans, Eddington, &c. &c.—but we find the forces of change emphatically at work. It was out of Ireland—where Jews are almost as happily scarce as snakes—that James Joyce's "Ulysses" came. The causes of vast cultural changes, be they renaissances or decadences, are buried deep in complex historical & psychological phenomena. Our present convulsion—which is probably a renaissance in some phases & a decadence in others—is far too big an affair to be traced to any one simple origin. Roughly speaking, the thing is due to the effect of sudden new doses of knowledge, & of sensationally rapid changes in ways of living, travelling, earning money, & making things. Personally, I think we're losing more than we're gaining; for of all the current changes only the matter of added knowledge & intellectual liberation seems really good to me.

Weiss & Harris write very interestingly—especially Harris, who is refreshingly intelligent despite a narrow aesthetic horizon. He'll expand with the years, I think.

Rather cool autumn hereabouts, so that I haven't been outdoors as much as last fall. I don't envy you up in the Arctic regions! ¶ Best wishes—& I eagerly await your second article on literary transvaluations.[1] ¶ Yr ob^t Servt HPL

P.S. Is the magazine you want *The American Poetry Magazine,* edited by Clara Catherine Prince, 358 Western Ave., Wauwautosa [*sic*], Wisconsin? The man who prints that is a friend of a friend of mine,[2] & is thinking of founding a pedagogical publishing house. If he does, I shall probably be his chief reviser.

Notes

1. WJC had published "Literary Torch Bearers" in *Driftwind* for November 1929. It appears there was no "second article."
2. HPL refers to Maurice W. Moe's friend Clara Catherine Prince, editor and publisher of the magazine. The publishing company was the Kenyon Press, which did publish a few booklets that HPL may have revised.

[36]   [ANS]

[Postmarked 30 January 1930]

[*Text unavailable.*]

[37]

10 Barnes St.,
Providence, R.I.,
Feby. 27, 1930.

My dear Coates:—

Well—here I am at last with that belated subscription which my chronic brokeness prevented me fron sending at the proper season! This, I trust, carries me over till next January; at which time I hope to be less tardy. I am looking forward to future *Driftwinds* with eagerness.

Incidentally, I am shooting along some recent metrical emanations of mine in case some of them may be useful as *Driftwind* fillers. Of these 33 sonnets, you are free to choose as few or as many as you with—or none at all, if they don't fit the magazine—of those which are not tagged with the name of some other periodical. Those so tagged have been sold—I think about 15 are thus disposed of. All these sonnets can be used separately & independently except the first three, which form a sort of progressive introduction. You might return the whole batch—whether or not you take any—letting me know the numbers of the ones you want, if you do want any. I will then make copies for you—leaving the original MS. intact for further lending purposes. But don't bother to take any—or even to read the stuff—unless you really feel like it.

Hope you still remain unfrozen—as you probably do if Vermont has had its share of our recent & highly welcome premature spring. From what Orton writes, I judge that the mildness has been felt as far north as Rutland.

Incidentally—I am interested in Orton's new "Tory Press", & in his expressed intention of reprinting our famous Declaration of Independence as a broadside. I like the name of his press—it reflects my own sentiments, & appears to endorse my own wish to return the independent republicks of New England to their loyal dominions of His Brittannick Majesty! God Save the King!

Do you hear from Cook frequently? I have had no word since his arctic sojourn with you, though Munn says he is actively back at the *Transcript* office—somewhat improved in nervous poise, though still woefully seedy as compared with his normal health. I surely hope the spring & summer will put him fully on his feet again.

I am hoping to patch up a sort of southward trip some time this spring—getting as far toward the equator as my anaemic purse, plus a motor lift from my young friend Frank B. Long—will let me. I surely need it, for this winter has drained nearly the last drop of energy out of me. Damn cold weather! I may have to live in the South yet, despite my intense hereditary attachment to old New England!

With best wishes, & hoping that the submission of the enclosed doggerel does not constitute an imposition,

I have the honour to remain, Sir,

Yr most oblig'd, most ob^t Servt,

HPL

P.S. Amidst many woeful interruptions, I am trying to get started on a new horror-story with a *Vermont* scene.

[38]

[26 April 1930]

[*Text unavailable.*]

[39]   [ANS]

[Postmarked 29 April 1930]

[. . .] the most utterly fascinating city I have ever seen![1]

Notes

1. HPL was in Charleston, SC.

[40]

[12 June 1930]

[*Text unavailable.*]

[41]   [ANS][1]

[Postmarked Providence, R.I.,
11 August 1930?]

is _____ interesting to _____, the weird _____. I had never before seen the _____, & am grateful indeed for this opportunity, _____ _____ To me it seems to have _____ England origin—though it is _____ that _____ are modifications make it an _____ British _____. Your introduction represents _____ & painstaking scholarship for which the bibliophile & literary student will be profoundly grateful. ¶ Have just been to the N.A.P.A. Boston convention, after which I made interesting side-trips to Salem, Marblehead, Quincy, &c. The _____ successful _____.

Best wishes—
H P L

Notes

1. *Front:* Main Entrance, Old Witch House, Salem, Mass.

[42]   [ANS] [*Nonconformist* 1, No. 3, 2009]

[Postmarked Providence, R.I.,
7 August 1931]

Congrats on the two latest Driftwinds—one of which arrived during my absence, & the other of which just came. You are surely the premier upholder of Vermont letters! The N Y Times last Sunday had a fine full-page review of the new Stephen Daye Vermont anthologies on p. 2 of the book section.[1] Yours stood at the head of the list! Best wishes—come down when you can & bring WPC along. Give him my regards.

Yr obt HPL

Notes

1. Uffington Valentine, "Green Mountain Literature" (a review of *Vermont Verse: An Anthology* and other books published by the Stephen Daye Press), *New York Times Book Review* (16 August 1931): 2.

[43]

[20 August 1931]

[*Text unavailable.*]

[44]

[27 September 1931]

[*Text unavailable.*]

[45]   [ANS][1]

[Postmarked Haverhill, Mass., 4 October 1931]

Greetings from an important assemblage—Tryout & Recluse[2] at the native village of Whittier. Glorious weather! Yesterday one of the amateurs took Cook & me to Hingham & the south shore—where we saw the Old Ship Church built in 1681. Now W P C & I are going to ancient Newburyport. Regards—H P L

Tryout

Notes

1 *Front:* The Gardens at Poet Whittier's Birthplace, Haverhill, Mass.
2. I.e., Charles W. Smith and W. Paul Cook (who did not sign the card).

[46]   [ANS][1]

[Postmarked Providence, R.I., 25 October 1931]

Glad to see the new Driftwind. The long poem[2] makes me wish I had the cash to head for the West Indies—which would be just the climate for me during the next few months. Had a glimpse of inland Connecticut this month—going to Hartford to meet Orton & discuss a book job, & returning via Norwich & Plainfield. Delightful countryside—& I had never seen it before despite its proximity.

Regards—H P L

Notes

1. *Front:* The Carrie Tower, Hope, Manning and University Halls at Left. Brown University, Providence, R.I.

2.. Caroline Parker Smith, "The Virgin Islands," *Driftwind* 6, special number (October 1931): 5–19, a collection of poems, each named after an island (such as "St. Thomas").

[47]

[1 November 1931]

[*Text unavailable.*]

[48]   [ANS][1]

[Postmarked Providence, R.I.,
17 November 1931]

Glad to see the interesting new *Driftwind* with its pleasantly varied contents! That frontispiece is fascinating—hope Montpelier hasn't changed too much since then.[2] Suppose Cook will be up to see you Thanksgiving week. If it were mid-July I'd surely envy him!

Regards—H P L

Notes

1. *Front:* New Industrial Trust Bldg. by Night, Providence, R. I.

2. "Montpelier in 1850," *Driftwind* 6, No. 3 (November 1931): frontispiece.

[49]   [Sotheby's]

[25 January 1932]

Glad you found some of the Fungi worth using.[1] "Recognition" & "The Canal" represent recurrent dream-types which I have encountered since earliest youth. Yes—I wish I could include the whole lot in a booklet some time. There are two or three more around here somewhere, which I never had the energy to type.[2]

Notes

1. Ten of the sonnets appeared in *Driftwind* (one after HPL's death, and perhaps not actually submitted by him). Notes written on the handwritten draft of the poem indi-

cate that four sonnets had been taken early. HPL submitted the typescript of the poem at the time of this letter. Three poems appeared in 1932, including "Recognition,"
one in 1934, and "The Canal" in 1936. It is not clear when and how WJC selected the
other five poems he eventually published.

2. HPL had not typed "Evening Star" and "Continuity" because he considered them to
be the closing verses of *Fungi from Yuggoth* and felt he would write other poems as part of
the series.

[50]

[17 February 1932]

[*Text unavailable.*]

[51]   [ANS][1]

[Postmarked Boston, Mass.,
2 April 1932]

H. Warner Munn arrived from Athol last night and Lovecraft came up today
and for the rest of the week we are to have a great time of going places and
seeing things. Tomorrow it will be Harvard University and museums.
Paul Cook

Gay life in the metropolis! Our standard speed is five museums per diem.
Too bad you aren't around, also! Regards—HPL

Together again.
H. Warner Munn

Notes

1. *Front:* Esplanade along Charles River, showing West Boston bridge, Boston, Mass.
[*Note with arrow by Cook:* "where I work."]

[52]

[8 April 1932]

[*Text unavailable.*]

[53]   [*Driftwind,* July 1932]

15 April 1932

I can't say I agree with your contributor about the merits of Joseph
Smith.[1] I've waded through the Book of Mormon, and find it—despite much
cleverness and occasional vividness—pretty thin and imitative stuff. I don't
know how much is Spaulding[2] and how much Smith, but the whole thing is a

pretty poor copy of the King James Bible. When the two are compared by anyone with the least literary discrimination, the Mormon stuff shews up pretty badly. Still, considering the limitations of its creator or creators, it is a pretty clever fake.

Notes

1. HPL refers to an article by Warren L. Van Dine, "Joseph Smith in American Literature," *Driftwind* 6, No. 6 (May 1932): 7–12, that claimed that Joseph Smith (1805–1844), founder of Mormonism, would become "the most important figure in American literature."

2. HPL's error for Solomon Spalding (1761–1816), author of two unpublished works that some scholars believed to have been appropriated by Joseph Smith in writing the Book of Mormon.

[54]

[21 April 1932]

[*Text unavailable.*]

[55]   [ANS][1]

[Postmarked New Orleans, La.,
6 June 1932]

Greetings! At the far end of one of my annual travel outbursts, & enjoying every minute of it! Shenandoah Valley . . . . . Tennessee . . . . old Father Mississippi (seen by me for the first time) . . . Vicksburg . . . . . Natchez . . . . & now ancient New Orleans, paradise of the architect & antiquarian. Right in the same class with Charleston & Quebec! Here for over a week, then Mobile, Ala. Have a *very faint* hope of getting to Charleston. Regards—& hope that spring is getting around to the Arctic regions at last!
HPL

Notes

1. *Front:* Old St. Louis Cemetery, New Orleans, La.

[56]

[6 August 1932]

[*Text unavailable.*]

[57]

[1 September 1932]

[*Text unavailable.*]

[58] [ANS][1]

[Postmarked Boston, Mass..
2 September 1932]

Greetings! Off on my one vacation of the year—to ancient QUEBEC, haven of the past! For once I'll be farther north than you are. This is the first time I've been in Boston since the time when I so tragically missed seeing you—last October. The old place looks much the same! Regards—H P L

No sooner do I arrive at what I facetiously call home than I begin to have distinguished guests. But this is only for a few hours, as Howard takes an evening train for Montreal and Quebec. The prints of the "poem" were received all right and many thanks. Have started the revision of the prose, and with cool weather may finish it.
    Paul

Notes

1. *Front:* Business Section of Boston. [*HPL's note on picture side:*] The festive scene [*pointing to Hancock Street*].

[59]

[3 September 1932]

[*Text unavailable.*]

[60] [ALS]

[17 January 1933]

[. . .] Cook nearly took my breath away the other day by sending me a copy of [Maturin's] "Melmoth" as a gift—a thing I've been looking for for years. [. . .]

[61] [ANS]

[Postmarked 14 February 1933]

[*Text unavailable.*]

[62]

[25 April 1934]

[*Text unavailable.*]

[63]   [AHT]

66 College St.,
Providence, R.I.
May 29, 1935

Dear W J C:—

Very glad indeed to hear from you! I enjoyed the May *Drift-wind*, as always, & must congratulate you upon its increasingly solid quality. It is surely gratifying to watch the progress of an institution whose birth—in amateur journalism—I witnessed nine long years ago!

Regarding the inclusion of my name in your list of "Associates"—I surely feel overwhelmingly complimented by this idea![1] I must, however, admit that our friend Culinarius was all too realistically correct in his belief that so obscure a nonentity would add no prestige to the enterprise. Actually, I am no poet at all—hence am not known to any considerable number of the circle that clusters round the poetry magazines. So far as they are concerned, "H P Lovecraft" means no more than "John Smith" or "William Brown". It is, then, up to you to decide whether your title-page ought to carry such a useless dead weight. . . .

Cook's general restlessness is another matter—& something which I hope will tend to diminish with the years. Evidently his long period of stagnation in Athol bred an insatiable discontent & longing for sheer change—change for its own sake, without any particular object or plan. When one is in that state, every environment except the existing one seems full of beckoning advantages— which disappear as soon as the new is sampled. Culinarius has pretty well summed up this type of temperament himself in the lines entitled "Rootless"[2]— but I can't help thinking that his own restlessness will tend to diminish in time. . . .

At last we have had something approaching warm weather, & I hope the North Mont-Polar region has been proportionately benefited. Sooner or later I hope to take advantage of that invitation so generously repeated! . . . .

At present I am writing absolutely nothing in the verse line. The fact is, I have not written a single serious couplet or stanza since my voluminous out-burst of 1929–30. Evidently I tend to sing in spasms . . . . but when the next spasm comes on I may inundate you! By the way—a new journal called *The Galleon* lately accepted two of my old "Fungi from Yuggoth."[3]

With all good wishes & appreciations—
Yrs most cordially & sincerely,
H P L

Notes

1. In 1935, WJC began listing Associate Editors on the masthead of *Driftwind*. When he added HPL's name in the June/July issue, he renamed the list "Editorial Fellow-ship." HPL was listed through the February 1937 issue.

2. "Rootless," *Driftwind* 9, No. 8 (February 1935): 242–43. In *Contradictions*. A T.Ms. signed "Willis T. Crossman" exists at JHL.

3. Lloyd Arthur Eshbach, editor of the *Galleon*, accepted "Harbour Whistles" and "Background," but published only the latter.

[64]   [Sotheby's]

4 February [1936]

Visited [Frank Belknap] Long in N.Y. around New Year's, & saw all the gang. Loveman's new book of poems was out . . . Have you seen the new book of Long's poems—*The Goblin Tower*—which Barlow & I crudely printed last summer when I was in [Florida]?

Nettie and Walter John Coates

Woodburn Harris in 1938

Letters to Woodburn Harris

[1]   [AHT]

10 Barnes St.,
Providence, R.I.
(Begun) Feby. 25, 1929
(Ended) March 1, 1929
(Thank god for a vernal-sounding
date to write!)

My dear Harris:—

I am certainly glad to hear that my preceding letter and its enclosures helped to relieve your gnawing ennui, and only wish it had arrived a day earlier, so that you might have been spared the dull evening you describe. I share your lack of interest in radio—in fact, I have never owned one of these devices. Barring plumbing and electric lights, I fancy I shun the new-fangled contraptions of the machine age fairly well! Speaking of boredom— why don't you try to accumulate a library which will furnish you with a solid reserve of intellectual and aesthetic pabulum? The expense—unless you are particular about the appearance of the books—is truly next to nothing; for one can obtain astonishing bargains on the 10¢ and 25¢ counters of second-hand book shops. I believe that a discriminating book-buyer could, in less than a year's time, assemble a really splendid library nucleus for not over fifty dollars, by making (or having made for him) careful selections from among the musty shops of any good-sized city. Any time that you especially want some standard work, you might let me know—for I could probably find you a marvellously low-priced copy either here or in Boston. I couldn't live a week without a private library—indeed, I'd part with all my furniture and squat and sleep on the floor before I'd let go of the 1500 or so books I possess. My collection isn't a notable one, but it represents my dominant interests pretty fairly; so that by piecing out with library books and private loans I manage to have something interesting on hand most of the time.

I'm sure that Ernest Boyd would be vastly pleased if he knew how his article had impressed you![1] He is really a critic and litterateur of phenomenal acumen and good sense—by birth and education a Dubliner of the Protestant circle, but for the last decade a resident of the United States. I have admired him for years—long before his advent to these shores, and ever since I read his collected essays.[2] He is surely a consistent individualist—even to the extent of sporting a full beard in the year of our blessed redeemer 1929. As for the article, I think your appreciation may be said to have earned it for you a permanent possession! Pray keep it with my compliments—though you might *lend* it to me when you return the other material, for your reaction makes me rather anxious to glance over it again! It is certainly a clarifying and sanifying influence amidst the platitudes and illusions of Babbittdom. "Boosters" and machine-age optimists, as well as the theologically-minded, naturally foster the notion that a cynic is merely a destructive sneerer; but one does not have to study philosophy long to discover that cynicism really means, instead, an analytical and intelligent sense of proportion—which is equivalent to a sense of humour. The only justification for the popular definition is an *historical* one—it being a fact that the actual Hellenic founders and disseminators of the formalised cynical philosophy—Antisthenes, Diogenes, etc.—were indeed rather unpleasant and eccentric worthies. The modern cynic, in terms of historic lineage, is really more of an Epicurean than a follower of the Athenian snarlers and tub-dwellers.

Now returning to our controversy—I don't quite see where you have me cornered regarding the matter of ethics. You deny an undue enthusiasm for this subject, averring that your feelings are akin to those with which you survey the fact of 2 and 2's constituting 4. Well—I shall be convinced when you shew as much *indignation* over a challenge to this belief—which future developments in relativity may conceivably provide—as you do over the idea of disenfranchising all the Protestants in the United States! Personally, I feel more irritated by a challenge to an accepted scientific theory than I do by an act of so-called "evil" or "injustice" amongst mankind; although I never allow my irritation to hamper my acceptance of the new theory as soon as positive evidence warrants it. Thus I have reluctantly exchanged the old nebular for the planetesimal hypothesis, and am beginning to accept the main points of relativity despite a profound intellectual distaste. What is, is—and our emotions regarding the cosmos and its phenomena are of no significance whatever, being wholly subjective matters dependent on individual accidents of neural and glandular physiology and of experience and environment. About my own attitude toward ethics—I thought I made it plain that I object only to (a) grotesquely disproportionate indignations and enthusiasms, (b) illogical extremes involving a reductio ad absurdum, and (c) the nonsensical notion that "right" and "wrong" involve any principles more mystical and universal than those of immediate expediency (with the individual's comfort as a criterion) on the one hand, and those of aesthetic harmony and symmetry (with the individual's emotional-imaginative pleasure as a criterion) on the other hand. I believe I was careful to specify that I do not advocate vice and crime, but that on the other hand I have a marked distaste for immoral and unlawful acts which contravene the harmonious traditions and standards of beautiful living developed by a culture during its long history. This, however, is not *ethics but aesthetics*—a distinction which you are almost alone in considering negligible. The mental and emotional forces behind this attitude, and behind the attitude of the religionist or abstract moralist, are leagues apart; as is clearly recognised by virtually all arguers on both sides. Before I get through I shall quote a very good description of my type of person, from the pen of a man very much on the other side. You can't gauge differences like this by one's daily personal conduct, because personal conduct is largely a matter of response to instinctive stimuli wholly dissociated from intellectual belief. We do what we do automatically, and then try either to rationalise it according to some theory, or to conceal it if it clashes too much with the particular theory which happens to be fastened upon us. We are mostly puppets—automata— though of course the theories we happen to hold may sometimes turn the scales one way or the other in determining a course of action, when all the other factors are evenly divided between two alternatives. So far as I am concerned—I am an aesthete devoted to harmony, and to the extraction of the maximum possible pleasure from life. I find by experience that my chief pleasure is in symbolic identification with the landscape and tradition-stream to which I belong—hence I follow the ancient, simple New England ways of living, and observe the principles of honour expected of a descendant of English gentlemen. It is pride and beauty-sense, plus the automatic instincts of generations trained in certain conduct-patterns, which determine my conduct from day to day. But this is *not ethics,* because the same compulsions and preferences apply, with me, to things wholly outside the ethical zone. For example, I never cheat or steal. Also, I never wear a top-hat with a sack coat or munch bananas in public on the streets, because a gentleman does not do those things either. I would as soon do the one as the other sort of thing—it is all a matter of harmony and good taste—whereas the ethical or "righteous" man would be horrified by dishonesty yet tolerant of coarse personal ways. If I were farming in your district I certainly would assist my neighbours—both as a means of promoting my standing in the community, and because it is good taste to be generous and accomodating. Likewise with the matter of treating the pupils in a school class. But this would not be through any sense of inner compulsion based on principles dissociated from my personal welfare and from the principle of beauty. It would be for the same reason that I would not dress eccentrically or use vulgar language. *Pure aesthetics,* aside from the personal-benefit element; and concerned with emotions of *pleasure versus disgust* rather than of *approval versus indignation.* This is a highly important distinction. Advancing to the question of *collective* conduct as involved in problems of government, social organisation, etc.—I fully see your side of the matter, and would be the last person in the world to advocate any course of civic or economic policy which might tend toward the destruction of the existing culture. In accordance with this attitude, I am distinctly opposed to visibly arrogant and arbitrary extremes of government—but this is simply because I wish the safety of an artistic and intellectual civilisation to be secure, not because I have any sympathy with the coarse-grained herd who would menace the civilisation if not placated by sops. Surely you can see the profound and abysmal difference between this emotional attitude and the emotional attitude of the democratic reformer who becomes wildly excited over the "wrongs of the masses". This reformer has uppermost in his mind the welfare of those masses themselves—he feels with them, takes up a mental-emotional point of view as one of them, regards their advancement as his prime objective independently of anything else, and would willingly sacrifice the finest fruits of the civilisation for the sake of stuffing their bellies and giving them two cinema shows instead of one per day. I, on the other hand, don't give a hang about the masses except so far as I think deliberate cruelty is coarse and unaesthetic—be it toward horses, oxen, undeveloped men, dogs, niggers, or poultry. All that I care about is *the civilisation*—the state of development and organisation which is capable of gratifying the complex mental-emotional-aesthetic needs of highly evolved and acutely sensitive men. Any *indignation* I may feel in the whole matter is not for the woes of the downtrodden, but for the threat of social unrest to the traditional institutions of the civilisation. The reformer cares only for the masses, but may make concessions to the civilisation. I care only for the civilisation, but may make concessions to the masses. Do you not see the antipodal difference between the two positions? Both the reformer and I may unite in opposing an unworkably arrogant piece of legislation, but the motivating reasons will be absolutely antithetical. He wants to give the crowd as *much* as can be given them without wrecking all semblance of civilisation, whereas I want to give them only as much as can be given them without even slightly impairing the level of the national culture. When it's an actual question of masses versus culture, I'm for giving the masses as little as can be given without bringing on a danger of collapse. Thus you see that the reformer and I are very different after all. He has a *spontaneous enthusiasm* for reform and democracy, thinking it imperative to *urge* these things. I, on the other hand, have no enthusiasm at all in this direction; thinking it the best policy not to *urge* concessions, but merely to grant such things when the safety of the civilisation demands it. He is a democrat at all times, and because he *wants* to be. I am one only occasionally, and when I *have* to be. Still—if you want to be so concrete and pragmatical as to ignore all emotions and motives, and judge persons by acts alone, I suppose you can say that the moderate reformer and I have *something* in common. We are both generally for a safe middle course, although each strains toward opposite boundaries of that course. In terms of the late campaign—all moderates were either for Smith or Hoover, though the reformer often wished the policies of Norman Thomas and the Socialists would work, whilst I would frankly prefer a landholding aristocracy with a cultivated leisure class and a return to the historic authority of the British crown, of which I shall always be spiritually a subject. But as men of more or less rudimentary sense, both the reformer and I know that we can neither of us get what we respectively want—hence last autumn he compromised on Smith whilst I compromised on Hoover. And that's the way of it. We want different things, but have enough sense of reality to take what we can get. He works for as democratic a government *as possible;* I for as aristocratic a one *as possible.* But both recognise the limitations of possibility. Incidentally, the developments of the machine age may conceivably make inevitable a third and altogether different sort of organisation equally dissatisfying to democrat and oligarch! As for the relative value or authority of the democratic and aristocratic ideals—there is not, cosmically speaking, a bit of preference to be given either side. It is all a matter of personal emotion. I happen to favour the system which permits the free exercise of the most complex and evolved vital forces, but I freely concede that there is just as much logic in advocating a system which keeps everything down to the animal level. I would, indeed, freely concede an equal cosmic standing to any design of the insect race to extirpate the mammalian world and bring to dominance the ideals and institutions of the disciplined and efficiently organised articulata. But I couldn't get exactly enthusiastic about it!

All this will shew you that I am not insensible of the various concessions which have to be made now and then to certain elements in order to ensure practical safety—so that in reality one phase of your argument was unnecessary. In the matter of disfranchising certain classes—I simply said *that it would do no harm if it would work.* The country was governed just as well as it is now when certain classes *were* disfranchised—women everywhere, Catholics and Jews here and there, and men below a certain property level in places. All that has happened is that such cases of disfranchisement *have not been found possible* as matters of direct legislation. There is nothing to crow about—nothing to get excited or complacent about. The change hasn't done anybody any good, and we are no better because we *do* grant universal franchise, than were our ancestors because they *didn't.* Each of us—ancestors and contemporaries—has really done exactly the same thing: 'gotten away with' as much as possible. If anything, our ancestors deserve the more credit, because they 'got away with' more. Certainly, we could make government a neater and more effective thing, and more of a preservative of our best culture, if we could apply the same restrictions that our forefathers did. Apparently we can't—but that's nothing to brag about. No need of spilling slush and sentimentality because we have to retrench. Our modes of life and feeling are very distinctly a product of the English Protestant culture—taken as a culture apart from matters of actual belief. It would be of infinite benefit to the tone of our national life and the growth of our legitimately hereditary arts and letters if none but the English-descended Protestant element were given a share in the government—and only the best and best-chosen part of that element. That we can't establish such a restriction at this date, after our abysmal folly in admitting all sorts of immigrant elements, I am willing to concede as a practical fact; but I am *not* willing to pretend that this condition is a *benefit* to the nation. I'm damned sorry that it's so, and would do almost anything to get rid of the non-English hordes whose heritages and deepest instincts clash so disastrously with ours, and do so much to frustrate the fruition of our 300-year-old cultural stream. Therefore I'm for *any workable policy* which will throw power toward the old-American stock and take power away from the immigrant stock. The longer we can keep the strangers from tangibly tampering with our culture, the better our chance of finally assimilating those which are here (provided we have the sanity to keep others out) and of making them conform to our standards of civilisation. I don't say I'm for any more circuitous measure which will accomplish something of the same thing. My reason is plain and concrete—that it's oppressively unpleasant to live in a country where the customs, folk-ways, literary and artistic tone, and governmental forms are markedly unlike those natural to one's own race and civilisation. English civilisation was here first, and established itself by virtue of its strength. If we beat off Indian influences, we ought to be able to beat off other alien influences. Constant strength and resolution are the price of racial-cultural integrity. Do I make myself plain? You say that the idea of Catholic-Jew-atheist disfranchisement is "monstrous". I say that it is merely *impracticable at this date.* The parallel of red-haired and cross-eyed massacres is not quite valid, because red hair and cross eyes have no symbolic significance in the composition of the civilisation—but so far as abstract principles go, I had as lief as not see carrot-topped and strabismic folk quietly put out of the way. I'd merely think it was *more impracticable* than Papist-Jew-infidel disfranchisement, and would languidly question the aesthetic status of such a violent measure—inquiring whether or not the incident had an artistically adequate object. Another thing—in the past, men *have* been disfranchised because of blood, heritage or belief, whereas adults have never been slaughtered en masse because of individual physical peculiarities. This would argue that the instinctive make-up of mankind does not necessarily protest against blood-culture-creed distinctions, whereas it does seem to discourage less clear-cut discriminations in matters of selection for survival. And so it goes. Nothing is "monstrous"—but some things will work while some things won't, and some things are aesthetic according to our cultural canon while some things aren't. There's really nothing to get excited about. Grant outsiders as little influence and privilege as we safely can, and let it go at that. If we *can't* make disfranchisement work, all right; but don't let's pretend to be glad about it, or egg the foreigners on toward still further demands. Incidentally—I think disenfranchisement ought still to be enforced on niggers in the Alabama-Mississippi black belt. What would happen if those gorillas were given the ballot and lined up by shrewd "white-trash" or carpet-bagging Northern bosses is something I don't like to contemplate—little though I care for the Baptist-Methodist illiterates forming most of the citizenry of the region involved!

Mussolini is a sharp leader, and knows his business. He learns more as he goes, as his recent Vatican concordat proves.[3] It is clear from his past record that he has no more use for religion than you or I have—but he knows what it means politically to enlist the aid of a force which will always come first with the superstitious rabble. Therefore the Dictator Mussolinus becomes the haloed San Benito—more power to him! Play intelligently on the emotions of the herd, and you can rule any country as an absolute monarch—but how few mortals know perfectly the player's art! I think Napoleon could have done it had he encountered no foreign opposition. If Mussolini falls, I feel sure it will be through outside pressure.

As for the Roman Empire—are you sure you have exactly the right picture of what *did* take place? Possibly you have, but I don't quite grasp your point. At any rate, you must realise that the Empire never "excluded immigration" in the modern American sense, and that by the time of the Antonines it was already more riddled with foreign blood than America is today. You recall Juvenal's lines—"Iampridem Syrus defluxit Orontes in Tiberim" etc.[4] At the time of the invasions there was no barrier against individual foreigners— and indeed, so many had been admitted that the army was almost wholly German. These barbarians were by no means despised—indeed, after Tacitus' time the superior strength and virtue of the Northern tribes became a byword at Rome. Many emperors, beginning with the uncouth Maximinus, were wholly or partly of barbarian blood—German, and in one case even *Arabic*. The wars of the period had a different cast along different frontiers. In the east, the Parthians and their successors the Sassanid Persians were warred with on very much of a plane of equality—the Parthio-Persians being the aggressors as often as the Romans. Neither wanted to make any wholesale penetrations of the other's country, (for after Trajan the idea of Roman expansion had vanished) but both quibbled about boundaries, or about such things as the protectorate of Armenia. The case of Palmyra was distinctly an exception—but even there the idea was not to keep foreigners out, but to drag foreigners (plus their territory) in! The fact is, that immigration was actually encouraged—especially in view of the dwindling Roman population— and that certain types of soldiers especially fitted for warfare were deliberately sought outside the guarded frontiers. Nor was there any wholesale tendency to exclude *even entire tribes* of outsiders, when the latter professed a desire to enter and a willingness to live peaceably without harassing their Roman or Romanised neighbours. Case after case of permission for tribal entry is on record, so that by the time of the great migrations there were whole provinces almost completely Germanic in blood—a circumstance which made the final German conquest easier, since kinsfolk could not help welcoming rather than resisting kinsfolk. The Romans had no clear notions of ethnic differences, and would never have thought of imposing a race barrier. Indeed, their heterogeneous empire absorbed so many outsiders by conquest that the total area within the frontiers included all sorts of nationalities. Those in the west, where no great civilisation had preceded Rome, took on a more or less complete Latin culture; though no attempt was ever made to supplant the Greek culture (recognised as superior by the Romans) in any area where it was established. In the end, the Greek culture outlasted the purely Roman—for as we all know, the Greek or Byzantine half of the Empire held out till 1453 with a constantly diminishing area, whereas the Latin parts began to go to pieces before A.D. 500, and were completely transformed into the various feudal Romance cultures by 900 or 1000. No indeed—the Romans of the Empire did *not* keep up any hard and fast barrier against the barbarians, and after the 4th century A.D. the influx was tremendous. This was the period when the Huns began to push the Slavic tribes from the East, whilst the Slavs transmitted the pressure to the Germans. In one sweeping gesture a *million* Visigoths were admitted south of the Danube in A.D. 376, being granted lands and even supplied with free food until their first harvest. That this venture did not end well was due to the laxity of minor officials; who neglected to disarm the newcomers according to treaty, and who practiced a species of graft in providing their food. This latter aroused the Goths to armed protest—whence the battle of Adrianopolis in 378, and the slaying of the Eastern Emperor Valens. Theodosius *subdued,* but did not attempt to *expel* them; and when after his death they rose again, it was altogether without provocation. They had been well treated as peaceful settlers, and it was their own proud blood and ambition—the proud blood and ambition of the unconquerable Nordic, whose day of supremacy was almost due on the stage of history—which stirred them up under Alaric, and drove them on to their spectacular career of pillage amongst the decaying towns of the dying classical world. After Alaric's death his brother Ataulf shewed signs of becoming Romanised and forming a defender of the Empire, and for that purpose left Italy and set up a dominion in Spain and Southern Gaul; (the actual ancestor of the present Spanish nation) but by that time the whole frontier had given way, and scores of tribes, under arms and wishing only to seize land for themselves, (*not* to become Romans) were rushing in to form independent kingdoms in which they ruled the conquered Roman inhabitants as overlords whilst retaining all their Germanic ways and organisation. You know the familiar catalogue—Burgundians, Franks, Vandals, Suevians, Ostrogoths, etc. etc., not to omit mention of our own respected progenitors the Angles and Saxons. Any of these yellow-bearded warriors would have been welcomed to the Empire as a peaceful settler and candidate for Romanisation. All that the frontier legions strove to exclude were armed conquerors who sought to seize land away from the Empire! It is this point, very clear to one who surveys the whole pageant of decline and fall, which it seems to me you do not stress sufficiently. The "wise policy of coöperation" which you suggest *was indeed tried*—but see what came of it! Actually, the empire had been pretty well doomed for centuries. The old vitality of the republic had been sapped by sophistication, standards of material luxury, wholesale disease, (some authorities call the devastating plague in Marcus Aurelius' reign the *greatest single factor* in the decline) and the pollution by foreign blood. The old hawk-nosed, tight-lipped Italian race was virtually extinct, and the existing mongrel stock could not possibly have the deep, vital fervour for national life and integrity which had characterised the real Roman people. Italy itself was lost amidst the provinces it had conquered. Half the empire was Greek, and the veneration given to Greek culture caused Latin culture to ebb very low. There is no Latin art or literature or feeling worth the name after the age of Pliny and Tacitus. The most cultivated Romans—including Marcus Aurelius—composed their literature in Greek, and Alexandria continued to be the intellectual centre of the world. The conquered Hellenistic culture had become a peaceful conqueror—so that, as we see, the Greek part of the Empire outlasted the Latin part by a thousand years. In the later stages of decay Christianity undoubtedly did harm through its exaltation of softness, justice, and universal brotherhood, and its demand for the renunciation of earthly ties and loyalties; but it is a mistake to consider this the principal cause of decline, as some do.[5] Rome would never have adopted this mawkish slave-religion if it had not begun to acquire the soft slave-mind and the subtle slave-religion of human equality. The nation, through other causes, had become psychologically unfitted for the traditional classic polytheism and the virile schools of philosophy. Itself decadent, it had begun to demand something like the slave-faiths and mystically consolatory cults of the long-decadent East; hence by the time of the Antonines was groping frantically for something new and soft and mystic. It was a gamble which of many faiths would win—Persian Mithraism (altars to Mithras have been dug up in parts of the Empire as remote as Hadrian's Wall in Britain) Jewish Christianity, Perso-Syrian Manichaeism, and Oriental-Alexandrian Neoplatonism being the main contenders apart from the Apollonian, Pythagorean, and Dionysiac mystery-cults whose appeal was too complex and aesthetic for the majority. It was pure accident that Christianity won—but once it did win, it undeniably did harm through its weakening effect on patriotism. It sapped at the vigorously nationalistic cast of the Roman mind, and made the people feel that the identity—or even the nature—of their earthly government was comparatively inessential. What it did was to *accelerate*, though not to *cause*, the ruin of the classical world. But in my opinion—as well as in that of a majority of modern students—the *prime source* of Roman decline was something wholly apart from any of the circumstances enumerated above. It was, indeed, *exactly the same thing which is now menacing our Western civilisation*—namely, **a growth in magnitude and complex administrative needs beyond the capability of the age's scientific, psychological, and economic knowledge to cope with.** The unwieldy imperial fabric, with its cumbrous finances, declining national spirit, heterogeneous peoples, and wide dissimilarity of conditions in different regions, had become unmanageable through sheer size and diversity. *It was almost impossible to find any effective way to get necessary things done.* All that anybody could do was to *tighten up*— subdivide all duties, create more officials, and make these hapless officials more and more rigidly responsible to their superiors and to the head of the state. In the absence of any scientific guide to the apportionment of responsibility or the creation of favourable public moods through social readjustments, the only thing to do was to look to the old Eastern monarchies for governmental precedents; so that in all truth the government was fast becoming Oriental in everything but name. Only the coming of the Teuton saved the civilised world from Orientalism. Diocletian devised a fine system of screws and a fine way of putting them on—but he couldn't think up a way of getting results after the screws had pulverised and destroyed those to whom they were applied! In the end, the only way in which the frontiers could be kept defended and the roads and public works kept in repair* was the virtual concentration of every administrative energy on the one task of ruthless and continuous *tax-extortion.* The nation that had once conquered blithely and lived in luxury had become so muddled up that it was narrowed down to one bitter and frugal defensive struggle for survival. There were, it was said, more tax-collectors than people taxed—and nowhere could any responsible amount of wealth either public or private be found. Since the officials were personally responsible to the emperor, and obliged to make up privately what they could not collect, they often became bankrupted and ruined; so that they sought in every way possible to escape the duties of office-holding. This tendency to escape was overcome by making the official's dignity *hereditary and compulsory,* so that the provincial curial nobility became in all truth an oppressed caste more miserable than the coloni or serfs. Instead of being sought by rich plebeians, as formerly, the local senatorial rank began to be shunned as the plague; so that once the citizens of a Roman municipium in Spain voted a statue in the forum to a man who *voluntarily* offered himself as a Senator to lighten the burthens of his fellow-townsmen. Local noblemen, though prohibited by law from so doing, often escaped by stealth into the church as priests, or sank quietly out of sight amongst the guilds of artisans in the

---

*and these began to decline after the beginning of the 4th century A.D. Everything fell into neglect—so that when Alaric invaded Rome he found half the aqueducts out of order and all the baths disused and decaying. The provinces were even worse.

towns. Some, even more desperate, deliberately destroyed their status by marrying a serf-woman and becoming peasant coloni to the barbarians. There was relatively little rebellious feeling, because in the main everybody realised the dire necessity of the struggle for survival. There was only one real peasant rising—that in Gaul in Diocletian's time, when the most rigorous features of the tax-extortion system were new and unaccustomed. Oriental caste institutions and rapacious taxation were all that could keep the Empire running and hold the Goths at bay—but the time came at last when a weary and bewildered people began to wonder whether, after all, the tax-collector were not at least as great an evil as washed-out roads, crumbling cities, and the rule of Teutonic kings! Regarding the latter point, it must likewise be kept in mind that the whole army was Teutonic already, and that even the civil population along the northern frontier was largely so. And so the end came—very gradually and imperceptibly. I suppose you realise that the notion of a sudden end of the Roman world in A.D. 476 is merely a schoolboy illusion. What the renowned Odoacer really did was simply to introduce a slight change in the technical status of things.[6] As far back as Honorius' time the German generals in Roman service had *contemplated* a seizure of the actual power. Both Stilicho and Aëtius were killed for harbouring that ambition. Then, in A.D. 456, the German Ricimer actually did take hold and set up and depose four puppet-emperors. In 472 the German Orestes took the power and set up *his own son* as "Roman Emperor of the West". It was *this* "Roman"—the poor, helpless little German boy "Romulus Augustulus"—that Odoacer deposed in 476 after slaying Orestes. Odoacer's only advance on his immediate predecessor was that he did not set up any puppet as emperor. He ruled Italy himself—*yet not, mark well, without keeping up the Roman Imperial fiction.* All he did was to *make himself a lieutenant of the Eastern "Roman" (Greek) Emperor at Constantinople*—declaring that the system of two emperors and divided territories was no longer necessary, and that he would rule Italy faithfully for *the one and only Roman Caesar*—Zeno, of the East. Technically the empire had not fallen, but had become unified again under the Eastern or Byzantine Emperor. Actually, of course, Odoacer was an absolutely independent German chieftain, living with his noblemen and warriors under Germanic customs and law though respecting the rights and liberties of the conquered Roman population. The same polite fiction was carried out in Gaul and Spain by the chiefs of the Burgundians, Franks, and Goths, so that *in theory* the mighty empire still lived on. Only our own forefathers* in Britain were perfectly frank. They indeed did not render any outside allegiance to anyone—for by the grace of Fortune they were destined to become the unconquered successors of the early, world-

---

*Our people were still pagan, worshipping Thor, Odin, etc., whereas the other Germanic invaders of the Empire had become Christianised.

swaying Romans themselves! When Theodoric the Ostrogoth deposed Odoacer, he did so under a nominal commission from the Eastern Emperor—being appointed a Roman "patrician" to "supersede" his fellow-German in the government of Italy. After his death, the great Eastern Emperor Justinian actually did reconquer a large part of Italy for the Empire, (we must remember that the Byzantine nation, though always Hellenised and fast becoming Orientalised, was actually a legal continuation of the eastern half of the divided Roman domain) ruling it from Constantinople as the exarchate of Ravenna. This state of things was partly broken up when the Byzantine General Narses invited the ferocious Lombards in, as a revenge for court intrigues against him at Constantinople. The Lombards, like the Anglo-Saxons, recognised no Byzantine-Roman overlordship; and would have eventually seized all the exarchate had not the Franks been invited in. What they did seize, was taken as a pure Lombard kingdom—'and nothing else but'—with its capital at Pavia. Their holdings were in several detached parts, the main mass (Lombardy) north of the dwindling exarchate, the other belts north and south of Rome and extending all across the peninsula. In between, the Imperial power continued; although on account of religious quarrels* the bishop or pope of Rome revolted against the exarch at Ravenna and claimed to hold the city in direct authority from the Byzantine Emperor. *Note right here the beginning of a fabric which still forms a live issue in these days of Mussolini.* The pope emerges as a temporal authority†, and begins to make negotiations with imperial and foreign courts. Still the Roman-Empire fiction persists, though—and we see the non-Lombard parts of Italy divided between imperial exarchs at Ravenna, and an Emperor-acknowledging pope at Rome. But the imperial hold grows less and less. Emperors depose popes and tax Rome, and in reprisal popes excommunicate Emperors. At length the popes take office without any *formal* sanction from the Emperor, and finally (A.D. 781) they cease dating events by imperial reigns and adopt our present Christian Era. Thus in the latter part of the 8th century we find three conditions of territory in Italy—the regions *actually* ruled by the Byzantine-"Roman" emperor through the exarchs of Ravenna, the region of Rome and vicinity ruled by the pope *in the shadowy name* of that imperial absentee, and the kingdom and various dukedoms of the Germanic Lombards, acknowledging no superior authority whatsoever. Then, as the 8th century drew near its close, the aggressions of the Lombards

---

*The Byzantine emperor's prohibition of image-worship as idolatry was not approved by the Latin church, hence the "Great Schism" which gave to posterity the separate Roman Catholic and Orthodox Greek churches.

†Temporal power for Roman bishops is not new, for they had been civil magistrates before. Revolt of Rome from the exarch, left the pope the natural ruler of Rome and vicinity. The only unique thing was the union of this circumstance with the universal extent of his spiritual power outside Rome.

against Rome became acute, and the pope saw that the only Roman salvation lay in the old game of playing German against German, and inviting in a Teutonic tribe who would be more amenable to the Roman Imperial faction. Otherwise the Lombards would swallow all, and Italy would be a German kingdom like England. In choosing a barbarian ally, Pope Stephen III had an unusually good opening; for the reigning house of the Franks—the Carolingian dynasty—was under great obligations to the papacy. Shortly before, Pope Zachary had used his spiritual authority to elevate Pepin, Frankish Mayor of the Palace, to the actual kingship in place of the puppet Merovingian dynasty; and Stephen himself had crowned and anointed Pepin. Thus the Franks stepped gladly in, reduced the now somewhat decadent Lombards to vassalage, and gave to the pope almost or quite outright (Catholics and Protestants interpret it differently) the Roman zone plus the belt from sea to sea which the Lombards had just seized from the Byzantine exarchs. This new territory, as formally received by Stephen's successor Pope Adrian, is the Papal State which existed unchallenged until the Italian unification of 1870, and which in reduced compass Mussolini has just restored. Its relation to the Byzantine-Roman Empire was very shadowy—as indeed that of the Frankish kingdom had become by that time—but it was nevertheless theoretically acknowledged. Whether the pope was in theory also a vassal of the Frankish king is the thing which has always been disputed. At any rate, the close friendship of the Franks and the papacy was again cemented—and in a way to produce far-reaching results. The rest is well known. Very late in the eighth century there came once more to Rome a friendly Frank to save the Pope from Lombard aggressions. This was Pepin's son Charlemagne, who had previously expanded the Frankish kingdom and unified the German peoples to a miraculous extent which makes him among the few who *possibly* deserve to be considered as personal influencers of history. (The fact that much of this territory fell apart after his death is what makes his historic place debatable) Charlemagne made short work of the Lombards—reminding them of their vassalage, deposing their ruling dynasty, and placing upon his own head the famous Iron Crown—and finally went to Rome to pray and receive the papal blessing . . . and something more. All this time the Western World had recognised the *shadow-authority* of the Eastern Emperor to an extent we can scarcely realise except when we look closely at mediaeval literature. *Rome had never fallen* in any outward sense, and the popular imagination still looked to it as the focus of all mystical splendour and authority, even though its customs had become changed, its language debased, and its *actual* sway limited to the narrow belt of Papal power. Now just at this juncture the imperial dynasty at Constantinople had become rather jazzed-up. With characteristic Oriental subtlety the fond Empress-Dowager Irene had put out the eyes of her young son Constantius VI and seized the power for herself—an act which went well enough with the

Orientalised Greek court by the Golden Horn, but which didn't 'go over big' at all with the unsophisticated Teuton chiefs who swayed the Western World. There were those who declared the imperial throne forfeited and vacant, and ready for a new dynasty of Caesars and Augusti, and among these was Pope Leo VI. Accordingly, on Christmas Day, A.D. 800, as the visiting Charlemagne knelt in prayer at Rome, the Pope placed upon his head a golden crown and saluted him as the true successor in world-empire of the blinded boy at Byzantium. Vivat Carolus Augustus, Imperator Romanorum! Ave, Carole Auguste! The surrounding multitude took up the acclaim, and the great King of the Franks became the legal heir to the glories of the Julii, the Flavii, and the Antonines. Roma Immortalis, Caput Mundi! But of course it was all a very splendid bit of theory. Charlemagne remained a great Frankish king only—albeit, with a title which helped him sway his domains far more effectively than he otherwise could. You will note that, throughout the west, all the mystical emotional allegiance hitherto given to the "Roman" Emperor at Constantinople was transferred en masse to the "Holy Roman" Emperor of the Frankish dynasty. This new empire was not, in theory, a western empire acting in concert with the Eastern; but a restored world-empire including both east and west, and forming the unbroken heritage of the Caesars. In cold fact, it did not try to meddle with the Byzantine empire which really was the de facto and de jure prolongation of the Roman fabric. It merely assumed *theoretical* supremacy and ensured a transfer of emotional allegiance from the east to the west—a healthy thing for Europe, since it centred all loyalties within the dawning Nordic civilisation. The eastern empire half-faded out of men's imaginations as a part of Europe, and we only hear of it now and then in connexion with the Crusades and with the temporary Latin occupation of Constantinople, until in 1453 we witness its collapse before the Turks. The "Holy Roman" Empire, which soon becomes a German Empire with the overlordship of most of Italy, shrinks into an Austrian dukedom and evaporates into legalistic-emotional theory; technically lasting until 1806, when it receives its coup de grace from Napoleon. But the important thing to consider is the prodigious vitality of the Roman idea. Rome was so mighty that it *could not fall.* It had to vanish in a cloud, like so many of the mythical heroes of antiquity, and to receive its apotheosis among the stars before men became fully aware that it had vanished from the earth! I hope you can pardon this long digression; but as I may have told you before, Rome has always been one of my special interests. It is my second country—and just as soon as I pass back of the existence of England in my survey of history, I find myself unconsciously and involuntarily a Roman in perspective and feelings. I have always hoped that there may be a drop of old Roman blood in me—left in Britain by the legions of Agricola, Ostorius Scapula, or Paullinus, and trickling down through the one or two Welsh lines in my ancestry. At any rate, I think I have shewn that the Roman Empire was not overthrown because it kept the barbarians out. It was never overthrown, but merely took in barbarian blood until it was itself barbarian, and gradually exchanged actual for theoretical authority until it was all a theory. And for this slow metamorphosis no one cause is responsible, though racial replacement and the unwieldy complexity of the imperial fabric stand prominent among the many parallel sources of decline. In a sense Rome has never died, for all the Western World is heir to its culture. We use its alphabet, most of its word-roots, and most of its modes of thought—and now America is duplicating its specific conditions and problems! Incidentally—it was *not* the bursting of the barrier in the 5th century which had the "awful consequences to civilisation". *Civilisation had already perished within the barrier*—that is, the high type of civilisation which we know as classic. Had there been no barbarian invasions, the culture of Rome would have petered out just the same—indeed, it *had* petered out, for the thought and life of the later Empire are substantially mediaeval. This is the more manifest because, as we see, a full half of the Empire *did not* collapse under the 5th century inroads. The Greek half lived on in slow decadence, and from that decadence in the once-Hellenic lands we may pretty well measure what the decadence within the Latin area would have been. The case was simply one of cultural old age—like that of the Western World today, or rather, in the generations just ahead. The old impulse to civilisation had worn itself out, and an hiatus was needed before the rise of the next and probably last Aryan culture—the Nordic. Meanwhile we have to look to the Saracens, fresh from the emotional stimulus of new-born Islam, to find a really vital culture amongst the Caucasian race. The glorious mediaeval world of the Caliphs of Bagdad and Emirs of Cordova was the true dominant civilisation of the Dark Ages, and we are damned lucky to have escaped being swallowed up in it and thus deprived of our normal racial culture of the future. All honour to Charles Martel! That Arabic Empire was the last of the great Semitic cultures, just as our Teutonic western civilisation is the last of the Great Aryan cultures. Both branches of the white race are getting toward the final sunset, and in another thousand or two years I fancy the Mongol will have his chance.

As for practical government today—of course a certain amount of the forms of democracy is necessary to keep the majority quiet, but one doesn't need to drag the device to unnecessary lengths. The majority are physically stronger than the minority, it is true; but their management is all a matter of influencing their psychology. It is conceivable that the herd will in time become overawed enough by the complexity of a machine age and its necessary administration to realise how silly the idea of a layman's government is; and that they will consent to sensible modifications of suffrage whereby special knowledge will constitute a requisite qualification for voting in the election of certain types of administrator. But of course there will always be a conflict of feelings and ideals between the two fixed types of human mentality—those who wish a general milieu favourable to the highest possible aesthetic and intellectual life, and those who seek a world standardised on the level of spiritual mediocrity and equalised physical luxury. It would be impossible to conceive of the diverse human race as working toward any one goal. What one seeks, another loathes. A constantly changing and more or less unstable balance or state of compromise is all we can ever expect. There's no use in getting worked up over the matter, one way or the other, for slow historic trends have a way of shaping themselves gradually and inexorably without much regard for the lilliputian struggles and pipings of the individual. I certainly don't intend to start any revolt against democracy, but merely say what I think when occasion rises. I have interests of my own to attend to—literary, antiquarian, architectural, and so on—and am perfectly willing to let the politicians do their own worrying. It amuses me to read over the heated civic sentiments in the essays of my adolescent period. I certainly was a militant old-school Tory then—but now I am a disillusioned, middle-aged cynic!

As for the *Saturday Evening Post*—don't let me be thought of as condemning it so far as its current information function is concerned. I suppose it is adequate enough in its transcript of daily facts and figures, though I myself prefer to get these through the *N.Y. Sunday Times* and the sanely balanced and disillusioned news-weekly *Time*. When I call it *superficial* I refer to its *analysis and exploitation* of these facts and figures, and to some extent to the policy of selection, proportioning, and emphasis followed in recording them. It looks at the world with the eyes of the shrewd, insensitive, hard-headed, unimaginative, well-fed, half-educated, materialistic Babbitt, catering to his interests, and interpreting the phenomena of the day in terms of his restricted and artificial philosophy. It is the organ of people whose gods are good business and prosperity, not beauty and truth. There are excellent articles now and then, but the prevailing tone is unmistakable. I never see it except at the barbershop, and even then it doesn't make the time until my turn seem conspicuously short. If I were more interested in business, politics, and economics, I might find more to it; but since my tastes lie in other directions I find it rather arid. Most of the fiction is hokum tinctured with optimism and sentimentality, although a few good things get in by accident. It prints none of the real literature of the day so far as I know—none of the stories of the writers who are really attempting a sincere interpretation of contemporary life. The tales have a brilliant, hard-surfaced cleverness, so that it really requires great skill and sophistication to land a piece of work with the editor; (I've never tried it!) but I haven't happened to see more than a few specimens (such as Hergesheimer's work)[7] of a grade likely to survive as authentic art. Of all the magazines I think *Harper's* is about the best. I'd have said the *Atlantic* a few years ago, but latterly it seems to me to be getting a little self-conscious—like the

Boston Transcript, if you know what I mean. *Scribner's* isn't bad since its bracing-up a year ago, but on the whole I don't think it quite makes the *Harper* grade. One doesn't have to be a *scholar* to exercise discrimination in magazine selection. Heaven knows I'm not one myself! But when there's a choice between sincerity and artificiality, or between soundness and superficiality, I want to be on the best side. I am disillusioned enough to know that no man's opinion on any subject is worth a damn unless backed up with enough genuine information to make him really know what he's talking about. I am not so free with opinions as I used to be, having outgrown the stage of the cracker-barrel senate. When I want to say something, I take darned good care to glance over my background-knowledge and see whether or not my opinion has any valid reason for existing. If it hasn't, I try to look up the "straight dope" on the subject—and if the subject happens to be modern, I want the most solid, thoughtful, and reliable possible periodical to furnish the information. That's why I turn to things of the Harper-Century-Scribners grade. I know from experience that these are the places where really thorough and intelligent presentations of the really vital topics are made. One can, of course, read of "the world's great figures" elsewhere—but I want to be sure that these figures are chosen rightly and emphasised rightly, and that their reasons for greatness are correctly, thoughtfully, and analytically stated. In other words, I want my view of the world to be as scientifically impartial, comprehensive, realistic, and objective a view as can be obtained. One never obtains such from the sketchy, emotion-tinctured, and quasi-sensational columns of the frankly popular press, for these columns reflect an artificial world, sentimentalised and oversimplified. However, as I have said, the *Saturday Evening Post* is by no means flagrantly bad in any respect; and really has much of excellence in it now and then.

About architecture—one *doesn't* have to study it to appreciate it, since a natural sense of beauty will help one to an opinion in eight cases out of ten. In aesthetics, we cannot say as we do in intellectual matters, that only the real student has a right to an opinion. Here the case is very different, and an inborn sensitiveness of organisation is worth more than all the study in the world. Aesthetes are born, not made. I've never seen a better proof of this than in your own recent letter, where you speak in one breath of your lack of architectural knowledge and of your dislike of the Albany state capitol—which I have seen. How you quite naively opine that a trained architect might disagree with you regarding this edifice. Guess again, my son!!! Take an old man's word, you struck it right the first time! In all truth, the Albany state capitol is recognised by every contemporary architect to be *one of the most unutterably hideous public buildings in the United States*. It was erected in the middle nineteenth century, during the utter Dark Age of American architecture, and would certainly have been pulled down long ago were it not so colossal and expensive an affair. Nothing good is to be said about it. All over the country, cities are tearing down the frightful caricatures put up during the corresponding period as fast as they can afford it. New York City's absurd post office in City Hall Park has been on the list for demolition a long while, and in Philadelphia some citizens are even thinking of trying to get rid of the loathsome City Hall, notwithstanding its vast cost and relatively recent additions. The truth is, that from 1830 to 1900 American architecture and decoration—like the costume of the period—represents a lapse of taste which still mystifies the student. *How could they do such things?* is all one can say as he stands aghast at the grotesque jumble of Victorian hybridism and caprice embalmed in wood, brick, and stone. The only half-decent things in all that bleak age are the Upjohn Gothic churches toward the beginning, and a very little—damn little at that—of Richardson's Romanesque work toward the close of it.[8] The World's Fair of 1893, which evoked some good classic and true Renaissance designs and attracted a host of architects from all over the country to see them, marked the dawn of better days. It took a long while to get the general taste reëducated up to the level from which it had so inexplicably dropped in 1830, but it has been done at last. Since 1900 a good proportion of our buildings have been very decent, and some of them are splendid. Classic and colonial motifs are used to immense advantage, and Gothic has almost regained its mediaeval magic under wizards like Ralph Adams Cram. Hybridism and collectivism are mercifully killed off, and the future is really very bright unless modernistic nonsense begins to spread and blight what has been accomplished. The *skyscraper* has a charm of its own in its proper place, achieving an exotic and almost fairylike effect when seen in masses from a distance; though its over-use, and its needless erection in small cities, are to be deplored extremely—as is also the silly attempt to carry skyscraper motifs into interior decorative art. That educational building at Albany which you praise is *very fine*—truly classic, and well adapted both to its purpose and to the landscape. I still recall the impression it gave me in the sunset last July. Thus you see that while professing to despise art (for to boast of ignorance of it implies contempt, conscious or unconscious) you have really proved yourself delightfully sensitive to it in a very typical and illuminating case! I wish you had extended your remarks on New York's Pennsylvania Station to include a comparison with the Grand Central. Actually, though far less ambitious in point of luxury and magnitude, the Pennsylvania completely eclipses the Grand Central—being done in a very correct Roman manner inspired by the Baths of Caracalla. Size and splendour, of course, are never the important things. Technique and proportion are what count—lines and curves, lights and shadows.

Your general estimate of aesthetics requires considerable discussion and clarification, because you appear to miss the point of the whole thing. Beware of missing points—such a habit makes the world look a lot simpler than it is, and leads one into snap judgments and prejudices which appear pretty odd and grotesque to the maturely informed. For instance, I am sometimes tempted to minimise the importance of *music* because I am not personally sensitive to it—but then I stop and think of its actual place and function in civilisation, and check my hasty utterance; knowing that it would be just as silly for me to *boast* of being unresponsive to music, as to *boast* of being colour-blind, deaf, or one-legged. The "hard-boiled" attitude which ostentatiously distrusts and despises the arts is really one of raw adolescence, abnormally prolonged into adult life. Where you miss the point is in your taken-forgranted assumption that the crux of art is the *literal imitation of nature.* How come? If that's so, why hasn't photography supplanted painting? And what kind of *nature* does a Greek temple or a Gothic cathedral imitate? The truth of the matter is, that the basis of aesthetics is still so deeply wrapped in mystery that no final definition of art's primary function and appeal can be formulated. We have clues, but only clues—and all these point toward a somewhat bewildering complexity. At least three separate factors seem to be involved— physical-sensory pleasure, mental-emotional association, and mathematical symmetry or rhythm; the last-named of these being most purely and characteristically aesthetic and differentiated from general sensations and emotions. I once participated in a controversy on the basis of aesthetics, and if I can find my copy of the text I'll enclose it herewith—for later return. I'm not sure, though, that I can find it. Besides these three static factors there seems to be a vague dynamic factor involving emotional intensity, whereby most art fails to be poignant unless it reflects a certain degree of concentrated ecstasy in the creator. Amidst all this, the mere copying of nature bulks pretty small—being of course directly connected with only one of the three major factors, that of mental-emotional associations, although it links up indirectly with all. Ultra-modernists banish it entirely, as did also the creators of certain schools of primitive art—Aztec, Egyptian, Minoan, etc. It does not figure in any art that is highly conventionalised or subjective; and when carried to excess degenerates into insipidity, as in the 19th century painting of men like Bouguereau and Alma-Tadema.[9] Clearly, *the bald copying of Nature is no true function of art.* What art—as connected with Nature—really is, is a matter of *interpretation.* We know that although all normal-sensed persons receive the same mechanical impressions of the external world upon their senses, there are great differences in the subtleties of individual sense-response; (just as there are great differences in the subtleties of our individual emotions) so that *no two people really inhabit the same world.* Each separate person reacts a little differently to what he sees, hears, feels, smells and tastes, according to the individual differences in his cellular, neural, and glandular organisation; so that there *is no one real aspect of Nature,* but merely an average of an infinite number of slightly different aspects as envisaged by the different individuals, past and present, of the human race. And even more than this—the background of individual mental and emotional experience which each of us brings to bear as association-material upon any impression of the external world, of necessity gives every separate person a *thoroughly separate set of emotional and imaginative overtones* when he looks at a given scene in common with others; so that no two persons could possibly carry away the same net result from a contemplation of the same material. What means cheerfulness to one (through associative memory) means melancholy to someone else; what calls up a picture of one set of scenes to Mr. A, calls up a wholly different picture to Mr. B. This associative differentiation is even more pronounced and important than the physiological sensory differentiation, and strikingly confirms the truth of the general axiom that *there is no Nature, as known to us; but only an infinite number of fairly closely related Natures, each one peculiar to him who experiences it.* Practically speaking, you and I would not experience the same picture if we were to stand side by side and look at any given landscape or street scene. True, the ultimate reality before us would be the same; but no one can ever guess what any ultimate reality is, except vaguely, by comparing the subjective impressions and dreams of many sensitive observers. We would not get the same impression because we are two different physiological machines, and it would be an inconceivable coincidence if our senses worked precisely alike in every detail. We would call what we saw by the same name, but who can say how close your concept of "tree" or "house" is to my conception of the same things? To start with, there would be differences in registration upon our physical senses—and beyond that, our different habits of emotion and attention would certainly pick different parts of the whole image for emphasis and subordination. No human mind, of course, can ever consciously take in the *whole detail* of a scene presented to the senses. Any mind that could would be a god's mind. Only a *part* of the thing seen can ever be recorded by the conscious mind—and certainly, no two minds could possibly be so alike as to choose precisely the same part. What you and I would select as material for a hasty and truthful sketch of the scene's "high spots" would be markedly different—for you would tend to register impressions overlooked by me whilst I would tend to register impressions overlooked by you. And beyond all this, our widely different streams of past experience and memories would give every detail of the scene such a widely different aura of associative glamour, feeling, and imagery in our respective minds, that we cannot for a moment suppose ourselves to receive identical pictures. Reality being beyond human vision, each of us receives a vague shadow of reality—wholly subjective on our part, and only roughly similar in the two cases. The resemblances will result from our membership in the same organic species, in the same race-stock, in the same civilisation, and in the same New England fabric. The differences will result from our differences in physique, tastes, environment, and experience. What you see will be nearer like what I see than what a Chinaman or an ancient Assyrian would see, but not so near as what a Providence man with tastes and experiences more like mine would see. From this principle arise the differences in style among different individual artists of the same age and group, the wider differences among groups which are in the same civilisation but which represent different ages or different mental and geographical milieux, and the still wider differences among different national and racial art-traditions. Diverse vision is everywhere—and beyond it all the absolute lies hidden. Now what about art's relation to Nature in view of all this—in view of the fact that every different human being carries around with him a separate and distinct version of what Nature is and looks like? Well, I'd say that good art means *the ability of any one man to pin down in some permanent and intelligible medium a sort of idea of what* **he** *sees in Nature that* **nobody else** *sees.* In other words, *to make the other fellow grasp,* through skilled selective care in interpretive reproduction or symbolism, *some inkling of what only the artist himself could possibly see in the actual objective scene itself.* You see we have gotten around to your point about seeing sunsets versus seeing pictures of sunsets. It took a long time to do it, but it's worth it if it shews you where you slipped up. Why rave, you ask, over the picture when you can see the real thing? Well—here's your answer! The picture can, if it be good art, give you something in the real scene which you couldn't have gathered for yourself—which only the particular artist who painted the picture could ever have gathered and preserved for other people to see. Of course, there is just the same inevitable diversity of vision when we look at a work of art—i.e., no two spectators see quite the same thing. But in this case the artist, through his knowledge of the difference between his especial vision and the average of mass vision, (as tested by a comparison of many artists' results) has been able to supply guide-posts to a very great extent; so that we cannot fail to recognise his emphasis on those features of the scene which he alone has beheld in the proportions represented. *That is what self-expression is, and self-expression is art.* A man is a true artist according to his ability to make other people see the visible or emotional or imaginative world *as he sees it,* without departing from the true basic outlines of the world he is delineating. In a sunset by J. M. W. Turner you get something you never could have got from a first-hand visual inspection of the natural sunset he painted. There's the answer to your somewhat hasty "why rave" question, and to your certainly superficial guess that the discriminating admiration of any artist's work is a mere tribute to his technical cleverness. We may admire the man too, but we take a pleasure in his work apart from its creator. Of course we know that there is a great deal of *feigned* appreciation among affected or parvenu types, but that has nothing to do with the *real* appreciation which it clumsily tries to imitate. Heaven knows I have no more patience with perfunctorily assumed art-enthusiasm than I have with crude art-contempt. Just as I would not for a moment pretend to despise music because I cannot enjoy and understand it, so would I never think of pretending to enjoy or understand music when I can't. But I don't make the childish mistake of calling *all* expressed appreciation a fake merely because *some* is. I don't go off at half-cock about anything that doesn't really get at my inner aesthetic tissue; but when I really *do* come upon a picture or poem or building or statue that 'packs the punch', I'm not sophistry-tangled enough to think that my strong emotions are a fake! And it tends to make me tired when bumptious Babbitts strut out of their Rotary meetings shouting noisily that "this art game is all the bunk—there ain't no percentage in it!" But one more thing. Conceding that real art *does* give us an authentic subjective interpretation of Nature that none but the particular artist could ever have given, I can picture some people as asking—"Well, wot de hell of it? Who gives a damn what some nutty bozo seen w'en he looked at a sunset? It may be diffrunt from wot I seen, but I ain't layin' awake nights over that, Big Boy! Not me!" The answer to this question is like the true answers to most questions about realities, essentially complex; though not beyond the point of tracing out and grasping. First, we may concede that only sensitively developed people are concerned in the matter. Colour means nothing to a colour-blind man, nor art to a calloused, undernourished, or insensitive spirit. In order to see, one must first possess eyes. So, having defined the type of person concerned, let us see where he gets his art-pleasure—his pleasure at seeing the crystallised revelation of another man's purely personal vision. Well—for one thing, the sight of the other man's vision, with its emphasis on the personally selective element, *tends to bring out his own subconscious memories of kindred aspects of vision*— that is, to drag up to consciousness impressions received and retained in the subconscious, but never before realised. This means the discovery of something new and unexpected in oneself—always a highly pleasurable phenomenon, and possessing a kind of dramatic vividness akin to that of some glimpse from an hypothetical previous incarnation. The new-found memory was always at the back of the mind, hence has the elusive charm of vague familiarity. Yet because it was never before consciously registered, it has all the striking fascination of absolute newness as well. The work of art has enlarged our supply of conscious memory-wealth—has shewn us to be richer than we thought we were. It has, in all truth, enriched and *developed* us. This enrichment is permanent, because the raising to consciousness of a new type of vision enables the spectator to exercise this new type in his subsequent contacts with Nature. *We see and feel more in Nature from having assimilated works of authentic art.* There is no question but that an artistically untrained or insensitive man is really groping half-blinded through life. He isn't 'hitting on all six', as it were—he's only partly developed and partly alive—only partly a human being in the finest sense of that term. What he sees around him, and what he experiences from day to day, form only a fraction of what the world has to offer to a fully developed personality. His capacity for pleasure is merely rudimentary, as we may perceive from the pathetically exaggerated importance he attaches to physical pleasures which form merely the beginning of a full personality's quota of pleasure. Mercifully, though, he is saved from corresponding extremes of suffering. Art is the gateway of life—and in the opinion of many, myself included, the only reason that any highly developed man of sense has for remaining alive. Life without art* is simply an animal or mechanical process, even when dully diversified by sterile thought. We only live as human beings in proportion to our receptiveness to impressions of beauty—thus I regretfully admit myself only partly alive, since the magic kingdom of musical exaltation, as well as substantial provinces of various other arts, is closed to my limited sensibilities. No one person, of course, is 100% developed. Most of us lead 25% or 50% lives, though some get as high as 75% or 80%. I don't know where I rank—about 50%, I guess. I'm dead to music, and I fear my response to large sections of prose literature is intellectual rather than aesthetic. I don't stand high amongst the genuine aesthetes of my acquaintance—and I've studied their reactions pretty thoroughly. To continue—I could cite many concrete instances to prove that a sympathetic familiarity with the best art makes a man see twice or three times as much in the visible world as he ever saw before, and extract twice or three times as much pleasure from it. Any scene means vastly more to the artistically mature man than it does to the man without such sensitiveness and experience. But we must pass on to other sources of the pleasure derived from good art. Besides the joy of discovering untapped wells in ourselves, there is *the joy of capturing another's vision*—the sense of expansion and adventure inherent in viewing Nature through a larger proportion of the total eyes of mankind. We derive from this process a feeling of magnification in the cosmos—of having approached the universal a trifle more closely, and banished a little of our inevitable insignificance. Instead of being merely one person, we have become two persons—and as we assimilate more and more of art we become, in effect, more and more people all in one; till at length we have the sensation of a sort of identification with our whole civilisation. This alone would make art worth our while. But the list of pleasure-phases is not yet exhausted. Another thing which art does is *to intensify and clarify our own personal and conscious reaction toward Nature*, by setting our minds definitely into the pattern of creative selection. This is a concrete way of stating the familiar abstract maxim that the spectacle of self-expression on anyone's part is a tonic and pleasant experience for us. By watching someone else 'be himself' intensively and skilfully, we ourselves are impelled to 'be ourselves' more thoroughly and poignantly

---

*by this, of course, I mean not only formal art but the instinctive beauty-perceptions of the sensitive though untutored person as well.

than might otherwise be possible. Specifically, the presentation of a view with only high spots or symbols stressed brings up to our mind the high spots and symbols which we would stress if we could paint what we saw—the high spots and symbols which for us represent the visible scene. This phase of pleasure is additionally acute when the type of art happens to be really very close to our own type of aesthetic vision. In such cases the work of art reca- pitulates with startling vividness what we actually did see—and recapitulates it more effectively than the scene itself would, since it does not contain any of those suppressed details which in the actual scene tugged at the subconscious and insidiously weakened the dominant image. Paradoxically, the work of art shews us more of the scene we saw than would that scene itself! Then there is still another source of art-pleasure—an outwardly intellectual source, (albeit based on emotional illusion) and the reason for many persons' identification of beauty and truth. To get at this, go back to Sheet XII and note the point I mention at the turn of the page—or better still, I'll repeat it here. *No one can ever guess what any ultimate reality is, except vaguely, by comparing the subjective impres- sions and dreams of many sensitive observers.* Now you see what this implies—that the constant discovery of different peoples' subjective impressions of things, as contained in genuine art, forms a slow, gradual approach, or faint approx- imation of an approach, to **the mystic substance of absolute reality it- self**—the stark, cosmic reality which lurks behind our varying subjective perceptions. I don't need to tell you what a tremendous force this conception necessarily is, in any maturely developed and fully civilised mind. The search for ultimate reality is the most ineradicable urge in the human personality— the basis of every real religion, and the foundation of all that nobly poetic body of philosophy which has its fount in Plato. Anything which enhances our sense of success in this quest, be it art or religion, is the source of a price- lessly rich emotional experience—and the more we lose this experience in re- ligion, the more we need to get it in something else. In stark intellectual truth, this experience is an illusion; since it is absurd to fancy that the narrow range of visions afforded by different artists within the human species could give even the merest hint of an ultimate reality known to us only from the restrict- ed point of view (or closely related points of view) of mankind with its local and limited range of sense-equipment. Absolute reality is for ever beyond us—we cannot form even the vaguest conception of what such a thing could be like, for we have no terms to envisage entity apart from those subjective aspects which reside wholly inside our own physiology and psychology. Solid, liquid, gas; size, dimensions, matter, energy, ether; time and space; eternity, infinity, finiteness, relativity; all are, in the last analysis, only shadows whose substance and nature we can never hope even to approximate. We have only extremely fragmentary and illusorily specialised projections to go by, and can form no idea of any principle of reference by which to define or envisage such a thing as absolute entity or reality apart from its few sensory manifestations. All we can do is to judge the relationships which those manifestations bear toward one another, and accept our fractional vision as having some fixed proportion or relationship to whatever the inconceivable whole may be. The mind of man can *never*—this is *the one absolute certainty in our knowledge*—get any further than this, since the limits of the five senses are a fixed and insurmountable barrier beyond which we have no possible avenue of access. Religion pretends to satisfy by assuming man's possession of mystic information-channels apart from the senses, but we are outgrowing the possibilities of this benign delusion. Only the subtler illusion of art is left—the illusion that our ability to command slightly different points of view within the human radius gives us a triangulation-base large enough to permit of mensurational guesses regarding absolute reality. This illusion we must keep as long as we can, for life without it would be sterile indeed for most of us; yet I do not think we can keep it always. Science is the great destroyer of beauty, and this phase will have to go in time. But that does not lessen its preciousness now, and we may still feel an emotional surge of approximation to the divine comprehension when a new artistic experience suddenly enlarges our horizon and shews us a familiar thing in the fresh, strange, and seemingly significant light of another man's vision. Now I suppose all this talk sounds like damned nonsense to you—but you must remember that the long-windedness lies wholly in the analysis and explanation, not in the complex phenomenon of art-pleasure itself! We feel all these phases instantaneously and simultaneously, and enjoy them without stopping to study them and pull them to pieces. I have had to be explicit here, simply because you profess a non-understanding and non-experiencing of these vital forces. In this explanation it is my hope that I have caused you to understand them, at least in part; and that I have proved to you that you are not really so insensible to them as you think. You are undoubtedly more alive than you imagine, as your reaction to the Albany state house and educational building amply proves; and it is possible that time will bring out in you still richer resources for the grasping and enjoyment of life. While for purposes of plain argument I have taken visual or pictorial art as a type of all aesthetics, you must realise that the principle as a whole includes every other branch of art-endeavour as well. One is just as impoverished through a dulness toward fine poetry and good literature, as through a blindness toward art. There is just as much defectiveness and undevelopedness in a failure to respond to exquisite word-imagery and tonal cadences in prose and verse, as there is in a failure to respond to a fine building—and I am sure that your instinct separated good writing from trash just as unerringly as it separates classic merit from Victorian rubbish in architecture. Surely, on reflection, you will see that the "mucker pose" regarding artistic perception and appreciation is a very absurd and illogical attitude for a sensible adult to assume.[10] There is nothing to be proud of in callousness, inexperience, or the state of being a cripple—yet the real substance of the Babbitt's or "hard-boiled egg's" boast 'that he cares nothing for art and beauty' is nothing more or less than a shrill and puerile exultation in his own defects. True, he does not know this himself; for he has never thought enough to realise what art is, and to understand how genuine and important a part of life its appreciation is. In his ignorance, he thinks that this major section of civilised life is a mere sham, and that he deserves credit for steering clear of it. But others see the situation as it is, and cannot restrain a smile as they see the honest soul screaming at the top of his voice the equivalent of "I am deaf and blind! I am crippled! I'm only a third alive, and damned proud of it! Half my brain is drugged, and I'm a better and harder he-man than the guy who lives with all his brain!" The best exemplar of this attitude now in the public eye is the deliciously comic-opera mayor of Newburyport—the redoubtable "Bossy" Gillis, of whose varied exploits you have no doubt read in the papers.[11] "Wot t'ell! I'll show dem guys w'ere dey gets off!" It's a good attitude to get rid of, for it hampers one frightfully in his attempts to make his life worth bearing. When one sinks into apathy toward art, the next step is one of apathy toward the intellectual life—and thence the road to complete animalism or vegetative futility is only too easy. To ask "what in hell's the use of art" is the next stage to asking "what in hell's the use of reading and thinking", and about two stages removed from asking "what the hell's the use of washing and dressing and shaving—why not live in dirt and disorder, or get taken care of at the work house?" No man who admits any good in anything beyond the satisfaction of the primal physical necessities can afford to sneer at art! Incidentally, you have a wrong idea of what real aestheticism is. For instance, you speak of your perception of a motor-car as a beautiful object as if you expected a confessed art-lover to deny the contention at once. How so? In truth, the aesthete is the very first to praise grace of line wherever he finds it; and there is no one who wishes to deny beauty to the more recent types of automobile-body. They are designed by persons familiar with aesthetic principles, and involve proportionings and adaptations to their function which bring them truly within the canon of art. They can, and often do, form high types of decorative beauty—lacking only the overtones of associative tradition in order to compete successfully in appeal with the finest specimens of old-time coach-making. I have not contended that the machine age cannot produce certain standardised types of decorative beauty, but have said that its net effect is imaginatively impoverishing. A beautiful motor-car calls up relatively few basic hereditary memories as compared with a fine coach of Georgian times; and one must remember, too, that the men who fashioned it had no part in the joy and feeling of creation. They carved no panels with the personal affection and distinctiveness of the old-time coach-maker, and had no subjectively clear vision of their task as a whole. They merely watched machines of infinite ugliness, and helped those machines give birth to a grotesque and heterogeneous progeny of parts equally ugly and even more meaningless in themselves. Beautiful objects may still be produced, but the processes of beauty are removed farther from life, and the sum total of beauty in life is infinitely diminished. What you say of the motor-car is equally true of the tobacco-tin. Surely you realise that small objects of utility—even the cheapest—have throughout history been sometimes so well made and happily conceived as to win a place in the field of art. Humble Greek and Roman lamps, the lowly commercial pottery of Corinth, every-day bits of Chinese and Japanese lacquer-ware—all sorts of things like this have always been highly esteemed as true, even if unpretentious, art, and have kept to this day an honoured place in museums. Your tobacco-tin undoubtedly belongs in greater or lesser degree to this solid tradition, and all one can say against it is that its widespread duplication is likely to lessen its hold on our aesthetic sense through sheer accustomedness. Being taken for granted, it may acquire something of the staleness of a hackneyed piece of music; though it will never be less beautiful, or less abstractly appreciated by the analysts of beauty. Incidentally—what you say about the deadening influence of museum display on one's art sense is only too true. You are not the first person to regret the lack of any other method for the exhibition of a large number of art objects in a limited space. Many museums try to escape this atmosphere in the case of a few special treasures; building a suitable environment around them and separating them from the bulk of the collection. Yet clearly, a vast majority must remain formally barracked in the old commonplace way. The only way to enjoy these things properly is not to try to study too many at once. Know what you're going to see on each trip, and make a bee line for it—paying no attention to anything else in the building. Only a fool—or somebody badly pressed for time—ever tries to "do" a museum in two or three days. I've been visiting the museums of Boston and New York for years, and don't pretend to have been through them. My favourite kind of museum display—early interiors with furniture and decorations—has fared very well of late years, insomuch as the modern tendency is to reconstruct whole rooms and furnish them exactly as they were when they were inhabited. Providence is very rich in this material, having the finest colonial furniture collection in the world; though the most varied and instructive exhibit of the kind is the one in the new wing of the Boston museum, which I visited last month. Altogether, it's too bad that the general average of museum-arrangement can't be raised—yet a man must be pretty primitive and childish in his non-analytical emotionalism if he allows the mere ennui of existing conditions to give him a prejudice against art. The really sensitive appreciator knows what he wants, and can't be scared out of his genuine personal feelings by the bogey-army of other marshalled objects all in a row. Art-love, to a sensitively developed person, is a natural major part of one's life, and not an extraneous accomplishment to be assumed with difficulty and lost with ease.

About the absolute aesthetic value of colonial architecture and antiques generally—we must not try to generalise, but must examine each type of design separately. A great deal of glamour is undoubtedly lent to such things by their history, nor ought we to despise that glamour or seek to restrain the pleasure it gives us. Linkage with the long continuous history of the race is a thing with a genuine poetic value in itself, and the joy we take in even the ugliest and most grotesque of traditional objects is *not* a false one. It is not *directly* aesthetic—that is, it does not proceed from the decorative beauty of line in the objects themselves—but it is none the less truly aesthetic in an indirect way; through the flood of unspoken poetic imagery and epic race-memory released in our minds by the historic and cultural symbolism of the objects. Such objects even when intrinsically unbeautiful, form an invaluable sort of springboard for the imagination. I can dream a whole cycle of colonial life from merely gazing on a tattered old book or almanack with the long f. Naturally enough, many surviving objects of the early days are commonplacely homely or even positively ugly. Puritan furniture—17th century—is heavy and stiff, and scores of household objects of every age have no actual beauty in themselves. Many colonial houses are drably plain or even poorly proportioned, whilst certain public buildings of the period are cumbrous and undistinguished. Yet this does not lessen their associational or symbolic value, or impair their capability of producing, in sensitive persons, a genuine ecstasy of secondary aestheticism. Moreover, though certain isolated objects may lack intrinsic beauty, their typical combination may contain that very quality to a marked degree. This is especially the case with an old town. The houses, each taken by itself, may be ugly enough; yet their arrangements in curving hill lanes and alleys, and the massed silhouette made by their blended roofs and chimneys against the sky, may possess a charm, poignancy, and absolute art value of the highest sort. Marblehead affords a striking instance of this. Few of the ancient houses are aesthetically distinctive, but their collective effect is truly overpoweringly lovely. Another similar case is the tiny hamlet of Guilford Centre in your own Vermont. Standing in its midst, I saw nothing extraordinary—yet what a vision of charm did I behold when I had walked far up the gradual slope behind it, and looked back at the huddle of spreading treetops, half-glimpsed gables, and the square, white church-tower rising above all it all![12] But so much for concessions. Now for the positive side. It is an actual fact that from about 1700 to about 1825 architecture and the decorative arts stood on a phenomenally high plane in England and America. The mediaeval-gothic tradition had gone out, and the Renaissance influence had reached the Anglo-Saxon world through sublimely gifted interpreters like Inigo Jones, Christopher Wren, Grinling Gibbons and their pupils; so that by the reign of Queen Anne we had fastened on as a sound neo-classicism adapted to English good sense and miraculously purged of the baroque Franco-Italian extravagances then reigning on the continent. Fine designers and craftsmen multiplied, and lesser artisans very widely and successfully copied their triumphs; so that the spread of the good taste was singularly wide and thorough. The British influences were not slow in crossing to the colonies; and though we built upon a more modest scale, we added to the tone of classic austerity rather than subtracting from it. By 1750 our best houses and furniture were genuine works of art—thoroughly classic in feeling, proportion, and decorative detail, and fit to stand on their own merits regardless of associational factors. The furniture of Thomas Chippendale and his cisatlantic copyists struck as high an intrinsic average as any school of furniture in history has ever struck, and the buildings of Wren, Gibbs, Hawkesmoore, Peter Harrison,[13] etc. cannot be surpassed except by a few monumental exceptions. Harrison came from England to Rhode Island, and designed some of the finest public edifices in New England. When one praises the house-proportions, doorway details, furniture, panelling, silverware, etc. etc. of this period, he is praising real beauty and not simply sentimentalising over the past. In the mid-century a change came, due to the fresh excavations at Pompeii and Herculaneum. Before then, renaissance craftsmen had not known how to apply their Graeco-Roman models to fine decorative details, insomuch as the world then possessed no classical reliques save monumental ruins. Pompeii and Herculaneum, however, yielded up abundant examples of the best Roman usage in interior finish and minute decoration generally; and the craftsmen of modern Europe were not slow to take the hint. About 1770 a whole new school based on the classical models arose—with slender straight lines replacing the curves and scrolls of the Wren-Chippendale period, and heavy rococo ornament ousted by the true Roman forms—wreaths, rosettes, and other fine conventional details—wrought in composition bas-relief. England again was lucky in her architects and cabinet-makers—the brothers Adam, Sheraton, and Hepplewhite[14] carrying the new style to exquisite heights. The transition reached America about 1780, and became general around 1800, giving the early Republican house and appointments their typical cast. We had some notable designers in this medium—Samuel McIntire of Salem, Charles Bulfinch of Boston, John Holden Greene of Providence, and so on. In absolute beauty this austere style probably eclipsed its predecessor, and we need no historic associations to make us appreciate the artistic triumphs produced under its influence. It was, indeed, too fine and austere to suit the coarse parvenu class then gaining ground through the spread of post-revolutionary democracy. Experiments in greater extravagance began to be tried—classic revivals, gothic adaptations, and so on. By 1830 the wreckage was well under way, and between 1840 and 1900 not a first-rate building was reared in the United States.

Europe, too, had its architectural and decorative decadence; though not so frightful a debacle as ours. They had more standard models and less new building over there. We, with our rapid material expansion, built like wildfire and plastered the landscape with hideousness. But the glories of the past remain, and we may be justly proud of our ancestors for their marvellously high and widespread standard of art exemplified by their best edifices large and small, and by their furniture, silverware, and craftsmanship in general. It was a great age—amidst which many a common carpenter had a better sense of form and design than did any trained architect of the Victorian dark age fifty years later. If you were interested I could lend you books and shew you significant pictures on the subject. Certainly, the Augustan period of American decorative art was that extending roughly between 1715 and 1830, and especially between 1750 and 1820. Actual specimens could not possibly break the spell formed by what you have read, and I hope you will have an early chance to go over a good exhibit of the sort—either at a museum or in one of the colonially furnished historical houses so abundant throughout New England.

I'm glad you've seen Salem—and wish you could have obtained still more of a "kick" from the House of the Seven Gables. Actually, ancient gabled houses like this, with diamond-paned lattice windows and overhanging second story, are extremely rare in America; since they ceased to be built about 1700, and since many were subsequently made over into the later gambrel-roofed style. These houses are an absolute continuation of the mediaeval European tradition in town architecture, and form something wholly apart from the more familiar colonial types which followed them. We almost forget that they ever existed, and that they once gave their characteristic mediaeval note to the early coast towns of New England—yet in truth many of them survived beyond the revolution, so that in 18th century days an average town would shew a great sprinkling of them (despite the frequent great fires of that period) amidst the newer gambrel-roofed and square Georgian houses. The fact that these peaked veterans represent a well-nigh forgotten chapter in our history, and that they are true contemporaries and symbols of the Puritan age with its dark hints of witchcraft, ought to give them a degree of charm obvious to all. Salem has about 5 specimens, two of which have been moved to the garden in the rear of the House of the Seven Gables and one of which stands in the grounds of the Essex Institute. Ipswich has a fine example, Gloucester one, Topsfield one, and Boston a rather poor specimen—the Revere house (1676) in North Square. I know of none in its original condition in Rhode Island. I have "done" Gloucester thoroughly, and have also shared your enjoyment of Plymouth. The great elms there are certainly magnificent, although I think Bristol, R.I. and Deerfield, Mass. (both also famous for colonial houses) could match them. I envy you Cape Cod and Martha's Vineyard, neither of which I've yet visited, and I likewise want to see Nantucket.[15]

Portsmouth, N.H., and Newburyport, Mass., are favourite old-timers of mine, and outside New England I like Philadelphia, (with its splendid old suburb Germantown) Annapolis, Md., and Alexandria, Va. I want to get farther south in Virginia on my next trip—especially to ancient Williamsburg, which is being restored en masse to its true colonial condition.[16]

Glad you enjoyed the enclosures—or most of them. That Howe item was put in as a sort of illustration of the tendency one ought to avoid—the tendency to be callous toward art and the subtleties of life, which has done so much to prevent Howe from developing out of a state of mere hard shrewdness into something like philosophic breadth. As for the Madariaga article—it seems to me on the whole to hit the existing situation fairly well.[17] Of course, as a cynic I agree with you that enjoyment is really the test of a workable system of life; indeed, in one of my youthful essays I dilated at great length upon the disadvantages of the human state, and pointed out the superior fortune and felicity of the four-footed creation, thus adopting a strictly hedonistic standard independent of mere biological or cultural development. I still think that there is no need of burdening a happy savage or immature race with cultural subtleties beyond its power of grasping; for surely the logical goal of any group is not the mere state of superiority and high development, but rather the state of harmonious adjustment to its own instincts, traditions, and environment. Therefore, if it could be shewn that the American people were really an undeveloped tribe of barbarians, happy in their infantile mass-culture and worship of size, glitter, and sentimentality, and finding in these imperfect mental-imaginative outlets a genuine and adequate expression of their hereditary and traditional feelings, I would concur with you in recommending that they be let alone to work out their destiny until they began to interfere with the civilised world. Surely, contentment is the chief of boons; and even though the Americo-barbarians missed the most poignant experiences of life through the atrophy of the better part of their faculties, I would say that they needed no remedy—since in their present state they know not what they miss, and are as happy as a log of wood or a kitten chasing its own tail. They are, I would say, ridiculous only to others; and so long as they do not understand how absurd they are, they will not suffer any humiliation. Thus fortified with philosophy, I would settle comfortably back as a survivor from an elder civilisation, and watch the children play. I would not be the first to adopt such an attitude; for as you probably recall, Dr. Johnson's old opponent Lord Monboddo was warm in his praises of the savage state,[18] whilst the romantic followers of Rousseau all effervesced over the virtues of simplicity and innocence. The fact is, however, that I fail to find any evidence that the thoughtful and sensitive part of the existing American people is in any way happy or contented, or that the present state of arrested mental development is in any way suited to the history and traditions of the race. A careful survey of the writings of the most vigorous and receptive minds of the country reveals a great and increasing sense of frustration and mental starvation, so that large numbers of the most desirable persons have been forced to reside in Europe in order to escape the deadening and devastating influence of a half-baked, commerce-ridden machine culture. In my next letter I will send you a magazine cutting (which I can't find now) very pertinent to this subject—a letter from an American in Paris, explaining why he cannot endure the ordeal of living in his own land. As I have told you before, the reason you enjoy life is that your section of it has not yet been drawn into the stultifying vortex of American mass culture. That is also why I find existence tolerable—because I keep aloof from the rising machine-culture and remain a part of the old New England civilisation which preceded it. But nothing good can be said of that cancerous machine-culture itself. It is not a true civilisation, and has nothing in it to satisfy a mature and fully-developed human mind. It is attuned to the mentality and imagination of the galley-slave and the moron, and crushes relentlessly with disapproval, ridicule, and economic annihilation, any sign of actually independent thought and civilised feeling which chances to rise above its sodden level. It is a treadmill, squirrel-trap culture—drugged and frenzied with the hasheesh of industrial servitude and material luxury. It is wholly a material body-culture, and its symbol is the tiled bathroom and steam radiator rather than the Doric portico and the temple of philosophy. Its denizens do not live or know how to live. They spend all their time devising ways of safeguarding life and making it physically comfortable, but once they get it as they want it, they don't know what to do with it. They have developed an elaborate technique for preserving and enshrining something which gives them no pleasure, and for which they can find no use. They mean well enough, but the effect of their ignorant blundering is a malignant one. Like the Indians, they occupy a highly desirable land and prevent civilisation from enjoying its benefits. And on account of their material wealth and physical strength, they may yet constitute a genuine menace to the civilised world. Children are always up to mischief, and matches, edged tools, and firearms are dangerous in their hands. Now all this wouldn't be quite so tragic if the pitiful mass-culture could become reconciled to itself. Even if modern America were impossible for civilised men to live in, these civilised men could return to England and let the barbarians welter in their own stupidity. That would be the logical thing if the biped fauna of 20th century North America were really barbarians by heritage—that is, if the existing barbarian culture were really a natural product of their blood and traditions, and could be depended upon to give adequate expression and satisfaction to the instincts of their coming generations. But—and here is the big point—*in all truth this degraded culture is* **not** *the natural culture of the American people, and can* **not** *be depended upon to give free play to the instincts and mentality of the race.* The Americans are not, by descent, barbarians, and their impulses and thought-patterns are not such as can be satisfied by the present artificial barbarism. This barbarism is not a normal product of the race's history, but a peculiarly unfortunate accident resulting from a complex group of circumstances incident to the settling of a new continent, the rash severance from the mother land, and the sudden appearance of the machine age before the social body is ready to exercise a mature sense of proportion in assimilating it and correlating it with the national life. Strictly speaking, this new barbarism is *not the American civilisation,* but a false and accidental blight which has chanced to fall upon America and obliterate its civilisation. Its worst phase is that it can never satisfy—for since Americans are *of civilised descent and traditions,* they cannot help producing minds of civilised sensitiveness and capacity in moderate proportions; minds which hark back atavistically to the old civilised state, and which must necessarily suffer conflict and anguish amidst the barbarous milieu developed by democracy and machinery. Thus the new barbarism is *not* the honest, happy, natural barbarism of a genuinely savage race. It is an artificial barbarism foisted upon the descendants of civilised people—descendants who remember just enough of the old standards and folk-ways to be vaguely dissatisfied with the trap into which they have fallen, and who inherit enough of the old cultural capacity to chafe, rebel, and suffer. Real America had the start of a splendid civilisation— the British stream, enriched by a geographical setting well-calculated to develop a vital, adventurous, and imaginatively fertile existence. Naturally the hardships of settlement might be expected to cause an hiatus and develop a certain crudeness, whilst the revolution dealt another woeful blow; but even so, the hardy growth was not perceptibly stunted in the early part of the 19th century. There was much philosophic naivete and crudeness of manners, but no more than was natural to the situation. Taste and thought, at bottom, were sound and vigorous; and the more intelligent classes had a healthily humorous realisation of the rawnesses of national youth which surrounded them. In New England and Virginia a continuous settled life of 200 years had caused real civilisations to sprout, so that life in these places held the rich harmonies of natural adjustment, mystic[?] mental coherence, and integrated folk-ways, whose total absence is such a salient characteristic of the new barbarism. In New York and Pennsylvania, too, real civilisation was growing; and all these cultural areas had enough in common to promise a composite future civilisation of the utmost soundness, vigour, and homogeneity—a civilisation staunchly English at heart, though with such local individualities and differentiations as were dictated by the geographical situation. That civilisation is the only one which ought properly to be associated with the United States. It is the natural and logical one, insomuch as it is the direct product of our blood and previous experience. It is not, strictly speaking, wholly dead even now; for it survives definitely in many non-metropolitan parts of the original colo-

nies (especially in your own Vermont) and among the older and more conservative families everywhere. Providence retains much of it—for the sleepy
old hill with its Georgian houses, ancient college buildings, shadowy Athenaeum, and unchanged old families, has a remarkable knack of resisting modern intrusions and keeping comfortably aloof from the seething polyglot
commercial life of the lower town on the flat lands across the river. You can
find it, too, in Salem and Portsmouth, and in drowsy, beautiful Concord. The
South has it, too, as a careful inspection of Annapolis or Alexandria will soon
reveal. This is a real civilisation, although perhaps not so brilliant and creative
as many in the old world. It might have surpassed most of its predecessors
had it been suffered to thrive and develop unmolested. Even as it is, it has the
great essential which distinguishes civilisation from barbarism. Its people are
not slaves of size, speed, and luxury, but are balanced human beings with traditionally developed capacities for intelligent adjustment to their environment. They know how to think, feel, and dream—in other words, they know
not only how to keep alive, but *what to keep alive for.* They know how to live.
What destroyed it as the dominant culture of this continent? Well—first came
the poison of social democracy, which gradually introduced the notion of dif-
fused rather than intensive development. Idealists wanted to raise the level of
the ground by tearing down all the towers and strewing them over the surface—and when it was done they wondered why the ground didn't seem
much higher, after all. And they had lost their towers! Then came the premature shifting of the economic centre of gravity to the relatively immature
west; which brought western crudeness, "push", and quantity-feeling to the
fore, and accelerated the evils of democracy. Sudden financial overturns and
the rise of a loathsome parvenu class—natural things in a rapidly expanding
nation—helped on the disaster; whilst worst of all was the rashly and idealis-
tically admitted flood of alien, degenerate, and unassimilable immigrants—the
supreme calamity of the western world. On this dangerous and unstable cultural chaos finally fell the curse of the machine age—a condition peculiarly
adapted to favour the crude and imaginationless and to operate against the
sensitive and the civilised. Its first results we behold today, though the depths
of its cultural darkness are reserved for the torture of later generations.
Whether an intelligent minority can still escape it, and keep alive real American civilisation as a parallel stream, is at this date an open question. I am not
pessimist enough to say that it cannot be done; indeed, I think that persons of
retiring tendencies (like myself) can always manage to eke along in a quiet antiquarian way—living imaginative inner lives based on the true hereditary civilisation. It is the man who is at once civilised and highly social or gregarious
who has the worst time. He will have to live abroad unless the prevailing
darkness can be modified. I thought the "mucker pose" article very apt and
well based, for it hits me now and then. Since coming into correspondence

with younger men I have picked up certain slang phrases, and have now and then used them for easy emphasis (as you can see occasionally in my letters) when as a matter of fact plain language would have done just as well. We are tempted to adopt bits of street patois as a species of pungent descriptive detail—and indeed I suppose the practice is not to be wholly condemned except when carried to excess, or followed lamely and unimaginatively instead of artistically and intelligently. So long as one can remain master of his slang, he is relatively safe; but heaven help the poor wight whose slang becomes the master of him! Many a wretch has awaked some morning to find that he has lost his mother tongue, and can utter only the vague and blunted vulgarisms and generalities of the slums and fish-docks! Thus far I have been thinking of *writing* only. In *oral discourse* a man must simply use his own judgment and good taste, while being careful not to lose his hold on the civilised language of his family and real friends. Personally I have no dislike of the illiterate; but since my work is home and mail work, I do not often have occasion to talk with them at length. However, even if I did, I don't believe it would be necessary to adopt an idiom very different from that of civilised Providence—indeed, if I tried to do so, I would have a sort of guilty feeling, as if I were *mocking* my uncouth vis-a-vis rather than really meeting him on his own ground. For after all, the *real* test of appropriate language is *naturalness*. The only sensible and graceful way for a man to talk is the way his family and friends talk—the way he was brought up to talk—and whenever he tries to adopt artificial dialects either above or below that natural level of speech, he is merely play-acting and making a fool of himself. Naturally, in casual conversation one doesn't use the precise and elaborate language of a book. The proper thing is a plain simplicity; and so far as I can see one seldom incurs the charge of affectation when he practices it, no matter who his audience may be. Would you say "Nice-a day, Beppo! Breeng-a me one plate spaghet' weeth meat-a sauce, pleece!" when ordering food of an Italian waiter, or "Yeah, Misteh Johnson, dis am de way down cellar!" when admitting a nigger ash-collector to the house? As for Yankee farmers—oddly enough, I haven't noticed that the majority talk any differently from myself; so that I've never regarded them as a separate class to whom one must use a special dialect. If I were to say "Mornin', Zeke, haow be ye?" to anybody along the road during my numerous summer walks, I fancy I'd receive an icy stare in return—or perhaps a puzzled inquiry as to what theatrical troupe I had wandered out of! I have never heard any marked dialect in any New England town, and even in the open country it seems to be obsolescent. In the village of Brattleboro, Vermont, the speech is just the same as in Providence, though the rustic reaches of neighbouring Guilford retain the *-aow* sound in "caow", "haouse", etc. Even this, however, does not apply to the younger generation of the more carefully educated residents. Whenever I talked with the *-aow*-sayers I did not think it was necessary, or that it would even be courteous, to imitate them. I soon ceased to notice the mannerism, and conversed just as I would with anyone else. Nor did they seem to notice anything conspicuous in my own speech—for the plain language I used is a sort of easy common denominator among all native-Americans, and will scarcely seem odd to any one of the old stock. The Guilfordites had heard speech like mine every time they were in Brattleboro, and in many cases among their own number. I'd have felt like an ass trying to say "daown" and "araound"! The same thing applied when I was travelling in the Annapolis-Alexandria-Washington region—and even the Philadelphia region. Also Cleveland, in the Middle West. There are distinct local idioms in all of these sections, yet it did not seem to me necessary to duplicate each one. Nobody thought my language strange, either. When I lived two years in New York I saw no reason for aping the ugly accents of the native proletariat and saying "momunt", "woild", "kerosene *etl*", etc.*, or for adopting the local habit (probably of German origin) of adding the word "already" to sentences where it doesn't belong. Nor did I say "Oi, Isidor, eh vunt yeh shood feegs id up deece suit—a'ready!" when getting repairs done at the Jew tailor's. Yet there also I did not find myself stared at as a curiosity. Altogether, I think it's safe to say that plain, simple, correct, and inconspicuous language will "get by" almost anywhere without friction if the speaker will preserve a sense of proportion and refrain from putting on airs. Certainly, it is very bad taste to *emphasise* one's differences from one's audience, but *being natural* somehow doesn't seem to do that. One must of course use tact—for instance, when the other fellow mispronounces a word, it is very bad form to use that word immediately with its correct pronunciation. In such a case it's best to avoid the word if possible—or to postpone its use till the connexion of the two pronunciations will not be obvious. It would be extreme, though, to feel that one must deliberately copy and adopt the error! As for *choice of subjects*—of course it would be ridiculous to try to talk to a person about things of no interest to him. That goes without saying. A man of sense does not try to "horn into" company where he obviously doesn't fit; but if circumstances force him to talk to incongruous people—or if special interests bring him into contact with people whose general interests are different from his—he will usually know how to steer clear of subjects which can only confuse and repel his confreres of the moment. I trust you don't think I burden grocery-clerks and street-car conductors with the kind of harangues, or the kind of expository language, which occur in these controversial letters of mine! But at that, I don't see where the "mucker pose" is really necessary. It's all right to liven up a long discourse with a little informality, lightly used, but making a cult and a habit of hackneyed and inexpressive vulgarity and plebeianism is another matter.

---

*a vulgar New Yorker would pronounce "Ernest Boyd" as "Oinest Bird"!

All poses are bad as a rule, and this one is no exception. I'll enclose a cartoon which touches rather cleverly on one phase of the "mucker pose". You needn't return this. I shall look for the errors you mention in the Adams article and see what I think of them. What you say of kindliness as an essential of good-breeding is undoubtedly true. I try never to get rough unless the other fellow starts it—and even then my controversial fulminations have no hostility or ill-will or desire to offend in them. However, I don't see but what other phases of good-breeding are also to be encouraged—or that such other phases need involve the least abatement of the kindness element. I do not think that the well-mannered people of earlier generations were less generally kind than are the "mucker posers" of today—for if the "old prigs" of Gen. Washington's time could be "meaner than Billy Hell", they were surely exercising no accomplishment unknown to the self-conscious boors of modernity! The truth is, no age is free from malignity and cruelty; but I'd rather have the given amount of cruelty mixed with good manners, than the same amount mixed with bad manners!

Your description of yourself is very interesting, and I congratulate you upon your retention of the youthful spirit. I am myself a great admirer of most of the qualities of youth—its keen imagination, unbroken spirit, intellectual adventurousness, and resilient buoyancy—and I envy you your retention of its temperament and attributes. It is a great thing to have—and when one can retain its advantages while developing beyond its crudities, he is a fortunate mortal indeed! Most of my correspondents are of the younger generation, since my own crop of minds has begun to get too fossilised to suit my cynical point of view. I am, you see, a sort of hybrid betwixt the past and the future—archaic in my personal tastes, emotions, and interests, but so much of a scientific realist in philosophy that I cannot abide any intellectual point of view short of the most advanced. Only the younger fellows seem to me to give proper treatment of my eternal question—"What is anything?" I like youthfulness in national spirit, too, if it is a normal youthfulness which properly fits the race. Nothing disgusts me more than the weary decadence of the Continental nations. But I myself am not much of a youngster in looks or point of view. All of my 38½ years show in me, I guess; and so far as my temperament is concerned, I was born an old man. I call my young friends my "grandsons", and lecture them sagely on the superior ways of the years before they were born. However—I am not quite such a solemn prig as you probably assume from my letters. It is part of the cynic's creed to unbend when he feels like it, and anti-democratic theory as applied to governmental policy does not prevent me from being as informal and free-and-easy as I choose. I would, I am sure, enjoy your breezy manner of argument; and certainly did *not* take offence at its appearance on paper. When I spoke of your attitude toward my point of view, I was merely trying to make sure that you were not missing any factors of the argument through a departure from scientific impersonality. I am, in truth, as offence-proof as the average cynic. I have no stiff-necked dignity at all. Just to prove the latter I will enclose a snap-shot taken on your own Vermont soil, and shewing me in a state of the most extreme informality. As Orton's guest last summer I got right down to Mother Earth, and the picture shews me (as well as my genial host) garbed in all the odds and ends which the combined resources of attic and barn could yield forth, and ready for the most arduous duties of the rural kind. I am the sour, cynical, lantern-jawed cuss on the right—yoked up to carry the milk or cider or bootleg whiskey to taown.[19] I'll have to ask you to return this photographic masterpiece, since I have no other print and the negative is lost. But anyway, it proves that the old man is really a vastly more harmless creature than he sounds on paper!

About the future of man—it is barely possible that in some respects we don't differ as widely as we think we do. For example; while I am not especially enthusiastic one way or the other, I think that "equality of opportunity" is by no means a bad general idea when it does not interfere with the best accomplishments of a civilisation. We all know, of course, that there is in nearly every culture a gradual renewal of the upper classes from the ranks of the lower, and that this condition is healthful rather than otherwise. Very few conservatives are such extremists as to wish to destroy this condition; the only object of those who urge caution being to prevent the rise of the plebeians to power *in such numbers and with such speed that they will carry their crude institutions with them and thereby make those institutions the dominant mores of the nation.* Nobody really gives a hang about existing aristocratic families *as such.* All that is desired is *to maintain the existing standards of thought, aesthetics, and manners,* and not to allow them to sink to low levels through the dominance of coarsely-organised, sordid-minded, and aesthetically insensitive people who are satisfied with less and who would establish a national atmosphere intolerable to those civilised persons who require more. Nobody wants to prevent any member of the race, as an individual, from assuming a high position in the civilisation; *but we do want to make it imperative that he go through a refining process and measure up to the best standard before he takes his place among those who represent the civilisation and shape its institutions, manners, and future.* The one important thing is how to make the application of this refining process imperative. It implies a necessary filtration, and a check on the sudden rise of vast parvenu groups. But it does not imply any wish to keep down any man who possesses the requisite qualities for elevation. It is perfectly sensible to give everyone like opportunities for mounting the ladder—although it would be far from sensible to raise the cry of meaningless abstract idealism and try to destroy the natural advantage of the man who happens to be born on the top. The latter is more fortunate, it is true; but it would be a waste of energy to raise theoretical objections to the accidental fact that he does not have to work for what someone else does have to work for. Since he happens to be born ready to participate in the cultural leadership, let him participate and be done with it. To thrust him aside would be to throw away the material needed for the maintenance of the cultural level. When the other fellow does work his way up, he will be glad enough to claim similar advantages for his own sons born at the top. The great idea is to keep the cultivated class in power, and see that its new recruits measure up to the requisite cultural level before they are allowed to exercise its privileges. *The maintenance of that high cultural standard is the only social or political enthusiasm I possess,* aside from my constant wish to see the Anglo-Saxon race and psychology remain dominant in America. In effect, I venerate the principle of aristocracy without being especially interested in aristocrats as persons. I don't care who has the dominance, so long as that dominance remains a *certain kind* of dominance, intellectually and aesthetically considered. Returning to the matter of the future—I enclose a short cutting touching on the subject of boredom in the machine age, which I think I'll ask you to return. This is a very real and vital question, as you may see from all the evidence at hand. As for your objection that the machine age's added leisure will be a boon rather than a curse—one may only say that such a hope is scarcely warranted in view of the fact that everything in the atmosphere and environment and conditions of the age tends to separate the individual from those memories and sights and experiences and living conditions which would give him the necessary background for enjoying his leisure intelligently.[20] The question is, as I thought I carefully explained in my last letter, profoundly intertwined with the subtlest and most complex emotional and psychological nuances. It involves the sources, and the relationship of our age-old adjustment to Nature, of our faculty of enjoyment and contentment; and takes into consideration the part played by excitement, uncertainty, non-repetition, and free and easy regularity in making life seem like something worth enduring. Do not forget that you cannot judge this matter from personal experience, since you still live in the familiar elder world and have not yet encountered machine culture. That goes for me, also. You and I must survey this matter abstractly and from a distance—and we can perhaps arrive at a more impartial verdict for that very reason. Granted that the machine-victim has leisure. What is he going to do with it? What memories and experiences has he to form a background to give significance to anything he can do? What can he see or do that will mean anything to him? If he takes an aeroplane trip to the country, what will such a glimpse mean to one whose natural connexion with the rural scene is hopelessly shattered? The few vigorous and original minds among the machine-slaves* will no doubt become scholars, aesthetes, and antiquarians; cultivating

---

*and they may not be many, for in a machine culture most brain-power is shunted

the art and literature of imaginative escape and feigning the atmosphere of a vital and natural type of life which has passed away. But even to them the whole thing will be hollow, artificial, and unreal. All their scholarship and art (for this modernistic decorative craze has obviously narrow limits) will have to draw upon past phases of environment and experience for its inspiration— they will be living in a world that is dead, just as Arthur Machen's hero in "The Hill of Dreams" lived in a dream life in the Roman Britain of 1500 years before his time. Yet even this small respite from reality will be denied to the majority, since there are relatively few persons of sufficient stamina, originality, and imagination to carve out for themselves an independent mental life apart from the dominant currents of their age. What has heretofore made life tolerable for the majority is the fact that their *natural workaday routine and milieu* have never been *quite* devoid of the excitement, nature-contact, uncertainty, non-repetition, and free and easy irregularity which build up a background of associations calculated to foster the illusion of significance and make possible the real enjoyment of art and leisure. Without this help from their environment, the majority could never manage to keep contented. Now that it is fading, they are in a bad plight indeed; for they cannot hope to breast the tide of ennui as the stronger-minded minority can. There will be, of course, high-sounding and flabbily idealistic attempts to help the poor devils. We shall hear of all sorts of futile reforms and reformers—standardised culture-outlines, synthetic sports and spectacles, professional play-leaders and study-guides, and kindred examples of machine-made uplift and brotherly spirit. And it will amount to just about as much as most reforms do! Meanwhile the tension of boredom and unsatisfied imagination will increase—breaking out with increasing frequency in crimes of morbid perversity and explosive violence. I enclose a book review which covers the topic of the early machine age pretty well, and which is an especially conservative document because it takes the case of the average *small city* instead of the metropolitan centres where the blight is at its worst. One sentence toward the end sums up pretty well the whole nature of the new barbarism which is supplanting civilisation in America. The typical machine-age city, comments the reviewer, *"is sophisticated in the mechanism of living and pitifully naive in almost everything having to do with the purposes of living."* It has not, in short, begun to ask itself my eternal question, *"What is anything?"* The result is that it feverishly frets around and works the treadmill, occupying its mind with meaningless material luxury, sports and amusements of the most pathetic triviality, and political and civic interests whose utter emptiness and fundamental futility and absurdity are a jest for the gods.

---

into technological channels; so that the brains of the country will be among the masters of the machines—industrial magnates on estates like Ford and Rockefeller. These people may enjoy themselves mildly, but their minds will be too technology-warped to allow them to live fully.

When you speak of the 'immense amount of *comprehended* work still to be done' in the machine age, I fear you miss the point of the argument about de-naturalised functions. The remaining duties which you list are *not* the *creative* fields of endeavour whose passing is viewed with such alarm. Rather are they *the very sort of maddening routine procedure which the machine age is multiplying.* It is true that this group of activities does not happen to have the one detail of *in-comprehensibility,* but you may easily see that in general essence—monotony, repetitiousness, colourlessness, regularity, and *absence of completion* (this last an important psychological detail)—it closely duplicates the atmosphere of the out-and-out machine job. This sort of work has *always* been the bugbear of life—this window-washing, floor-cleaning, machine-oiling kind of thing—and has hitherto been endurable only because of other palliative influences exist-ing around it. Now these palliative influences—those contacts with the free-dom and variety and excitement and irregularity of a natural life—are slowly disappearing, and are being replaced by bugbears just as bad as the original routine bugbear. This point ought not to be difficult of grasping. You can see that drab *routine and care* functions are not in any sense the kind of *creative* la-bour which genuinely gratifies the performer. Nothing of the emotional satis-faction of *self-expression and construction* can go into these patterns of monotonous motion leading nowhere. Every element of interest and stimula-tion is absent from them, for they *make nothing, offer no latitude or variety, involve no element of personal originality and individuality,* (I will not believe you platitudi-nous enough to cite the old saw about "doing *any* work *well*" as a medium of self-expression) and *leave the performer at the close of each day exactly where he was before.* Of course, it is naive and foolish to speak of any tendency in *absolutes,* hence no one wishes to claim that *every individual being alive* will be chained to repellent monotony. There will always be *a few* persons less monotonously occupied than others—especially those connected with *transportation* by land, sea, and air. Research scientists, artists, (such as there can be) antiquarians, archaeologists, and other intellectual workers will get a trifle of the old sense of variety and adventure, but it is easy to see that such an infinitesimal minor-ity can never give its stamp to the age as a whole, or determine the prevailing emotional milieu of civilisation. The kind of work whose decline is so univer-sally lamented, is that which we may class as *creative*—the work in which a definitely individualised person bends his faculties to the shaping of sur-rounding materials and forces to some concrete and visualisable end, and into which he puts a substantial proportion of personal feeling and original and independent choice of design. Every genuine craftsman of the non-machine type has a distinctive personal touch in his work which corresponds to *style* in the artist. It may be the making of shoes or the building of furniture or the planting and harvesting of crops—but the feeling of creation and the joy of adequate technique and completion are the same as those experienced by the poet in moulding a sonnet or the prose-writer in sculpturing a paragraph of exquisite imagery, rhetoric, cadence, and tone-colour. What really counts is the vital relationship of the creator's mind and feelings to the pattern and process of creation. As long as freedom of choice, opportunity for subtle variation, (I suppose you know that the real inner magic of the best Gothic architecture involves a kind of inspired and insidious asymmetry) and personal control over a gradual growth toward a foreseen end are present, the process remains an adequate form of emotional expression. When, however, authority and design are removed from the fashioner; when mathematical adherence to a standard is substituted for the adventurous independence of possible variation; when demands for speed and inordinate quantity destroy the old balance of emotion toward perfection of accomplishment and substitute new and alien ideals of procedure; and when even the sight and conception of any definite goal are denied the quasi-blindfolded worker; it is easy to see that nothing of true creative feeling and emotional satisfaction can remain. The process of making things ceases to be an art and becomes an applied science. Creation gives place to technology. And the artisan finds at last that he has ceased to be a personal craftsman, but has been made the discharger of a mere *routine and care* function; a slave of repetition and monotony, and a sharer of the plight of the window-washer, street-cleaner, and floor-sweeper whose sterile bondage he once so acutely pitied! As for the growing *standardisation of intellect,* I don't see how you can fail to grasp the actual situation. You allow yourself to be misled by superficial resemblances, and wholly overlook the underlying phenomena upon which *real* likeness or unlikeness depends. In truth, general thought and feeling were never so lethally crushed into uniformity as they are today. The individual cases of conscious persecution for unusual opinions which you cite, have to do with extremes almost wholly outside the question under discussion. Certainly, bold flights of speculation contravening the utmost limits of the illusion-sphere of any age are always opposed by the majority, and fought desperately with whatever weapons may chance to be in fashion. This always has been, is, and always will be. But the question of individualism versus standardisation which we are considering, does not involve any such basic and momentous matters as these. It involves those lesser and more familiar attitudes, idiosyncrasies, and folk-thoughts which are so much closer to our daily lives and actions; and which affect our immediate opinions and policies infinitely more than do the soaring hypotheses and deductions so gravely feared by the reactionaries of all ages. Common sense must tell you that, within the formal limits imposed by theology and convention, there has always been an enormous amount of intellectual and cultural diversity; a diversity which has made the contact of different minds a never-failing adventure, and which has led, through intelligent discussion, to the creation of a piquant and ever-fresh field of mental experience whose effect is not only to banish boredom but to evolve fruitful ideas and innovations in the technique of life, society, and government. Differing environments, traditions, and streams of experience have bred differing schools of thought and differing types of personal attitude; thus ensuring a rich interplay of idea and opinion, and a vital fabric of enlivening, stimulating, broadening, and sanifying speculation. That certain remote limits were fixed to the field of permissible difference has mattered relatively little, since after all only a very few have ever cared to branch out toward those flaming ramparts. What has really mattered to our daily lives, is that freedom and individuality *in the small intimate concernments* have never known a serious curb. The world can never be dull when a trip to the next village, or the next state, or the next country, can provide a change of mental climate and give us a chance to compare notes with some fellow-thinker whom differing geography, customs, and opinions have cast in a different mould. Well—you see what the machine age with its easy transportation, standardised living conditions, daily routine, and merchandise, uniform educational methods, worldwide change from diverse natural environments and climates to one standard artificial environment and climate, and so forth, has done to all this. Conscious persecution of diversities of thought would only have served to enhance them, since individuality thrives on opposition. What has really happened is far more deadly than any conscious persecution; since it is a subtle, persuasive influence which sets up no healthy reaction. It is, in truth, nothing more or less than *a quiet and imperceptible withdrawal from life all over the world of those natural environmental and experiential differences which have hitherto caused different groups and persons to form differing standards, attitudes, and opinions in the ordinary concernments of daily existence.* The old individualism is being killed, not by any deliberate persecution, but by a wholly different and impersonal process which happens to destroy the causes that make men individual. Don't be misled by the fact that there are still strong individual differences left in the world. No process, of course, is ever quite complete; and there will always be a few detached souls original enough to break through all barriers. But this slender minority will not count for much with mankind as a whole. What we shall see is a gradual and insidious ironing out of the small, personally-determining idiosyncrasies which now keep a group of thinking men from being like a bushel of peas; and the eventual crystallisation of thought into a few standardised schools of immense proportions—schools determined by those vast emotional cleavages (such as that between your set of sympathies and mine) which are basic, inborn, and sometimes hereditary, and beyond the power of any environment to influence. Within each of these schools—aristocratic, conservative republican, liberal, radical, protestant-religious, catholic-religious, materialistic, idealistic, conservative-aesthetic, radical-aesthetic, commercial-realistic, industrial-scientific, speculative-scientific, etc.—there will be few if any individual differences. Each will have its standardised set of tenets and forms, to which all adherents will generally subscribe. All the forms of habit and social opinion will be favourable to uniformity; so that men will come more and more to be described and classified not as separate personalities, but as members of this or that group. Everyone will wear a tag—or rather, a set of tags covering the different facets of personality where schools of opinion are concerned—and will be spoken of not as 'a man who believes this or that or the other thing' but as *'a this-ist'* or *'a that-ist';* the standard group idea being inseparable from the popular conception of human thought. The sad mutation will be all the easier because man's cruder impulses are all toward standardisation anyway. Savages, peasants, and workmen are naturally standardised, that being one of the reasons that they count so little as actual human beings. It is only the mental-aesthetic or finely developed side of man that is naturally independent and individualistic—the ethereal and relatively fragile side which is so much easier to crush and kill than is the coarser, more basic side. Thus stands the case. Does the current complaint about standardised intellect still seem to you as you so vividly and originally express it, "all bologna"? Remember that this whole question is apart from the larger question of the tolerance of radical innovators. This larger problem will never be solved, for the psychological factors entering into it are basic and constant. It is the old question of the irresistible force and the immovable body. Incidentally, it is curious to note that the respective conditions behind each of these two questions are *precisely opposite.* The problem of the radical innovator argues *the force and survival of human individuality,* insomuch as it shews it as an element so potent that naturally homogeneous majorities (majorities homogeneous at least on the large issues involved) have to unite to stifle it. The problem of the standardised intellect, on the other hand, shews *the weakest side of human individuality,* insomuch as it displays that element as unable to stand up against the environmental unification brought about by the deterministic influences of the machine age. The effect of this standardisation is to *lessen rather than increase* the frequency of the other sort of clash, since instead of *crushing the original intellect* it merely operates toward *the prevention of its formation* in the first place. But the lessened conflict implies a net life on a lower intellectual plane.

As for religion—of course there is a great deal in what you say about its "dog-in-the-manger" attitude, and I have often dwelt upon the same point in arguing with those who insist on the attempted fostering of faith amongst the intelligent. The only point on which we differ, is that you try to carry the same principle down to cover the unintelligent as well. My contention is that religion is still useful amongst the herd—that it helps their orderly conduct as nothing else could, and that it gives them an emotional satisfaction they could not get elsewhere. I don't say that it does either of these things as well as it used to do, but I do say that I believe nothing else could do them so well even now. The crude human animal is ineradicably superstitious, and there is every biological and historical reason why he should be. An irreligious barbarian is a scientific impossibility. Rationalistic conceptions of the universe involve a type of mental victory over hereditary emotion quite impossible to the undeveloped and uneducated intellect. Agnosticism and atheism mean nothing to a peasant or workman. Mystic and teleological personification of natural forces is in his bone and blood—he cannot envisage the cosmos (i.e., the earth, the only cosmos he grasps) apart from them. Take away his Christian god and saints, and he will worship something else. Many a crude man has been talked into thinking himself an atheist, so that he loudly denies Jehovah and the Virgin and carries a load of Haldeman-Julius blue books in one pocket—yet in his other pocket he is likely to have a rabbit's foot, and the chances are 9 out of 10 that he wouldn't walk under a ladder or stop in an hotel room numbered 13! Where the Father, Son and Holy Ghost don't flourish, voodoo and witch-whispers stand ready to engross primitive emotions. Spiritualism, magic, luck-charms—all this stuff shews how irrevocably the crude human mind is chained to its hereditary illusions. "Life as an end in itself" doesn't form much of a substitute for supernatural illusion, because it isn't what the primitive mind is reaching after when it turns to prayer and mumbo-jumbo. Not but what primitives want all the life they can get; but after they have drained the cup, as they understand it, they are still looking for more. What that "more" is, as I have intimated in an earlier part of this encyclopaedic document, is undoubtedly *an approach to the mystic substance of reality itself*—the hidden reality which our senses only imperfectly apprehend. Naturally the herd do not understand what it is they are looking for. Indeed, they have not the faintest notion of any difference between phenomena and noumena. But the troublesome feeling that the senses are imperfect informers continues to lie at the back of their brains, and without knowing it they are just as restless in their search for ultimate reality as in the highly evolved theologian, philosopher, artist, or scientist. This emotion *must* be satisfied in some way—either by the crude illusion of religion, by the highly refined illusions of philosophy and art, or by the hard certainty of science that the question is absolutely settled by being absolutely unanswerable. Now it is plain to see that the satisfactions of philosophy, art, and science are hopelessly and abysmally beyond the capacity of the herd mind. Only supernaturalism is left. And since the gnawing urge of the primitive personality absolutely demands supernaturalism of some sort, it is better to let that sort be the traditional Christianity than to shift the avid emotions to snake-worship or spirit seances. As for the more intelligent classes—they *are indeed* adopting your recommended attitude of "life as an end in itself." When they cling to the outward forms of religion it is merely as a refined and traditional decoration or social custom. They don't waste much of their serious thought and emotion on the graceful rituals they chant through, and it will be found that their hereditary observances don't constitute much of a motivating force in their lives. Religion doesn't do much harm today, although one must admit that there are cases where it becomes a trifle ridiculous and annoying. What really satisfies the reality-seeking impulse in modern civilised folk is either philosophy, science, or art. Incidentally, though, one can't truthfully say that these diverse media of satisfaction are all antagonistic. Art and religion, in particular, are certainly the very reverse of enemies—so much so that there are whole schools and movements in art which depend altogether upon religious fervour for their inspiration. Religion would be gloriously justified if it had never done more than evoke the Gothic cathedral and the painting of Renaissance Italy. It is only Protestant Puritanism which tries to choke off art and absorb the feelings that ought to go into an appreciation of beauty, but even Puritanism hasn't held that pose very vigorously since the 17th century. The most beautiful thing in Providence is the steeple of the 1st Baptist Church, put up in 1775; and if you saw the half-finished Baptist Church on Riverside Drive, New York, you would have a new revelation of what soaring, pinnacled Gothic loveliness can be. I will, however, concede that the sterner sects, especially in the less populous districts, hold more to the 17th century ideal; hence am ready to sympathise with you regarding the absorption of your youthful appreciative faculties by devotional illusions. I would add, though, that a mind as exceptionally vigorous and presumably resilient as yours ought not to feel that its future is irrevocably settled by the past. Your reaction to nature and to the Albany buildings proves that your aesthetic sense is by no means atrophied; and I have no doubt but that, once you become intellectually convinced of the importance of enlarged sensitivenesses toward life and beauty, you will soon find yourself in the midst of an emotional and imaginative unfolding which will leave you marvellously enriched and more satisfyingly adjusted to the human scene. About *relativity*—I see your point regarding the "immortality" implied in the conception of the cosmos as a fixed unit in which time is merely a dimension. The idea had, indeed, occurred to me before—so that I had even thought of basing a weird tale on it. I do not, however, believe it will have much emotional or philosophical effect; since it is so purely theoretical in its relation to life and the stream of cosmic history as visible to us. Time and sequence are, for us, phenomena so inseparable from our situation in the universe, that they cannot help becoming actual noumena in all but the remotest objective academic sense. All that we can ever subjectively understand as entity, in its opposition to absolute nullity, is coincidence with certain time-sections of space; it being utterly beyond our mental and emotional capacity to envisage the relationship of an attribute of one time-section to a corresponding place in another time-section. "Beginning" and "ending" are as inalienably real to us as if we had never heard of Einstein; and without question the only conception of *immortality* which can have any meaning for us is that of a limitless diffusion through *all* the time-sections of space. That is, our minds work only with what they really experience; and we have found time and sequence to be too vivid a proximate reality in the history of our planet to allow us to consider life, entity and duration independently of them. Unless a given thing can co-incide in all its dimensions with every time-section of space which from our standpoint lies in the future, our subjective intellects refuse to grasp it as immortal; for to us existence is measured only by participation in the visible stream of time-space glimpses which our sense-equipment and point of observation lead us to recognise as proximate reality. In other words, the sight of a world on which our forefathers cannot be found, and the realisation that there will some day be a world on which we cannot be found, prohibits us from conceiving perpetual existence on an Einsteinian basis. Possibly astute theologians will devise some subtle interpretation which the masses will swallow—using the idea of relativity to rehabilitate the doctrine of supernaturalism. Indeed, they have already started to do this, as well as to accept the newer ideas of intra-atomic physics as evidence of a spiritual world. But whatever new emotion the world may derive in this way will be due to the cleverness of the theologians rather than to the convincingness of the material. In bald truth, the notion of a relativity-immortality is just as remotely abstract in one direction, as the principle of cosmic futility in another direction!

I read with interest your explanation of your attitude toward my atheism and its clear-cut negations, and can well understand how you feel. Aesthetically I feel the same way; indeed, it is my chief delight to weave verbal images of unreality, in which I can flout, rearrange, and triumph over the impersonal cosmic pattern at will. I am no less impressed than you by the magnitude, complexity, and essential beauty of the cosmos; nor am I less sensible to the veil which separates us from the grasping of ultimate reality. The great difference between us in these matters is that you like to colour your philosophic-scientific speculations with your aesthetic feeling; whilst I feel a great cleavage betwixt emotion and perceptive analysis, and never try to mix the two. *Emotionally* I stand breathless at the awe and loveliness and mystery of space with its ordered suns and worlds. In that mood I endorse religion, and people the fields and streams and groves with the Grecian deities and local spirits of old—for at heart I am a pantheistic pagan of the old tradition which Christianity has never reached. But when I start *thinking* I throw off emotion as excess baggage, and settle down to the prosaic and exact task of seeing simply what is, or probably is, and what isn't, or probably isn't. I love to dream, but I never try to dream and think at the same time. Like the boy in your argument, I would pause a moment in awe and admiration before great whirring wheels—but I fancy neither the boy nor I would stand there gaping for ever. Sooner or later we'd "snap out of it" and try to understand the impressive spectacle before us. The same goes for natural beauty. The morning frost scene which you describe takes hold of my imagination tremendously, (with the room temperature at +76°) and creates a genuine thrill of aesthetic mysticism. I can grasp the wonder and perfection of those complex and delicate crystals; for I have seen many, and seen pictures of many more. If confronted by such a scene, I would (in my dying fancy, as the 10° below drew me up toward the gates of heaven) surely harbour no thought of scientific laws or philosophic deductions; but would instead feel poignantly the mystic beauty, and would commence to weave dreams of faery workmanship or interplanetary magic around the exquisite objects before me. Not until I got back to the library or the laboratory (assuming that the temperature lets me get back at all) would I employ the things I had seen as data in intellectual research or speculation. It is the same with the sky. I am, as I may have told you, rather an astronomical devotee; yet these evenings when I tread the narrow ancient streets on the brow of the hill and look westward over the outspread roofs and spires and domes of the lower town to where the distant hills of the countryside stand out against the fading sky, I do not scan that sky as a measurer or an analyst. Resplendent Venus and Jupiter shine close together, hanging over the great beacon-tower of the terraced Industrial Trust Building as they used to hang 2000 years ago over the towering Pharos in Alexandria's crowded harbour; and as I watch them and compare them with the great red beacon and the mystic twinkling lights of the dusk-shadowed city below, I surely hold no thoughts of their objective nature and position. I do not say to myself that Jupiter is a cloudy belted sphere 1300 times larger than the earth and situate some 480,000,000 miles from the sun, or that Venus is a globe slightly smaller than the earth, perpetually veiled by a cloudy atmosphere, and about 66,000,000 miles from the sun. I do not reflect that Jupiter's orbit is outside the earth's while Venus's is inside, and that this circumstance determines the vastly different apparent motions they display in the terrestrial sky. The fact is, I do not say or reflect anything—I merely watch and dream. I dream of the evenings when these orbs did indeed hang over cryptic and seething Alexandria—and over Carthage before it, and over Thebes and Memphis and Babylon and Ur of the Chaldees before that. I dream of the hidden messages they bring down the aeons from those distant and half-forgotten places, and from those darker, obscurer places in the still older world, whereof only whispered rumour dares to speak. As I watch them, I feel that they watch me, and that the beauty they cast upon the thickening night and the candle-pierced, crepuscular town is a symbol of primal glories older than man, older than earth, older than Nature, older even than the gods, and designed for my mystic soul alone. This, indeed, is *feeling*—but when I approach the same objects as an astronomical student I do so very differently. Then I leave my dreams behind and take along my telescope; and instead of glancing at the lighted town below, I curse it for the smoke and heat-vapours it sends up to obscure telescopic definition. I note the phase of Venus and the curve of the terminator, and reflect how far past greatest elongation it is; and when I turn the glass on Jupiter I regret its long distance past opposition. I don't couple the two planets at all now—the pattern vanishes with the aesthetic mood—and would much rather have Jupiter over in the east, where it is on the evenings when it is nearest the earth. As for my story—the idea was not that a world of dream and beauty is meaningless, but that a world of thought is meaningless. I was merely advising people to be poets instead of astronomers. It didn't especially occur to me to stress the liberating side of cosmic meaninglessness, because I think that side has been somewhat overrated. Only a minority, I think, felt really chafed by the mythical demands of theism; whilst vast numbers acquire a very uncomfortable sense of anchorless drifting as a result of modernity's removal of fixed, objective values and points of reference. "Life as an end in itself", as I have opined before, seems to me a trifle beyond the development of the average citizen. Physical and aesthetic sensation are not enough to give him the comfortable illusion of significance.

As for the question of the comparative birth-rates of cultivated and uncultivated classes—that is a genuinely hard problem whose only solution would seem to be the spread of suitable information amongst the uncultivated, and perhaps the compulsory enforcement of sterility amongst certain unassimilably alien and hereditarily defective types. Certainly, under existing economic conditions, it is illogical to ask any but the definitely wealthy groups of the intelligent stratum to cultivate a higher fecundity. A smaller but better-proportioned population is the sensible goal. I can see your point about the deleterious effect of religion in this matter, though hardly fancy a whole type of illusion can be condemned for this one point alone. Catholicism is the chief offender here, although it is possible that a certain amount of unconscious Protestant feeling also goes into the maintenance of the existing absurd barriers against widespread information. However, I don't think the checking power of religion will prove permanent. Protestants all practice birth-control, and so do millions of Catholics, and sooner or later theory will be squared with reality. But of course, I concede your point that at certain stages of history religion is often anti-social. Incidentally—I also liked that recent pronouncement of Harry Elmer Barnes.[21]

Well—I *think* I've answered your appreciated letter! It is now March 1st, for I've been writing a little each day, diary-fashion. Pardon the length—but how else can one deal with topics of the greatest magnitude and most infinite subtlety and complexity?

With compassion and best wishes—

Yr Obt Servt

H P L

Notes

1. Possibly "In Defense of Cynicism," *Harper's Magazine* 157 (July 1928): 195–200. Ernest Augustus Boyd (1887–1946) was a well-known Irish critic best known for his studies of the Irish literary renaissance and also for translating the works of Guy de Maupassant.

2. Probably *Appreciations and Depreciations* (1917), which contains Boyd's essay on Lord Dunsany.

3. HPL refers to the Lateran Treaty, signed on 11 February 1929, whereby the Italian government recognized Vatican City as an independent state and compensated it for the loss of the Papal States. The treaty was ratified by the Italian parliament on 7 June 1929.

4. *Iam pridem Syrus in Tiberum defluxit Orontes* ("Long ago did the Syrian [river] Orontes flow into the Tiber"). Juvenal, *Satires* 3.62.

5. This was the view of Edward Gibbon in *The Decline and Fall of the Roman Empire* (1776–88).

6. Flavius Odoacer (433?–493), a barbarian statesman, deposed the last Roman emperor, Romulus Augustus, in 476.

7. Joseph Hergesheimer (1880–1954), popular and critically acclaimed American novelist of the period.

8. HPL refers to the British-American architect Richard Upjohn (1802–1878) and the American architect Henry Hobson Richardson (1838–1886).

9. William-Adolphe Bouguereau (1825–1905), French painter; Sir Lawrence Alma-Tadema (1836–1912), Dutch painter who worked mostly in England.

10. HPL apparently refers to "The Mucker Pose" by Philip Curtiss, *Harper's Magazine* 143 (October 1921): 662–65. Curtiss argued: "The mucker pose is that curious state of mind which induces well-bred, intelligent people to disclaim superciliously any refinement, education, or natural good taste which heredity or opportunity may have given them, and to set themselves deliberately to the worship of the coarse or the commonplace" (663).

11. HPL refers to Andrew Jackson "Bossy" Gillis (1896–1965), who was elected mayor of Newburyport, MA, in 1927. When he attempted to open a garage and gas station at the corner of State and High Streets without a permit, he was sent to jail, conducting municipal business from his cell.

12. HPL visited Guilford in late June 1928.

13. HPL refers to the architects James Gibbs (1682–1754; Scottish), Nicholas Hawksmoor (1661?–1736; English), and Peter Harrison (1715–1775; American). Harrison designed several important buildings in Newport, RI.

14. The British architects Robert (1728–1792) and James Adam (1732–1794) and the British furniture makers Thomas Sheraton (1751–1806) and George Hepplewhite (1727?–1786).

15. Frank Belknap Long and his family took HPL to various sites on Cape Cod, including Onset and Sandwich, beginning in August 1929; HPL visited Nantucket in September 1934.

16. HPL visited Williamsburg in May 1929.

17. Possibly an article relating to Salvador de Madariaga (1886–1978), a Spanish diplomat and historian who had just written a book, *Englishmen, Frenchmen, Spaniards* (1928), on national psychology.

18. James Burnett, Lord Monboddo (1714–1799), Scottish judge and philosopher, and author of *The Origin and Progress of Language* (1773–92). In *Journal of a Tour to the Hebrides* (1785), James Boswell notes that Monboddo and Samuel Johnson had a debate as to whether the "savage" or a London shopkeeper had the better existence, Monboddo purportedly arguing for the former.

19. The photograph is no. 44 in the H. P. Lovecraft Archive's "Photo Gallery" of all known photos of HPL (hplovecraft.com/life/gallery.aspx?PhotoID=44).

20. In a few years HPL changed his tune. In proposing that working hours be reduced so that more people can be employed, HPL remarked in "Some Repetitions on the Times" (1933): "Education [. . .] will require amplification, in order to meet the needs of a radically increased leisure among all classes of society. It is probable that the number of persons possessing a sound general culture will be greatly increased, with correspondingly good results to the civilisation" (*CE* 5.93).

21. Harry Elmer Barnes (1889–1968), American historian and professor at Columbia University (1918–29). He was about to publish *The Twilight of Christianity* (1929), a treatise that maintained that Christianity must give up adherence to outmoded dogmas, accept the latest findings of science, and must lend its weight to moral and social advancement.

[2]   [ALS]

Vergennes, Vt.
Oct 28, 1929

My dear Lovecraft:

An interview with Einstein[,] "What Life means to Einstein", Sat Eve Post Oct 26 is well worth a nickel.[1] For a lover of architect [*sic*] an article in Chicago setting forth the claim of being the most beautiful city of America might be interesting.

I am making progress but have been alone all the fall and compelled to work Sundays and all. If you feel the machine age getting you come up and swing the pick and shovel a few day[s]. Practically the same way they did it hundreds of years ago. That should revive your drooping spirits.

Sincerely yours
Woodburn Harris

P.S. Will have to revise somewhat my judgement of Krutch's "Modern Spirit"[.][2] I find his treatment of the Paradox of Humanism remains in my mind and threatens to take up permanent abode there.

Notes

1. "What Life Means to Einstein: An Interview with George Sylvester Viereck," *Saturday Evening Post* 202, No. 17 (26 October 1929): 17, 100, 113–14, 117.
2. Harris refers to *The Modern Temper* (1929) by American critic and biographer Joseph Wood Krutch.

[3]   [AHT]

10 Barnes Street
Providence, R.I.
November 9, 1929

WARNING! Don't try to read this all at once! I've been gradually writing it for a week, and it comes to just *70 pages*—being, so far as I recall, the longest letter I have ever written in a lifetime now numbering 39 years, 2 months, and 26 days. Pax vobiscum!

My dear Harris:—

In point of laborious engrossment, my recent congestion of revisory work has proved a close rival to your water-piping enterprise! I have been dead to the world, with not an ounce of energy to spare—and only last Saturday, a week ago today, did I get the accursed stuff out of the house. Then came piled-up correspondence and minor revision items—so that today is my first chance to sit down argumentatively with any prospect of continuous time ahead of me. May gawd keep important matter out of the morning mail, which is due to arrive in a couple of hours! Amidst this rush I must regret to say that I couldn't pick up the Satevepost issue which you recommended. I had it in mind, and tried to get it the first time I could get down town; but by that time the Oct. 26th number was off the stands. So, alas, it is only at third-hand that I shall ever know what life means to Herr Albert Einstein! As for Chicago's beauty—that is probably all a matter of standards. It certainly would not be beautiful to me, for it lacks all mellowness and charm—all subtle shadings and marks of gradual growth—but in a hard, synthetic, geometrical way it is undoubtedly achieving a studied sumptuousness and elegance of design, and a monumentally imposing quality, which other towns are slow in parallelling. Of course I have never seen it, but I rely on pictures to tell the story. I don't especially care to see it—although I shall "do" it perfunctorily if ever I make a long-planned trip to see some friends in Wisconsin.[1]

I regret to hear that progress on the water-works has been so laborious and single-handed, but am glad it has at least been tangible. I surely would enjoy helping if the weather were warmer—pick and shovel could have no terrors for me after my struggles with a revisory fountain pen! The piped water will undoubtedly prove a great asset—that kind of convenience represents the beneficent side of mechanicalism; a mechanicalism still under man's control, and not yet controlling him and disintegrating his values and folkways. No—I would never have advised the Romans to give up a single aqueduct!

As for the art question—I guess that by this time each of us has some idea—at least a rudimentary one—of what the other is talking about. I can see how current criticisms of American "civilisation" might easily irritate you, and must admit that they are too frequently overdone by those imperfectly qualified by taste or knowledge to make them; yet one must discriminate carefully betwixt the sound and the unsound, and see whether, after all, the criticism concerns the genuine hereditary culture-stream to which we belong. The way it looks to me is that American civilisation is almost extinct, but genuine so far as it does survive—in certain groups of people all over the country, and in certain geographic areas, especially Eastern Virginia and parts of New England. What conservative people are deploring and fighting is not our ancestral culture at all, but a new and offensive parvenu-barbarism based on quantity, machinery, speed, commerce, industry, wealth, and luxurious ostentation, which has sprung up among us like a noxious weed since the rise of the tasteless multitude in the 1830's. It has no more to do with our civilisation—the main stream of English and classic thought and feeling established in these colonies by over two centuries of continuous life, 1607–1820+—than have the barbarisms of Polynesia or the Sioux Indians. It is simply a plague to stamp out if we can, and to flee from if we can't. But it would be a libel on our ancestors to call it "American civilisation." It is "American" only in a geographic sense, and is not a "civilisation" at all except according to the Spenglerian definition of the word.[2] It is a wholly alien and wholly puerile barbarism; based on physical comfort instead of mental excellence, and having no claim to the consideration of real colonial Americans. Of course, like other barbarisms, it may some day give birth to a culture—but that culture will not be ours, and it is natural for us to fight its incursions over territory which we wish to preserve for our own culture. We would fight if the Japanese tried to spread their undoubtedly high culture over the United States— and so do we fight when we see another alien system trying to establish itself on the soil that has known New England and Virginian influences. In the late 17th and early 18th centuries we fought the French culture as it crept toward us from Canada and the Mississippi Valley. Today we fight the machine "culture" as it creeps toward us from the hives of artificially nursed industry and stunted taste. That we are probably foredoomed to defeat, does not alter the essential aspect of the case. The impending victory of the intruding order does not alter its intrinsic status. What is to be, is to be, but we are not obligated to grin and pretend we like it. Personally, we can do all in our power to stave off the calamity, and then step aside with the resignation of a dying man, or of a 6th century Roman confronted by the Dark Ages. We can still choose as places of residence those parts of the country least affected by decay, or we can return to England, the source of our culture, where its death will be slower than in this colonial region.

As for France, and the crudeness of peasant life there—of course peasant life is crude anywhere. The squalor you ran up against is no more typical of cultivated French people than is the squalor of an Alabama nigger settlement or an urban Dago colony typical of the cultivated American people. The fact that the French peasants are biologically related to the French civilised classes, and that their numerical proportion is rather great, signifies nothing at all. It does not make real French culture any less, because this crude lumbering fabric happens to coexist within the same national boundaries. It is all very well to preach—but the hard, cold fact remains that the civilised classes of France have managed to reach levels of intellectual insight, sensitive living, comfortable disillusion, and evolved appreciation of beauty, substantially beyond those of any other contemporary people. That is a thing in itself—a definite, tangible thing which no milk-and-water moralising or ethical theory will shake. If you don't like it, all right. Many do like it. Many think that such a definite, tangible thing—an intrinsic extension of the human evolutionary process—is of more importance than the meaningless question of giving cheap cinemas and modern plumbing to a few more million dolts who had just as lief grub along without them, and who wouldn't achieve any real imaginative enrichment through their possession. Frankly, it doesn't make any more difference whether French peasants live in dirt, than whether Alabama niggers do likewise. We don't have to go and live with them—except in a war emergency such as couldn't come more than once in fifty or a hundred years—so why not let them alone in peace and judge France by its real civilisation, just as we expect France to judge us by our real civilisation . . . . our orderly streets and homes and colleges instead of our nigger huddles and ghettoes?

I can certainly shake hands with you about the Albany capitol, and hope we both live to see it torn down and replaced by a classic structure like the educational building. It's a real puzzle how such junk could ever have been put up by a generation who had known tasteful Georgian architecture in childhood—but I think the old bugbear of democracy is largely to blame. The new moneyed class of the 1830's—a parvenu tribe without taste or traditions—came to the fore between 1830 and 1860, and fixed the idea of change, lawlessness, and costly ostentation on all the decorative arts. They had the peasant's dull resentment against taste, and subconsciously hated the harmonious and simple classicism of the older cultivated classes even when they attempted to merge themselves with the upper element. They vaguely wanted to pull down their superiors by creating a new standard of lavishness, according to which the real beauty of the old order would appear inferior. Also, they had the tasteless ignoramus's instinctive love of tawdry overdecoration and grotesque proportion. The real wonder is that there was less "comeback" from people who truly knew what was what. Even now I can't understand how the decadent forms managed to get "put across" and stay "put across" so long. The illusion of progress, then fostered by the immediate conveniences of the early machine age, may have aided in the evil outcome by creating a deep feeling that all change *must* be in a "forward" direction. Of all the writers in America, Edgar Allan Poe is the only prominent figure who stood out against the newer ideals and ridiculed them. By the way—your poignant reminiscence of the Albany state house is amusingly similar to an anecdote which a Rabelaisian ex-member of my literary "gang" once related; an anecdote of which the younger James Gordon Bennett (of *Herald* fame) was the "hero", and in which a friend's parlour and an ornamental vase played the respective parts of the state-house attic and the silver cuspidor. Alas—according to this tale, the subsequent discoveries of Mr. Bennett's host, and the tracing of these revelations to Mr. Bennett's call, led to an abruptly terminated acquaintance. It is likely that Mr. Bennett had not the excuse of dire necessity, since a timely word to his friend's butler would surely have provided suitable guidance.[3]

About Spengler—of course he is as revolutionary *as anybody dealing with historical causes can be,* but my point was that the soundest thinkers have *never* possessed any absolute dogmatism in regard to trends and causes; so that he is not overturning any *fundamental* fabric of belief in the sense that Einstein is. And by the way—*Galileo* is *not* the one who first promulgated the real facts about the solar system, as you seem to imply in your illustration. The Polish priest Kopernik—or Copernicus—did that neat little job almost a century and a half before Galileo. What Galileo did was merely to *confirm,* through the earliest application of the newly-invented telescope to the skies, the theories which Copernicus had previously formulated from purely abstract and mathematical data. Discovery of planetary satellites and rotation-periods, and of the moon-like phases of the inferior planets, formed physical and ocular confirmation of the Copernican doctrine and placed it beyond dispute—but it didn't invent that doctrine. What is more—you are of course aware that the Greeks of both Ionian and Alexandrian schools speculated widely on the solar system, and at times approached the real facts quite closely. The accepted Ptolemaic theory of the Middle Ages was a product of the Alexandrian decadence. Returning to the main theme—the illusion of continuous progress and achievement is by no means so deep-seated as you seem to imply. It was absent in mediaeval times; and although set on foot by the expansive psychology of the Renaissance, did not attain a virulent absurdity until the 19th century. It was never taken wholly seriously by the totality of scholars—in fact, I don't think there has been any period of modern history in which a certain number of historians have not proclaimed Periclean Athens as the true apex of human development. It is only the second-rate philosophy of the popular stream that Spengler so violently overturns. In general—no really thoughtful analyst ever takes any broad historic *interpretation* more than tentatively, so that there is really nothing to overturn in the philosophy of history. However—this is not to say that Spengler isn't bold, original, and distinctive! He is indeed very remarkable in the *extent* of his freedom from hampering precedent—in fact, he closely approaches my absolute ideal of sound scholarship; i.e., the man who gets *face to face with the cosmos itself* and forgets what other people have been saying and thinking about it. His is really the only way to avoid the perpetuation of misleading historic myths and errors.

About the lack of time-sense in classical antiquity—I don't quite "get" your point unless you have misinterpreted Spengler and taken him as *literally* claiming that the Hellenic culture knew nothing of the past or of its own place in the historic stream. Assuredly nobody could ever make such a claim as that—look at Herodotus and his chapters on Egypt etc! Spengler's real point is that the Greeks *were not emotionally influenced and motivated by the time sense as we are.* Of course they knew what time is, and that other nations were older than they; but it remained an aloof and abstract knowledge remote from their sense of immediate reality. Their sense of the past was *not absent,* but was infinitely *vaguer and more tenuous* than ours. We think of the past and future as vital parts of the real world—as things just as important as the present, or even more so, since their quantitative extent is so vastly—infinitely—greater. To us, the present is just a dot lying midway on an infinitely long dotted line; and we shape our thoughts and feelings in conformity with that instinctive conception. It is the distinguishing habit of the type of culture to which the modern Western World belongs. Now with the Greeks it was all different. They thought of the present as a self-sufficient, all-engrossing reality; and were not especially interested in how it came to be, or what it was headed for. They knew, of course, that it must have a beginning and an ending; but they were so little impressed with the importance of knowing and thinking about such things that they suffered them to lapse into neglect, ambiguity, and myth. Thus they traced the descent of their early culture-heroes—the heroes of the Trojan War cycle—from the gods in an amusingly slight number of generations; though knowing at the same time that Egypt must have existed for untold ages. It simply never occurred to them to compare their own chronology with Egypt's—although they knew perfectly well in an academic sense what scientific chronology was. They had the example of Egypt—a culture as time-conscious as our own—spread out amply before them. It was simply a case of alien emotion—of frank uninterestedness. To them, the living Hellenic world presented a panorama so emotionally satisfying, that there was no incentive for cultivating the emotion of time-consciousness. There are people like that—individuals—in our own Western civilisation; though to us they seem superficial and freakish. And there are still-existing cultures—like the Hindoo—which equally lack a time-sense. It is very possible that the coming machine-culture will return to the timeless conception—the idea of historic placement fading out, and immediate time-sensations being translated into the one sense and goal of physical velocity in daily motions and events. It is true that the Greek calendar was a typical product of a timeless culture, since the very idea of detached units like Olympiads argues an undeveloped sense of continuity. It is curious to see how the transition to the modern system of continuity developed. The earliest Romans reckoned time by the reigns of their Kings, and afterward by the terms of their consuls. Instead of giving a year in terms of some fixed point, they would say or write something like "P. VARRONE. CN. SAUFEIO. COSS."—i.e. "Publius Varro and Cnaeus Saufeius being consuls", or "in the consulship of Varro and Saufeius." But as time passed, the Roman culture began to acquire a chronological sense in advance of the Greek—paving the way for the modern conception. Little by little we see a growing practice—especially among formal historians—to have recourse to a second *and continuous* cycle, based on the year of the founding of Rome as commonly calculated. Thus by the Augustan Age the term A.U.C.— "Anno Urbis Conditae",[4] or "In the year of the founding of the City"— became as frequent a way of designating a date as the mention of that year's consuls, so that there was no novelty of principle in the present continuous Christian era, which began to be used increasingly from the 6th century on. In the Middle Ages it was often customary—while recognising the Christian Era as the Romans had recognised the Era of the City—to date events by the reigns of monarchs—"the third year of Louis XI," and so on; a vague survival of the Roman practice of consular reckoning. This survives *even now* in legal and judicial phraseology—so that you'd find this year's London chancery documents dated *"XIX Geo. V."* But of course it is the *continuous* era which has won out in our general consciousness—steadily gaining vividness since the days of Caesar and Cicero. Whether it will decline again, and give way to some system of detached units in the coming timeless machine-culture, we cannot venture to predict. Our own civilisation is as far as we can answer for. But it seems a good guess that, as long as the scientific spirit survives, philosophic *historians* will never drop the convenient habit of reckoning from a fixed point—even if they change from the birth of Christ to the establishment of the Russian Soviet State or the invention of the steam-engine!

By the way, though—there's one point in your letter which perhaps shows a wrong impression of a statement of mine. You seem to think that I place a high intrinsic value on the time-sense, and that I said I was *pleased* at discovering my own possession of it in distinction from the classical attitude.

Such is *not* the case, and I thought I made the point clear in my former letter. Basically, it is impossible to give preference to either emotional attitude toward time, so long as one's scientific sense remains uninjured. We know, indeed, that the greatest of cultures to date—the Athenian culture—was a timeless one. I was **not** pleased, but bitterly **disillusioned and disappointed**, when I discovered a major emotional barrier betwixt myself and the Graeco-Roman world which I love so well; for in youth I delighted in regarding myself as an absolute Graeco-Roman, preserving the attitude and psychology of the ancient world amidst an alien civilisation. To find that there were points in which I had to stand aligned with modernity against classicism was a cursed bitter pill for me to swallow—but I swallowed it because my sense of *truth* is always stronger than my sense of *emotional preference*. I couldn't reasonably deny the sense of chronologic pageantry which has always ruled my attitude toward existence.

As to Shakespeare versus the Greek tragedies—it is possible that Spengler overshoots the mark a trifle in his sensational contrast, since in truth art cannot always be measured by its precise relation to life. Rather must we say that the authenticity of art depends on its relation to *the prevailing emotions about life*—a test which permits Athenian tragedy to fare a little better than Brother Oswald would have it. There is no question but that the classic Greek feeling toward the universe differed from the naturalistic modern or post-Renaissance feeling; so that the highest artistic expression of that feeling must necessarily differ greatly from ours. The Greeks envisaged a tight-woven rhythm and overshadowing conscious fatality in life which we do not so poignantly feel. To them, the outcroppings of this universal pattern and law were of greater emotional import than the varied play of surface events about which the modern mind is chiefly concerned—hence in order to be true to human feeling, Greek tragedy had to be more ponderous and patterned and artificial than modern (i.e., *historically* modern, and including Elizabethan) tragedy. That these *apparently* conventional qualities were in truth vital reflections of the contemporary emotional life, and *not* mere sterile crystallisations of expression, can be seen from the whole course and history of Greek tragedy. Tragedy was never static, but moulded itself unerringly to the changing feelings of its age. Beginning at a period of intense ceremonial devotion not far removed from archaic naivete—and indeed originating in religious ritual—it is inevitable that early tragedy should have been ponderous and artificial and naive. *Nothing else would have expressed the sincere feelings of the people about the universe and its relation to them.* Observation shews us that the art was indeed adequate, and that the earliest generation of tragic writers (as surviving in its chief figure Æschylus) captured with perfect and perhaps matchless authenticity those feelings of awe and majesty and thunderous grandeur which characterise a simple race's response to the thought of infinity. Any other sort of expression would, at that time, have been bad art; because it would have be-lied the real feelings of the culture out of which it grew. As Athenian civilisa-tion broadened, tragedy altered to match it—the change of tone from the thunderous to the merely stately and from the stately to the pathetic being clearly observable as we look through Sophocles and Euripides. Now it is very obvious that the main difference between Æschylus, Sophocles, Euripi-des, and Shakespeare—or if you wish, between the three Greeks on the one hand and the Elizabethan on the other*—is simply the fact *that they worked from different backgrounds of knowledge and feeling about the cosmos and about life*. You can't say that any one was greater than any other—for each interpreted su-premely well the reservoir of feeling within and around him. As artists, the four men stand almost on a level; for it is clear that Shakespeare's greater sig-nificance *for us* is due merely to our greater closeness to the world of thought and feeling which was his. The Greek culture is *not* our own, but the Elizabe-than culture is—that is, it represents the opening phase of the era in which those of us who are forty or more are still emotionally living. The reason that the Greeks never produced as naturalistic a dramatist as Shakespeare is that, unfortunately, their art-impulse began to fade before their general under-standing of life was as broad as that of Elizabethan England. It was the ill luck of the Greeks to have their age of art come before the climax of their experience—and our good luck to have our art-apex and experience-apex come closer together. Of course, even with us the coincidence is *not perfect*—for obviously the Elizabethan age knew less about life than our own present moment. But it is at least a better approach to a coincidence than the Greeks had. If the Greek art-tide had run high a century or two later—thus coincid-ing with the disillusioned and naturalistic Alexandrian age—there might have been some approximate equivalent of an Hellenistic Shakespeare. Likewise—if our own art-tide were running high now, amidst our exact knowledge of human motives and values, we could get an utterly unprecedented pitch of humanistic tragedy from any artist of the calibre of Æschylus, Sophocles, Eu-ripides, or Shakespeare. But before leaving this topic, let me correct your *dia-metrically wrong* impression that Shakespeare was a "highbrow" in attitude or method. Great God! Don't you realise that the fellow was the **exact opposite** of all this—a careless, non-academic, spontaneous, hit-or-miss, uneducated poet who thought he was following the popular fashions and who used the commonest and most colloquial language of his period? Shakespeare, as an immortal artist, was a *pure accident of genius*. He was gifted with a natural com-bination of language-sense and insight into human motives which few men have ever had—but he didn't know it himself, and lived all his life as a cheap ham actor and literary hack—taking the popular tales he found around him

---

*For of course, the periods of the three Greeks overlapped and half-coincided,

(cheap ballads, catchpenny historic chronicles, and popular translations of classic and foreign authors) and doctoring them up in the racy idiom of the day for mass consumption. He was a great artist *in spite of himself, and without meaning to be*. All his ambitions were social, not aesthetic. He simply wanted to rise above the burgher-yeoman class and found a country family with a coat-of-arms. It was toward nobility and place, not toward art and scholarship, that he was looking. It would have pained him to be taken for a serious scholar or aesthete—gentlemen never pursued learning or art beyond the dilettant level in his time. Analyse any of his works and you'll find more absurd mistakes per square inch than in any other accepted author in our language. And compare his diction with Jonson's or Webster's or Beaumont's or Sidney's to see how far he was from the literary or academic in style. He was as free-and-easy and colloquial as Sherwood Anderson or Ring W. Lardner—the only reason we find him abstruse today is because the language has changed. In his day, he spoke the plain accents he heard around him—allowing of course for the well-understood and popularly acknowledged difference between literal prose and metaphor-coloured verse. He was, in truth, regarded as very slovenly and unscholarly by his precise contemporaries. Can't you see the difference between the racy carelessness of his "Julius Caesar" or "Antony and Cleopatra" and the heavy exactitude of Jonson's "Sejanus" and "Catiline"? Hell! If there's anything poor old Bill wasn't, it's a *highbrow!* Before quitting the Elizabethan age, let me remark in passing that we often do its general sophistication and intelligence an injustice because of an historic accident which spoils our perspective—the intrusion of a duller and less balanced age between it and ourselves. Undeniably, the flowering of the Protestant Reformation and the reign of a Puritan culture in the middle 17th century put a tremendous check on the culture-stream set in motion by the Renaissance; so that when we look back to 1650 or so we find a very dull state of things in existence. But that was only a transient eclipse. Go back a little farther—to 1620 or 1600 or 1580—and you'll find the vigorous youth of the same persistent enlightenment-stream which burst to the surface again in the 18th century after its brief course underground. In a way, the transient Puritan period was a fright-reaction against the disconcerting new knowledge which the Renaissance had fished up to pit against the set ideas of mediaevalism.

Returning once more to the main argument—I don't think we can justly assume, as you suggest, that the successive relapses to quasi-animal simplicity after the death of world-cultures are less and less complete as the ages roll along. Remember that we cannot go back indefinitely into palaeontologic time for data, since behind a certain point the *physical evolution* of the existing species was not complete. We must confine ourselves to the period during which the given animal—*homo sapiens*—has existed in his fully differentiated form. All fully recognised human races possess a certain minimum of basic accomplishments—tenacious anthropological attributes—which indeed seem never to be lost. These things—like the use of fire, domestication of animals, making of stone tools, the use of articulate speech, possession of a certain tribal organisation—seem to be ground into the fabric of instinct in a virtually permanent way. But the line of demarcation betwixt this group of habits and the more complex accomplishments of barbarism and civilisation continues to be very sharp—so that there is no real comparison between a basic folk-way like club-wielding and an extraneous acquisition like gunpowder. Men may conceivably forget how to make gunpowder, (since it depends on complex, interrelated processes involving vigorous memory and careful technique) although they will never forget to pick up or fashion a big stick when they want to deal a hard blow. This latter process involves so little complexity, memory, and conscious method that it could not readily be lost so long as the race's intrinsic mental capacity remains on anything like the normal level of *homo sapiens*. Accomplishments which depend on *quantitative strength of purpose* (i.e., on the fatigue-defying phases of *will*) can easily be lost in the exhaustion of cultural senility; though accomplishments which depend on the simple, untrained, and merely survival-purposed mental capacity cannot be lost without true biological-physical decadence. It doesn't do to confuse one group of accomplishments with the other.

In practice, of course, no lapse of culture is ever really *complete*—i.e., *all* the way back to animal simplicity—because odd bits of accomplishment survive by chance, and are fostered by the parallel streams of culture which environ the exploded one and contribute to its eventual replacement by a fresh culture. When Sumerian culture waned, in the Tigris-Euphrates Valley, a Semitic culture was rising to take its place; and when that culture itself waned, the culture of Persia was there to pick up the pieces. Persianism gave way to Hellenism and that had not completely sunk to animal simplicity when the Parthio-Persians overran the region with their inferior culture. Then it was not long before the vital flame of Islam gave the region a fresh start and produced cultivated and many-domed Bagdad. In none of these cases had the dying culture had a chance to get completely downhill to a biological minimum. Of the *crests*, the Semitic (Babylonian-Assyrian) probably exceeded the Sumerian, whilst the Persian scarcely parallelled it. The Hellenistic towered above all others, while the Parthio-Sassanid was frankly barbaric and inferior. The Islamic at least parallelled the old Persian level. *In this matter of crests, no large continuous trend either backward or forward can be discerned.* Now as for *troughs*—Sumerian-Babylonian was very slight—Semitic culture fusing into the Sumerian almost without a break. The Semitic Persian lapse was also relatively mild—for soon after the fall of Babylon we see a flourishing Achaemenian culture along the Tigris and Euphrates. Nor had this sunk very far when Alexander knocked hell out of Persia and founded the dynasty of the Seleucidae. Rome didn't put much of a cultural impress on this region, so we see the Hellenistic culture getting down rather low by the time the Parthians appeared. The supplanting of Parthians by their kinsfolk the Sassanid Persians hardly forms a culture-break—we can lump them together like Babylonians and Assyrians despite great minor differences in both cases. They didn't amount to much except in a military way, and they hadn't fallen off very notably (though they were weakening under Byzantine pressure) when the hordes of Mohammed's followers wiped them out and established an almost instantaneous Islamic culture. That culture, at various times in the hands of Arabs, Persians, Tartars, and Turks, is still the reigning culture of the region; but it has sunk (because of time-opportunity) to a *trough deeper than any which the region has known before*. The state of the people is as low as in mediaeval Europe, and lower than in contemporary China. Dirty, ragged, ignorant, mentally sterile— and from now on open to exploitation by Western outsiders. *This region itself is now culturally lower than at any time within recorded history;* probably lower than at any time since it has had a civilisation at all. The only records of an inferior state are palaeontological, and involve races either imperfectly evolved or, in any case, unfamiliar with prior civilisations. A graph chart of this cradle of civilisation—the Tigris-Euphrates valley—would run something like this:

Sumerian	Chaldeao-Assyrian	Achaemenian-Persian	Hellenistic	Partho-Persian	Mohammedan

Now how about *Egyptian* culture, where Pharaonic, Ptolemaic-Alexandrian-Hellenistic, Coptic, and Islamic cultures have followed one another? Here is a rough graph:

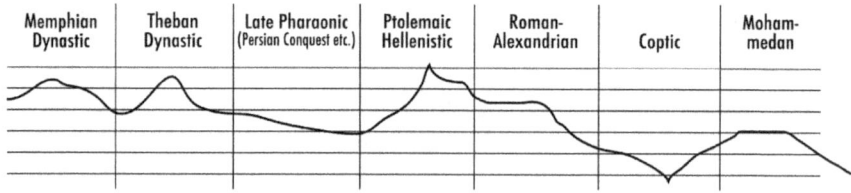

Memphian Dynastic	Theban Dynastic	Late Pharaonic (Persian Conquest etc.)	Ptolemaic Hellenistic	Roman-Alexandrian	Coptic	Moham-medan

Or take Greece under the Minoan, Achaean, Dorian, Classic-Hellenic, Roman, Byzantine, Turkish, and Modern-Greek influences:

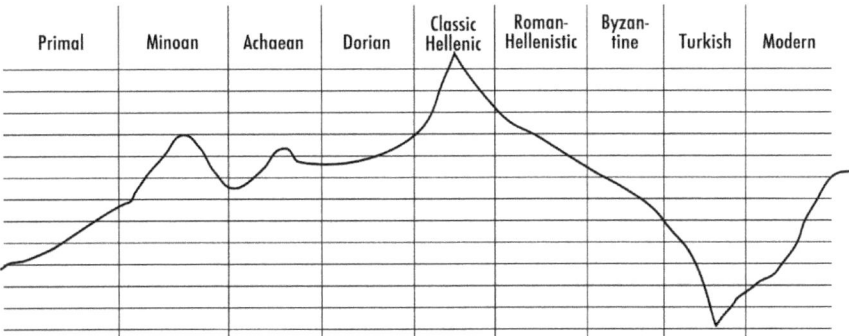

Primal	Minoan	Achaean	Dorian	Classic Hellenic	Roman-Hellenistic	Byzan-tine	Turkish	Modern

No regularity at all—and as in the case of Mesopotamia, shewing low points in relatively recent times. And how about our own home territory under Celts, Romans, Saxons, and Norman-English?

Primal	Celtic	Roman	Saxon	Norman	Planta-genet	Tudor	Cromwell	Georgian	Victorian Modern

No use—you can't make any laws of progress. Our real crest was probably the Elizabethan age—judged by general mental, emotional, and aesthetic vitality. General taste had a crest of its own in the Georgian period, certain branches of taste in the 19th century, and intrinsic knowledge is at or even before a crest at the present moment; but adding everything up, the real crest was the Tudor age.

The trouble with reckoning collapses is the difficulty of finding any specimen in which some alien civilisation didn't step in at once and provide a fresh culture. Really, there has been only *one* total collapse in known history—that of the classical world in the west after the decay of Rome. And when we consider the depths to which the Dark Ages sank, immediately after the glory of a high Roman civilisation and within easy reach of both the Arabic and Byzantine cultures, we must admit that the idea of retaining more and more material from prior cultures rests on a pretty slim basis. *There has never been any period in the life of Western man, since his history opens in primitive Homeric legend and Italian folklore, when his best-existing culture has been lower than in the years 700–1100 A.D.* In that period our mental life had few or no advantages over the mental life of the primitive European tribes—the Gauls, Britons, Saxons, Germans, Slavs, etc.—whilst even our physical lives, in point of comfort, cleanliness, and security, were scarcely removed from the simple folkways of prehistoric times. The sole feature which separates the Dark Ages from primitive savagery is *the material setting of architecture and tangible inherited articles*. There were a few buildings and towns and simple utilitarian and military devices which came down from classical times, but which were no more a part of the circumambient barbarism than are the muskets the red Indians adopted or the silk hats and glass beads that African chieftains wear. In general mental life and creativeness, and in most physical methods, standards, and ideas, the soldiers of Charlemagne had few if any advantages over the soldiers of Arminius, Vercingetorix, or Cassiovelaunus. If you can think up a more complete collapse, bring it on! Lest you think me an exaggerator, let me add that of course the state of *animal simplicity* is by no means so utterly low a thing, for Aryan white men, as the term—or the analogy of non-white savages—would seem to imply. The Caucasian has quite a little bag of tricks ground into his instincts; so that as long as he keeps his blood pure, he will never get very near the gorilla, or even the nigger or Esquimau. The ancient savage Gauls and Germans were nobody's swine or grovelling foot-mats; but were in reality bold, fairly orderly, rational, and beauty-loving men. They had many accomplishments, and sometimes dwelt in villages of permanent homes. But naturally, in spite of this, we'd rather keep up the more intelligent and highly sensitised lives of civilised and cultured beings if we can manage to do it.

Now about the autochthonous American cultures—it isn't correct to assume that there was any one continuous decline which would have reached a final petering-out if the Spaniards had not come. The real case was highly complex, and involved the successive conquests and cultural stuntings of civilised groups by fresh waves of warlike invasion from the north. The Mayan culture—the highest and oldest—had been reduced to a state of subjection by various Nahuan cultures of the Mexican plateaus, of which the Aztec is the best known. The Mayans were a *defeated* rather than *decayed* race when the Spaniards came; whilst the Aztecs appear to have been barbarians on the upgrade rather than civilised people on the down-grade. They had taken over countless Mayan folkways and art-forms, and would probably have established a mighty culture as solid as the Egyptian of Chaldaean if they had had a career of unhampered isolation—or had been strong enough to repel the white man. And—pardon my saying so—you are all wrong in saying that a culture can't flourish in perfect isolation. We need look no farther than *China* to see a perfect example. China, until very lately, admitted no external influences whatsoever; yet enjoyed a long and full term of existence, with periods of cultural flowering equal to any which any nation has ever known. Bertrand Russell believes the Chinese culture is the greatest which this planet has ever produced—that its chief period excelled even Periclean Athens in that full grasp of life and beauty which is the only rational measure of cultural status.[5] There was no contact with the outside world—all foreigners were "foreign devils"—yet you can't deny that "the old Chink who tooted the cornet" sure did puff a mean set of blues! Greece itself was likewise unusually isolated. It *knew* of the outside world, but knew only to repel and reject. The term βάϱβαϱος (barbaros) served alike to designate a foreigner and a savage. No— in cold fact, it is pretty clear that the *most isolated and most aristocratic* races are always the ones to climb the highest on the ladder that leads out of animal dulness, ignorance, and insensitiveness. Track down any opposite theory, and you'll find that it springs from ethical, religious, or political sophistry—not from an impartial survey of the facts.

You mention the present tendency to amalgamation and levelling amongst existing races, and argue that future culture-collapses—affairs of mental-aesthetic boredom—will involve increasingly large numbers of people until at last one will come which will involve all the human species. The principle is certainly sound, although it may be doubted how literally far it can be carried. Repulsion between certain racial extremes is still very strong, and in some cases unconquerably so. A White-Mongolian fusion is barely conceivable, but an inclusion of blacks is less so. Even a mulatto-touched group would avoid fusion with pure blacks, so that the disappearance of a separate black race except by massacre is hardly probable. In practice, it is very probable that Western, Mongolian, Hindoo, and negroid streams will never meet, and that conflict will be their only form of contact. The Mongolian will ape the Westerner but will not be received except by force. Of course, a Mongol conquest of Aryandom, a consequent forced fusion, is conceivable; but even then I doubt if the resultant mongrel would care to mix with Hindoo or black. There might, though, be a Mongol-Hindoo mixture at some stage of the game—or part of the Mongols might line up with the Hindoos and part with the Western World. There is some trace of a pan-Asiatic feeling, overriding race-lines, in the air; and a mixed Mongol-Hindoo-Semitic grouping against the Western World is not inconceivable. This would at first preserve its internal race-lines, but might later suffer them to be dulled. The only Aryan recruits to such a coalition would be the Soviet Russians, who are Asiatic in thought and feeling.

However—this is all a matter of speculation. Assuming that at some future period *all* mankind's culture *does* collapse through ennui, we can by no means say that the end of human civilisation will have been reached thereby. Remember that cultural old age is probably due more to *psychological boredom* than to physical deterioration. What, then, shall we expect a few generations *after* the final relapse of mankind to animal simplicity—when the memory of former cultures and ancient ennuis shall have been totally erased from the globe's barbaric population, or shall have become etherealised into fascinating legends of gods and heroes? Well—what happened *before* when the earth was filled with physically sound barbarians with no thoughts of previous civilisations behind them? Cultures were gradually born here and there, weren't they? Well—that's about what will happen again under similar circumstances. There will be other cultures—and they will never know that ours ever existed except through vague folk-myths, and later through archaeological discoveries of concrete foundation-walls, bridge piers, subways, and such monuments of still earlier cultures as the Pyramids and the Chinese Wall. A new world—new groupings into tribes and races and civilisations, and the whole farce of organised life over again. Kingdoms—empires—priesthoods—wars—aristocracies—revolts—democracies—machine ages—and a second general decay and collapse and oblivion. And so on . . . and so on . . . and so on . . . . until something radical happens, through accident or attrition, to the biological stock of *homo sapiens,* and he becomes again subject to the physical evolutionary process, upward or downward.

You err in stating that the continued existence of mankind proves that the idea of biological senility in race-groups is a fallacy. Remember that the scientists who promulgate this idea know as well as you that a few human beings are still alive! What they say is merely that *any isolated group, long deprived of fresh fertilisation from other groups who have been bred under different physical conditions,* tends to become listless, devitalised, de-energised, and ultimately sterile. They do not speak without a close study of isolated groups and races. According to their theory, no race experiences this physical old age except by living for countless generations without external admixture, so that there has been no chance as yet for the collective senility of all mankind. Not until the whole race becomes homogeneous, and thus deprived of the possibility of any cross-fertilisation, could any collective decline and sterility occur from this cause. For my part, I don't call the idea of biological senility thoroughly established as yet—but I present these incidental points to shew you that it is not so flagrantly absurd—not so easily waved out of court by the jaunty gesture of a layman's hand—as you seem to imagine. Neither you nor I can speak competently on a theme demanding profound biological erudition.

It seems to me rather superficial to claim that the Spenglerian drama cannot be enacted again. Despite the vast *mechanical* progress of mankind, the amount of intelligence capable of being applied to non-immediate and non-concrete problems is no greater today than in Caesar's time. Thought is never the motive-power of the herd—only *feeling.* There aren't enough intellectually *governed* (as distinguished from intellectually *informed* or intellectually *endowed*) people living in this or any other age, under this or any other educational system, to produce so much as a dent in the blind deterministic course of world-history, as shaped by the irrational feelings of the vast emotional majority—both cultivated and uncultivated. The kind of mental energy that plans dynamos and selling forces is not the kind that can weigh imponderable values and make dissimilarly-emotioned groups all want the same thing and work toward the same goal. To fancy that all likelihood of war can be abolished merely because we know of its disastrous results, is to be as naive as to fancy that a heavy gambler will stop gambling merely by pondering on his previous losses. When a group of people want something which another group—or the majority—doesn't want them to have, they will listen to pacific arbitration just as long as they think (a) that they can get what they want by strategy, without combat, or (b) that they haven't any decent chance of winning in a passage-at-arms. But if they want the thing badly enough—as undoubtedly they will from time to time—and feel that they can't get it without a fight, they will certainly be on the lookout for chances, and start a fight the moment they think they have a good likelihood of defeating such forces as are liable to oppose them. It is useless to fancy that individual independence will ever make such group-greed and daring impossible. There are group-objects which no amount of individualism and democracy on the one hand, and no amount of abstract internationalism on the other hand, can ever really obscure. Once in a while the objectives of different groups will conflict—and then, hell to pay! The closer contact of races will *aggravate rather than palliate* this tendency, since it will magnify the possibilities of friction as points of overlapping increase. The international traffic jam will grow more acute as the nations get oftener and oftener in each other's way through the increased spatial expansion of their activities. And there's no use in hiding the fact that different race and culture groups have ideals and standards and values and goals so fundamentally different that homogeneous coöperation toward a common end can never be more than a political pretence or moralistic myth. With care and coolness, it seems distinctly possible to *reduce the number of wars* considerably below the former average—by investigating causes of friction and adjusting rival claims. But there are deeper and greater troubles once in a while, involving profound attitudes toward life and momentous struggles for supremacy and survival, which cannot well be imagined as having any outcome but physical combat. And *what* combat, as the deadly devices of the machine age multiply! Each new one, of course, will be worse—and it may well be predicted that repetitions will not be likely to come during the lifetime of the generation which has suffered from one of them. But of course, as a war-surviving generation dies off, there arises another group of leaders who have not had the personal experience to give them a really acute and motivating war-dread. This new and unscathed generation will again relegate the problem to the abstract, and hold warfare in reserve as a possible means of getting what can't be got otherwise.

No—the problems of the present and future differ from those of the past only in *relative magnitude,* not in *nature.* The Spenglerian cycle still works—and of course, once we are back to animal simplicity after the next full smashup, the whole show begins all over again exactly as it began between 10,000 and 30,000 B.C. Then all our prophecies based on scientific sophistication and the machine age will be reduced to nullity and irrelevance—because the shepherds and hunters of that future time will never have heard of science or machinery save in the form of religious myth woven around certain grass-grown and ivy-clad ruins.

You can't well dismiss in a sentence the question of a *culture-damaged* (nobody has said *absolutely cultureless*) machine age, because history has shewn that an inferior culture often follows a superior one. Just as you try to dismiss my apprehensions about the coming machine culture, so did the forward-looking exponents of mediaevalism try to dismiss the apprehensions of the Romans about the coming non-classical culture . . . . but did that make the apprehensions absurd? Line up the Rome of the Antonines against the Frankish kingdoms of Clovis and Charlemagne and see which you think superior. Did Boëthius and Symmachus and Cassiodorus and Rutilius Namatianus deserve a jackass hee-haw for plainly seeing that the coming order of things wasn't going to be as good as the old order? And another thing—it ought to be clear to you that a good part of the current hate of a machine culture has *nothing to do with the relative merits of that culture and ours,* but is based altogether on the *radical alienage of the intruding order.* I thought I made that plain in a dozen concrete illustrations! For instance—we know that right now the Japanese culture is every inch as good as ours, and that the French is decidedly superior . . . . but do you mean to tell me that you wouldn't fight like hell, and to the very death and beyond, to keep the Japanese or the French from spreading their cultures over the territory that belongs to us? It wouldn't be a time for the weighing of abstract values, but a case of normal, healthy, primitive instinct reacting to an insufferable stimulus. We'd postpone our analyses of the merits of Japanese or French culture until we had wiped the last god-damned yellow squinter or jabbering frog-eater off of Anglo-Saxon soil—or gone down to death in the attempt. We despise people—like the Jews—who purchase life at the price of a resigned heritage, and consent to live in a world which has stamped out their culture as a geographic reality. As Aryans and regular white men, it is our instinct to fight blindly on until we either defend our own heritage or are extirpated to the last man. Well—you can't tell me that machine culture is any less alien to the culture we have grown up in, than is French or Japanese or Arabic culture. It may or may not be worth anything to people born within its influence, but to us it is simply an intruder and destroyer. It means the end of everything which **we** consider worth anything, and the negation of every life-value which makes existence worth enduring **for us**—and believe me, I don't need any further reasons to determine my attitude! The intruding fabrick may have any number of excellent points as envisaged by its own components, but to us it is an alien and antagonistic thing to be fought to the limit while life lingers within us. To us, it is the equivalent of death—to be fought by all who would fight against national death or foreign conquest. From *our* point of view there might as well be *no world,* or a French or Chinese or Arabic world—as a machine world. We needn't get needlessly harrowed up or spend our time tilting against windmills, but if we have any respect for ourselves—and for the culture that is the expression of ourselves and our ancestry—we will quietly and effectively do *what we can* to check the engulfing death. Probably we can't do anything—but we shall at least not surrender tamely. To the moderns who repudiate patriotism, we may merely point out the length, painfulness, wholesale value-destruction, and *absolute futility* of every major culture-replacement in the history of the world. It is always a nuisance—and never gets anybody anything—so why not check another such wasteful force if it can be done? Probably we can't check it—but we can at least avoid making ourselves absurd by *welcoming* a poisonous and annihilative nuisance.

By this time it ought to be clear to you that the force and fervidness of my opposition to the machine age do *not* arise from any question of the latter's relative *merit* as compared with our age. My feelings are based primarily on its *difference*—and take for granted that it can manage to possess some *sort of a culture* in an alien way. At the same time I must continue to insist—not necessarily as part of my anti-machine argument, but as an academic probability of historic interest—that the coming era is likely to be as much inferior to existing western civilisation as the Middle Ages were inferior to Graeco-Roman civilisation. After all my letters of the past, I ought not to have to re-catalogue my reasons for holding this opinion. I have not said that *no culture* will exist, but simply that no culture *comparable to ours* is conceivable. You say, very sensibly, that a certain fabric of *new* memory-mellowed folkways is likely to grow into existence; and I agree that a certain number of such palliatives may quite reasonably be imagined. But I tend to look deeper into the structure of a mechanical culture and to note its rate of change *within itself.* Then I ask if it is not conceivable that the conditions of such a fabric (where all usage rests on invention and is subject to revision with each fresh discovery) are so constantly shifting that *no permanent re-crystallisation and tradition-growth can ever be effected* until the culture collapses and gives way to a recurrence of animal simplicity. Say what we may, a rapidly mutable machine-culture is never likely to bring out so much of the human personality—to utilise so many of man's possible sources of pleasure and possible points of removal from animal simplicity—as a slower-moving humanistic culture. It is perfectly naive and absurd to fancy that the new culture *must* be as good as the old—for how often do we ever see a culture replaced by a *precisely equal* one? There are high cultures, which utilise a great many possibilities of the human brain-structure, and low cultures, which utilise relatively few. It isn't hard to tell them apart when our eyes aren't blinded by modernistic theorising—we know that Greece and China and France and Italy have built up marvellously fine edifices, and that our own Anglo-Saxon edifice isn't much below them in many ways—and we also know that the Arabs, Hindoos, Mayans, Egyptians, Persians, Babylonians, etc., built up edifices with greater crudities and limitations, which left more or less extensive tracts of human thought and feeling unutilised and wasted. Life with the first group functioned on a high, full plane; with the latter group, on a distinctly lower and incomplete level. Well—it is the belief of most who coolly analyse the probabilities of the coming machine age, that such a culture essentially belongs to the lower group—the group which utilise only a fraction of man's mental sensitivenesses, and let the rest go to waste. It will be a half-ration culture—a culture which will let only part of a man live. And that isn't the sort one ordinarily welcomes. I don't see that any of my points have been successfully answered or refuted—and there are rafts more where they came from. I won't try to pile on any fresh arguments in this epistle, but will enclose some recent cuttings—asking you to return them, though not necessarily in any haste. I haven't yet read O'Brien's "Dance of the Machines,"[6] but want to when I get a chance. I'll sum up my position by saying just what I've said dozens of times before—that I think machine culture is inferior to ours because it exalts an *absolutely meaningless* group of qualities—speed, quantity, industry *per se*, wealth, ostentation, etc.— to the position of primary virtues, because it destroys normal memory-relationships with environment and folkways, because it emphasises uniformity in place of individuality, and because its net effect is a vicious circle of activity leading nowhere and sapping continuously at the normal ideals of quality, adventure, personality, and the full expansion of the human spirit in poignant and complex realms remote from animal simplicity.

About Krutch—I'm surely glad you were able to get hold of "The Modern Spirit", and that you found so much food for solid reflection in it. He is one of the most significant thinkers of the present generation; and his fearlessness in the face of his own emotional reluctance is truly remarkable. It is agreeable to contrast him with the timid souls who take refuge from devastating truth in puerile ostrich-acts and weak-kneed sophistries . . . . the unctuous Millikans and Eddingtons who think there *may* be *something* deep and divine in the purposeless cosmos, and the fantastic Bellocs and Chestertons who *repudiate* thought altogether and flop back into the perfumed slough of orthodox neo-Catholicism.[7] Krutch is a regular guy, and dares to think things through. I don't share all his overdone heartburnings about our lost ideals, but I surely do admire his clear vision and unflinching gaze. "The Paradox of Humanism" and "The Tragic Fallacy" are both quite sound, and there's really more to that chapter on "Love: the Birth and Death of an Ideal" than your cocksure snap judgment seemed willing to acknowledge at the time you wrote your letter. Let us grant that Krutch now and then strains a point in his effort to lend emphasis and obviousness to an obscure but basic truth. What arguer hasn't done the same in his day? All discounting aside, Krutch's case is good enough to win him a verdict from the impartial and disinterested reader—as I am in this case, since nothing cosmic or humanistic vs. mechanistic is at stake. You base all your adverse conclusions on the superficial observation of a few organic species, forgetting that Krutch's conclusions rest on the observations of scientific biologists who have studied the behaviour of every conceivable organic species under every conceivable sort of environment. Your contention is that Krutch errs in describing non-human and savage sexual phenomena as being in the main limited and seasonal, and you cite cases in the realms of fowl, dogs, and deer to establish the theory that the male is perennially active, and restrained only by the reluctance of the female. Now of course all this sounds important until it is analysed; but you must remember that you have dealt with only a few species, and that you have not taken measures to gauge (a) the relation of the time of observation to the breeding season, (b) the absolute intensity of purpose on the male's part, and (c) the absolute intensity of reluctance on the female's part. Scientific biologists *do* take measures to gauge these things, plotting out seasonal graphs of erotic restlessness on the part of both male and female, and gauging the absolute intensities of desires in each case by the degrees of restlessness shewn by isolated males and isolated females over long periods. Now it is conceded that breeding seasons are not perfectly fixed periods, that different species differ in the restriction of their erotic phenomena to such seasons, and that very few species are wholly incapable of extra-seasonal eroticism under special stimuli. So far, so good. But the fact remains, as proved by an overwhelming bulk of data, that *most* animals have *relatively feeble* sexual feelings outside season; and that sexuality certainly does *not* motivate their ordinary daily life to anything like the extent that it motivates the daily life of the average civilised human being. There are exaggerations and exceptions, but the general law holds good. In season, some animals are more furiously erotic than human beings ever are; but when the season is over they tend to forget all about it—to an extent that the average human being seldom tends to forget it. And as for the reluctance of the female as the sole check on all-year-round eroticism—that is a fallacy which a little detailed research would soon prove. Let it be granted that the ordinary biological mating-process calls for male initiative, and a slightly greater sexual intensity on the male's part—or rather, a slightly *quicker* response to a given sex-stimulus, and a *considerably greater freedom from the fear-reaction accompanying sexuality*—than on the female's. Well and good—and a sufficient explanation of the fairly universal phenomenon of male pursuit and female flight. But have you stopped to ask *how much* greater the male's intensity is than the female's . . . . . or *how sincere* is the female's apparent flight from his advances? Scientists have to stop and ask such things. They have to observe the comparative discomfort of males and females in isolation, the amount of trouble a male will take to gain a female, the conduct of a pursued female when steps are taken to make her flight successful, the question of a male's successful conquest of many different females *all of whom have been proved in previous racing tests to be radically fleeter than he* (or his conquest of *stronger* females in cases where resistance depends on considerations other than flight)—etc. etc. etc. Well—the result is almost invariably to prove that, in general, the erotic intensities of male and female are nearly equal; and that the male pursuit and female flight are mere pattern-phenomena determined by the respective functions of the two sexes in coition, and in no way dependent upon vast differences in erotic ardour. These courtship-patterns differ in different species, and are bound up with other secondary mating-rituals in many cases; but they do not imply a constantly raging male and constantly frigid female. Let the male be held back in any way, and the almost equally ardent female will do all she can to facilitate his pursuit, lure him on, or find another male pursuer. Her flight is one of Nature's innocent hypocrisies—an insincere gesture whose insincerity comes out whenever there is any grave danger of the gesture's success. You must know the familiar lines about the fleeing nymph who glances behind at the pursuing swain and hopes that he will overtake her. That's the way throughout the animal world. If the swain slowed down, the nymph would too; for she has meant to allow herself to be caught all along. And if for any reason he failed altogether to pursue, she would turn about and put herself in his way—or even go so far as to pursue him. There is no question about this—all biologists who have studied the female in isolation and under restricted pursuit attest the fact. The amorousness of she-cats and mares in season is well-known—both to those who own them and to those who have seen the many literary allusions to their fury. Virgil's Georgics speaks of the erotic mares who dash neighing over the hills in the spring— and I guess Yankee farmers could produce similar data. No—the male pursuit and female flight is merely a superficial and easily reversed pattern; albeit a persistent one under usual conditions, and one which is naturally duplicated in the light and playful *imitations* of the courtship process—"flirtations", so to speak—which occur outside the breeding season among many species. It may be this feeble and sportive imitation courtship which you have so often noticed among dogs. On some of the occasions you have seen, the amount of *real* sexual ardour involved may have been very small—the seeming rage of the male being merely a casual and aimless rehearsal of what he is in earnest about only once or twice a year. And so it goes. Krutch may exaggerate the freedom from all sexuality which the average animal enjoys between seasons, but the general principle is correct beyond a doubt. And it isn't any female reluctance that causes the hiatus, either. Now when we ascend the evolutionary scale to the mammal primates, we find about the same general grouping of forces involved—both above and below the technical line between "man" and "ape"—until we strike human beings within the defining area of *artificial civilisation*. This is not to say that no primal savages ever mate except in season, or that orgiastic ceremonies are always needed to make them mate even in season—but merely to say that they think a lot less about sexuality than civilised people do; that the dominant events and values of their lives are motivated and determined by sex to a much lesser extent than the corresponding events and values of average civilised life. I don't think you can find anything "outrageous" about a claim of this sort—I've really forgotten just how Krutch puts it. Of course savages vary according to race and climate. Negroes are highly erotic, while American Indians and Nordic whites are exceedingly non-erotic. As to the Indians—don't be misled by a few accounts of one branch of them. The existence of promiscuity is not a valid proof of high eroticism, since the origin of such customs is very diverse. A non-erotic tribe may practice—listlessly and sparingly—a complete promiscuity; whilst a highly erotic tribe, guided by taboos, may confine itself to very restricted sexual channels—intensity and frequency of indulgence being scarcely measurable by the extent of its scattering amongst different objects. As a matter of fact, however, promiscuity was never general or universal among the different Indian tribes; the Algonquins of the east being wholly monogamous so far as our observations extend. Our Puritan ancestors, who were of an acidly inquiring turn of mind in such matters and who had close contact with the domestic life of the Indians, failed to find any standards of sex very different from those of their own exacting theology—indeed, I leave it to you to imagine the sanctimonious yowlings and missionary paroxysms that the Massachusetts-Bay Elders would have staged had they found that the redskins were living in "divellish fornicaciouns" as well as in (white-induced) "drunken beastlinesse" and "heathen idolatry". In bold fact, the colonists found the Algonquin tribes so non-erotic that they often mentioned their cold sluggishness. And it is a matter of record—unwillingly wrung from redskin-haters who would have been glad to fasten any sort of crime on the "daemon salvages"—that *no female prisoner of the Indians was ever subjected to the least sexual outrage, insult, or indignity*. There is no mistake about this—you can't suspect a Puritan "conspiracy of silence" when scores of chronicles all the way along the Atlantic coast tell the same story in every possible aspect. The fact remains, that although the Indians took female as well as male prisoners, they treated them as though the fact of sex did not exist. They beat them, burnt them, stabbed them, scalped them, tortured them, made pack-animals of them, or sold them as slaves to other tribes and to the French in Canada—but there is not a single recorded case of ravishment. Knowing the unrestraint of the savage mind, and the absence of any scruples of delicacy among these Indians who beat, scalped, tortured, and enslaved men and women alike, we can come to no other conclusion than that they simply weren't interested in the erotic possibilities of their female captives. Each warrior had his squaw, and didn't bother any further about sex in a world so full of more interesting things like conquering and torturing and hunting and fishing . . . . . and keeping alive amidst the stern inclemencies of a northern climate. That white women were *not repugnant* to Indians we know from the occasional cases of *marriage* between female prisoners and their captors. These marriages were made on the usual Algonquin basis—the husband treating his white squaw like any other squaw, and neither exalting nor depreciating her because of her white blood. It would be hard to shake these facts about the Algonquins—especially by means of any data from the culturally and racially dissimilar tribes of the West. Evidently the Eastern Indian was of that well-defined anthropological type whose physical eroticism is moderate to start with, and whose emotional life has been too preëmpted with other things to cherish sex as a major value. We ought to understand this type, because our own Germanic and Celtic ancestors belonged to it. Classical testimony from a vast body of hostile sources—testimony as full and as little liable to biased colouring as the Puritan testimony anent New England Indians—pictures our savage blond forefathers as an erotically sluggish and extremely chaste (not only naturally but by tribal taboo) race of hunters and drinkers and warriors, whose emotional energies were almost wholly expended in warfare, the chase, and the alternating hilarity and oblivion of intoxication. Climate, customs, mode of life, and the absence of provocative beauty in either sex all joined to make eroticism a less successful candidate for our daily thoughts than many another phase of life. You can trace this emotional proportioning in many of the earliest recorded works of Teutonic literature. Glory—conquest—adventure—the spurt of foeman's blood or the lure of the unknown seas—the magic of black oaken forests and the terrific realms of a long drunken slumber—the sense of kinship to the gods and the hope of a long hereafter of Valhallan fighting till the day of Ragnarok, when Bifrost the rainbow bridge shall break and the horn of Heimdall shall sound the Twilight of the Gods . . . . . yes, indeed, our revered progenitors had a lot to think and feel about besides the softer Paphian problems which held first place south of the Rhine and Danube!

Now as to the ideal of "romantic love"—of course it was a thorough illusion as envisaged by mediaevalists and Victorians, yet it would be hard to say that the illusion didn't have as many artistic and pleasurable possibilities as the parallel illusion of "god" and the current popular illusions of "justice" and "democracy". None of these things have any real meaning and all are essentially absurd; yet from each one of them it is possible to extract certain thrills (as long as we can believe the illusion) which are not only sincere while they last, but which are often the basis of authentic art-expression . . . . an art, however, which unfortunately loses value and becomes absurd in the eyes of later and disillusioned generations. It would be erroneous to say that a certain emotional value did not exist in the year 1300, or (somewhat modified) in the year 1850, which was unknown alike to the age of Horace, Tibullus, and Propertius, and to our own modern age. That value, based on a series of fallacious associations and assumptions, was of some mystic significance and promised happiness of exalting nature in the emotional reaction of one person to another of opposite sex; and is what we have termed romantic love. Its merit, if any, lay in the sense of wondering and inspiring *expectancy* which it bred in those who harboured it—the sense that life held something strangely lovely and poignant just around the corner, awaiting him who should persevere long enough in seeking it. This sense of expectancy, like the illusion of religion, helped to foster the comfortable delusion that life's boredom is really worth enduring. The fact that nobody ever found the priceless boon of "perfect love" is quite immaterial—for as long as the possibility of its achievement was conceded, it continued to furnish a motivation for the really empty and wearisome existence-process, and it really did heighten the attractiveness of the courtship process—investing eroticism with a mystic and pathetic beauty which it never had before and has never had since. It was an immense stimulus to the always shaky and unsatisfying convention of monogamy, for some of its ramifications directly fostered the naive myth that certain "souls" are "destined" to dwell together in "spiritual love". (cf. the maundering loveletters of Poe and Mrs. Whitman) It was, perhaps, more vital and tangible than religion, because it had more apparent and accessible pseudo-proofs, chief among which was the occasional accident of lasting wedded love—a feeling which in reality arises from the real mental and emotional compatibility of two persons plus the domestic associations productive of family loyalty and the sentimental residue of the originally motivating eroticism. Of course it led to many a bitter disappointment and disillusionment, yet on the whole it probably contributed more to the zest of life than it subtracted from it. The chief trouble with it was that it was so contrary to fact as to be ridiculous to almost everyone not under its influence or hoping to be under its influence. It never could last very continuously, and we can trace many periods since its birth in the Middle Ages when it was not taken very seriously. It was more of a literary convention than a really believed thing among the Elizabethans, and the Restoration virtually put it out of business for a century and a quarter. It crept back during the Romantic Revival of the later 18th century, and attained its zenith of extravagant swallowing in the Victorian period. The late 19th century clipped its wings, and psycho-analysis and the 20th century have put it out of business for good so far as the present Western Civilisation is concerned. Apparently no other culture than the Aryan-Western stream ever produced anything of quite the same sort—and perhaps no other ever will. We may be pardoned for gently regretting an illusion which was undoubtedly very vivid and very beautiful in our grandfathers' eyes—though our regret may well be tempered by the thought that classical antiquity got along very well without it. In time it is likely that various non-erotic matters will take up our emotional attention to such an extent that we shall not miss the excrescences whose removal has again lowered the value of the sex-element to normal. Krutch is undeniably overexcited about this loss, as he is about other cultural losses—but he doesn't demand that we all share his feelings. He perhaps overrates the good which the lost illusions conferred, just as you undoubtedly overrate its evil side. In cold truth, most enlightened people took it with just enough subconscious reservation to rob it of its worst effects. It was mostly the naive and the simple-minded that it injured. You are, I fear, carrying your constitutional *concreteness* a bit to excess in fancying that Krutch's attitude must have been determined by his own *personal* experience. A lifelong student of human values and motives like Krutch doesn't depend on any *one* person's experience, but draws cautious conclusions from as full an array of historic, biographic, literary, medical, philosophical, and sociological data as wide reading, observation, and questioning can provide.

As to the limited value of eroticism when divested of its romantic aura—certainly the process ceases to be anything worthy of *primary* exploitation in life and art, as we may easily see by noting how secondary it was in the great human classics of antiquity. When sex is non-mystical and common, it ceases to be a matter of prime concern as in the literature of romantic times; but steps down and takes its minor place among other feelings, thoughts, and motives. Power, glory, pity, fatality, achievement, death, struggle, failure—a thousand basic human things stand out in equality to sex as motive-forces in life and literature, and the ancients made full use of them. It seems to me that both you and Krutch err in different ways—you in imagining that sex amounts to more than it really does, and Krutch in fancying that its admitted subordinateness is anything to regret or worry about. We cannot yet predict what form its expression will ultimately take—either in the machine-culture or in any real culture which may survive in any part of the world—but we may safely say that with the decline of *mystery* in connexion with it, it will not be the live issue that it was in the 19th century. Of course it will always amount to a good deal, especially in relation to the appreciation of beauty; but it won't be any great motivating force capable of making adults swallow the delusion that life is worth living. Made familiar to youth at an earlier age than formerly, and expressed more freely at every period of life, it soon gets to be "old stuff"—just a little too hackneyed to fill its older place, though of course as much of a diversion as it was to Greeks and Romans. The "kick" of abridged feminine garb will last only as long as that garb remains a novelty; for there is really no *intrinsic* erotic value in nudity. Among many savage tribes it is considered the commonplace thing to wear no clothes, and the alluring thing to wear any. Nor does it take a career of libertinism, as you seem to assume for granted, to make the trifles of sex appear rather a stale subject for major exploitation. Sheer repetition and non-mysteriousness are the great slayers of interested emotion, and you'll see quite a let-up in the commercial publicising of "sex-appeal" as soon as the older and youthfully-repressed generation has died off. The sensible thing is not to depend so much upon this one senescent motivation-element, but to cultivate a wider array of life-interests and emotional stimuli.

As to the future of erotic customs in the Western World—as I said before, no person now living can venture a valid prediction. The present age of transition is too unformed and too chaotic to furnish any reliable guide; and *two* generations of biassed thinkers (the old guard of Victorians and Edwardians, and the first post-war generation of irresponsible rebels) will have to die off before any signs of stable recrystallisation can appear. Other commentators—especially Bertrand Russell—can prophesy better about this than I can, since I am less interested in this one trend than in the general collective trend of Western Civilisation. My guess would be that society will experiment with a combination of promiscuity and marriage, in which marriage will play a decreasing part until eventually it disappears. Paternity, however, will always be registered; and the state will fix responsibility for the rearing of such offspring as are born—although there will be a disconcertingly small number of the latter, perhaps necessitating a subsidy on births in those nations where small population implies military disadvantages. Among the lower orders promiscuity will in all probability be widespread and absolute—as indeed it no doubt is already. In higher circles the element of aestheticism will probably boil it down to a more or less rapid succession of liaisons—consecutive rather than simultaneous. In general, the many and complex causes of change in erotic standards would seem to include the following:

a)   decline of illusions of religion and romantic love.

b)   discovery of effective contraceptive methods.

c)   economic independence of women.

d)   custom of apartment-dwelling, with prepared foods and mechanical conveniences; which eliminates need of home-making in its hitherto understood sense, and renders the family a redundant institution.

e)   availability of automobile as means of popularising and facilitating promiscuity during its early period of necessarily furtive practice.

f)   modern intellectual fashion of ignoring and despising tradition.

g)   effect of democracy in substituting an ideal of cheap physical comfort and sensual pleasure for one of aestheticism as applied to life.

h)   machine-age dulling of sensitive emotional capacity and promotion of a need for simpler, more primitive, and more stupid life-incentives.

i)   fact that *homo sapiens* is a naturally promiscuous rather than monogamous primate.

j)   impossibility of inducing men to live erotically with women over forty except under compulsion of strong aesthetic and ethical obligations which vanish with the economic independence and relinquished chastity of the modern female.

k)   decline in regard for children as principle of hereditary tradition succumbs to machine barbarism; coupled with increasing tendency of state to assume socialistic guidance of such children as are born.

l)   rise of a sense of ennui and futility, in the absence of belief in cosmic values and life after death, which induces a wish to crowd life with as much violent and ecstatic sensation as possible.

m)   increasing medical control of venereal diseases, and diminishing dangers of promiscuity arising therefrom.

n)   general machine-age sentiment of collectivism and paternalism in social-political organisation; dulling the sense of individuality, independence, and privacy on which family life is founded, and substituting a quasi-publicised, communised life in which state-licensed promiscuity will be much more natural than marriage.

o)   almost certain reign of complete promiscuity in youth, owing to decline of belief in religious-ethical barriers against indulgence of powerful precocious sexuality at ages below that at which old-time marriage is economically possible—and the subsequent reluctance of men to assume legal responsibilities toward females whom others have enjoyed without such responsibilities.

p)   unwillingness of the aesthetic-erotic male to feel himself debarred from company of young women as he grows older. Present custom of infidelity to aging wife likely to be held clumsy and needless by a generation devoted to candour and directness—abandonment of the marriage custom likely to be held greatly preferable.

q)   acceptance of the Freudian doctrine with its implications of the importance of sex, and consequent sense of unfairness at the erotic restrictions and unrealisations of wedlock. Marriage without fidelity-obligations will soon be followed by the death of the institution as a whole.

Personally, I don't welcome the changing code; for I am a traditionalist of the old order, with a high aesthetic regard for the ancient New England ideals of chastity and domestic affection. I wish to Heaven the social and economic basis promised enough continuity with the past to ensure the cherishing of these exquisite and delicate phases of art-in-life—but as a realist I have no such illusions. The handwriting is on the wall, and anyone who does not wish to make a naive fool of himself must prepare to witness strange ethical metamorphoses and transvaluations. One may dislike the trend, just as one may dislike the coming of the machine age—but what the devil is one going to do about it?

Here I come upon your argument that a relative coolness on the female's part tends to regulate human eroticism—an extension to mankind of your general (and *undoubtedly erroneous*) theory of vertebrate sexuality. Now I hate to be constantly dynamiting your beliefs, but I really must say a word about this one. My god, man! but where is your medical and sociological reading and classical knowledge? Do you mean to tell me that you are, at your age, still taken in by the hackneyed feminine pose (forced upon her, of course, by masculine taste in the Middle Ages) of coldness, which she adopts in order to seem delicate and superior, and to egg the male on to greater heat? Holy hades—read Havelock Ellis or Bertrand Russell or Lindsey or Forel or Robie[8] or somebody who knows something about the question! Great guns—if you ever pulled that naive theory of female coolness in public discussion, you'd never hear the last of it!!! Of course, there may be two or three couples in every dozen or so where the wife is cooler than the husband in fact as well as pose, for considerable inequality exists in *both* directions—but the *opposite* side! My god, the *opposite* side! *Read*, man, *read! What* a perspective on the whole situation you must have! For Pete's sake get an intelligible slice of data by seeing what competent specialists—physicians, sociologists, anthropologists, historians, psychologists, biologists, etc—have to say from their wide, deep, careful, and accurate observations! That tendency to go only by what you can smell and touch in your own farmyard will be the philosophic ruin of you if you don't shake it off pretty soon—take off the blinders, boy, and see what the world is thinking and discovering—*read, read.* Pardon my vehemence, but I can't help seeing in this *one* instance a tendency which will hamper your grasp of truth in *all* the various fields of investigation. You are blandly assured and dogmatic . . . but from no adequate data at all! And in this case, *what* a different story the *real* data tells!

First. Far from the female's desiring eroticism "for propagation only", it is *absolutely certain that no animal except man above a certain state of savagery has any idea of the connexion betwixt sex-desire and reproduction.* None of the animals who mate in season have the least notion that their excitements and pleasures are connected with the young which the females later bring forth, nor do they dream that the male is connected with the young he breeds. This is true even of those monogamous birds whose males guard the nest in the female's absence. These males know that the young belong to their mate, but do not link them with the bygone mating. *And the same ignorance is true of mankind below a certain stage of savagery.* Anthropologists can deduce from many tribal customs that early man did not know, until long after his conquest of fire, that the burgeoning of the females in late winter and later summer had any connexion with the wholesale pleasure-orgies to which nature moved the tribe each spring and fall. In very low races like the miserable Tierra del Fuegians *this ignorance still exists.* No Fuegian today knows why the females bring forth young. Pleasure and reproduction have no linkage in their minds. Moreover, it is an almost certain fact that even among civilised races the thought of offspring is always remote and secondary in moments of pleasure—for the female just as much as for the male, despite her transparent pose of reluctance and idealism. See Havelock Ellis's "Little Essays in Love and Virtue", and also an article in a recent *Harper's* exploding the myth of a continuous maternal instinct and an intrinsic female desire for young.[9] Don't be taken in by hokum. No living creature *of either sex mates because it wants children.* All creatures mate *to please themselves*—this being the bait that nature sets to ensure propagation. But it is *only nature,* and not male or female, that wants young. As soon as the male and female learn that their pleasure produces young, they at once begin to look out for means of defeating nature.

So much for that! Don't think I'm handing out any arguments of my own—hell, no! I'm only telling you what is as much a matter of commonly accepted scientific fact as the earth's revolution around the sun or the evolution of man from the amoeba!

Now as for human female desire—the plain facts are almost certainly these and just these:

a) the desire is *more slowly excited* than in the male;

b) but, once excited, it is *certainly just as strong,* and according to a large group of physiologists, much stronger.

c) eroticism is *more of a motivating force* in the female than in the male—and there is a more persistent tendency to regard it sentimentally or cosmically.

d) females, in the absence of the male, experience desires and frustrations just as intense as those of the isolated male—hence the savage sourness of old maids, the looseness of modern spinsters, and the infidelity or tendency thereto of wives left alone by husbands for more than a week or two. (cf. Ellis, Fielding, Collins, Overstreet,[10] Forel, etc.)

e) but, due to traditional reasons arising in the Middle Ages and culminating in the Victorian period, refined women of the older generation have thought it necessary to pretend a coldness which only an accidental few of them can really possess—a coldness which they sometimes feign so well that they fool even themselves; sublimating their desire into the psychological field and thus establishing a repression which soon produces a neurosis and in some cases ends in insanity.

Now again—don't think I'm launching any notions of my own. I'm no special-ist, and I'm simply repeating the findings of the standard authorities as I've run across them in miscellaneous biological-sociological reading and controversy. Look 'em up for yourself—it may be disillusioning, but you must know the real facts about these things if you are to form intelligent opinions of your own, or apply intelligent criticism to treatises involving the debated matters.

I should think that your college Latin studies would have dispelled your il-lusions about female frigidity—for of course you realise that, prior to the medi-aeval birth of "romantic love" and the age of the trouveres and troubadours with their conventional stanzas about "my cold and cruel ladye faire", all poets and satirists and historians and essayists united to describe and deplore the burning and savage lusts of women—which impressed them as being more lawless than their own masculine desires. Can you have forgotten the univer-sally known Sixth Satire of Juvenal, and all the brief quips in Horace? Ovid sums up the matter in the first book of the Ars Amatoria: (ll. 275–282)

> Utque viro furtiva Venus, sic grata puellae;
> > Vir male dissimulat: tectius illa cupit.
> Conveniat maribus, nequam nos ante rogemus,
> > Femina iam partes victa rogantis agat.
> Mollibus in pratis admugit femina tauro:
> > Femina cornipedi semper adhinnit equo.
> *Parcior in nobis nec tam furiosa libido:*
> > *Legitimum finem flamma virilis habet.*

Dryden translates this as follows:

> To secret pleasure both the sexes move;
> But women most, who most dissemble love.
> 'Twere best for us if they would first declare;
> Avow their passion and submit to prayer.
> The cow, by lowing, tells the bull her flame;
> *The neighing mare invites the stallion to the game.
> *Man is more temp'rate in his lust than they;*
> *And, more than woman, can his passion sway.*

I could quote dozens of things of similar import from the Greek and Roman poets and prose writers—but what's the use? You see the facts. The writers of antiquity all recognised woman as a being with very strong and assertive

---

*Dryden's custom of inserting these redundant Alexandrine lines in his pentameter verse always makes me tired—as indeed it did Pope!

lusts*, and no one ever hears of any *coolness* on her part until the Christian-romantic myth-weaving of the Dark Ages begins. There is no reason to think woman less naturally promiscuous than man—as the lives of the Renaissance Italian ladies, and the Frenchwomen of the 18th century, well attest. Eros was their god, and they worshipped him at many masculine altars. In 18th century France, birth-control methods were known—hence the prevailing feminine pleasures. In Thibet and Tartary the institution of polyandry exists—one female simultaneously marrying a whole family of brothers and deeming herself ill-served if the number be too small. In Roman Imperial times Messalina, Agrippina, the two Faustinas, and other similar matrons shew the natural bent of their sex with the mask off. They practiced the crude birth-control methods of abortion and infanticide, in which certain Greek and Egyptian practitioners were especially adept. You can judge from Juvenal, Persius, and Martial how vast and widespread this state of things was. Christianity checked it prodigiously—indeed, this faith has been the greatest of all historic curbs upon sex-license—but it did not prevent Theodora, wife of the Byzantine emperor Justinianus, from being a very gallant lady! Since the Middle Ages custom and precept have tried to ensure the monogamousness of woman, and have perhaps made her imagination temporarily less roving than man's—especially since her economic and social security has hitherto depended upon strict monogamy. But in liberal ages the truth has burst through, and as late as the 1740's Pope wrote in his "Moral Essays":

> "Men some to business, some to pleasure take,
> But ev'ry woman is at heart a rake."[11]

You'd understand the background with which he was familiar if you knew the 18th century through contemporary memoirs, Walpole's letters, etc. etc. Well—the present age is liberal beyond the wildest dreams of the 18th century, and the future age is likely to be more so. And it won't be women who will check the tendency. I don't suppose you are ignorant of the fact that female freedom has now reached such a pitch that even *old* women are trying to recapture youthful thrills as their husbands do amongst the nymphs of the chorus. Hence the 20th century institution of the sleek *male* prostitute, or *gigolo,* to whom elderly and unattractive females are resorting in greater and greater numbers in the larger cities. In Paris they are now licensed and medically inspected by police surgeons like their professional sisters of more ancient standing. No—I can't say that I have much hope for monogamy in a traditionless, non-aesthetic, practical, concrete, materialistic, democratic, and me-

---

*cf. the *myths,* where the Greeks embodied their conceptions of character as fables. Note tales of Pasiphaë, Byblis, Myrrha, Phaedra, the Maenads, the nymphs who ravished the youth Hylas, Circe, Calypso, Salmacis, etc. etc.

chanicalised world. But the new system will fit the new age, and it won't be considered inferior by those who grow up under it. Actually, it will mean the depression of sex to the position of a minor issue; for with all the mystery and taboos gone, eroticism will signify no more than eating or drinking. Another thing—the change won't actually be quite as great as we fancy; since all along there has been an enormous amount of furtive licence practiced. Statisticians may some day try to compute the numerical extent of the resistance to monogamous standards in the various ages preceding the present. Hell of a time they'll have, with fragmentary and evasive data, and ambiguous literature, on every hand!

And that's about all I know of the poor, hackneyed, overdone old "sex question"—standby of standbys for callowly modernistic debate in Greenwich-Village basements and attics!

As for Walter Lippmann—I must read that book of his![12] Of course I am not so much interested in the question of *what people do*, as in that of *how the cosmos is constructed;* but it is nevertheless always interesting to get an intelligent sidelight on the question of relative values in a purposeless and valueless world. There's a whole list of books I want to read when I get a chance—but gawd help me, I don't know when that leisurely moment will ever come! Some of the recent things in my mind are the following—and if you can beat me to them, so much the better for you:

> The Nature of the Physical World—Prof. A. S. Eddington
> The Universe Around Us—Sir James Jeans
> Our Knowledge of the External World—Bertrand Russell
> The Dance of the Machines—Edward J. O'Brien

As for a *name* for the code of sensible conduct best adapted to ease one along through life—I suppose there's nothing better than just plain *sensible conduct* or *rational conduct*. Of course the terms *ethics* and *morals* could conceivably be used, since the thing described serves, in an age of reason, the same purpose which ethics and morals used to serve in a world of theological and teleological beliefs; but as I have pointed out, the survival of many of the old beliefs, and the consequent continued employment of the terms *ethics* and *morals* in their former sense, creates a somewhat troublesome ambiguity unless one establishes a distinction.

About abstract aesthetics—I rather thought you would find that matter of the modernists' objection to the concrete on steel-frame buildings a bit extreme, despite your respect for the contemporary utilitarian ideal! It is a good example of the *reductio ad absurdum* of a roughly sound theory. I hardly need to say that the holders of this doctrine are scarcely taken seriously—but the existence of the doctrine itself is a fair indication of how far art has removed its frontier from the purely decorative realm. This extreme theory must not be confounded with the love of many far-from-eccentric artists for the linear harmonies of structural steel. Even the late Joseph Pennell[13]—conservative and academician that he was—loved to draw the spidery lines of the girders in downtown Manhattan's new skyscrapers as he watched them from his lofty window in the Hotel Margaret, across the river in Brooklyn. Others, too, have praised the structural steel roof of the train-shed in New York's Pennsylvania Station. But this liking does not imply any contempt for the finished product. For my part, I can't say that I'm inordinately fond of structural steel or unfinished work of any kind. It is possible that I am somewhat calloused toward purely abstract aesthetics—i.e., the pure rhythms of line and mass.

About books—I'm going to send you a bunch of tempting catalogues the next time I can get out to parcel-post the package. These needn't be returned—my name is on dealers' lists as a collector and I get whole baskets full every week. This will sort of introduce you to the field—shew you what sort of books are floating around. But of course these items aren't as cheap as some of the commoner ones which you'd want first. As I said before, you'd be astonished at the stuff you could pick up for a quarter, fifteen cents, a dime, or even a nickel, at the vast second-hand book joints of Providence, Boston, New York, or Philadelphia. If you seriously decide to begin a working-library, I'll make you some tentative lists of titles and send them (the lists, not the books!) on for your approval or veto; then, later on, I'll be glad to purchase the books (or such as I can find on the cheap counters here for you at rock-bottom prices, and have them shipped to you by parcel post or express. But before I make up the lists, you'd better give a few *directional* suggestions yourself—as to the especial *side* of the intellectual and aesthetic world which you want to cover first. Since your library ought to express your own personality, and since you seem to lean more toward history and philosophy than toward other fields at present, I'd suggest that you begin with these subjects—and the sciences necessary for their understanding, such as biology, anthropology, psychology, etc. etc. At the same time you'll want to brush up on general literature, in order to understand the thoughts and images which have been motivating people and groups and cultures down the long centuries of history. You ought to have a few of the Graeco-Roman classics on hand for reference—in translation, even if you know Latin, since the form ought to be close to your daily thoughts, and without mechanical retardations to ready consultation—as well as certain popular books about Greek and Roman thought—like Prof. Capps's "Homer to Theocritus" or the Chautauqua texts on Greek and Roman literature, art, and life. You also ought to have representative English literature—poetry and prose—say Chaucer, Spenser, Marlowe, Shakespeare, Jonson, Beaumont and Fletcher, Herrick, Milton— and so on, and so on, down the line. And of course, a few good manuals of English literature as well—both to explain and place the authors you have, and to suggest more authors for you to look up. I'll give you plenty of titles to choose from as soon as you decide to start in seriously. Then, too—you want a few volumes of *literary criticism* to get you on your feet aesthetically; not only old volumes, but some new ones illustrating contemporary trends. I'll suggest you a lot of the latter from recent Haldeman-Julius and Modern Library lists. What you need is *an understanding of the aesthetic attitude, and its share in motivating the life of high-grade civilised men.* One great source of good books when you feel able to pay about a *dollar* each, rather than a *dime,* is the steadily increasing array of reasonably-priced "libraries" or issues of uniform editions of standard books. I'll get you the catalogues of most of these if you wish. They include not only such newly prepared reprints as those of Everyman's and the Modern Library, but also many reprints from the original plates of standard books only a few years old. The Doubleday-Doran "Star Dollar Books" are of the latter sort. You certainly must look over a list of these, since they include some almost *incredible* values. The paper isn't much to brag about, but the binding is neat and convenient, the type legible, and the text full and accurate. This series has just included Wells's "Outline of History"—the latest edition of over a thousand pages, with diagrams and illustrations in full, all in one volume for only a single buck! My god, what more could one ask? Truly, it's so easy to acquire a sound and vital library nowadays that nothing but sheer indolence can prevent a man from having one! I say "nowadays"—although that's really giving the present too much credit. As far back as Poe's time—in fact, as soon as *stereotyping* became a common process—these cheap editions became a common thing. In Philadelphia such firms as Lea and Carey and Carey and Hart struck off thousands of sets of the best poets and novelists at low prices in the 1830's and 1840's—while you of course know of the famous cheap Harper editions of the same period in New York—Harpers Classical, Family, etc. Libraries. I have scores of these Philadelphia and Harper Editions on my shelves, bequeathed to me by thrifty Yankee forbears who knew a good thing when they saw it, yet were careful of their cash. You can still pick up some of these old-timers on the stands—I have myself from time to time. Then in a later generation came Burt's Home Library—still issued by the publishers. That used to come at a half-dollar per volume, though it's probably more expensive now. That had many fine titles—though it also included some mediocre material. The biggest bargain of all, probably, was Cassell's National Library—published in paper covers in Great Britain and reprinted by the cheap-book house of Munro in New York. It was edited by the eminent scholar Henry Morley—and you can hardly believe the titles it included at a dime each. Not only well-known stuff, but curious, out-of-the-way things like Lobo's treatise on Abyssinia, (from which Johnson got the idea of Rasselas) Lucian's Trip to the Moon, and Gonzales' "London in 1731". My father used to get these to carry in his pocket and read on the train, just as I get

Haldeman-Julius stuff nowadays, and I have dozens of 'em—including Walton's "Compleat Angler", White's "Natural History of Selborne", Marco Polo's and Mandeville's Travels[14]—etc. etc. etc. I wish to hell they were still issued—for they were really far better bargains than the H-J Blue Books—standard-length texts, ably edited and free from gross misprints. I gave away all of my family hoard of those that duplicated bound books on my shelves—but now I wish I hadn't, for they are admirable things to tote around for idle moments. Once in a while you'll find a few in second-hand shops now—I'll send you a sample the next time I come across a good title on a five-cent counter. Another regular gold-mine for non-wealthy library-gatherers is the god-given boon of *publishers' remainders.* When a new book doesn't sell profitably, the publisher generally dumps the edition on wholesale dealers at veritably give-away prices, and these dealers market them for damn near nothing. Now, since popular sale is no indication of the merit of a book, it naturally follows that some marvellously fine things get "remaindered" every little while; so that a lynx-eyed library owner can sometimes pick up for a song a book he has ardently wanted ever since it was published—pick it up in the expensive original edition, at that! And you'd be surprised at the *newness* of some of the books you can get in this way. Right now I'm patting myself on the back over a buy that comes close to the miracle class—Hervey Allen's magnificent 2-volume life of Poe, issued in 1927 and including all the recent data on Poe discovered in 1925, for only *$2.98.* Its regular price 2 years ago was ten berries, and the custodian of the Poe Shrine in Richmond tried to sell me a set last spring at that figure—but I was too broke to fall for it. The cause of this particular case of "remaindering"—since the book is a widely acclaimed and definitive text—is really something of a mystery; but my guess is that the publishers mean to put out a new edition with revised text and better proofreading, so that this edition will soon be a back number. The book was *rushed out* in 1927 to forestall the sale of a very inferior biography then just published.[15] It had been under careful and scholarly preparation for years, and it would have been a cursed shame to let this upstart careless concoction capture the market and saturate it for a decade. So the Doran Co. speeded up on the scholarly Allen text and got the book out before its mediocre rival achieved any headway—incidentally succeeding, and reducing the competitor to an almost total oblivion! But all this entailed careless and hasty mechanical work at the last moment, so that the text is not in the most polished shape, and the typography subject to occasional misprints. However—all this doesn't worry me; since the facts are there in perfect fulness and accuracy, and the slips of style and presswork are so minor that they don't catch the notice of the reader who is out for the story rather than the details of form. This, of course, is an extraordinary case. Most "remainders" are simply books issued in the ordinary way which haven't met a good sale. I have picked up lots of these—things like Maurice Hutton's "Greek Point of View," Wake-field's first series of weird stories, Kostolanyi's novel about Nero, etc. etc. etc. There are certain bookselling firms which specialise in large remainder de-partments—both for personal shopping and mail-order purchase—whilst many bookshops and department-stores carry counters of remainders either occasionally or all the year round. In Boston you can always find a colossal variety of remainders—priced from a quarter up—at the Goodspeed branch in the basement of the old South Church, as well as at Lauriat's around the corner in Washington St. Lauriat does a large remainder mail-order business, too—you ought to send for their catalogue—*Chas. E. Lauriat Co., 385 Wash-ington St., Boston.* In New York you'll find oceans of remainders in the book department of Macy's—at Herald Square—and in the Liggett drug store in the Grand Central Station. Also in many of the bookshops along East 59th St.—they're so numerous I can't remember their names. And a vast mail-order trade in them is conducted by the *Union Library Association, 118 E. 25th St., N.Y. City*—for whose catalogue, as well as Lauriat's, you ought to send. Providence, unfortunately, is not a very good town for remainders—but once or twice a year some of our large department stores have sales of them . . . . God help my purse! Right now I'm praying not to be led any further into temptation by a Lauriat remainder in the latest catalogue—Charles G. Har-per's "Haunted Houses" for only two beans . . . . . but a two-spot is 200 whole copper cents to a poor deadbroke guy! As I say, I'm no sentimental bibliophile—but hell knows I'd be pretty damn lost if I couldn't put my fin-ger on something interesting and stimulating and liberating and motivating now and then without trekking down town and going through with the red tape of the public library. You simply can't be fully alive unless you have a decently easy access to the general imagery and thought and feelings and do-ings and perspectives and pageantry of the world and cosmos, as provided by the printed records of the race. It's no use for you to *say* that you don't expect ever to indulge in 'research, argument, or opinion worthy of the name'—for, damn it all, it's easy to see that you are at all times simply naturally bursting with perspectives and opinions in need of adequate formulation and expres-sion! I wouldn't urge reading and literary-ownership on anybody that didn't need such things. Hell, no—if a goof can get enough of a kick out of life by eating and earning and cinema-gazing and radio-listening and tabloid-sopping and baseball-arguing, so much the better for him! But *you* can't do it, as your constant urge to philosophic thought and argument and rational conduct prove. You have too energetic, keen, alert, and restless a mind to be content on quarter-rations. Your mind is too ceaseless in its grinding not to need some sort of a substantial grist to work on. Else why do you worry over the manifold absurdities of the circumambient world? No use, old top—just as your judgment of the Albany capitol and of stream-line tobacco-tins proves you more of an aesthete than you want to admit, so does your disgust at reli-gious-sentimental hokum, and your wish to pound your way to reality, prove that you are more of an intellectual than you'd like to appear. Much as you may enjoy the pose of the soil-bound, pedant-baiting, culture-jeering barbari-an; the solid fact remains, that you'll never be really contented—never feel really placed or at ease in the world—until you've brushed away the cobwebs and gotten down to the vital essentials of truth and beauty and motivation—the what's what of life—in a way that nothing but the poor, despised pro-cesses of reading and general fact-gathering and fact-sifting can help you to do. Ridiculous and affected as it may *now seem* to you to be cautious about da-ta and to require a lot of reading and opinion-comparing before accepting an idea; the stern, unpleasant fact remains, that there's absolutely no other way of getting the straight dope about anything. Either you've got to go after the facts and values in a full, clear, accurate way, or you'll have to wander in a tantalising haze of half-knowledge and put up with mirages, blurred outlines, and eternal uncertainty and bafflement all your life. In the cultivation of per-ception, it's about the same as in the cultivation of artistic sensitiveness and responsiveness—a man has to take his choice between vegetating along with only a small fraction of his brain and pleasure-capacities in use, and waking up to a fuller employment of the powers and senses with which nature has provided him. For one who hates the idea of deliberate *waste,* it would pay to get busy and begin to hit on all six cylinders instead of merely one or two. And that's all that reading and study really amount to among men of sense. There's no pose or affectation or pedantry in it, heaven knows! It's merely a question of squeezing the lemon of life dry—of cracking the oyster fully open—of walking in sunlight instead of a fog—of knowing where you stand instead of being lost in the woods—of steering by real vision instead of play-ing blindman's-buff. There's a lot more pose and affectation about the fellow who wears an ostentatiously jaunty front and elaborately clowns along with a studied battery of colloquial flash words and intricate wisecracks, than there is about the man who simply goes after the facts and fundamentals, acts like himself, and talks in the first plain words and phrases that occur to him. You may call the latter a "highbrow" because he now and then uses a word which is neither common nor monosyllabic, *but if you stop to analyse his use of the longer and rarer word, you will see that the motivation behind it is not one of ostentation, but one of boldly practical efficiency and naturalness.* If he uses a "five-dollar word", it is merely because that word expresses something real and important *more briefly and accurately than it could otherwise be expressed.* To avoid the use of the "high-brow jawbreaker", it would be necessary to beat around the bush in a clumsy and verbose way involving *far more pose and artificiality* than the concise, clear-cut, straightforward use of the exactly right word. The only reason that the herd despise and reject such precise words, is that their blurred vision *never grasps the exactitudes which these words express.* They don't know anything about the real facts and distinctions which these words concern—such things do not exist in their limited radius of sight—so that they imagine the accurate thinker is inventing notions and talking nonsense just for effect. It is like the case of a savage and a white man with a spy-glass looking at a distant ship. The man with the glass can see the ship's name and describe the rigging precisely—which of course the naked-eyed savage can't. And the savage laughs at the white man and thinks he is making up things in order to appear like a great god . . . for the simple reason that the savage doesn't know what a telescope is! No—the really plain and sensible and unaffected man is not the low-comedy lowbrow, but the fellow who simply goes after real facts and values, and speaks of them in the clearest and easiest words that come to hand. It doesn't argue any pose or insincerity if these words sometimes include a few which aren't common in conversation—for how can a guy get the facts without reading the books where they are stored, and how can he read many books without picking up a few of the precision-words which the authors have to use in order to put across their facts in the fullest, shortest, easiest, and most accurate way? Hell! a man would be *artificially posing* if he stopped to think of his speech all the time, and elaborately pruned out every word that hadn't the 100% endorsement of corner-drug-store and cracker-barrel lexicographers! There's no use in pulling the old "highbrow" grin about the plain words that a person unstudiedly and unconsciously uses to get his message across in the quickest and best way, even if those words happen to be drawn—through natural necessity—from printed sources outside the radius of Broadway slang or crossroads gossip. It's the motivation and attitude that count—and you can't tell me that a decently cultivated plain-speaker isn't more of a he-man and regular guy than is the trick mucker-poser who stands on his head and walks on his ear in order to be a properly certified member of god's great common peepul. Not, of course, that all decorative or metaphorical jocosity and colloquialism are to be placed under the ban—for of course they have a substantial graphic quality and art-value in their place. The only foolish thing is to regard them quasi-pedantically (for there are pedants in ignorance and frivolity, as well as pedants in primness and learning!) as sacred and exclusive linguistic standards, any departure from which is to invite a general jeering out of court as involving pose, pompousness, and heresy. Really artificial and ridiculous pedantry and scholastic affectation do exist, of course—but common-sense can soon distinguish this cheap stuff from straightforward realism. You can't talk with—or correspond with—a man very long without seeing whether he's really interested in ideas and beauty, or merely anxious to raise himself in his own and others' eyes by a display of the external and superficial paraphernalia of learning and taste. The fake will show out in his language, mood, handling of subject, and so on, before many words are exchanged. It's dead easy to tell whether one's interest be in *matter* or *manner*. When a bozo is too precise and solemn on the one hand, or too loftily jaunty and flippant on the other; when he is long on rhetoric and lists of scholarly names, and short on specific facts, arguments, and sources—then look out for the faker. But for hell's sake don't laugh at the real truth-and-beauty-hound just because this mongrel imitation exists! Don't punish the innocent for the guilty! And—to carry the moral of all this to your specific case—don't be afraid to go out after facts, and read and collect books, and cultivate the sense which makes you hate the Albany state house and like the Educational Bldg., merely because you think it may make you a solemn pedant to do so. Cheer up! It won't hurt your manner and speech as badly as you think—and if it ever gets you in wrong with any crowd, it's a safe bet that such a crowd isn't worth being in right with! Go ahead—it'll never make a bespectacled Clarence or lisping Reggie-boy of you! And more—don't worry because you can't find people at hand to talk substantial things with. Thousands are in the same boat! Depend on correspondence when you feel like discussing things—I can put you next to lots of live-wire minds with whom you'll be glad to exchange letters. Just now I've lent one of your epistles to a fellow—*Frank B. Long, Jr., 230 West 97th St., New York City*—who is keenly appreciative of all the things which interest you, and who could argue with you by the hour on Krutch or Lippmann or Eddington or Spengler—or anything else in philosophy, art, or literature that you might be keen about. You may hear from him in time—or if not, why not drop him a line yourself about "The Decline of the West" or "The Modern Temper" or something like that? He has, as I have myself, a very high regard for your intelligence; and agrees with me that you have unsuspected pleasures ahead, to be derived from ampler data and more effective standards of accuracy and validity in art and thought. Oh, yes—one thing more. If the problem of book-storage is a psychological deterrent to library-gathering on your part, why not *build your shelves or get your bookcases first?* A set of empty and inviting shelves, fairly crying to be appropriately filled, will quite reverse the psychological situation. And depend upon me for suggestions! I'll pick up a set of Brown University reading-course slips the next time I pass the college library, and will shoot 'em along to you. Remember—I'm not trying to force reading on anybody who doesn't need it, but am merely recommending what I think you need for your peace of mind, judging by your undoubtedly genuine and intense zeal for argument and opinion-holding in matters of philosophy, history, science, and so forth. And suppose a wider outlook *did* check your material prosperity a bit? What of it? What is material prosperity, that its commonplace physical comforts are to be compared to the vital and fundamental pleasures of a keener cosmic grip? To resign the pleasures of full living for those of fat living is to resign the substance for the shadow. And are you so sensitive to the opinion of clods and machine-age barbarians that you would be worried by the myopic jackasses who might bray the old peasant standby—'he made a good start and was a good worker, but got to reading and began to let things slide until now he doesn't amount to a damn'. Truly, my own opinion of the mental attitude involved in such a criticism is one of such amused contempt that I could not even be ruffled by the censure. To me, the holder of such a view is *not a person*—not a person in the sense of a member of the civilised community. He is just a mindless voice from the animal herd—monkey's chatter, ox's lowing, peasant's mouthing—all the same. What, pray, could a *good start* be toward, if it did not involve the full life of the mind? And of what value were the things the reader *let slide*, in comparison to those which he *gained* by reading? And if a conscious and humanistic life doesn't constitute 'amounting to a damn', what is there about a machine-age "life" of physical repletion or a peasant existence of animal simplicity that can be said to amount to anything? The truth is, that for natural clods—the kind of people who make such criticisms—a physical mechanicalism or state of animality really *is* better than a state of humanistic realisation and conscious contact with the sources of human stimulation. But what the hell does all that mean to *you*, or any other person naturally reflective and sensitive enough to be a real human being? It doesn't follow that *you'd* get anything out of a purely peasant round, merely because *they* can. Get rid of the democratic fallacy! I'm not one to deny that we might be happier as cats or oxen or monkeys or peasants or savages than as civilised men—indeed, I think the lower orders are greatly to be envied; and that it might be wise to choose membership in them if one could have a set of emotions to match. But given the emotions of civilised man—and a certain percentage of every highly-organised race-stock can't help possessing such evolved emotions as a matter of biologic accident—are we not fools if we think we can get any peace or comfort from the tinsel gewgaws of physical repletion which form the goal and summum bonum of clods? Then why listen to the advice, or resent the jeers, of clods who don't know what they are talking about when they apply their homely platitudes to you? What in hell do those swine know about *your* mind and feelings, and the eternal restlessness of a sensitive and highly-organised personality whose only possible satisfaction is in the perilous adventure of humanism? *Their* heaven would be *your* hell. In trying to grasp *their* kind of happiness, you would be losing the only kind which could ever be real happiness to you, like the dog in Æsop, who dropped the bone for its reflection in the water. Do you mean to say that you seriously fancy the dull life of a successful, unimaginative worker or business-man holds any true reward for *you* or for any other sensitive and civilised person? If you do, then I can't explain the urge which makes you need to argue and hold opinions about reality. But I don't think you do, when it comes down to close analysis! So I advise you to start a library. You can't imagine how much it will enrich your life—give you a sense of command over gates and doorways of escape from stifling physical limitations into infinite avenues of imaginative freedom and magnificence. My whole idea of a book is that of a *doorway*—as you'll see from the bookplate which I chose in preference to the heraldic one used earlier in my family. I had the artist make it a graceful *Georgian* doorway in order to bring it still closer to my personal tastes and milieu—for the Georgianism expresses both the atmosphere of Old Providence and my own individual antiquarianism. You can keep this sample bookplate—I own the die, and can always have as many as I like struck off. You may want a bookplate of your own later on, if you accumulate a library and get attached to it—and it's very easy to get attached to one's library, even when one doesn't lapse into the artificial affectation of binding-worship and first-edition-mania, or the Charles-Lamblike sentimentality of extravagant bibliolatry and print-and-paper apotheosis. If you ever do want a bookplate, I can put you next to some artists who'll turn out a good job without ruining you financially—I know one who'll give you conservative decorative effects as in my own plate, and another who can furnish a more impressionistic modernism—or give you the address of a company which furnishes a wide variety of graceful stock designs with any name printed on the paper plates. But first, the BOOKS! I appreciate the force of your baseball-game-and-knothole metaphor, but can't help feeling that it implies limitations on your part which are only imaginary. Just begin gradually with a few lines of reading, and you'll find the price of full admission to the game will gradually accumulate in your pocket . . . . and that your suit will slowly get pressed into such quietly correct lines that you won't feel any oddities or shabbiness of costume. You don't have to sit in the front row—god knows I don't myself!—but you can at least get a regular bench in the rear and sit beside my gang . . . . me and Coates and Orton and Long and all the fellows you've heard me talking about. We're no shining lights, but we simply feel that the outsidest kind of outsideness is a little too chilly for comfort. Back seats suit us plenty; but in general we feel that the *reverse* of the old coon song is true of the Temple of Enlightenment—and that 'it's better to be on de inside lookin' out than on de outside lookin' in'!

As for what you consider 'fraudulent' in my attitude—i.e., the fact that I hold a few strong personal preferences despite my principle that one's view of the cosmos should be objective, uncoloured, and impartial—hol' yo' hawsses, man! Have I ever objected to personal bias *so long as it does not colour one's perception of the external world?* Haven't I confessed to strong prejudices and enthusiasms in a dozen odd directions here and there? Didn't I freely say that I think Anglo-Saxon culture is worth fighting for, that I'm intensely fond of cats, that ancient Rome arouses my enthusiasm, that India gives me a pain in the neck, and so on, and so on? Hell! Everybody has his personal likes and dislikes—but the point is, that a man of sense doesn't let these things make him believe what ain't so, and disbelieve what is so! There's where I try to be impartial. For instance—I think the old culture with its idea of quality versus size is worth fighting for—perhaps the only thing on earth worth fighting for—*but I don't think it's going to win.* I have as much belief that a blighting barbarism of machinery and democracy is inevitably coming, as has any imaginationless sausage-trust financier or ethics-drunken parlour socialist. I hate it like poison, but I see it ahead. Here is a case of not allowing the very strongest of feelings to sway my intellectual opinion in the least. Another thing—I hate a jabbering Frenchman with his little affectations and unctuous ways, and would defend the English culture and tradition with my last drop of blood. But all the same I can see clearly that the French have a profounder culture than we have—that their intellectual perspective is infinitely clearer than ours, and that their tastes are infinitely farther removed from animal simplicity. What Anglo-Saxon could have written Balzac's Comedie Humaine or Baudelaire's Fleurs du Mal? It is only in *poetic* feeling of the main stream that we excel the French, so that in point of civilisation it is only figures like Shakespeare and Milton and Coleridge, Byron, Shelley, and Keats, that we can hold honestly above them. They are the Greeks of the modern Western World, as we are the Romans. *But*—for all that, my blood is eternally on the other side, and my memory full of ancestral images of Old England's hedged fields and willowed brooks, village steeples and abbey chimes. I shout as loudly as any Anglo-Saxon for the stout long-bowmen of the Black Prince, and for the glory of Crécy, Poictiers, and Agincourt. God Save the King! The Frenchman is our superior, god damn him, but he'll never set foot on an inch of English soil—not while Wellingtons and Nelsons, Phippses and Wolfes, hold the frontiers of our race in the old world and the new! . . . . not while the Georgian steeples of Boston and Providence ring with joy at the fall of Louisburg and Quebec!—not while Rhode Island breeds men and ships like Capt. Daniel Fones and the sloop *Tartar!*[16]—and so it goes. Do you see any interference between emotion and intellect? I shout at every French prize that Capt. Abraham Whipple (my collateral ancestor) brings into Providence harbour and delivers to His Majesty's prize court of admiralty at Newport—but all the same I coolly concede that the French are more deeply civilised than ourselves.

As for democracy—I don't really see much to add to what I said before. The whole thing is as much an illusion as "romantic love"—only it happens to be the illusion of the 20th century instead of the 19th. It is a mere deification of the ethical abstraction of "justice", plus the crude modernistic devotion to quantity as opposed to quality. If made a cardinal principle, it can do nothing but harm to civilisation—and yet, as I said before, I don't let my opinion interfere with my estimate of the situation. The evil is very definitely on the increase, and will probably spread until it has lowered our culture to a level scarcely endurable to a civilised being—unless, by chance, a counter-movement of intellectual-aesthetic aristocracy can somehow manage to coexist with a state of social-political democracy. The social-political future of the United States is one of domination by vast economic interests devoted to ideals of material gain, aimless activity, and physical comfort—interests controlled by shrewd, insensitive, and not often well-bred leaders recruited from the standardised herd through a competition of hard wit and practical craftiness—a struggle for place and power which will eliminate the true and the beautiful as goals, and substitute the strong, the huge, and the mechanically effective. I'd hate to have descendants living in such a barbarism—a barbarism so tragically different from the old civilisation of New England and Virginia which rightly belongs to this land. Thank God I'm the last of my family—*requiescamus in pace!*

Once again you get misleadingly *over-concrete* when you say that my ideas about democracy would have been changed by army experience as a private soldier. Do you think I have so little power to reason abstractly that I'd have let transient personal experience—the personal experience of one mediocre individual *in an essentially non-typical, emergency situation*—interfere with my general conception of values as applied to the normal course of whole nations and cultures? I knew just as well as you, before hand, that an enlisted man has to undergo ordeals of devastating repulsiveness and humiliation which of course a gentleman won't endure *in times of peace*. But does not a state of general warfare alter all standards? In times of peace nobody but a maniac would live in a dugout or stand in the path of flying missiles—but temporary needs breed temporary measures. One braces oneself for horrors both of the flesh and of the spirit—and it has never been considered a social stigma to serve in the enlisted ranks *in time of war*. Of course, one wouldn't want to get in a regular army or drafted outfit unless some transfer made it obligatory later on—for the majority of the best citizens of the community, who are not officers, are usually found in National Guard units. But even there one expects very irritating things, and naturally prepares to submerge his own personality for the duration of his service—with the sole exception of that part of the will which touches on the single ideal of victory for one's own civilisation and hatred and extirpation for any force opposed to that civilisation. If a person be of such a temperament and tradition as to base a large part of his emotional life on the image of his race and culture as a proud and dominant group, it is very easy to see how he might manage to hold his other emotions in abeyance for a while—accepting his daily lot in the ranks as if it involved another person, and submitting to an ignominy of personal status with some grace because of the compensating exaltation of feeling inherent in his symbolic identification with the conquering forces of his racial and cultural fabric. He would so thoroughly separate this transient experience from the normal current of his life as a whole, that it would scarcely occur to him to associate military indignities with corresponding indignities of civil existence. To have one's military personality insulted by a crude non-commissioned officer or tactless or parvenu officer would seem like a temporary unreality—to be endured like cooties, shell-dodging, and trench squalor in general; all the more so because one would realise that as soon as service concluded, one could freely kick the offending sergeant in the buttocks as a clod and inferior, socially cut the parvenu officer and send him back to his chain-store counter, and give the tactless social-equal officer a clout on the chin that would make him fight back like a man or be ostracised as yellow. Not but what one would often find philosophy difficult during service—or but what one might easily have many bitter passages-at-arms with arrogant military superiors; but I can hardly picture these things as producing anything but a personal hatred of the individuals abusing their emergency-conferred status and privileges. I can't picture myself as hating the *cultural ideal of aristocracy* merely because a plebeian or anybody else gets a temporary advantage over me and rubs it in. I would realise, in the first place, that my presence in the given situation was the result of voluntary choice; so that the symbolism of the whole affair would be different from that of actual membership in a permanent lower class. I would know that my outwardly tame compliance meant *no permanent relinquishment of my claim as a gentleman and freeman,* but was instead only a part of *my own dedication* to the purpose of wiping out the enemy of my culture. The final right of choice would always rest with me—and if, in the course of some sudden political overturn or mutiny, the army ceased to represent its original purpose of extirpating the foreign foe, I would no longer consider myself bound morally to my former acquiescence. In the event that such an overturn involved the use of the army *against* my own culture—as the armies of Russia in 1917 ceased to fight for Russian civilisation and turned about to destroy it—I would refuse both obedience and service, and accept the consequences as philosophically as I could manage—just as the decent French accepted the guillotine as philosophically as they could when offered a choice betwixt death and mob-truckling. There are things a gentleman *can* do, and things he can't do. He *can* bow to ignominy in the service of a purpose *which is his own and his race's,* but he can't accept that same ignominy when the system involving it is imposed *from outside his own will.* He *then* prefers to relinquish life, rather than to relinquish the proud *unbrokenness* which makes him a gentleman and distinguishes him from peasants and plebeians and Jews. In the ranks of my own nation, fighting that nation's foes, I would keep my temper down and make the best of a bad situation whose possibilities I would have perfectly foreseen. But in ranks dedicated to any *other* purpose, I would tell any insulting superior to go back to the kennel where dogs of his breed belong—realising in advance that it would involve fatal results. Those results I would consider inevitable—since a further existence at the price of *outside* humiliation would be intolerable to an *unbroken* spirit. I cite all this at length, because it expresses *precisely what passed through my own mind in 1917* when I tried to get into the service. I'm no romanticist, and I never had the least thrill of dress-parade glamour about the matter—any more than I had any use for the current hokum about "a great moral crusade for liberty, democracy, the great heart of all mankind." Bullshit! I no more pictured the Central Powers as devils and baby-crucifiers and the Allies as winged saviours than I pictured Santa Claus as an annual reality. The fact is, I deeply *respected* the Germans in an abstract way, as I respect all proud and unbroken Nordics. But the fact remained that I happened to be an Anglo-Saxon myself, with an emotional balance and sense of normal placement wholly dependent upon a mental image of membership in a world-dominating fabric. The idea of belonging to anything but the world's ruling civilisation is so outrageous to me—so devastating to my feeling of personal dignity and even personal identity—that a challenge to that civilisation has all the force of an individual insult in my consciousness. The preservation of Anglo-Saxon world-supremacy is essential to my personal immunity from insults, indignities, and humiliations. This—remember—is something all apart from my objective philosophic views; a mere personal condition of no importance to anyone but myself. Well—the result of this condition was, that I of course felt deeply disturbed at the war's challenge to England's power—and doubly so when the chances of German success seemed to grow. I tried to work off my emotion in verse, for as a cynic I hardly cared to risk hardship and suffering if others could do it for me; but with the lapse of time and the stimulus of America's entrance—involving visible preparations all around me—the literary medium became inadequate, and I felt a sense of constant emotional repression and unfulfilment—just as I feel today, in a more hopeless fashion, over the menace of the machine-age which I have no power to avert. It seemed desirable, in the interest of adequate aesthetic values, to achieve a fuller symbolisation of my ardour for Anglo-Saxon conquest—hence my endeavours to enter the companies of Coast Artillery which the R.I. Natl. Guard was forming to swell the collective forces. I realised, as I have said, the hardships and humiliations inseparable from the lot of a common soldier—but the emotional reward seemed to me adequate. Of course I intended to study for a commission the first thing after getting in—but knew that, being non-practical and non-mathematical, and with no executive experience, my chances for success in that line weren't good. Thus I was prepared for the worst—including transfer, through replacement drafts and reorganisations, to regular-army and conscripted units whose personnel might be expected to represent the nadir of heterogeneous rabbledom. I was prepared to accept the experience as a fantastic, Dantesque dream . . . . . wholly apart from the previous and subsequent course of my life, and involving a temporary confusion of all values save the one representing the victory of my kith and kind . . . . . St. George and Old England! Rhode-Island Invincible! Death to all who oppose the dominant Anglo-Saxon! As it happened, a couple of repulses put my design on the blink[17]—and today I don't know as I have enough regard for the objective world and the incidents of a decaying Western Culture to try such a thing at all. But if I had succeeded, I don't think the result would have been to make a democrat of me. It might very conceivably have altered my emotional life in this way or that, as I gather from the war-narratives of many sensitive men—the exact sort of alteration depending on my particular set of experiences. But I do not think, on the whole, that I could ever have woven antinomian and democratic generalisations out of my own experience. It would have been too clear to me always that my own case was a purely isolated and non-typical thing—that my position in the ranks was the result of my own dulness and failure to win a commission—that thousands of other well-born men were enduring just the same thing—that my own peace-time place and personality were not affected at all—that stern authority was a necessity in an emergency, and that one in a subordinate place *ought* to be subordinated. That last is a very strong point, and perhaps too subtle and abstract a thing to seem plain at first to a predominantly concrete and non-analytical mind; but to me it is almost paramount. In a word, my aesthetic devotion to a given system is so complete, that I can easily imagine myself *siding with the system against my own individual body*. It would not be siding against my own *mind,* because my mind—or collective personality—has no complete existence except as the sum of certain emotions including the love of the system. The system becomes an inseparable part of my own sense of identity and existence. I reflected on this point very thoroughly—and, I think, self-understandingly—in 1917. It is my one dominant wish that an *Anglo-Saxon culture exist, that it be paramount in the world, and that it be so organised as to retreat as far as possible from the primitive toward the fullest utilisation of the manifold and delicate cosmos-exploring and pleasure-experiencing capacities of the human species.* Compared to this, all my other wishes are minor ones. I expected my emotions on this matter to override and block out any other emotions which the vicissitudes of military service might breed, and I still think they would have had at least a chance of doing so. But for all that, I wish I had had the experience of service. There is no question but that it would have aided in the breadth and realism of my conceptions of human values, emotions, and motivations. As a last word on this argumentative illustration—let me point out that your parallel of army-tyranny and aristocratic political-social organisation has two grave defects. First—that even a democratic civilisation could never abolish army-tyranny, since in time of war the present and traditional system of complete subordination is *absolutely necessary* to the operations of a military unit—so much so that soldierly obedience could not in any way become a legitimate symbol of non-democratic civil life. And second—that no civil aristocratic system desired by philosophic aesthetes involves any such absolute and physical checks upon the freedom of any individual as does the emergency discipline of an army. It is impossible for an habitual logician to connect the two ideas—and I don't see how I could have done so.

Returning to the general aristocracy-democracy argument—you say that my motivating idea of the fostering of the highest intellectual and aesthetic expression ought to lead to a system with equality of opportunity rather than one with fixed castes. Well—did I ever say I wanted fixed castes? On the contrary, all I'm interested in are fixed *standards,* and the best methods of keeping them at the highest possible level. It seems to me I've often said that I don't believe in closing all the channels between classes. *Most certainly, there ought to be a steady recruiting of the upper classes from the lower. But this recruiting mustn't be so rapid as to swamp the delicate and highly evolved intellectual-aesthetic standards of the highest existing class,* as it would certainly do if carried to excess. Nobody wants to push anybody down if the person is really qualified to enter into the harmonious life of the dominant stratum; but a good many *do* want to see that the rapid up-climbers don't bring their crude ideas and feelings with them, and thus give a cast of rawness and crudity to the dominant life and thought of the civilisation. If everybody in a nation could be given the mellow culture that characterises the nation's highest thought, there would of course be no need for social classes. But it simply can't be done. There's no way of establishing a set of influences calculated to ensure the high education, emotional refinement, and civilised living of uncounted millions of people doing thousands of different things. Obviously, if a civilisation is to exist, a certain number of individuals must be given a training and environment above the average, with more than the average opportunities for freedom, influence, and self-expression. This is virtually axiomatic except among utterly irrational and ethics-mad communists and I.W.W.'s.[18] The only question is how to determine a principle of selection. Now there is just *one* basic quality of real weight in this question as practically envisaged, and that quality is simply this: *the relative ease with which the material can be moulded to the desired type.* We want certain types to exist—and we don't care where they come from. We have no energy to waste—and therefore must select the candidates for the desired type from those *closest to it already*—from those who can become the desired thing with the least expenditure of effort on the community's part. Now the most logical candidates are clearly the children of those already belonging to the type—children whose heredity and infant environment do more than half the necessary work of adaptation. To neglect this ready and predisposed material and waste energy in the forced cultivation of promiscuous elements with no natural or acquired adaptation for civilised life and feeling, is sheer idiocy, sentimentality, extravagance. There is no rational excuse for such criminal weakness of policy. Every dictate of sense, and of regard for the national welfare in matters of cultural status, demands that our best qualified elements be conserved—at comparatively slight effort—in their present status, rather than that they be neglected in a mad and wasteful attempt to force unsuitable and unqualified elements into equal influence and articulateness—and at so rapid a rate that much of their unsuitability and non-qualification will inevitably be carried upward with them into the dominant national life. Amidst such a forced process there can never at any time exist the sort of serene stability and settledness of custom and feeling which the development of a true culture absolutely demands. Some group of people has got to be *let alone* to evolve that sort of integrated mental-emotional life which only mellow, continuous thought and custom, plus reflective leisure and absence of economic problems and motivations, has any chance of evolving. They must be let alone, without the constant handicap of competition with alien, half-digested material calculated to vitiate and nullify all that they achieve. Not that they need to be a wholly hereditary group, but that they ought to be just hereditary enough to ensure the continuity of hereditary refinements and sensitivenesses. They can accomodate newcomers, but only so far as the newcomers are such as have previously modelled themselves to the desired pattern. Good outside material ought to have a chance of so modelling itself—but the process should not be forced, or made a wholesale sentimental obligation on the community's part. The important thing is not *who shall be in the civilised class,* but *that a civilised class shall exist.* Don't worry—your Burns's and Lincolns couldn't be kept out of this class in the end. There are no 'mute inglorious Miltons'—that was just Mr. Gray's urbane literary sentimentality. It would take a *literal* "caste" system—such as no Western nation has ever had or wished to have—to keep down such naturally able sons of the people as the astronomer Herschel, the poet Keats, the scientist Faraday, the late statesman Stresseman,[19] etc. Ability, by a process of natural selection, always finds its way up—indeed, the natural inclination and adaptation of brilliant minds to membership in the dominant culture-group *is in itself that very thing* which forms the basis of logical candidacy as previously mentioned—i.e., *the relative ease with which the material can be moulded to the desired type.* These superior plebeians may well be considered as just as eligible for a rational aristocracy as are the children of aristocrats—and indeed there has always been a tendency to regard them as such, even under the least democratic of regimes. But there aren't many naturally superior people in the world, so that if a nation is to have a cultured class large enough to make a suitable audience for its artists and thinkers, it must necessarily include a vast number of more mediocre minds within the circle of the cultivated. It is here where heredity and predisposition so greatly simplify matters. Of two ordinary minds, one born and reared under good influences is so *overwhelmingly* closer to the desired type than one of crude origin and early surroundings, that it would be imbecility and crime to try to boost the latter into a position of competition with the former. Real culture springs only from the continuous existence of a group who develop their sensitivities to the full, express themselves without ulterior motives, and reflect the mellow influence of an unhurried and undisturbed experience-stream—a group secure enough not to be worried by greed or material ambition, and large enough to have a collective life in a real sense; a set of natural mores and traditions, and a reading and appreciating element substantial enough to work out rules of taste and applaud and inspire the genuine artist. In this group there ought to be much of the hereditary, though of course no barrier against rising outsiders fitted to assume the traditional standards and folkways. What is wanted is *not any rigid caste fixed by law,* but simply an economic system rendering existence less competitive to persons able to conform to the highest cultural standards; and—*vastly more than this*—a national psychology willing to accept as its goal and standard *the philosophy of quality rather than quantity in achievement and life,* plus a political system which allots influence on the basis of intellect and taste rather than on the basis of numbers. Make no mistake about this. *Nobody wishes to place the lower orders under a Bourbon despotism, or to make their lives and acts subject to the will of any other class.* All that is wished is *to give the evolved life of the cultivated an ampler field of development and influence*—a larger voice in the national life, and a greater share in the moulding of national policy and standards. This is to be accomplished in subtle and gentle, rather than rigid, ways. It would be done through the arrangement of educational systems[*], the governmental attitude toward art and letters[†], the distribution of tariff, industrial taxation, and other economic advantages in favour of small business at the expense of large, and of agriculture instead of manufacturing and commerce; the decrease of money in circulation, and discouragement of the vicious circle of overproduction and forced consumption—inculcation of greater thrift, and more modest standard of material living for all classes—breaking down of quantity ideal by increased difficulty in excess profits—decrease in permissible profits on capital in purely speculative and non-essential industries, but unlimited freedom of profit in small basic industries and in every form of agriculture or other activities involving permanent land tenure; the establishment of moderate provisions for primogeniture and entail of property, and abolishment of all inheritance taxes—heavy taxation of luxuries and amusements of non-cultural value, with no taxes on cultural or educational enterprises and amusements; the skilful moulding of public opinion in the right direction by judicious educational

---

[*]liberal for sons of gentry—specialised industrial for various branches of working class.

[†]subsidies to artists, a national academy with awards, a bureau of fine arts and education, etc.

propaganda*—efforts toward the discouragement of cheap or industrial standards of constant work and heavy gain, and toward the acceptance of a standard of *being* rather than *doing*—a little excellence rather than much mediocrity; franchise by educational and racial-ancestral (to ensure the growth of a culture homogeneous with our 300-year-old Nordic civilisation) tests—limited to Nordics (as scientifically defined by statute) plus the scions of any ancestors in the U.S. before 1820 or so; the limitation of office-holding of every major sort—executive, legislative, judicial, diplomatic, etc., and all minor offices above the municipal—by general custom, and as far as practicable by law, to men of the definitely cultivated class; etc. etc. etc. It would be worth any amount of money and effort and patience to get the people of the United States reconciled to such an ideal as this—for it would restore to the country that most precious of all boons; the possession of sufficient rewards for the ordeal of living, to justify the pain and monotony and travail of that ordeal. At present it cannot be said that the life of any civilised and sensitive man in America is really worth living—except so far as he is able to make an imaginative escape from the encroaching milieu, either into the past of his culture-stream or into a fantastic and hypothetical future of his own dreaming. Clods can stand the usurping barbarism very well—it quite expresses their utilitarian minds and stunted personalities—but fully evolved human beings will have to return to the old world unless something can be done toward restoring the civilisation of the new. Already, the exodus of sensitive men to France and England is becoming marked. The quantity ideal of the overspeeded machine "civilisation" of this continent is too utterly sterile to make the process of consciousness bearable to anyone of evolved imagination and delicately attuned emotions. There is no reward for keeping alive—no food for the myriad spiritual hungers of the civilised personality. It became that way in later Imperial Rome, and sensitive men had to flee to the Hellenistic East—to Alexandria and Athens, Pegamus and Antioch—in order to find an air that they could breathe. And yet, as I have pointed out, the alternative course which civilised men desire for America does not mean the reduction of the lower orders to serfdom or villeinage. In cold fact, they would probably be far better off than under the present and future "democratic" system, since the chief object of an aristocratic culture is to check not *the peasant and artisan, but the grasping burgher and industrialist.* Generally speaking, the industrialist-financier is always a worse enemy to culture than the outright plebeian—indeed, it is only in China and Mediaeval Italy that a merchant class has ever really fostered civilisation over any long continuous period. We

---

*Idealisation of *cultivated* rather than *financially successful* life; honours paid to men of *pure* science (like Millikan, Hale, Shapley, Michelson, Osborn, etc.) instead of men of *industrial* science like Edison; praise of thrift and *competence* rather than ceaseless industry and quick wealth; honours to poets and artists, not engineers and business men.

know, alas, from abundant historic precedent, what a commercial "civilisation" is like. Carthage had one! Simple peasants and labourers are at least closer to nature and the fundamental realities than are middle-class traders and hagglers—parasites who deal with money as a commodity in itself—and all aristocratic cultures draw more from their artless ways than from the sterile existence of the bourgeoisie. It would be an excellent policy to enforce higher wages for the simple workman and lower profits for the grasping merchant and manufacturer. Let the way up to financial independence be just enough harder than now to weed out the parvenu profiteers and subject the climbers to such a discipline that their rough corners will be smoothed off by the time they reach the heights and seek to enter the civilised class from which leaders and public officials are drawn. And let the *material* incentives for this entry be diminished, in order to discourage material-minded persons from attempting it in great numbers. This might be done by letting the estate of aristocracy involve *no financial advantage*—or as little as could possibly be arranged. Likewise, it would be well to discourage peasants and workmen from trying to become burghers and traders, by making their wages as high and their lot as comfortable as possible. With more favour and comfort for the plebeian, and less for the trader and industrialist, the foundations of a much firmer cultural structure could be laid. And of industrialists, the agriculturist ought to have first favour, as one whose land-tenure and economic place most closely ally him to the traditional historic structure of our civilisation. The greatest of all changes would have to be a subtle and spiritual one, instilled by education and propaganda—namely, the teaching of that vast fundamental truth, that size and "prosperity" mean nothing in themselves, and that the only good of permanent value in all life is the leisure and freedom to develop an intelligent and imaginative personality. To change the popular objective from speed and ready money and wealth to thrift and security and tasteful leisure; and to eradicate the plebeian's envy of the leisured aristocrat by demonstrating the value of that aristocrat's existence in establishing standards which make the long burden of life worth carrying. Then, too, it must never be lost sight of that the door to aristocracy is always open to the really qualified aspirant. Many official and unofficial ways of helping the assimilation of likely material could be devised, and some valuable recruits might undoubtedly be gained—more, in all probability, from the lower classes than from the merchant-manufacturer class. For after all, the essential quality of the real aristocrat and man of taste is simply a first-hand and disinterested contact with thought and beauty—a contact independent of personal ambition and thoughts of material profit and usefulness. This absolute directness is virtually impossible with the bourgeois type, but it does frequently occur in the peasant and workman. In this affinity betwixt top and bottom lies a possible hope of abating the obstacle of plebeian envy. It is mostly the plebeian, *not* the trader and industrialist, who envies the leisured and cultivated gentleman; because the trader is too eager to ape the externals of gentility himself to envy the class he copies. If we can alter the alignment enough to let the plebeian feel that he and the aristocrat stand together spiritually—as men who value *things in themselves*—leisure and pleasure—and not the empty commodity of financial rating or industrious speed and quantity—we can possibly achieve a balance of forces favourable to mutual toleration. There is no question but that the existence of an aristocracy and an aristocratic standard of taste is really of great value in giving all classes a goal to live for. When you praise your plebeian heroes—Burns and Lincoln and so on—you forget that *a thoroughly democratic environment would probably never have called them forth.* In a system favouring mediocrity it is not likely that *anybody* would be moved to supreme effort. The mute inglorious Miltons would remain mute—or become cinema subtitlers and advertising men—and the Burns's and Lincolns would never be heard from except as syndicate columnists and corporation presidents. It is the existence of an aristocracy above them which makes people wish to get out of the common rut and live instead of commercially and materially vegetate. Lacking an emulous motive, they would stay as they were before, or follow the standard pattern of achievement dictated by an inferior civilisation. However—don't get the idea that persons of genius are as frequent among the existing lower orders than [*sic*] among the upper classes. So far as physical and biological capacity goes, the present upper classes are distinctly superior through natural selection—because the grade of men likely to have climbed their way up, or to have been chosen originally by historic circumstance, is of course higher than that now remaining at the bottom. They are physically and biologically higher, and of course certain to breed a higher grade of offspring. This is no mere theorising—army psychiatric tests in war time shewed the conditions plainly, and did much to send the democratic fallacy to oblivion, along with god and Jesus and romantic love, in the minds of disinterested and non-ethical scientific observers. There is no myth about selective breeding. Mankind has its thoroughbreds and its Percherons;[20] and if one is looking for exceptional specimens, one will certainly find an overwhelmingly greater number in the thoroughbred class than in the Percheron class. Nor can a democratic system turn Percherons into thoroughbreds overnight, or make Percheron sires and dams breed thoroughbred colts. *The fact that what equalitarians want is a general lowering-down instead of a general raising up is shewn by their characteristic manners and attitude. Democrats invariably ape the grotesque crudities of the lower orders and make conspicuous clowns of themselves; jeering at civilised speech, manners, and standards of accuracy and beauty instead of respecting these things and urging their beloved masses to work up toward them.* As long as they persist in this position, they will win nothing but the distrust and hostility of men well-disposed toward civilisation and the fullest realisation of the human personality.

I trust you see by this time that what I advocate is *not* a despotism of the Czaristic or Oriental order, but merely a well-balanced civilisation of the traditional Western pattern, which shall permit society to crystallise naturally into its accustomed strata in such a way as to bring out the highest potentialities of the race-stock. Nature *is* "in cahoots" with me in this matter, contrary to your jaunty offhand assumption—for it is only unnatural artifice which tries to drag down the flight of the strongest by clipping their wings and burdening them to make them as handicapped as the weakest. You say that 'exceptionally sensitive men and creative souls are as common in hovels as in castles'— but even if this were so, which as previously mentioned is undoubtedly *not* the case, it would not make the democratic argument valid. *The case is not so simple as all this*—you are eternally trying to *over-simplify and dogmatise on insufficient data.* Suppose individual geniuses *were* as common in hovels as in castles. Would that mean, at the same time, that the hovel-population in general could yield the cultivated non-genius body of appreciators, critics, and audience-elements necessary for the successful functioning of genius, as numerously and as readily as the already-well-adapted castle-population? Do you not see the absurdity of trying to train up an additional appreciating-body—at the expense of infinite wasted energy—*when one already exists?* We must grant that it is impossible to make *every* element in a complex community as capable of tasteful and appreciative living as a selected class can be—and only an enemy of the civilisation would wish to drag down the standard of the highest to match the highest possible collective standard of the entire body. Because some people must be trained to be mechanics and salesmen, it does not follow that everybody ought to be trained in a fashion tinctured with the spirit of the garage-helper and drygoods-drummer. We find by experience that the level of taste in an hereditarily aristocratic class is far above anything it could possibly be amongst a parvenu element. *Try as one can to stop it, crude standards are always dragged up to the surface of society when a crude element climbs up in overwhelming numbers and displaces an old aristocracy instead of being assimilated into it gradually. Here is where the castle has it all over the hovel.* Now I hope you have followed my arguments closely enough to see what I mean—*that even if the few actually creating geniuses could be drawn as frequently from the hovel as from the castle, it would be no sign that the cultivated appreciator-class as a whole could be of hovel as easily as of castle origin.* This ought to have been clear in the first place, but idealists are damnably slow in grasping a truth so hostile to their theories. In reality, of course, the contrast of classes in a culture needn't be as wide as the hovel-castle figure implies. Class ought to be a matter of heritage and standards and point of view rather than of *economic* distinction. In the last analysis, being a gentleman is a state of mind—whether it be birth or other circumstance which brings it into being. Real aristocracy is a worship of things in themselves without ulterior considerations—a pursuit of individual experience and self-realisation as

ultimate ends, with a corresponding regard for leisure and freedom, and contempt for material gain and physical utilitarianism. I know many absolute gentlemen of humble birth, and many insufferable mental plebeians who inherit a
coat-of-arms—but one can't calculate systems from exceptional individuals.
The humbly-born gentlemen I know wouldn't have had the qualities they
have, if a background of actual and recognised aristocracy had not existed in
the past to create the standards they follow. The machine age will never produce such men. It is hardly necessary for me to refute in detail the fallacy you
seem to imply in your complaint about certain aristocrats' wasted opportunities for life on a high plane—opportunities wasted in liquor, wenching, and
gambling. Aside from the case of a certain decadent element in Continental
Europe, with which we Anglo-Saxons have nothing to do, you must have
common-sense enough to know that the percentage of dissipated wasters is
no greater among gentlefolk than among any other class, and that it is probably far less than among the lower orders of the urban community. Every class
breeds its rebels against human and civilised restraint, and habits of even the
cautious small-merchant class are nothing to brag about. As for the town
rabble—gawd! The idle aristocrat may have his vices, but for sheer wholesale
swinishness—well, read any modern sociological study, consider the growth
of the underworld as symptomatised in Chicago racketeering, and then calculate percentages! Evidently you group *all* aristocrats—a class which of course
rightly includes all gentlefolk—country planters, professional men, the higher
grade of semi-leisured business men, etc. etc.—with that particular section
which the Hearst press singles out for vulgar exploitation; the decadent froth
of underbred and over-rich American bounders of the "400", plus the head-
line-gaining scum of fortune-seeking European nobility. You ought to have
sense enough not to make this mistake. The real aristocrat is the man of quiet
taste and responsibility—the New England professor or man of means, the
Virginia planter, or the traditionally sober and solid English country-
gentleman. I have enough good data—*concrete* as you please—on all of these
types to know *that they, and the refinement they reflect, are indeed no myths;* and that
only the machine-age destruction of the background which produced them
can ever alter or deteriorate their type. It is this alteration and deterioration
which I now fear—for malign and sinister social forces are at work. As a sort
of footnote to this topic I can't help appending a comment which is really
scarcely germane to the immediate issue, and which your emotions and point
of view may make it hardly possible for you to understand. It is this: that
since evolved self-realisation, *and not material gain or civic service,* is the only absolute goal of the free man of sense and culture; *there is really no more barbarism
in the decadent's pursuit of wine, women, and chance, than in the callous and non-aesthetic
industrialist's pursuit of money, physical splendour, and activity and quantity for their own
sake.* Indeed, the quest of the industrialist is even *less* sensible than that of the

decadent; since the former is denying true values and pursuing false values, whilst the latter is merely pursuing inadequate values without expressly denying the true or taking a wholly anti-civilised position. It is only because of several minor considerations, prejudices, and associations, that the decadent seems to us—in certain moods—more repulsive than the industrialist. Actually, he is not so great an enemy to our civilisation and to our task of maintaining genuine values in life. I now draw toward your vehement climax, in which you assert that democracy is inevitable *because* (as per Krutch) it is the *human* tendency to test each value and experience of life by the criterion of "what do I get out of it?"

God, man *what* a tangle you're in!

Why won't you try to sift and discriminate in handling ideas? *How* can we ever get an idea of what the other is talking about? Listen, 'bo, if you want to hear a seeming paradox.

1)　you are, alas, right in saying that democracy is inevitable.
2)　you are also right in endorsing Krutch's view that the humanistic tendency is toward individualistic seeking.
3)　BUT you are WRONG in thinking that (2) is the cause of (1).

Actually, the humanistic I-exaltation of the individual is the *one deadly enemy of democracy* as a permanent system, and would make democracy even temporarily impossible if it were highly developed and coupled with strength in many people. Each I tries to get all he can, and sooner or later *the strongest ones* build up a system favouring themselves and those they choose to succeed them— which lasts until *another* group of I's becomes strong enough to challenge it. Then the new group wins and reigns until another group gets strong enough to depose and supplant it. Groups follow one another, *as long as the humanistic I-element remains strong in the race*, like a succession of prize-fight champions— Sullivan to Corbett, Corbett to Fitzsimmons, Fitz to Jeffries,—Burns—Burns to Johnson, Li'l Artha to Willard, Jess to Jack, Jack to Gene[21] . . . . . *As long as the humanistic I-element remains a motivating force, democracy cannot exist.* **What is now making democracy not only possible but sadly inevitable is the decline of the humanistic I-element as the growth of the machine age destroys humanism and splits up the life of men into robot mechanicalism and animal simplicity. Humanism and democracy cannot coëxist.** Democracy means decadence—the triumph of the machine over the individual. The corollary to your curious misinterpretation of this matter involves another curious misinterpretation—that by which you seem to think I am unique in opposing democracy. Hell, man, read *The American Mercury* and the series of essays by H. L. Mencken entitled "Prejudices."[22] FIND OUT WHAT'S GOING ON!!!

You say 'that I ask the majority to resign humanism in order to permit a few to develop humanism highly', (or words to that effect) and that "even Krutch never thought of that." Good god, man, but what are you driving at? What am *I* 'thinking of' that millions haven't 'thought of' before? What am *I* enunciating except the ordinary and universally known arguments and value-estimates enunciated by *all* advocates of an aristocratic social-political system? Actually, of course, only a few are even human beings to the fullest extent. More may vaguely want to be, but there is no use in encouraging their feeble, futile stirrings, since such encouragement on a large scale would merely make it impossible for anybody to become human to the fullest extent of the race's capacity—that is, to realise and improve their humanism to the full. When a man of a subordinate class *does* possess a large amount of natural humanism in combination with sheer intelligence, he doesn't stay down long. He finds ways to rise, and the civilisation soon recognises his worth and helps instead of hinders his progress. All society is a struggle. You are naive and artificial when you assume that I fancy the lower elements could be *persuaded* to stay down in order to give opportunities to the higher. It is not a case of *persuasion* but of *management*. Only a few are generally strong enough to break through a system which they have been gradually worked into, and which really is capable of giving them as many boons as they are likely to get from a democratised system of their own. That the herd *can* be kept down under certain conditions is shewn by the history of the past, in which sporadic revolts have always been followed by re-subjugations. At present, it seems likely that mechanicalisation, and the consequent de-humanisation of the upper classes, is making democracy a fact; but if you will look closely you will find the *principle of subjugation still at work*. What modern industrial democracy does mean and will mean, is what you call *equality of opportunity*—the constant rise of the shrewdest lower-class *individuals* in large numbers to the places of power and wealth, and the consequent importation of lower-class standards into the general "civilisation". *But does this mean the end of the principle of subjugation?* Not on your tintype, kid! After all is said and done, and despite the isolated magnificent gestures of a few industrial profit-sharers like Ford, *what really IS the status of that industrial lower-class composed of individuals too stupid to work themselves upward in the democracy and therefore still functioning as a lower class?* Why, my dear boy, *it's becoming more and more the absolute pawn and football of the ruling intelligent stratum* . . . . and what does it get from the fact that that ruling stratum is only recently risen from its own ranks, and that some of its present ranks will some day rise into the ruling stratum? Think it over, son! Why, damn it all, if you were to talk to a *real communist,* as I have many a time, you'd think that your own democracy was Bourbon aristocracy! Try to pull your arguments about nature and opportunity on them—oh, boy! And try to tell them that the subjugation of the workman is a modern impossibility! This reminds me—I can put you on the trail of a roaring communist right now—an interesting bird whom our mutual friend Coates sic'd on me last year. He is *Henry George Weiss, Box 196c, Route 2, Tucson, Arizona*—a transplanted Bostonian with tuberculosis. He is a bright but emotional chap of 28, and he certainly can argue and rhapsodise like a professional. He ought to be the Russian Soviet Ambassador to the U.S. If you'd enjoy a hot argument in precisely the opposite direction from that you're now having with me, drop this kid a line of politico-philosophic opinion and await results. I like him very much. He contributes weird scientific stories to the magazines under the name of Francis Flagg—and you must have seen some of his stuff both signed and pseudonymous in *Driftwind*. There's no question but that these communists are right enough in saying that the workman is the slave of the industrialist. He is—and more than the peasant was ever the slave of the landowner in the old days. Can't you see what lies ahead of your democracy of opportunity? At present *the intelligent plebeians are climbing freely into the ruling class of industrialists*. But what of the **future,** *when* **all** *the intelligent stock will have climbed into the ruling industrial class, leaving the working class composed wholly of biological morons and mental defectives incapable of climbing or of mastering the increasingly complex technique of an industrial civilisation?* Look at the situation for yourself—*avenues open, but impossible of transit because of the low intelligence of a herd drained dry of their intelligent individuals through democratic natural selection.* The trouble with you is that you spend all your energy crowing over the immediate advent of something you like, and neglect to look ahead to the *next* step. Democracy, we agree, is inevitable *in the early machine age*. **But what then?** Here is the situation in a nutshell—2100 or 2200 A.D. Huge machine barbarism with incredible physical luxury and a vast ruling class of highly intelligent men trained to think in terms of money, size, speed, profit, and activity for its own sake. Technique and machinery so perfected that there are *too many intelligent men for the number of directive jobs requiring them;* a wealthy surplus trained to think so materially that aesthetic and intellectual traditions will be virtually closed to them. *A new aristocracy without the souls of aristocrats.* Here is where your common-peepulism breaks down. This aristocracy will be open to all—but who save its own members can mentally qualify? Remember that it was produced by the selection of all the first-rate brains (never a great percentage) in the race. What of the surplus? To me it looks very much like the old story of wine, woman, and chance—just what you object to in the baser elements of the present aristocracy! You see, history has quite a repetitive tendency, and you can't dodge the order of nature—which is essentially stratified—no matter how many ethical illusions you pile on! Of course it is conceivable that even in a machine age a new aristocratic culture might be worked out by the leisure class. That would bely both your wishes and my anti-machine predictions, but it is possible. Given a few generations of *enforced* leisure through lack of jobs, the wealthy surplus may at last turn to ways of cultivation and try to recapture the art of life—the art of *being* instead of *doing,* and of enjoying quality instead of quantity. But it will be up-hill work, for the lack of traditional background and the standardisation of a mechanised world won't be any myth or joke. Below this administrative and surplus ruling-class there will naturally be a fairly large *subordinate-executive* or *manager* class composed of moderate, third-rate intellects. This may be an in-dependent stratum made up of rising proletarians belted by limited brains, or it may be a social appendage of the ruling class, recruited from the occasional inferior minds which the superior stock will breed. And below this, infinitely varied within itself according to occupation, but virtually brainless because it will be the residue of a selective process, will be the vast industrial proletari-at—well-fed, well-housed, well-amused, well-clothed, well-medicated, well-treated, well-flattered; living its half-animal, half-vegetable round in perfect physical comfort, and with ample leisure for as much diversion as its brains will enable it to enjoy. It will have the privilege of rising as high as it can, but its potentialities of ascent will have long been exhausted. It will be the utter and implicit property of its intelligent masters. Free in law and tradition—but in fact completely and benevolently enslaved. What lies ahead of it? Conceiv-ably it may remain unchanged, once it has finally crystallised, until the grow-ing ennui of the upper classes causes a relaxation of the system and a Spenglerian end of the Western World. Then it will, of course, become a *sepa-rate race* in the ensuing barbarism; and may conceivably be slaughtered off by the virile and warlike tribes descended from the former ruling class. But this, of course, leaves out the complications which the existence of *other* cultures than the Western machine-culture may imply. There will be wars all along—fought by the intelligently offered hordes of brainless workmen—and it is possible that some Asiatic culture will conquer Western machinedom before the final ennui-collapse. Then again, it is possible that the machine world will be rent by civil warfare. A spontaneous revolt of the well-fed brainless class is unlikely, but it is very conceivable that they may sometime be stirred to revolt by discontented demagogues of the intermediate *manager-class;* especially if that class be composed of rising proletarians rather than inferior upper-class specimens. Or the demagogues might be one of those rare biological freaks—a superior type atavistically evolved by the brainless class itself, or perhaps a bastard begotten into the brainless class by men of one of the two higher classes—or perhaps an eccentric ethical doctrinaire from the surplus element of the ruling class. A revolt, if provided with intelligent leaders, might con-ceivably *succeed*—and what then? One or two things, probably. Either a com-munist state in which (as in Russia now) your favourite principle of *non-subjugation and equalisation* is extended to industry as well as to opportunity, with the result that all technology and commerce and administration above the low capacity of the brainless class under the ban* and gives rise to a stagnant, low-potential proletarian state; or else an utter chaos marking the end of the civilisation and the hastening of that new dark age and fresh start in tribal or feudal life which would have come soon anyway from Spenglerian causes. It may be toward this sort of collapse that a proletarian state would also lead; although such a state would have a chance of evolving a fresh stratification and possessing a sort of second mind as an opportunist democracy and finally an oligarchy again.

Well—I suppose that by this time, if you're not asleep over the tedious verboseness of my arguments, you're pleasantly rocking with Homeric laughter over the absurd abstractness and queer notions of that ridiculous old back number down in Providence . . . hee, hee, hee, haw . . . . Which is quite all right so far as I'm concerned! I've already made it plain that I don't think the sort of social political structure I favour has any chance of adoption in this decadent period, so you needn't charge me with being an 'impractical doctrinaire' and all that. Hell! nobody knows better than I do that there's no chance for the adoption of any consciously advanced individual theory of government in a world where everything is governed by a profound, hidden, deterministic trend beyond the reach of all deliberate action or reform. And just now, we both agree, the trend is toward a democratic organisation—which will muddle along for a while until the final Nietzschean master-and-slave arrangement comes in. At the same time I can't resist pointing out that my idea of an aristocratic culture may not be at all what you imagine as a result of half-formed concrete associations with the word "aristocracy". What I want to see is the element of mellow taste given supremacy in government and tradition-moulding, but this does not imply any stiff and grotesque aloofness or snobbery on the part of the ruling class. On the contrary, the upper orders in a publicly recognised aristocratic society can afford to be very democratic personally, since their positions and the safety of their civilisation are so securely assured. The perfect snob, cautious and timid about whom he can socially recognise or speak to, is essentially the creation of an insecure order, amidst which he has to assert what position he has through a pusillanimous self-assertion. Which leads me to remark, somewhat sardonically, that if snobbery is what you hate, you are wasting your time in advocating political democracy—since exclusive snobbish cliques will continue to persist even in the most democratic civilisation. They exist everywhere today, and will continue to exist in any order short of Soviet Communism. Now and always such cliques will set themselves apart from the rest of the vulgar rich class, and

---

*just as your present democrats seem anxious to place a ban upon all arts and refinements and traditions above the capacity of the rabble

through the practice of certain meaningless manners, and the harbourage of certain empty traditions, proclaim a factitious superiority to which neither birth nor cultivation entitle them. And just because of the loudness of their proclamations, most of the rest of the community will take them at face value, truckle to them except in the granting of political and economic power, and pay them the perennial compliment of imitation. They will have no aristocratic culture worthy of the name, because their position is too artificial and unconnected with continuous and recognised tradition to permit of their fostering one. They are too close to the speed-and-size ideal of the trading rabble, and too remote from the real aristocratic tradition of old New England and Virginia, to achieve any standard of taste other than an imitative affectation tempered by a pallid reflection of the mucker pose. Extravagance and lavishness—the typical ideals of the age—will be their distinguishing marks; and they will tend to that state of decadence before ripeness which is characteristic of all parvenu patriciates—all codfish aristocracies.[23] They will set themselves on parade, conciliating the rabble and lulling their envy through a pretence at industry or civic usefulness, and becoming the idols of a naive and imitative democracy. Admission to their circle will, as now, be prodigiously difficult to secure; and the heavens will ring with their assumptions of superiority. With their taste debased to suit the rabble's as the purchase-price of their regard and tolerance, their influence on the civilisation will be evil rather than good; so that the basis for their self-esteem will be doubtful and mysterious. They will be—and already are—what may be considered the *demagogues of the social world;* or in more succinct language, the perfect embodiments of the eternal genus *snob.* Personally I don't think these people do any extreme harm—and certainly they aren't as offensive as the industrialists—but I can't say that I consider them adequate successors to a *real* aristocracy whose dicta and assertions were designed to uphold *standards and traditions and motivating links with thought and beauty* instead of merely to boost the prestige and glamour of certain more or less commonplace and overdressed individuals with an exhibitionist complex. There's the essential difference between real aristocrats and democratic parvenu snobs—the aristocrats fought primarily to safeguard certain basic things *outside themselves,* whereas these parvenus fight merely for a cheap personal recognition. To my mind, your dear democratic system has not even the virtue of abating what is undesirable in aristocracy. Instead, it fosters and coddles a class which has all the drawbacks and none of the virtues of a true aristocratic group. However—I'll give you ethical idealists the credit of not relishing this side of the matter personally. You don't even need to explain to me that *you,* as an *individual,* have no use for the snobbish parasite fringe. All very well—but your system can't help nourishing them just the same. The instincts behind such groupings are deep in the blood of the human species, and when the *natural* stratification of a culture is interfered with, all sorts of grotesque, anomalous, and paradoxical *artificial* stratifications will spring up to take its place.

Altogether, it is not likely that you and I could ever agree about the structure of society; because the question is primarily one of *preference* rather than of *fact*. What one thinks on a subject like this is conditioned by his *wishes*—his individual set of emotions and imaginative leanings—and not by any of those rules of *reason* which are binding on all alike. In other words, it isn't a plain *is-or-isn't* matter, but a matter of *opinion* wherein we can say no more than "every man to his taste". All of our natural standards, inclinations, emotions, sympathies, points of view, habits of thought, instinctive enthusiasms, symbolic associations, and so on, are so utterly antipodal and antithetical in every way— as revealed in all our emotional reactions and habits of logic and language— that eye-to-eye vision in fields like this may be regarded as definitely impossible for all time. There are subtleties and overtones on my side that you can never "get", and subtleties and overtones on your side that I can never "get". Emotionally, neither of us is a good receiving set for the other's emotional and imaginative wave-lengths. The difference is basic and architectural and physiological—we're simply not built the same way, and our glands simply don't function the same way. And because all mankind is made up heterogeneously of individuals with just as great and greater dissimilarities, there can never be any unified body of opinion about anything, or any single collective goal or ideal for the entire race. Some people will always be working and fighting heart and soul for the very thing that other people are working and fighting heart and soul against. That's life. Utopian harmony? Hell!!

As for Krutch and Boyd, and their relative moods; Boyd is certainly the man of greater superficial sense, whilst Krutch is just as certainly the man of deeper insight. Boyd skates along the surface of things with many of his emotional sensitivenesses atrophied, always avoiding a full glance at the essence and meaning of the whole sorry jest of life. Krutch, on the other hand, is absolutely fearless; and almost alone among well-known philosophers has the guts to give a really square look at my eternal question of *"what is anything?"* I'd hardly say that Krutch is *trying* to bring about a reign of pessimism—it seems to me that he's really only expressing his own reaction to things as they are now and seem to be. Really, there ought not to be any such inclusive term as *pessimism*. "Pessimism" argues the existence of fixed and universal values which cause a certain outlook to be *intrinsically bad* as judged from every point of view. Actually, so dissimilar are the wishes of different people, there is no kind of "pessimism" which is not somebody's "optimism"—even the chaotic, purposeless, and standardless cosmos which so disturbs Krutch may mean for some people a happy irresponsibility and liberation; whilst the coming machine age, a curse to the highly evolved man, is no doubt very welcome to the callous and insensitive man of practical physical tastes and no imagination. Undoubtedly Krutch is over-disturbed about the present situation—shewing too little emotional adaptability, and too little stoicism in the face of the inevitable—yet he is really a far more acute and serious thinker than Boyd. Boyd's attitude of causeless joviality, in a world where nothing particularly exists to cause joviality, hints somewhat of forcedness and artificiality. Of course he is facetious in this recent article—in literal life you probably wouldn't find him (or anybody else) quite so bland as he theoretically appears to be. It isn't quite natural to keep such a constant hee-haw level when one has a keen imagination and still bears the impress of solid tradition. The goddam cosmos simply keeps on in its own way, as predetermined from eternity, without paying attention to the wishes of any of the conscious organisms which may flash up negligibly now and then on some of its material atoms. Since these organisms are cast in all sorts of different forms, with all sorts of different wishes and perceptions, it follows that some of them naturally tend to find pleasure in the immediate way they think their part of the cosmos is headed, some tend to find pain, and some don't give much of a damn one way or the other. These are, respectively, the "optimists", "pessimists", and "cynics". An "optimist" and a "pessimist" may sometimes *believe exactly the same thing*—differing only in their *personal feelings about it*. That's largely the way with you and me. Or an "optimist" and a "pessimist" may differ because they have the same goal, but differ in their belief about the world's ever attaining it. Thus you can't tell whether a man will be an "optimist" or a "pessimist" from a knowledge of what his intellectual beliefs are—you've got to know how he feels about them. And conversely, you can't tell what his beliefs are merely by noting whether he's an "optimist" or a "pessimist". It's a great world—and a cursed complex one!

I now get to your point anent not giving a hang about future cultural and racial dissolution on the same principle that most of us—of the generation under fifty—don't give a hang about personal dissolution. You make much of this point, but I don't think it weighs quite as heavily as you imagine. In the first place, possibly reasoning wholly from your own personal case, (you *must* temper your utter concreteness with a bit of abstractness if you want to know what's going on in the mental-emotional world!) you say that the idea of individual dissolution must always outweigh that of racial-cultural dissolution—an idea which is obviously a fallacy in any general sense. You leave out altogether the *associative and symbolising emotions* of the normal human mind, which cause all men of fully developed imagination to identify themselves with their general blood-and-folkway stream—both family and national-racial—to a greater or lesser extent. There is hardly a man living who hasn't *two* distinct pictures of his own ego—the individual picture, comprising his single personal self, and the panoramic picture, comprising his ancestry and posterity either physical or cultural, in which his personal self figures as one of a continuous series of manifestations, all of which possess a poignantly-felt relationship, and which collectively form a kind of physical or cultural immortality very satisfying to the emotions and wholly independent of the myths of supernaturalism and individual post-mortem soul-survival. To minimise this feeling from the point of view of cynicism is perfectly useless—for it exists just the same, whether or not it fits in with our theories to admit it, and has exercised the most powerful influence possible on the history of every race and nation. It is, of course, the basis of all family feeling and patriotism; and has functioned undiminished in many of the most materialistic and disillusioned of races—such as the French, Chinese, and the Graeco-Romans even amidst their greatest scepticism. There is hardly a materialistic philosopher who has not dwelt upon the gratifying nature of the idea of *immortality in one's descendants or in one's national future*. Whether, in its most acute form, it be in part a *secondary* instinct based on illusion, is a relatively minor matter. It is strong and real, and has to be reckoned with in practical life no matter how it came into being. Boyd minimises it, of course, for the sake of his own argument—but the real philosopher or man of science must take it into account. If an illusion, it is at least a far more solid illusion than those of democracy and romantic love, and probably more so than the illusion of justice. When the humanistic man asks of life, "what do *I* get out of it?", he instinctively includes in that "I" whatever is, for him, associated with the idea of his personality; and in more cases than not, his family and his race come into this larger *associative ego* somehow. He cannot feel personally placed without reference to the background which gives his thoughts and feelings the illusion of motivation and significance. We may say that every man's ego—the thing he fights to exalt and preserve, is a sphere with his body at the centre, and with its density rapidly diminishing as it extends outward. He cares intensely for his individual self; a little less so for his immediate family; a little less so for his social group; a little less so for his nation or race-stock; a little less so for his major culture-unit; (i.e., Western World, Asiatic World, etc., as the case may be) a little less so for mankind as a whole; a little less so for animal life as a whole; a little less so for life (both animal and vegetable) as opposed to the inorganic; a little less so for the terrestrial as opposed to the non-terrestrial; a little less so for the solar-systemic as opposed to the universal; a little less so for the galactic as opposed to the Einsteinically cosmic; and a little less so for the Einsteinian as opposed to the hypothetically infinite, unplumbed, and unimagined. Of course, the individual ego is at the base of it all—altruism as a principle is a myth and a joke—but in the course of nature the ego cannot avoid having symbolic associations with its environment; associations less and less poignant as distance increases, but all very vivid and real and practically motivating to the man of highly evolved personality and sensitive imagination. One can come to regard the total extirpation of one's individual part with comparative equanimity—that is, the present generation can—but the idea of the extirpation of all that gives one placement and significance is an altogether fresh pang; intrinsically much greater, since it wipes out the *last remaining* moorings to the cosmic stream, and requiring a whole new process of emotional readjustment comparable to that which we and our parents experienced when confronted with the death of the personal immortality idea. As we know, it costs the older people many a bitter pang to lay aside the dream on which they had based all their ideas of a desirable adjustment to infinity. Many cannot accomplish this renunciation even now—as a questionnaire-census among even the most cultivated and intelligent people over fifty or sixty would soon convince you. How, then, can *our* generation be expected to accomplish the *next* step with utter suddenness, and survey the idea of the death of all we cherish with perfect blandness? As a matter of fact it would be absurd and unscientific to imagine that we can do so. Because we are more used to scientific overtures and the scientific habit of thought than our parents and grandparents, we can of course accomplish the *intellectual* transition more easily than they could accomplish the corresponding one. We can *believe and realise* that our civilisation will end*, more readily than they could *believe and realise* that man does not possess an immortal soul. But we can't *like* the new idea any better than they could *like* the new idea which was thrust upon them. The next generation—the young fellows now in college—will get used to the new idea better than we; but it'll take still another generation to breed thinkers who accept a transient orientation and constantly shifting order as an absolute matter of course. They'll do it, no doubt, in the end—but that doesn't do *us* any good. And of course there *really is* a great emotional and aesthetic loss. *True or false,* any given imaginative stimulus or form of beauty-feeling *is a thing in itself;* and there's no denying that we've *actually lost* large slices of the heritage of feeling and vision which enriched the imaginative lives of our forefathers. Our emotions have to function on a lower potential—the net amount of energy which flows through them is less, and the net amount of pleasure we get out of them is less. The blasting of our *immortality-faith* is a *real loss,* and so is the end of our belief in a racial future. Romantic love, even, was something really gained and really lost between the Dark Ages and the present time. Don't fall for Keats's poetic fallacy that truth and beauty are one! Your own personal view of immortality as a *curse* from which you are glad to be free, is *not* a typical attitude in the Western World, hence you can't apply it as a philosophic generalisation. It occurs, indeed, in the *Hindoo* culture; but so few Western men can harbour such an attitude that with us it must be philo-

---

*i.e., end in a known and calculable way immediately connected with present trends. Philosophers have always looked ahead to an *ultimate* end of their civilisations, but it has always been in a vague, abstract way—so remote as not to involve personal patriotism. Just as young men are vague and abstract about death.

sophically negligible. The best we can do, emotionally, is to be *indifferent.* Of course, many of us prefer oblivion to *our present lives,* but relatively few Europeans prefer oblivion to *some possible life.* I myself could have a very fair time living on indefinitely if I had plenty of money, and if a congenial civilisation existed around me. There is so damn much to read and enjoy in the world, that no one mind *could* milk it dry in a thousand years. The ennui which overtakes most, *is itself merely a physical deterioration due to the same causes which later cause death.* Life is not worth living as we know it, but it *theoretically could be.*

And now I'll shut up at last. I've been at this ponderous document a full week—and gawd help you if you've tried to swallow it at one gulp!

With profoundest apologies—

Yr obt servt

H P L

Notes

1. HPL knew Maurice W. Moe (Milwaukee) and August Derleth (Sauk City) in Wisconsin. Alfred Galpin had gone to college in Appleton, but was now living in Paris.

2. HPL refers to Oswald Spengler (1880–1936), German historian and author of *Der Untergang des Abendlandes* (1918–22), translated into English as *The Decline of the West* (1926–28; 2 vols.), which proposed the successive rise and fall of civilizations throughout history. HPL read the first volume in early 1927; he does not appear to have read the second volume.

3. James Gordon Bennett, Sr. (1792–1872), American newspaperman who founded the *New York Herald* in 1835.

4. In fact, A.U.C. stands for "Ab Urbe Condita" (from the founding of the city [i.e., Rome]), canonically dated to 753 B.C.E.

5. HPL had probably learned of Russell's views on China by reading *Selected Papers of Bertrand Russell* (New York: Modern Library, 1927), which contains sections on "Chinese and Western Civilization Contrasted" and "The Chinese Character" (from *The Problem of China,* 1922).

6. The book was an exposé of the hollowness of literary work in the machine age. HPL did read it later, and purchased a copy for his library.

7. Robert Andrews Millikan (1868–1953), American physicist who attempted to reconcile science and religion; Arthur S. Eddington (1882–1944), British astrophysicist; Hilaire Belloc (1870–1953), British author and historian; G. K. Chesterton (1874–1936), British novelist and essayist.

8. Havelock Ellis (1859–1939), British sex theorist and author of *Studies in the Psychology of Sex* (1897–1928); Benjamin Barr Lindsey (1869–1943), American judge and coauthor (with Wainwright Evans) of *The Companionate Marriage* (1927); Auguste Forel (1848–1931), Swiss psychiatrist and author of studies on the sexual behavior of animals; Walter Franklin Robie (1866–?), American sexologist and author of several treatises on sexuality.

9. Dorothy Dunbar Bromley, "The Maternal Instinct," *Harper's Magazine* 159, No. (September 1929): 423–33. Bromley was also the author of "What Risk Motherhood?" (June 1929).

10. William J. Fielding (1886–1974), author of *Sex and the Love Life* (1927) and other treatises; Joseph Collins (1866–1950), author of *The Doctor Looks at Love and Life* (1926) and other works; Harry Allen Overstreet (1875–1970), American psychologist and author of numerous books on society and conduct.

11. Alexander Pope (1688–1744), *Moral Essays* 2.195–96.

12. HPL probably refers to *A Preface to Morals* (1929) by American political and social commentator Walter Lippmann (1889–1974).

13. Joseph Pennell (1857–1926), American artist who made numerous etchings of modern buildings in New York, Philadelphia, San Francisco, and elsewhere.

14. There does not appear to be a volume of Sir John Mandeville's travels in the Haldeman-Julius series. But HPL may have been referring to *The Voyage and Travels of Sir John Mandeville, Kt.* (New York: Cassells, 1886; *LL* 637).

15. The work in question was Mary Elizabeth Phillips, *Edgar Allan Poe: The Man* (1926). The Allen biography was first published in 1926, not 1927.

16. Daniel Fones (1713–1790) was captain of the British warship *Tartar,* which was part of the British fleet that captured the French city of Louisbourg, on Cape Breton Island, in 1745.

17. HPL alludes to the fact that his mother pulled strings to have him declared unfit to join the R.I. National Guard after he attempted to enlist in May 1917.

18. The Industrial Workers of the World, a radical leftist industrial labor union founded in 1905.

19. Gustav Stresemann (1878–1929), chancellor (1923) and foreign minister (1923–29) of Germany. He was the son of a beer bottler.

20. A breed of draft horse cultivated in what was formerly the Perche province of France.

21. HPL refers to the boxers John L. Sullivan, James J. Corbett, Bob Fitzsimmons, James J. Jeffries, Tommy Burns, Jack Johnson, "Little" Arthur King, Jess Willard, Jack Dempsey, and Gene Tunney.

22. Mencken published six volumes of miscellaneous essays on literature, politics, and society titled *Prejudices* (1919–27), chiefly taken from articles and reviews he had written in the *Smart Set* and the *American Mercury,* which he coedited with George Jean Nathan.

23. The social aristocracy of Massachusetts families enriched from the trade in codfish; any parvenu aristocracy based on commercial success.

[4]　　[ALS, JHL, verso page in ms. of "The Whisperer in Darkness"]

Vergennes, Vt

Jan 11, 1931

Dear Lovecraft:

I have neglected you for some time. No indeed I haven't been drunk all this time, truth is I seem to have swung into a very reasonable temperate course. But I have had a rather hard month. Early last month I had a rib broken in my back. I was hitching up my team and foolishly got in between the rack and a post so that if they started I was bound to be caught. They started and the heavy rack lunged into my back and the whole stopped dead on my body. It hit me low down—kidney region where there is a good deal of give. Well I have had ribs broken so many times I don[']t pay much attention. A rib up in the breething [*sic*; area] should be strapped up because the ribs move with breathing. But this one didn't bother me. Of course my side was pretty sore for over a month. I don[']t even know it was broken but I judge so after knowing how my other ribs have felt which the Dr has tended to. Then I am without help chores filling the day up pretty well and I have had two pretty bad spells with colds. I do detest being sick under conditions where I must keep right on working. For several days each time I was accutely [*sic*] afraid of pneumonia. From morning until about two P.M. I would have had hard work to do. Then come in and lay in a stupor with covers enough piled on to warm me then at it again. But I am feeling pretty good now.

We had a fine December for weather. Just recently we have had a blizzard. Did you know they make a real attempt to keep roads open for cars all winter now? The other night was very cold. 10° below zero next morning. I had to go down town to have my grange books audited—I am treasurer— Drove down in my truck entirely warm and comfortable inside the windproof cab. Had to walk a block from where I left my truck to the house we were visiting and damn near froze to death. A four mile drive wholly comfortable sitting still, and all the rigor of winter in walking one block in the city. You see we farmers are becoming the favorites of nature as well as the U. S. govt. Incident[al]ly it is quite a sight to drive at night with the huge snow banks on each side. Winter oil in the crankcase so refined that the starter works as well as in summer. $5.00 for a set of chains on the rear wheels. $5.00 for glycerene [*sic*] to fill the radiator (nonfreezing) a shovel in back to shovel yourself out if you get set in a drift, and there you are. Better than crawling inside a steam radiator with just a hole for your nose to stick out.

Business is rotten. Terribly low prices for eggs. But grain is as high as usual because Hoover let the farm board spend millions to keep up the price of wheat. He asked for [$]150 million more. Next day Coolidge's little piece was about the government fixing prices saying it was the wrong way and would not work. Hoover is going to be in bad by 1932. Hell will start popping once the

G.O.P. assemble in convention. I want a nadir then for I want to be in on that fight. I wonder if the Wickersham committee will get to report by then.[1] Have not yet tried any of Mrs. Willebrandt's grape concentrate[2] but I understand it is fine. Well I will end this foolishness and answer your letter.

Now as to the main body of your letter—your careful analysis of what you call the "emotional letdown" of the current era. I have just finished rereading it, a careful rereading as it held me engrossed from first to last same as it did seven weeks ago. Yes you present a real argument. I am more inclined to value it as a brand new peep hole upon the modern scene, than I am to argue with you. Especially seeing that at the close you refer to a future peak of experience, in which education has been reconciled with actual thought and experience, which will undoubtedly be far superior to the present but yet remain inferior to the previous peak.

After all I am not sure but that this last admission embraces most of what I was contending for. I don't mean that I contended for it at all well. No doubt your careful analysis boles [*sic*] me over at many points. But after all much argument is merely an attempt to rationalize a definite emotional state. So let me put it this way—your final admission, as I read it, makes me feel like I did before I started arguing. In other words after demolishing my faulty attempt at rationalizing, you then proceed to restore my self[-]respect. As for the comparative heights of the two peaks, that to me is wholly uninteresting. I can follow you when you speak of devitalized emotions in the present era, because to me the clash of belief and experience looms large.—a chronic, ever present, source of confusion. But when you move the clock ahead to where education and experience are reconciled, why then I refuse to argue. Admitting still all you say of the deep significance of the belief in cosmic purpose, even then I would claim we simply cannot know for sure as to the state of mind of these moderns. We can point out, as you do, a lot of things valuable to us which they will *not* have. But that is all. Can you with certainty for[e]cast the resiliency of the human spirit? Is it not possible that it will discover satisfaction for itself which we can scarcely for[e]see. You once put it to me that the future race would be so totally unlike us that you could scarcely feel any interest in them. Well my argument is as good for your side as for my own I admit. I admit it tends to become meaningless. But I again contend we are not justified in pronouncing judgment upon the future with too much certainty.

Well to leave this line in which I seem to have lost myself there is one definite point upon which I would like to question you. I wish I had Krutch's chapter on the "tragic fallacy" here so I could read it once more. I quote you. "There is a high sense of zest in *foreordained tragedy*, provided we believe the tragedy to be *real*, with elements closely involved in some great & purposive cycle. We can go down to doom, or to twilight, or to shadow, with an exquisite titillation of macabre satisfaction if we can only believe that the acts we have performed have had a true and mystical relationship to the will & conscious purpose of some vast power controlling the eternal destinies of the universe & the ultimate future of our race."

Now I am not arguing I am honestly asking for information. Some things I get easily, some come pretty slow. I would like to be able to discuss the classical idea of tragedy. And here I find you picturing it very different than I had it in mind. True the Greeks believed in the Gods! Fate surely loomed large. But did they believe in cosmic purpose? What purpose? Did they believe the race was pointed toward a glorious future? That is optimism man, not tragedy. You have got me all balled up. "A soldier of the Legion lay dying in Algiers. There was lack of woman's nursing, there was dearth of woman's tears. But a comrade stood beside him as his life blood ebbed away. And bent with pitying glances, to hear what he might say."[3] You doubtless recognize the exhibit. Tragedy yes but let us say the soldier died gladly realizing the glory his country is acquiring—I admit your emotional letdown here as this glory stuff is pure bullshit to me—in which process he has willingly had a part. Why do I introduce this? Because you have put the Greek tragedy exactly upon this basis. Not merely death of the battlefield but eternal twilight gladly embraced for the sake of the great cosmic purpose which a cosmic power was working out in the destiny of the race.

Why goddamit man I fully realize the absurdity of me challenging a classical student like yourself. But what can I do? My idea of the Greek was utterly different than this. Cosmic purpose! cosmic destiny for the race! I thought Spengler's denied them the time sense in the Egyptian way. Yet this is exactly what you picture. A purposive, beneficent power? Then where does Prometheus come in who sneaked up and stole the fire and gave it to mortals and suffered eternal agony at the hands of the vengeful outraged Zeus. A cosmic sense, yes indeed! But a cosmic sense of *injustice.* An injustice utterly monstrous and capricious. And the Greek loved to see the hero paraded upon the stage only to be struck down in a sense by meaningless way by an wholly unjust fate why? Because of the flare of defiance with which he marks his exit. "Yes they got him, but he told 'em what he thought[t] of 'em anyway." And when he gets to Hell they will frame him O.K. but he'll *put up a defence which will make hell cheer."* Briefly that was my idea so now prepare to scorch the ignorant son of a b——. My idea was that the Greeks' idea of the gods' part in human life made for a chronic sense of injustice, utterly unrelieved by by [*sic*] anything. That he enjoyed the life of the senses and regarded the gods as more or less his enemies. What else does Krutch mean in picturing the satisfaction of realizing that at least a god had to lean out of Heaven to strike him down. You will immediately seize upon this and say it is the difference to the ego, the difference of feeling you at least attracted attention instead of being the victim of a purposeless blind cosmos. Yet tho I appreciate this difference it seems trivial to me in comparison with the tragedy itself.

Why man for a long time I have been comparing modern tragedy to Greek tragedy making them somewhat similar. We cannot have the satisfaction of seeing a god leave heaven—get up out of a warm bed—in order to strike down our hero, it is true. But a clearcut example of tragedy today produces *in me* a feeling which I had imagined was somewhat similar to the classical feeling.—A flaming sense of outrage, amounting to a defiant affirmation of the incomparable superiority of the human spirit over the senseless cosmic forces which in some mysterious way so inexorably hold the which! Have you read Hemingway's "Farewell to Arms". After a series of romantic adventures together the girl finely [*sic*] dies in childbirth. I guess Hemingway's idea was merely to show up life as disgusting in that such dreams, such heights of spirit could so casually be cut short by a trivial accident of a slight misplacement of the foetus (cord around neck or some such damned inconsequential item). Yet to my mind it soars at the end. It stirs one. It is the sense of injustice. The sense of revolt and disgust against the cosmos which is to my mind only another way of proclaiming the magnificence of the human spirit, of human aspirations. Why man take your own self or Joseph Wood Krutch. I should say your strongest ultimate emotion is exactly this sense of tragedy, this keen awareness of the utter hopeless monstrous discrepancy between the aspirations of the human spirit and the evident cruel facts of human destiny. I had pictured this as a resemblance to the classical idea—minus of course the cheap ego excitement of being able to feel you got somebody[']s goat—but on average far stronger rather than weaker. When you read Harpers did you ever read anything of Alicia O'reardon Overbeck,[4] a woman who writes of life in the South American mining camps? About a 6 mos. [*sic*] ago she had one which gave me a tremendous thrill. I have been calling it a modern version of the classical tragedies. A young girl comes to ask for a position as household servant. It seems she is a half breed, the souvenir of a German engineer who once happened by. Well the girl's white blood shows in an exquisite sense of beauty, personal adornment, a natural art in the matter of making herself agreeable. This engineer's wife takes a liking to her but realizes at once that the girl will in all probably [*sic*] end in a brothel. However she shields her for a time and is rewarded by the half breed's love. You can easily guess as to how circumstances come about so that the girl is compromised and is forbidden privelage [*sic*] of remaining upon company property. Has to leave engineer's wife. Victim of system and predatory man of course. Passes downward and end comes when she is brought to Hospital all cut to pieces by a jealous Indian woman. But at the end the Dr. gives this commonplace theme a touch which lifts it into real cosmic significance. "What a waste!" he exclaims "Yet she was headed for this end from the very day she was born, with her Indian mind, her gringo soul, and her beautiful body. It could not possible [*sic*] have come out any different." At this moment the dying girl opens her eyes which light up upon seeing her former benefactress and she dies with the expression of regard she had used so often in happier days.

Well you will be disgusted by my falling for such a yarn but it was good. It came shortly after I gave my talk on astronomy. I had my wife read it and then I said "With which view of life does that story click, with the view that the hairs of your heads are all numbered or with the astronomy I was giving them. [*sic*] She felt exactly as I did.

Well I will be taking back admissions I made about letting down of feeling. I can't discuss the younger generation. I don't know any of them, I mean any who think. But I wonder if quite a lot of your letdown cannot be explained on the basis of rational shifting of emphasis. I mean if it is not a case of the former emotional attitude having rested upon an irrational bias. Valour! At the charge of Gettysburg, Pickett's men advanced as on a drill ground. They had to cross a rail fence when quite near the enemy, which necessitated breaking ranks. Then they calmly dressed the ranks (halted and resumed exact formation etc) before going on. Nerve! Yes indeed. But also goddam foolishness! Bullshit ad nausea! [*sic*] The theory was to be brave, not to even admit that death was striking around them at will. In the world war we would have charge[d] as follows. An officer would blow a whistle and a line of men would jump up and run say 30 feet and then the whistle would blow and they would drop prone, etc. etc. etc. Utterly different. No idea of pretending indifference to bullets. And had Picket[t']s troops charged in that way there would have been a hell of a lot more of them when they finally joined hand to hand fighting. Well as I said the old idea of valor was shot through and through with bullshit. Of course we can't thrill to something we can only half respect. But I would contend that in our own day in our own way things are somewhat similar as far as fundamentals are concerned. (Ambiguous. I mean human nature is somewhat the same.) I read a fine article "Blind All[e]y" in December Harper's.[5] Author quoted Krutch as mournfully claiming that the essence had been stripped from our ideas of honor, courage, self[-]sacrifice, restraint etc. Then he went on to challenge Kru[t]ch to live through once [*sic*] single day without basing his actions on exactly those things. I called him good. He voiced a sense of modern tragedy somewhat similar to mine. But it does seem to me you allow yourself to be carried too far from *actual human experience*. I tell you all the arguing about the cosmos which a whole generation of cynics may do does not change the fact that people *have to get along together*. Murder may be viewed in a different way but it is still *murder*, the crime which must *at all costs* be held in check by society. You don't want to have any tough free to hold a gun on your stomach and give you the choice of doing his bidding or having several leak[s] suddenly develop in your intestines. The modern complacence as to murder gangs in our large cities is simply a sign of degeneracy on our part, a dimming of the *social intelligence* Society simply cannot tolerate it!. [*sic*] But the individual who feels a gun shoved in his ribs finds his horror of murder revives damned quick.

You told me your friend in Kingston[6] *"was not the stealing kind."* I tell you morality is all bound up in intelligence. It is a pure matter of *intelligence*. Look at the road hog business. A real problem sometimes. Yet up here we have had a blizzard. Snow plow leaves great banks of snow each side of road[.] Utterly impossible for two cars to pass. Situation immediately adjusts itself upon a basis of pure intelligence. No laws or rules necessary. As two cars approach first one to see a place where he can get out of road immediately does so and waits for other car. Utterly senseless to insist in half the road or to do anything at all except exactly this. Were people intelligent many questions of morale would adjust themselves in this way.

Well it is a hard matter to discuss this attempt to shade emotional attitudes. "What you can get away with." I suppose you have reference to this attitude rather than my own of seeing the universality of an act. But I contend it is after all a matter of intelligence. Our education is at fault. I don[']t mean merely the schools. You yourself are to my mind an excel[l]ent example. You effect to speak lightly of murder, of breaches of morality, placing manners above stealing etc. Yet you react most violently to the aesthetic affront presented by a disgustingly intoxicated person. In this attitude you are entirely in accord with the whole American psyc[h]ology. Walter Lip[p]man[n] (that guy ranks in my mind much as Krutch does with you) in the December Forum has an article on "The Underworld".[7] He argues this large army living entirely at variance with statu[t]e law is the direct logical outcome of our American psyc[h]ology of hypocrisy. Great numbers of men in our cities will pay for sex gratification. That is a fact. European countries recognise this and allow for it in their law system. The respectable element in America finds this impossible. They prefer to pretend that "it aint so". They outlaw the whole business. Is human nature thereby changed? Of course not. A whole illicit industry comes into being. But the precious aesthetic feelings of the Godsakers [?] are safe guarded as it is kept out of sight. Ditto gambling. Ditto a thousand times prohibition. Hence a great underworld existing to supply those things which respectable people like to pretend don't exist.

It is a fine article and to my mind he is right. America actually elevates smug hypocrisy above security. Or rather say instead of regarding *violence* as the one great social enemy, America grows complacent of violence and saves all her finest enthusiasms for rendering the world safe for moral aesthetes. Is it any wonder violence waxes strong and fat and parades naked and unashamed in all our large cities. I tell you violence is the one great social evil, more horrible by far than all the drunks or prostitutes in civilization. When a man shoves a gun in another man's ribs and says "stick em up" right then something happens which should cause every intelligent civilized man to burn all over demanding that this simply must be prevented. He should by proxy feel exactly the same sense of outrage as the victim (For purely practical reasons of course). But we are educated to shrug, feel a moment[']s relief that it was the other guy not ourselves, and then sit down and discuss the advisability of using flogging for prohibition offenders. What can you expect in the way of correct emotional attitudes from a generation growing up under such a goddam mess as this.

I am wondering if you enjoyed the Outlook I sent. Perhaps I was wrong about that, but at least I was greatly amused. I took it a case of a millionaire producer, fancying himself upon an equal plane with educated men, breezing in in a patronizing manner, expecting to receive the usual flattery, and then finding himself calmly held up to public ridicule. And he asked for it! That letter amused me no end. They merely gave him exactly what he asked for. I have always heard the movies were deliberately made for morons. It would seem they are also made by morons. Question: did Carl Laemmle[8] expect any such letter as this? Did it affront him? Or is he even capable of perceiving the depth of contempt with which real intellectuals must regard him and all his works?

I enjoyed your analysis of the Arab-Turk question. I gave it to our librarian to read as we had had some argument on the subject.

Am reading Ludwig[']s "Napolian [*sic*] Bonaparte" and enjoying it very much.

Have received several letters from Weiss. He is quite interesting. However I don't think anything will shake his faith. He is as safe as my young theological student.

This fellow resumed the assault. He sent me a book by Montague "A Promethean Religion for the Modern World". I read it—it was a very interesting book—and wrote him my opinion. I told him Montague was no more a "Christian" than I. I proved to him that Montague had far more in common with Joseph McCabe[9] than with even the Modernists. Well he fooled me by sending me that book. I took it he must be getting pretty modern. He wanted his mother to read it. But after my analysis he wrote her he had somewhat changed his mind about the book and asked her not to take it too seriously. In two letters he invited my shafts in all frankness. He got them. Did he come back and argue? Not at all. He merely went polite on me. Not an inkling of any kind as to his reaction to all my stuff—and I discussed many things entirely outside of assaults on his faith—such as correcting his impressions of the beliefs of materialists etc. Spengler's cycle theory—the problem of tragedy—optimism vs cynicism—did he even read it? I do not know. A false alarm entirely. I have concluded he is a tiny bundle of pious emotionalism entirely incapable of even appreciating the fact that there are problems. So the joke is on me for I really extended myself in those letters.

[*In margin:*] I note what you say of scene of recent story. I often wish I might see Weird Tales. Not on sale here. So I never get to see your stories of [*sic*] those of Weiss.

Sincerely yours

Woodburn Harris

Notes

1. George W. Wickersham (1858–1936), former attorney general of the U.S. (1909–13), was head of the National Commission on Law Observance and Enforcement (usually called the Wickersham Commission or Wickersham Committee), which was tasked with assessing the criminal justice system under Prohibition. Its report was released on 7 January 1931.

2. Mabel Walker Willebrandt (1889–1963), former assistant attorney general of the U.S. (1921–29), personally opposed Prohibition but vigorously enforced it. After she left office, she represented a California company, Fruit Industries, that made a grape concentrate called Vine-Glo that could be turned into wine.

3. Caroline Elizabeth Sarah (Sheridan) Norton (1808–1877), *Bingen on the Rhine*, ll. 1–4.

4. Alicia (Barrington) O'Reardon Overbeck (1888-1935), "Encarnación," *Harper's Magazine* 160, No. No. 959 (April 1930): 587–94.

5. By Ludwig Lewisohn. The issue also contained "The Three R's on a Mountain Top" by Alicia O'Reardon Overbeck.

6. Bernard Austin Dwyer.

7. Walter Lippmann, "The Underworld, Our Secret Servant," *Forum and Century* 85 (January 1931): 1–4, the first of three articles on the subject.

8. Carl Laemmle (1867–1939), German-American film producer and the founder and (until 1934) owner of Universal Pictures. He is remembered primarily for such horror films as *Dracula* and *Frankenstein*. In a letter printed in the *Outlook and Independent* 156 (17 December 1930): 612, Laemmle asks readers to present "an analysis of present day American 'taste' and entertainment 'appetite'" as pertains to movies. In a lengthy and sharp reply, "A Letter to Hollywood" (pp. 612–13, 632–65), Creighton Peet states that the public wishes a higher level of entertainment than what movies have generally provided.

9. Joseph McCabe (1867–1955) was a well-known philosopher, historian, and free-thinker, author of such works as *The Evolution of Mind* (1910) and *The Story of Evolution* (1912). He also translated Ernst Haeckel's *The Riddle of the Universe* (1900).

[5]   [AL, verso page in ms. of *At the Mountains of Madness*]

[n.d.; February or March 1931?]

I must have forgotten one bunch of clippings you sent. Hope my negligence will not discourage you as I always enjoy them. First I ever read of Freud. He certainly has a clear direct style. I read of Einstein's latest effusions in my paper. If he can actually prove his proposition about curved space it will be the culminating joke. "Reasoning in a circle." An old expression. "Chasing the devil around a stump." When they find that a straight line projected into space eventually returns upon itself they will merely have demonstrated what thinkers have known a long time; viz, that you can't get anywhere. I can't make my self clear but some how the proposition sets me chuckling. If only they could change the whole Western philosophy so as to recognize this fact! Regard life merely as an incident which comes to an end. Regard death as man's best friend. Then invent some form of alcohol which wouldn't make a man's breath smell, why then life would be worth living. This last is imperative. Even an old oak like me. I always feel a wave of repulsion when I smell alcohol on a man's breath. In my cups that is the last regret to pass. How many times have I persisted in turning my head to exhale knowing and regretting the offense the fumes must give. [*sic*] If you can solve this problem you will no longer need to spend your winters in the north.

[5]   [AHT]

May 19, 1935

Dear Harris:—

Well—I'm glad that at least a few signs of midwinter's passing are manifest in the arctic! Hope the new poultry venture turns out well—and that the recent narrow escape from fire will lead to redoubled caution.

I haven't read Wells's new autobiography, but hope to get around to it in the course of time. His attitude toward religion seems to vary somewhat.[1] At one period he published a book affirming his belief in some sort of local cosmic consciousness subject to struggle and defeat[2]—but possibly he has shed that vestige of superstition by this time. Certainly, goodnatured amusement is the only logical attitude one can take toward the faith of the fathers. As for prejudices—we all have them, and one could better appraise H G's after reading his book. I would say that the attitude to take toward Marx is one of respect for his solid achievements—but not one of gullible idolatry regarding all the ramified and dogmatic theories which he spun out from the rough general principles he discovered. The same with Newton or Einstein or Freud or Pavlov or Darwin or Lamarck—each is a tremendously important figure, and has unearthed something new and authentic. But that feat of discovery does not make all the minor and elaborate speculations of the discoverer necessarily true. No one person ever envisaged a whole system correctly. It takes generations of research, observation, reflection, and correlation to interpret and fit together the results of any new major discovery. Regarding the monarchy—Wells evidently allows an early bias to blind him to realistic psychology and blunt his sense of proportion. A pure scientist would realise the value of a specific rallying-point for the blind loyalties of the herd—be it

King, Flag, Duce, Ghazi, Fuehrer, God, Justice, or what have you. Indeed, he would see that the tendency toward personal exaltation is so great that all the nations seem to be reverting to it (Lenin—Stalin—Der Schön Adolf, etc. etc.) under the stress of modern disorganisation. No doubt too much cash is spent on keeping a whole royal family in style—but a King is really a damn'd good figurehead to have around.

Regarding social and economic change—I don't think my belief in the possibility of a non-cataclysmic solution is as extravagant as you think. Germany has got a new system with no greater overture than a parliamentary coup d'etat—and it is possible to conceive of many degrees of actual revolution without the wasteful and repulsive overturn and wholesale deification of fallacy which have prevailed in Russia. We can't tell just how much violence and irregularity will be needed to clean out the clutching plutocrats. They are badly scared now; and unless the present administration bends their way, they are slated for still further shocks. At the same time, the Long-Coughlin influence is present as a warning to the administration not to veer too far rightward. The real job is to educate the herd to accept some system other than unsupervised capitalism. They won't accept it now—look at what happened to Sinclair![3] They've got to see one half-way measure after another fail, until they get it through their thick heads that *only government ownership of large industries, on a non-profit basis,* will give them any fixed assurance of steady work and decent living conditions. Even now I think they realise that *laissez-faire* capitalism is dead. They seem largely uninfluenced by even the loudest of Republican wailings and ululations. They know that nothing but governmental control of industry will ever restore to every man the likelihood of getting a job . . . which is quite a grasping-feat for the herd mind. One more step, and they'll realise that private profit probably can't or won't stand the strain of governmental control—which means of course that private profit must go, since governmental allocation of labouring opportunities is an obvious future necessity. By the time this is realised, the people will be really ready to elect a leftist administration with open and intelligent socialistic aims. But that's a long way from the barbarism and ignorance and false science and grotesquely inverted values of the orthodox Marxian communists. Intelligent socialism involves no such crazy gesture as exalting factory hands at the expense of high-grade planners. As before, simple work will command modest pay while high-grade service will command substantial pay. The world need not be turned upside down. What will disappear will be the vast private accumulations which do no one any good, the waste of resources in unearned profits, and the barbarous and criminal practice of leaving employment uncertain and dependent on the accidental profits of transactions whose object is not public service.

This, of course, isn't a *prophecy*. It is only a *possibility*. Nobody knows what will really happen, since all sorts of imperceptible and unforeseen factors may in the end prove the pivotal and decisive ones. When I speak of *sober evolution* I don't necessarily mean a thoroughly tranquil and parliamentary process. All sorts of coups d'etat, local riots, fascist marches, etc. etc. may be involved. Even a moderate revolution like those in Spain and South America would not be outside the category. But anything within sane limits can be called "sober evolution" as distinguished from the savage and destructive extravagance and stultifying fallacies of bolshevism. However—don't get me wrong. I merely say that I think evolution has a good chance . . . not that it is in any way certain. If necessary changes are too slow in coming, and if Republican madness and criminality hold up relief to any marked extent, there's no telling what may happen in the way of an hysterical explosion. I'd hate to see bolshevism come—but there are limits to the extent of my surprisedness in the event of such a disaster. After all—the Dark Ages did come, even though civilisation did its best to keep alive amidst the chaos of alien impacts and destructive philosophies.

As to this Buddha business—I'm frankly puzzled by the extent to which such a purely *verbal* concept impresses you. No one doubts the general rough *similarity* of mental processes among animals of the same or closely related species—a similarity, by the way, more marked among savage than among superior specimens. It is of course vastly overrated by those who think they have a point to prove—but that does not matter. This question of similarity *has nothing to do with the question of individual identity* . . . nor would it even if two or more organisms were *actually identical in type of construction and reaction.* Why not? It ought to be very clear. A *personality* is not merely a certain *kind* of construction. It is, on the contrary, a *compound* of (a) the kind of construction, (b) the specific experiences of the separate unit in question and (c) *the ability of some unified central consciousness to register sensation and experience as encountered by every part of the unit.* Point (c) is the most important of all. Nothing is a single personality unless it can know what is happening to all its parts. If an apparently single organism possesses sections whose experiences can never be known to the consciousness which knows the experiences of other sections, then it is *not* a single organism. It doesn't matter a damn whether one section or group of sections is or is not precisely the same as another section or group of sections. If we have 2 or 3 similar units side by side, and find that when we touch Unit A, *only Unit A is aware of being touched,* then we cannot sanely say that Unit B or Unit C is *the same unit* or *part of the same larger unit* as Unit A. To say such a thing is *merely irresponsible verbalism.* Who in his right mind could claim that *even perfect similarity* is tantamount to *being the same thing* or *being parts of the same thing?* We may have, on a mantelpiece, two identical vases turned out by the same mould. There is *no difference* between them. But are they indeed merely one object on that account? If we drop one, do both break? The inference ought to be obvious.

Really, though, no analogy betwixt the conscious and the unconscious is of any basic significance. That is why the flame allegory is merely a bit of decorative cleverness. A flame has no realisation nor memory, hence *has no identity in the sense that a conscious animal has*. What *would* determine identity, *if there were* consciousness, would be merely *the extent to which the flame was aware in one stage of what happened to it in a former stage*. Consciousness and personality in mankind resemble a flame to a certain extent—in that they persist despite a gradual replacement of the molecules involved in their oxidational or electrical process. But the *extent* of this persistence is clearly defined . . . . the definition being a matter of actual observation and not of theory. We see, empirically, *that we cannot transfer this consciousness to another set of oxidising or electrically discharging molecules after the breaking down and disintegration of the original set.* This is laboratory fact—not empty speculation. When the body of John Smith dies, there is no way to keep alive the individual memories of John Smith. If nobody but John knew where he placed a certain paper, then *nobody ever will know* unless the paper is found by accident. *And these individual memories are what constitute a human personality.* In the domain of organic life, there is no such thing as duplicating a personality as a flame may be duplicated through burning the same sort of oil in the same lamp under the same conditions. We lack a perpetuating lamp . . . . and a flame is not the same thing as *a set of individual memories*.

Remember that the only actual things which correspond to the concept of a personality or identity are continuity of memories and ability of some unified consciousness to register sensation and experience as encountered by every part of the given units. If we try to leave the facts and pretend that some other qualities—such as mere similarity—mean participation in a single personality we are simply playing with words in a childish way. The words don't mean anything. Suppose the same things did please Sam Pepys and H P L . . . does that mean that I know what Sam said to this or that clerk at the Admiralty office on such and such a date, or that Sam ever did feel or ever will feel the pain I suffered when I burned my finger with phosphorus in 1907? Unless these questions can be answered affirmatively—as they certainly can't—it is simply frivolous to try to pretend that Sam and I are the same person, or parts of the same person. I've never suffered when Sam has stubbed his toe, nor has he ever suffered when I've stubbed mine. Sam is not H P L, nor is there any such thing as a composite animal equivalent to Sam plus H P L (plus W H etc. etc.) Don't forget that the word "identity" or "personality" cannot have any meaning when separated from the real facts or actual conditions (i.e., continuous memory and unified registration of sensation and experience) which it was invented to describe. It is only facts and conditions which mean anything. Words in themselves mean nothing. When we try to inflate and transfer such a word as "identity" or "personality" so as to make it cover some new conception alien to the original one, we do not really show any new condition. We merely destroy the value of the word. The fact behind the word (in this case, that unit which is determined by the possession of continuous memory and unified registration of sensation and experience) remains precisely the same, however we juggle and confuse and devolve the language. It changes nothing to say that the real unit-which-is-determined-by-the-possession-of-continuous-memory and-unified-registration-of-sensation-and-experience shall henceforward be officially considered as negligible and unimportant, and that its name shall be withdrawn and given to something else . . . some shadowy collection of many units, or some abstract category to which such a unit logically belongs, or some fixed generative background out of which such units are formed in rough duplicate. We have merely switched words. The unit is just as distinct and important as it was before, and the shadowy generalisation does not really mean a damn thing more because of its acquisition of the name of something else.

But of course this talk of "importance" really means nothing. There is no such thing as "importance" in the cosmos. Neither the real unit-which-is-determined-by-the-possession-of-continuous-memory-and-unified-registration-of-sensation-and-experience, nor the shadowy abstract aggregate or generative principle of such units, has any absolute qualitative status. If we speak of the "importance" of either, we must speak only relatively, with some local scale of reference in mind. We may say, rightly, that the unit is of no "importance" to the aggregate; and we may likewise say that the aggregate, or any *other* unit, is of no "importance" to any given unit except so far as these external things may act upon that unit during the period of its existence (i.e., period of continuous memory.) Such things as "egotism" do not figure at all. The fact that a unit is a separate thing does not enhance its "value" or "importance". The fact that John Smith means nothing to me does not make me out any greater person than as if John Smith *did* concern me. For, by the same token that Smith is unimportant in *my* life, so am *I* unimportant in *John's* life! John, myself, and the whole species to which we belong, are all equally unimportant in an absolute sense. In a *relative* sense, each unit is important only to itself . . . . John to John, H P L to H P L, and species to species. Organised society exists as a practical device because both John and I know that we can individually get what we want only by making such things easy for all to get. John advocates measures for my protection not because he gives a damn what happens to me, but because that is the only way he can be sure of getting protection for himself during his lifetime.

The (not very) "exact similarity of consciousness in all men" is a far cry from the identity of all men as a single personality, the deeds of one of whose parts have certain inevitable consequences of significance to that part. Just what Gautama meant, no one but a very advanced scholar could safely say . . . but there is certainly no sense in the way most eastern thinkers have interpreted his meaning.

As for the whole question of human similarity—I think a survey of all mankind, and a comparison of the motives of different salient persons like Alexander, Gandhi, Democritus, Plato, Archimedes, Cato, Tamerlane, Herschel, Keats, Savonarola, Heliogabalus, Leonardo, Cromwell, Balzac, Stylites, Nero, Pythagoras, Swedenborg, Amundsen, and Tiberius Gracchus, would make it clear to you that resemblances concern the semi-automatic lower attributes a good deal more than they concern those more complex attributes which mean personality in the fullest sense. The commonplace man of the herd has far less personality in a *quantitative* sense than a fully-developed man of genius—though of course (since personality is equivalent to mnemonic continuity and unified sensation-and-experience-registration) he is just as *separate* as an organic unit as Aristotle or Shakespeare himself. *Separateness* and *dissimilarity* are by no means interdependent. Things may be fully separate, yet alike as two peas.

About 'western aggressiveness'—I am no champion of its extreme forms. Indeed, I abhor excessive pushing and insistence on material luxury and "progress". My protest is simply against an *opposite extreme*. There must be a balance. I favour a civilised and permanent adjustment to nature as opposed to a typically western restlessness—but I think a decent adjustment ought to be secured before we sit down amidst our fixed order of things. The Oriental sits down—or lies down—too damn soon!

You'll enjoy both Tom Moore and Arnold's "Light of Asia".[4] I can lend you both if local library facilities let you down. As to Tom's alcoholism—I was merely presenting commonly known facts. Apologists for alcohol are by no means new—but the bulk of physiologists know its effect on heart, blood-vessels, liver, nervous system, and cortical tissue. Just how little the *sparing* use of alcohol would harm a *perfect* individual is an interesting academic question, but not an especially relevant one in a world whose inhabitants represent varying degrees of unrestraint and imperfection. Practically speaking, the relation of alcoholism to deterioration and early senescence is so marked as to require no comment. As for the notion that alcohol has *improved* mankind by killing off subnormals—that is too absurd for consideration. Actually, its degenerative effect is so *slow* that it generally permits its victims to do all their reproducing before it kills them—and likewise with the inferior progeny (born under unfavourable circumstances) to which its effects give rise. Trying to defend the use of alcohol is a pretty fruitless proposition. If it is a necessary escape from intolerable conditions of reality, then the thing to do is to remedy the reality. As a substitute for decent living, it's pretty costly, disastrous, and degrading!

Well—Spring is here at last, with feathery verdure on shrub and tree, and forsythias a yellow blaze. My second and (I hope) permanent outing season began with a visit from the same young chap (Robert Moe, son of my old Presbyterian friend and adversary) who opened the temporary season early in March. He came in his 1928 Ford April 27–8—and we certainly put in an active 2 days! On the 27th we visited old Newport—seeing 2 ancient windmills; a flock of sheep with small and sportive lambkins in the best pastoral tradition; "Whitehall", home of Dean Berkeley in 1729–32; the Hanging Rocks where the good cleric wrote his famous "Alciphron" (don't get this mixed up with the poem by our friend Tom Moore!);[5] the lofty cliffs; the strange rock cleft called "Purgatory" where the ocean pounds thunderously in; the Overing farmhouse where a small rowboat party of rebels under Col. Wm. Barton captured Genl. Prescott in 1777; and the venerable town itself—with 1726 Anglican church, 1739 colony-house, 1749 library, 1760 market-house, 1763 Jews' synagogue, and private dwellings as old as 1675. Glorious hot day . . . up to 82° in Providence, tho' not quite so good in Newport. Sunday the 28th we went to ancient New Bedford of whaling fame, exploring the quaint waterfront in some detail. We then set off southward for the Round Hills estate of Col. E. H. R. Green (old miser Hetty's son) in South Dartmouth, where the old whaling barque *Charles W. Morgan* (built 1841) is preserved at a realistic-looking wharf—but solidly embedded in concrete as a permanent exhibit. We went all over the vessel—which is tremendously fascinating. On the Green estate is also an ancient windmill moved from Rhode Island. We then explored a region—where southern Mass. adjoins southwestern R.I.—which, despite its proximity, I had never seen before in my life. Splendid unspoiled countryside with rambling stone walls and idyllic white-steepled villages of old New England type. Of the latter the best 2 specimens—Adamsville and Little Compton Commons—are both in R.I. Adamsville contains the world's only known monument to a *hen*—perpetuating the fame of the Rhode Island Red, a breed evolved in this village from East-Indian and Chinese gallinaceous forbears. At Little Compton Commons can be found the home and grave of Elizabeth Alden Pabodie—daughter of the famed John Alden and Priscilla Mullins of Plymouth, and first white woman born in New England. This region was once the seat of the Sakonnet Indians—whose squaw-sachem Awashonks was persuaded by the noted old warrior Capt. Benjamin Church not to join King Philip's conspiracy in 1675. It was settled from Plymouth about 1673, and came into Massachusetts in 1691 and into Rhode Island in 1747. Capt. Church lies buried not far from Little Compton Commons. At last we turned north through Tiverton, where on our left we had some marvellous vistas of low-lying fields and blue water. Here we passed the home of the navigator Capt. Robert Gray, who in 1792 discovered the Columbia River in the far-off Oregon country . . . naming it after his good Rhode Island brig. Then back home via Fall River and Warren . . . at which latter ancient seaport we paused for a dinner consisting entirely of ice cream—a pint and a half (involving 6 varieties) each. Finally back to 66, after which I regretfully guided the guest out of town and took a 4-mile rural walk before returning home. Quite a session!

The next week-end—May 3–4–5—my luck was lousy! Went to visit Cole in the Boston zone, and was continually dogged by chill winds and grey skies—though Saturday afternoon was sunny. Explored old Marblehead as usual—though it wasn't much fun outside Cole's heated Chevrolet. Fortunately, I was able to borrow an overcoat from him—he being not so far from my size. Damn this climate! Then—just as a bit of irony—the day *after* my visit was delectably warm . . . around 70°—so that I took my work to the idyllic woodlands north of the town!

Future events undecided . . . though there's a distinct possibility that I shall visit Barlow again in De Land after he returns thither from Washington in June. Going to Florida for the summer seems as bad as Cook's going to Vermont or New Hampshire for the winter—but there's really no time of year that I don't prefer a subtropical environment with its genial and dependable warmth, its live-oaks, and its (to me) peculiarly invigorating atmosphere. Naturally, if the project turns out well, I hope to pause in Charleston, St. Augustine, and other favourite spots of mine.

Well—On māne padme on![6]

—Ec'h-Pi-El

Notes

1. *Experiment in Autobiography* (1934).

2. HPL may be referring to Wells's *God the Invisible King* (1917), in which he affirmed belief in a finite God "of the human heart."

3. HPL refers to Upton Sinclair, who in 1934 waged a campaign for governor of California as a Democrat advocating the EPIC (End Poverty In California) movement, but was opposed by many businesses and lost to the incumbent Republican, Frank Merriam.

4. HPL refers to the Irish poet Thomas Moore (1779–1852). Sir Edwin Arnold's *The Light of Asia* (1879) is a versified account of the teachings of Buddhism.

5. George Berkeley's *Alciphron; or, The Minute Philosopher* (1732) is an attempt to refute contemporary attacks on the Christian religion; Thomas Moore's *Alciphron* (1839) is a long poem and a rewriting of the semi-weird novel *The Epicurean* (1827).

6. Typically rendered "Om mane padme hum," the Buddhist mantra means "The jewel is in the lotus."

[6]   [ALS, by Harris, verso page in ms. of "The Whisperer in Darkness"]

TAKE YOUR Time

Am desolated to have to ask you to do it the second time.

However: The railroad, especially for points south, cannot tell the difference between coin earned the first time and that earned on the second trip.

Don't imagine I can fuse the matter of professional services with that of personal interest and criticism. Naturally mere money, filthy lucre, can never command the latter[.]

In a few minor instances I have rejected your revision. My only criterion is that of the elocutionist. If the thing jingles well in real rendition then I am satisfied. I recognize the great improvement in nearly all of your changes.

Your point about inserting 15th Amendment was a good one. That is a favorite argument of mine. Springfield Republican only last week published my letter along that line. This time I use 15th Amendment but deemed it more effective put in at close so have cut it out from where you inserted it.

I trust only a couple of pages will have to be retyped.

Just recently public statements have appeared by Roosevelt, Dr. Doran, and ex[-]senator Butler—especially ex[-]senator Butler, which I use making my article right up to the minute.[1]

If this doesn't convince you you are as hopeless as my W. C. T. U.[2] example.

I think the title as I now have it is A. No 1.

Paragraphing is a blind mystery to me.

Notes

1. J. M. Doran was the Commissioner of Prohibition William M. Butler (1861–1937), U.S. Senator from Massachusetts (1924–26) who briefly sought the Republican nomination for president and asserted a determination to carry out strict enforcement of the Volstead Act.
2. Woman's Christian Temperance Union.

Zealia Bishop c. 1945

Letters to Zealia Brown Reed Bishop

[1]   [ALS]

10 Barnes St.,

Providence, R.I.,

May 10, 1927

My Dear Mrs. Reed:—

Your letter & two accompanying MSS. (stories) arrived yesterday, but I have not so far received the *article* you mention. If I do get it at any time prior to the mailing of this reply, I will make a note of the fact on the outside of the envelope—I trust that it is not lost, but that you merely deferred or omitted sending it.

I have read both stories with care, & believe—after the fullest consideration—that there is really an excellent chance for you to get a foothold in professional writing by means of diligent technical practice. To me the tales seem to possess unmistakable fluency & facility, & a visual directness which removes them altogether from the mechanically imitative class; though at the same time there is a need for cultivating literary form for form's sake—for learning the exact & inevitable word to fit every case, & the finest subtleties of construction to make the most of every image & situation. These qualities are to be gained in a twofold way—first by constant study of some authoritative rhetorical handbook such as Woolley's*, with a minute attention to the rules & principles there given, & second by a dominantly *analytical* perusal of the best English stylists (eschewing all purely ephemeral magazine writing) with an almost microscopic eye for turns, tricks, & niceties of style & language—quite apart from any consideration of plot or broader trend. Without a doubt *literary form*—the art of language as a delicate & complicated tool for fastidious handling & precise effects—is your greatest immediate need. It is very natural for your creative capacity to vary from day to day as you mention—it is so with all save the most prosaic writers; whether in regard to language, or merely to ideas & imagery. The only thing to do is to improve those hours when the mood is naturally on one—the dead of night being a time which many nervously sensitive authors find especially favourable. As to matters of vocabulary—in treating realistic themes no extraordinary range is necessary or even desirable. The simpler words are incomparably the better—not only because they have picked up more overtones of association, but because they are less grandiose in sound & therefore less prone to that element of half-felt incongruity on which bombast & ridiculousness are based. On the other hand, a vocabulary ought of course to be large enough to provide the *precise* & *inevitable* word for every occasion; thus giving a quietly simple strength to the

---

*Handbook of Composition, by Edwin C. Woolley, Ph. D. Pub. by D. C. Heath & Co.

style, & involving no distracting evidences of groping or duplication.

As to the two specific tales submitted—"When a Woman is Tempted" is in better shape technically than the other, but is not nearly so strong or so original in conception. The Easter morning part could be easily removed, but on the other hand there is not much need of removing it, since seasonal stories are bought six months or more in advance. A story for next Easter ought to be "landed" by September at the latest, & allowing for the inevitable rejections of beginners' work, the present is none too early to start sending out a tale with September "landing" in mind. As an illustration of what sending means, I may mention that an acquaintance of mine—& a veteran rather than a novice—lately had a short story accepted on its 32^d trip out! Your tale is very good light work, but is of a general type fairly well known to popular readers—hence would not be snapped up as quickly as would something with an absolutely unique twist. It is 2550 words long, hence at low rates—if accepted—it would probably bring about $25.00. This is a comfortably low estimate, although there are cheap rural weeklies which do not pay so much. On the other hand, most urban monthlies pay much more—even the wretched Macfadden rags of New York pay 2¢ per word, which would make this tale come to $50.00 instead of $25.00. The revision needed by this story is only elementary—no radical changes in arrangement—hence at its computed length would come to $3.85 (typed complete with one carbon) at my regular rate of 50¢ per 330-word page. I will go ahead on this item, sending the typed text as soon as it is done. Payment is usually in advance, but in regular work payment on delivery will do. If I find that I have wrongly estimated the length, the typed pages will show my error & permit of correction—but I do not think I am far out. Incidentally—in order to protect clients, I never charge *over* the first price I quote, even if the work turns out to be longer than estimated. I merely credit the client when the length turns out *less*. (Usually I can tell at once, because most MSS. come typed) As general remarks on the story—I might say (1) that the French name *Marie* has no accent over the "e", & (2) that care is necessary in avoiding the erroneous use of "lay" for "lie". If any more specific points occur to me I will mention them when sending the typed copy of the story.

Now as to the longer story—this is really quite a fictional achievement. The plot is unhackneyed, the developments are not prematurely foreseen, & the characterisation is in general very lifelike & convincing. The central figure certainly succeeds in commanding the reader's instant sympathy & comprehension—& I do not think her unusual qualities are so far "rubbed in" that an unpleasant after-taste of smugness, self-righteousness, or untruth to life is left. On the contrary, one feels that the very element of repression forms a defect or "human touch" ample enough to make up for such adumbrations of saintliness as the absence of resentment toward the faithless husband & Daphne forms. Yes—on the whole, the tale strikes one as both unusual & admirable in its conception & development, & I would be by no means surprised to see it "land" somewhere after a course of the requisite technical grooming. The length—nearly 6300 words—would make it very lucrative if it could stand at that figure without padding—but this is still a problem.

Technically, this tale is not nearly so finished as its lighter companion, & would require something between extensive revision & actual re-writing in order to "make the grade" professionally. I would be willing to call it extensive revision altogether & avoid the very high rate quoted for re-writing, but at its present length even the revision rate would come to $19.00; (which would leave you $44.00 net profit if you sold it at the 1¢ per word rate of $63.00) hence I think I will seek further authorisation before doing anything. There is really no haste in the matter, & it is always advisable to avoid unconsidered steps. In giving the MS. its careful perusal I made certain numerical notes at places where comment seemed to be in order—recording the data on a separate sheet. Since these comments give a fairly comprehensive idea of the *type* of change needed, I believe I will return the MS. with the note-sheet appended; so that you may give the whole text a second survey & decide whether you wish to make further changes yourself, or let me handle the entire revision along lines roughly marked out by the notes. Naturally it would be *quickest* to leave the whole thing to me; but on the other hand the process of further self-revision would be excellent literary practice for you, & might possibly put the text into such shape that only an elementary revision—at lower rates—would be subsequently necessary. It would not do, however, to *promise* this latter, since the scope, subtlety, & seriousness of the plot demand a high level of technical development & an absolute sureness of form. But in any case I am sure there is no haste. Time-considerations are utterly immaterial where perfection & only perfection is the goal.

Regarding details of the story—I'd make a serious effort, if I were you, to cut down the early parts. (This is disinterested advice—for it cuts down my fee correspondingly—but I really think it would improve the tale artistically. . . . & commercially as well, for editors shun & fear long introductions, even when aesthetically necessary. I shall attempt such cutting if the matter is left to me—restoring the text, however, if I find the excision doesn't work.) As you probably realise, the direct action does not begin till after 13 pages of the entire 37 (longhand)—nearly a full third into the tale—which is distinctly slow motion as modern technique goes. What is wanted prior to the incident of the mountainside is simply a very full exposition of Ella's character, environment, & place in the story—& many parts of this might be accomplished by retrospective statement rather than by dialogue & preliminary action as at present. The one early incident which ought to be *kept* in dialogue-&-action form is the porch discussion of Ella—with Lane's defence of her & her own overhearing. But of course one can't tell how smoothly a "cut" could be made until one tries, hence what I offer are merely suggestions. But I think, on the whole, that the attempt at early condensation is very much worth making.

I would also advise an elimination of everything *grandiose*—Clotho, Lachesis, Atropos, & all the cosmic implications. Only the starkest of ruthless realists—& only mature & acknowledged masters of the craft at that—can "get away" nowadays with the grand manner. To my mind even Hardy overdoes it—classic though he be—so that I cannot help joining George Moore in calling "Tess" distinctly bombastic & melodramatic.[1] In other words, all *visible* attempts to link up the fortunes of human individuals with large universal forces such as Fate or Destiny strike a false note in the consciousness of the contemporary sophisticated reader. Of course, the cheaper magazines no doubt teem with this sort of thing even now, for their especial clientele has not yet outgrown the twilight of Victorian mawkishness—but it is not well to select this milieu if any other is accessible. With a civilised modern audience, cool & impersonal detachment is the correct attitude for a fiction-writer. Do not try to be a footnote as well as a narrator—keep all inferences & subjective associations well out of sight, & let the scenes, characters, & events tell their own story. It is for the reader alone—as prompted by the sheer force of what he sees objectively unfolded before him—to make speculations about the powers behind the puppets. For one naturally inclined toward visible Æschyleanism & the sententiousness of the Dickens tradition, there is no better antidote & general model than the short tales of de Maupassant, with their truly admirable impersonality & economy of sentiment.

Then, too, one must always be on guard against the *stock phrase*. It is hard to weed these out at first, but one soon comes to recognise & shun them when an effort is made. In general, avoid any metaphorical, associative, or allusive group of words which careless common usage has degraded to thoughtless mechanicality & robbed of all *real* vitality or connexion with our image-forming faculties. One might broaden this precept to the extent of demanding *that no words be written, which do not suggest an actual image distinct from the shopworn images which a thousand others have seen.* In Woolley's little handbook, which I recommend to all beginners (despite an over-finical tendency—which is perhaps wholesome at the outset) there is a long list of trite expressions & quotations which have now become ridiculous & meaningless from over-use, & which are therefore *absolutely debarred* from the writings of mature & civilised authors today. A few specimens will illustrate the general idea—

render a vocal solo	Method in his madness
in a pleasing manner	Monarch of all I survey
specimen of humanity	Sadder but wiser
in evidence	Variety is the spice of life
the student body	All work & no play
made a pretty picture	All is not gold that glisters
like sentinels guarding	When ignorance is bliss
	Music hath charms—

This mention of a handbook reminds me of certain other aids which all beginners ought to have by them. A good dictionary—& freely used—is a *sine qua non,* & a *thesaurus* (Roget's is the standard—if not actually the *only* one extant) is scarcely less essential as a means of attaining verbal variety. For learning the exact distinctions between cognate words—or at least for learning that such distinctions *do* exist & appreciating their importance—it is well to get a dictionary of synonyms—such as Crabb's old standby, still printed from the original electrotype plates of fifty or so years ago.

But to return to the story—the title certainly needs changing, not only to get away from the pomposity of the "Fate" idea, but to express more directly the central theme of the story, which is the suppression & final release of Ella Brent's emotional energy. Something indicative of *bursting, liberation, or unshackling* is what the tale demands, & as a tentative heading I suggest "The Unchaining", or "The Key to the ⎫ Chain ⎫ ⎫ Probably you can Prison ⎬ &c" Cage ⎭ devise some similar title of still greater appropriateness, but I thought I'd map out the general direction in which one must search. In devising titles, one ought to emulate the better grades of current writing rather than the extremely popular romance & slush of the "confession" type.

Such, then, is the situation concerning the longer story. You can use your own judgment about further revision on your part—& of course I would be glad to furnish any additional suggestions during that process, should specific developments make such suggestions desirable. Or, if you prefer, I will take the text as it is & deliver it in as good shape as I know how for a fee in no case exceeding $19.00 & perhaps (especially in case of excisions toward the beginning) running substantially under that. And, as I said before, if you do make further revisions & later submit the result to me, the fee might or might not be cut in half on account of the non-necessity for extensive changes. That one could not tell in advance. On the whole, I would say that the tale is distinctly worth pushing through to completion & professional trial. Its especial combination of elements seems to me distinctly unhackneyed, & that is surely what editors want. At the same time, no such thing as quick acceptance can be looked for in these days of literary over-supply; when the woods are literally full of smooth & facile magazine-writers, & editors are so overwhelmed with floods of tolerably good material [i.e., tolerably good from the commercial standpoint—literary merit is another thing, & of no importance in any magazine of the popular type] that they are obliged to limit their acceptances, *caeteris paribus,* to their own small circle of dependable veteran contributors—who were on the ground first.

The foregoing, I think, covers all the particular points brought up. The lighter tale, which is pretty good in conception & moderately finished in diction, will receive slight revision & typing at once (I may even enclose it herewith, if a lull in other work gives me a spare forenoon) at a rate not exceeding $3.85. The serious tale, which is really excellent in conception but unfinished in workmanship, is returned with notes for further decision on your part—its probable revision-rate being that of $1.00 per 330 words—in no case more than $19.00 for the entire story.

There is certainly no need for you to feel anxiety about your writing as a general thing; for although it requires technical improvement, it undoubtedly possesses a fluency & vividness which will get it somewhere if you work ahead with the requisite minuteness & fastidiousness—keeping always in mind the paramount importance of fluent & sophisticated *form*, & the necessity for wide reading amongst all the classics of literature. I am sure that this is not false encouragement, because no matter how critically I view the defects & immaturities in the longer tale, I certainly can't find the dull imitativeness & soggy imaginative deadness which characterise the type of futile groping that says nothing fresh or new & deserves a disillusioning extinction for its writer's own good. And I have seen much of that type—for although I don't handle it myself, I know a man who does tinker with such things after frankly warning his clients to expect no success.

As I have said, you will need to work hard in absorbing *the subtle exactitudes of fine literary usage;* but at the same time I would urge that you do not take the process of composition & the fate of your MSS. *too* seriously; that is, seriously enough to worry about the matter & thus defeat your own ends through destroying the calm detachment necessary for artistic composition. The fullest results are obtained when one resolves to do nothing save the best, yet does not care too extensively whether or not he does anything at all. To my mind, the pleasure element rather than the task element is the supreme motive force of real literature. Your trend, I think, will be toward the semipopular. You are fortunate in being able to develop interests which are widely shared, & which are therefore acceptable to more editors than would consider material of a strongly analytical, purely decorative, or uniquely exotic cast.

Leaving further decision on the long story to you, & hoping you will like what is done to the short one, I remain

Sincerely yrs—

H P Lovecraft

P.S. Later. After completing the revision of the humorous story—which you will find under separate cover—I am inclined to speak still more highly of it than I have done in the body of this letter. It is certainly very adroit—situations well handled, & hinging with extreme cleverness upon one another, motivation devoid of jarring extravagance, & whimsical characterisation well developed. The incidents ensue with plausible naturalness, & the atmosphere is good. On the whole, I think it an excellent performance, & believe it ought to have a distinct chance with editors.

Notes

1. The Irish novelist and critic George Moore spoke harshly of Thomas Hardy's *Tess of the d'Urbervilles* in *Conversations in Ebury Street* (1924).

[2]   [ALS]

> 10 Barnes St.,
> Providence, R.I.,
> May 11, 1927

Dear Mrs. Reed:—

Enclosed are the revised & typed copies of "When a Woman is Tempted". The text ran a little over what I had calculated, but as I said, I will not exceed the originally quoted price of *$3.85* for the complete job, payable by cheque or money-order at your convenience. As I prepared the final version I was impressed anew by the cleverness of the handling & excellence of the workmanship. With persistence I really think you ought to be able to place it somewhere—I assume that you take one or more writers' magazines & therefore keep track of the market, knowing just where best to send each particular type of MS. You will find this text accurate, I think—for I have just given it an additional reading & correction.

I am now ready for any other work you may care to send—if you like this specimen. And, of course, if this does not suit, I shall be glad to make any further changes desired—until it does suit you.

Hoping the enclosed may ultimately find professional acceptance, I remain
> Very sincerely yrs
> H P Lovecraft

P.S. I return your original MS. under separate cover.

[3]   [ALS]

> 10 Barnes St.,
> Providence, R.I.,
> May 18, 1927.

My dear Mrs. Reed:—

Your letter of the 12th, with article & enclosures, safely arrived; & I greatly appreciate the promptness of the remittance for the previous revision. It was especially considerate of you to make the extra allowance for postage—but let me assure you that it has always been my custom to include postage in my quoted rates. I owe you, then, some forty cents for the generous overplus in money-order & stamps—which I am duly crediting on the job just completed.

Coming to the matter of this job—whose fruits I am herewith sending in completed form—I looked the article over with extreme care & decided that the proper treatment would be *extensive* revision, of the sort which your longer story will probably require when it arrives. ($1.00 per typed page averaging 330 words) I could, of course, have merely typed it as it was, for your personal archives; but concluded upon mature consideration that you would probably prefer it in a form which might have a chance for publication—either for profit, or in some less ambitious way which would at least give your ideas the desired diffusion & furnish you a source of printed copies for scrap-book & distribution. The only reason there might be difficulty in "landing" it for pay, is that the subject has been pretty widely covered already—& your data does not involve any startling novelty in subject-matter & point of view. Incidentally—I may say that there need never be any doubt of my ability to put any piece of writing into a technically acceptable form. If slight revision will not do, I can try extensive revision; & if that also is not enough, (as is sometimes the case when great faults of synoptic order & development—absence of unity, coherence, &c—are present) I can perform the operation of complete re-casting & re-writing at the higher rates quoted. In any case, no matter what I receive, I can return a piece of writing in rhetorically correct & polished form; so that the author's decision must simply be whether or not he wishes his idea developed at any cost. It would be well to furnish separate instructions with each MS. sent—telling me the highest rate-arrangement you would be willing to adopt in case a lower one cannot be applied; that is, setting a limit, so that if you do not care enough for an item to have it revised extensively, I can be duly warned & return it unrevised if it does not prove amenable to slight revision. Incidentally—you might also mention whether your desire for revision is contingent upon the professional acceptability of the MS., as determined by my closest scrutiny. In this way I can assist many times in avoiding the expense of a revision which is unlikely to bring ultimate returns. On the other hand, I shall always be glad to go ahead with a revision whether or not I think it professionally acceptable; provided you wish it for some non-professional purpose, or wish to hazard your independent judgment as to its possibilities. All I wish is to have the exact nature of the transaction understood in advance, so that no disappointment may be involved. I always endeavour to be very liberal in making the distinction between slight & extensive revision. Usually, the criterion is that of large-scale *re-wording*—whether because of looseness in the grammatical & rhetorical flow of the text, or because of weaknesses in the dramatic limning of the theme. In short, I call a case of revision *extensive* when the substantial exercise of the creative process is necessary—but when the need falls short of that complete rearrangement & original composition from a fresh synopsis which I treat as *re-writing* under the highest rate arrangement. In this connexion I must hasten to quote a reduction of rate which I have just made in the department of *re-writing;* a reduction planned in the interest of those desiring to market totally rewritten products. Up to this week I had been charging $3.25 per page, typed—which is about the same as the cheaper magazines pay for finished stories, & which therefore left the beginner no profit unless he placed his MSS. above the 1¢ per word rate. Realising this fact—& selfishly perceiving that more novices will wish to have crude work re-cast if they can count on some slight gain in the end—(for I always give warning that *re-writing* will profit them only educationally) I have come down to $2.50 per page with typing. (& $2.25 without) I mention this mostly as a matter of record, since after looking over your three MSS. I doubt very much whether anything of yours will need treatment as drastic as a complete re-writing. What you will require, in all probability, will be either *slight* or *extensive* revision; & a careful comparison of the two MSS. I have already done—the story a *slight* job & the enclosed article an *extensive* one—will show you exactly what I mean by each of these processes. It is perhaps well that you have the opportunity of seeing this short example of extensive revision before laying out a larger sum on a longer example. You can now understand precisely what—in general nature—is done under such circumstances, & decide whether you consider the results worth the quoted price of a dollar per page, typed. Personally I am rather prouder of this grade of revision than of any other grade I practice, because I have not so far encountered any other reviser who furnishes it. Generally a critic will insist on *re-writing* if he cannot put a MS. in shape by the process which I call *slight*—& I may add that all too many are content to accept fees for a mere straightening-out of spelling, grammar, & punctuation which they call a "slight revision" but which I do not consider *revision* at all—including it in the plain service which I quote as *typing*. But enough of explanatory data.

As to the article—it is a case of *extensive revision* amounting to 5½ pages, typed. This, at a dollar per page, comes to $5.50—but deducting the extra postage previously remitted I might as well call it an even *$5.00*, payable by cheque or money order at your convenience. I enclose the usual carbon.

Concerning the article itself—its arrangement was about right, but it badly needed strengthening in two ways—the flow of the language in the non-concrete parts, (you handle simple description & conversation more fluently than abstract or argumentative passages) & the precise marshalling of images & expressions at important points of the development—beginning & ending, especially. You can see what I mean more exactly by studying your original draft—as herewith returned—with my corrections on it. The main question at issue was not merely one of good grammar, but of *subtle form* as a matter of polished stylistic maturity & as a force in realising all the possibilities of the various claims & instances brought up. As the text stood, your arguments failed to gain headway. Note particularly the first page, where the exact connexion of each new idea with its predecessor needed an enormous amount of clarifying & tightening up. Every new turn of an argument or exposition ought to have an appearance of *inevitability* as a result of the turn immediately preceding. Only when this smooth development is carried out with maximum clearness & trimness, does the article seem really powerful, competent, & convincing. There ought not to be any doubt or vagueness about anything stated or cited—no doubt as to why it is set down in just the form & place observed. This quality of unerring precision is perhaps more important in essays than in stories—but it ought to be very prominent in both. Allied to it, of course, is that careful modulation of ideas which avoids extravagance, bombast, & grandiloquence, & sustains an atmosphere of quiet assurance & accuracy. Thus you will see that I have toned down the somewhat inclusive claims on page 1 to a form which historians & anthropologists would be less likely to challenge. On page 2 I have sought to give greater clearness to your obvious meaning. From there onward for about four pages, concreteness & conversation allow more of your original wording to stand—after which some renewed clarifying & tightening ensues. As the conclusion approaches, it is necessary to strengthen—or rather elucidate—a course of argument which tends to lack massed force & convincingness. The threads must be woven together more carefully, so that each example & precept may appear to have a direct bearing on some one proof or contention whose utterance or upholding is the main purpose of the article. Previous dominant lines of argument must not be sidetracked, but must be correlated with whatever new lines may follow them. In particular, a greater & more concrete emphasis on *the principles you advocate* had to be introduced. As the article stood at first, all the difficulties surrounding marriage were stated with great clearness & explicit detail; whereas the announced truths & proposed remedies were touched upon in only the vaguest & most general fashion—thus leaving the impression of a case inadequately maintained, or an array of unfavourable facts too strong for any defender of permanent & harmonious marriage to overcome or controvert. There was a suggestion of petering-out; of losing ground & assurance when the task changed from a description of existing evils to a statement of correct principles & remedies. To the removal of this whole effect I devoted considerable care; introducing several strengthened & more concretely assured forms of expression, & combating the noticeable lack of peroration & climax by two steps—first the modified gradation & correlation of your own text as far as possible, & then the addition of a wholly original conclusion whose rhythm & rhetorical colour might harmonise with the spirit of the whole essay & give it an ending appropriate to its entire tone—rounding it out at the adequate emotional & oratorical level, & avoiding all suggestion of groping, fumbling for words & images, or "letting down" in assurance & tension. I think, sincerely, that the article is now in about as good a shape as possible—though I shall of course be glad to make further changes at any time if you so desire. As now presented, it is a clear & fluent enunciation of a sound & conservative attitude; & would have difficulty in professional acceptance only because it covers a field often covered before in the same way by others. I trust the appearance of the typed copy may please you—& here let me remark that the manner of *folding* which I follow, *is* the correct method as ordinarily practiced by authors in mailing MSS. of slight & moderate thickness. Only the long MSS. of books & extended articles are mailed flat—anything up to 30 or 35 sheets is usually folded twice if the paper be reasonably thin. In furnishing typed copies I always give as thin a paper as is consistent with durability & good appearance, since most authors find *postage* a very troublesome item. I assume you are aware of the fact that all matter submitted to professional editors must be accompanied by a self-addressed envelope bearing full return postage. If the MS. is accepted, this return postage never comes back—& I have often wondered what becomes of the stamps in cases of heavy MSS! Perhaps the editors soak them off & use them!

I regret that the weighty envelope of my previous letter gave you a shock of alarm before you opened it—but must warn you that returned MSS. are things always to be reckoned with—even after many years as an established author. Writers whom I know—men who have been more or less successful with magazine writing for five years & more—tell me that they feel lucky if they *ever* place more than perhaps one out of every three manuscripts they send out. And of those MSS. which *do* "land", probably a full half are forced to traverse long rounds of submission & re-submission to various editors. Indeed, most MSS. become worn out before they succeed in finding a kindly haven—so that authors are constantly compelled to re-type their tales lest a dilapidated aspect reveal too plainly their many fruitless visits. In sending out MSS. it is well to add a heavy blank page after the last typed page—or perhaps it needn't be so heavy. When one writes much, it is quite necessary to own a typewriter, for the expense of having fresh copies of old MSS. made is really too great a burden to be sensible. Good typing costs about a quarter per page, (and poor typing is a great handicap with editors—i.e., inaccurate typing, or work which shows ignorance on the typist's part. The *author* is often silently saddled with the *typist's* crudenesses!) whereas the literary beginner can much better afford to furnish the time & energy himself—these items counting for more than the direct outlay in machine, ribbons, paper, carbon-paper, & repairs. A good machine can now be obtained for fifty dollars—the new portable Remingtons & Coronas being perhaps the most practical & satisfactory sort to get. Learning is very brief & simple if one is content to waive the touch system & rely on his eyes & two forefingers as most authors do.

As for the long story—let me make it especially clear that its corrected & erased & interlined form did *not* constitute any ground for objection on my part. I *never* ask an author to make a neat copy for purposes of further revision; for since my own corrections will soon be defacing whatever MS. I tackle, an attempt at mechanical neatness would be a criminal waste of energy on the writer's part & a barbarous thing for me to demand. When I speak of a MS. as in "rough form", I refer solely to its rhetorical or literary qualities, & not to its external appearance. Thus a neat MS. of an unrevised story is "in poor condition", whereas an almost illegible mass of corrections is "in perfect shape" if its text (as traced through all the revisory hieroglyphics) has attained its final & polished literary form. No thought need ever be devoted to the neatness or appearance of a MS. sent for revision—common legibility being the only desideratum.

However—I gather that the renewed attention you are reluctant to give the tale is rhetorical as well as mechanical. Distaste for revising one's own work is by no means new in literature; even Lord Byron saying that, like the tiger, he must finish his achievement at the first leap or not at all.[1] Most writers, though, find it very profitable to adopt a more philosophic attitude—not only because of the critics' fees it saves them, but because of the educational value of analysing & annulling one's own mistakes & tendencies to weakness. Repeated revision of one's own work gives one an intimate insight into one's own style, & helps the advanced author in the greatest of all literary tasks— that of making language respond unerringly to his every need & subtlety, till it becomes as perfect an artistic medium in his hands as is painting in the hands of the limner or music in the hands of the organist. Cabell says that the author's task is "to write perfectly of beautiful happenings", & long before him Flaubert remarked that "the inexpressible does not exist".[2] This high standard, however, presupposes a deep & critical knowledge of language as related to one's individual nature—& that can be gained only through the most drastic, alert, minute, & disillusioned self-criticism.

You yourself are probably the best judge as to whether or not you could improve a given MS. by further self-revision, so that I will leave altogether to you the decision regarding the long story. I will await it whenever it arrives, & will act as its condition & accompanying instructions may dictate. As I said before, it has the material of an excellent tale—its freshness & originality being unmistakable. It is worth revising, & if the matter is left to me I will do all I can to realise its possibilities. "The Unchaining" strikes me as a very appropriate title, & I think you do well in provisionally adopting it. I rather thought the *Slaughter* nomenclature was involuntary, & am interested to hear that it was suggested from real life. I noticed it in particular because puns were made on Gov. Henry Sloughter of New York, who in 1691 signed the death-warrant of Jacob Leisler & his associates, after Leisler's seizure of the gov-

ernment during the chaos following the fall of King James & the imprison-
ment of Sir Edmund Andros. Leisler's acts were undoubtedly fanatical & ille-
gal, but he meant well & has been much lauded by the partisans of
democratic government—who are naturally quick to make the most of Gov.
Sloughter's vulnerable patronymic.

I am glad you have Woolley's handbook, which is as good & concise as
any current manual I know of. The author is now & then amusingly over-
precise—but that is the safer side for novices to lean toward. As for the
shorter story whose typed MS. you have—yes, I see no reason for not starting
it out if you have the proper markets clearly in mind. I assume that you keep
track of these through some writers' magazine—if not, I'll recommend a few
periodicals of the sort.

I will duly note your change of address when informed. Too bad Cleveland is uncongenial—it seemed very pleasant to me during my one fortnight's
visit of five years ago, but the call of nostalgia is not to be denied! If I am in
New York during your visit I would surely be very much pleased to meet
you—though I don't get there very often owing to the 200 miles of distance
& the formidable size of the railway fare as measured by my lean purse. Oddly enough, most of my friends live there, & I tried staying there on that account for over two years; but the stridor & foreignness of the place finally
grated on my nerves, & I decided to return to that native New England soil
whose ancient atmosphere & architectural reliques accord so well with my
essentially antiquarian temperament.

With every good wish, & hoping that the enclosed work may prove satisfactory,

I remain

Very sincerely yrs

H P Lovecraft

Notes

1. In a letter to John Murray, Byron wrote: "I am like the tiger (in poesy), if I miss the
first spring, I go growling back to my jungle. There is no second; I can't correct; I
can't, and I won't. Nobody ever succeeds in it, great or small."

2. The James Branch Cabell quotation is from his "Auctorial Induction" to *The Certain
Hour* (1917). HPL errs in attributing the other quotation to Flaubert; it was written by
Théophile Gautier in conversation with Charles Baudelaire.

[4]   [ALS]

10 Barnes St.,

Providence, R.I.,

May 23, 1927.

My dear Mrs. Reed:—

The long MS. with its parallel versions arrived safely, & I shall get to work on it at the earliest possible moment. At present a very heavy job of verse revision has prevented my giving it more than a cursory survey, but as soon as that is off my hands I shall set to work in earnest. I feel quite certain that I can have the revised version in your hands within a week. Meanwhile I trust the revised article safely reached you.

As to titles—I believe that "The Unchaining" is the only really suitable one yet devised; since the climax of the tale is not merely the circumstance of inhibition, but the dramatic cessation of that circumstance through the agency of the child. The title therefore ought to hint at this dynamic element, & allude not so much to *captivity* as to *liberation*. It may be useful, as a general indicator of values in this field, if I comment briefly on all your other suggested titles, explaining why they do not seem as effective as "The Unchaining":

> The Restless Beast—a little florid, & non-indicative of liberation
> Chained ---------------------------------- "   "   "   "
> Denied the Power to Love—suggesting ultra-cheap romantic melo-
> drama—also *misleading*, since the heroine is denied
> only the power to *display* love.
> The Depths of Love—vague, & slightly suggestive of cheap ro-
> mance
> * ⎰ The Imprisoned Emotions ⎱   —dry & prosaic—suggests a
> ⎱ The Tempest of Emotions ⎰   treatise or essay rather than a story
> Chained Within—theatrical & non-indicative of liberation
> The Raging Tempest of her Soul—*extremely* melodramatic—to the point
> where conscious burlesque might be suspected

Regarding writers' magazines—I believe that the most helpful is *The Writers' Digest,* 22 East Twelfth St., Cincinnati, Ohio. $2.00 per year[.] This is very reliable & conservative, with full lists of current literary markets brought down to date. Nearly every author & critic recommends this strongly. *The Writer,* Boston, Mass., (I can't recall the street address, but I'm sure the city would be enough—you could make a tentative inquiry) is also very highly regarded, & has recently undergone radical enlargement & improvement. I am

---

*The word *emotion* is so quasi-scientific & utterly descriptive in its function, that I do not think it can be effectively used in any fictional title.

not sure of the new subscription rate, but fancy it's around the two-dollar mark. Another magazine which some don't like so well, but in which I have found some highly helpful material is *The Author & Journalist,* (formerly *The Student Writer*) 1837 Champa St., Denver, Colorado. ($2.00 per year) *The Writers' Monthly,* published by the Home Correspondence School, Myrick Bldg., Springfield, Mass., is $3.00 per year. It is very popular, but emphasises the selling side of the craft more than the creative. Some writers take many or all of the current authors' publications—& of course, the more one takes, the more useful hints one is likely to pick up. Under separate cover I am sending some specimens of this type of publication—which you may retain. Old issues, but typical of the average number.

Regarding markets on which to try "When a Woman is Tempted"—I believe that *Marriage,* 220 West Jefferson St., Bloomington, Ill., might be a good place to try—not only with this story but with your article as well. Another possible haven is *Marriage Stories,* Dell Pub. Co., 46 West 24th St., New York City. One might also approach *People's Home Journal,* 80 Lafayette St., New York City, or *People's Popular Monthly,* 2nd & Centre Sts., Des Moines, Ia. Other conceivable markets are *Woman's Home Companion,* 250 Park Ave., New York, N.Y., & *Woman's World,* 107 South Clinton St., Chicago, Ill. The Sunday Magazine of the *Boston Post* (George Brinton Beale, Editor) is a good place to try—& in the daily edition of the *Post* there is a prize short story department (for women writers only, & leaning strongly toward the domestic themes in which you evidently specialise) involving prizes of from $2.00 to $10.00—not a profitable market, but a good source of publicity & practice. *The Designer,* 12 Vandam St., New York City, is also in the market for feminine short story material. If—as is usually the case with a new writer—you have difficulty with these regular magazines, the somewhat more unpretentious *rural press* offers an excellent & hospitable start. Good specimens of this type to try are *Everyday Life,* 337 Madison St., Chicago, *Farmer's Wife,* St Paul, Minn., *Good Stories,* Augusta, Me., *Comfort,* Augusta, Me., *Holland's Magazine,* Dallas, Tex., *Home Friend Magazine,* 1411 Wyandotte St., Kansas City, Mo., *Household Guest,* 141 West Ohio St., Chicago, Ill., *Household Journal,* Batavia, Ill., *Chicago Ledger,* 500–514 N. Dearborn St., Chicago, Ill.[,] *Vaughan's Family Visitor,* Lawrenceburg, Tenn., *The Wright Magazine,* Kansas City, Mo., Farm & Home, Springfield, Mass.[,] *Western Home Monthly,* Winnipeg, Manitoba, Canada, *Farm Life,* Spencer, Ind., *Ohio Farmer,* Cleveland, *Pennsylvania Farmer,* Philadelphia, &c. &c. You can readily obtain other names, together with bulletins of recent requirements, from the various writers' magazine I have mentioned. *Good Housekeeping* & *The Cosmopolitan* would hardly be advisable for any beginner to try, since the chances for rejection are almost 100% except for the veteran writers habitually contributing. *The Cosmopolitan* demands a tone of great superficial sophistication together with very mature craftsmanship—although there is not much psychological subtlety or artistic distinctiveness in its pages. It is distinctly a market for the experienced writer only—for the writer intimately versed in the situations & mannerisms of urbane popular fiction, & viewing life from an angle of considerable worldly insight & disillusion.

As for the method of sending out—it is best to accompany each MS. with only the briefest & most businesslike of notes, stating that the story in question is submitted for consideration at the magazine's usual rates. A stamped & self-addressed envelope must go with the contribution—& in sending this it is most convenient to get one slightly smaller than the one in which you do the sending. It is easy to get envelopes of the two required sizes—& most authors keep on hand a stock of both. Return envelopes are just big enough to hold the 8½ × 11 MS. folded twice, & sending envelopes are just enough larger to hold the return envelope comfortably without folding. There is no rule, however, against folding a return envelope if you don't happen to have any variety of sizes on hand. Some do it constantly. Be sure to have your return address plainly written on your outside envelope, for some of the smaller magazines go out of existence & disappear with disconcerting suddenness.

Trusting to get at your story very shortly—I remain
  Sincerely yrs
   H P Lovecraft

[5] [ALS]

        10 Barnes St.,
        Providence, R.I.,
        May 28, 1927.

Dear Mrs. Reed:—
    The two recent MSS. have safely arrived, & I will give them the most careful possible consideration at the earliest available moment. Perhaps a week—or not much more—ought to see them safely back in whatever form I find best for them. Meanwhile I trust you have received my note of a few days ago, listing possible markets & recommending certain authors' magazines. I enclose some circulars from one of the latter which arrived yesterday, & which may contain some helpful hints. Almost any of the technical books advertised by these periodicals will be found to contain useful bits of data of one sort or another. I also sent some back numbers of authors' magazines—which give a better idea of them than descriptions can.

My pressure of work is phenomenally heavy just now, (what makes revision such an unprofitable business is the enormous amount of time & energy one has to put into even the smallest of jobs in order to produce really thorough & conscientious results) but I have at last begun actual verbal work on "The Unchaining". It required extensive revision after all, & I am finding it simpler to write a wholly new rough draught myself, rather than to interline your MS. The revision is based on version *#2*—which is incomparably better in every phase of technique; especially its immediate presentation of a crucial scene which touches the central subject of the tale—the emotional limitation of Ella Brent. I shall work slowly & well rather than hastily & superficially, but at the slowest ought to have the finished version in your hands by the middle of next week. I am glad you like the final form of the article, & hope that it can find a place somewhere in print—even if not in highly remunerative print.

I can understand your dislike of the typewriter, & am absolutely unable to comprehend how any living being can perform original literary composition on it—although many, including friends of mine, habitually do so. To me the process of typing is a torment, & I dread it far more than any other phase of revisory work—though ironically enough, one can't charge prices commensurate with one's dread, since it's manual rather than cerebral labour. Two long novelettes of my own—110 & 150 longhand pages, respectively[1]— remain unseen by the editorial public because of my sheer inability to face the ordeal of clicking them off on my antediluvian Remington. I am of course absurdly slow, being only a forefinger-artist in this department of craftsmanship.

Assuming that you now have the lists of magazines in my note & in the accompanying periodicals, there is no reason why you should not begin sending out the two MSS. you have on hand. Most authors keep their MSS. constantly on the move, having vast numbers out at the same time, & keeping track of them by means of a card-catalogue system. (which records previous rejections in order to prevent accidental repetitions in sending) One good guide in sending MSS. is to study the different magazines & see which ones are accustomed to use material of the type of each MS. in question. Also, digest well whatever individual advice & comment an editor deigns to mingle with his rejections. Occasionally one will get such comment, though of course the traditional "rejection slip" is much more frequent. *Delay* in consideration is a *favourable* sign; for a MS. is kept waiting only when it has been approved by the preliminary reader who decides what shall be saved for the scrutiny of the editor or editorial staff. A hopelessly bad or diametrically unsuitable MS. generally comes back at once. This rule breaks down, of course, when one gets to be favourably known—at which time most editors order their readers to refer all of one's MSS. directly to them—for decisions which are occasionally quite prompt. Two months is an average editorial wait for a new author's MS.

As to the possibility of profit on your part—it will of course be a matter of long waiting & diligent perseverance. You have perhaps heard of the almost maddening rebuffs received by the young Kipling forty years ago, & of the now classic fact that Joseph Hergesheimer sent his work unavailingly to editors for fourteen years before meeting the success which eventually rewarded him. It is, at the start, well-nigh impossible to predict the manner or degree of success which any given beginner will achieve; for the elements & qualities leading to popular acceptance are so infinitely subtle, elusive, & intangible that no description or detection of them is possible on any accurate scale. Actual experience—the test of writing & sending, & writing & sending again—is all that will give a final verdict; & even then, as the cases of Kipling & Hergesheimer show, there is much chance for a spectacular reversal of verdict after discouraging stretches of time. What one *can* tell is whether or not an author is hopelessly unfit at the start—unfit, as it were, to take part in the preliminary elimination skirmishes. Given a favourable answer to this question, the next thing is to see how apt & adaptable the writer is—that is, how well he responds to suggestions & how well he catches the atmospheric essence of what is required. If he does not take readily to moulding, he had better not continue; but if he does, it is a good indication of his comprehension of what is needed—of his realisation of his own equipment in relation to the given task, & his conscious mastery of the situation. That is presumptive evidence of success ahead, although of course only the test of experience can be final. So far as I can judge from your three earlier MSS., (I have not yet been able to go over the new pair) you have the aptitude which justifies further experiments; hence I would advise you to continue trying unless you feel very conclusively that all changes & suggestions represent a type of process beyond the power of your art-sense to grasp. And from a survey of beginning #2 in "The Unchaining" I would say that you appear very receptive rather than impervious to constructive comment. Indeed, you seem to have grasped the spirit of the revision very intelligently. I'll report later on the new MSS.

    Sincerely yrs
    H P Lovecraft

Notes

1. *The Dream-Quest of Unknown Kadath* and *The Case of Charles Dexter Ward.* Both remained unpublished in HPL's lifetime.

[6] [ALS]

        10 Barnes St.,
        Providence, R.I.,
         June 4, 1927

My dear Mrs. Reed:—

    The money-order & additional MS. safely arrived, as did the two other notes. There was really no necessity for going to the trouble of special delivery—the time saved is scarcely worth the added postage. I would have acknowledged some of these items sooner, had my programme been less desperately crowded. In yours of June 2nd you evidently refer to another story on the way. If this arrives before I mail this letter I will note the fact on the outside of the envelope.

The revision of "The Unchaining" was finished last Wednesday, but I have not yet been able to do the typing. That is the disadvantage of a one-man bureau over a large organisation with a constantly available staff—a disadvantage which may or may not be outweighed by the factor of uniform revisory style & individual familiarity with the entire output & characteristic literary tendencies of each client. I shall make every effort to type the story at once, perhaps having it in your hands by next Tuesday or Wednesday. I shall accompany the MS. with some critical observations, but the best way to profit by the change is to give a close parallel reading to the new version & to the version (#2) from which it was made. Example is better than precept. Since I have written a new longhand rough draught (which I'll later send with the rest, to give you an extra—if not very legible—duplicate) I am able to return herewith the original MSS. sent, bearing some marginal comments which I made on my first reading, & which may be of some instructive value to you. Although these take the form of *directions,* they are not to be acted upon now, since I have acted upon them myself. The tale is done, & you will see in the final copy the embodiment of these suggestions. I also return the very first draught, as well as the unused version #1 of the second writing. All these items, when correlated, have a certain educational value as evolutionary steps.

Regarding the holding of your MSS. by the International Magazine Co.— that would seem to indicate that the first readers liked them well enough to pass them on to powers higher up! It may be taken as a source of encouragement rather than of anxiety, although of course one must not have keen hopes of first-time acceptance by magazines of such standardised prominence. Two weeks is *not* a long wait for MSS. with any ordinary magazine—indeed, I recall mentioning that two *months* is much more typical. Patience—or philosophic resignation—is the one attribute without which a novice cannot even begin to buy his fortunes with the editorial brotherhood. If, however, you are highly anxious to get the MSS. off to another periodical, a note from you would undoubtedly bring them back at once. About that one's own judgment must be used. I never hurry an editor myself, being callous & phlegmatic enough to let nature take its course without auxiliary worry on my part.

As to an agent or agency for placing MSS.—I do think it would be an excellent idea to utilise one; for the fees are rather reasonable, while their knowledge of current market conditions is of course infinitely wider than that of anyone who does not make such knowledge his dominant professional specialty. At the same time, one must take care to deal only with reliable & punctiliously honourable agents; since the other sort are filled with schemes for unfair advantages & ill-gotten gains. For one thing, never sign any contract tying up future work. When this is demanded, the agency may be set down as undesirable. I am not very familiar with agents' names, but I know of one whose fair methods & helpful advice have been found eminently satisfactory. This is Robert Thomas Hardy, 25 West 42nd St., New York City. I don't know whether he cares to handle beginners' work, but he is certainly worth looking up.[1] It also occurs to me that a friend of mine—a professional author of long standing—has a very thorough knowledge of responsible agencies & could easily furnish you with the names of those which have benefited him. I will give his name & address here, & if you will inquire of him—enclosing a self-addressed envelope or postal—I am certain he will be glad to send the information at once as a matter of courtesy. He is Everett McNeil, 457 Fifth St., Brooklyn, N.Y.—author of about fifteen successful boys' books. As to the various writers' magazines—of course the market information in each individual issue differs in importance. One must have many issues on hand in order to possess a really full working background of data. I would certainly advise your subscribing to one or more of these periodicals.

Now taking up the recent story MSS.—I have given each one a very careful reading, & believe that their order of merit is as follows: 1. "Under Cover", (tentative title for unnamed MS. on yellow paper) 2. "The Silent Voice", 3. "Out o' the East." On the principle of elimination, it will be well to speak of these in reverse order, beginning with that whose market chances would probably be least.

"Out of the East" is at a disadvantage because of the essential *artificiality* of virtually all the elements involved. The setting itself is a great handicap, for even the popular reading public is beginning to feel the basic unreality & theatricality of the cinema Wild West with its stereotyped stock characters—the Dead Dawg Saloon & Gambling Parlour, the mysterious tenderfoot, the honest, open, hearty $\left\{\begin{matrix} \text{cowpuncher} \\ \text{rancher} \\ \text{miner} \end{matrix}\right\}$, the malign villain, (horse thief or road-agent of any but the sentimental Robin Hood type) the Big Near-Lynching scene, the eleventh-hour rescue, &c. &c. The trouble is, that this depicts a milieu & reflects an atmosphere based entirely on popular literary precedent & not on life. No such west exists, & only in sketchy outlines did such a west ever exist. In its details & glamour it is purely a fictional (& wholly Eastern) creation, so that it has not the deep appeal of anything taken out of life. In your "Unchaining", the western setting *does* ring true. That—so far as an Easterner may judge—really represents the west in something of its natural colours. But this other MS. has the flicker of the screen & the click of the camera somewhere in the offing. The world it shows is not a real one, & there is no chance for that sincere unfolding of human character against an authentic background which gives permanence & fundamental vitality to literature. The various events & figures appear to share the atmosphere of the scene, & the plot itself is based on an artifice not much in favour at this date—i.e., the deliberate deceiving of the *reader* (as distinguished from the deception of the *characters*) concerning the status of one of the protagonists. I may add that even the deception of the characters has its aura of stiltedness. These "sealed-lip" mysteries & complicating inhibitions are not characteristic features of real life, & therefore have a very doubtful value in that system of glorified symbolism which is literature. To sum up—this tale errs in staking everything on *plot*. The mechanism is so dominant that it cannot escape visibility. As to the structure—it would have to receive an enormous amount of toning-up & reapportionment of parts. It is topheavy—the beginning ought to be the landing of the cryptic lady from the train, since that is the crucial or keynote incident which starts off the action. In matters of language—i.e., ways of presenting antecedent events, twists of current narration, modes of introducing scenic & dramatic effects, & modelling of general structure in order to achieve maximum results from each word,—a considerable re-casting would be required; with great attention paid to the subtle associational value of each word, sentence, phrase, & paragraph. In particular, there would have to be an elimination of cases of *obvious explanation*. This is one of the fictionist's greatest problems—how to tell a thing not directly represented in the continuous action without having it appear that an effort is being made to tell it. It must always be either by indirection—implied in some *convincingly* casual act or remark in the natural flow of the events—or by retrospective statement so **utterly** brief, lightly interpolated, & glancing that it fails wholly to obtrude itself on the contemporary setting or to give the impression of heaviness or clumsiness. In my opinion, one ought to keep as much of this explanatory matter as possible out of *conversation*. Dialogue is a ticklish thing at best, & becomes altogether hopeless when the characters are burdened with an historical mission—when they are forced to say explanatory things which would not ordinarily have been said in the given situation. And in this connexion it is fitting to remark that there is only one really sound criterion of dialogue, either in stories or in the drama. That criterion is **absolute** *fidelity to life*—& we may see, as its corollary, that no one ought ever to attempt dialogue without first acquiring an accurate & intimate familiarity (either at first-hand or through literature conceded by the best critics to be faithful) with the type of character & environment treated of. Returning to the story specifically—I really don't think it would be fair for me to revise this item (& it would require the most extensive treatment) with any expectation of sale, since the vital fault is in the setting & plot essence, apart from the technique. It is not by any means a discreditable performance, & has undoubtedly furnished splendid practice in fluency & narrative deftness; but the material is too well-worn to warrant elaborate development according to the original plan. I would advise keeping this manuscript in reserve for possible later development in a lighter way—

for the central deception could be made very ingenious if a less serious & conventional set of events were attached to it. I believe I will return it under separate cover for your future consideration—your consideration at a more advanced stage, when you will be able to bring a greater fund of technical experience to bear upon its problems—& hope that this circumstance may not prove in any way discouraging so far as your general output is concerned. I would have picked it to pieces less minutely, had I not formed a preconceived standard through the excellent characterisation in "The Unchaining" & the fluent technique of "When a Woman is Tempted."

Now as to "The Silent Voice"—here we have an authentic human situation with infinite literary possibilities; the case of the jealous son, so masterfully handled by Booth Tarkington in "The Magnificent Ambersons." Technically, however, there is an enormous need of radical revision—perhaps the actual re-writing which I have mentioned as a last resort, & which is of only educational—never commercial—value to the client. The great defect here is *scattering*—material & time-lapses enough for a novel being crowded into the compass of a particularly short short story. This instance makes it apropos for me to emphasise very definitely some almost essential attributes of the *short story* as a fixed & well-differentiated form. The most inclusive quality, perhaps, is *incidentalness* of subject-matter. By this I mean that the short story, on account of its limited length, ought never to attempt the portrayal of whole *lives* or long chains of events. These things are the province of the *novel*, & all attempts to make a short tale a "tabloid" novel are foredoomed to artistic disaster. It is true that a short story may often *suggest* whole lives & long chains of vital events. Perhaps the very greatest of them always do. But this suggestion must perforce be accomplished through isolated, typical *incidents* in the stream of life or events concerned; effected by means of whatever *symbolism* the selected fragment may possess. It was Poe who first discovered the great aesthetic truth that the sine qua non of a short story is *singleness of impression.* A short narrative must tell of brief events, & must be draped definitely around *one scene or happening.* Lapses of time & shifts of scene are not forbidden, but they should be cut down to a minimum; & all should hinge vitally & inescapably upon one central point—thus giving a basic unity which is psychological, if not in all ways chronological or geographical. The way to lay out a short story is to select some brief, culminating moment in the life of a person or group of persons, (or in any dramatically potent sequence of events) & present this in high light & detail; working in the necessary supplementary elements as compressedly & inconspicuously as possible.

There are types, of course, which necessarily contravene this rule— notably those in which *a fragment of motion* itself occupies the position of a central idea. That state of things occurs mostly in the sort of fiction where plot predominates over character & atmosphere—not the highest type, by any means. "The Silent Voice", I take it, is meant to be a story of human character rather than of plot; the boy's stratagem being merely a device for the enhancement of the impression. This being so, it becomes necessary to see how the conflicting elements of big theme (remember that Tarkington took a whole novel to develop the same basic situation) & brief length may be reconciled. To me two courses occur. One is to create one central scene—such as Philip's sight of the emerald ring on Clare's finger—& group everything around it as prologue & aftermath, respectively, & the other is to adopt the Continental mode of letting the *idea* of the son's jealousy form the working nucleus; adopting a very objective & detached point of view, & narrating the whole thing in very dry, laconic prose with utmost economy of space & connected action or dialogue. By this I mean the removal of all reflections on the part of the characters themselves, & the paring down of all continuous scenes & bits of conversation. The idea would be to tell the story very markedly *from the outside,* with no sentimentality or emotional sympathy with any of the actors, but with a touch of polite cosmic irony at the essential impersonality & purposelessness of the universe. The effect of this, if adroitly done, is to rouse the reader's sympathy & emotions *more* than could be effected by any appearance of sympathy or emotion on the writer's part. Of course the length of the whole must be kept rigorously down to the Continental standard—as fixed by almost any modern French short story of typical form. Your great guide & model in this field is De Maupassant, who really is a supreme technical master despite the promiscuous rabble applause which would lead one to doubt it. Every writer of short fiction ought to know the whole of De Maupassant virtually by rote—indeed, if I knew that any beginner was not thoroughly familiar with these tales, I'd advise him strongly to defer all further writing until after a close perusal & mature assimilation of them. Like Poe's tales, they are an absolutely essential & indispensable part of any modern fictionist's background. I shall probably say more concerning necessary reading in answering a later question of yours. Just now, I'll merely observe that I would myself advise a Gallic treatment of this particular story, with De Maupassant as a model & with a much less melodramatic title—such as "The/An Emerald Ring", "Reward", (meaning, ironically, Clare's reward for maternal devotion) "An Abnegation", or anything of crisp, graphic brevity without the element of mawkishness or melodrama. In rewriting, beware of hackneyed word-uses, stock phrases & incidents, & artificial conceptions of life, feelings, manners, & customs generally. Be as simple & realistic as it is possible to be, for the basis of the tale is stark, relentless life. In writing about the stratagem of the emerald ring, go slowly & carefully. These deceptions are not, on the whole, very typical or symbolic in their relation to real life. They are insidiously stagey & artificial in their general suggestion; & although sometimes spectacularly effective in a popular & mechanical way,—just as

Christmas-tree ornaments are effective—are not on the whole very good art or literature. The story would, I am sure, be much more powerful if Jack could alienate Phil in quieter & subtler way—perhaps by circulating rumours of his mother's engagement to another—endeavouring to make Philip believe that her hesitancy was not really due to material solicitude, but to the rival attractions (either personal, social, or financial) of another suitor. Don't go ahead till after reading "The Magnificent Ambersons" if you're not already familiar with that book. Remember that a story of deep emotions like this cannot be handled in a simple or superficial way. You must realise that the conflict of aims & feelings is infinitely profound & complex, & must take care to utilise a vision, background, & subtlety commensurate with the depth of the theme. The opportunities for fine & penetrating work are really very considerable. It is well to keep always in mind the essential extent & seriousness of the author's task. No progress will ever be achieved if one contents oneself with the false motivation, artificial values & types, & deceptive simplicity of characterisation found in the popular type of magazine. Cheap fiction does not even begin to tell what human beings actually think & do—it merely parrots a mock-world of absurd simplifications, distorted proportions, & conventional hack illusions which commercial experience has found to be palatable to an enormous public of mixed intelligence & negligible cultural or scholastic depth. One may, by chance, hit on financial success by bowing to these cheap traditions—for do not "Dr." Frank Crane, Fannie Hurst, Eddie Guest,[2] & a host of other facile surface-skimmers wax fat on the cheques of businesslike editors & the praises of dull-witted boors? But this isn't literature, & the beginner who really has serious things in mind must establish the distinction clearly at the start. Let the cinema & the *Peoples' Home Journal* & the Sunday supplement retreat forgotten to their native caverns of darkness; & let the policy of the future be the study—not of tawdry artificialities & false stock-images—but of life itself, as seen directly in fragments, & reflected in really standard literature. The English & Continental classics, as recognised with some unanimity by all competent authorities, ought to be studied in detail as an indispensable groundwork; while the current American scene (if that be the writer's chosen province) should be learned through no interpreters less solid & truthful than Edith Wharton, Theodore Dreiser, Sherwood Anderson, Kathleen Norris, Willa Cather, Thomas Boyd, Joseph Hergesheimer, Frank Norris, Ben Hecht, or Robert Herrick. These people are telling about life for its own sake & for the telling's sake, & you can depend to a reasonable extent on the truth of what they say. Anything more flashy or popular than this grade may be considered as bearing a greater or less tincture of meaningless & commercial "hokum". *Borderline* types—with good groundwork but dubious leanings—are (for example) Sinclair Lewis & Edna Ferber. Apostates—men educated for real things but subsequently bowing to the Golden

Calf & showing only accidental & fugitive flashes of the "real stuff" are Rupert Hughes & Robert W. Chambers. Anything below this level ought to be left severely alone—as mental & artistic poison. But this is merely a digression to accentuate the need of wide observation of real life, & perfect fidelity to it. Returning to your story—the least thing I could conscientiously do to it is absolute re-writing at $2.50 per page, typed—& this would come to the formidable figure of about *$25.00* for only *ten* or so typed pages of text. Candidly, I don't think the educational value would quite warrant the expenditure—especially since at this early stage you would probably get much more benefit from the practice of re-writing it yourself, with the incisive impersonality & tragic beauty of De Maupassant in mind. *After* you have done this, I might be able to give it a final form through either elementary or extensive revision at the lower rates quoted. With precisely the right touch, the tale might sell—although of course one must realise that the theme is very old & repeatedly used. Its success would all depend on freshness, vitality, & realistic originality of treatment—so that really it might be well to postpone re-writing till after the acquisition of more technical facility through practice on lighter themes. But I will leave that to you. All I can justly present are the facts as I see them. Since you will probably decide against the costly re-writing by me, I will re-enclose the tale with the western one. Don't forget, however, that it is infinitely better than this more artificial envelope-mate. Incidentally—I am not charging the advisory critical rate for the foregoing remarks, since they are not as detailed as I would have made if such treatment had been advisable. In what I have said there is very much of the *general,* as applicable to all that you write, hence I think it is most fairly included as a gratuitous appendage to the revisions I am giving your other manuscripts.

At this point I find it necessary to turn to another long-deferred piece of work, hence will divide the matter I had meant to include in this letter; continuing tomorrow on the other subjects brought up in your letters. Suffice it to say in concluding this instalment that I think the new (yellow) MS. can be made into a popular tale through extensive revision, (abt. $21.00 in all for the 6970 words) although it has in general a certain artificiality & superficial conception of human emotions which rather militates against its art value. (though not against its possible salability.) If you'd prefer to have it back for more touching-up, I'll send it; but on account of the involutions of plot (requiring technical experience) I couldn't absolutely guarantee that such a procedure would enable me to finish it at the elementary-revision rate. I will not, however, start in on the more costly process without a further authorising word from you—& I suggest that you defer deciding until you receive my preliminary critical remarks on the tale. Your technique is certainly progressing—this story is much better-written than either of the ones I am returning, although it doesn't equal "The Unchaining". Incidentally, I may say that your *technical* high-water mark appears to be "When a Woman is Tempted"—a thing which possibly suggests that *light* themes would do well for immediate practice. In the next instalment I shall answer whatever questions about general prospects &c. were not answered in my note of a week ago, & shall perhaps be able to include the typed version of "The Unchaining."

One point more—as to an article on child-character, I may say that such a thing would have to be very original in angle or content in order to "land" remuneratively. As with the marriage article I revised last week, the subject is an old & oft-thrashed-out one, & the chances are against anything new turning up in it. However, many "home" magazines might be glad of it on an unremunerative basis, so if you wish to get on record in print, there is no harm in sending it where it might have a chance. At any rate, you might let me see the MS., & I will give whatever opinion I can regarding its possibilities. Your basic idea of early character-formation is now pretty universally shared, so that the trouble would probably be too much public agreement rather than too little.

I will, then, continue my remarks at an early date. Your new MS. is safe, as will likewise be the one you say is now en route. It is unfortunate that prompter service cannot be furnished—but the combination of one head & many streams of MSS. from diverse quarters presents insurmountable obstacles to speed; so that I can only offer my apologies & my regrets.

Hoping that the foregoing remarks may be found of some utility, I remain

Yrs most sincerely,

H. P. Lovecraft

[P.S.] Please pardon possible mistakes—absolutely no time to re-read!

Notes

1. Robert Thomas Hardy (1873–1935), American editor, agent, and writer of poetry, short stories, and silent movie scripts. He worked as an editor at Lippincott, Street & Smith, the Frank A. Munsey Co., and others.

2. Frank Crane (1861–1928), Presbyterian minister and author of numerous volumes on religion, ethics, and society aimed at a popular audience. Fannie Hurst (1885–1968), popular novelist and short story writer. Edgar A. Guest (1881–1959), poet whose work was widely featured in newspapers but was held in low esteem by critics.

[7]　[AHT]

10 Barnes Street

Providence, R.I.

June 5, 1927

My dear Mrs. Reed:—

[. . .]

I come at length to the matter of your literary prospects, and to the procedure which—so far as anyone can decide from the necessarily very incomplete data at hand—I would be inclined to suggest as best suited to your present ambitions and your present state of development. Naturally, you will realise that no outsider can conclusively do anything more than conjecture; since to appraise an authority profoundly, one must know not only what he is momentarily doing, but what he is trying to do, how long he has been trying, and what background of scholastic knowledge and imaginative life he is drawing upon for the creation of his present effects. These things, on the whole, can seldom be perfectly gauged except by the author himself.

First—as to what an author is trying to do. Now there are many motives for literary creation, but to my mind only one—and that the one least admitted by commercial-minded people—is of enough validity to warrant a person's going ahead with systematic writing. We may, then, dispose at once of the people who wish merely a source of income. These may succeed if they have a large endowment of natural technical proficiency, but they will always be essentially mechanical. They will never produce anything which—to employ your own words—is "worth while" or "has any depth", and could probably realise their ambitions sooner and more pleasantly in some other field of enterprise. We may likewise dispose of those merely restless souls who write as a relief from boredom or from unsatisfactory living conditions. These people merely want something which they haven't, and think that the easiest way to get it is to make up a simple play-world on paper; in which they, in the person of their heroes, can enjoy all the things that real life doesn't furnish. They care nothing for literature or craftsmanship for its own sake, nor does the world possess for them any golden wonder or glamour which they feel they must record. Their thoughts are limited, commonplace, and twisted in the direction of their own particular source of mundane discontent; and there is little prospect that their writings can have any real power, beauty, grace, or universal symbolism and appeal. They would be far better off if they could find something else to interest or satisfy them—as they occasionally do after authorship has begun to bore them. A third class to be eliminated is the mere pastime scribbler—the languid and unoriginal recreation-seeker who finds amusement and gratified vanity in more or less laboured imitations of books and stories he has read and admired. He takes a childish pleasure in achieving a certain resemblance to his idols—or in accomplishing a certain reflection of their false, simple world (or their true, complex world, in the rare event that his tastes are classic)—which may be compared to the pleasure of the successful crossword-puzzle solver of 1925, or the high-score questionnaire-answerer of the present year of grace. This sort of person may now and then attain a level which is not half bad—but there is no vital motive force behind his work, and he will eventually veer off to something else. What literature is to him now, baseball or politics or foreign missions may be next year. Another unlikely set is the stern-faced, vociferous legion of People With A Purpose. These good folk write because they want to make others do or believe in something which they believe in, and of course their main purpose is propaganda and persuasion—and not that reflection of real life or exaltation of sheer beauty which is authentic literature. Of course, if these people are by any chance gifted with culture and natural eloquence—as, for example, Plato, Lucretius, and Ralph Waldo Emerson were—they may really produce literature through sheer accident; but this blending is not a common phenomenon, and we may quite safely advise the Burning Band of Idealists and Serious Thinkers to confine their writing to essays and tracts on their own respective subjects. They won't get much of anywhere in any other literary direction— for the very excellent primary reason that they aren't particularly anxious to!

Well, the significance of all this is that any beginner who can identify his motive force with any of the foregoing types ought to think twice before wasting further time and energy on literature.

Now, what is the one real aesthetic impulse which *does* justify an arduous and devoted pursuit of letters—the impulse which every serious author ought to be able to discover in himself? It is monstrously hard to define, for its very essence is vagueness, elusiveness, and intangibility; but I think it has enough definite earmarks to make it distinctly *recognisable,* even if not accurately describable or neatly classifiable in the businesslike filing-cabinet of modern psychology.

The impulse which justifies authorship—the quality which lends dignity and reasonableness to a human being's insatiate wish to spread himself out on paper—is *a kind of heightened vision which lends strange colours to the universe, and which invests the pageant of life with a mystic glamour and veiled significance so poignant and potent that no eye may behold it without a resistless wish to capture and preserve its essence; to hold it for future hours, and to share it with those who can be made to see it with kindred perspective.* No person without this tense feeling of wonder and pageantry as connected with the world of reality or the world of dreams can ever hope to create real literature. If the events of life—or the fantasies of thought—appear in no mystic colours; if they remain mere earthly effects and illusions without ecstatic and unplaceable suggestions of vast cosmic patterns and boundless gulfs of breathless mystery, then one may as well turn to something more wholesome and normal and practical than hen-tracking good dollar-a-ream paper. One can test oneself in the late afternoon, when the slanting sunlight throws strange mantles of golden enchantment on roofs and spires, groves and gardens, fields and terraces, shaven lawns and the ripples of lilied meres. If such a scene does not produce a quick tightening of the throat—a wild certainty that some strangeness lies just beyond the blazing west, or a singing sureness that some marvel lovely and incredible is about to blossom—then one ought not to feel obliged to write down such thoughts and impressions as may chance to inhabit his cranium. All the common, una-dorned things have been thought and said and repeated a thousand times be-fore. The dull, prosaic world of usual feelings and events is so well "written up" that nothing vital remains to be added. The time to begin writing is when the events of the world seem to suggest things larger than the world—strangenesses and patterns and rhythms and uniquities of combinations which no one ever saw or heard of before, but which are so vast and marvellous and beautiful that they absolutely demand proclamation with a fanfare of silver trumpets. Space and time become vitalised with literary significance when they begin to make us subtly homesick for something 'out of space, out of time.'[1] There is no real author who has not stood in awe and expectancy before some fragment of earthly scene—some gap in quiet hills at dawn, some bit of city pavement glistening with rain and reflecting evening's lamps and lighted win-dows, some line of distant roofs or balustraded garden terraces—whose glori-fied contours bring up with sweetly maddening poignancy a haunting, ineluctable sense of cosmic memory; of having known that scene and others akin to it in other lives, other worlds, and other dreamlands. *To find those other lives, other worlds, and other dreamlands, is the true author's task.* That is what litera-ture is; and if any piece of writing is motivated by anything apart from this mystic and never-finished quest, it is a base and unjustified imitation.

Well, so much for motive. Motive alone will never make an author; for thousands of restless souls share these dreams and mystic longings without ever being able to communicate them. The second essential—the element which, joined to the proper vision, makes literary competence a *certainty*—is a *keen sense of beauty as applied to language*. A natural author thinks of words solely in their aesthetic relations—in their power to grasp delicately and exquisitely his every shade of meaning and emotion, and to sing forth his dreams in mu-sic of surpassing loveliness. To him language is no haphazard, utilitarian thing, but the conjoined marble and chisel of a sculptor, wherewith perfect things may be bodied forth afresh in perfect beauty. No one need try author-ship unless he feels himself able and inclined to treat language as a fine art—as a thing of complex and delicate laws, of hidden meanings, and of a thou-sand potent subtleties of sound, rhythm, force, vividness, tone-colour, and associative values. He must be willing and eager to bind himself in a long and toilsome apprenticeship to the gods of speech—and must never be impatient or rebellious. He must come to love language so much that it will form al-most an end in itself—he must love it till the mere handling of beautiful words and rhythms becomes an exquisite pleasure. And that is that. It isn't really as grandiose as it sounds—but that's the kind of dual feeling it is. One must feel strangeness and significance and expectancy in scenes and events, and must take a delight in telling about them in lovely singing words. That is authorship. Naturally, as one cultivates this real faculty, he becomes more and more impatient with the hokum and artificiality which tries to pass itself off as the genuine article. By degrees he turns away from the hackneyed commonplaces and falsified simplicities of charlatans, and searches humbly among the rocks for some trace of the real wonder and essence of things. He discards all that is cheap and popular, and seeks the real sources of truth. Weary of copying poor copies, he searches diligently for some vital and transcribable fragment of life itself. And when he can't find this he keeps quiet.

Thus I have turned your question back to yourself, for only you can answer it. Have you the right motive force? Well, you can only ask yourself whether or not you are really searching for 'the light that never was on land or sea'.[2] If you are, you're on the right track. Have you the right material for technical development? Well, if you regard words as things to be treasured and caressed; as the sacred notes of melodies and rhythms; I'd say that the presumptive evidence is all in your favour. I would add, that it's a good sign, if you don't care very much about your material results, and don't dramatise or sentimentalise your own possible position as an author. A real creative artist is so absorbed in the enjoyment of the images he discerns and perpetuates, that he doesn't give a hang what pay he gets, or what the lousy rabble thinks about him. He ceases to exist as a person among persons. He is dissolved, etherealised, and sublimated to an external cosmic eye whose only god is symmetry and whose only passion is beauty. He is abstract and impersonal—his life and soul are what he sees and dreams.

As to external evidence—as I said before, your second version of "The Unchaining" appears to me to indicate a very keen ability to progress in the mastery of literary form. Your self-revision of "Under Cover" will shed still further light. Exact judgment cannot be made without knowing how much you have studied technique in the past, and what your background of reading and scholarship is. The ambition you express seems a very encouraging thing, and many passages in your tales display a pictorial force and sincerity far removed from amateurishness. You select incidents well, and have a very good eye for interesting plot developments. A sense of fitness is unmistakably present—as exhibited in your choice of names for characters. So far I have found no inept or inappropriate personal names in your manuscripts—counting out "Dr. Sloughter" as a pardonable associative accident. This innate perception of obscure congruities is a very cheerful augury, and promises fine results when extended through training to a larger field. And more—your desire for sincere depth and merit is itself a sign of teachable discrimination, as are the shivers you experience from utterly tasty work. The finely drawn character of Ella in "The Unchaining" is also a good omen. As for the drawbacks—I'll reverse my previous order and treat language before vision here, because that factor is more easily dealt with. To be brief, you are really in need of systematic drilling in the subtleties of verbal usage—both syntactical and rhetorical. The practice may make you impatient, and seem to interfere with your flow of thought, but it's overwhelmingly worth your while. If it interferes with thought, then *separate it* from your thoughts. Do your rhetorical practice in exercises that you care nothing about—you'll find it a pleasure in itself if you have the prose artist's second essential. Let the serious authorship wait till you've caught up technically—get the right books or courses and plug everlastingly; and later on, when you turn to serious authorship again, you will find your thoughts unconsciously and automatically taking the most correct and beautiful form. There's nothing to be discouraged about in lacking technical skill. Everybody was unskilled once—William de Morgan didn't quit ceramics and learn literature till he was about sixty,[3] so no one need feel that it's too late to make a dignified beginning. Don't be too proud to learn—start in and let other considerations take care of themselves! Of course it is for you to decide what mode of instruction best suits you. My own recommendation would be dual—on the one hand *a close and analytical reading of the very finest English stylists,* with detailed attention to the precise way in which they achieve their various effects; and on the other hand *a systematic study of some standard textbook of composition and rhetoric.* Woolley's is a very good manual, but it sometimes seems to me that the old, thorough books of eighty or a hundred years ago laid the foundation of a truer and firmer sense of beauty. At any rate, we haven't the true stylists today that we had thirty, forty, and fifty years ago. Donn Byrne, James Branch Cabell, Arthur Machen, Lord Dunsany, Walter de la Mare, William Butler Yeats—all living, it is true, but every one middle-aged or old. The younger set is falling behind. What little I know of style was gained primarily through two yellowed volumes printed in 1797 and 1845, respectively; the latter book—Parker's famous *Aid to Composition,* is in my opinion the best rhetorical text-book ever published.[4] I buy all the duplicates I can find at the second-hand shops to lend to clients and literary students. If you would care to look over a copy I'd be pleased to send it on for as long a period as you wish. But after all—*it is the reading and not the formal text-book study which does the supreme good.* That and only that can nourish the instinctive sense of beauty in language. Read Walter Pater, Oscar Wilde, Lord Dunsany, Thomas De Quincey, Washington Irving, Lafcadio Hearn, and the old Queen-Anne essayists—Addison, Steele, Swift, Defoe, and so on. Style— style—style—nothing but beauty of style really justifies any work of literature. It is to be understood, of course, that this dual regimen must be accompanied by copious actual practice in rhetorical composition. Write, write, write! Read, read, read! Study, study, study!

Now as for the second drawback—simple, but involving a possibly more difficult combination of imponderables. This is *a somewhat uncertain grasp of the realities of life and human feelings,* as evidenced by an occasional acceptance and serious treatment of the artificially simple stock world and characters of ephemeral popular fiction. This does not argue a lack of literary depth and insight in yourself. The character of Ella in "The Unchaining" shows that you can give life and people the right treatment when you have the right material. The trouble apparently is that you haven't excluded superficial modern fiction rigorously enough from your daily reading—that you've allowed cheap magazine matter to exert an unconscious influence on your image of life and human nature, so that you are at present unfortunately able to take seriously—and feel an interest in—certain simple, flabby unrealities of stock romance which under other circumstances you would laugh at! Here is the "brutal frankness" you asked for—but the brutality is very easily tempered by the obvious corollary that if wrong reading has given you a false world, right reading will quickly and easily give you a true one. It is always so—for truth has a certain convincing quality of its own, and nearly everyone is quick to shed false perspectives when real ones come in sight. We are all very largely what we read, and the one thing for an aspiring writer to do is to cut all connections with the cheap, the hackneyed, and the tawdrily false and simple. Even if you write for the cheaper magazines you can't afford to read them. Put an absolute ban on everything below the *Saturday Evening Post,* and accept even that with extreme circumspection and reserve. The only group of magazines one can afford to take as indices of contemporary life is that including *Harper's, Century, Scribner's, Atlantic,* etc. But magazines are poor fodder at best. Books—books are the things! That's where you'll find human life as it is! It's a fallacy to think that personal experience is an author's most helpful key to life. It might be if one person could live the lives of all mankind in all ages—but so far one has been able to do that only in books. Those are the keys to the magic casements! That's where humanity has stored its essence and its soul! But for Heaven's sake read the *right* ones! Of course, all this *positive* advice as distinguished from the negative injunction to keep clear of popular magazines and best sellers may be supererogation. Of that I can't tell. Possibly you've read all the standard books in an average cultural curriculum and are merely allowing their influence to become overlaid with a stratum of popular hokum. Indeed—if Ella Brent didn't come from life, the chances are that she came from real literature rather than from *Sobby Stories!* [5] Then, if you need no suggestions on what to read, just take my suggestions on *what not to read* and let time do the rest. The real perspective will come back, and you'll find your standards of emotional significance and importance readjusting themselves. You'll soon cease to find any poignancy or validity in eleventh-hour lynching rescues, callow-love-at-first-sight, or any of the strained stock scenes and falsified human simplicities of the Charles Garvice or Harold Bell Wright tradition;[6] and will be looking instead for such authentic reactions of human soul with human soul, or of human soul with scene and heritage, as contain some elusive element of the unique and the awesome—some hint of unfathomable cosmic deeps, or some imminence of remembered and ethereal vistas. That is literature—and given the proper vision, wish, and word-mastery, you'll not be reading it long (provided you keep it purged of cheap adulterants) before you'll be unconsciously writing it. And there'll be no question about the status and quality of what you'll then produce. If, on the other hand, your acquaintance with the classics has not been thorough, you ought to lose no time in starting in. Begin with standard American things—Irving, Hawthorne, and such poets as Longfellow and Bryant and Poe. Work back into England, through the great psychological novelists (Meredith, Thackeray etc.) and the eighteenth-century Titans—Fielding, Sterne, Smollett, Gold-smith, Richardson. Don't miss the minors—Jane Austen, Fanny Burney, Charles Lamb etc. etc.—and dwell long on the greatest poets—for in poetry is distilled all the sublimest essence of all literature and all art. Trace the great poets backward—Swinburne, Tennyson, Browning, Byron, Shelley, Keats, Coleridge, the suave eighteenth century versifiers—Thomson, Pope etc.—Dryden—back to Milton—then the great Elizabethans, and immortal, dawn-fresh Chaucer. Read the drama—the essay—everything that mankind has had to say about itself—for how else will you ever know life as it is?—and if you don't know, how are you ever going to write anything vital about the depths of human personality and feeling? Of course you don't have to read every-thing that everybody has ever written—follow any high-school or college his-tory of literature, and temper the whole process with your own judgment and common-sense. And don't confine yourself to English letters, either. Read the great translations—Balzac is the greatest of all interpreters of human life except Shakespeare, and only the Russians know the depth of human mad-ness and despair. Gautier and Flaubert and de Maupassant are absolutely es-sential, while Ibsen is scarcely less so. Read the great picaresques of continental literature—"Don Quixote" above all. And always keep close to the poets—they are the true vanguard. Include, by all means, the Graeco-Roman classics in good translations. Everyone *must* know Homer and Virgil and Ovid and Horace, and the immortal dramatic trinity of Aeschylus, Soph-ocles, and Euripides. Learn the polished poise of calm antiquity from the golden paragraphs of Plato, Cicero, and Seneca—remembering always that it is wholly upon this classic heritage that our Western civilisation is founded. And of course don't limit your reading to mere belles-lettres. To know man-kind intelligently enough to write about it one must have some sort of histor-ical perspective. Read the *Story of the World* in such simple outlines as Wells's, enlarging the field through fuller works at points where your interest is unu-sually keen. And too, don't neglect the scenic setting. Man is only a negligible grain in the universe, and to envisage him clearly in all his insignificance one must learn his relation to space and time and matter through the reading of simple little books on astronomy, physics, chemistry, geology, geography, biology, psychology, and so on. Get an inkling of the inwardness of science—of cosmic proportion—and you can't get very much excited again over dime-novel courtships and cinema weddings. Great Scott! A mere moment ago in time the very principle of organic life didn't exist on the earth, and in another mere moment, relatively speaking, it will have disappeared again without having left in the universe any sign of its forgotten existence. Humanity—poof! And yet dime-novel heroes still make tinsel vows by the eternal stars in their courses. Depth—insight—proportion—perspective—those are the roads to sanity and substance in the literary reflection of life. To reflect a thing, one has to get a decent idea of what it is and where it stands! Incidentally—if you wish some simple and fairly representative course of reading, calculated to give quick results in a balanced knowledge of life, I'd be glad to furnish suggestions—or a public library could do better than I. Books ought to be owned, too—and I fancy Cleveland has as good shops as any—some of them almost literary centres. Laukhof's in the Taylor Arcade, Eglin's in E. 9th St., Powner's—etc. etc.[7] Also—the five cent Haldeman-Julius booklets have some splendid titles, while the *Modern and Everyman Series* (about a dollar) contain the very best classics old and new.[8] As a drastic and immediate means of breaking up the false tinsel world of cheap-fiction mawkishness and sentimentality, I'd recommend the always pyrotechnical and sometimes extravagant outbursts of H. L. Mencken and George Jean Nathan.[9] They are sharp and often disagreeable medicine, but they are necessary purgatives to a sentimentalised America just pulling clear of the drooling, ghastly nonsense and flubdubbery of the 1900 period. Read Mencken's "Prejudices"—four books of pertinent critical essays—"In Defence of Women", "A Book of Prefaces", etc. etc. And in particular his (and Nathan's) superb collection of silly local folk delusions—"The American Credo". (I think there's a new volume of this by Nathan alone which I haven't seen). That sort of exposé virtually blasts the ground from under the tame delusions and stock assumptions of conventional provincialism. As for other suggestions—to break up commonplace falsities about family affection read Samuel Butler's "Way of All Flesh". And don't neglect the study of *Philosophy*—which may have a dry sound, but which contains the whole record of the human spirit's beliefs and aspirations. Fortunately you can get a surprisingly decent perspective of the whole subject in one simple, popular book of recent date—"The Story of Philosophy", by Will H. Durant. Philosophy has done surprising things to mankind. We all think and feel differently because Arthur Schopenhauer and Friedrich Wilhelm Nietzsche lived and suffered and thought. A stiff programme? Not at all! One at a time, and with your keen interest in human life and feeling you'll be so interested that the suggestions won't come fast enough to keep up with you! You want to write about life—well, here's the way to get a vital background to harness that writing-energy to! I'm sure the inclination—with its obvious sincerity and intensity—deserves no less truthful and ample material to feed on. And of course keep writing constantly. Don't be in a hurry to place the stuff—but everything you write improves your technique just so much more. Since the deeper emotions are so closely connected with basic truths that their accurate presentation requires the most finished skill and background, it might be well to let the earlier stories revolve around lighter themes—which you seem to handle notably well, as judged by the unusually good technique of "When A Woman is Tempted". By eliminating all deep problems of motivation—choosing homely and trivial themes whose threads are not deeply linked with complex, mysterious forces—you can be free to concentrate all your skill and attention on the technical problems of expression—of making words work intelligently for you, bowing to your conscious mastery and saying with maximum completeness the precise thing—in the precise shade of meaning—that you want them to say. These problems are very real, for there is a definite best way to say anything; and an accomplished author knows just the most effective handling of ideas and the most adroit amenities to use in outlining and disposing of any given situation. All the characteristic problems of saying things—of narrating events, introducing conversations, describing characters, managing scenic effects, handling moods and emotions, etc. etc., have been worked out in literature by a long line of artists and craftsmen beginning with Chaucer; just as all the problems of *painting* things—of massing and mixing colours, marshalling masses, conquering aërial perspective, distributing chiaroscuro, rendering characteristic forms, perfecting draughtsmanship, etc. etc. were worked out by the painters of the Italian Renaissance from Cimabue to Raphael. It is the job of the 1927 craftsman to profit by the skill which has gone before—and this can best be done when the subject is not complex. But don't fancy that homely little themes are to be despised. Only the cheap cinema-addict demands huge grandiose spectacles all the time, or fancies that the central feature of life is a sickish, artificial romance symbolised by two callow and imaginationless young animals pawing and slobbering over each other. Epicures and connoisseurs in living—aristocrats and aesthetes—delight supremely in the quiet minor themes and lightly delicate grace-notes of cosmic rhythm; the little by-ways of action and feeling which have not the harsh stridency of intenseness or the essential vulgarity of obviousness and commonplaceness. Studies in quaint character, situations based on patterns in habit, manners, heritage, and tastes; all these things make excellent practice work for a beginner. This is the sort of thing which drags down the prizes in the *Boston Post*. Do in prose what the skilful genre painters—the Dutch and Flemish masters—did in the seventeenth century in line and colour. I enclose a typical *Boston Post* first-prize winner which you can keep as a sample of modest but competent work in homely theme and elementary craftsmanship. This sort of thing is the miniature-painting—the gemmary—the cameo-

carving—of prose art. The mildness of the theme leaves full leeway for supreme workmanship and the untrammelled development of the decorative
element.

Sincerely yrs

H P Lovecraft.

Notes

1. Poe, "Dreamland" (1844), l. 8.

2. "The light that never was, on sea or land." William Wordsworth, "Elegiac Stanzas," l. 15.

3. William de Morgan (1839–1917), British potter and tile designer who began writing novels late in life, beginning with *Joseph Vance* (1906).

4. The other book HPL refers to is Abner Alden's *The Reader* (1802, not 1797). HPL had an 1808 ed. (*LL* 25).

5. Fictitious; presumably a parody of the actual magazine *Snappy Stories*.

6. Charles Garvice (1850–1920), prolific British writer of romance novels. Harold Bell Wright (1872–1944), best-selling American novelist and essayist.

7. HPL frequented these establishments when visiting Samuel Loveman and Alfred Galpin in Cleveland in the summer of 1922.

8. HPL refers to two separate series of inexpensive reprints of classic literature, the Modern Library and Everyman's Library.

9. At this time, Mencken and Nathan were coediting the *American Mercury*. Previously (1914–23), they had edited the *Smart Set*, for which Mencken wrote a monthly book review column and Nathan a monthly column of drama criticism.

[8]   [ALS]

10 Barnes St.,

Providence, R.I.,

June 11, 1927

My dear Mrs. Reed:—

At last I am able to return "The Unchaining" in typed
form, & I hope very much that it will not disappoint you after your long wait.
As I prepared the final copy I was impressed anew by its excellence, & I cannot help feeling rather optimistic about its ultimate magazine placement—
although of course I don't wish to extend delusive hopes. I have exercised the
greatest care in revising—catching two small points at the very last moment,
as you will see by changes in the typed text. The MS. came out with 23½
double-spaced pages, somewhat in advance of my original estimate; but as
usual in such cases I will not charge in excess of the maximum first named.
The bill for this item, then, will be *$19.00*, payable at your convenience.

As to the various points of revision—to begin with, I used one paragraph
from the rejected version (#1) to outline a scenic background for the open-

ing. A tale of this length ought to be touched off with some dramatic effect, & I think that your sunset picture fitted in finely. The playful bears furnish a sort of smoothly symbolic keynote for the discussion of emotion—& then the action begins. Casual incidents & pictorial effects ought to have as much bearing as possible—though in a subtle way, & without the cheap artificiality of stage thunder for the Big Murder Scene—on the narration & characterisations. In the "mental throwback" scene—convent & funeral—it was necessary to make the pictures a trifle more concrete & visual than they were. The dry, descriptive forms of the scientific treatise must be assiduously avoided in places like this. In the twilight scene after the return of Will's party the pictorial values must be well maintained—each person's place in the scene being made perfectly clear. When the first time-break comes, (on p. 6 of the typed copy) that circumstance must be prepared for—both rhetorically & psychologically. It is well to let the mountain scenery have a certain symbolic value here—always taking care not to become melodramatic & grandiose. The subsequent description of Ella's chained emotion was rather too concrete & elaborate, & has been suitably toned down. In the discovery scene—pp. 7–10—there seemed to be a slight lack of pictorial definiteness, making the scene rather hard to visualise. I have sought to remove this inadequacy as fully as possible. One must always be careful to make scenes live—visually—else the result will be a synopsis rather than a story in the fullest sense. In the dancing scene on p. 10 I note that Ella still wears a walking costume. In the East, even in a summer camp, the guests usually put on formal attire for evening diversions—though I assume you have the Western data right. If the matter is an oversight, you can merely change the phrase *trim hiking togs* to *well-cut evening gown*. This is so easily done—if necessary—that I did not take the liberty of altering the passage in the MS. Later you have a *nightingale*, which is a European songster not found in America. Many—familiar with the traditional literature of the mother-continent—make this slip, but it is just as well to be accurate. I have seen similar slips regarding *yew-trees*. On page 15 I have eliminated one of the many breaks in the narrative, for there ought not to be too many. There is no reason why the story cannot be continuous here, & I have so made it. On page 16 there is a matter which came to my notice at the very last moment—after the manuscript was typed. You have the telegram—& its dramatic consequences—occur *on the very day* that Ella brings up the subject of the Lanes' return. This is one of those *improbable coincidences* which the author must always shun. Fortunately the coincidence can be broken by the addition of four words & the change of a pronoun to a proper noun, as you will see in the MS. In dealing with the nurses you again employ the device of *overhearing* used three times before. (pp. 1, 7 et seq., & 12) This had to be eliminated—although I did not change the three mentioned because their dissimilar circumstances removed the principal objections. Never employ the same literary trick too often, lest it become a mannerism. In treating the whole matter of the illness, keep the time-element well in mind. Make the sweep of the months clear, & quicken the tempo as the end nears. You will see how I have tried to do this. Here & elsewhere pay close attention to the words used—seeking variety, precision, pictorial & associational value, &c. A tensely unfolding scene needs language handled with all the finesse of a plastic art. Avoid above all the too frequent repetition of the same word. On pages 20 & 21 the heavy sententiousness had to be removed. Also—as I saw at the last moment—Ella would never have left the book & telegrams *under her pillow* where any maid might find them while she was away. They must be locked in the desk. Let the reading of these telegrams form a time-break—for they have the appropriate significance. From there on certain changes of order were needed to make the effect smooth & powerful. The telegram-revelation must be deferred—& the melodramatic burning must not take place in Lane's presence at the moment of the proposal. The natural & dramatic time for this holocaust is in private just afterward—the incident forming a fine culmination just before the ultimate & climactic "unchaining" scene. That scene itself needed considerable remodelling—especially the removal of the final anticlimactic speech. I have taken extreme care here, & believe the climax is set off in just about the right sort of way. You are, of course, aware that the beginning & ending of a story are the two points requiring the most careful treatment of all.

I sincerely hope you can place this MS. Meanwhile, to get the maximum educational value out of the revision, study carefully the changes & types of change made; comparing even the smallest details in original & revised versions—& never hesitating to ask questions concerning any alteration whose cause does not seem clear. I trust I have preserved throughout the essence of your style & mood.

I am now ready for any work you wish done on the tale tentatively titled "Under Cover"—whose MS. with advisory criticism I trust you safely received. The enclosed specimen of extensive story revision may aid you in deciding what type of service you wish the later MS. to receive.

Very cordially yrs

H P Lovecraft

P.S. I am sending the carbon & rough draught of the final "Unchaining" version under separate cover.

P.P.S. It is of course understood that any points in this revision which do not satisfy you will be altered free of charge. The fee for extensive revision implies continuous service till the client is absolutely satisfied with the result.

[9]   [AHT]

10 Barnes St.,
Providence, R.I.,
June 12, 1927

My dear Mrs. Reed:—

[. . .]

It is interesting to note the basis of reality in the Western tale—a circumstance which makes especially vivid the literary axiom that truth is stranger than fiction can ever afford to be. Daily life has a thousand odd incidents so grotesque, undramatic, absurd, and devoid of universal symbolism or significance, that their embodiment in a story (supposedly typical of some deepwoven emotional symmetry) would be either extravagant or meaningless. And the same is true of certain trite or melodramatic situations which, though barred from art through over-use, nevertheless turn up now and then by accident in actual life. Since art is at bottom *a treatment of life* rather than life itself, we cannot justly take factual reality as an absolute criterion of fictional availability. Paradoxical as it may sound, many real happenings are far too improbable for a story. What fiction demands is a fragment of reality typical and universal enough to arouse myriad associations in the reader and suggest the hovering nearness of things even outside and above reality. However, there are ways whereby an adroit author may frequently "get away with" a trite setting or incident when it is absolutely necessary—the best perhaps being a prompt and open direction of attention to the hackneyed quality, followed by a half-humorous, half-apologetic asseveration that the thing was really so, even though it ought not to be according to all the laws of probability, credibility, and good art! This will often "go" well—although of course there are limits to the length to which it can be pushed. The difference between a mature and immature craftsman is that the former *knows* the ticklish nature of a trite theme, and acts accordingly; whilst the latter drones on simply and seriously, as if he did not know how well-worn and even comic his subject-matter has become. A semi-humorous start, and a little less melodrama and stage mystery, might yet make that Western tale into a good light adventure or riddle story.

The vitally important thing, as I have said, is the formation of a clear, wide, authentic, and analytically penetrating notion of the world and of mankind for use in literary exploration. This involves, first of all, a thorough demolition and clearing-away of all the stock-pictures and false simplicities of the cheaper writers; and secondly, a discriminating sense of relative values in selecting, from the vast body of real events and feelings, such particular fragments of life as possess the drama, significance, symbolism, and universality to make them legitimately art material. This part of authorship is perhaps the hardest part of all—the greatest test of sheer aesthetic insight as distinguished from mere fluency, correctness, and cultivation. What is an aesthetically significant situation, character, or emotion? A hard thing to answer positively, though one may venture a few broadly inclusive suggestions. We may, for example, say that very simple and obvious things are hard to use effectively; since they are so well-worn, and so destitute of the subtle lights and shades necessary for a richly developed art. The sort of character and emotion one must portray is one in which overtones, confusions, mixtures, and contradictions exist—just as they exist in real life. Actually, human feelings are never straightforward—we are never so fond of a person that we don't sometimes wish he were in hades or Nicaragua, and never so interested in a subject or purpose that we aren't occasionally bored to death by the very mention of it. Single passions that influence whole lives are exceedingly rare—and when these seem to exist, it will often be found on analysis that the permanence is in the effect—as produced through subsidiary causes set in motion by the initial emotion—rather than in the pristine motivating force itself. Now it is the writer's business to untangle all these complexities, divine the element of drama (almost always based on *conflict*) in them, and set forth this bit of cosmic symmetry in perfect language. The conflict may be physical in the lower forms of fiction—the "action" story—but in the higher forms it is mostly mental and emotional. Tales of character rather than of plot are what all the better grade of magazines demand. The romantic writer must take extreme care lest superficial glamour distort for him the actual relative potency of various motive forces as operating in various types of human character—also, lest he acquiesce in the false valuations and partialities affected by older writers of the same type. The most common of these illusions, of course, is that of the paramount importance of "love" (a complex synthesis of dissimilar forces perversely regarded as single and homogeneous) as a permanent factor in life, and of the *culpability* of allowing any other consideration to outweigh it. The best example of this, of course, is the stale situation of stern parents and daughter about to contract a mesalliance with an honest shepherd lad. All cheap novelists write in condemning the "worldly" and "calculating" parents and exalting the silly, transient infatuation of two young fools so fundamentally dissimilar that a lasting union would lead either to joint infidelity or mutual murder; whereas the real artist looks closer and recognises that there are environmental and temperamental considerations far more important than romantic attraction in the adjustment of any sensitive and well-balanced person to the universe. One could make long lists of complex human conditions—social, intellectual, imaginative, geographical, aesthetic, national, and so on—far more potent and influential than "love" in the life and happiness of any normal person of culture and evolved mentality. And of course, the transience and mutability—the capriciousness and dividedness—of "love" itself do much to subtract from its importance as a unified driving force. Therefore, unless a writer wishes to appear very naive, or to cater wholly to an unsophisticated public, he will beware of the exaltation and apotheosis of the thin, unimaginative, falsified Romeo-Juliet theme. Instead of gullibly assuming an artificial state of things and monotonously rehashing the milk-and-water triumphs (inevitable triumphs!) of a mythically omnipotent "love" over all obstacles, any solid writer of *real* love-stories will tell of *conflicts* and *compromises* betwixt *various phases* of love in *various stages of completeness or intensity*, and other environing conditions of equal, greater, or lesser importance, as the case may be, or with decreases or contradictions in the fabric of the love itself. He will tell of defeats, hard-headed adjustments, absurdities, disasters, peterings-out, and boredoms, as well as of victories; and he will not try to take sides in a play of cosmic forces which matters but little either way. It is this drama of *life*—not of the cinema imitation—which is the proper groundwork of literature. The romanticist must learn to distinguish, then, between what is vital and significant and what is merely wooden and conventional and meaningless. There is absolutely no art in a tale of how two simple souls conquered all the Fates and lived happily together ever after; but there would be art in a graphic portrayal of how two souls started out with the illusion of perpetual romance, sickened of it eventually, (on one or both sides) and spent the residue of their lives in preserving the outward forms of the passion in order to satisfy their sense of dignity and fitness. Art, too, could enter into a tale of environmental adjustment—a straightforward, Ella-Brent sort of person marrying (for example) a New York "colyumist" of the sophisticated literary set, and having a wearisome conflict betwixt a genuine affection for her husband on the one hand, and on the other hand an absolute inability to endure, comprehend, or participate in his falsetto-keyed world of learned pretence, dramatic pose, and worship of nimble paradox and epigrammatic smartness as supreme values. In moulding such a story the pendulum could swing naturally and uncertainly in either direction—the final victory, compromise, or defeat depending upon the exact conditions and upon the exact balance of feelings in each of the characters concerned. And one may add, that the birth of a dear little chee-ild would *not* solve all problems in glib nickelodeon fashion! Rather, it would be a complication provocative of even more misery. One of the first essentials of real literary training is the eternal destruction of the puerile illusion that Life (that sort of conception carries its own redundant capitals!) is neatly divided into the Big, Wholesome, Vital Things, and the false, superficial, frivolous things. Actually, the importance and significance of everything is purely relative—all values being matters of transient circumstance and perspective, and nearly always occurring in a state of ridiculous and incongruous mixture. All life is essentially *ridiculous* as a matter of fact—as no one has shown quite so well as the late Anatole France. Which reminds me to add Anatole to the list of authors who ought to be read—either in the original or in translation. Nothing is quite so exquisite in its revealing irony as the end of his "Penguin Island."

Perspective, proportion, variety, depth, accuracy, sanity, impersonality, humour—these are the qualities which the natural romanticist should cultivate assiduously as safeguards against artistic pitfalls. Do not fancy the result will be extreme *realism*—natural bias will take care of that; and of course there are moments when the illusion of romance is poignant and dramatic while it lasts, so that such a thing as glamour *does* exist in the world. What will develop, is a more lifelike, tempered, and convincing romanticism.

I am very truly yours,
H P Lovecraft.

[10]   [ALS]

10 Barnes St.,
Providence, R.I.,
July 13, 1927

My dear Mrs. Reed:—

I trust the Parker's Aids duly arrived—I meant to acknowledge your letter of 18ᵗʰ ult. long ago, but have been delayed by an almost unprecedented press of work,—including the preparation of a Greek literature course (in translation) for a private student—curiously aggravated by a session of out of town company, to whom sights must be shown & amenities extended.[1]

Meanwhile I am glad to note that you are settled in a more familiar & congenial region, & that the revision of "The Unchaining" proved acceptable. I hope that editors may regard it with equal favour; though as I said formerly, the road to editorial recognition is a very long & arduous one. There is no real haste about payment if the process of interurban migration has made funds difficult of access, & I trust that eventually the revision fee will be more than refunded by magazine placement. I must remark in this connexion that ultimate placement sometimes occurs years after an early rejection of the same item. The wise author always saves his early work, no matter how widely rejected; & is often able to place it to great advantage in after years, when an entreè [*sic*] to the magazine field is definitely secured. As to the rejection of the other MSS.—from the periodicals in question, that was to be expected; and the long period of retention ought to encourage you as to the amount of consideration their first reading secured for them. This matter of early rejection is good discipline for the literary novice; for it helps him learn to accept philosophically a type of incident very frequent in the nascent stages, & never wholly absent even in one's successful later career.

I hope sincerely that Parker's Aids are living up to their name, at least to some degree. The soundness of these old manuals has always had the strongest appeal to me, although I realise that nowadays many do not care for their manner of approach. It is interesting to learn that you have tried the Home Correspondence School, & I fancy that its shortcomings may be due to its lack of individual criticism & mode of instruction. Each pupil has characteristics of assimilative power peculiar to himself—individual aptitudes as to method & mode of presentation which the oral instructor or personal teacher by mail is quick to recognise & heed, but which of course can scarcely be allowed for in a correspondence course. I don't know of the Home School, of course, except by reputation; & it may well be that they are quite deficient in the amount of individual care which their critics & correctors give to any one student. I am sure that Uzzell would be better—that he wouldn't undertake to teach a student unless sure that he had the time to make his instruction really personal. Even so, however, there are many who learn from experience & from actual specimens of revised work better than from abstract precept either oral or by correspondence. In that case it is best to follow the policy which experiment proves most profitable; though a conscientious re-reading of the old textbooks & correspondence lessons would undoubtedly work well in the long run—smoothing away technical difficulties now & then, warning against pitfalls, & suggesting many avenues & felicities of expression which would not be likely to occur to the unguided novice. A correspondence school won't, it is true, make a fiction-writer to order where no native ability or deep inclination exists—& this probably accounts for the keen prejudice which most successful writers appear to entertain against such institutions. For my part, however, I do not see how this fact can affect the very substantial benefit which reasonable guidance cannot help conferring upon such beginners as *do* have ability. Technical skill does not descend like manna from heaven. The novice must pick up the rules somewhere—& why can't they be given as effectively in a correspondence course as in anything else? But naturally, correspondence schools must differ in merit. There are different degrees of force & clearness in putting forward any given idea, & different degrees of conscientiousness & persistence in the matter of seeing that it is thoroughly assimilated by the individual pupil. Certainly, there's no reason to feel discouraged merely because one school fails to produce the desired reaction—& in your case, much ground for optimism is afforded by your very intelligent use of constructive advice in recasting "The Unchaining". I would advise your persisting in the field until you shall have had a chance to test the response of your style to the broader & more sincerely analytical outlook on human phenomena which you are now cultivating. Let the immediate present be a period of growth & storage rather than of expression as a predominant factor; & let the deepening tone of the few choice things you do write serve as an index & proof of your progress. One thing which I've perhaps neglected to mention specifically heretofore, but which I really think is very helpful to a novice in learning what the extent & status of style's problems are, is *the practice of reading books of literary criticism.* Mencken's are good, & from another point of view there is much soundness in the less homiletic of the utterances of the late Stuart P. Sherman.[2] Of the more exotic writers Arthur Symons writes illuminatingly, & there is great value in old standbys like Lowell's "My Study Windows" or the various critical essays of Edgar Allan Poe. The primary worth of these things is to define the province & plumb the complex depth of the author's art—to point out vividly the enormous degree of sincerity & accuracy & fastidiousness needed to make the transcription of life a beautiful or glamorous or convincing thing. I am enclosing a little Haldeman-Julius booklet which I frequently send to fictional aspirants without charge—I meant to send it before, but my supply was exhausted at the time. In the matter of straightening out the beginner's artistic perspective I have found this brochure admirably effective, & hope that it will prove markedly helpful to you. It is interesting to note that the author has no great use for correspondence schools. There's lots in this Blue Book series that a novice can use to great advantage—both standard classics which ought to be read, & concise treatises of value in a technical way. I was astonished at the variety & excellence of the latter when I examined the stock at a local shop yesterday. Most emphatically I'd advise you to get a catalogue & make some selections, undeterred by the curious atmosphere of cheap sensationalism & quasi-charlatanism which hangs about the way the books are advertised & marketed. Address Haldeman-Julius Co., Girard, Kansas. They'll be only too glad to supply catalogues & other printed matter.

After about two weeks—for a succession of visitors has quite automatically determined the present period as the nearest equivalent to a vacation on my part—I shall be ready to work on "Under Cover" if you wish it developed further. There is of course no haste about this, & it is perhaps a fact that the tale will be better, the more preliminary study you pursue before giving it its final formulation. In preparing a last synopsis, note well all the subtleties & probabilities touched upon in my comment on the tale, & be careful above all to let the prime conflict or interest hinge upon some point more or less removed from the obvious or the artificial.

Hoping, then, that both Parker & the enclosed will prove of genuine aid; & congratulating you again upon your return home from alien soil, (a thing I can appreciate poignantly by recalling my own joy at regaining ancient Providence after two years in roaring, mongrel New York!) I remain

Most cordially & sincerely yrs—

H. P. Lovecraft

Notes

1. Donald Wandrei visited HPL in Providence on 12–29 July 1927. James F. Morton also paid a visit for part of that period.

2. Stuart P. Sherman (1881–1926), American critic and author of *Criticism in America* (1924) and other volumes. He was a coeditor of *The Cambridge History of American Literature* (1917–21).

[11]   [ALS]

10 Barnes St.,

Providence, R.I.,

July 14, 1927.

My dear Mrs. Reed:—

Your letter, cheque, & manuscript arrived only a day after my own tardy epistle, & I must hasten to acknowledge the communication. The amount of the bill was only *nineteen* dollars, but I will credit the excess on the next order. I am just now combining business with the vacational activities to which I referred in yesterday's note, & am writing this in what is probably one of the finest scenic spots in the United States—a lakeside bluff in the exquisite & celebrated Lincoln (or Quinsnicket) Woods four miles north of Providence. If a rocky seat & unconventional posture works havoc with my never too praiseworthy penmanship, I hereby ask pardon for the circumstance. I expect to do a good deal of work in this open-air way during the summer—& am just now able to do it despite the presence of the first of my guests; since that youthful individual has just discovered that my library contains two Dunsany books which he hasn't read, & is consequently dead to the external world until he shall have read them through! Incidentally, this young man is just beginning a writing career, the first of his professionally published stories appearing in next month's issue of *Weird Tales*.[1]

I am glad that Parker's Aids have really justified their name in your case, & hope you will feel free to retain the volume as long as you like. I hope also that you may find some helpful comment in the booklet I enclosed yesterday—you may have heard elsewhere of this Charles J. Finger, who to some extent fills the place of the late William Marion Reedy.[2] Parker is valuable on account of his explicitness. They don't teach that way now, I'm sorry to say—indeed, my present young guest tells me that he & his fellow-students at the U. of Minnesota find great difficulty with technical problems which, in the old days, would have been solved & relegated to the subconscious long ago by boys as far advanced in their studies (he has finished his junior year) as he. The younger generation may have a fuller, sounder, & more disillusioned perspective on life, but there is no question about the superiority of the older generation—the generation who are old men now—in the sheer art of grace-ful & facile expression. I would certainly like to see a return to the earlier—even if more formal & empirical—method of rhetorical instruction. It was the faddish attitude of Victorian pedagogy which killed the old American tra-dition of sound, precise, & classically grounded rhetoric.

I have examined the new MS. with great care, & believe that a course of *extensive* revision ($7.00, since its approximate 2300 words will come to 7 typed pages) would put it in shape for serious consideration, although the frequently used nature of the subject would limit its professional acceptability except in relatively unsophisticated magazines of the "Farm & Home" type. The changes would be greatest at the *beginning* (the opening must concern the dress more or less directly) & at certain of the "joints"—where the flow & tempo of the action ought to show a transitional element. I think I can adjust all this without any further work on your part, but will not begin operations unless you expressly authorise them—in case you do not care for extensive revision on a piece whose professional acceptability has so many limitations. If you think the process would be of value pedagogically, I'll begin work im-mediately upon authorisation—for of course a parallel study of the versions "before & after" would naturally shed light upon the methods of disposal of several specific fictional problems. As I have said, the main professional mar-kets for such a tale would be the semi-rural periodicals affecting honest homespun characteristics. Their rates, on the whole, are much lower than those of general publications. Let me know at your convenience what you wish done. In a revised version the opening action would be the original plan of Mother Martin to b[u]y a *foullard*. (And incidentally—are you sure this word has two l's in its Anglicised form? I'll look it up.) Changes in the tempo would occur when each of the sacrifices is introduced, & the later parts would hurry toward a finale of rather careful construction & elaboration. The whole action might perhaps be shortened, & the tone might be shifted just a little from conventional American amiability & cheerfulness to that of dry & slightly sardonic Gallic irony. Oh—& by the way—is the name of that *collar* BATANBOURGE or BATENBOURGE—& is it what is commonly known as "BATTENBURG"?[3] As a linguist I am deplorably naive, unimaginative, & ill-informed. [At this point my hat departed on a wind-borne excursion into the glen behind the cliff. My sentiments, after an Alpine descent & ascent of damaged retrieval, are not conducive to urbane or coherent rhetoric—inclining rather toward interjections of a racily Elizabethan colloquialism!]

I shall give due consideration to any further material which may arrive, & trust that results may be as satisfactory as before. Meanwhile I hope for good editorial luck with "The Unchaining" & its predecessors. The time taken for consideration surely proves that no hasty dismissal is contemplated. As to *nov-els*, there are really no specific rules which differentiate them from other forms of fiction; save that they handle broader segments of life & longer periods of time, & adopt a leisurely movement & detailed treatment in consonance with their scope. More digressions are permitted, (though they are not to be encouraged) & the tense linkage of parts need not be quite so unfailing as in the short story—although of course a continuous current of development must be maintained, & every incident must contribute something to the theme & the outcome. I say *outcome* rather than *climax* or *denouement*, because in a novel this "big moment" effect is not emphasised with quite such theatrical force as in the short story. Novels, with their wider field, require much greater skill & knowledge of life than do short tales. You cannot draw a character once & for all—but must have it grow or change or react to its environment as the long course of the events affects & modifies it. The best preparation for novel-writing is the closely analytical reading of standard novels. Tarkington is good, & any of the recognised classics will contribute. Edith Wharton, Arnold Bennett, Joseph Hergesheimer, H. G. Wells, John Galsworthy, Kathleen Norris, Leonard Merrick, William McFee, Joseph Conrad— these names are recited at random, & selected from the modern age because contemporary technique is the best sort to acquire by habit & instinct. In the domain of the novel, the ages have undeniably brought artistic progress. But novel-writing is usually best deferred till after considerable progress in short fiction. A novel is a serious & difficult proposition!

As to your rate of progress—the new story certainly shows an encouraging toning-down of background, & I really think you have no reason to feel deterred. A year is too soon to expect perfection, though it will surely test your rate of adaptability. With best wishes, I remain

> Most sincerely yrs
> H P Lovecraft

Notes

1. Wandrei's "The Red Brain" appeared in the October 1927 issue of *WT*.

2. William Marion Reedy (1862–1920), St. Louis–based editor best known for promoting the poets Sara Teasdale, Edgar Lee Masters, and Carl Sandburg in his newspaper, *Reedy's Mirror*. Charles Joseph Finger (1869–1941), British-American writer and musician, became acting editor of the *Reedy's Mirror* upon Reedy's death. The book HPL sent to ZB was probably Finger's *Hints on Writing Short Stories* (1922).

3. Battenburg lace is used in making decorative collars and cuffs.

[12]   [ALS]

10 Barnes St.,

Providence, R.I.,

July 27, 1927.

My dear Mrs. Reed:—

Yours of the 15th & 21st duly arrived, & I shall proceed as soon as possible to give "The Blue Foulard" an extensive revision ($7.00) as suggested. In stating that the plot-idea was a frequently used one, I did not refer so much to details as to general tone & atmosphere—the basic theme of domestic sacrifice & tribute rendered too late. I shall re-cast the paragraphs with my usual care, & would suggest a close parallel examination of original & revised versions when you receive them—since perhaps you find concrete example the best method of learning what is needed in the technical formulation of fiction. This job will receive my very early attention, though I cannot promise record speed because of a new & heavy task on my hands—the editing of a deceased poet's posthumous work in a volume which *must* be in his family's possession by Christmas.[1] However, I think it is safe to say that you will probably see the finished story (which is only a third as long as "The Unchaining") within two weeks. After that I shall be glad to see the new story, as well as the amended version of "Under Cover". Meanwhile I follow the fortunes of "The Unchaining" with keenest interest—hoping to hear not many months hence of its acceptance & publication.

That Greek literature course I mentioned was wholly a matter of English translations—for my own study of the language is a three-quarters-forgotten thing of twenty years ago, & never went beyond the Anabasis[2] & the first seven books of the Iliad. I could no more teach it (nay, nor read it!) today than I could teach Sanscrit or Chinese! But as a matter of fact, the best road to the Hellenic spirit is through a good set of translations—unless one possess a really phenomenal linguistic gift—since otherwise the mechanical mastery of the medium comes to occupy a dominant place, & detracts from the aesthetic enjoyment one would normally derive from the ideas & imagery. It is safe to say that one can best grasp the spirit of the living Greece from a text which one may read in the natural mother-tongue of his childhood. Keats, the supreme Hellenist of our literature, knew not a word of Greek. One sees the pathetic reverse in the dry, dull, mechanical conception of Caesar & Virgil, Cicero & Horace, Xenophon & Homer, & so on, which ordinary students form after wrestling with them in the usual academic manner. They miss all the charm because they have confronted these authors under trying conditions of grammatical routine—& come to hate the very beauties of thought & description which they ought to admire. No translation, of course, is as good as an original; but when one is not a really phenomenal linguist the question is one of relative evils, & to my mind translations are the lesser evil as compared with syntactical struggles. In these days there are some very fine & faithful translations (like the Lang prose Homer) which preserve a remarkable amount of the original spirit. A fair knowledge of Hellenic life & literature—the sole source & eternally supreme inspiration of all European civilisation & art—is really quite essential to any author or student of humanity & its expression today. Fortunately some excellent books exist, so that one might almost guarantee a proper cultural grasp of the theme to anyone who would intelligently read such an assortment as the following—which formed the basis of the course I prepared:

Preparatory
History of Greece—J. Dorman Steele (in Barnes' series—Am. Book Co.)
Age of Fable—Bulfinch (obtainable almost anywhere)

General Outlines
Homer to Theocritus—Capps (splendid history & interpretation of the literature. Am-Book Co. (I think))
Masterpieces of Greek Literature—Wright. (selections with notes. Houghton-Mifflin Co.)

Translated Classics
The Iliad—Lang, Leaf, & Myers (prose—literal & magnificent. Full of true Homeric fire & spirit)
The Odyssey—Lang & Butcher.   "   "   "
And later on one ought to read good translations of the dramatists—Æschylus, Sophocles, Euripides, & Aristophanes.

I shall later have the task of preparing an equivalent Latin course—a field scarcely less essential than the other, since all the Hellenism in modern civilisation has come to us through a Roman filtration.

I am glad that Parker's Aids is proving useful. To my mind the fulness & explicitness of these old books give a far sounder rhetorical foundation than anything published today. At the same time a parallel reading of the best contemporary material is greatly to be desired, lest one's style (like mine, when I am off guard) tend to fall into heaviness & archaism. A prose style—or a verse style, for that matter—ought to show as few marks of immediate date as possible. The cheaper & more trivial the style, the more infested it is with ephemeral forms & constructions peculiar to one brief period alone. What one should aim at is *universality* in the highest degree.

As to the revision of one's own work—I quite comprehend how tedious it is in comparison to fresh composition, yet cannot escape the fact that it is often absolutely necessary. Personally, I avoid it as much as possible by spending an infinite time on my first rough draught—so that when I have finished a tale or essay my MS. is usually too scratched-up & interlined to be legible to anyone but myself . . . . & often too much so even for me, after a lapse of time. But there are cases where later revision is imperative, as fuller perspectives & broader moods reveal grave basic defects in style or structure. When this is so, there is nothing to do but grit one's teeth & pitch in—& in this connexion I may add that I have generally found the task less repellent after a *long* interval than after a *short* one; since in the former case there is less monotony & more of the sense of fresh creation—to say nothing of a lesser sense of futility & wasted labour in contemplating the discarded original version.

I am pleased to hear that you have availed yourself of the Little Blue Books, for they are really a prodigious boon to the impecunious student. I have no patience with the bibliophiles who scorn them because of their lowly exterior—indeed, I have no patience with bibliophiles of any kind, since to me there is nothing of value in a book except the ideas & images behind it. Give me a correct & legible text, & I ask no more. I can't see any more sense in first-edition collecting than in collecting postage stamps or cigarette-box pictures. I never go anywhere without a pocket full of Blue Books to read at odd intervals, & probably own about half the entire series. Just now I have bought ahead of my reading needs, since I hear that many numbers (including the Harvey translations of classic drama)[3] are to be dropped. For a literary beginner there are several titles which ought not to be missed. According to my catalogue the following would be well worth your purchasing:

Handbooks
1131—How to Write for the Market[4]
1143—   "   "   Prepare MSS.[5]
764—Hints on Writing Book Reviews[6]
822—Rhetoric Self-Taught[7]
823—Eng. Comp. "   "[8]
821—How to Improve Vocabulary[9]
708—Romance of Words[10]
734—Useful Phrases[11]

Books of Literary Criticism—useful in forming ideas & standards of style

448
449
450   Critiques of English & French men of letters by John Cowper Powys
451
452
453

Classic Short Stories—models of style or structure

15	6	570	} Flaubert
143	199	617	
318 } Balzac	292		
344	887	198	} Anatole
1042	886	219	France
1043— } Balzac	915	828	
1044	916 } De Maupassant		
1045	917	178	
1046	918	345 } Gautier	
1047	919	230	
1067	920		
	921	865 } Sherwood (modern)	
	922	866 } Anderson	

12	1054	745	
108	1055 } Ambrose	746	Frank
162	1075 } Bierce	923 } Harris	
186	1080	924	(modern)
290		1176	
939 } Poe	693[12]		
940	699		
1154	1163		
32	1164 } Ben		
356	1165 } Hecht		
144[13]	1166 } (modern)		
	1167		

Of course this is only a taste. The more widely one reads, the more one understands life & the better able one is to reproduce reality in literature.

Second-hand bookshops offer opportunities as great as the Blue Books—with the added spice of uncertainty & the possibility of phenomenal "finds". Quaint learned characters like the one you have discovered were by no means unusual a generation or more ago, though today they are becoming less numerous as social flux places the trade in the hands of increasingly low-grade persons. New York's immense array of bookshops, including the book centres around 4th Ave, 59th St, & 125th St, where they cluster in dense groups, are nearly all in the hands of repulsive Jews; while in New England the tendency is to place them in the hands of shrewd business people whose scholarship concerns bindings & editions rather than literature & philosophy. The present age is, unfortunately, not leisurely enough to develop on a large scale the ancient type of spectacled, erudite bookseller, quaint & crotchety, & grown wise on his own wares as sampled in odd moments. The nearest approach to the species I have ever seen is an old man in this city—but even he is sadly one-sided & more or less contemporaneously cheap in his literary inclinations.[14]

If you make the New York trip you will surely have countless opportunities for literary replenishing, for one of the few good things I can say about the place is that its bookshops offer an infinite variety of material for almost nothing. If one is not particular about bindings, one might almost stock a standard library with bargains from the five & ten cent counters. In case you make the Providence side-trip I hope you will not be disappointed—for I fear my oral criticism would not be much clearer than what I write. With me the pen is a much more natural medium than the tongue, & when I am through writing on a subject there is not much left in my head to surprise or edify the face-to-face listener! The one real advantage of conversation is the possibility of instantaneous reply, which ensures the quick disposition of any one point without delays in transmission. This no doubt formed the crux of the Socratic method, & the guiding principle of the great schools of Plato, Aristotle, Zeno, Epicurus, Aristippus, & their ilk. At any rate, whether or not you derive any actual literary benefit, Providence would well repay a visit if you enjoy the charm of ancient & beautiful towns. Much of the past, architecturally & scenically, remains here in a way impossible to a Western city; so that you would probably be reminded of the larger towns of the Carolinas if your memories of that region be vivid & firmly fixed. This archaic charm is a leading factor in my own enjoyment of life—indeed, I soon learned in New York that I cannot pretend to exist without the imaginative stimulus of a quiet, reposeful Colonial setting.

I think you would find Uzzell a very effective instructor if you should decide to take a systematic course in authorship. His courses inculcate in a very direct way the technique demanded by modern editors—as a proof of which I may mention that the friend of mine who attended his classes has just had two stories reprinted from magazines in a short-story anthology. Of course, no teacher can make an author of a novice without hard work & coöperation on the student's part—to say nothing of original literary gifts. But teachers can certainly facilitate the learning process by pointing out characteristic pitfalls & recommending effective methods.

As to your literary attitude—alternations of tragic & comic mood, &c—I fancy that is common to all writers save those of the most narrowly specialised sort. What will come in time is a characteristic outlook on the universe—a more or less fixed & individual perspective on life & the dramatic significance of its events—which will cause any given subject to assume a certain colour or pattern in your eyes, & to evoke from your pen a certain sort of response, whose style will glow with the particular kind of wonder or ecstasy which the scene—as you envisage it—will inspire in your imagination. (In this connexion, do not fail to read the critical volume by Arthur Machen entitled "Hieroglyphics.") So far as I can see, the secret of all authentic art is the quality of imaginary glamour or artificial significance which a certain type of mind—the aesthetic type—succeeds in reading into an essentially meaningless & purposeless universe. Without this special mental quality—a quality altogether distinct from intellect or commonplace emotion—artistic or literary creation is an absolute impossibility. When it does exist, the possessor ought to spare no pains toward its cultivation; for he will never be contented till he can exercise it in perfect aesthetic expression. The test of authentic aestheticism is one's response to any given scene or event or sequence of events. If such things seem to imply more than they show—if they seem to call up strange vistas of wonder & drama & beauty & fatality reaching far beyond themselves into the illimitable gulfs of starry aether—then one may legitimately assume that he is an artist by temperament, & that his literary treatment of life is likely to have in it something besides the obvious & the usual. ¶ When this temperament is joined to a keen scientific insight, one usually becomes a realist & a prober of thoughts & motives. Superficially acknowledged values & attributed motives become puerile & ridiculous to him, so that he soon progresses beyond the state in which he can take popular fiction—or anything like it—seriously. Joined to strong elementary emotions, this temperament produces the lyrical romancer—but even he distrusts & disavows the superficial, & weaves unhackneyed beauties into the high-spots & intensities with which he deals. When the temperament is linked with a sensitive imagination, we behold the cosmic or fantastic writer like Poe, Dunsany, Machen, or Algernon Blackwood. And finally, when it stands quite alone, with all energies bent toward the purely decorative, we have the *stylist* par excellence—the Oscar Wilde or Gautier or Flaubert or Lafcadio Hearn or Walter Pater who exquisitely adorns everything he touches, but who is comparatively indifferent to what he does touch. It will be seen that the different genera of authentic artists are pretty widely separated—yet they all have the common quality of repudiating the superficial & the hackneyed in dealing with life. In other words—the secret & essence of their temperament is that they see & feel imaginary things which others do not see or feel; & on that account demand a strictly first-hand, individual contact with their respective themes.

My present influx of guests—almost a literary convention—has surely been an exciting & enjoyable experience; & I shall be distinctly sorry when the last one departs. Providentially for me, they are all informal & comprehending fellow-strivers in the field of letters, who appreciate my straitened circumstances & realise that a host who merely has rooms in a sedate Victorian backwater for the genteelly reduced cannot be expected to entertain as he might have done in more affluent & domestic years gone by. Thus the gastronomic responsibilities of your quondam sable servitress have not been imposed upon me—since each guest has shared my luck & pay-check at the modest restaurants of my frequenting, as well as attending to such petty details as his own lodgment fee! A benignant patron deity whom I could not affront with the term of "landlady"[15] has enabled me to stow four visitors beneath this very roof, whilst others have distributed themselves about a neighbouring tavern. The total 'attendance' so far has been *eight*, including a local writer who has participated in some of the sessions. Of all these, *five* are authors in the same vein which claims my own unambitious efforts—the Poe-esquely weird & fantastic—& it would doubtless have amused a cynical commentator to watch the naive manner in which four of us spent the greater part of Saturday night—seated on a flat-topped tomb in the ancient hidden churchyard on the hill, through which Poe used to wander during his visits here in 1847 & 1848.[16] Our discourse was of ghosts, ghouls, & other appropriate phenomena—& it was really a pity that none of us happens to believe in any of these colourful things which so poignantly haunt our respective imaginations! If you follow to any extent the magazine *Weird Tales* you may recognise some of my guests as more or less regular contributors—Frank Belknap Long, Jr., (this is the Uzzell student I spoke of) Donald Wandrei, H. Warner Munn, & C. M. Eddy, Jr. all being known to the reading public through that rather cheap but unique medium. These, plus an ex-weird-author now trying his hand at publishing, a museum curator specialising in mineralogy,[17] & the parents of Frank B. Long, constituted the maximum personnel of this epoch-making conclave. The scenic spot north of Providence which I described is surely worthy of any amount of encomium, & in my callow years evoked from me many a pastoral in rhymed heroics, with suitable motto from Virgil or Theocritus. Upon my next visit I shall anchor my headpiece more securely!

I shall, then, attend to "The Blue Foulard" as soon as possible, striving to have it reach you in final form within two weeks. After that I shall be ready for "Under Cover" or the other new story you mention. Meanwhile I trust that Parker & the Blue Books may be of assistance in preparing the background for future work of greater & greater fluency & assurance.

With best wishes, I remain

Yrs very sincerely,

H. P. Lovecraft

Notes

1. HPL was preparing John Ravenor Bullen's posthumous poetry collection *White Fire* for publication. It appeared in 1928.

2. The *Anabasis,* or the "March Up-Country," was an account by the historian Xenophon of the march of 10,000 Greek mercenaries (of whom Xenophon was one) from Persia to Asia Minor. It is in seven books. Elsewhere HPL declares that he never read beyond the first six books of the work in Greek (*A Means to Freedom* 583–84).

3. Alexander Harvey (1868–1949), who translated Sophocles, Aeschylus, and other classic dramatists for the Little Blue Books.

4. By James Oppenheim.

5. By George Milburn.

6. By Leo Markun.

7. By Lloyd E. Smith.

8. By Lloyd E. Smith.

9. By Lloyd E. Smith.

10. By Clement Wood.

11. *1600 Useful Phrases.* Selected and arranged by Lloyd E. Smith.

12. So written. HPL meant to write 698.

13. Pocket Series Book No. 356 is Edmund Clarence Stedman, *Edgar Allan Poe.* Ten Cent Pocket Series Book No. 144 is Sarah Helen Whitman, *Was Edgar Allan Poe Immoral?* HPL omitted from his list Book No. 941 by Poe, *Tales Psychological and Gruesome.*

14. Arthur Edwin Eddy (1860-1933), brother of Clifford Martin Eddy (1873–1937) who was the father of of HPL's friend, C. M. Eddy, Jr. He ran a bookstore on Weybosset St. in Providence that HPL and his friends frequented.

15. HPL refers to Florence Reynolds, the landlady at 10 Barnes Street.

16. St. John's Churchyard, the churchyard of St. John's Episcopal Church on North Main Street (1810).

17. Referring to W. Paul Cook, who was publishing books under his Recluse Press imprint, and James F. Morton.

[13]   [ALS]

> 10 Barnes St.,
> Providence, R.I.,
> July 29, 1927.

My dear Mrs. Reed:—

By again combining business with vacationing, & taking a portfolio of MSS. into the country, I am able to report on "The Woman Who Came Back" (which I would re-title "The Return" if aimed at high-grade magazines) considerably sooner than I had expected.

I am very glad to say that, in my opinion, the present tale represents a very perceptible advance over the average of your former work. The tone is soberer & maturer, & the construction of individual sentences & paragraphs distinctly surer than was the case with earlier productions. The absence of a conventional happy ending is especially to be commended. I shall—unless the order is countermanded—give this tale (which comes to 4200 words) an extensive revision amounting to *$12.00* complete, & hope I can have it in your hands within a month; after, of course, the completion of "The Blue Foulard", on which I shall begin work today.

The points of emendation will, of course, be best displayed in the corrected MS. itself. Just now I will mention a few outstanding points where changes will occur:

(a) The tale will begin with the supper scene where Gloria demands the divorce—antecedent data being retrospectively introduced.

(b) I may, with your permission, make Philip something other than a *struggling inventor*, since this type has become frightfully hackneyed in popular fiction. I presume you realise that the greatest tendency you have to fight is an acceptance of certain conventional types & scenes & moods as workable reality.

(c) After the conclusion of the supper scene a break must be introduced—manifest in the style as well as in the substance—in order to provide for the changed time-element. Hitherto there has been only one scene—now the action skips over much ampler chronological units. The revised version will illustrate the necessary mutation in tempo.

(d) In narrating Philip's success a less prosaic tone is needed. When one has bare facts to state, one must handle them with all the greater art & rhetorical adroitness.

The later parts of the story are, I think, the best ones; although the very ending will need some dramatic development. If the note of real life is to be struck, each character will have to show some progressive evolution according to his or her original bent—Philip toward business absorption & disillusion, & Gloria toward material engrossment & candidly indifferent selfishness. It must be emphasised that what the later Gloria wants is not her particular husband, but any steady & solvent husband who can give her a comfortable anchorage now that her days of attractiveness & excitement are waning. Her rather indifferent & cynical resignation upon learning of Philip's second marriage should be emphasised. After all, each is better off as he or she is—a shrug of the shoulders, a stifled yawn, & Philip turns to his second weary compromise whilst Gloria looks about for a freer & more unsophisticated marital refuge.

As I have said, this tale shows a distinct advance over the bulk of your previous work, & amply justifies you in a policy of hopeful perseverance. The best advice which you could follow would be to continue in the same direction—breaking down with relentless vigour & persistence the novice's common conception of a romantic, artificial world in which simple motives, single-phased characters, (i.e., heroes & villains—all good, all bad, all odd, or all normal characters) deep & undeviating emotions, & melodramatic situations are the rule. The great thing is to purge oneself once & for all of the tawdry, the superficial, the deceptively simple, & the romantic. Don't deal in a tinsel world of obvious types & patterns & prettinesses—take the mixed & confused arena of life as it really is, & the result will have infinitely greater vitality despite the lesser percentage of strong, manly heroes, impeccably exquisite heroines, & idyllically enduring passions & sentiments. Most people are ugly & commonplace—boresome when not actually repulsive. Let this dreary truth be reflected in the general average of your fictional characters. Most successes are only partial, & most failures are too indefinite to possess even the redeeming note of authentic tragedy. Keep this in mind—as I shall do in revising "The Return", where Philip's success will be only a *tolerable*— not a brilliant or spectacular—one. Also—life is never a simple choice between alternatives. Because one road leads to disaster, there is no reason to assume that the opposite road would have led to success. In "The Return" I shall make it clear that Gloria would have gained nothing by remaining with Philip. She would always have been bored, & would always have felt that she had chosen wrongly. Each person does just about the only thing he could have done under the given conditions. When we think we have made a definite mistake, it is normally true that we simply lack the capacity—emotional, intellectual, or imaginative—for following the alternative course which we wish we had followed. A deterministic synthesis of heredity, accident, & individual quality really governs our every thought & act, & blindly impels us to whatever course we take. Free will is an illusion—we have no real choice or freedom in the shaping of our lives. Everything is relentlessly shaped for us by the infinite & ineluctable natural forces of the cosmos. Another artificial convention to be discarded is that domestic happiness bulks supreme in the average full life. It is an important detail, of course, but it ought not to form the absolutely paramount element which it tends to form in cheap fiction. With a world full of varied phenomena & interests, it is absolutely absurd to suppose that the whole or even the principal happiness of an intelligent being depends on the question of whether his wife appreciates him or not, or whether he has or will have any wife at all. In the present story, all the narrated events are probably the merest trifles in the life of Philip—though doubtless less so in the case of the narrower & more primitive Gloria. As an intelligent & sensitive man he has all the mental & aesthetic stimuli in the world to absorb him—the pageant of history, the loveliness of nature & art, the wonder of science, the drama of unfolding ideas, & so on—so that the really vital story of his true inner life would be very different from the mere external narrative of his marital mutations, which superficial romanticists take for granted as constituting his essential story. This is not to say that the external story of these mutations lacks suitability as art material. It is merely that such phases must not be handled with too great seriousness, as if they were more vital than they are. Perspective should be retained, & the external should not *too often* be selected as subject matter.

The best road to a mature appreciation of the relative proportions of things in life is a constant & diligent reading of the best standard literature— with a leaning toward *realistic* writers (Joseph Conrad, William McFee, Theodore Dreiser, Edith Wharton, Ben Hecht, Sherwood Anderson &c) when one's natural tendency is toward excessive romanticism. The most useful reading of this sort is generally in novel form, & will of course be of vast use in building up a subconscious sense of form & style for later employment in novel-writing. For the nonce, however, it is to be considered purely as a *substitute for life*—vicarious experience, as it were—which one must have as a background for translating life into the magical symbolism of art.

Above all in importance is *the complete destruction of the artificial cheap-Sunday-newspaper & popular-fiction world of simple romance & melodrama as a factor to be taken seriously*. Only when one can dismiss with a bored laugh the hectic or saccharine poses & sentimentalities & tritenesses of the cinema & the popular magazine—only when one ceases to have even a passing interest in such grotesque & conventional infantilities—can one be said to have achieved artistic adulthood or to have laid the foundations for a really clear vision & really intelligent authorship. Before we can understand or delineate life, we must get absolutely & finally rid of such banal music-hall attitudes as Christmas-carol sacrifice, home-&-mother twaddle, nonsense about undying love & devotion, rags-to-riches blah, triumph of truth & justice, success of the weak & upright & downfall of the strong & evil—& all that damned tinsel & vulgarly accepted falsehood. I think that Samuel Butler's "Way of All Flesh" ought to be prescribed reading for every incipient author. I would recommend the plays of George Bernard Shaw if it were not that their very unconventionality has become a convention. Almost anything by Oscar Wilde—essays like "Intentions", for example—is good, so long as one does not lose touch with the quintessential lightness of his attitude.

However—this is all general suggestion, & is straying far from the specific matter of "The Return". One can't stick to a subject well in the teeth of a woodland wind—& especially when surrounded by besieging legions of small & nimble red ants. I think I shall make a change of encampment before commencing work on "The Blue Foulard".

Suffice it to say, as a summary, that I believe "The Return" really does show a very encouraging advance both in theme & technique; & that further development along the same lines is certainly worth pursuing. Comparison of original & revised versions later on will serve much better than abstract comment in pointing out details connected with individual problems of artistic expression. Just now your task is twofold—to get rid of any remnants of acceptance of the artificial-romance world, & to cultivate technique as a much finer & more *precise* art than you have been accustomed to regard it. In well-selected books you will find talismans potent to unlock both gates.

With best wishes,

Yrs very sincerely,

H P Lovecraft

[14]   [AHT]

10 Barnes St.,
Providence, R.I.,
August 2, 1927

My dear Mrs. Reed:—

[. . .]

The opening of a short story must always strike the main keynote—an irrelevant digression cannot occur without ruinous consequences.

To achieve *atmosphere,* one must *visualise* very clearly every scene about which one is writing—and must exercise extreme care and art in deciding just what details are of maximum significance and symbolic value. The whole notion of *fiction* must be banished as far as possible—the author must think of his characters and situations as occurring in real life, and must test their essences and accessories by the same rules of naturalness and appropriateness which he would use in judging the soberest narrative of fact. The whole plot must be surveyed and analysed with the utmost seriousness—and absolutely nothing must be added through mere artificial literary convention. Don't write a thing unless you *see* it with almost painful clearness—indeed, the only excuse for authorship at all is the resistless outward pressure of a mentally-limned world whose sharp outlines frantically demand the crystallisation and permanence of the written record.

Rhetorical correctness and felicity are largely a joint matter of mental attitude and artistic sense. The first thing of all is to adopt the very highest grammatical and rhetorical standard, and never think of being satisfied with any other again. This of course means hard study—but it is amply worth it. The idea is to dig unsparingly into such textbooks as Parker's *Aids,* Roget's *Thesaurus,* and Crabb's *English Synonyms* until one realises the finer and subtler qualities of words—their nice distinctions, and the precise need of one certain word for each particular place; a need which no substitute can possibly supply. This is aided, of course, by a diligent analysis of classic English authors with a view to noticing how they manage to achieve their respective effects—and I need not say how different this process is from any mere skimming or casual reading. Once the best books are mastered, it is virtually *impossible* for any observant student to write in other than a tolerably correct style. The important thing for the beginner is to realise at the very outset just how much he has to learn—just how far he is from possessing the art of perfect expression, and just how little he may rely on any standard he has ever possessed before. A natural sense of words is of course an infinite help in this matter, but experience has proved that it is by no means essential to correctness if only the student be serious enough.

As to *felicity*—the knack of producing musical and rhythmical prose whose images glow with the happy touch of perfect aptness in wording and selection—this is undeniably a matter of artistic instinct. It is quite a necessary thing for all minor authors, though a few of the intellectual and imaginative titans whose *ideas* are of overwhelming weight have managed to do without it. Among realists Theodore Dreiser and Sherwood Anderson have both succeeded without possession of any inherent charm of language or description, whilst in the domain of fantasy the same may be said of Algernon Blackwood. Ambrose Bierce, too, was not notable for either vividness or harmony in his diction. But everyone should be as felicitous as his nature will allow, hence all authors are urged to spare no effort in mastering the countless tricks, niceties, and subtleties whereby the telling of an event can be removed from the sphere of bald statement and lifted to the level of dramatic pageantry or pictorial illustration. Correspondence courses try to teach these tricks, but the appreciative reader of literary classics will eventually come to recognise and assimilate so many of them that his need of further instruction is doubtful. What to assimilate from these classics is the spirit, not the letter. That is, we must not merely learn a specific set of devices and copy them, but must rather absorb the artistic spirit which impelled their creation in the first place, and let that spirit weave us a set of new devices to meet the needs of our own particular plot-incidents. In trying to envisage the artistic demands of the narrator's art there are few books more helpful than Prof. W. F. Webster's "English Composition"; published about 1900, and still possibly in print, although I'm not sure. I lent my only copy to a student about five years ago and it was never returned—otherwise I'd be glad to let you look it over. I'd get another one if I could find it cheaply. It has a very full and comprehensible text, as well as many peculiarly valuable study outlines. Also—the more I think of it, the more I feel that you really ought to have that book ("Short Stories Analysed"—or something like that)[1] of annotated and dissected short story classics which I mentioned some time ago as published by the American Library Association of New York. I can't recall the precise name or price, but am sure the publishers would be glad to supply information. That thing—of which I had a rather extended glimpse five or six years ago—struck me as being about as valuable to a beginner as any one book possibly could be.

  Yrs very sincerely,
      H P Lovecraft.

Notes

1. Robert Wilson Neal, *Today's Short Stories Analyzed.*

[15]   [ALS]

<del>W. PAUL COOK</del>
<del>The Recluse Press</del>
<del>Box 215, ATHOL, MASS.</del>
Home Address—
10 Barnes St.,
Providence, R.I.,
Aug. 21, 1927

My dear Mrs. Reed:—

Your latest letter & MS. have been forwarded to me in Athol, where I am visiting the publisher of the posthumous poetic book I am editing; & serve to remind one of the frightful extremities of negligence to which this latter devastating job has reduced me! In all truth, the editing of this book has proved arduous beyond all expectations; so that I have had to work* day & night in order to meet the time schedule imposed by the "angel" who is financing it.[1] It has been necessary for me to go to Athol to superintend the printing & do the proofreading on the spot—& as a result all my other work has been thrown into chaos. You can get some idea of the magnitude of the task—& thus of the validity of the excuse—when I say that about 100 poems were submitted in wholly unclassified & unrevised form; out of which it was necessary for me to make selections, classify as to mood & theme, perform needed revision, &c—writing a biographical & critical preface & putting the whole business into shape for the printer, with all details attended to. Only 39 of the poems were good enough to use even with revision, & these had to be arranged with particular care to make the finished work an artistic unit. The carbon enclosed illustrates what I have done to date—though the preface is still to be completed.

In view of all this, I am sure you can excuse my dilatory tactics. I duly received the $6.00 cheque for "The Blue Foulard", & the previous letter with several points on which I will touch fully when able. Also the new MS. of the Indian agent article; which I think will be excellent, & which will probably need no more than extensive revision. I shall assume, unless I hear to the contrary, that you prefer this article to be revised *ahead of* "The Return"; & will get at the work as early as I can. I shall probably return home a week from today, & can perhaps get the article to you a week later, with "The Return" another week later. Again let me apologise for my inability to fulfil the earlier time-schedule mentioned before this book matter so hopelessly engulfed me.

Scenically this trip has more than repaid me for the hustle & anxiety, for it has brought me to a region of magnificent landscapes & colourful antiqui-

---

*pardon blurs—a small, coal-black kitten with large yellow eyes insists on walking over this sheet & playing with the fountain pen as it moves!

ties which I have always wanted to see. My publisher-host has diversified business with some rural motor-rides after my own heart, including one to Amherst & historic Deerfield, & another to Lake Sunapee, N.H. The enclosed cards convey some idea of the general cast of the circumambient terrain.

Your own trips must have been highly interesting, & I fancy the article will have an excellent chance of landing somewhere. Glad you are reading Flaubert—I'd advise you to get the whole text of "Salammbo", for it's well worth reading through. As you rightly point out, Flaubert's painstaking technique ought to form a model & inspiration for the beginner. About the number of words in "The Unchaining"—I really don't remember, but fancy there were about 21 pages in the typed text. This would mean about 21 × 330 words—6930—which you could call approximately 7000. As a short story, the tale is of medium length.

Upon my return—or possibly in some lull before then—I will answer in detail your recent letters & furnish an estimate of what the article job will be. I'd say on a guess that the article will come to 8 double-spaced pages, 8½ × 11— hence forming an $8.00 job under extensive revision rates. You are wise in getting the typewriter, though such things aren't much for original creative composition. I must get mine (a rebuilt "blind" Remington bought in 1906) overhauled soon, for its neurotic recalcitrance is making work doubly hard for me.

Best wishes—

Sincerely yrs

H P Lovecraft

Notes

1. Archibald E. Freer (1862–1943), a doctor in Chicago.

[16]   [AHT]

Providence, R.I.

Aug. 28, 1927

My dear Mrs. Reed:—

[. . .]

When I was seven I encountered *Poe*[1]—which fixed my taste for all time, so as far as the subject-matter and approximate mood of fiction are concerned. Somehow I cannot become truly interested in anything which does not suggest incredible marvels just around the corner—glorious and ethereal cities of golden roofs and marble terraces beyond the sunset, or vague, dim cosmic presences clawing ominously at the thin rim where the known universe meets the outer and fathomless abyss. The world and all its inhabitants impress me as immeasurably insignificant, so that I always crave intimations of larger and subtler symmetries than those which concern mankind. All this, however, is purely aesthetic, and not at all intellectual. I have a parallel nature or phase devoted to science and logic, and do not believe in the supernatural at all—my philosophical position being that of a mechanistic materialist of the line of Leucippus, Democritus, Epicurus, and Lucretius—and in modern times, Nietzsche and Haeckel.

As to the length of time required to collect a scholastic background suitable for literary purposes—do not for a moment be discouraged by my chance reference to early studies! If I had indeed been studying continuously with one object in view for twenty years, I would surely be either an established success or a proved failure; but the fact is, that I have always been too indolent and vacillating—and too cynically convinced of the ultimate worthlessness of all human effort—to apply myself long or conscientiously to any specific field in a serious or professional way. In other words, I am a victim of changeable dilettantism in its most virulent form; and will amount to no more in the decades to come than I have amounted to in the decades past. When I was very small, I was all for fantasy—as I am now. Then came a period of science—chemistry, astronomy, biology, anthropology, etc.—during which I despised all literature and aesthetics, although continuing to write tales. Then at eighteen I turned to poetry and criticism, not returning to weird fiction for nine more years. And now, at thirty-seven, I am gradually headed for pure antiquarianism and architecture, and away from literature altogether! Heaven knows where I'll end up—but it's a safe bet that I'll never be at the top of anything! Nor do I particularly care to be. Thus you may see that I am to be counted out in any calculation of time and concerted effort in literary progress. As a matter of fact, I believe five or six years ought to see anyone through the apprentice stage—my young friend Long has been about that time in his development, (he is an Uzzell pupil) and is now placing a small number of manuscripts regularly. Others are even quicker. A youth who began writing only three or four years ago in High School has just placed at least three fantastic yarns with *Weird Tales*,[2] while a friend has recently told me of a boy *still in High School* who has struck sudden success through a novel of High School life. It is all a gamble—depending on a vast number of separate factors such as native ability, natural sense of words and style, ambition, energy, rightness of direction, leisure time, state of public taste, coincidence of subject-matter with popular demand, opportunities and influence, and so on. It is virtually impossible to predict the future course of anyone, since only experience tests the real proportion of the various factors. The boy for whom I predicted the quickest success of all—a veritable infant marvel whose cerebral gymnastics left me beaten and amazed—has dropped literature altogether and is desperately studying *music* in an effort to become a composer; meanwhile, teaching French in Northwestern University as a bread-and-butter side-line![3] The vitally important thing is *not to care* about progress as such, but merely to assimilate and express for the pure pleasure of assimilating and expressing. A watched pot, says the old adage, never boils—and the best way to cover ground is not to think about the goal, but to tackle each step for the sheer joy of the immediate process. *Spontaneity* is the greatest of all qualities not only in art but in learning as well. It is to some extent the secret of all aesthetic life.

As for the use of pseudonyms—I don't see either any good or any harm in the practice. It's all a matter of taste. Commercially, of course, one must expect to stick to whatever he adopts—he must do all his deciding beforehand; for when one name gets known, it is folly to use any other. Editors generally insist that a popular contributor continue to use the name under which he gained his recognition—although they don't care whether the name is genuine or assumed. The only objection to a pseudonym is the possibility that one may after a long time regret that he did not bring his own name to celebrity. It is possible for an author to become jealous of the fictitious personality he has built up—resenting the homage which critics accord to "Fitz-John Neville Rockingham," whilst plain Wilbur J. Brown is unknown to fame's eternal beadroll.[4] Perhaps an eighth of the recognised American writers of today—none, however, of the very topmost rank since "Mark Twain"—use pseudonyms or contractions. "Anthony Hope" is Anthony H. Hawkins. "Fulton Oursler" has dropped the praenomen of Charles. "Murray Leinster"'s real name is Jenkins, and Ernest Seton Thompson is now sporting the curiously transposed designation of Ernest Thompson Seton. Theodore Dreiser has always stuck to his real family name, but his elder brother Paul— the song-writing idol of the 'nineties—affected the variant form of Dresser.

No one can advise another regarding the choice of a nom de guerre, since only one's self can fully grasp all the sentimentally associative factors concerned. When an author especially cherishes and wishes to honour a particular line of his ancestry which his surname does not express, I think he is eminently justified in effecting some transposition or interpolation better fitted to his state of mind. But once he does it, he must stick to it. If I were you I would use the name which subtly seems to you the most natural—the most ingrainedly your own—whether it be Haslett, Brown, or Reed. There is surely no logical basis for disliking the latter—for it is tasteful, euphonious, and by no means undistinguished. In Portland, where I have just been, there is a statue of Speaker Thomas Brackett Reed[5] in one of the principal park-like promenades; and all the guide-books point out his birthplace as a shrine to visit! For my part, I have always used my own name as a matter of course——for sheer lack of any reason to use any other—except for hack work too poor to be acknowledged.[6] When an author produces only one kind of work he can use any one name he likes—though it is sometimes advisable to employ another designation for work conspicuously out of one's own line. Thus the mathematician and text-book writer C. L. Dodgson found it advisable to become "Lewis

Carroll" when writing "Alice in Wonderland". My only general objection to pseudonyms is that they tend to imply a sort of self-consciousness or self-dramatisation on the user's part, which is somewhat foreign to the process of impersonal, disinterested artistic creation. They imply that the user stands off and thinks of himself as an author, instead of being so wrapped up in his aesthetic vision that he never regards himself as a person at all.

 With every good wish, I remain
  Most cordially and sincerely yrs
   H P Lovecraft.

Notes

1. Elsewhere HPL dates his discovery of Poe to the age of eight: "Then I struck EDGAR ALLAN POE! It was my downfall, and at the age of eight I saw the blue firmament of Argos and Sicily darkened by the miasmal exhalations of the tomb!" (*Letters to Maurice Moe and Others* 431).

2. HPL presumably refers to August Derleth, who landed stories with *WT* beginning at the age of seventeen.

3. HPL is referring to Alfred Galpin.

4. A catalogue of people whose souls are to be prayed for. A catalogue of names; a pedigree, a long respected series.

5. Thomas Brackett Reed (1839–1902), U.S. representative from Maine (1877–89) and Speaker of the House (1895–99).

6. HPL neglects to mention the numerous pseudonyms he used when publishing poetry and other matter in the amateur press.

[17] [AHT]

                                          10 Barnes St.
                                        Providence, R. I.
                                          Sept. 8, 1927

My dear Mrs. Reed:—

        I'm glad the cards proved entertaining—and enclose another set covering the latter half of my vagrant itinerary. From Newburyport—after a side-trip to see a friend in Haverhill—I proceeded through ancient Ipswich to Gloucester, the last of the really unchanged New England fishing ports. Here—despite a growing Portugese and Italian invasion—one may actually get a lingering taste of old New England's maritime past, along a waterfront filled with sail-lofts, ship-chandleries, and seamen's missions, and with an old-fashioned tangle of spars and rigging rising above the blue harbour beyond. The old houses, too, are numerous and fine—I went through two of them, one built in 1704 and the other in 1768. After "doing" Gloucester I visited some of the still quainter suburbs—such as Rockport—and obtained a bit of natural grandeur on the cliffs at Magnolia, where the ocean pounds in supreme splendour at the historic rock of Norman's Woe. Subsequently I worked down the coast through Manchester to Salem and Marblehead—these last two the absolute nuclei and quintessences of the American colonial tradition. Salem—the town of Hawthorne holds many a relic of the 1692 witchcraft; whilst Marblehead is the most unchanged colonial town in the United States—narrow, curving, hilly streets, unpaved and sidewalkless, and brown, crumbling lines of quaint houses which have stood unaltered since the early 1700's. After Marblehead anything else would have been anticlimax, so I hastened unobservantly home through prosaic Lynn and hackneyed Boston—reaching here Friday midnight and subsequently reaping[1] the whirlwind of massed labour caused by previous neglect. But the trip was worth it. I gathered enough impressions to make another year endurable, whether or not they come out as crystallised images in any tales I may write.

Concerning reading—if you don't like *Flaubert*, there are plenty of other classics to try; although no one ought really to give up either *Flaubert* or *Gautier* till he has tried them in Lafcadio Hearn's magnificent translations. But there's an abundance of good material at large, so one need not try too hard to acquire a liking where it doesn't come naturally. A notebook is an excellent thing to keep—and the best of all is a habit of *close attention* whereby the minutiae of rhetoric and style may be noticed with enough clearness to ensure *thus* gradual and intelligent absorption into one's work.

As to the matter of gratuitous contributions to the Oklahoma paper—I'd send things, if I were you; since at an early stage it always does an author good to have a ready medium of publication, pay or no pay. It will give you abundant copies for distribution, give you the knowledge that you are writing for a real audience, possibly elicit helpful critical comment from various sources, and furnish the truly great psychological stimulus of seeing your name and work frequently in print. I would surely try the book review—for reviewing is an occupation which stimulates one's analytical and critical sense, and reacts favourably on one's own creative work. What is more—I would make a practice of reading the various current reviews in some reliable journal like the *New York Times Literary Supplement*[2] or the *New York Herald Tribune Book Section*. Both of these things can be subscribed for separately from the newspapers they are designed to accompany, and I strongly advise your taking them. The constant reading of good criticism cannot but be an enormous help toward a full realisation of the high-grade author's province and problems.

As for fumiferous indulgence on my part—let me express a very keen appreciation of your kindness in proffering a nicotinic tribute ere I remark that the odour on that carbon copy must have come from the desk which my genial Athol host placed at my disposal! The fact is, that I've never smoked since donning long trousers; since the fragrant weed is to me no more than a choking nuisance. When I was small, I smoked because it was the grown-up, masculine, and forbidden thing to do; but as soon as I could present a reasonably grown-up appearance without it, I relievedly suffered it to become a none-too-cherished memory. I naturally have to tolerate clouds of mephitic vapour from most of my friends, and I flatter myself that I do it without complaint. But at least I don't have to thicken the cloud of tear-gas by any voluntary exhalations of my own! But again let me thank you for a kindness which I appreciate none the less because of my un-chimney like predilections.

I remain

Yrs very sincerely,

H P Lovecraft.

Notes

1. For "reaping," AHT reads "escaping." Cf. Hosea 8:7: "For they have sown the wind, and they shall reap the whirlwind"; i.e., to suffer now because of mistakes made in the past.
2. HPL has confused the *New York Times Book Review* with the (London) *Times Literary Supplement*.

[18]   [AHT]

10 Barnes St.,

Providence, R. I.,

Sept. 22, 1927

My dear Mrs. Reed:—

[. . .]

I am making no charge for this analysis—but if desired will later on furnish a regular and minute analysis of the whole plot and style at the usual rate of $5.60 (for 5600 words). This will apply only if you wish to do the rewriting yourself. If you have me do the correcting—either the $28.00 extensive revision or the $56.00 re-writing—there will be no additional charge for critical analysis and advice. The case, indeed, closely parallels that of "Under Cover"—to which I gave the full analysis. As for which course to choose—I'd really advise waiting altogether (unless you are in haste or feel that the specific comment would be of additional value) until you can have profited by the Uzzell instruction. There is no use in squandering cash on fragmentary helps when a systematic and intensive course looms ahead; and of course Uzzell's advice would be much more to the point, commercially, than mine. My maturest judgment—the uncommercial impersonality of which you can appreciate in view of the revision-fees which it denies—would be inclined to advise a course of study and reading only, or at least mainly, until the January term of organised class work begins. There is great need of a wide and deep foundation—a clarification of taste and training in the art of close and precise attention to details—on which to build the subsequent structure of technical proficiency; and the intervening three months offer great possibilities in connection with the *Blue Books* or with such carefully-chosen reading courses as most of the public libraries furnish. The thing to seek is the right orientation and point of view—a clear knowledge of the problems faced and the standards demanded, and a cultivation of the habits of instinctive accuracy and facile research in matters of fictional setting, colour, and plausibility. I would recommend, in particular, a very thorough and reflective reading of as many critical essays as possible—things in which there is enough discussion of literary standards and problems to give a concrete idea of the field ahead. Then, too, there is the element of philosophic patience to be cultivated. The infinite slowness of really solid progress must be recognised and accepted, so that there will be no disappointment when mere weeks or months fail to display a sensational advance. One must become resigned to the fact that all real development occurs in the subconscious mind alone, so that a substantial period of incubation must always elapse between the reception of a new impression and the successful utilisation of that impression in the field of creative art. Each new idea must be absorbed, correlated with all the rest of one's cerebral possessions, and assimilated to such an extent that it can mould spontaneous thought, feeling, or imagination without one's conscious or calculative effort. Only then can it operate perfectly through the medium of aesthetics—though of course it can be used before that in anything of a purely intellectual cast, such as historical, philosophical, or scientific effort. It must likewise be realised that serious authorship as a whole is not a matter of any sudden and joyously glamorous inspiration which seizes mind and hand without scholarship or close thought, and luminously writes itself into art through some vague, mystical, temperamental channel. No idea could be more false than this. It is true that an author must have certain inborn gifts of perception, selection, and symbolisation; but these things are the merest raw material. The successful craftsman must be a sober and diligent student of all things, a temperate and philosophical thinker and analyst, and a keenly alert, observant, and intelligently self-critical workman at every stage of the process—knowing precisely the effect he is seeking, consciously moulding all his material toward that effect, and accurately drawing his setting in such a way as to satisfy all the historical, geographical, scientific, philosophical and artistic perceptions of the critical reader. Writers who are "aesthetically" proud of their ignorance of certain branches of knowledge which they call "prose", (as are at least two young men of my acquaintance) or who fancy that they can "get by" with an imperfect or fragmentary acquaintance with life and literature, would do well to watch the methods and attainments of any successful author and note how completely he scorns all evasions, poses, or "temperamentally" irresponsible "bluffin". Take the matter of local colour or historical colour, for example.

To deal with this rightly, there is only one course to follow—*absolutely correct and intimate knowledge of the place and period described.* I know an old fellow who writes historical novels for boys,[1] and it is an interesting thing to see the special shelf of library books he always has beside him—all pertaining to his present subject, and each one filled with bookmarks indicating topics bearing on the field he is to cover. Never does he set down a statement possessing historical or geographical implications without verifying every detail from the authorities at his side—and as a result his books ring so true that they unconsciously fill their young readers with a vivid sense of reality, to say nothing of eliciting the appreciation of the most careful parents. Accuracy, attention, alert and conscious scholarship, and minute fidelity to details have helped him to accomplish his purpose—to re-create fragments of life, in their authentic setting, in such a way that the reader cannot help being swept off his feet, away from reality and into the glamorous world of the story.

This reminds me of another point—that no story can be truly potent unless it mirrors or suggests larger segments of entity than its mere characters. There is nothing new or interesting in the pitiful fretting and mating and quarreling and killing and parting of a few commonplace human beings. Cheap newspapers and dime novels have so fed the public upon this sort of thing that nothing of freshness or novelty is left—everything is known or expected, for it has been told a thousand times before in one guise or another. A story becomes arresting and significant only when its elements stand out as well-linked components or symbols of some larger cosmos, either by artistic treatment or by a faithful and scientifically individualised depiction of the various characters. Ordinary characters ordinarily treated do not make a story. If the characters are to possess only the commonplace, unimaginative emotions and motives, then the events must be handled in so poetic a fashion that the very commonplaceness of the folk will form a brilliant symbol of their helplessness in the toils of fate. And if the events are to be tame and usual, then each character must be drawn with highly individualised skill;—so that his particular attributes will be his own and not shared by any other—the whole tale to form really an analysis of the given events, just as the other sort of tale may be said to form a synthesis of the infinitely commonplace. In determining *just what forms a commonplace or unimaginative character* one must be sure of one's standards. Some authors are themselves so circumscribed in vision that they draw tame and painfully ordinary puppets without realising the tameness and ordinariness at all. The way to test one's perception of depth and uniqueness—or conversely, of shallowness and commonplaceness—in human character is to read a few books describing types which are truly and extremely unusual in one way or another. I would advise no person to write a word of fiction without having attentively studied at least a few of the nineteenth century French decadents, (notably *A Rebours,* by Joris-Karl Huysmans, or the poetry of Baudelaire) some Celtic aesthete like Yeats, Synge, or Arthur Machen, ("The Hill of Dreams" absolutely demands perusal by any cultivated person) a morbid Slav or two, (such as Dostoievsky's "Crime and Punishment"—Tolstoy is not so good, being homiletically mawkish beyond even the Slavic average) and a good dose of our own Anglo-Saxon mysticism as exemplified in Poe, (every story by whom is vitally essential for every short fiction writer) Algernon Blackwood, ("Incredible Adventures") and Walter de la Mare. Books like this open up vistas of complex thought and character which make one realise the flabbiness, tameness, and utter unoriginality of many types which may previously have seemed quite distinctive. It is not that these extreme books need be imitated, but that they are necessary for the acquisition of a perspective capable of showing who's who and what's what in the realm of characters and events. One might also add that it is necessary to correlate characters and events to some extent in space and time in order to make them vital. Mere puppets commonplacely (and by commonplace we mean ordinary violent things—unimaginative murders and usual amatory phenomena and all that—as well as ordinary tame things) jangling in a void mean absolutely nothing. Only when they are shown as symbolic outgrowths of a period, nation, race, or some other unit do they gain any vitality or significance. That is why the historical or geographical element is so important. Moreover, they must not act their drama on an empty stage. After all, the human figures are the least important details of a good landscape—and by the same token we must realise that in a story the composition of the background (time, place, colour, details of exterior and interior settings) is at least of almost equal importance with the drawing of the characters. It is this which imparts unity and meaning to the action. After all, the events of isolated human lives are of the smallest possible interest or purport. *It is only the collective life of some larger unit, of which the human beings form parts and symbols, that is of any moment;* wherefore we must see that the picture is complete—that the human elements are not unduly magnified at the expense of their locale. One of the reasons I recommended Flaubert was his splendid command of his settings—how Carthage lives again in "Salammbo". That novel is the epic of a certain chapter in Carthaginian life as well as of the lives of Hamilcar, Salammbo, and Matho—and is so amply and accurately written that it will almost serve as a serious textbook of Punic archaeology—as the recent explorer Count de Prorok eloquently attests.

I thought you'd realise, after reading "Pickman's Model", (one of my very tamest and mildest effusions) that not much of my own style gets into my revisions. Incidentally, the setting of that tale was very close to fact up to this year, and I was tremendously mortified last July when I tried to show the district to one of my guests (the Donald Wandrei whose "Red Brain" appears in the current *Weird Tales*) and found the whole scene torn down for two blocks around! I imagine the building inspectors must have found those ancient houses as sinister as I did, albeit with a different sort of perception. That is the perennial grief of an architectural antiquarian—in a city as large as Providence or Boston something quaint is always being demolished in the interest of alleged progress. As to whether I am comic or serious in temperament—I fancy the balance stays most on the comic side, since I have too poignant a sense of the futility of the universe and the insignificance of mankind to view life as other than a trivial and ridiculous spectacle. At the same time my devotion to beauty and tradition is sincere, so that my creative writing is not of the flippant or sophisticated sort. I realise the emptiness of everything but externals, and for that very reason value externals and illusions for what they are—thus viewing all cosmic phenomena in a purely decorative light, and writing of strange wonders and ethereal marvels with a breathless absolute—even though mentally discounted—naivete. Dunsany, Poe, Machen, de la Mare, and Blackwood are my literary congeners. Weird literature as a form interests me prodigiously, and I have written a short historical article (25,000 words) on the subject which W. Paul Cook is shortly to publish in his privately printed magazine, *The Recluse*.² Of weird stories I must have written forty or fifty, over half of which have appeared in print—generally the worst ones, which professional editors like best.

  I remain
     Yrs very sincerely,
     H P Lovecraft.

Notes

1. Everett McNeil.

2. HPL devoted Chapter VII of "Supernatural Horror in Literature" to Poe; Chapter X, "The Modern Masters," is given to the others.

[19] [ALS]

        10 Barnes St.,
        Providence, R.I.,
        Novr. 12, 1927

My dear Mrs. Reed:—

    I duly received yours of the 4ᵗʰ & 6ᵗʰ, & am indeed sorry to hear of the continued illness of your son. Anxiety on your part surely needs no excuse; though I feel certain that in this case, as in most others of the kind, the resiliency of youth can be relied upon to throw off the infection with reasonable promptness, & without any permanent after-effects. The assiduous care he is receiving, too, cannot but be in his favour; so that, altogether, an outside & impartial observer would probably find very little of a really alarming or depressing nature in the situation. His physician, no doubt, has already given many assurances to this effect.

The New England floods, I am glad to say, have not affected Providence in the least—the coastal situation of the town making it easier for surplus water to seek the sea than to overflow the land. The northern & western parts of Rhode Island, however, have not shared our immunity; many villages being partly inundated, & an exasperating number of highway bridges washed away. But of course even this damage is mild as compared with the cataclysmic fury of the streams in northern New England. Several of the places which I visited on the earlier part of my August trip have tasted deeply of the disaster—indeed, I'm rather anxious to hear from my publishing friend in Athol, from whom I haven't had word since the flood, despite the presence of some rather important business on the docket. Enclosed are a couple of newspaper views of the deluge—though possibly your local papers have published even more vivid glimpses. The contrasted violence & tranquillity of the Vermont & Rhode Island scenes forms a good index of the relative force of the phenomenon in the two regions.[1] These views, by the way, need not be returned. The papers are full of them.

I am glad you found the local scenic views of interest—certainly, nowhere else can one find such a perfect realisation of the poet's conception of *rus in urbe*.[2] Whether or not a first-hand sight of the place would repay you, depends of course upon the degree to which your imagination is sensitive on the side of venerable, the quaint, the picturesque, & the beautiful in its landscape & architectural phases. Persons whose sensitiveness lies in other aesthetic fields—as music, painting, or the more abstract element in poetry—would no doubt hold that I overrate the town; interpreting its scenery as I do in terms of my own visual & antiquarian imagination. But you have plenty of time in which to decide for or against a 200-mile-&-return detour from your regular itinerary. The motoring time is about 9 hours each way from New York—over predominantly good roads, & through some finely typical New England scenery . . . . which will appear to best advantage, naturally, in the spring & summer.

I'm sorry to know that the scenic beauty of Kansas City is menaced by shady politics—& hope the menace is merely that of neglect & undevelopment, rather than that of irrevocably destructive suburb-spreading & factory-rearing. Only two weeks ago I came across a highly extraordinary case of the *opposite* sort of change, & am still perceptibly exhilarated by the effect it had on my imagination. I was taking an afternoon's walk, for old times' sake, through a semi-rural region in East Providence which I had not visited for twenty years—its decay & cheapening having spoilt it for me—but whose extreme beauty of meadow-land, grove, & river-valley once made it a favourite haunt of my boyhood. The focal point of this area, a woodland waterfall & island-dotted rapids near a picturesque old ruined mill, had become the site of a vulgar amusement park—cluttered with detestable sheds & roller-coasters & dance-halls, & with still more detestable patrons—so that all the charm was submerged & destroyed. On this recent occasion I hoped but little for anything more than a chance relic or two of the old days—hence one may imagine my astonishment upon beholding, as in a dream, a perfect restoration of the quiet 1900 landscape, lineament for lineament, with not so much as a trace to show that any cheap near-Coney-Island had ever been there! In the golden magic of sunset I had to rub my eyes before I could credit the reality of the miracle, yet on closer thought it was not hard to see what had taken place. The original ruination was wholly one of *addition*, & had not really involved the destruction of any of the natural graces of the spot. Then, when the resort failed or moved, (& it must have gone fully a decade ago, to judge from Nature's complete & settled return) the intruding buildings were torn down; leaving the topography precisely as of old, & thus inaugurating a restoration which became perfect as soon as the revolving years brought back the grass & the flowers, the mosses & the underbrush, & narrowed down the paths to their pristine trail-like proportions. Not often does one behold a triumphant reconquest of beauty as clear-cut & spectacular as this. It was a perfect realisation, on a small scale, of the theme of Dunsany's "Prayer of the Flowers!"[3]

I am glad that the "Return" MS. safely arrived, & that it proved satisfactory to you. It is, I think, wise on your part to postpone further composition (except, of course, informal practice work) until after receiving the benefit of Uzzell instruction. That instruction, I feel sure, will be of substantial value to you—& I trust that you may not permit any of the brusquenesses of Mr. Uzzell to discourage you at the outset. No matter how purely commercial & matter-of-fact his point of view may be, it is no less true that his methods in teaching the basic elements of prose fictional form are of equal value to those whose ultimate aims are widely different.

With best wishes, & trusting that you are even now beginning to note a heartening speeding-up in young Jimmie's recovery,

   I remain,

     Sincerely & cordially yrs

      H P Lovecraft

Notes

1. HPL later used the floods in New England, especially Vermont, as the trigger for the events in "The Whisperer in Darkness" (1930).

2. I.e., countryside in the city.

3. Dunsany's "The Prayer of the Flowers" (in *Fifty-one Tales,* 1915) tells of a world beset by pollution and industrialization. But Pan reassures the flowers, stating: "Be patient a little, these things are not for long."

[20]   [ALS]

10 Barnes St.,
Providence, R.I.
Novr. 15, 1927.

My dear Mrs. Reed:—

I looked over the Hardy letter with considerable inter-
est, & was rather surprised to see how summarily "The Unchaining" is la-
belled 'unconvincing'. I know, however, that all delineations of unusual or
peculiarly situated characters are at a disadvantage with the public; hence can
scarcely say that I do not grasp the principle on which the verdict is based.
Editors are not responsible for this condition, for they are guided in every
detail by the likes of their readers, as expressed in the numerous letters they
receive. That is why most of the cheap magazines have voting departments,
in which the intelligent & cultivated reader is invited to seize his stubby pencil
& five-cent ruled pad & scrawl out his preferences & prejudices amongst the
current contents. The tales & authors that poll a maximum of votes are taken
as standards to follow in accepting future work—so that the editor really has
no voice in the matter at all—his only optative task being the selection of
what he thinks comes nearest to the expressed ideals of his choice clientele of
brachycephalic stevedores & lymphatic kitchen-wenches. But of course editors
& agents can't work indefinitely under such standards without picking up—
unconsciously or otherwise—something of their public's point of view. Hence
one need not wonder when they occasionally proffer advice & appraisals
founded on the psychology of the popular & the commonplace. They are not
judging with either art or life in mind. The majority have no use for these things
as sincerely presented. Their criterion is a certain simple & conventional pattern
which they know will please the obtuse multitudes who relish such a pattern.

Now as to "The Unchaining"—I have studied it with renewed care, &
doubt very much if it could be made to fit the Hardy–Uzzell pattern of salea-
bility without a re-writing equivalent to the creation of a new story. This is
because the objected-to features are all integral parts of the plot & characterisation, & so completely merged & interdependent that the removal of even
one of them would destroy the entire motivation & cause the plot to collapse
hopelessly. If it were the technique or space allotment it would be different.
These could be changed. But as it is, I don't see a thing to be done save to
normalise the two leading characters—& that would naturally mean the creation of a whole new set of consequences based upon the altered personalities
. . . . . in other words, a new & entirely different story. Whether or not you
care to write such a story, of course, rests wholly with you. It would, as you
can see, be little more than a trite & ordinary "eternal triangle" tale if deprived of its present individualities—its only possible salvation being some
particularly new or clever incident or mood or atmospheric touch on which

you might hit by accident or design—& without contravening the rigid canons of artificial simplicity which seem to prevail so universally in the popular magazine world. The only conceivable way to modify the characters which I can see—i.e., to modify them & yet preserve some trace of the existing plot—is to portray a *resentment* of the Daphne–Will situation on Ella's part—a resentment held in check by her regard for Will, perhaps, but nevertheless sufficiently strong to develop a substantial emotional conflict & to destroy that undivided pity & affection for Daphne which she never appears to lose. Such a state of things would, of course, be much closer to the average of human nature than the phenomenal abnegation now depicted—but it would be very difficult to introduce without a complete recasting of Ella's character & emotional problem from the very beginning. Still more difficult is the question of changing Will. To kill him off by some means other than worry would involve too much *coincidence* for the purposes of even popular fiction, while to let him live would require a complete alteration of the climax, with the loss of such dramatic values & surprises as now reside therein. The best compromise, I suppose, would be to have Will less violently ill, & to have Ella give him a divorce for his own—or her own—or the editor's—good after nursing him back to health. Also—to avoid the rather hackneyed device of universal marrying-off at the end, you might have Ella adopt the child without wedding the apparent father—although this is a point about which the editors would not be likely to be particular . . . . in fact, they might even prefer the existing end. However, it is clear that any sort of change means a vast degree of overhauling—equivalent even at best to the writing of another tale. I assume that you would not wish to have me do this at present, involving as it would the highest of all rates—that of actual re-writing (and this after extensive revision has already taken place!)—hence I am returning the MS. untouched. If you would like to attempt a re-casting for purposes of literary experiment & exercise, the process might not be without its value—although I'd advise its postponement until after you can have reaped some results from the Uzzell course. But in any case it would not be well to destroy or lose the story in its present form. In the event of success & recognition with other work, an author is often enabled to place, later on, material which met only with repeated rejection when originally written.

I trust, by the way, that you may not regard as mercenary my practice of treating such re-submitted work—re-submitted after an originally completed transaction—as an entirely new job not covered by the first fee. While I do undertake to change work repeatedly under the first fee until it suits *the client,* a moment's thought will reveal why it would be suicidal for me to prolong this privilege of free alteration to cover later ideas of change suggested by *editors.* As you can see, there are likely to be as many different opinions of a story as there are different editors, agents, & critics; so that if a reviser undertook to change & re-change a tale under the first fee until it finally ceased to evoke editorial suggestions, (if such a state can be imagined!) he might be compelled to devote all his time & energy to the lifelong rewriting of one tale, for which he had been paid but once! And under these circumstances it is not likely that his life *would* be long—unless substantially eked out by the State Board of Charities or some benevolent medium of analogous cast. Therefore revisers have to make it a rule to confine free re-alterations to such as *the client himself* feels necessary for the expression of what he wished to say in the manner he wished to say it.

I endeavour to be as liberal as possible in interpreting this provision—never hurrying a client into the acceptance of any work which does not seem to satisfy him perfectly, & never being reluctant to make suggestions or minor corrections even after the completion of the original bargain. But you can readily appreciate why a basically re-opened task of revision or rewriting—demanding precisely as much time & care as a wholly new task—has to be regarded financially as a new & distinct transaction. If this be miserliness, let the public make the most of it! I am lenient enough to call it self-preservation.

Turning to the matter of "The Return", I find Hardy's criticism less baffling than in the other case. You will recall that I myself called attention to the triteness of the theme, & expressed doubt as to the professional marketability of the story. Of the two objections Hardy makes, the first appears to me less unreasonable than the second. While to my mind the division of the tale into equal parts—justifying the detailed action of the second by an ample & intimate preparation in the first—seems the more artistic arrangement, I realise that the plot would lose nothing by a condensation of the preparatory & retrospective section. Accordingly I have gone ahead & done this—boiling down 13 pages to 7, & thus reducing the whole story to the compass of 5600 words. I enclose the condensed version—the new pages assembled with the old, & the latter properly re-numbered—herewith, but am likewise returning the thirteen discarded pages of the earlier version in case you wish at any time to restore the text. The seven carbon pages can be similarly joined to the later re-numbered pages of the earlier carbon. This job involves *light revision,* which I perform for 50¢ per page, typed with carbon; hence (7 pp) comes to *$3.50** in all, payable at any time. As for Hardy's later suggestion—'more feeling' in the latter part of the tale—I so strongly doubt the advisability of the change that I am not undertaking it, even though it forfeit me the profit I might derive from the revision. I took considerable care, when drawing the scene, to maintain exactly the emotional atmosphere which seemed suited to the occasion & characters; & upon studying it a second time I must say that I fail to envisage the matter any differently. I really believe that the Hardy criticism is

---

*making the *entire* current bill *$22.50,* or *$27.00* if the "Under Cover" analysis is included.

an individual one—one person's opinion—which need not be taken as an absolute criterion. If, however, others make the same comment, & you decide to continue work on the tale, I shall be glad to do what I can in the usual way. The present condensation of the first part will not be affected by any later work on the second—so that in any case what is done now represents permanent progress & does not involve any waste of cash or of labour.

As a final word on "The Return"—I do not think that any *further* condensation of the first part would be advisable. A certain amount of preparation is necessary to give the events of the main scene a background & dramatic significance, & I think the present seven pages form an absolute minimum. *Change, reversal, & surprise* are the elements on which the story hinges, & these can have no force unless there is a clear picture of something to be *changed from* or *surprised about.* Hardy, I may remark, has a very high standing professionally; & will be an excellent & honourable person for you to deal with when your tales have assumed such a popular-professional cast as to encourage his handling them. He was formerly a reviser & teacher of fiction by correspondence, & those who have dealt with him have nothing but praise for his kindliness & conscientiousness. I am returning his letter herewith.

I am glad to hear that young Jimmie is at last definitely on the up-grade physically, as indeed I felt sure he would be by this time. It is really too bad that you did not have a nurse before, so that the tax upon your own strength might have been less. Now, however, you & your son can have an opportunity to recuperate together.

My first word from Athol came this morning, & I was pleased to learn that the flood did no damage there. If it had drowned the still unassembled sheets of that book I am editing—& which has already been paid for—I would have been in a very trying predicament indeed . . . . . it's bad enough as it is, since a stupid press-room error caused the edition to be printed before my final proofs reached the office—leaving three misprints in the text, & necessitating (because of the arrangement of the folios) the reprinting of 24 pages—three sheets of 8 pages each. The financial loss will have to be borne by Cook, since he was responsible for the premature printing; but the incident is extremely provoking to me as well, since it involves additional proof-reading & imposes a dangerous delay in the face of an ironclad arrangement calling for delivery well before Christmas.

Hoping that the enclosed condensation of "The Return" may prove satisfactory to you, & to some editor, in turn; & regretting that a revision of "The Unchaining" to cheap popular standards would be such a precarious & fundamental proposition,

I remain,

Yrs very sincerely,
H P Lovecraft

[21]   [ALS]

10 Barnes St.,
Providence, R.I.,
Jany. 10, 1928.

My dear Mrs. Reed:—

I must hasten to express my sincere sympathy concerning the various trials you have been through—in particular the sudden bereavement which must have been so great & so unexpected a shock. It is difficult to offer any consolation which can seem adequate at such a time, though one might perhaps point out how much more poignant & devastating the grief would have been had the blow fallen years later, after a long married life would have supplied a thousand additional ties & tender domestic associations which now have the vaguer & less sharply definite status of intangible aspirations. It is, too, some consolation to reflect upon the obvious esteem in which Mr. Henry was held, as judged by the ready offers & really exacting sacrifices of so many loyal friends. There is a clear beauty about such a memory which has power to mitigate, or at least to transfigure to something closely approaching glory, the sharpness of the pain which must attend it.

I am sorry, likewise, to hear of the wider spread of illness in your household—though pulmonary troubles seem very rife this autumn & winter throughout the country; no less than five or six of my friends & correspondents having suffered grippe or influenza in one form or another. I trust that Junior's illness was reasonably light, that his cough will soon vanish, & that young James's convalescence passed into full recovery without a setback. Your own attack was especially to be regretted—but it was fortunate, in view of so many household responsibilities, that it did not turn out still more severely. I trust that you may be able to rest as much as possible, till recuperation has advanced to the stage where change & activity outweigh quiet as curative forces.

I am glad the matter sent last November arrived safely, & hope that "The Return" may yet be able to avoid living up to its name after some editorial visit. Naturally the recent weeks have not been much of a season for work or study; but there is surely nothing lost thereby, since in reality time is not nearly so important as the artificial standpoint of ultra-modernity would have one believe. It is well, I think, that you have been brushing up on Mr. Uzzell's methods in view of your coming course with him; & I am still certain that you could not have chosen a better source of instruction. You have doubtless heard details from him by this time, & I trust a satisfactory time-schedule & programme of studies has been arranged. If you are used to travel, so that the stress & routine of the process do not wear too heavily upon you, the experience of the trip will probably be a tonic & beneficial one. I hope it may proceed without a hitch, & that you may find your interviews with Uzzell an ample repayment for the effort & expense. I did not know that his personal instruction was ever as brief as a two-or-three-week period—it having been my impression that you were to spend a full term of three or four months under his eye. But possibly he finds the shorter stretch sufficient in connexion with a highly individualised correspondence programme. I am under the impression that my young friend Frank B. Long Jr. went to him for many seasons—first encountering him at Columbia, and following him after his severance from that institution. I regret, by the way, that I shall not be likely to be in New York during your sojourn—although I can assure you that you miss very little, since I am one of those colourless individuals whose most important (or least unimportant!) utterances are those occurring on paper. The present winter has brought a devastating grind of especially arduous editing & revision which makes travel seem as formidable in point of energy as it always is in point of finance—& only last week I was forced to tell Long that I was unlikely to be able to take advantage of his cordial urgings till the spring thaw. *Cold* is my deadly enemy—I am hardly yet recovered from being caught out in it (+14°) the evening of Jany. 1st., on which occasion I had to summon a cab to get home. I would spend my winters in Jamaica or somewhere if I had the cash—& would live in the tropics were I less inextricably welded to the scenery & atmosphere of my native soil. On some more leisurely occasion, even if not now, I trust you can see Providence. Our winter cold—scarcely ever below +15° or so—(-3° is the coldest reading in the history of the local weather bureau) sounds very mild & trivial to one accustomed to mid-Western subarcticism, but it is surely *enough* for me.

You showed genuine courage in providing such a festive Christmas for the younger generation, & I am sure they must have had enough concentrated delight to compensate you. There is nothing quite so poignant in its mystic joy as this archaic festival of the Saturnalia & the solstice—immemorially ancient & ground into human consciousness aeons before the Christian date was made to coincide with it—in the naive & atavistic eyes of childhood; & I am not yet too old to retain a touch of the enjoyment in a reminiscent & vestigial way. The present year, I am glad to say, was no exception to the rule.

That book of poetry is off my hands at last, & turned out well despite the many setbacks. It makes a fine appearance mechanically, & seems to me well worth the $2.00 charged by the publisher. My present burden is mainly a revisory one—the alleged fiction of an old fellow—a former associate of Ambrose Bierce—whose learning & standing make me wonder how he could possibly write anything so utterly bad![1]

Again extending my sincerest sympathy, & hoping that your Uzzell trip may be productive of the very best results, I remain,

Most cordially yrs

H P Lovecraft

P.S. The enclosed folder of the juvenile productions of a friend of mine may be of interest to the Jimmy-Junior duo. McNeil is a delightfully ingenuous old chap of over sixty, but with the zestful psychology of a small boy. His work is really excellent.

Notes

1. HPL refers to Adolphe de Castro.

[22]   [ALS]

10 Barnes St.,
Providence, R.I.,
Jany. 25, 1928.

My dear Mrs. Reed:—

I am indeed sorry to hear of the additional worries & ordeals superadded to those you have been enduring, but am glad you are now able to secure some compensating changes of scene. Although I am myself very fond of the country & its quiet, I can imagine the desolation of a type of country which lacks the beauty & traditional associations of rural New England, as Oklahoma must. I noticed the desolation of the flat Ohio fields when going by train to Cleveland—my only experience in the Middle West. It is fortunate that your sister is recovering, & that you are no longer chained to a depressing landscape & milieu.

Since you will not be in New York long enough to have its exterior wear thin, I fancy your impressions will be pleasant & stimulating. The intrinsic magnitude & glitter have a certain fascination as long as they remain a novelty, while the sheer aimless stir of feverish activity is generally exhilarating for a while. There are many features of genuine beauty—such as the skyline of Manhattan from the Brooklyn shore, [don't fail to see it at night from the parapet at the foot of Montague St.—early in the evening, when all the office windows are alight & the whole thing looks like a constellation fallen from the sky] the line of roofs at 59th St. seen from some distance within Central Park, & various bits of 5th Avenue at a twilight hour when the scarlet of the western sky blends curiously with the purple of the shadows & the mellow, timid yellow of the new-lit lamps—while the older sections (Greenwich Village, the tip of the island below Wall St., St. Paul's church, Jumel, Dyckman, & Van Cortlandt houses, &c) have a wealth of tradition that any first-rate guide book can point out. A ride up Riverside Drive on a 'bus roof at sunset is worth anybody's dime—while of course one must not leave the museums (Metropolitan, Am. Mus. of Nat. Hist., N.Y. Hist. Soc., Hispanic, Am. Indian, Brooklyn Mus. &c) unvisited. To pick up the general traditional colour of the whole town, the best guide book I know of is the tiny *free* brown leather volume distributed by the Bowman hotels & obtainable at the desk of the Biltmore, Commodore, Belmont, Ansonia, or Murray Hill. It is called "The Sidewalks of New York",[1] & sums up the atmosphere & colour of the place with remarkable vividness & conciseness. Little guide maps help the visitor to find his way about. The best thing is to read it through once at your hotel, & then take it along to consult as you explore the various quaint sections in person. If the N.Y. hotels are out of copies, I can let you have a duplicate.

By this time I presume your momentous first interview with Uzzell has taken place, & I trust he was not reluctant to offer encouragement. He still seems to me the best & most thorough teacher of short story method, & I firmly believe that a conscientious following of his course cannot fail to work vast improvement in the style of any literary beginner. With best wishes—

Most cordially & sincerely yrs—

H P Lovecraft

P.S. I trust you don't intend to overlook the excellent book-buying opportunities which N.Y. affords. The principal belts of 2nd hand bookshops are in 4th Ave. below Union Sq., & in 59th St. east of 5th Ave. Samuel Loveman, once of Cleveland, to whom you wrote last spring, is now proprietor of the Rowfant Book Shop, 165 William St., in downtown Manhattan.

Notes

1. By Bernardine Kielty.

[23]   [AHT]

10 Barnes St.,
Providence, R.I.,
Feb. 13, 1928

My dear Mrs. Reed:—

I was very sorry—and not a little surprised—to learn that my telephonic voice seemed in any way inhospitable! It was merely the ordinary voice which, despite its lack of musical overtones, I am compelled to use every day in the year; and its intention was most surely not to discourage any trip which would be likely to repay your trouble in taking it! I suppose the Yankee timbre sounds thin and dry to Western ears—but I had no idea I was seeming ogreish and formidable! I surely expected to see you if the weather made travel in any way enjoyable, and would indeed have found a chat or discussion delightful. Only common conscientiousness made me leave the matter to your judgment and convenience—for it surely would have been nefarious indeed to exert active pressure toward influencing a busy person with limited time to journey two hundred extra miles and return, unless the compensation either in scenery or in scholastic aid could be very certain! I am no sight at all to see—for my antiquarian eccentricity does not make me exteriorly or conversationally picturesque—and I still fancy that you would have felt rather disappointed had you essayed the trip in weather offering no advantageous by-products. However, I believe the Tuesday you tentatively selected was in fact a rather good day; so it is really too bad that you didn't get around. The train-ride is nothing marvellous—too much in a coastal flat-land region to be picturesque—but the motor or omnibus ride through the old roads and white-steepled villages of rural Connecticut is truly exquisite. As I said, it takes nine hours; but not a second is lost. One only wishes there were more if it—filled as it is with the very essence of lovely and archaic New England. I can certainly urge the trip as emphatically as any temperament might wish, when it can be taken in that manner!

But in any case, pray let me offer whatever apologies are necessary in view of the absolutely altruistic and thoroughly cordial spirit motivating my non-coercion! During your spring trip you must certainly make the Providence extension; and in that sort of weather I can guarantee an exquisite scenic setting which even my own garrulously guidebookish commonplaceness can only partly impair. You can decide beforehand—with the aid of pictorial and descriptive matter which I shall send—just what things you most wish to see; and I can weave these into an itinerary whose time-element will fit whatever span of leisure you may have at your disposal.

Meanwhile I am greatly interested to hear that you met Mr. Loveman—whose keen poetic genius, lovable generousness of character, and unfadingly boyish verve and spontaneity have endeared him to all the members of our almost-literary "gang". Although his modesty probably prevented his mentioning it, he is one of the finest and subtlest lyric poets alive, with a curious dual mixture of the Hellenic and the Elizabethan in his aesthetic makeup. His long poem, "The Hermaphrodite", recently issued as a thin book, is perhaps the most authentically Greek in spirit of any sustained utterance of recent years; and we all regret that the chaotic standards of modern taste have denied him the wider recognition he could have secured a half-century or more ago. I have not heard from him lately, but am sure he must have enjoyed your call. I have not seen his shop, either; since he was a rare-book expert and cataloguer with the large firm of Dauber & Pine in lower 5th Ave. when I was last in New York. In the matter of valuable books he is a connoisseur of the very first water.

I shall indeed be glad to write to the youthful James if you will give some idea of the topics most likely to interest him—or better still, if he will let me know his tastes himself. I'd hate to weary him with material which might not appeal to him at all—for despite what Mr. Loveman may have said, I am not by any means an expert in juvenile psychology. What Loveman was probably referring to was my circle of "adopted grandchildren"—young prodigies whom I have occasionally come across in various parts of the country through correspondence, and whose growth into men of genuine artistic and intellectual ability I have watched (rather than aided) with the indulgently complacent eye of a theoretical grandsire. These, however, have been boys of a little older growth—in high-school or college—who have happened to possess literary, philosophical, historical, scientific or aesthetic interests more or less akin to my own. My epistolary discourse with these hopeful scions has not been that of a guardianly adviser or self-conscious "good influence", but has adhered usually to the topics of common interest; in which I have tried to avoid the atmosphere of patronage or pedagogy, and to live over my own remote youth by viewing the field of thought and art once more through young eyes and along young perspectives. There is thus in my correspondence a sort of free and easy equality preclusive of the really didactic—I don't pretend to be much wiser than the boys, and offer such opinions as I do offer on a "take-'em-or-leave-'em-alone" basis. With my basic cynicism and essential indifference to mankind and all human institutions I couldn't very well pose as a Helpful Person with a Mission. The most I can say is that my influence is at least not a bad one. I am primarily an aesthete, to whom beauty and harmony are the only illusions worth cherishing in an absolutely purposeless and valueless cosmos; and am therefore keenly sensitive to that harmonious continuity of traditions and culture-streams which to any mature mind must necessarily constitute one of beauty's most poignant phases. Thus whatever comment of mine ever approaches the ethical is always delivered from the standpoint of rational conservatism—a conviction that the only valid standards are those which centuries of veneration by our forefathers have established as potent emotional factors; and that the only type of life, thought, and feeling which can be considered beautiful, is that which takes them into account as much as expanding science and more complex environmental conditions will permit. I am thus a sort of half-way link betwixt my fellow-ancients and the "young moderns". I don't believe any more in religion or *cosmic* moral values than the latter do; but I do believe in a degree of *taste* which prescribes, in the interest of that minimum of beauty and dignity without which life is an empty and directionless nightmare, a general code of manners and conduct quite identical with what the old religious-moral system would prescribe if it were still valid with the vanguard of thinkers. Naturally many of the young fellows deem me a hopeless fossil—but with my characteristic cynicism I am not greatly disturbed by that fact. Nor am I at all certain but that their more hectic world is, at this particular stage of world-decadence, far closer to the scientific normal than is mine. I let them enjoy themselves in their own way, while I enjoy myself in mine; and when I express an opinion it is optional with them to accept or reject it. Their own natures and the age as a whole will mould them far more than any one person's preaching could—and perhaps it is just as well that it is so. Certainly, I don't worry about it! I have taken quite a grandfatherly pride in seeing some of the children blossom forth as authors and men of brains; for there is satisfaction in having recognised genius in youth. It has also gratified me that none of my "adoptive descendants" has become a very notorious reprobate or popular hold-up man. Many of them are represented in the table of contents of *Weird Tales*—the real star, perhaps, being "Little Belknap"—Frank B. Long, the ex-Uzzell pupil—who is now a semi-moustached person of nearly twenty-six, with a volume of verses to his credit. I have been thus explicit in outlining my general attitude toward youth in order to dispel any illusions of sacerdotal and evangelical didacticism which Mr. Loveman's passing reference may have created. It may be that you would not deem wholesome the influence of an open atheist, materialist, and philosophic pessimist who believes in nothing and complacently looks ahead to the decay and passing of civilisation and of all mankind in succession. I do not, however, ever attempt to shake religious faith in the few youths whom I find still possessed of it. I find a great deal of beauty in religion although I don't believe in the supernatural, and it is my policy never to disturb or destroy beauty when it can be helped. As a cynic, I don't consider truth of sufficient importance to warrant the shattering of a beautiful illusion for its sake— my general attitude being much like that of George Santayana in this respect. I really wish this generation did know less, so that it might return to the unperplexed tranquillity of former times—the tranquillity of simple loyalty to King and Church, amidst which those idyllic figures, the country 'squire and the parish vicar, could regain something of their olden significance. Certainly, the acquiescent, dogmatic, and well-ordered life of simpler ages had, with all its glaring defects, a fundamental harmony and good taste that we seek in vain amidst the excesses of that "jazz period" to which the invention of complex machinery and the spread of democratic fallacies have jointly given birth. Thus I am, whilst utterly radical in such departments of sheer intellect as science and philosophy, thoroughly and cynically conservative—even reactionary—in social and political matters; a Tory, Czarist, Junker, patrician, Fascist, oligarchist, nationalist, militarist, and whatever else of the sort you can find in Webster's *Dictionary* or Roget's *Thesaurus!* My idea of modern democratic and humanitarian ideas simply can't be printed. I'm for old cultural standards, and ruthless, aristocratic efficiency in government—as sadly out of tune with our modern sociological Messiahs as with our modern hip-flask hounds! So much, then, for my philosophic position. Of course, not much of this would appear in letters addressed to a gentleman of twelve or thirteen; but I thought I ought to mention it in case it might subtly colour later comments on this or that phase of life and art, and in case you prefer to give the sprightly Jimmy as much of a chance as possible to grow up among influences favourable to the faith of his fathers. I will leave it wholly to your judgment whether or not the young man would find interest and constructiveness in the sort of thing I would be likely to write—and as before mentioned, would like to hear more of his tastes in advance, in case you deem such epistles wholesome rather than corrupting. Incidentally—don't let me convey the idea that I disapprove of—or look down upon—commercial writing. Far from it! It's a legitimate business, just like insurance or banking or engineering, which somebody has got to do; and it takes absolutely first-rate brains to do it. My hat is off to the person who succeeds at it! The case with me is simply that this industry doesn't happen to be my natural specialty. I lack—much to my own material detriment—the commercial type of mind; hence cannot put my real fund of energy or purpose into anything with a commercial object. I am truly interested only in the creation of strangeness and beauty for their own sake, and in the recording of truth through new and poignant harmonies.

As to my theological views—or absence of such things—I don't see that my position is a particularly humble one; since if it makes an aimless atom out of *me,* it likewise does the same for everyone else, from Caesar and Shakespeare down! However—scientific questions aren't to be decided by considerations of egotism and emotion; wishes or aspirations. Such things furnish absolutely no evidence one way or the other. All we can do is to look at nature—the earth, the universe, and the phenomena thereof—and study its workings in the light of such tests of truth and pointers of probability as we know how to apply. When we do this—setting aside all traditional preconceptions and misleading emotions—we cannot help seeing that there is not a spark of genuine evidence or even likelihood of the universe's being anything but a perpetual cycle of mutually interacting forces, whose regular rearrangements always have been going on and always will be going on. There is no reason to assume any central consciousness, purpose, or direction; but a great deal of presumptive reason to assume the contrary. In this infinite welter of alternate building-up and breaking down our earth and the organic life upon it—including the human species—form only the most transient and trivial incident. A second ago—as eternity is measured—they did not exist. A second hence their existence will have been forgotten. Any other assumption involves extravagant improbability and sheer fiction of the most flagrant sort. This realistic facing of the purposeless void is not new, but has come down through a long line of Graeco-Roman thought including Leucippus, Democritus, Epicurus, and Lucretius. Its widespread diffusion, however, is distinctly a feature of the present age; since it is only the enormous strides of contemporary science which have rendered it such an utterly inescapable attitude for any dispassionately analytical thinker. The younger generation cannot regard the old theistic teaching as anything but out-and-out mythology—and the more thoughtful wing of oldsters has been forming the same estimate during the last seventy-five years.

Haeckel and Huxley are practically unanswerable, despite all the obscurantist mysticism brought to bear on them by desperate adherents of the dying faith. And yet the popular mythology has had an excellent sociological value in its day—so that I cannot sympathise with the violent anti-Christian agitators and "debunkers" of the *Truth-Seeker* and *Haldeman-Julius Weekly* type.[1] It was a perfectly natural and inevitable phase of uninformed man's reaction to the scenes around him, and will always have a retrospective beauty which no impersonal aesthete can fail to respect. I think the organised church will last for many generations to come—as a social pose and artistic gesture on the part of the educated, and as a focus of ignorant faith—as always—on the part of the emotional herd. The greatest changes will come within the next quarter-century, when the world's positions of influence and thought-moulding begin to be filled by men whose intellectual life was developed in the scientific enlightenment of the period we now dub "post-war". In some ways the coming change is to be deplored, for it will probably dry up many of the well-springs of art and culture at the same time that it augments our grasp of truth and improves our intellectual understanding of the universe. Spengler is right, I feel sure, in classifying the present phase of Western civilisation as a decadent one;[2] for racial-cultural stamina shines more brightly in art, war, and prideful magnificence than in the arid intellectualism, engulfing commercialism, and pointless material luxury of an age of standardisation and mechanical invention like the one now well on its course. It would be better if we could still be naive, beauty-loving, and ignorant—yet we cannot turn the clock back. Memphis and Nineveh, Babylon and Persepolis, Carthage and Ctesiphon, Athens and Lacedaemon, Rome and Alexandria, Antioch and Tyre—all these have had their day and their sunset; their grandeur and their fall. In the face of such a pageant of history it would be folly to expect anything else of the existing civilisation. This age in America corresponds quite startlingly to the luxurious and disillusioned age of the Antonines in the Roman Empire—when Rome, Alexandria, Antioch, Athens, and New Carthage blazed in the sunset that was to mark the death of the ancient world. A gradual death, of course, which took many centuries in dragging itself out. If I were at all a mundane person—at all disposed to identify myself with one age any more than with any other—I would probably be greatly depressed by the existing phase of European culture; since I have no respect whatever for the hectic mechanical world which is supplanting the simpler tradition-anchored world into which I was born. Fortunately for me, though, I am not greatly engrossed in external reality; so that my imagination is as free to live in another age as in this. It is only these broad, historic sweeps of life which interest me. I prefer to think in terms of centuries and dynasties than in terms of years and individuals. The proud, austere Roman republic of the Punic War period,—the Rome of Scipio Africanus, Lutatius Catulus, and Fabius Maximus—and the periwigged eighteenth century in England and America, are my two favourite periods. Mentally I live in either one or the other—or both!

As for being interested in forms of life "not beautiful"—I am only so far as their gruesomeness or tragedy contains rhythms of picturesqueness equivalent to beauty. What I call beauty includes the *strange* in almost any form—and of course the quaint and grotesque. I don't think I care much for 'life just for itself' except as expressed in long and dramatic stretches of history. I don't belong to the pitying, very-human school of the late Thomas Hardy and the estimable Victor Hugo. I like many individuals well enough, but I can't get excited over humanity in the mass—save as an incidental element in the drama of history. I am above all else *scenic and architectural* in my tastes—it might quite justly be said that the only genuine motivating element in my existence is a quest for novel adventures in landscape, panorama, and lighting-effects: new combinations of hill and river-bend and wooded valley, new juxtapositions of winding road, stone wall, and half-embowered farmhouse roof, or new effects of slanting late-afternoon sunlight over the spires, roofs, and terraced gardens of some marvellous city I have never seen before—these things, and the constant recalling of the picturesque past in glimpses of archaic countryside and vistas of ancient urban quaintness. I ought to have been a pictorial artist instead of a would-be writer—but unfortunately I have even less talent with pencil and brush than with pen, ink, and paper. My theory of aesthetics is a compound one. To me beauty as we know it, consists of two elements; one absolute and objective, and based on rhythm and symmetry; and one relative and subjective, based on traditional associations with the hereditary culture-stream of the beholder. The second element is probably strongest with me, since my notions of enjoyment are invariably bound up with strange recallings of the past. It may be this out-reaching toward earlier ages which has given me my general taste for the literary overleaping of the bounds of the material universe—or it may with equal probability be exactly the other way around. I don't know yet whether I'm a fantaisiste because I'm an antiquarian, or an antiquarian because I'm a fantaisiste! Nor do I fancy that it matters extensively.

As for the matter of drinking—I have never tasted intoxicating liquor, and never intend to; having a strong aesthetic disgust at anything which blunts or coarsens the delicate natural equipoise of the evolved human intellect and imagination. Of course I am not "modern"—indeed, I said some time ago that my only point of contact with the younger generation is in abstract philosophical and scientific perspective. My mind recognises the accuracy of their abstract view of the universe—but my tastes and habits remain true to the traditions of a long line of conservative country-gentry. I refuse to be dictated to by the superficial customs of any age and place. Drinking excited my personal repugnance, hence I don't drink—let the herd do what they will. I am rather in favour of prohibition—the prohibition of any one anti-social force as well as of any other. Prohibition of murder can't be enforced—see any day's news as evidence—yet I haven't heard of any movement for the repeal of laws against homicide. Of course this parallel is an overdrawn one, but I think it is at least theoretically true. The existence of intoxicating drink is certainly an almost unrelieved evil from the point of view of an orderly and delicately cultivated civilisation; for I can't see that it does much save coarsen, animalise, and degrade. Any step to get rid of it is to be welcomed—just as any step to get rid of murder, robbery, and forgery is to be welcomed—and the only criticism one can make of prohibitory legislation is that which pertains to its effectiveness and enforcement. Here, of course, the "wets" have the best of it; for obviously the application of the present law has not even begun to approach the expectations of its proponents. Apparently the alcohol-sponges craved their "hard likker" far more desperately than less habit-chained persons could realise—or else alcohol-dispensers craved their financial profit more desperately than less commercial souls could understand. At any rate, be the motive force, thirst, or lucre, it is clear that legislation has been resisted far more stubbornly than one could have foreseen. This, to a cynical soul, brings up the question of whether or not the law is worth the trouble of enforcing. Granting that alcohol is an anti-social force, is it anti-social *enough* (as compared with murder, robbery, etc.) to warrant the expenditure of infinite money and energy without securing any better results than have so far appeared? This I am beginning to doubt. In 1919 I was a whole-hearted prohibitionist, but in 1928 I am more or less of a neutral. First let someone—if possible—get at the real facts of the legislative results, without obscuring the mock-data so profusely supplied by the partisans of both sides. Then, if no marked sociological improvement is disclosed, let the law pass into peaceful obsolescence. In a matter of alternative evils like that of legalised liquor versus futile and troublesome prohibition, one may merely choose the lesser—after deciding which is the lesser. I don't think the cheap slogan of 'personal liberty' means much one way or the other. 'Liberty' to drink rum is theoretically indistinguishable from 'liberty' to take narcotic drugs or set fire to one's neighbours' houses. The law ought to be able to prohibit any practice whose degree of harmfulness makes it worth prohibiting, if we make any pretence of having an orderly civilisation. As to this question of degree—in my opinion the evil of liquor is amply sufficient to justify at least one large-scale prohibitory experiment. It is useless to point out that *some* people can use liquor without harmful social results; since for every one who *can* there are a hundred who *can't*. The only conceivable way to stop the trouble is to cut off the whole supply of the provocative material. But as I have just admitted, the practical difficulties of enforcement seem well-nigh insuperable; so that no cynic could now be a dogmatic prohibitionist. With so many other destroying agencies at work, liquor may well be classed as a minor evil—and after all, it does not greatly matter whether or not civilisation decays—or at what speed it decays. I am no longer interested in the question except through reminiscences of my own former interest. It is an aesthetic matter with me. I think drink is ugly, and therefore I have nothing to do with it. This aesthetic position, by the way, may sound odd for one who professes to be a conservative; since of course all our respected forbears indulged in the flowing bowl to such an extent as to make fishes seem land animals by comparison. I think my own paternal great-great[-]grandfather could have drunk any "young modern" cake-eater under the table without shaking a bit of powder from his Albemarle tie-wig; nor do I think any the less of him for it, though it did no good to his fortune. But conservatism admits of a slow aesthetic growth and subtilisation along with the retention of time-honoured essentials; and I cannot but feel that the finer-grained life of the nineteenth century represented in many ways a normal and wholesome advance over the bluff coarseness of my beloved eighteenth, despite the dulness and hypocritical extravagances of Victorianism in its extremest form. One phase of that refinement was a radical *moderation* in the consumption of strong drink; and while many persons and households were content to let the evolution stop at that point, my own aesthetic theory cannot help carrying it onward to the ideal of total extinction. Let the graces of wine live in literature—its function in the life of a delicate and fastidious civilisation would seem to me definitely outmoded. In my own family, wine has been banished for three generations; and only about a quarter of the conservative homes of this section retain any regular use of it. Any person with the least character or independence in his voice can manage to be a total abstainer without giving anybody offence or creating any social contretemps. Of course I don't know much about the younger generation en masse—but at least three of the youths of my acquaintance are total abstainers despite the much-advertised flamingness of their contemporaries.

[. . .]

[last sheet (VII) of a long letter, possibly 13 February 1928:]

As for intruding my personal aesthetic views into literature or revision—perish the thought! I am the most abstract & impersonal of mortals, & have even written drinking-songs in the typical 18th century manner—one of which begins:

Come hither, my Lads, with your Tankards of Ale,
And drink to the Prefent before it fhall fail;
Pile each on your Platter a Mountain of Beef,
For 'tis Eating and Drinking that give us Relief.
    So fill up your Glafs,
        For Life will foon pafs:
When you're dead ye'll ne'er drink to your King or
    your Lafs![3]

Many of my heroes drink, though I do not—just as
many of them are ghouls & wizards, though I have
never personally consumed a cadaver nor summoned the emissaries of Abaddon out of the Great Abyss. Nor do I venture to criticise those who drink in real life. It is a question of taste, & I would as soon think of condemning a man because he liked Marcel Proust or Walt Whitman, or failed to like Dunsany or Arthur Machen! After all, nothing in the universe greatly matters.

I shall certainly write Iacobus Parvulus[4] very shortly—& was very much interested to hear of his tastes. I share his penchant for bicyclic locomotion, & was never more woeful than when increasing years & changing customs made it seem inappropriate for me to trundle about the highways in pneumatic-tired independence. Meagre fortune, alas, did not permit me to indulge in the cycle's petrol-pushed successor. I envy the inhabitants of Europe, where the bicycle is not yet obsolete for adults of conservative cast. I also share the young James's love of faery tales—a branch of literature from which my taste for the weird probably grew. Before I could read I avidly drank in all the mythic lore which oral narration supplied; & when at the age of four I mastered the printed page, it was good old Grimm who served as an intellectual teething-ring. From Grimm & the Teutonic myth I progressed at the age of five to the Arabian Nights in Lang's translation;[5] & was thereby so enchanted that I renamed myself "Abdul Alhazred", burnt-corked a Saracenic beard upon my visage, & forced my mother to fit me up an Arabian corner in my room, with Eastern tapestries, lamps, jars, & objets d'art from the Damascus Bazaar downtown. In another year, however, I stumbled upon Bulfinch's Age of Fable & a volume of tales from the Odyssey; & thereafter forswore Bagdad & Cairo & Granada for the more classic glories of Hellenistic myth—the magic of green meadows & boskage, vivid blue seas & skies, & the gleaming white of temple columns & clouds blown on Ægean winds. I now saw fauns & dryads in every oaken grove, & built altars to Zeus & Athene & Artemis, & Apollo of the gleaming Bow. From that mood I have never fully emerged, since the substructure of all my imaginative & intellectual life is still purely Graeco-Roman. Before I was seven I was an art-museum-addict, had begun reading the standard 18th century classical translations, & had commenced crude experiments in myth-weaving of my own. Then I stumbled on an old schoolbook of my great-grandfather's in the attic, (Abner Alden's "The Reader"—1797—with the long ʃ)[6] & began learning the rules of "Rhetorick & Poetick Numbers" as taught to a generation still under the spell of the Pope–Addison–Johnson tradition. My first "poem" was composed at the age of 7½, & bears the impress of my mythological tastes. It is called "The Adventures of Ulysses; or, the New Odyssey"[7]—& begins as follows:

> The night was dark, O Reader, hark! and see Ulysses' fleet;
> All homeward bound, with Vict'ry crown'd, he hopes his spouse to greet;
> Long he hath fought; put Troy to naught, & levell'd down its walls,
> But Neptune's wrath obstructs his path, & into snares he falls.

I read "The Rover Boys"[8] with great interest, though I've completely forgotten what they were all about. The series was interminable—& I'm greatly interested to hear that it still survives! I also note with interest young Jimmy's familiarity with the work of good old Mac. Tell him to write the naive old duffer—Mac would be tickled to death to hear from any of his young admirers. He is one of the quaintest Victorian survivals outside a museum—if I were a gently humorous realist I'd give him such immortality as his own books may not themselves supply. His address—in case the young man wishes to write him—is *Everett McNeil, 457 Fifth St., Brooklyn, N.Y.* James's maternal devotion reminds me of Little Belknap. That child gets worried if his mother is as much as fifteen minutes late home, & she is the same way about him. But all his tenderness is hidden as carefully as possible beneath a bored, George-Mooreish exterior—which deceives nobody. He'll never grow up—no real artist ever does.

But this epistle seems to have lapsed into senile rambling! Next time I'll have more to show for the space consumed—including the snake story, if all goes well. Meanwhile see what you think of my handling of "Red Blood". If you like that, I'll be glad to handle any other MSS. of the Uzzell course which you may submit. Most sincerely yrs

H P Lovecraft

Notes

1. The *Truth Seeker* (1873f.) was a leading freethought magazine of the period; it continues to be published today. The *Haldeman-Julius Weekly* (1922–29) was published by E. Haldeman-Julius. It printed two letters by HPL in its issues of 10 January and 17 March 1923 (see *Miscellaneous Letters*).

2. HPL refers to Oswald Spengler's *The Decline of the West*. He apparently read only volume one of the English translation.

3. This is the first stanza of the poem "Gaudeamus," inserted (without title) in the story "The Tomb" (1917).

4. The child James; i.e., ZB's son.

5. HPL must have read another translation of the *Arabian Nights* at the age of five, for Lang's translation only appeared in 1898, when HPL was eight. The copy in his library was given to him by his mother.

6. Alden's *The Reader* was first published in 1802. HPL owned an 1808 edition.

7. The surviving ms. gives the title as "The Poem of Ulysses; or, The Odyssey."

8. The Rover Boys appeared in a series of books for young adults written by Arthur M. Winfield (pseud. of Edward Stratemeyer, 1862–1930). Thirty books were published between 1899 and 1926.

[24]   [ALS, fragmentary: sheet VI]

[February 1928]

Her mind filled with ophidian images, she now falls to the floor & expresses the only thing she knows how to express. She hisses & hisses & hisses . . . . . Thus the man has died—in a way—from snakes, as he felt fated he would do. And upon the woman who killed the snakelets has been visited the long-legended curse of the snake-devil. She has been—mentally, at least—'turned into a snake' because [in *actual* linkage—see preceding] of what she did that bygone day with the musket-butt!

In this plot you will note a *completely connected chain of motivation*. The denouement has the quality of *inevitability*, which editors generally seek with much avidity. The pioneer atmosphere suggests some of the tales of Ambrose Bierce, [cf. "The Boarded Window" in "In the Midst of Life"] & I believe the tale ought to have a style not unlike the dry, metallic, paragraphs he was so fond of. If you decide to have me do the story this way, you might send back the sheets of this letter containing the plot outline; (IV & V) although I fancy I have most of the essentials either in my head or jotted down on your note pages. It will not be necessary for you to write out any more than the notes—I like plenty of latitude in working up a story—but you might send some more notes on points of local colour. I seek *accuracy & realism* above all things, [cf. my comment on the Austrian story, & certain amplifications in "The Return"] & even though I may not use any of the colour I get, I want it at the back of my head just the same. It is my opinion that no author ought ever to write down so much as a sentence unless he can see clearly & visually with his fancy the scene he is writing about. I made rough notes of the data I need when first examining the synopsis several days ago—& rather than waste time in copying them I'll send them along as they are, in the hope that they may be found decipherable. Like all too many Easterners, my knowledge of the West is of the vaguest & most sketchy kind; so that it is no exaggeration to admit that I have a great deal more definite knowledge of Ctesiphon & the Parthian Empire, Samarcand & the Sogdianian plains beyond the Oxus, or Timbuctoo & the mysteries of the Saharan Hoggar region than I have of the history, life, topography, & general colour of 19th century Oklahoma—or any realm thereto adjacent, so far as that goes! Some day I really must brush up—I suppose a library information desk could pass out lists of suitable source material in short order.

Such then, is the case. (a) I'll need the additional notes whatever plan I follow. (b) I'll write up the anecdote literally for $2.00 per page, total not to exceed $20.00. & (c) I'll prepare & try to place a story written from the above amended plot for half the proceeds, no advance fee. Let me know at your leisure which plan you prefer to have followed.

In case you care to try more in the macabre line, & would like reading recommendations toward that end, I will try to find a copy of my "Supernatural Horror in Literature" (in W. Paul Cook's privately printed magazine *The Recluse*) which I can spare. If I succeed, I'll send this along for your permanent retention. You don't have to wade through it till you wish hints on books for background-reading—though here & there there may be a useful abstract suggestion or two. Cook prints this magazine wholly through love of literature—for free distribution. Possibly Loveman told you of the *amateur* organisation to which most of our "gang" once belonged—& to which many of us still technically belong despite its moribund state. Ten or fifteen years ago I'd have recommended this society (or rather this pair of half-interlocked & half-rival societies) (The United & National Amateur Press Associations) to you as the best possible source of literary encouragement at this stage; but the thing is now so listless & decadent that I couldn't conscientiously urge anybody to plunk down a $1.50 entrance fee in view of the almost negligible returns. It may revive some time, but just now it is a very pallid spectre of the "amateur journalism" of my day. I think I'll enclose a circular—for there might be enough of it left to amuse & interest small James (if he writes) even if it has now fallen off a bit from the adult level. Any of the officers listed could tell you more about its *present* state than I could.

As to writing in general—I certainly think that Uzzell's opinion of the advisability of your continuing is to be held as more authoritative than any contrary opinion held by laymen—even laymen as solicitous & kindly as one's own family. It is a specialist's appraisal of such a case which surely ought to prove the deciding factor. However, one needn't feel that there is any sharp line of demarcation between writing & non-writing; between being 'settled down' & continuing to read, study, & practice with a view to increasing stylistic & psychological power in the art of fiction. A certain amount of writing can form an ingredient of any sort of career, & I fancy it is really better for a writer not to get the habit of regarding himself as a special being with an unique mission & personality. The closer he keeps his life & personality to the cultivated norm of the surrounding civilisation, the better he can reflect his setting & period in his chosen medium. If anything on earth is at once contemptible & pathetic, it is the average small-time, Windsor-tied, unshaven, falsetto-lisping, self-conscious "I-am-an-Artist" hanger-on of Greenwich Village & its analogues. The first thing I advise my artward-bending 'adopted grandchildren' to be is *plain, solid citizens.* Paraphrasing what Dr. Johnson once said of a very worthy bookseller, I tell them not to consider themselves as *Writers*, but as *gentlemen who write*—among other suitable pursuits & interests.

In conclusion, let me express again my extreme regret that I seemed to freeze up the long-distance wires with inhospitality! During your next Manhattan pilgrimage you surely must make the side-trip—for vernal Providence is well worth seeing, no matter what sort of a dreary old bore its least conspicuous citizen may be!

> With all good wishes,
>   Most sincerely yrs
>   H P Lovecraft

[25] [ALS]

Thursday [23 February 1928]

Dear Mrs. R—

I must offer a thousand apologies for the delay on this Ms., but can assure you that the present date of delivery is absolutely the earliest possible moment with my programme in its present shape. I would have returned it or passed it on to my new revisory colleague—Frank B. Long, whom I am breaking in as a critical fellow-slave—had I thought any time would be saved thereby, but upon reflection I decided that the quickest thing—& the most advisable thing—was to go ahead after all & do it as best I could, whether or not the date come exactly right for your Uzzell schedule. So here it is—with the apologies above mentioned.

This job, I am pleased to say, is one of *light or elementary revision*—hence comes at the lower rate of 50¢ per page. This 26-page MS., therefore, amounts to only **$13.00**, payable at your convenience.

You will note that this is the first MS. since that early comic sketch which I have been able to handle as *light revision*. This indicates a *highly remarkable improvement* in your style—a phenomenal testimonial to the Uzzell methods, in view of the time-element involved. Apparently Uzzell has found your metier for you—at least, your present metier—light, domestic fiction in the popular vein; with spirited conversation & jaunty details of the externals of life as dominant elements. This in a way bears out my own advice not to tackle too profound themes during the early stages—& also explains why so little had to be done to the style of that old MS. ("When A Woman is Tempted") at a time when other work required such radical readjusting. Obviously, this style is a natural one for you—which is probably lucky, since the field is lucrative.

At any rate, let me assure you that the technical progress represented by this MS. is *enormous*. I don't know what could possibly be more encouraging!

I shall answer yrs. of 13th & 17th very shortly, & handle weird theme as soon as possible. ¶ In extreme haste—

Sincerely

H P Lovecraft

P.S. Am sending my article on weird fiction under separate cover. Your Okla. notes are just what was needed. The Indian tom-tom element is *splendid*—it will furnish an atmosphere dominating the story.

[26]   [ALS]

10 Barnes St.,

Providence, R.I.,

Feby. 24, 1928.

My dear Mrs. Reed:—

I must reiterate my apologies of yesterday regarding the delay in your work. As I re-read your letter of the 12th I see that Uzzell wishes "Red Blood" by the 28th—which will surely be a woefully close call under present conditions. All I can say is that it couldn't be helped—& I might here remark that *two weeks* is about as short notice as I can absolutely guarantee for any piece of work just now. I was never so crowded with interminable drudgery before—& I may soon have a book job on my hands to increase the doubtful merriment still further!

As I said in my note, "Red Blood" represents an *amazing* technical advance on your part; & surely justifies the Uzzell theories & methods. I think on the whole that the advice not to have the hero die is sound. Fiction ought to have something of the universal in it; hence it is really truer to life as a whole to present *general probabilities*, than to transcribe the particular details of any one actual case. Though the hero died in real life, his death would sound a note clashing somewhat with the mood & tone of the story as here told—& Uzzell is undoubtedly wise in forbidding it. This is not to say that deaths ought always to be barred—but merely to say that in this especial plot it is best to preserve the hero. Regarding Phyllis's having another beau at the end—i.e., having her attachment to Glynn as transient & superficial as his to her—I fancy it would be truer to the majority of cases than having the sudden & unexpected serious turn. It would not wholly ruin the story, either, since the main action is undoubtedly Janet's campaign. However—it would do much toward reducing the whole tale toward the absolutely commonplace, & would certainly take a great deal of vitality & interest out of it. The anomalous seriousness of Phyllis is by no means so utterly rare a phenomenon as to be grotesque or freakish, & it gives the action a heightened colour & firmer foundation which I would certainly not advise sacrificing. In passing, it is well to remark that questions like this cannot be decided merely by what actually happened in the chain of events on which the tale is based. The real life nucleus can at best be no more than a nucleus or point of suggestion & departure. Art & invention alone can determine just how a given thread of plot may best be spun.

It seems to me that Mr. Uzzell ought to find a vast amount of promise in this tale. I thought it better to administer only *light* revision; since it is excellent as it stands, & since Uzzell, in order to help you, ought to see your work very largely as you produce it yourself. What is more, I greatly doubt if I could have improved the tale by even the most extensive of changes; since it represents a psychology & treatment so far from my own revisory & creative specialties that its moods & turns form virtually a foreign language to me. I can doctor up the mechanics of such a tale well enough, but it would be useless for me to try to tamper with the tone as a whole, as in attempting to introduce radical new doses of humour or pathos. Incidentally—I regret that I could not consult that *Red Book* which you mentioned. It is a back number, & public libraries in this part of the world don't handle periodicals as frankly & unclassically popular as the one in question.

On the whole, I think that what I have done to the tale is the best which could be done under the circumstances, & I trust that you may find the work satisfactory. Pay especial attention to details of paragraphing & arrangement, & to points noted on the original MS. I hope Uzzell may find it as remarkably encouraging a thing as I do, & that after a final revision by him it may bring in the corpulent fiscal receipts at which he so alluringly hints. The cost of the present job is *$13.00*. This, together with the amount due on previous work, (12.00) brings the total current bill to exactly **$25.00**, payable at any time. [Of this 4.50 will be credited on any future work on "Under Cover"]

Your opinion of my work on this MS.—but more especially *Uzzell's* opinion after seeing it—ought to serve as an index as to whether or not such revision is really beneficial at this stage. Uzzell's opinion of the style of "The Return" ("large words"—"rhetorical"—&c) impresses me afresh with the notion that for this commercial type of tale I may not be by any means the best type of reviser. I cannot enter into the spirit of commercial writing, or indeed think at all of authorship in a fundamental way except as a disinterested medium of aesthetic expression without regard for cheques, fame, approval, or the brains of any particular sort of reader; so that in catching whatever mood or vocabulary of the moment Mr. Uzzell may recommend, there will naturally be a sort of alienage, rustiness, or *creaking mechanicality*[1] about my work. There can be no spontaneity—no actual element of the creative—in the process.

Now it may be that this is entirely all right—I can reduce chaotic matter to orderly form, & prune away many crudities; which is perhaps sufficient when the author himself provides the tone & tempo with marked distinctness. But at the same time it hardly seems as though this is the ideal sort of criticism to pay out good money for when the def[ini]te[2] object is development in the popular commercial manner.

[Balance missing]

Notes

1. The phrase is underlined, but it is uncertain if HPL himself indicated the emphasis.
2. The ms. is torn here; the word has been conjecturally restored.

[27]   [AHT]

10 Barnes St.
Providence, R. I.,
March 9, 1928

My dear Mrs. Reed:—

Enclosed—as you may see—is the completed snake-tale, which I have decided to call "The Curse of Yig". The deity in question is entirely a product of my own imaginative theogony—for like Dunsany, I love to invent gods and devils and kindred marvellous things. However, the Indians certainly had *a* snake-god; for as everyone knows, the great fabulous teacher and civiliser of the prehistoric Mexican cultures (called Quetzalcoatl by the Incan-Aztec groups and Kukulcan by the Mayas) was a feathered serpent. In working up the plot you will notice that I have added another "twist"—which I think increases the effectiveness of the impression. I took a great deal of care with this tale, and was especially anxious to get the beginning smoothly adjusted. This accounts for the frightful condition of the manuscript—a condition which I hope will not make it utterly undecipherable to you. For geographical atmosphere and colour I had of course to rely wholly on your answers to my questionnaire, plus such printed descriptions of Oklahoma as I could find. I hope very much that I have avoided grave errors, and that I have not altogether failed to catch something of the general aspect of the region. In typing this manuscript be on the lookout for geographical blunders, (almost inevitable in the case of an absentee chronicler) and let me know when you find them. I will correct any which may be pointed out to me. Certain points were rather obscure—such as the source of lumber used in building cabins, etc. I think I am right in deducing from various descriptions that Oklahoma is quite hilly in the east, and not wholly devoid of rich forest areas; the vast dusty plains being mostly characteristic of the western half.

As for the price—on account of the congeniality of the theme I said I would make a cut rate and promise not to exceed $20.00 typed. By the same arithmetical process the untyped job ought to cost $17.50, at which figure it may be considered to stand. This, plus the $25.00 on previous work, brings the total bill up to $42.50, payable at any time. Needless to say, the existing rate provides for as many further changes and re-revisions as you may think desirable in order to make the story thoroughly convincing and true to its geographical locale.

 I remain most cordially and sincerely yrs—
   H P Lovecraft.

[28] [ALS]

            April 7 [1928]

My dear Mrs. Reed:—

     Well, here is the second instalment of my febrile epic of repeated apologies & partial performances!

 Have never been so overwhelmed with indifferently-paying work in my life—unexpected 2nd edition of that book I edited last fall, & now the prospect of collaborating on an important biography of Ambrose Bierce if I'm not too particular about advance pay—but I think I'll turn that down, for a gamble with royalties in a non-best-seller proposition *is* a gamble![1]

 I shall very shortly answer your letter of 14th ult. & attend to the Uzzell suggestions on "Red Blood", but just now I must get you the synopses of those two novel plots which you desired, & which I have just finished. As I said, I will make no charge for the first one. That much is really due you in view of my repeated delays; which, though unavoidable, really constitute very poor service.

 The second plot, which I have developed with some fulness in two alternative forms, I will submit at my usual rate of *$2.50* for outlines of average length. I shall, of course, be glad to change both of these as may be desired, or to submit additional advice & suggestions in reasonable quantity, without additional charge.

 The former bill—after the cashing of yesterday's cheque—came to $25.75. This, plus the $2.50 fee for the present Outline #2, bring the current bill up to *$28.25,* payable at any time.

 I trust you found "A Matter of Management" satisfactory, & that Uzzell may regard it with approval. Also that you got it typed without too much trouble. I shall be able to handle typing again in about a couple of weeks.

 Pray tell the sprightly Iacobulus that I still mean to write him as soon as I can see daylight amidst all the massed toil now engulfing me. Just now my personal correspondence is simply piling up into a mountain before me!

 With best wishes, & trusting that the two current plot-synopses may be of genuine future aid to you, I remain

Yrs most sincerely,
H P Lovecraft

Notes

1. A second edition of Bullen's *White Fire* reached the proof stage but was never issued. HPL also refers to Adolphe de Castro's desire to have HPL revise his *Portrait of Ambrose Bierce*, but HPL insisted on $150 in advance, and de Castro was unable to accept those terms. He persuaded Frank Belknap Long to revise the text; in exchange, Long wrote a signed preface to the book.

[29] [AHT]

395 East 16th St.,
Brooklyn, N. Y.,
May 1, 1928

My dear Mrs. Reed:—

When you perceive the foregoing temporary address, and correlate it with what I have quite frequently expressed as my unvarnished sentiments toward the New York region, you will probably appreciate the extent of the combined burdens and nerve-taxes which have, through malign coincidence, utterly disrupted my programme this spring, and brought me to the verge of what would be a complete breakdown if I did not have a staunch and brilliant colleague—my young "adopted grandchild" Frank B. Long—on whom to lean for coöperation and assistance in getting my tasks in shape.[1]

It is amusing to reflect that such coincidences, though barred as "artificial" and "unconvincing" in the composition of a story, really do occur now and then in actual life. It was bad enough when all my work piled up beyond the possibility of prompt and orderly performance. That, in itself, was a coincidence "improbable" enough; since hardly ever have so many imperative tasks assailed me with such diabolical simultaneousness. But when, upon this proximate chaos, there was suddenly superimposed the ultimate chaos of a necessary sojourn of indefinite duration in the New York region; the stretching of coincidence surely began to transcend all literarily admissible limits! Like the cautious rustic who, upon beholding a rhinoceros for the first time at a menagerie, gave vent to the classic dictum: "there ain't no such animal!"; I am tempted, as I view the combination of circumstances which have just now "balled up" my critical output, to parallel his canny incredulity by exclaiming: "Hell! there ain't no such situation!" And yet my piled-up desk here (the piling-up of my home desk conveyed hither in an all-too-capacious valise) tells me with melancholy finality that the situation is indeed a very real insistent entity.

Nothing but strong domestic pressure could ever have induced me to waste a spring in this accursed metropolitan pest-zone. What occurred was the unexpected commercial need of my wife's wish that I join her for a time. Her business affiliations usually take her to different sections of the country for indefinite periods; and when these sections are far away, there is of course no thought of my interrupting my quiet Providence life (I room on the lower floor of a sedate Victorian backwater, with my elder aunt rooming on the second floor and furnishing a reminiscent touch of old-home family atmosphere) in order to follow. New York, however, is so fatally *near* to Providence in a geographical way—'so near and yet so far', as it were—that this time my wife really thought it only right for me to transfer a little of the domestic background to her present scene of action. Impartially reflecting, I could not help conceding the essential justice of the opinion; hence decided that the least I could do would be to conquer my anti-metropolitan repugnance for a season and avoid that depressing household inharmony which forms the theme of so many works of fiction! Fortunately the present quarters are in the very *least offensive* part of the whole greater New York area—a part so home-like, village-like, and old-American, indeed, that there is really very little in the immediate environment to complain of. This benign oasis is the southwestern section of the ancient village of Flatbush, Long Island, now overtaken by and incorporated in the Borough of Brooklyn. The particular district in question, protected by real-estate restrictions and by mutual agreements among the old-time property-owners, has resisted the encroachments of decadence and modernity to an astonishing degree; so that it is even now a place of separate wooden houses, green lawns and back yards, quiet streets with generous shade-trees, and sleepy churches whose chimes weave music and magic on Sunday mornings. One of the enclosed postcards gives a fair idea of it—as you will see, the terrain could very well be mistaken for a fairly modern residence section in almost any small American city. From this unique vantage-point, New York seems remote and incredible indeed—and it is difficult to believe that the howling bedlam of 42nd St. is only a half-hour away on the subway. That is the one mitigating thing which makes it possible for me to remain here for any continuous time. I have not yet—during this visit—been above ground in the crowded mid-town district, save for one trip to the public library. I fluctuate altogether between the somnolent oasis of Flatbush and the far uptown section of Manhattan where my youthful colleague Belknap holds forth. I have twice seen Mr. Loveman—who, by the way, has recently moved his Rowfant Book Shop from the downtown section to the famous bookstall colony in 59th St.—103 East 59th St., to be exact, opposite the Anderson Galleries. I've not yet had a chance to examine this place with care. One thing I'm going to do as an antidote to this metropolitan ordeal is to take advantage of my two-hundred-mile-greater proximity to Philadelphia and Washington to accomplish some antiquarian exploration I've long wished to undertake. I hope to snatch a look at many colonial sights—perhaps as far south as Williamsburg, Virginia—before returning to Providence, and to explore certain old towns like Annapolis and Alexandria with the same thoroughness I have been able to exercise in exploring Salem, Marblehead, Portsmouth, and the other old towns of New England.

The small apartment I am in is very tasteful, and the apartment-house is the only one in a neighbourhood of old-fashioned lawns and homes. My greatest immediate hardship is the absence of my library—but this will not hamper my research-work for such clients as need it, since all the public libraries of New York are at my command, and former residence here has taught me how to use them. I have no typewriter with me, (my old Remington has just been repaired, and now awaits my return in good shape) but my little colleague Belknap will attend to all the typing which may be required of our newly-organised "firm". This "firm" has been organised in such a way as to give each member the type of revisory work to which he is best adapted, and we believe it will enable each of us to cover more ground than he could possible cover if working alone. Work may be sent either member, and will be performed by the one best able to handle work of the specific kind in question—unless, of course, the client wishes some exception made. Remittances had best be sent to the member who actually performs and returns the work paid for, although if any client prefers to adhere to a system of unified payment to one especial member, his wishes will be heeded. We are planning to insert advertisements in one or two magazines—believing that our new arrangement will enable us to handle a radically greater amount of work than at present.[2] Rates will remain exactly the same as those I've been charging.

I remain most cordially and sincerely yrs

H P Lovecraft.

Notes

1. HPL's wife Sonia had requested that HPL spend some time with her in Brooklyn to help her set up a new hat shop. Though separated, HPL stayed with her from late April to early June.

2. Only an advertisement in *Weird Tales* (August 1928) is known.

[30]　[ALS]

still abroad ———>　　395 East 16th St.,
Brooklyn, N.Y.,
May 18, 1928

My dear Mrs. Reed:—

I am reprehensibly tardy in acknowledging yours of the 4th, but can scarcely be expected to function normally till I am home again on good Providence soil—as I hope to be by the middle of next month at least.

Meanwhile I feel comfortably certain that my small grandchild Belknap is act-ing very capably as a literary substitute for the Old Gentleman. I saw his revi-sion of "Red Blood" day before yesterday, & was impressed with the depth, assurance, & competence of his emendatory work. He certainly has a far pro-founder grasp of the modern popular spirit & technique than I have, & I be-lieve you will find Uzzell reacting much more favourably to his results than to mine. Henceforward—now that Belknap & I are acting in partnership—I be-lieve that I shall assign to him all new jobs of modern-fiction revision, (except when otherwise specified) taking care of the more conservative & traditional work myself. That, of course, is the object of the partnership—to "pool" or-ders, & let each member take such items as may best suit his particular special aptitudes. In this way we can probably cover infinitely more ground than we could working separately & coping with all sorts of work, whether or not it be of our especial species. By the way, though—Belknap exaggerated somewhat when he said that I was ill. I've not been really down at all, but merely under a nerve-strain from accumulated work & absence from home which presents some of the external aspects of illness. Once my literary calendar is a bit cleared up, & I am again ensconced in my retirement on Providence's ancient hill, I shan't need to worry in the least about health! Providence is I, & I am Providence. It is there that I shall live & end my days, whate'er betide! I couldn't possibly remain sane & work anywhere else. God Save His Majesty's Colony of Rhode-Island & Providence-Plantations!

Meanwhile I am indulging—as during my long two-year exile of 1924–26—in such antiquarian peregrinations as the New York environment makes possible. There is much more of the past left here than most realise, & I have some claim to being a walking guide-book where such matters are concerned. Enclosed are a couple of cards illustrating the old Morris or Jumel mansion on Washington Heights—a fine specimen built about 1760 & preserved in excellent shape as an historical museum. The curator of this place—William Henry Shelton—is 88 years old, but still active as an administrator, author, & artist.[1]

I hope that Little Belknap's work is by this time producing the proper impression on Mr. Uzzell. We concur in our amazement at some of the Uzzellian dicta—especially as regards "The Unchaining", which Belknap ad-mires as much as I do, & does not hesitate to class as your best production so far. Our long-standing confidence in the superiority of Uzzell methods is be-ing put to the critical test as never before, so that Belknap is almost inclined to adopt a new policy of recommendation & henceforward direct literary be-ginners to the correspondence department of Columbia University—with which U. used to be connected. It remains a fact, however, that Uzzell *does know* how to teach the practical side of fiction-writing—wherefore I still think that you can get some satisfaction out of him if you will not hesitate to prod him with questions & requests for *specific* information. At any rate, don't get discouraged. Belknap's estimate of your work & progress is very encouraging, & with his experience & training he certainly ought to know.

I am glad your reading goes on steadily. Sonny agrees with his grandpa that this phase of literary development is most important of all. The public library will make this procedure very easy & inexpensive, while the Haldeman-Julius Blue Books will give you many useful items for permanent possession at a relatively insignificant cost. I am asking the H J co. to send you their new large catalogue in case you have not already received a copy. When I see Loveman I'll tell him to tell his partner of your eventual concurrence in his views on scientific psychology. I saw the partner in question the other day, & fancy he is decently well-read despite his hesitant foreignism of demeanour. Whether a scientific background is good or bad for a literary beginner would seem to me to depend largely on individual temperament. I value it highly—indeed, I place a very high valuation on all the sciences as ingredients of a well-rounded culture—but can see how it might prove an imaginative check in many cases. Belknap hates science—the little rascal almost assassinated me three years ago because I tried to explain to him what causes a total solar eclipse!

We've had quite a colloquy over your plan for obtaining books in N.Y., & by this time Belknap has probably told you the result of our deliberations. What do you think of his alternative plan of sending *library* books at a nominal fee? He insists that you are referring mainly to books of *criticism* in your plan; in which case he is overwhelmingly the logical person to make the choice. If, on the other hand, it is *general literature* which you desire; either he or I could serve tolerably well as agents. He assumes that permanent possession is not a prime object with you. If it is, you might let us both know—furnishing us each with a list of the volumes already in your library (including dictionaries & reference works) in order to prevent duplication on our part. We could build you up a valuable—i.e., valuable *to you*—working library at a surprisingly slight cost, & would be glad to do so without a service charge in spare moments. Let us know—& be sure to send a list of the books you already own—if you wish us to begin building up such a collection. I assume that the external appearance & condition of the books would be a secondary consideration if the text were accurate & complete & the price low. Incidentally—I could do this buying nearly as well at home as here, since the bookstalls of Providence & Boston are ample & excellent.

About the *re-revision* of your work—much as you hate it, I really think you will find it of more actual educational value than any other procedure. The two-stage work on "Red Blood" & "A Matter of Management" will prove—if you study the various changes, comments, & marginal notes involved in each successive metamorphosis—a profoundly valuable exemplification of current fictional standards & technique; & I hope you will preserve the crude & intermediate versions as well as the final result, so that you may keep before you a concrete illustration of what to avoid, & how to avoid it. With careful study of the different versions you will soon acquire a quick eye for what is naive, trite, inexact, awkward, confused, or otherwise inadmissible.

When I speak of your liking people too much & literary form too little, I do so only in a *relative* sense. What I mean is that the first-rate author must be one who loves *words, rhythms, niceties of imagery,* & *the process of literary craftsmanship* for their own sake—independently of his interest or lack of interest in people & events. The magic of expressive language must be venerated as a precious thing apart from all else—for only with such an attitude may one attain that ideal of authorship so vividly summed up in James Branch Cabell's phrase—"to write perfectly of beautiful happenings." One ought to read books on *words*—things like Trench's or Anderson's—& to browse pleasantly through dictionaries, thesauri, & treatises on synonyms.

As to *life*—the great thing to do is to learn to discriminate by instinct between what is essentially trivial & commonplace & what is essentially significant & symbolic. A combination of ample reading, acute observation, & sound common sense is usually sufficient to effect such a sharpening of the faculties.

"The Curse of Yig", of course, went to Wright long ago; but I have not yet received word about it. I fancy he is overrun with work during this post-vacation period, for another client of mine sent him a MS. last month & has not yet heard from him. It seems to me that "Yig" stands an excellent chance of acceptance. If W.T. doesn't take it, I advise you to try it on *Tales of Magic & Mystery* & *Amazing Stories*—though the latter is very slow—& slight—in matters of payment. Loveman tells me that Brandt—the literary editor of *Amazing Stories*—wants me to get in touch with him before I go home; but I am surely in no hurry to do so after the wretchedly tardy & trivial returns I gleaned for "The Colour Out of Space."[2]

As to further work—I shall surely be able to handle some in the near future, especially after I get home; & shall give first attention to the weird plot-nucleus submitted some time ago. I am certainly glad if my services have been of substantial benefit to your progress, & trust that they may continue to be so—even though my small Belknap-grandson is likely to shew more up-to-date intelligence in coping with contemporary fictional problems. The best type of work to be submitted to me, I fancy, is *idea-material* for elaboration into proper aesthetic (rather than immediately salable) form; whilst Belknap can best handle the red-hot romances of the jazz era.

Regarding financial matters—in view of the chaotic state of your own exchequer I can't feel justified in being unduly insistent about bills, hence will assure you that any time during May will be sufficiently prompt for the transmission of that residual $28.25. Belknap, too, will not prove a peremptory Shylock—although I believe a steady trickle of funds would hearten him vastly just now, in view of his desire to show his father (a practical, hard-headed professional man, & one of the finest dentists in New York) that he can earn at least a modicum of real money. Belknap Pere is inclined to be the least bit impatient about the monetary unproductivity of his youthful scion & namesake, & now & then remarks wistfully that a man of 26 (for Sonny is that, although it's hard for his old grandpa to believe it!)[3] ought to be able to do more than merely keep himself in clothes & tobacco!

I don't wonder that the canine tribe are at present personae non gratae with you! My mother was chased & bitten by a dog when she was four years old, & could never really like dogs after that to the day of her death. I don't care over much for dogs myself, though I've never been menaced by one. With me it's an aesthetic preference—I hate nosy sloppiness & yelping, parasitic fawning, & admire the cool, aristocratic independence, neatness, & self-sufficiency of the cat tribe. When I get home I'll send you an essay on the relative merits of cats & dogs which I once wrote as a contribution to a literary club programme.[4] I note with pride that I share my ailurophilic tendencies with many eminent persons of letters from Poe & Baudelaire down to the amiably discursive William Lyon Phelps.

I'll tell Loveman that you received his list—whatever it was. I did not see his William St. place, but fancy I might have liked it better than his present location, since I am always fascinated by quaint, narrow lanes & archaic buildings. William St. is a finely historic thoroughfare. In Colonial times it was known as "Golden Hill" & formed a place of residence for persons of the best quality. One of the earliest skirmishes of the Revolution was fought in its vicinity, & it is further distinguished by being the birth-street of Washington Irving. The transplanted Rowfant (103 E. 59th St.) is in a more prosaic book district—at the corner of Park Ave., just across the street from the celebrated Anderson Galleries. You will see all this, no doubt, when next you are in N.Y. The city is by no means devoid of interest if one does not have to live there—& before you visit it I will send you one of those little leather guidebooks I spoke of, plus a few individual observations on especially choice antiquities.

I am conquering my literary congestion only by slow degrees, but am closer to seeing daylight (thanks to Belknap's aid) than I was a month ago. The big Bierce-memoirs job still hangs uncertainly in the offing. Its author, an old man of great learning & equal egotism who was closely associated with Bierce for 25 years, seems frantically anxious for to me to do it, & pesters me with telephonic & other calls. He is, however, unwilling to pay cash in advance—without which I could not think of tackling such a proposition. Whether or not he'll "come around"—& a 350-page job at top rates naturally makes him pause—yet remains to be seen. If he does, I shall have a three-month period of slavery on my hands—during which I can do nothing else. Of course, it will have to be done at home, since I can only command about a quarter of my normal mental efficiency in the neighbourhood of this beastly metropolis. As an illustration of how much I love New York I may state that during the present sojourn I've been above ground in Times Square only *once*—on a necessary trip to the public library. My tentative plan for the Bierce job—if I get it—is to devote the whole of next November, December, & January to it. I *will not* be cheated out of the summer—the only time of year that my cold-hating constitution can really be said to be alive. I want to get a few tales of my own written—& I am furthermore rushed by the task of proofreading my story "The Shunned House", which is being published as a book by good old Cook of Athol—who published Belknap's "Man From Genoa."[5]

Before I go home I mean to take an antiquarian trip to Philadelphia, Baltimore, Annapolis, Washington, Alexandria—& perhaps Richmond & Williamsburg. I am especially anxious to see Annapolis, which has some of the finest surviving colonial antiquities in the country.

Pray give my regards to Parvulus Iacobus, & tell him I shall surely get around to that letter some day. When I write I'll send him some juvenile fantasies by a correspondence friend of mine (whom I expect to meet personally for the first time this month) which may greatly stimulate his literary interest.

With best wishes—

Most sincerely yrs

H P Lovecraft

Notes

1. William Henry Shelton (1840–1932), American painter, printmaker, etcher, illustrator, and author.

2. C. A. Brandt (1879–1974), associate editor of *Amazing Stories,* had urged HPL to submit more stories; but when HPL was only paid $25 for "The Colour out of Space" (amounting to ⅕ of a cent per word), HPL refused to submit anything to the magazine.

3. In fact, Long (b. 1901) had turned 27 on April 27. HPL mistakenly believed Long to have been born in 1902.

4. "Cats and Dogs," written for a meeting of the Blue Pencil Club, a Brooklyn amateur press group, in September 1926. HPL had just returned from New York to Providence in April, and therefore could not attend the meeting, so he wrote the essay to be read by James F. Morton.

5. Sheets for Cook's edition of *The Shunned House* were printed but not bound or distributed.

[31] [AHT]

10 Barnes St.,

Providence, R. I.,

July 28, 1928

My dear Mrs. Reed:—

My trip—which at the time I saw you was to include only a jaunt southward to Washington and intermediate points—finally expanded into a Grand Tour of unprecedented length, extent, and variety. The change of plan began when a friend of mine—now resident in New York but spending the summer in his ancestral Vermont—fairly kidnapped me into a two weeks' visit at a lonely farm he had hired in the exquisite countryside near Brattleboro. In this half-fabulous paradise of endless green hills and wild, brook-haunted glens, it is needless to say that my nerves recovered very substantially from the strain of New York. My first glimpse of Vermont, obtained last August, had whetted my appetite for more; and I now drank in to its fullest extent the miraculously preserved early-American life of the region. Literary companionship, too, was not absent; for the gentle rustic poet Arthur Goodenough (who wears a rusty frock coat and inhabits an unpainted farmhouse built in 1783) dwelt close by, and one week-end the indefatigable Walter J. Coates of Montpelier (editor of *Driftwind*) came down nearly a hundred miles to mingle in the throng. W. Paul Cook (publisher and critic) also came up from Athol twice. On Sunday, June 17, a whole crowd of literati (both actual and would-be) assembled at the ancient Goodenough farm for a session of general discussion and fraternising—the event being written up quite extensively in the local Brattleboro press.[1] I think I will enclose a clip full of Vermont matter in case it is of any interest, but which need not be read if it is not. This stuff can be returned at your convenience, although nothing else in the envelope need be. The article is what I wrote about the region after my brief glimpse of last year, but I don't take back a word of it after my second and more extended survey. The newspaper stuff is from the *Brattleboro Reformer*—the puff of myself being by my host, Vrest Orton of the *Saturday Review*.[2] The snapshots give a faint—very faint—notion of the beauties of my environment both interior and exterior. Orton is a stickler for the old-time furnishings and ways when he is on his native Vermont sod, as you may see by the views of his living-room. He even insists on archaic oil lamps.

But Vermont did not form the end of my visiting; since W. Paul Cook, on his second trip up, repeated the process of kidnapping a helpless old gentleman and bore me away for a week's visit in Athol, where I had the honour of seeing him send to press, with his own hands, the sheets of my story "The Shunned House", which when published will form my first cloth-bound book, (albeit only a thin affair of sixty pages, with a brief preface by my Belknap-grandchild). My sojourn in this sightly village was exceedingly pleasant, for I had as an associate not only Cook himself, but the young weird writer H. Warner Munn, who was one of my guests in Providence last summer. Nor was *this* the end of my visiting programme! Whilst in Athol I received an invitation, too cordial to resist, to spend a week at the home of a delightful old lady authoress some distance south of there, in the town of North Wilbraham, near Springfield, (home of the Home Correspondence School). This veteran of the art (Mrs. Edith Miniter, author of the successful novel "Our Natupski Neighbours") was a Bostonian during her more active years, but has now retired to her ancestral region for a tranquil sunset period; residing with an equally elderly cousin[3] in an ancient house of considerable size (a tavern in colonial days) whose capacious rooms are absolutely stuffed with antiques of the most valuable sort—none for sale, but all destined for the museum in Springfield upon their venerable owner's demise. Other objects of interest on this delightful estate are seven cats, two dogs, two horses, two kine, and one hired boy. Far to the west, across marshy meadows where at evening the fireflies dance in incredibly fantastic profusion, the benign bulk of Wilbraham Mountain rises purple and mystical. The region, being very old and remote, is full of the most extraordinary folklore; some of which will certainly find lodgment in my future stories if I ever live to write any more.[4] The scenery thereabouts is magnificent—as I can testify after a walk around the mountain and almost over its crest.

But at last I put visiting behind me, and embarked upon the more kinetic part of my irresponsible wanderings. Glancing cursorily at Springfield—but without calling on the redoubtable Dr. J. Berg Esenwein[5]—I rapidly ascended the Connecticut Valley by trolley and omnibus, passing through Holyoke, paying my respects to Mt. Tom, saluting Northampton, home of the Emperor Calvinus I,[6] and revelling in ancient Deerfield—which I visited last year, and had also visited earlier this year on a side-trip from Vermont. At quiet Greenfield I took a west-bound stage-coach over the celebrated Mohawk Trail, and was forthwith enraptured by a greater display of scenic magnificence than my fancy had ever theretofore conceived. Endless leagues of hills and winding rivers outspread—and the ineffable sense of mountain mystery as the coach wound down precipitous slopes into the bowl-like valley containing the town of North Adams. I kept on to Albany, N.Y., at which point I took a boat down the river, through the storied and scenic Catskill region so dear to the heart of Washington Irving. At New York City, compulsion being absent, I did not tarry except to exchange greetings with Little Belknap and young Donald Wandrei; (the latter weird writer being now emigrated to Brooklyn, and living only two blocks from the accursed scene of my own weary exile of 1925!) but kept on southward to my dearly-loved colonial haven of Philadelphia. There I communed as usual with the past; in the form of endless rows of Georgian brick, and endless alleys of labyrinthine archaism and mystery in the sinister, half-forgotten regions near the Delaware water-front. Finally I moved on to Baltimore—travelling by omnibus through a region rather tame scenically except for small spots around Elkton and Havre-de-Grace. I had never seen Baltimore before, and therefore proceeded to give it an exceptionally thorough exploration. I saw Fort McHenry, birth-place of Mr. Key's celebrated ode to the tune of "Anacreon in Heaven", but delighted chiefly in the melancholy grave of Edgar Allan Poe, in a neglected corner of Westminster Presbyterian Churchyard. I tried to purchase pictures of it, but could not locate any during the short time I had at my disposal. I regretted not having brought along a kodak. After Baltimore came historic and colonial Annapolis; and there I was forced to give vent to an almost childish enthusiasm over the marvellously preserved archaism of the place. It is utterly and vibrantly a part of the eighteenth century, redolent of the court-ly life which after 1694 centred around the capital of the Proprietors' Colony of Maryland. The town itself is as purely Georgian as Newport, R.I., or the coast towns north of Boston; whilst the country-seats adjoining show the true southern type of colonial architecture, (steep roof, flat end chimneys, wings and arcades on each side of the main edifice etc.) as distinguished from the middle-colonies type prevailing in Pennsylvania and as far south as Baltimore. I also went through the naval academy buildings—of which the golden-domed chapel, with the body of John Paul Jones in its crypt, is by far the most interesting.

After Annapolis came Washington, D.C., which I made a base of opera-tions for many side-trips into the adjacent parts of northern Virginia. Alexan-dria, with its venerable Christ Church and endless rows of colonial brick houses, was my favorite goal. In places like this, and Annapolis, one finds more of the old royalist spirit than in New England, where the sentiment for sedition was stronger in the unfortunate period of 1775–83. It did my ancient Tory soul good to walk along such thoroughfares as King St., Prince St., Roy-al St., King George St., Duke St., Prince George St., and Duke of Gloucester St. I have no sympathy with rebellion, but am still a loyal subject of His Bri-tannick Majesty's Colony of Rhode-Island and Providence-Plantations. *God Save the King!*

But I did not permit my loyalist sentiments to deter me from visiting Mt. Vernon, country-seat of the late rebel leader General Washington. I have a hearty respect for the gentleman, who was a true Virginia aristocrat and man of taste for all his disaffection from his rightful sovereign. I left no part of the mansion or the grounds unvisited, and must express my most unqualified admiration and approval of the whole estate. Another trip of mine was to the quaint valley hamlet of Falls Church, Va., of whose venerable fane General Washington was a vestryman. Washington itself—mostly the older Georgetown section—claimed considerable of my attention. Of the newer buildings I think I was most impressed by the imposing temple of the Scottish Rite Masons at 16th and S. Sts. I saw this first at night; and something about the Cyclopean windowless facade, with its guardian Sphinxes and cryptical twin braziers burning beside the great bronze door, gave me an ineffably poignant sense of brooding, transmitted mystery—of terrible secrets and obscure arcana of an elder earth, handed down in nocturnal incantations amongst the ancient and privileged group whose meeting-place the temple is. I could understand the sensation of awe, sometimes amounting to fear and aversion, with which the masonic fraternity was generally regarded by outsiders in naiver ages than the present.

But the climax of the whole Odyssey was my excursion, by train, to the *Endless Caverns* in the exquisite Shenandoah Valley. Despite all the fantasy I have written concerning the nether world, I had never beheld a real cave before in all my life—and my sensations upon plunging into one of the finest specimens in the country may be better imagined than described. For over an hour I was led spellbound through illimitable gulfs and chasms of elfin beauty and daemonic mystery—here and there lighted with wondrous effect by concealed lamps, and in other places displaying awesome grottoes and abysses of unconquered night; black bottomless shafts and galleries where hidden winds and waters course eternally out of this world and all possible worlds of mankind, down, down to the sunless secrets of the gnomes and night-gaunts,[7] and the worlds where web-winged monsters and fabulous gargoyles reign in undisputed horror. I could not begin to describe the place myself, but fortunately there were some excellent descriptive booklets at the office—to be had for the taking—with which I enthusiastically inundated all my friends forthwith. I trust your copies reached you safely.

After the caves there was absolutely nothing else to do but go home. Any other course would have been the sheerest anticlimax . . . . especially since I was dead broke and travelling on borrowed funds. Accordingly I veered northward, travelling both day and night to save time and hotel bills. I had intended to take some time for a leisurely exploration of ancient Connecticut as I reached the final lap of my journey—perhaps zigzagging from New York to Hartford, Hartford to New Haven, New Haven to New London, New London to Norwich, and Norwich to Providence over the old Plainfield Pike. Upon reaching New York, however, I found letters awaiting me which told of the illness of my elder aunt; (with lumbago—not serious, but requiring a nurse and the constant performance of errands) a circumstance which made my immediate presence in Providence advisable. Therefore I took a night train at once, and landed in the town of my birth at eight a. m., Wednesday, July 18, 1928. It was with a thrill of loyalty and affection that I beheld the familiar spires and domes of the ancient city once more; and when I mounted the quiet, sun-drenched, village-like streets of the colonial hill—fragrant with many gardens that have blossomed unchanged through the centuries—I could not but concede in all impartiality that Old Providence is lovelier than all the exotic spots to which my wanderings had taken me!

And here I have been ever since, vegetating in my accustomed fashion. I have had scarcely a moment to breathe in, since duties have been very numerous, and I have tried to read up all the papers and magazines that accumulated during my long absence. Moreover, I have had to straighten out all my files of papers, cuttings, and magazines as the result of a plumbing accident which occurred whilst I was away, and which caused the upheaval of everything on my carefully arranged alcove shelves. But at last I am getting reassimilated in my own home, and becoming able to think of tackling work again—both revisory and creative. I shall go a bit easy on the revision just now, since I absolutely must get some more things of my own written. Wright, as you may see by the enclosed note, is becoming politely clamorous. But there will be time for a moderate amount of critical labour, and with the coöperation of my small grandson (who stopped by last Monday with his papa and mamma and aunt en route for Cape Cod) I expect to keep up with my programme rather better than I did last winter.

I remain
        Yrs sincerely,
            H P Lovecraft.

Notes

1. [Unsigned], "Literary Persons Meet in Guilford," *Brattleboro Daily Reformer* (18 June 1928): 1.

2. Vrest Orton, "A Weird Writer Is in Our Midst," *Brattleboro Daily Reformer* (16 June 1928): 2. Rpt. in *A Weird Writer in Our Midst: Early Criticism of H. P. Lovecraft*, ed. S. T. Joshi (New York: Hippocampus Press, 2010), 51–54.

3. Evanore Olds Beebe (1858–1935).

4. HPL used several bits of legendry told to him by Miniter in "The Dunwich Horror," written later that summer.

5. J[oseph] Berg Esenwein (1867–1946) was the author of *Writing the Short-Story: A Practical Handbook on the Rise, Structure, Writing, and Sale of the Modern Short-Story* (New York: Hinds, Hayden & Eldredge, 1918; *LL* 320), which HPL read shortly after he resumed the writing of fiction in 1917. Esenwein was at this time the editor of the *Writer's Monthly*, based in Springfield, MA.

6. I.e., President Calvin Coolidge.

7. HPL's childhood coined name for creatures who haunted his dreams, meaningless to ZB; hence his explanation in the following letter.

[32]   [ALS]

10 Barnes St.,
Providence, R.I.,
August 25, 1928

My dear Mrs. Reed:—

I would have sooner acknowledged yours of the 16th, with cheque enclosed, but for a sudden & unexpected accession of duties which would brook no delay. Let me express my appreciation, belatedly though it comes. Meanwhile yours of the 18th is at hand, & I can assure you that Belknap will not send mail to Nevada, Mo. I was only able to forward your envelope to him yesterday, for it came just too late to catch him at the Thousand Islands. Now he is at home, & 230 W. 97 is the correct address once more. It has not, alas, been my privilege to act as his host during these weeks—my humbler privilege being merely to act as the forwarder of his mail. Each summer the Longs close their home & make a rather extended tour in the family Essex; & since their location is constantly changing, they have hard work keeping in touch with the world. It would obviously be impossible to telegraph everybody each time they pause at a post office, so they have adopted a plan of centralisation which seems to work fairly well. All of their mail is sent in my care, & I am constantly notified by telegraph of their temporary whereabouts. The moment I receive a wire, I send them by registered mail everything which has come for them. Then, as soon as they receive the consignment, they move onward along their civilisedly gypsified trail. But, as remarked above, that trail for 1928 has returned to its starting-point; so that 230 W. 97 is the proper formula henceforward.

Your account of the mildly touched old lady with extra-terrestrial vision & affiliations is indeed extremely interesting, & I have no doubt but that the case could—with some modification & elaboration—be made into a distinctly powerful tale. It would take the greatest care & subtlety, however, to handle the subject effectively; & I fear that the inherent pathos of the theme would make impossible a full exploitation of its comic side. I would say, in general, that it seems like material for a rather sombre or wistful tale—or else an out-&-out weird one. Just how salable it could be made is rather a question. Editors might look askance at the "blasphemousness" of handling the Saviour's name in such a familiar way—but that feature might be averted by making "John" the pseudonym of John the Baptist, St Peter, St Paul, or some other demigod less potent than Christus in the popular mythology. Of course, the case as observed is only the *nucleus* or *idea* of a story. The story proper—with plot, suspense, development, & climax—is yet to be written, & you have yet to decide just what sort of an emotion you wish to create in the reader. As I say, it seems to me that your only choice is between *pathos* & *weirdness;* for the *comedy* could be used only in a tale of the most iconoclastically cynical &

sophisticated sort—in the manner of Anatole France—& you have not so far seemed inclined to gravitate toward this type of composition. If pathos is decided upon, I would recommend a light, wistful touch such as was used in "The Blue Foulard". The emptiness of the character's life could be brought out by suitable wording, & the pitiful relief of the hallucination could be made very vivid. Of course, the logical *climax* is the heroine's *cure*. But the crux of the pathos is that this "cure" is merely the source of fresh emptiness & misery. Knowing the truth only adds to the subject's woes, for now she has *nothing* to live for. She has been too long out of normal touch & sympathy with those around her, to have them form any real or satisfying world for her. The hallucination was her only emotional reality; & now that this has gone, she is an alien among her own kind—disillusioned & detached from all sources of interest. At this point a melodramatic romanticist would have her commit suicide, but that is too spectacular & *mechanically* appropriate to be real life or (which is the same thing) good art. Instead, merely have her sigh & resign herself to the monotony of empty & endless days—with the freshness of spirit gone, & the visible marks of old age quickly appearing. In detailing this individual tragedy, it would be well to adhere to a somewhat concrete, rather than diffusively sentimental or philosophically sententious style. Let the *atmosphere* only suggest that the individual summarises & symbolises the universal. The futility of all life & of the universe can be told better by implication than by direct statement. And yet the subtle atmospheric note of the universal ought to be there. Only day before yesterday a correspondent of mine—a very gifted young Irishman in rural New York state who is just breaking into *Weird Tales*—phrased the matter very appropriately in a letter.

> "In writing which pleases me", he writes, "there is always an indefinite something—an aura, or atmosphere, or implication of something infinite & all-embracing—which has nothing to do with the plot of the story, or with mere words at all. I do not know how this aura is to be attained—perhaps no one does—but I think in all real literature or art it must be there."[1]

So much for the possible *pathetic* handling. If *weird* treatment is desired, the obvious thing is to have the afflicted lady's illusion slightly more *real* than the actual working world permits. The *revelation* of this alarming genuineness would form, of course, the obvious climax; & this might occur in one of two ways—either the possession of knowledge on the heroine's part which could come only through supernatural linkages, or the manifestation of "John" or some other celestial denizen to one or more persons other than the patient. This revelation, I think, ought to occur amidst distinctly (though not overstrainedly) dramatic circumstances; [for a *weird* tale allows of more drama & effect than does a realistic tale] & ought to concern grave & important rather than relatively trivial matters. The death hour of the subject would be a good time to have the revelation come. One sort of thing which would be rather good would be to have the ghost-world bring about the hanging—under similar circumstances—of the one whose bygone deeds caused the son to hang himself. The kind of atmosphere to use in the weird handling of this theme would be the lighter, touch-&-go manner of Montague Rhodes James rather than the heavy, cumulative rhythms of Poe or the half-poetic sorcery of Arthur Machen. As for comic treatment—I'd scarcely recommend it to you at this stage. Later, if wider & more iconoclastic reading comes to give you a more ironic & analytical outlook on the mockery of life & human feelings & objects & efforts, it might do—but not now. The only innocuous or non-cynical way

[Leaf II missing]

I am glad that the James–Junior duo continues to enjoy itself in manners appropriate to the divergent tastes of its respective components. Club affiliations are always important & pleasing to the young, so I presume that Iacobulus is distinctly in his element at present. I doubt if the susceptible Junior will really perish of a broken heart, despite the spatial removal of the diminutive light of his life. The necessity for correspondence—which may last as long as a whole month or two—will give him practice in the art of literary creation, so that his present trial may prove the source of many blessings . . . . if indeed literary inclinations may be regarded as blessings rather than afflictions. I think that the acute James may be accounted fortunate in his freedom from premature romance—nor do I believe that such immunity is in the least indicative that he will be hopelessly enslaved by the luminous orbs of some one charmer of the future. That latter idea—that one who is not an amateur sheik is likely to become the ultimate prey of one consuming passion—is purely a stock invention of popular literature. James is wise, too, in avoiding weird fiction if it causes him nightmares. In my own youth I was a prey to the most devastating glimpses of unholy nocturnal chasms & beings of sleep—ugh! I shiver *now* when I think of them! When I was about six I used to be afraid to go to sleep because of the lean, oily, hairless, horned, bat-winged, tailed, & *accursedly* **silent** beings which used to snatch me up as soon as I closed my eyes, & bear me away through the night to inconceivable abysms of blackness, where grey, jagged peaks bearing hieroglyph-graven fragments of elder ruins reached vaguely up into a sort of hellish grey twilight. No one had ever told me about such scenes & beings, but I invented the name "night-gaunts" for my voiceless captors. Probably they arose from my youthful porings over the Doré illustrations in "Paradise Lost" & Dante's "Inferno"—great flat books that I used to absorb by the hour stretched out on the bearskin rug before the unused fireplace in the red parlour at the old home. The night-gaunts do not harass me nowadays, but I have put them into a short novel which I wrote two years ago[2]—& have never typed because I can't endure the prospect of such a long typing job. If Junior likes weird stories yet is not ready for Poe, why not give him the tales of Montague Rhodes James—that learned antiquary & Provost of Eton College whose skill with simple ghost yarns is so phenomenally great? These, indeed, are merely the elaborations of the yarns which Dr. James habitually spins to the juvenile part of his family at Christmastide. The titles are as follows: "The Five Jars," (this is avowedly juvenile) "Ghost Stories of An Antiquary", "More Ghost Stories of an Antiquary", "A Thin Ghost & Others", & "A Warning to the Curious." Junior might not "get" a few of these at first, but the majority are fairly obvious. The ghostly element is finely handled—so finely that the books had better be kept out of young James's way!

I am indeed delighted to know that you are finding Belknap's literary coöperation of substantial value—as I certainly thought you would. The little imp surely knows his art, & knows how to tell others the fine points of it. I can't compete with him in brevity—it takes me ten pages to say what the child can say in ten words! I am so conscious of the difficulty in conveying exact shades of meaning, & so anxious to have no mistake about the right shade, that I ramble on indefinitely—fancying that I clarify; whereas in truth I may be only compounding obscurity! Sonny just strikes out in epitome—yet probably hits the mark oftener than his aged grandpa does. You are making no mistake in placing *reading* before writing at this stage of the game, for nothing will increase your fictional power more than a mental background saturated with good style & realistic ideas of human thought, conduct, & motivation. I note that you mention Ben Hecht. His work is a good antidote to the sickly, artificial, & falsely conceived popular novel, though his style may be a bit too choppy to serve as an ideal model. He knows the vulgar, strident modern world from the inside, & has created in "Erik Dorn" the best single picture of a typical modern that contemporary literature (or what I know of it) can afford. "Humpty Dumpty" is a better-written novel, but it is only a repetition in substance. "Erik Dorn" is the real cerebral document.

I am glad the article by John B. Watson proved of interest.[3] He is one of the soundest psychological thinkers in existence; & though not primarily an aesthete, his views on literature cannot help being very sound & valuable so far as the handling of human character goes. As I said before, the Jackson & Salisbury book[4] is very highly regarded—& I really think I will look it over if it is obtainable at the local library. When I do, I'll let you know what I think of it. As for the incidental fracture of "ideals"—that's really a very healthy process, for it means merely that one is shaking loose from a puerile & mythological system of folklore which taught a vague & artificial set of false notions regarding cosmic values, man's place in the universe, & human thoughts, acts, reactions, & motivations. Modern psychology knocks the bottom out of all this nonsense, & shows pretty frankly & honestly what people really are, why they think & do as they do, & why they hide their thoughts & motives even from themselves under the cloak of the ancient myth-system. A writer, if he is to depict human character accurately, must know the actual ruthless facts; for otherwise he will perpetually be having his characters do the wrong thing at the wrong time, & react impossibly to the various events brought up by the plot. All this doesn't strip the drama from life—indeed, in many ways that drama is enhanced by the futile complexity & deterministic helplessness amidst which the poor human animal is now seen to be struggling. Beside the truth, the old mythic idealism seems vapid, mockingly childish, flimsy, artificial, & thin-blooded.

I have, regrettably, been delayed in getting at the weird tale of the Indian, but hope to report substantial progress next time. When I do finish it, I hope to have a real story with all the necessary elements of plot & atmosphere.

With apologies for the loquacious length of the present epistle, & best regards to yourself & the Jacobus–Junior duo,[5] I remain

      yrs most sincerely
      HPLovecraft

P.S. And of course I'll report anything regarding the publication date of "Yig" which I may hear from Wright.

Notes

1. The correspondent in question is almost certainly Bernard Austin Dwyer. He had just sold a poem, "Ol' Black Sarah," to *WT;* it appeared in the October 1928 issue. It was his only contribution to *WT.*
2. *The Dream-Quest of Unknown Kadath,* unpublished in HPL's lifetime.
3. John B[roadus] Watson (1878–1958), American psychologist and founder of behaviorism.
4. Josephine Agnes Jackson and Helen M. Salisbury, *Outwitting Our Nerves: A Primer of Psychology* (New York: Century Co., 1921).
5. Referring to ZB's son James and to his friend of nearly the same age, Watson Stains, Jr., as though they were inseparable.

[33]   [ALS]

                10 Barnes St.,
                Providence, R.I.,
                Aug. 30, 1928.

My dear Mrs. Reed:—

        I am adding this postscript to my letter of the 25th at the urgent insistence of my small grandchild Belknap, who has just received the letter from Uzzell which you sent him, & is bristling with chivalrous indignation down to the very extremities of each of the seventeen separate down-wisps comprising his tenderly coddled moustachelet!

What the child wants his grandpa to do, is to back him up in his advice to you regarding the dropping of Uzzell instruction. He recalls my original favourable impression of U—gathered from U's articles in various magazines, his speech, his general high standing in his Columbia days, &c—& is afraid I will advise you to continue with him despite the ineptitude & commercial rapacity he has shewn in his dealings with you. Accordingly, he is haranguing me most eloquently—portions of his S.O.S. message to me reading:

> "Uzzell is obviously a faker—he does not intend to help & is primarily interested in the cheques. He never even pretends to criticise *style*, & is so horribly, hopelessly Babbitesque in his predilection for trite conventional plots that I cannot work with him.
>
> "Mrs. Reed will be merely throwing her money away on Uzzell. I would have suggested that she give him up sooner, but could not conscientiously do so as long as I thought he might help her *sell* stories. But this letter is a revelation! *For heaven's sake tell her the truth before it is too late!* [the italics are Belknap's! I can see that moustachelet bristle!]
>
> "One hundred thousand dollars, forsooth! And his fourth paragraph is the crudest, most unspeakable—my Gawd! is Mrs. Reed a horse? 'probably a delicate feeder &c' Ugh! It is horrible that such creatures as Uzzell exist in the universe!"

Well—Sonny needn't have been so alarmed about the old gentleman's advice, because a perusal of the Uzzell letter gives me, in my elderly way, about the same reaction that it gave Belknap in his youthful way. I give in—my Uzzellian disillusion is complete, although the fact remains that during his Columbia days he must have been a very effective teacher. It is clear that he has thrown conscientiousness aside, & is now merely one of the multitude of literary parasites who absorb a constant stream of cheques without giving any real thought or service in return. I wouldn't have thought it of him—& I'm very slow in turning against one of whom I have entertained a favourable opinion; but this last letter of Uzzell's is too much. Even before that I'd have hesitated advising you to pay *more* to Uzzell, but I thought your original course fee covered everything. Now that I see his plan, I don't hesitate in joining Belknap in advising you to 'quit him cold'.

Uzzell's letter is a very strange document indeed. The presence of at least two gross grammatical errors & the repeated citation of Kathleen Norris's name as "Katherine" are enough to prove the carelessness with which it was written, while the general tone & statements testify abundantly to the hollow commercialism of the writer's whole attitude. The advice & recommendations seem to me singularly irresponsible, & in some ways contradicting previous advice of his. His present idea seems to be to encourage you to write flimsy romance for the gum-chewing Woolworth-clerk & telephone-girl public—though I'm not sure that his idea can be very definite, since he couples authors as widely separated as the superficial Temple Bailey & the conscientiously artistic Kathleen Norris.[1] Possibly he couples them because of the anatomical resemblance he cites. It would be rather interesting, even if scarcely relevant, to make a scientific study of the 'feeding' habits of the literary profession. One might write learnedly on the effect of pork & beans on the poet's sense of rhythm, or the etherealising influence of corned beef & cabbage on imaginative imagery. Possibly I might have amounted to something if I had not reduced in 1925—though even as it is, I consume considerable meat & potato without getting very spectacular cerebral results. Perhaps the cumulative effect of a potato diet in Ireland since 1848 is the cause of the Celtic renaissance that produced Yeats, Synge, Dunsany, A.E., Lady Gregory, Padraic Colum, & all the rest! What a thesis for a Ph.D. degree! But further—Uzzell seems very careless & obtuse in grasping plots & plot-elements, as witness his misconception in the case of "The Unchaining". In this letter he says he fails to "get" "Ice Music," yet Belknap assures me that the plot is very good (I have not seen it) & perfectly comprehensible.

Uzzell's *prices* are utterly indefensible, & apparently more than what he outlines in his advertisements. I am very sure that in the cutting I sent you he said that $10.00 was his fee for *collaborating* on a story—i.e., what I would call "extensive revision" & perform at $1.00 per typed page. *Now* it appears that this is simply the fee for *reading*—which I do for nothing when the job of revision isn't given me—without any appreciable advice or collaboration at all! Such inconsistency is beyond my power to analyse—I can only say that it looks as if Tom were cutting loose from all standards & absorbing all the cash he can get while the absorbing's good. Maybe the game will play out when everyone becomes aware of his latter-day tactics—then he'll have to go back to work; a punishment which, though terrible, is perhaps not incommensurate with his offences.

But at any rate, I must advise you not to sink any more cash into Uzzellian promoting schemes & get-rich-quick plans to make $100,000.00 & retire to a stout old age! Belknap is surely right in opposing such a returnless waste, & I would have said the same before, had I not fancied the payments were already made. I still think that a course of systematic instruction in the mechanics of narration—style, handling of incidents & plot turns, &c., choice of words, &c &c—would be of the highest benefit to you in addition to revisory aid; but after recommending such a "dud" as Thomas H. I feel guiltily hesitant about making any further recommendations. Belknap thinks that the Columbia College course is about the best thing available by mail, as I believe he told you last May. It occurs to me that Belknap himself may have enough special technical knowledge to make a good teacher—since he took magazine-story technique for several years at Columbia—hence I am asking him whether or not he would feel capable of giving you a course at suitable rates. I myself am not a good teacher. I can get results on paper, but don't know the ropes of pedagogical method; hence I couldn't conscientiously charge any ordinary fee for lessons which at best would be inexperienced & amateurish. But you really do need lessons—clear, explanatory, regular lessons in the art of handling words, images, associations, & narrational twists & turns—& if Belknap can't furnish them I'd strongly advise the Columbia course. This is the sort of thing which Uzzell *used* to give when he was on the Columbia staff, & what he is *supposed* to be giving now. It is, as I have said, a shock & a surprise to me to find that he isn't living up to his pretensions.

Again I must apologise for having caused you to incur the expense & futility of this Uzzell course. I thought my advice was good when I gave it—but unfortunately I lack the convenient qualities of prophecy, clairvoyance, & omniscience. If I weren't so accursedly impecunious, I'd reimburse you for wasted cash by taking off of future revision bills—alas for the ignominious position of the deserving poor! At any rate, the best I can do *now* is to back Belknap up & advise an adieu to Trifling Thomas. ¶ Apologetically yrs—

H P Lovecraft

P.S. I enclose a reference to your city which I found in last night's paper. This outlander's point of view may seem amusing to a resident.

Notes

1. Irene Temple Bailey (1869–1953), American popular novelist and screenwriter who reportedly sold more than three million copies of her books during her lifetime. Kathleen Norris (1880–1966), American novelist and journalist who, although prolific, was highly regarded by critics. Her best-known novel is *Saturday's Child* (1914).

[34]   [AHT]

10 Barnes St.,
Providence, R. I.,
Oct. 2, 1928

My dear Mrs. Reed:—

[. . .]

One application of modern psychological knowledge which you may have noticed is the new "stream-of-consciousness" school of literature, which has undoubtedly gained surprisingly within the last decade. This school recognises as a fundamental principle the newly discovered fact that our minds are really full at all times of a thousand irrelevant and dissociated threads of imagery and ideation; and that our acts are in truth determined by the sum total of all these heterogeneous, unconscious scraps, rather than by the one thin line of connected ideas which we outwardly recognise by virtue of its position at the top level of our consciousness. Accepting the implications of the newer psychology to the utmost extent, the new school of literature strives to mirror life accurately and logically by laying bare the whole subconscious and conscious hodge-podge of impressions, feelings, and memories which flows irresponsibly through the mind from moment to moment; and by tracing the obscure connections between these random sources and the *seemingly unrelated* results in the domain of action and outward expression which are in truth their *direct and inevitable outcome.* The principal exponents of this advanced school are James Joyce in prose and T. S. Eliot in poetry. Naturally its products strike the uninitiated as mere jumbles of senseless incoherence, so that Joyce, Eliot, etc. have had to meet a devastating amount of ridicule. Actually, it seems to me still an open question whether stream-of-consciousness literature may by classed legitimately as a vital and workable art-form. There is much to be said for it; but against it we may argue that art concerns only *results* and harmonic impression-patterns—a definition which would classify stream-of-consciousness writing as mere prosaic *science* or *philosophy* rather than genuine *aesthetic* creation. I myself think that the extreme methods of Joyce, Eliot, and their congeners (E. E. Cummings, Hart Crane, Aldous Huxley, Wyndham Lewis, Dorothy Richardson, The Sitwells, D. H. Lawrence, Virginia Woolf, Gertrude Stein, Kenneth Burke, Ezra Pound, Marcel Proust, etc. etc.) do indeed transcend the limits of real art; though I believe they are destined to exert a strong influence upon art itself. Literary art, I think, must continue to adhere to the practice of recording outward happenings in consecutive order; but it must from now onward realise the complex and irrational motivation of all these happenings, and must refrain from attributing them to simple, obvious, and artificially rationalised causes. Just how much of the subconscious hodge-podge behind any outward event ought to be recorded by a literary artist is still a very perplexing question. It must be decided independently in each particular case by the author's own judgment and aesthetic sense—and I for one believe that it can be done in such a manner as to leave the main current of Western-European literary tradition undisturbed in its aesthetic essentials. It occurs to me that you can find this whole question of modern psychology in literature discussed with admirable clearness in the *Atlantic Monthly* for December, 1927, (Vol. 140, No. 6) which you can consult in bound form at any first-class library. The article is "Past and Present", by Edwin Muir, and I really think you ought to read it as a valuable aid toward the formation of a clear-cut literary perspective. Muir cites five different passages from representative fiction ranging from Jane Austen to James Joyce, and illustrating the several different stages between completely old-fashioned surface fiction and the analytical stream-of-consciousness fiction of the modern experimenter. He also points out the limitations of the new method as practiced by Joyce and Eliot—showing that these moderns, despite their attitude, do not really succeed in establishing a significant relationship between the acts and the subconscious image-jumbles of their characters. It might be a good idea for you to read some of the moderns as an element in background-building. The important thing is to realise how profound, complex, sincere, and exacting an art real literature is; and consequently, how utterly trivial and beneath contempt—how completely *non-existent* as factors in real creative effort—such flashy superficial money-seekers as Zane Grey, Eleanor Glyn, Temple Bailey, Harold Bell Wright, and the rest of the herd of popular slush-purveyors are. The first step toward responsible artistic effort is to sweep one's mind clear of all ideas and standards connected with this pitiful tribe of commercial fool-pleasers—to banish for ever all remembrance of the cheap commercial magazines of the day, the cinema, the current best-sellers, and all that, and to buckle down to a study of the real authors and their methods. There is no possible point of contact between the world of ten-cent news-stand romance—the world of James Oliver Curwood, Phyllis Bottome, Carolyn Wells, J. S. Fletcher, Mary Roberts Rinehart, and the scores of even flimsier authors whose names I don't pretend to note or remember—and the actual world of honest literary creation as typified in our day by artists like James Branch Cabell, Edith Wharton, Walter de la Mare, Thornton Wilder, Ernest Hemingway, Morley Callaghan, John Galsworthy, Sherwood Anderson, H. G. Wells, and others of equal or lesser ability who write with the same standard of pure aesthetics uppermost. Uzzell doesn't advocate emulating the sincere artists . . . . . . but I, on the other hand, don't advocate emulating Uzzell!

Turning at last from didactic verbosity—my dominant failing—I note your inquiry as to how my Milwaukee teacher-friend reacted to the fourteen-page travelogue I sent him. Amusingly enough, my reply can quite truthfully take a somewhat spectacular form—for a chain of circumstances operated in a highly peculiar way to give a portion of the letter a wider publicity than was anticipated. The fact is, that one paragraph of the travelogue is about to be incorporated in a seventh-grade school reader which the Macmillan Co. will issue next spring! It all comes about through the circumstance that my friend—Maurice Winter Moe—has been collaborating with Profs. Moffett and Leonard of the University of Wisconsin on a new series of Macmillan readers—the ninth grade book being wholly under Moe's editorship. When he received my letter he thought so favourably of it that he showed it to his colleagues; and among them they hit on the idea of using my description of Sleepy Hollow and Tarrytown as a note to Irving's "Sleepy Hollow" in the seventh grade book. It will there appear, Moe tells me, with due credit given to the lowly author.[1] Of course it's nothing but a small-type appendix note, yet it is rather amusing in a mild way to think of oneself as a real "classic" permanently represented in a standard school reader! My name, as it were, will live upon the tender lips of infant generations yet unborn . . . *exegi monumentum aere perennius*,[2] and all that sort of thing!

I remain yrs sincerely,

H P Lovecraft.

Notes

1. HPL's "Sleepy Hollow To-day" (an extract made by Moe from the travel essay "Observations on Several Parts of America" [1928], which HPL circulated in typescript to his colleagues) appeared in Sterling Leonard and Harold Y. Moffett's textbook *Junior Literature: Book Two* (New York: Macmillan, 1930), 546–47. Moe assisted in the compilation of the volume.

2. "I have erected a monument more lasting than bronze." Horace, *Odes* 3.30.1.

[35]   [ALS]

10 Barnes St.,

Providence, R.I.,

Oct. 28, 1928

My dear Mrs. Reed:—

I had hoped to be able to send along the weird Indian tale when replying to yours of the 11th, but once more the Fates were against me. It is fortunate that you are in no haste for it, & I surely hope I can produce a good piece of work when I am at last able to undertake the construction. No—there is not any other story-nucleus in my possession. The only one is of the cryptic Oklahoma mound & its taciturn guardians.

Let me congratulate you upon the sale of the renamed "Red Blood".[1] Sonny Belknap surely does know how to bring out the salable potentialities in modern fiction! But what on earth was that $51.00 deduction of Uzzell's? No conceivable *commission* could amount to such a figure! Was it not applied to some fee-payment connected with the alleged course & service? In any case, though, it was piratically rapacious, & serves to confirm my disillusion regarding the astute Thomas. Never again shall I recommend such a literary privateer turned pirate! However—you ought not to let the incident mar your delight in your first regular sale. That in itself is such an encouraging milestone in your career that it really ought to overbalance any less pleasant accessory circumstances. I am glad that Belknap has provided a good literary manual, & am asking him particulars about it—since I have always wanted to know of a good book to recommend to prose beginners with the same assurance that I recommended Brander Matthews' "Study of Versification" to poetic beginners. The only Hearn I know of is the illustrious Lafcadio, & I was not aware that he had written a volume on the author's craft.

Thanks very much for the photographic glimpses of the youthful Iacobus—which I enclose herewith as per request. Truly, he is a delightfully prepossessing & attractive young man; & has an aspect of poise, seriousness, & competence not often to be expected in one of his tender years. I was hardly prepared for the long trousers—yet upon reflection recall that I donned such symbols of maturity myself at the age of 13½. The rapid shifting of Iacobus' interest from one subject to another is, I think, a perfectly healthy sign of an active & nimble mind; & a matter for congratulation rather than for worry. It is this which will ensure him a comfortable breadth of mind; making him familiar with many things instead of merely one or two, & guarding him against bias & pedantry. Another & older James whom Belknap & I know has always had much the same tendency, & it has led him to the curatorship of an important city museum![2] I'd enjoy seeing snapshots of Iunior when you have some readily available. His aversion to writing is nothing to lament, for literature is only one of many forms of adequate self-expression. It is not remarkable that both Iacobus & Iunior are predominantly interested in mechanics & electricity; for if anything is typical of this age, it is surely the supremacy of power & mechanism in daily life & thought. There is no question but that the bulk of the world's brain-power is now concentrated upon science & invention, being largely withdrawn from philosophy, literature, government, & the arts. I do not welcome this transition, for it is producing an artificialised civilisation of new forms, values, & folk-ways so little connected with any traditional roots that it lacks all the charm & mellowness of memory & familiar association. But welcome or not, it appears to be inevitable; & it is only natural that the newest generation is growing up thoroughly saturated with its spirit. Only small groups of boys like Belknap & Wandrei & my other grandchildren & semi-grandchildren will remain as atavistic nuclei of the old order. No doubt the newer civilisation will have a tradition & aesthetic of its own after a while, as indeed is prefigured by the awkward & grotesque forms of so-called "modernistic" art & furniture & decoration. But all this will merely constitute an outlying province of the ruthless Empire of the Machine, & will rest upon so complexly artificial a basis that it cannot have the really ripe strength & emotional convincingness of an aesthetic which springs from unbroken inheritance & the overtones of thousands of years of basically similar life & fixed relationships with the sky, the soil, the seasons, & the landscape. It will be an alien civilisation to us—as alien as ours is to the civilisation of Babylon & Nineveh.

I am surprised to hear that Wright has delayed his report so long, though surely there is no occasion for worry. He is in execrable health, & given to contradictory & unaccountable moods & decisions; but one soon comes to excuse all that in view of his unfailing generosity & punctiliously honourable methods. By this time I trust you have heard from him. I hardly see how his opinion of "The Unchaining" can help being favourable, though he may not be able to suggest any professional market for it just now. It will interest me to see how the "Husband pro Forma" fares under Little Belknap's guidance. He may be able to give it a salable cast, but I still feel that other stories of yours are freer from artificiality & closer to the spirit of artistic creation. "The Return" is very good, & I hope it will ultimately attain publication. As for novel-writing—it would, I suppose, be somewhat more enjoyable than short story writing; but it is infinitely more exacting, & requires a technique & mental tempo markedly different. It is a maturer art, & ought really to come after one has attained considerable experience in the shorter forms. Still, I do not think it would harm your short story technique to try a little of it. Indeed, it would afford some very salutary exercise in the general art of narration & character-delineation. Altogether, it might be well to commence the ministerial novel some time soon; working on it in a leisurely & intermittent way. Novels are harder to market than short stories, but you would not trouble yourself with extravagant hopes the first time.

The autumn hereabouts has, until the last few days, been marked by the most extraordinary mildness; so that I have taken my work almost every day to the primal woods & ancient countryside north of Providence. Now that chilliness has come, I feel quite cramped by my indoor setting.

With best wishes,
Yrs very sincerely,
H P Lovecraft

Notes

1. The story was published under the title "One-Man Girl."
2. I.e., James F. Morton, curator of the Paterson (N.J.) museum.

[36] [ALS]

10 Barnes St.,
Providence, R.I.,
Jany. 22, 1929.

My dear Mrs. Reed:—

Yours of the 13th with enclosed story duly arrived; & I have sent "On the High Places" to Wright, together with a note expressing the hope that he can use it. As I said before, it is just as well to make this use of the tale at present; since that in no way impairs the later fortunes of "The Unchaining" in book form or otherwise. Of course, this special version is not the real story—but its existence does no harm, provided you fully realise its frankly altered-to-order character & its obvious limitations as a piece of spontaneous & homogenously balanced art. Wright's criticism, as quoted by you, is a typical commercial-popular reaction. It was quite absurd, from the point of view of real literature, to complain of the overstressing of Ella's emotional peculiarity, when that thing formed the main theme of the whole story & gave point to the title! I don't think that Belknap fancied the tale was sent to Wright for professional acceptance or rejection; & if he advised the present adaptation it was probably because he interpreted Wright's letter as indicating a receptive attitude on the latter's part. As for the attempted-suicide interpolation—I don't think Belknap could have had any illusions about its aesthetic status, but imagine he inserted it consciously & reluctantly as a sop to the public's undeveloped taste & the typical editor's mania for "action" at any cost. I did not remove it, you will note; but merely wished to warn you that it really violates the sound principles of sincere & authentic art. I am glad you like the altered conclusion & new title of the story—the latter being really necessary in view of the modified subject-matter. There is no fee for this— since no ponderous reconstruction was called for, & since your original fee to Belknap may be considered as covering the job. These added touches are, in effect, incidents in the process of completing Little Belknap's revisory "break-ing in"—you have doubtless seen, on the street-cars, an old motorman "breaking in" a young recruit; yet you have not been asked to pay an extra fare in such cases! In any event, the stamps which you so generously enclosed may well serve as a cancellation of all possible indebtedness to date. My next real bill will come when I deliver the Indian ghost story, a thing I intend to do as soon as I recover enough mental & nervous energy to resume creative work. If all goes well, I hope to be able to get various matters adjusted by spring or summer, so that I can map out a programme with something of the unharassed equilibrium of earlier years—& indeed, I may be able to get at the ghost story much before that season.

Belknap is destined, I think, to make a splendid teacher; & whatever literary advice he offers is certain to be sound. Judging from the samples cited, his reading recommendations are just the thing to give you an enhanced realism of perspective; while I have no doubt but that he urges with equal force a *stylistic* development on your part—that is, an increasing interest in the beauty of language itself as an aesthetic medium, with its rhythms, precise descriptive & atmospheric powers, & artistic proportioning & balancing of phrases, pictures, & ideas. I can see that your outlook on psychology, motivation, & general events is becoming closer to life—& consequently to art—& assume that you are preserving the faculty of scepticism & aloof analysis which you are winning; applying it to your new "brutal" books as well as to the older artificial romances, & realising that as a matter of fact life is seldom as vivid as in *any* novel. The old romances worked with false motivations & artificial values; whereas the new "brutal" narratives take human motives & values more or less as they are, but exaggerate certain elements & proportions for dramatic effect—so that the characters say & do, on the whole, much more extravagant things than is usual in common reality. Actually, life is dominantly a flat, tame affair composed of unrealisable aspirations, endless dull frustrations & futilities, & an overpowering monotony which saps at all values & makes peace & quiet one's only final ambition. To most people, not much of importance ever *happens;* so that the main keynote of human existence is really that of a simply mental unrest & emotional or imaginative conflict. The highest grade of literary artists recognise this, so that their novels tend to be cerebral chronicles in which relatively few objective events occur; but most writers fall below this standard & introduce a heightened emotionalism & greater plenitude of happenings for the sake of the reader's interest. Of course, these things may be admirable in the delineation of individual types of occurrence; but they depart none the less from the real atmospheric keynote of practical existence—frustration & monotony. As for love-scenes—I enclose an article from last June's Harpers which may aid in giving realism to your style.[1] It seems unusually sound & scientific—& its French author understands the difference between his own psychology & the Anglo-Saxon's surprisingly well. This need not be returned, since I am dismembering & discarding all my piles of old magazines. Incidentally—in reading "brutal" books I trust you do not allow yourself to be misled by differing national psychologies. Continentals think & feel very differently from Anglo-Americans, & many of the Continentals differ widely from one another. Foreign books are all right regarding basic human instincts, but are not to be relied on regarding the proportion & manifestation of these instincts. You can't really interpret American life in terms of Schnitzler[2] or de Maupassant, or judge the feelings of a German or a Scandinavian by an Italian novel.

Before I forget it, let me enclose an advertisement of a writers' handbook which came the other day, & which seems to describe something of remarkable merit. I'd almost advise your getting this, for it seems to contain many concrete specimens of extremely instructive calibre. It must be something like that book of analysed & annotated short stories which I have often recommended so highly, but whose exact name I can't recall.

I'll look up tourist information on Japan, China, & India the next time I'm down town—at the moment I'm confined to the house with the last end of a bad cold. I imagine that of the three regions mentioned, Japan would be the most satisfactory to a traveller; since it is both intrinsically & architecturally beautiful in the extreme, & has enough of Western conveniences to make travel easy. China certainly has enough of beauty & tradition, but I imagine that owing to unstable governmental conditions it is less easy to explore than Japan—except in the immediate neighbourhood of the European treaty ports. India has a good Anglo-Saxon administration, hence is admirable for convenient travel; yet I do not seem to gather the same impression of beauty & interest from books & pictures of it that I do from accounts of the Far East. The architecture & scenery are certainly not comparable to those of China & Japan, & I fancy the hot climate would be a deterrent to many— although it would not be for me, since cold & not heat is my implacable climatic enemy. In going to the Far East I think one ought to improve the chance to see as many of the Pacific Islands as possible—certainly Hawaii. I myself would like to see some of the prehistoric cyclopean masonry on some of the less known islands—notably Ponape in the Carolines—which is probably a relique surviving from a forgotten civilisation that flourished aeons ago when much more land was above the waves than at present. All these stone remains link up curiously with the colossal stone images of Easter Island.

I myself did some travelling early this month, albeit in my vastly humbler & more local way! Samuel Loveman decided to begin the year with a business tour of New England bookshops, & I took the opportunity to guide him among some of my favourite antiquities. His time in Providence was limited, so that most of the sightseeing here had to be done by electric light; but I accompanied him when he marched onward to Boston, & spared no pains to initiate him into the archaic mysteries of the Novanglian metropolis. We stopped at the venerable United States Hotel in Beach St., which was built in 1826, & was once the temporary home of Daniel Webster. Here, too, Charles Sumner once entertained Dickens. With such an headquarters, the rest of the antiquities came naturally. I shewed Loveman the historic old South Church, the old State House built in 1713 as a market, the ancient (1723) Christ Church (erroneously called the Old North) where Paul Revere's celebrated signal lanterns were displayed, the Georgian magnificence of King's Chapel (1749) with its hoary churchyard, the magnificently preserved Georgian streets of Beacon Hill, the hellish & crumbling North End which formed the scene of my "Pickman's Model," & many another characteristic sight— including sedate, quiet old Cambridge, with the centuried brick halls of Harvard Yard. I enclose a few of my inevitable postcard views. The one shewing the Common & Beacon Hill is especially typical of Boston, insomuch as it gives an idea of the city's refreshingly traditional skyline, kept free from skyscrapers & modernistic towers by a rigid zoning law. The church at the extreme right, at the bottom of the hill, is the graceful old Park St. church, built in 1816; whilst the golden-domed edifice crowning the crest on the left is the famous new (1795) State House, whose glittering dome is popularly held to be the Hub of the Universe.[3] The Common itself, shewn in the foreground, is one of the most celebrated & historic spots in America. We also visited the Museum of Fine Arts; where, as may be imagined, Loveman went wild over the Greek sculpture & vases, whilst I experienced corresponding ecstasies at the newly opened wing of decorative arts, which contains the largest & choicest array of typical furnished interiors (European & American, ranging from an authentic panelled Tudor room of 1490 to a McIntyre[4] interior of 1805) in the United States. But on the final day of our Massachusetts sojourn the real climax came—in the form of a trip to those twin Meccas of my fancy, witch-haunted *Salem* & incredibly ancient *Marblehead*. Time was limited, so I could shew Loveman only the "high spots", but we managed to make a fairly representative & infinitely colourful itinerary. At Salem we went through the Hawthornian "House of the Seven Gables," (the Turner–Ingersoll house, built circa 1650) saw Hawthorne's birthplace & the "Old Witch House", traversed stately Chestnut St., (conceded to be the finest Georgian street in the U.S.) & picked up atmosphere generally. Then we took the trolley to Marblehead—& left the present age altogether behind us! I have told of the charm of Marblehead in *summer,* but that is only half of the magic one finds in *winter*—when all the frivolous vacationists are out of sight, & all the silly modern gift "shoppes" closed! It is then that the ancient, unbroken life of centuries comes to the surface, & one sees the real fishing village of old, peopled by none whose fathers have not dwelt there 200 years & more. How shall I describe the fascination of the little climbing lanes & the archaic fanlighted doorways, & the alluring lines & clusters of mellow gambrel roofs & crumbling chimneys? It can't be done! All I can do is to enclose a few more of my perennial postcards & let it go at that! Incidentally—I'll add an old Providence inn-yard drawing which occurs on the cover of an art exhibition catalogue & rather well typifies the spirit of our ancient hill. ¶ Glad to hear that Iacobus Parvulus liked the card. I shall certainly appreciate his epistle when it arrives, & hope my reply thereto may not bore him! ¶ With best wishes—Yrs Sincerely, H P Lovecraft

P.S. I'll discuss "On the High Places" with Belknap the next time I write him. He'll be glad to have an added opinion on it.

Notes

1. André Maurois (tr. Henry Longan Stuart), "Past and Future of Love," *Harper's Magazine* No. 157 (June 1928): 69–74.
2. Arthur Schnitzler (1862–1931), Austrian dramatist and novelist, notorious for his frank descriptions of sexuality.
3. See EB 5n5.
4. Samuel McIntire (1757–1811), American architect who designed many Federal-style buildings in New England.

[37]   [ALS]

10 Barnes St.,
Providence, R.I.,
March 4, 1929.

My dear Mrs. Reed:—

I duly received yours of 17th ult., & was sorry to learn that "On the High Places" had been rejected. That circumstance, however, was not so great a surprise as it would have been in the case of "Yig"; since as I said in a former letter, no tale can be inwardly & convincingly weird unless it is written so in the first place. Only this—or a re-writing thorough enough to amount to the same thing—will give the text as a whole that brooding atmospheric quality which paves the way for the climax & makes the unearthly element seem, for the time being, natural & inevitable. I had hoped Wright would not be acute enough to recognise this lack of homogeneity in the altered MS., for heaven knows he can be obtuse to a record-breaking degree at times! Unfortunately he did catch the jarring note, as his comment proves. However, the process of adaptation has not been without its educational value—illustrating as it has so many stages & conditions of literary construction—hence I do not think you need view the matter with unqualified regret. You might try the MS. on that wretched Macfadden thing—*Ghost Stories*—if it is still issued.[1] I haven't the Macfadden address at hand, but you can no doubt find it in some current authors' magazine. Meanwhile, of course, the original "Unchaining" still exists in reserve for later use. That is a far finer tale than any artificially altered version could be, & ought to find a typographical haven some day, when your entree to the magazine press becomes more complete.

I was especially able to appreciate your anecdote of my small grandchild's transient fit of petulance, because it came almost simultaneously with a letter from the child himself, in which he quite similarly sputtered over the alleged stupidity of his aged grandpa & of the universe in general! This latest attack was due to a somewhat belated letter of criticism from me, concerning those points of revision in "On the High Places" which I mentioned to you last December. It seems that you were wiser than I in advising that the second revision be not mentioned to Sonny, & I really must apologise (that is, I must if the incident has earned you as sharp a letter from the little rascal as it earned the Old Gentleman!) for the grandfatherly solicitude which made me anxious to have him reap the benefit of my suggestions. For in all truth, & most unexpectedly to me, my youthful colleague really was rather nettled at the thought that his emendation of the tale had not been final; a feeling which was increased when I told him of the Wrightian rejection. By now, however, I feel sure that the juvenile wrath has somewhat subsided; insomuch as a good part of it was based on sheer misapprehension. I am inclined to think that Sonny didn't read all his grandpa's letter of criticism—perhaps rage choked off his assimilative power—for when writing me he laboured under *the mistaken notion that I had removed the near-suicide incident,* which of course I did *not* do, although I violently objected to it as bad art, & uttered my objection to Belknap as I did to you. What especially galled him in my criticism was *the fact that he perfectly agreed with it,* & that he detested the melodramatic interpolation as heartily as I did. As I half-thought, he inserted it against his own will & artistic judgment, acting on the suggestions in Wright's letter as he interpreted them. He did it solely to improve the story's chances of professional acceptance—& after such an heroic procedure it was only natural that he became provoked when he thought I had removed the passage & perhaps destroyed the sale of the story. I don't blame the blessed lambkin a bit for thinking his meddlesome old grandpa an unqualified idiot, for I would have been had I removed the passage without substituting some carefully evolved bit of equivalent sensation or action. The only point is that I *didn't* remove it—& when Sonny re-reads my letter & the MS. of the tale itself (which I have now sent him) he will regret having prematurely exploded. Misapprehensions, though, seem to have been general all around—beginning with Wright. When I sent "The Unchaining" to him in the beginning—before its revision—I *specifically told him* that it was **not** submitted for professional consideration, but merely for his friendly personal opinion. Evidently he did not read my letter, for Belknap informs me that the long letter of advice which he wrote you about the tale (& which I have not seen) was distinctly a professional rejection. I recall now that, after receiving this letter from Wright, you asked me whether I was sure he understood the story was *not* sent for acceptance or rejection. I *was* sure, or *thought* I was, because I had been very careful to make the matter clear in my note accompanying the tale; but it seems that he did not heed what I said, (or that he forgot it) & that he wrote his advice under the impression that the story was designed for the magazine. From this error on Wright's part—which is very difficult for me to understand—came the suggestion which prompted the preparation of the altered version. Sonny took Wright's advice very seriously & carefully, & did his best to answer the specifications even when they went against his sense of aesthetics. Therefore I don't blame him for resenting his grandpa's tirade against that extraneous bit of "hokum."

[*Balance missing.*]

Notes

1. *Ghost Stories* (1926–32), a pulp magazine that featured confession-style weird tales. It was published by Constructive Publishing Co., a company operated by Bernarr Macfadden.

[38]   [ALS]

[H. P. LOVECRAFT
10 BARNES STREET
PROVIDENCE, R. I.]

March 7[, 1929]

My dear Mrs. Reed:—

I can't resist enclosing the inevitable & expected "follow-up" message from Grandpa's Precious! Bless his little heart, but he means to be a good boy! And surely Grandpa must pardon his irritation when he retracts it so naively & officially, signed & sealed with the family arms! No doubt he has sent you a similar apology—that is, if he previously wrote you anything to occasion it. Needless to say, I am assuring him that no shadow of harshness or resentment ever crossed my aged mind!

Best wishes—
Hastily—
H P Lovecraft

[Enclosure]

[Postmarked New York, N.Y.,
Mar. 4 1929]

Dear Howard:

Just a line to assure you that I have permitted it to "sink in" that you did not omit the disputed incident! But even if you had excised it my letter was an inexcusable performance. Please ascribe my momentary irritability to post-flu depression. The entire affair did not justify so much hectic excitement, and I made *several chains* of mountains out of an anthill.

I shall return commonplace book, and write at length soon.

As ever,
Francis Lord Belknap

Pieux quoique preux[1]

Have just finished *Primitive Hearths in the Pyrenees*—a gorgeous account of exploration in haunts of the Aurignacians, Magdalenians and Azilliars[.]

[*P.S. on envelope:*] Visited Mac last week. He read me opening chapter of his new book re Cortes and the Aztecs[.]

Notes

1. The Long family crest. The motto means "Pious though valiant."

[39] [AHT]

10 Barnes St.,

Providence R. I.,

March 20, 1929

My dear Mrs. Reed:—

Let me hasten to assure you that my recent observations on commercial anchors for literary aesthetes were *not* designed to apply to you as well as to my small grandchild Belknap! I am not much given to inter-linear suggestions, and in the present case I thought I had made it clear that I was speaking of poets and other artists for art's sake whose serious work is never—even in its ultimate perfection—likely to be of commercial advantage. This leaves you out entirely, since your chosen field is one in which you have many chances of striking the popular fancy and reaping the rewards thereof; but it does apply both to Belknap and to myself, whose aesthetic ambitions alike follow channels where the material rewards are meagre to the point of nothingness. In other words, what you spontaneously wish to do is some-thing potentially remunerative, so that you can throw all your emotional ener-gies toward what may be a paying goal; whereas in Belknap's case and in my own case, all serious creative emotion is tightly bound up in non-paying direc-tions, so that we have to face the commercial problem—whether it be a branch of writing or something totally different—coldly and reluctantly, and without the driving force which goes with real enthusiasm. On this account, it makes very little difference to our aesthetic lives what we do for a living, since both hack-work (whether original or revision) in literature and business out-side literature are equally remote from the type of vision-seeing and vision-recording which to us means life and creation and serious self-expression. With us—and with me perhaps even more than with Sonny—the chance of producing anything profitable in the course of serious artistic work is so slim as to be almost negligible; whereas you, on the other hand, appear to resem-ble that more fortunate group (like Booth Tarkington or Sinclair Lewis) whose serious interests happen to come closer to the popular (and therefore remunerative) field. Not, of course, that any writer's future can be predicted with certainty—for chance plays a tremendous part in commercial success, and thousands of diverse and intangible factors determine which of many equally qualified (or unqualified) authors shall come to the surface as a "hit" or best-seller. Merit has something, but not a great deal, to do with it; the cru-cial essence of popularity being rather some subtle and unconscious mental sympathy or understanding between the author and the type of public for whom he writes. A superlatively great artist—that is, one of a calibre far beyond anything which our "gang" is likely to develop—can always get a hearing, a little appreciation, and possibly a little money, even if he does not suit the general public; but he cannot reasonably expect more. On the other hand, the veriest idiot and ignoramus can sometimes bring down fame on a luckshot, as the cases of Edgar A. Guest, Edgar Rice Burroughs, Harold Bell Wright, and many others show. Usually, though, the successful commercial writer (outside the dime-novel class) stands somewhere midway in merit—with a moderate cleverness of thought and a fairly glib technical assurance; the technical skill being perhaps the more necessary of these two qualities. What really determines his success is a third and wholly different thing—an unexplainable and imponderable rapport with the mental and emotional processes of the larger reading public—which has no relation to literary skill and which is found equally among the greatest geniuses and the dullest dolts. Of the three major factors—literary inspiration, literary technique, and popular sympathy—none can be wholly absent in a successful author; although many do "get by" on a very small modicum of the first-named, whilst the use of revision and collaboration enables others to succeed without the factor of technique. But when popular sympathy is slight or nonexistent—as it is with Belknap and me—there is no use expecting more than the meagrest material profit except through rare accident. Either of us could view the future more comfortably if sure of modest positions as bank-clerks, accountants, or something like that. I am old enough to see this fact clearly, and to regret that I did not provide a safeguard for myself when I was younger; but Sonny has not yet reached the stage of disillusion at which the wish for security outweighs the natural horror of an artist for settled prosaic bondage. That is the difference between youth and middle age—when a man passes over that intangible mental line he has undergone the greatest psychological climacteric since the earlier loss of his fantastic childhood world. Of course, no artist ever passes over so completely that he is willing to relinquish his art altogether. For my part, I wouldn't even now consider anything which would subtract mental energy from creation or leave me totally and permanently without time for aesthetic writing. What the aging artist is willing to concede to the world is not his brain or major aspiration, but his brawn, his good faith, and a reasonable though limited portion of his time and attention. When he has to give more in order to survive, the mere circumstance of survival becomes worthless; so that the revolver or the laudanum-bottle becomes the appropriate solution.

With Belknap, therefore, the question is not one of giving up his sincere artistic creation—for no one would ask him to do that—but of exchanging the thankless labour of revision and hack-writing for the scarcely less truly literary field of non-auctorial commerce. The change is not so great as it

sounds; for he has as little time for art while revising or writing stories to order, as he would if he worked in a bank or office. Believe me—I know! . . . .
for revision hasn't left me with enough time or energy to write anything of
my own since last August![1] Therefore I am urging him to accept any necessary change as something far from bad in itself, although of course it is not so
pleasant to contemplate as absolute creative leisure would be. Personally, I
would jump with almost indecent avidity at any really steady job short of the
absolutely ridiculous, artistically destructive, or conspicuously humiliating—
for I know that if given the chance I could earn a far more dependable wage
in that manner than by putting the same amount of time and energy (or rather, a *greater* amount of both!) into the nerve-draining and ill-paying ordeal of
revision. The only way to make a good thing of revision is to discard conscientiousness and adopt an Uzzellian charlatanism—but unfortunately both
Sonny and his grandpa are too full of old-fashioned inhibitions and code-
loyalties to prosper at that game! Calculative business, confound it, is no place
for a gentleman. Whether it would be better in the end for Belknap to develop his revisory-pedagogical activities slowly and solidly, or to try something
altogether different, is a point very hard for anyone but himself to decide. I
myself would choose the altogether-different, but it is of course possible that
he has a greater aptitude than I in the revisory-pedagogical field. I know that
it does not take him as long as it takes me to prepare a manuscript, and he is
seemingly less exhausted by the application. Moreover, he has indications of
being a more successful instructor than I. Since he has only been at revision a
year, I would naturally advocate letting him try it a year or two more before
turning to something else; but his father—being totally outside the literary
field and bunching all the years of literary struggle together without separating
the seven or eight years of story-writing from the single year of revisory
work—has an equally strong impression that writing has been given a sufficient trial, and that the child ought to begin to get entrenched in something
solid for his own future good. The thought of one's son in actual want—and
totally unfitted to cope with the world—long after one is dead is not a pleasant one; and I can thoroughly understand the fears and feelings of Dr. Long,
for whom I have a vast liking and respect. It is hard to say what the future
holds, and very conceivably some gradual compromise or adjustment may be
made; but meanwhile I try to reduce Belknap's anxiety and sense of frustration by assuring him that commerce can't be so *very* much worse than revision
and hack-writing, even if these latter things are easier for him than for me. Of
course, the strident arena of competitive business would be a fearsomely incongruous place for a sheltered and naturally home-keeping and unworldly
boy like Sonny; but if the change were necessary, it seems as though there
might be fairly quiet niches open to one who would never expect to specialise
in business or do more than eke along in a very modest manner. When age

tones down some of his youthful tastes—as for new suits, cigarettes, plush hats, and carved dog-headed canes—he will find that business need not mean a frantic attempt to chase extra cash above all else. A modest clerkly salary will go a long way with a person whose tastes are quiet either naturally or through cultivation—I myself scarcely ever spend more than fifteen dollars a week including room rent and food—except of course when I kick over the traces and "blow in" a cheque on antiquarian travel regardless of consequences—yet twenty years ago, before hereditary prospects exploded, my serenely careless extravagance would have made Belknap's present programme look like Coolidge economy. What the old man learned without acquiring permanent melancholy, the young man can learn when necessity impels. Adjustment has its pangs, but is eminently worth while in the end; hence I don't think that Sonny's future prospects need be regarded as exactly stark tragedy. Still—they must seem that way to him now, so that he needs all the encouragement and all the constructive suggestions which older, soberer people can give him. My own share is to cheer him up, show him that commerce can't be worse than revision, congratulate him on his youth while urging him to improve its opportunities, and keep reiterating the sage and ancient advice not to do as I *do,* but to do as I *say.*

This, however, is rambling a long way from my original point—that my reference to a non-popular author's need for other sources of income was most emphatically not meant to apply in your case. While no one ought to count absolutely on any future prospect—so complex are the factors of existence and so great is the function of chance—I see nothing in your progress to date which would imply the advisability of discontinuance. It appears to me that you have a very good encouraging foundation on which to build, and my advice today would be the same as in the past—to put all energies into the *twin* fields of *accurate life-knowledge* and *subtle language-mastery;* substituting for a romantic interest in a limited field of outward human actions a profound curiosity to get at the roots of conduct and events and to detect hidden rhythms, ironies, and inclusive truths behind the external mask—this, and a carefully cultivated love of *the art of written expression for its own sake,* involving a passionate interest in words and phrases and cadences at least three-quarters as great as your interest in what you write about. Cultivate *accuracy, profundity,* and *scholarship*—remembering that the popular tastes and perspectives are all false things of the surface unworthy of a sober thinker's attention, and that the proportionate importance of the different factors in life is never even approximated by romantic popular literature with its artificial, catchpenny standards based on the dull comprehension of the brainless majority. Learn to lose interest in the tawdry and tinsel things exalted by cheap novelists, and to gain interest in the only two things worthy of a high-grade adult mind—*truth and beauty,* as exemplified by a searching and unbiassed glance into the real nature and proportions of life, and a single-minded devotion to the processes, harmonies, and niceties of art as practiced only for its own sake. Substitute the specific for the general, the scholarly for the careless, the accurate for the inexact, the true for the pleasant or conventional, the analytical for the empirical, the serious for the trivial, the painstaking for the casual, the conscientious for the dashing, the objective for the subjective, the impersonal for the personal, the gradual for the sudden, the profound for the swift, the effacing for the ambitious, the unworldly for the worldly, the settled for the restless, the relentless for the ennuied, the patient for the impatient, the sceptical for the credulous, the ironic for the romantic, the calm for the excitable, the deliberate for the random, the sharp for the blurred, the conscious (in *craftsmanship only,* however) for the unconscious and haphazard, the well-planned for the vague—and so on and so on. Readjustment of interests and perspectives and standards is the idea—readjustments which will subordinate the superficial and bring to the fore in most artistically available form the driving energy which makes you wish to write at all. Make the goal that of *satisfied curiosity and perfect achievement*—that is, choose as the only suitable aim in life the feat of spying out truth so far as it can be spied, and of pinning it down to paper in the most vivid and beautiful of all possible forms. Adopt the goal envisaged by James Branch Cabell—"to write perfectly of beautiful happenings"—and in doing so be sure to select happenings which are *truly* beautiful and significant and true, rather than those which popular literature and uncultivated taste assume to be beautiful and significant and true. Beware of hasty surface beliefs and standards and judgments. If you are told that a certain thing is true or beautiful or important, ask *why* it is so, or why your informant thinks it is so—whether your informant be a book or life itself as seen at first-hand. Let all your interest and enthusiasm go into the process of selecting the true and significant from the false and irrelevant, and of crystallising your selection in the most perfect language and imagery which art can provide. There is a goal worthy of an indomitable driving-power. Read, read, read, and read—endlessly! Science, history, philosophy—you are helpless as a serious author without such aids to a sense of reality and proportion. Not merely quack psychology as Uzzell would recommend, but the general background of knowledge against which all life has to be scaled and analysed. See how constantly Belknap reflects such a working-fund of necessary facts—as when in his ending to the altered "Unchaining" he spoke of Trivil ape-men and so on. A decent stock of information is not hard to obtain—things like Wells's "Outline of History", Thomson's "Outline of Science", or Durant's "Story of Philosophy" are a marvellous help. The important thing is to *understand, assimilate, and correlate*—to bring the general background of facts into so usable a part of the subconscious that it can condition your daily views and judgments of life. Often a beginner has all the requisite knowledge to start with, and needs only to learn how to correlate it and apply it to the task in hand. And of course *literary* training must go on by the side of this. Language as an art and source of intrinsic delight must be constantly worshipped, both in form and in spirit. Different modes of thought and presentation, imagery and tone-colour, must be perceived and mastered until their command becomes second-nature. One must learn to think and talk in symbols as well as in factual statements—a thing which demands poetic as well as prose scholarship. No one should attempt to write prose without studying poetry and writing a certain amount of it for practice in the imagery and rhythms involved. All good language is rhythm—and only through the study of poetry can we learn how to cast and modulate it. I have always congratulated myself that I first started Belknap writing poetry—a thing which has been of incalculable benefit to every phase of his art. And all the while one must read, read, read—and *analyse* what one reads, not only in ideas but in *language*. When a particular image or passage strikes you with extraordinary force, stop and inquire *why* it does so— why the *idea* is significant, and why the *language* is significant, and how much the visible significance of the idea owes to the cast and rhythm of the language. Write out the same idea in your own words, probing for the secrets of expression. Then go back and write out a different but parallel idea in language as close as possible to that in the book. Search, search, search—curiously, relentlessly, slowly, intelligently, and indefatigably—for the fascinating secret of language; the cryptical, complex, marvellous relationship betwixt ideas and images and the verbal medium through which they reach the reader. Cast aside all interests and ambitions in life save this one alone—"to write perfectly of beautiful (and significant) happenings." Get all your driving force and restlessness into one deep channel and steer it faithfully and enthusiastically—that is the way to make it take you somewhere! Authorship is not a careless overnight job, but a lifetime engrossment needing absolute devotion and years of apprenticeship. And yet, if one have a strong and unmistakable urge toward it, it is abundantly worth while—worth while because it is the only thing which will ever bring peace and satisfaction to the authentic possessor of such an urge. Whether such an urge is a blessing or a curse, only the blind, bland and bodiless Mana-Yood-Sushāī, whose idle dreams the gods are, knows—and Mana-Yood-Sushāī speaks never to man, nor to the gods whereof he dreams.[2]

Best wishes

Yrs sincerely,

H P Lovecraft.

Notes

1. HPL completed "The Dunwich Horror" in August 1928. He would not begin another story until February 1930, when he started writing "The Whisperer in Darkness."

2. Mana-Yood-Sushāī is the chief of the gods of Pegāna in the writings of Lord Dunsany.

[40]   [ALS]

10 Barnes St., Providence.
March 29, 1929.

My dear Mrs. Reed:—

Bless my soul, but Grandpa's Boy never told any of these wistful sentimental reminiscences to the Old Gentleman! What strange arcana of a long-dead past are coming to the light of day! Ah, me, but it is indeed a token of the sunset years when one's very tiniest grandchildren look back through a haze of romance at *their* departed youth. Sonny always did want to be grown up—I recall a bygone meeting up at George Kirk's old room in West 106th St., when the child was just 22 years of age. We were discussing our reactions to Swinburne; & after the grey-bearded element had delivered itself of its dicta, there came a sage & thoughtful verdict from our grave little infant colleague—who had some fifteen less pounds in his weight, & some 5⅛ fewer down-wisps in his even-then-cherished moustachelet, than he has now. *"When I was a young man,"* began Sonny, "I considered Swinburne . . . . . ." but I have forgotten the rest! Probably it was drowned out by the general chorus of laughter from the cracked throats of the senile majority. At any rate, we were given to understand by our young friend that he considered his best & most fruitful years as long departed, & coloured with all the glamour of remote memory. I'll send you a snapshot of the precious imp as he used to look when I can find one amidst my chaotic files—or possibly you noted many such reliquiae last year in the maternal gallery at 230 W. 97. Well, anyway, it's a wonder to me that the 28-year-old charmer of that long-vanished time could resist kidnapping the blessed child & adopting him! In those days he was turning from a scientist—a butterfly-collector & natural history authority in general—to an aesthete, & producing such promising masterpieces as "A Cagliostro of the Northland", "Dr. Whitlock's Price", & "The Box of Horror."[1] It was the "Whitlock" tale which so impressed me with his remarkable potentialities.

No—I won't mention any other MS. which may reach me for critical consideration, though I doubt if Sonny's pique about the "Unchaining" business is as deep as you imagine. What really galled the child was his mistaken notion that I had removed the near-suicide incident & thereby wrecked a sale to Wright. His recent suggestion about the weird sketch was probably made in good faith—though of course it can't help pleasing him subtly to have such confidence expressed in his work. That surely ought to erase any sense of unpleasantness which may have developed over the recent incident. Glad you are able to keep his fees well paid up—prompt & regular cheques will be a good argument to convince Longus Pater that there may be something in this revision game after all! Belknap's collaboration in the novel will certainly be worth the price—& much more. Yes—I'd be glad to look over the opening chapters later on, though in work of a modern vein I don't pretend to compete with Sonny. He, by the way, seems to have picked up something of your style. He has just sent his Grandpa a new tale to look over—a light contemporary piece aimed at the popular market—& were it not for his statement I'd think it one of yours! All I criticised in it was his lack of differentiation of the characters—he made them all use the language & sentiments of a smartly cynical & ironic arm-chair man of the world—in other words, they were all disillusioned & prematurely middle-aged Little Belknaps!

Glad to hear that the Gemini are prospering—but Lud, I vow those examination weeks come around as unbelievably swiftly as an old man's birthdays! But no doubt the present victims, aided by their other instructions, are able to dance away their troubles. I could never be made to take dancing-lessons despite the direst threats & most frantic entreaties of a fond mother these thirty years & more ago. Thus I have grown into a stiff, awkward, & uncouth old age, though I can't truthfully say that the deficiency worries me exceedingly. I don't think Belknap dances either—though whether his infantile resistance to instruction was as complete as mine, I am not sure. But dancing is a good accomplishment to have, if it comes naturally; & as an aged philosopher I no longer have the tendency to quote, as I did in my more formal & dignified youth, the hackneyed Ciceronian precept—"Nemo fere saltat sobrius, nisi forte insanit."[2]

What Wright has done with "Yig" is more than I can say—for I long ago gave the Farnsworthian mentality up as one of those ultimate cosmic mysteries between us & which the principle of the quantum theory sets an eternally impassible barrier! All I can say is that I know he is honest & well-meaning in every way, & that he will certainly publish the story in the end at the full price agreed upon.

I may see Little Belknap before another fortnight is over, for the pleas of my friend Orton that I visit him have taken on a pathetic insistence & impatience too complimentary for elderly vanity to resist. Orton is in Yonkers, on the northern metropolitan rim, but I fancy I shall beat quite a path between there & 230 W. 97th. Too bad these congenial gangsters can't leave the decadent miasmata of neo-Babylon & take up an abode in a civilised country like Rhode Island!

With best wishes, I remain

Yr most obt Servt

H P Lovecraft

Notes

1. Frank Belknap Long, "Dr. Whitlock's Price" (*United Amateur,* March 1920). The other two stories appear to be unpublished and are probably now nonextant.

2. "Scarcely any sober person dances, unless by chance he is insane." From Cicero's *Pro Mureno* 13. HPL claims that he spoke this line to his mother when he was eight years old, as she was seeking to enroll him in a children's dance class. See *Letters to Rheinhart Kleiner and Others* 66.

[41]   [AHT]

10 Barnes St.,

Providence, R.I.,

June 3, 1929

My dear Mrs. Reed:—

[. . .] After my two weeks with Orton—whose Yonkers farm is so rural and unspoiled that one can scarcely believe it is on the threshold of Manhattan—I spent a week in that latter abyss itself as the guest of my small grandchild Belknap. During this period I saw most of the old "gang", and was pained to witness the seizure of good old Everett McNeil (whose books I believe you said young Iacobus had read) with a severe illness, based on dietetic errors of long standing, which is still confining him to the hospital. I enjoyed many motor trips with Belknap and his parents, and indulged in the usual aesthetic, philosophic, and scientific discussions with the child. He is flourishing in his accustomed way—with perhaps a pound or two more of avoirdupois, and an extra down-wisp or two in the moustachelet. A woolly and rather lethargic Scotch-terrier has been added to the House of Long, and is the idol of the young heir—but I, with my inveterate catly preferences, remain a faithful devotee of tawny, regal Felis. [. . .]

[. . .] Richmond is a place I have always wished to see and absorb, and I lingered several days amidst its reliques of former times. This was the real "home town" of my idol and model Poe, and I missed none of the places with which he was associated—both during his youth with the Allan household, and in his later period as editor of the *Southern Literary Messenger.* An old house—the oldest in Richmond—has been fitted up with reliques and mementoes as a "Poe Shrine", and I spent a very contemplative two hours amongst its contents. Nor did I neglect the city's other attractions—the old State House built in 1792 from Jefferson's designs, the 1813 Governor's Mansion, the ancient church and churchyard of St. John's, the Confederate White House where Pres. Davis resided, the homes of John Marshall, Genl. Lee, and other eminent characters, and the many scenic vistas afforded by the bluffs above the yellow James—especially Gamble Hill, which was visited in 1607 by Capt. John Smith. One day I extended my frontier still farther south by making an historical excursion to Jamestown, Williamsburg, and Yorktown. Jamestown, though now deserted and harbouring only a ruined church tower, (with church restored) a few ruined walls, and some crumbling foundation-stones, was perhaps the most impressive spot on which I have ever stood—the cradle of English civilisation on this continent, and the genesis of that Virginian culture which forms the high-water mark of social development in the western world. As a feast for the eye, Williamsburg offered the most; for here was a perfectly preserved Colonial town—the former capital of the colony—with all the surviving earmarks of the 18th century life. Financed by the younger Rockefeller,[1] the restoration of Williamsburg to its complete pre-revolutionary state is now going on; so that in a few years it will be even more of an antiquarian delight than it is at present. The original building of William and Mary College in this place, erected in 1698, is the only structure in America designed personally by Sir Christopher Wren. It has survived the centuries well, and is now being restored to its precise pristine condition. The town as a whole centres in one immensely broad street—Duke of Gloucester St.—with a strip of greenery down the middle. Throughout its extent vivid reminders of colonial times are thickly scattered. Yorktown is a typical southern village of the sleepier type—to me a very melancholy spot because of the surrender on the part of His Majesty's forces which took place there in the autumn of 1781. It is little changed since that time, and reflects the 18th century with as keen fidelity as Williamsburg. The York River which flows nearby is of a clear blue—a singular rarity in a region where most of the streams are yellow from the prevailing clay of the soil. After my tour of the peninsula I proceeded north to Fredericksburg, the boyhood environment of Gen. Washington. Here is another fascinating 18th century town with reminders of royalist times—the main thoroughfare being Princess Anne St. I threaded the sleepy lanes of this place with the utmost appreciation and delight; visiting the splendid Georgian mansion of Kenmore (built by Gen. Washington's brother-in-law) the home and tomb of Gen. Washington's mother, the ancient Rising Sun Tavern, the law-office of James Monroe, and countless other objects of interest. I also crossed the wide and shallow Rappahannock to the curious and still older hamlet of Falmouth. Fredericksburg dates from 1727—Falmouth from 1720. The next point on my route was Washington, of which I am always very fond, and where I explored numerous galleries and museums. The prehistoric Easter Island colossi in the Smithsonian Institution formed one of the most imaginatively stimulating sights I have ever encountered. After Washington came my other favourite town of Philadelphia, where I went my usual colonial rounds and likewise visited the new art museum at the end of the parkway. This latter is positively the most impressive piece of contemporary architecture I have ever beheld—a magnificent Grecian temple of tinted marble on an Acropolis-like height, approached up broad flights of steps flanked by artificial waterfalls. Its wings enclose a vast tessellated courtyard with a central fountain. The interior is not yet completed, but even now contains some notable material—especially a chain of English Georgian and Colonial rooms, the latter including the only

Pennsylvania-German specimens I have ever seen. From Philadelphia I reluctantly approached New York again—but did not pause at all, since the Longs gave me a delightful motor lift on my up-river course. My design was to proceed to ancient Kingston, at the foot of the Catskills, and absorb the historic colour of the region whilst visiting a friend there—the artist-fantaisiste Bernard Austin Dwyer. All developed as planned, and I had a truly delightful time. Kingston—founded by the Dutch in 1658 and once called Wiltwyck—is a splendidly stately and reposeful place, full of the old stone houses built between the years 1660 and 1730. It was burnt by His Majesty's forces in October 1777, only one house (still standing) being spared; but the stonework and heavy beams of the houses prevented total destruction. At that time the N.Y. State Senate met there—the capital (then N.Y. City) being in the hands of the royal troops. I did Kingston very thoroughly, and also explored two very famous neighbour-villages, Hurley and New Paltz. Hurley, founded in 1660, is an absolutely unchanged bit of the old Dutch civilisation—surviving just as it was about 1700; stone houses, spreading fields, original families, local customs, and all. Dreaming against its purple mountain backdrop, it has defied time altogether; and a visiting Dutch diplomat not long ago declared that it is more truly Dutch than anything left today in Holland itself. Only the language is English. In the old days Hurley was famous for its cheeses, and many an old Dutch jingle about them existed in the vast fund of colonial Hudson Valley folklore. It was to Hurley that the rebel colonists and State senate fled in 1777 when Kingston was burnt. New Paltz, founded in 1677, was originally a French Huguenot settlement; and most of the present inhabitants are descended from the founders. It is apart from the world in the peaceful Shawangunk Valley, about 16 miles south of Kingston. It is a larger and busier place than Hurley, but fortunately the newer parts lie on a hill some distance from the original settlement; so that the straggling stone houses of the pioneers (average date 1700) still remain much as they were. The abodes of these old-time Frenchmen are highly distinctive, though generally following early Dutch designs. Architecture in this region kept its primitive characteristics long after the Dutchmen of southern New York developed such later features as the gambrel, the curved roof-line, and the porch; so that the atmosphere here is far different from that of any other Dutch district I have visited. New Paltz has experienced two changes of language and custom—French to Dutch, and Dutch to English—the first between 1730 and 1750, and the second between 1790 and 1810. The first change was bitterly fought by the elders of the place; and there is an amusing anecdote of a child sent to a neighbour's to borrow some bread, and refused the desired commodity because she could not ask for it in French! Another sidelight is the will of the schoolmaster Jean Tebenin, who died in 1730, leaving his French Bible to the church with the provision that it be sold for the benefit of the poor whenever French should cease to be spoken in the village.

Having glutted myself upon Dutch and Huguenot antiquities, I ascended to Albany and crossed the Berkshires to the well-loved fields of my own New England—to the rolling hills, stone walls, narrow, winding roads, white farm-house gables, pine-girt lakelets, and embowered village steeples of my heredi-tary soil. It was good to be back—and I celebrated my return by dropping in on W. Paul Cool at Athol, Mass. before taking the final leap to Providence. Cook has a farm for the summer, so I was treated to an intensive bit of primi-tive Novanglian life—and I also saw the young *Weird Tales* author H. Warner Munn. Before I left, Cook took me up to Brattleboro in his car, so that I had a glimpse of the exquisite Vermont countryside which so enthralled me in 1927 and 1928. Then at last my host motored me down to *Providence*—the sight of whose sunlit spires and domes from a distant hill gave me the most poignant thrill I had experienced since leaving them nearly two months pre-viously! It was a great trip, and a marvellous enrichment to my imagination; yet I was glad to be back—for Providence is exquisite in the late spring. Now, after a grim tussle with accumulated mail and magazines, I am beginning to pick up the threads of vulgar industry again. [. . .]

Yr Obt hble Servt

H P Lovecraft

Notes

1. The restoration of colonial Williamsburg was largely funded by John D. Rockefel-ler, Jr. (1874–1960) and his wife, Abby Aldrich Rockefeller (1874–1948).

[42]   [AHT]

10 Barnes St.

Providence, R.I.,

August 25, 1929

My dear Mrs. Reed:—

I recd. your note some time ago, and would have acknowledged it sooner but for a seething vortex of work—a textbook on poetic appreciation which had to be in shape for the author before the open-ing of the school year.[1] I regret to hear of the illness in your family which has kept you so busy, and hope that by this time your sister is fully recovered.

Meanwhile my small Belknap-child is worrying his little moustachelet in-to a drooping decline over your impression that his revision devitalised your novel! It's none of my official business, of course; but I really must say that—judging from various sections in both versions which the child has shewn me—I get a totally opposite impression. The fact is, that had I been revising the book myself, I would undoubtedly have made even greater changes than

he did in the same direction . . . . and I say this in complete artistic impartiality, unbiassed by the sentiments of a doting grandparent! In fact, I even scold-
ed Sonny once or twice for not revising with sufficient thoroughness when he
sent certain sections for my opinion. It is my opinion that the reviser serves
best when he gives the text the *absolutely best form possible,* no matter how much
he has to alter the wording. Belknap, on the other hand, feels it to be a sort of
duty to stick to the original copy as closely as he can. Such being our difference in belief, it quite astonished me to learn that Sonny's work struck you as
changed too much. To my mind, it followed the original with almost excessive
closeness, widely departing only when it became absolutely necessary to clear
away some case of sentimentality whose extravagance seemed to belie probability and the facts of life, and to introduce an element of hollowness seriously injurious to the narrative.

According to Belknap, your criticism of his version is that it is *too "flat",*
especially at the conclusion. Now to my mind, this criticism argues a somewhat artificial and romanticised view of life and literature; and confirms my
old-time estimate that you ought to spend much time in getting rid of popular-magazine psychology, and grounding yourself in actual human motivations and sound literary values, before attempting creative work on a serious
scale. In other words it reveals the same need which I pointed out in 1927—
of a wholesome readjustment of perspective on your part, in which you may
shake off the superficial mock-world of the light magazines by *beginning at the
beginning;* investigating human thought and motives through life itself—or
through **standard** literature—and attacking the problem of linguistic expression *at the correct end*—the end involving basic principles and rudimentary critical laws. Much study, much **standard** reading, and much careful forgetting of
cheap current literature must of necessity precede any effective excursion into
serious authorship—or any successful attempt to understand serious literature
and appreciate relative values in aesthetic expression. This grounding is *basic
and essential*—one can't beat the game and 'get by' without it unless one has a
virtually superhuman natural instinct for realities of thought and symmetries
of language. That is why I was so insistent in recommending that you follow
Belknap's **lessons** before essaying any long-distance flights—the success of
the flights being dependent on the thoroughness with which the lessons have
been mastered. Another indication that a wholesale rectification of outlook is
needed is furnished by your statement that my own recommendations of
former years were incomprehensible to you. They certainly ought not to have
been, for they did not involve any matters beyond the rudiments; and I would
have been glad to make them clearer had you requested additional explanations. But the fact that they were not clear proves very amply that a thorough
grounding in the *complex shades* of human feeling and action, in the principles
of sincere expression versus cheap sentimentality, and in the fundamental

problems of language as related to subject-matter, was sorely needed. This I hoped Uzzell could supply—and after the explosion of that bubble I imagined that Belknap's lessons could do it. The latter, indeed, I *still* think—if you will stick to the lessons before attempting major creations, and if Belknap (whose nerves are all on the jump this year) has the strength to keep up his work. At any rate, I fancy you can gather what I am trying to convey—that you really must get a thorough grounding in *methods and standards;* in knowledge of what people **really** think and say and do under different sets of conditions, and of how language best presents such thoughts and words and actions; before you can either write a serious story which *rings true in every part* or pass serious judgment on a piece of writing and its relation to actual human experience and emotion. As I have said before, I don't think you'll have the least difficulty in doing this once you make up your mind that it **must** be done. Your energy, steadfast purpose, and quick grasp of whatever you *try* to grasp all point toward probable success once the campaign begins *in the right direction.* But you must not place the cart before the horse—or the tail-light before the radiator, if one must be contemporary! The first thing is to get rid of the idea that serious attention to the details of life, nature, the historic stream, and the principles of art is something boresomely "highbrow" or reprehensibly affected. Not a bit of it! There is nothing boresome, arrogant, or affected about plain *truth*—and that is all careful scholarship amounts to in the long run. It is, rather, the commoner pose of superficiality, artificiality, and romantic sentimentality which is really affected and hollow. There is only one sensible way to view the world—and that is with an impartial, minute perspective which correctly registers the *relative importance of things* and *declines to envelop phenomena with emotions out of proportion to their significance.* The whole essence of ridiculous sentimentality is an attempt to interpret phenomena in terms of excessive or irrelevant emotion. Let your whole survey of life concern itself only with the question of *what is* and *what isn't.* Be accurate and conscientious, and nature will supply the colouring needed to weave your pictures of real life into the tapestry of literature. When the process seems difficult or complex, don't quit in disgust and impatience and say something must be the matter with the process. That gets no one anywhere! *Stop and think*— meet and conquer the problem instead of running away from it or denying that it exists! Only by such a policy of courageous confrontation and conquest can anybody fight his way to a real comprehension and mastery of life and literature. Shirk, and you'll always be baffled by realities—always bewildered, confused, and under-appreciative when faced by some *genuine* literary presentation of life as distinguished from the artificialised romantic slop of the quarter-of-a-dollar magazine press.

And it isn't as difficult a matter as you may imagine from a hasty skimming of these paragraphs of senile verbosity. I'm only trying to get you *to real-*

ise what the problem is. Once you do that, a good course of reading and study will seem as clear to you as my recommendations now seem muddled!

What you want is a reading-course in several parallel lines, mapped out with care by some competent scholar and followed attentively and conscientiously by yourself. I'd say, offhand, that about five parallel streams would be about right—*elementary science,* to give you an idea of man's place in nature; *psychology and philosophy,* to shew you how people think, why they do what they do, and what they do under given conditions; *history,* to give you an intelligent perspective on possible fictional backgrounds; *literary method,* (critical essays, textbooks on writing and appreciation) to teach you how to translate thoughts, events, pictures, and moods into language of the greatest possible advantage; and *literature itself*—in its most *standard* form—to enlarge your *authentic* knowledge of life, and at the same time to accustom you unconsciously to the most effective devices of linguistic expression. Of these five streams, the last-named is by far the most important and necessary. Above *everything else* comes *good* literature. And of course, a concomitant to all this would be a complete swearing-off of the cinema and of cheap magazines. You can't bury that stuff too deeply out of sight and memory for your own artistic good!! I may add, that these reading courses aren't by any means difficult. They only *sound* so when described in advance. There are pleasant popular manuals and outlines covering all the needed subjects, which are a delight rather than a burden to read. I could send you the printed reading-course leaflets issued by Brown University library if you had any trouble about getting hints nearer at hand.

This, then, is the writer's fivefold problem:

1. To get the facts of life.
2. To think straight and tell the truth.
3. To cut out maudlin and extravagant emotion.
4. To cultivate an ear for strong, direct, harmonious, simple, and graphic language.
5. To write what one really sees and feels.

One thing I'm going to do is to see that my present client sends you a complimentary copy of his book on poetic appreciation when it's done and published. Although it's supposed to pertain to poetry, it really covers prose as well; and is the most marvellously clear exposition of the difference between real literature and insincere sentimentality that I've ever seen in brief compass on paper. I wish this chap had time to give private correspondence lessons—if he had, I'd recommend him to you in a flash—but unfortunately his school work and authorship take all his hours . . . . and more energy than he ought to spare.

Well—what I'm getting around to (for I really *do* get around to things in the end, no matter how long I take!) is this: that I swear upon my personal and professional honour that Belknap's revision of your novel is *not only not a "flattening", but a 100% improvement, without which the MS. could never be considered professionally.* You'll have to take this on trust just now—accepting the joint word of Sonny and his grandpa—but I'll guarantee that if you'll faithfully follow the background-enlarging course I recommend, you'll agree with us whole-heartedly inside of six months, and bless the child for the painstaking and intelligent job he has so conscientiously done. I give this assurance with the utmost impartiality, and with the fullest confidence in my own correctness. Wait and see if I'm not right!

Just to take one specific instance of your complaint—the ending. In the first place, all deathbed scenes are lamentably hackneyed stock devices—so much so that I'd undoubtedly have cut the whole thing out as artificial and theatrical. Secondly—it's **entirely fallacious** to assume, as you apparently do, that a man under strong emotion at a deathbed would do cheaply theatrical things—pull out an old engagement ring, picturesquely kneel and attitudinise, mouth the old melodrama-gag "forgive me", and all that sort of thing. Also— no real dying person would ever talk popular-magazine language and give the stale old 'one-I-have-always-loved' line. Frankly, this is **not life** but **artificial novel convention;** and you must realise that your *ideal of naturalness* is in need of readjustment. Again, as in 1927, I must insist that you *forget about cheap-fictional convention* and begin to adopt the moods and reactions *of real life,* as reflected in *standard* literature, as your working criterion. Belknap was very quick to spy the essential weakness of this artificial and theatrically sentimental conclusion, and was really a little wizard in the way he substituted *real, deep emotion* (whose natural language is always of profound, cruel directness and tragic simplicity) for *mere magazine sentimentality.* My only criticism is *that he did not go farther in the same direction*—for instance, he has this hackneyed bit:

> "Arthur nodded, and gathering her tenderly in his arms imprinted a kiss on her half-parted lips"

whereas I think he ought to have deleted the old hokum altogether and used the simple language of **real** emotional tensity—something like the following:

> "Arthur nodded and reached for her gropingly, tender and tense at the same time as the situation worked into his consciousness. Almost spasmodically, yet very gently, he kissed her squarely on her half-opened mouth."

Note how *this* version avoids the traditional stock language—unrelated to reality and derived merely from convention—of the cheap romantic novel. I don't say "tenderly in his arms" or "imprinted a kiss on her half-parted lips", because those old phrases have been so worn to death by repeated use at the hands of penny-a-line romancers that they are purged of all vitality and individual significance—only raising a laugh when read by a cultivated and sophisticated audience. If you take my advice, you'll write this change into the copy. Belknap would have done a similar thing if he had dared—but he didn't want to depart too radically from what he found. Imagine his puzzlement, then, at being told he had gone *too far* instead of *not far enough!*

The thing you object to most—Colby's tragically simple speech "Deon is dead"—is really *the one flawless touch in the whole ending,* and a vivid illustration of Belknap's fine sense of fitness and knowledge of starkly powerful expression. You believe that this is something which a deeply moved man in Colby's position *wouldn't* say—whereas I must assure you with the most profound sincerity that this is *exactly* the sort of brief, unadorned sentence which such a person **would** utter under the given circumstances. *Real* and *deep* emotion strips away all the furbelows of language[2] and reduces a speaker to stark, naive, barren elementals of speech—as you could not help realising after a sufficient familiarity with life and *authentic* literature. If you don't believe me, read any accepted classic which deals with profound, unveiled emotion—say Synge's "Riders to the Sea" or any Shakespearian tragedy. Analyse the diction and see if I'm not right! Only in the cheapest of trash are strongly-moved people made to spout flowery platitudes. The fact is, you're blaming Little Sonny for what is really a *master stroke* on his part; a master-stroke *which alone saves the whole deathbed scene from ineffectiveness and artificiality.* Make no mistake about this—it is the cold aesthete and not the fond grandsire who speaks! If you can't see the point now, wait six months and read the passage over again after an enlargement of your literary background. In a way, your appreciation of a point like that will serve as a kind of *test* of your literary progress—it is really very much like the carefully worked-out appreciation tests in the book I am revising. *When you begin to understand* **why** *an ending like Sonny's is more authentic than an ending like your own, you will be on the high road to that independent mastery of literary art which you are seeking.*

Belknap has also done marvellously—in this case, better than I would be likely to have done—in the very last paragraph of the book. I won't point out the especial crux of effectiveness just now, for I think it will be good literary exercise for you to try to find it yourself—remembering all the pictorial, associative, symbolic, and connotative qualities of good literary expression. Discuss it with the child, and don't rest till you grasp the essence of this and other points. That's the one way to get the background you need—be **thorough**—discuss things **fully**—thrash them out—don't be so afraid of many words and full descriptions, for sometimes they are needed to convey subtle points and distinctions. If you had been more peremptory in your demands for *clear explanations of every doubtful point* you might have extracted more enlightenment and usefulness from Uzzell's spasmodic outbursts and my own long-winded but well-meant dissertations. There's no use in doing anything with literature unless you take it seriously enough to probe to the bottom and get all the working principles and inside information you can. When you pay for criticism and revision, get your money's worth! Nobody is more conscientiously eager to give full—and more than full—value than Little Belknap!

And now I hope you'll pardon this spluttering torrent of explosive explanation and pompous old-gentlemanly advice! Really, I oughtn't to be so boresome and didactic; but I can't help letting loose for once, because I am so profoundly and sincerely impressed with the masterly excellence of the job Sonny has done. He knows psychology, and he knows literary expression; and he has really dealt with the problems of your characters in a marvellously genuine and effective way. I don't know of a qualified critic under the sun who wouldn't agree with me after a comparative survey of "before and after" versions—so you can easily see why I get sort of excited and pedantic when I meet with an adverse criticism of what are undoubtedly strong points! If my asseveration of my conviction seems over-abrupt, pray accept my sincerest apologies here and now. I certainly haven't *meant* to insist on my point beyond the limits of good manners; and if I've done so in spite of that benign intention, I am properly regretful and humiliated. More than this—I sincerely trust that my efforts to [be?] clear regarding your literary needs have not conveyed any sort of a discouraging impression. Had I wished to discourage, I would not have expended so many words on the subject of your future progress—and I again assert that the course I recommend is neither difficult nor unpleasant to follow. It is simply one of those things which must come at a certain stage of normal progress—natural and easy and delightful, but a necessary stepping-stone to the heights. Lessons first—then large-scale creation. And I am certain that your zeal and indomitable energy will see you brilliantly through both stages!

Such, then, is the object of the present harangue—to call attention to the really fine quality of the job Belknap has done, and to give you clues toward seeing it in the same light that I do. It would be a pity for work like that to go unrecognised, and I am inclined to hope that your point of view has even now—in the light of the foregoing attempted explanations—become somewhat more favourable. Remember that non-extravagant diction is the surest sign of true artistry, and that stark simplicity is the natural language of strong emotion. Incidentally—it just occurs to me to ask pardon if Belknap's description has caused me to overestimate your objections to his revision. I haven't seen your letter to him, and he is so easily depressed by adverse opinions that he may very possibly have exaggerated your verdict—giving it as it *seemed to him,* rather than as it actually was in black and white. But anyway, you have my opinion of his job; and I can vouch that it's a sincere one, and one in which I feel myself very securely correct!

I have been in a desperate whirl of revisory work all summer—such a whirl that my own creative work has had to go neglected altogether. I must shake clear of this revision long enough to write some more stories, but heaven only knows how I am going to do it! Every spare second I get, I am too mentally exhausted to indulge in any pursuit save my favourite pastime of antiquarian exploration. My trips since the great springtide jaunt have been limited but pleasant. In June I accompanied my guest Morton to various ancient villages along Narragansett Bay—but I think I mentioned that before. In July I had another guest—a young man from St. Louis,[3] in your own state—and initiated him into the mysteries of colonial Newport. Early August witnessed a solitary jaunt on my part—a Massachusetts trip with twofold goal—(a) the old Fairbanks homestead in Dedham, built in 1636 and the oldest house in English America, and (b) the celebrated Red Horse tavern in Sudbury, built in 1686 and famous as Longfellow's "Wayside Inn". The Fairbanks house, built in the same year Providence was founded and only 6 years after the founding of Boston, is the most fascinating edifice I have ever seen. It is built of massive timbers from Old England—probably parts of a ship dismantled in Boston Harbour—and has undergone no changes since the early 18th century. Wings were added to the original part in 1641 and 1648, so that the structure has a quaintly rambling aspect, and exhibits an infinitely picturesque line of sagging roofs as seen from the road. I enclose a view. The house has never been out of the Fairbanks family, and is now operated as a museum by a society of descendants. The atmosphere of the place is beyond description—*antiquity—hoary antiquity—immemorial ancientness and kinship to elder and forgotten worlds*—your house at the beginning of your novel is a mere mushroom growth of yesterday compared to it! The walls and roof are in places oddly sunken, but have been safely strengthened in recent years. Here it stands—unique in its age, fascinating in its colourful irregularity—cobwebbed attics, staircases everywhere, steps up and down from room to room, vast beams, wooden-pegged and marked with the vestiges of hand-hewing, great fireplaces, titanic chimney of old English brick, massive woodwork blackened by smoke and long centuries, curiously slanting floors, archaic latches, queer half-forgotten kinds of furniture and household utilities—in fine, all the subtle earmarks of long continuous living; bringing down to the present the faint, strange, stirring echoes of 1636, when New England was a frail infant colony clinging to the seacoast, and this house was a bold outpost set on the edge of black, unknown woods, haunted by shadowy daemons and reaching none knew whither. Verily, this was the most poignantly imagination-rousing house I had ever seen—I could hear the sound of the builder's axe in the nighted woods three hundred years ago, when the lone, questing canoe of Roger Williams and his companions dug its prow into the sand of Moshassuck's pathless shore, not four squares downhill from the spot where I now am seated!

The famed Wayside Inn—now owned by Henry Ford—was a bit tame after the old Fairbanks house; (it is half a century younger) but was good for a first-class "kick" none the less. It has been restored as nearly as possible to its colonial condition, and its neighbourhood has been kept in a very pristine and traditional state. Within, the colonial taproom, dining-room, kitchen, parlours, and bedrooms are all outfitted as in Georgian times, as if ready to accomodate a generous company of periwigged travellers or roysterers. There are some quaint details which only a full-length travelogue could enumerate, and which ought to be written up in a guide book. The famous parlour described in Longfellow's poem is fitted up exactly as in his day—all the articles mentioned in the verses having been reclaimed from the various owners to whom they were sold after the last landlord's death. Longfellow and his friends were extremely fond of the inn, and visited there at sundry times; though they were never assembled all at once under its roof as in the poem. The vast structure was built in 1686, and from 1714 onward was a public tavern conducted by successive generations of the Howe family—till the extinction of that line at the close of the 19th century. Across the road is the stable mentioned in Longfellow's poem—now harbouring sheep, oxen, horses, and a collection of curious old vehicles. Not far away can be found a fine old stone water mill with blithely turning wheel, and a small schoolhouse of the late 18th century—moved from Sterling, Mass., and celebrated as the scene of the incident which created the well-known juvenile doggerel of "Mary's Lamb". This schoolhouse—which I am sure Iacobus–Iunior would find more picturesque than the urban institutions they attend—is fitted up with old fashioned benches and teacher's desk, and is situate in a pine grove just off a winding by-road, in a manner very suitable and natural to colonial seats of instruction.

My final outing of the season was a week with Little Belknap and his parents at Onset—at the head of Buzzard's Bay near the base of Cape Cod, some 50 miles from Providence. The Longs had been on a vast motor tour reaching as far north as Quebec, and were edging southward along the New England coast—hence invited me to share their last halting-place with them. I had a very pleasant time; (vide cards) for although Onset itself is merely a sprightly beach resort of no especial quaintness, it is within easy reach of all the antiquarian colour of Cape Cod and New Bedford. We did ample justice to all these places—being especially captivated by New Bedford's historic waterfront and famous whaling museum. At the latter is a half-sized model of the old whaler *Lagoda,* accurate in every part, and open to visitors. Belknap, his father, and I clambered over it till we were about ready to go to sea as sailors or harpooners! At Onset I made enough of a concession to modernity to take my first aëroplane ride—a highly exhilarating experience giving a splendid sense of cosmic freedom from the map-like blue and green world outspread far below. No sense of *motion*—merely an impression of *high wind*. The Longs motored westward through Providence, and are now safely back in Manhattan's depressing dump.

Hoping that my comment on the revised novel may not be thought impertinent or officious, I remain

Yr most obt Servt

H P Lovecraft

Notes

1. I.e., Maurice W. Moe's *Doorways to Poetry*. Whether the book was ever completed is unknown. It was scheduled to be published by Macmillan, but the book was in fact never published and is now nonextant.

2. Something that suggests a furbelow—a pleated or gathered piece of material, esp. a flounce on women's clothing—especially in being showy or superfluous.

3. I.e., Victor E. Bacon (1905–1997), amateur journalist and editor of *Bacon's Essays,* which published work by HPL, and Official Editor of the United Amateur Press Association (1925–26).

[43]   [AHT]

10 Barnes St.,

Providence, R. I.,

Sept. 11, 1929

My dear Mrs. Reed:—

[. . .]

That is why the really high-grade artist has no "temperament", affectations, or mannerisms—at least, in later life. He knows that nothing on this cursed planet really matters.

Yes—I did manage to work in some fairly piquant and variegated trips during the summer, despite the unprecedented rush of work which gave each one of them the semblance of truancy. Only two weeks ago my younger aunt and I took a one-day excursion which compares well in interest with any of the others—to the western Rhode Island countryside which formed the abiding-place of my maternal forbears during the 18th and early 19th centuries. It was the second of a series of trips in quest of early homesteads and family burying-grounds; for I have an ambition to see all the houses and landscapes that my progenitors inhabited, (so far, of course, as the houses are still standing and the landscapes still unaltered) and to copy all the existing epitaphs from their tombstones. Three years ago I covered the scenically lovely Moosup Valley region where Places, Tylers, Caseys, and Perkinses came from; and where still stands the rambling old house where my mother, grandmother, and Place great-grandfather were born. This time I chose the Howard Hill country just southeast of the Moosup, which is the old seat of the Howards, and where my great-great-grandfather Asaph Phillips settled just after the Revolution. For scenery this place surpasses even Moosup Valley; presenting the typical New England landscape at its absolute best—green rolling meadows, mysterious woods, narrow, stone-walled roads, sloping orchards, hilltop vistas of far plains, purple horizons, and white village belfries embowered in distant valleys, alder-fringed brooks with moss-grown, centuried water-mills, quaint chimneys and farmhouse gables peeping through tangles of gnarled apple-boughs—in short, everything connected with Rhode Island's poetic yesterdays, and saved by some miracle from change, sophistication, mechanisation, and foreign invasion. I told my aunt that I don't wonder at my pastoral landscape tastes—for with an ancestry nurtured in rural shades, I surely come honestly by them. I found the site of the Asaph Phillips house—now burned down—and copied all the epitaphs in the hillside burying-ground; which has been well maintained, and has a modern annex in which are laid many migrated Phillipses from Providence and elsewhere, who wish to rest at last under the waving grasses and calm skies their fathers knew. Asaph has an old-fashioned slate slab with weeping willow and epitaph,* for he died in 1829. My great-grandfather Capt. Jeremiah—Asaph's son—has a white marble slab of the austerer design of the late '40's; for he was killed in his own mill in 1848, when the skirts of his voluminous frock-coat caught in a belt or wheel. His epitaph is merely the polite fiction "This mortal shall put on immortality." Collateral descendants of the family still hold the land and inhabit the house, (a clever archaistic reproduction incorporating woodwork taken from neighbouring old houses) and I had a very interesting session of genealogical note-comparing with them—incidentally gaining full directions for reaching that older Phillips country (with still-standing houses and burial-places of my great-great-great-grandfather James Jr. (died 1807) and my great-great-great-great-grandfather James Sr. (died 1746)) which will form the terrain of my third ancestral pilgrimage; a thing I hope to make before cold weather sets in. James Sr.'s father Michael (1642–1686) lies at Newport, but I have never found his grave in the old Farewell St. burying-ground, and fear the slab is now undecipherable. Mike's father, the Rev. George, (1596–1644) rests where he preached, at Watertown, in His Majesty's Province of Ye Massachusetts-Bay, but I have never visited his grave. And George's father Christopher will take me farther afield—for he sleeps in the blessed soil of Norfolk, in that dear ENGLAND which he never quitted in life, amongst the bones of his fathers beneath the ivied parish church of Rainham St. Martin's, in the hundred of Gallow. God Save the King! Some day I must get back to the loved old land and see the tombs and homes (such as are standing) of all—paternal and maternal—who have gone before me. Minster-Hall in Devonshire, seat of the Lovecrafts till 1823, is demolished; but their bones dream

---

*The sweet remembrance of the just
Shall flourish when they sleep in dust.

conservatively in the churchyard at Newton-Abbot. I have never set foot on the old sod of Mother Britannia, but every fibre of my being thrills with loyalty to the ancient scenes and ancient ways. Devon, Cornwall, Norfolk, Cumberland, York, Northumberland, Wales—even one strain from *Ireland,* which entered in 1656—all live in my blood and heart and memory; the one remaining sentimentality of an unsentimental cynic. God Save the King! But even though I have not yet been back to the *oldest* home, it is a great delight to trace time backward through the meads and groves of the *next-oldest* home— ancient New England. On this occasion I walked over Howard Hill to Moosup Valley, reentering the territory of my first expedition and renewing my acquaintance with the Place homestead—whose picture (a crayon-drawing by my mother after an oil-painting by a great-aunt who was also born in the house) has always hung in my room as an object of affectionate reverence. It is in rather shiftless and mediocre (though not foreign) hands at present, and I wish I had the money to re-purchase and restore it. I hate to think of what is happening to the mellow old panelling, mantels, and doors under the existing regime. Behind the house a shady valley slopes down to a winding brook, and across the terraced hills to the northwest one may spy the white belfry of the Moosup-Valley village church, whence float tuneful harmonies at evening. All told, we had a great day—retracing our steps to the high-road and stage-coach in the glamorous golden light of late afternoon, and arriving at Providence as the first lamps of evening glowed through the violet dusk. I surely hope I can work in another trip this autumn. The older Phillips region is rather far from any existing transportation line, so that my aunt will not be a participant in this final pilgrimage. There will be strenuous foot-work—and, I hope, proportionate epitaphic rewards! I am become a veritable ghoul and mould-burrower in my old age! The old tavern you mention sounds exceptionally interesting, and I wish I could see a view of it some time. The colonial and later Georgian structures in the West are so few, that each one of them merits particular notice. In Ohio, a few good houses were built during the early settlement days, and of these several survive—mostly in the southeastern part of the State. In Indiana the town of Vincennes had much colonial material, including some early French specimens. The old French court house from Kaskaskia, Illinois, built in 1780, is still preserved, but removed to Chicago. One colonial house remains in Detroit, and my St. Louis friend mentions a village not far from his city where traces of the first French traders are found. I think he has mentioned your Daniel Boone tavern—though vaguely, inexactly, and from hearsay only. It will naturally interest me greatly to see your story based on the old tavern, and I'll gladly put into shape any antiquarian parts submitted skeletonically. No—I won't tell my sensitive grandchild about it, and will be interested to see how many of his grandpa's sentences he will revise!

Too bad about Loveman's commercial debacle—though I think he needed the lesson. Commerce *sounds* so easy till one tries it! He will soon be as profitably situated on a salary as he was before the experiment, and this time he'll know enough to let well enough alone. It's an exceptional aesthete who can do business—for the whole psychology of trade is antipathetic to the creative imagination. A case right now is that of another of my "grandchildren"—young Donald Wandrei, the *Weird Tales* contributor, whom Belknap and I have probably mentioned to you. On graduating from the University of Minnesota a year ago last June, Wandrei went to try and took a position in the advertising department of Dutton's, secured for him by our fellow-gangster Vrest Orton. He succeeded brilliantly, and for a time had visions of giving ten years of his life to intensive commerce; 'cleaning up a pile', and then living the rest of his days amidst the aesthetic leisure of a scholar, an artist, and a gentleman. But the nerve-strain proved too great—and only day before yesterday I received a note saying he had resigned in sheer desperation, lest the cross-trading atmosphere and utilitarian psychology drive him mad. He is going back to writing and writing only—starve or not—and tells me he has 'a novel of age-old horror' well under way.[1] He may visit Providence for a couple of weeks before winter—taking a vacant room in the attic of this house, as he did in the summer of '27.[2] Last Sunday another of "the gang" passed through Providence with his wife in the course of a New England motor tour— George Kirk, whose New York bookshop I once advised you to visit for choice items, but whom I don't recall whether you met or not. His commercial venture seems to succeed—though from past knowledge of his happy-go-lucky generosity and irresponsibility I imagine that Mrs. Kirk must be the business brains. Good old Georgius has to be held in check, like Loveman, lest he give away his stock to friends!

> Yr obt Servt
> H P Lovecraft.

Notes

1. I.e., *Dead Titans, Waken!* (first published as *The Web of Easter Island*).
2. Wandrei visited HPL again only in 1932.

[44]   [AHT]

> 10 Barnes St.,
> Providence, R.I.,
> Dec. 19, 1929.

My dear Mrs. Reed:—

[. . .]

By the way—you will be pained to hear that good old Everett McNeil, whose books Iacobus–Iunior have read, and from whom I think you once received some data, is no more—having succumbed to his illness last Saturday after crossing the continent to Tacoma to rest at his sister's home. Poor old Mac—it is a pity he could not have had a longer and more reposeful evening of life after his forty years of struggle and poverty in the New York slums; but at least one must reflect that he emerged from the worst phase of squalor three years ago. Belknap and I feel frightfully depressed, for Mac was one of the most distinctive and flavorous ingredients of our "gang". I cannot think of the New York terrain without his gentle, grey, plodding presence—for he is inextricable bound up with my fresh, first glamorous impression of the metropolis; the fascinating impression of fantastic wonder which preceded the period of familiarity and distaste—the early, wondering impression of Cyclopean, flowerlike pinnacles rising out of violet mist, of strange landscapes glimpsed from balustraded plazas and tiers of titan terraces, of glittering twilights that darkened into cryptic ceilings of night pressing low over lanes and vaults of spectral phosphorescence, of alien life surging bewilderingly out of unknown eastern steppes, and of the vast sunset expanses of flat lands and marshes in Southern Brooklyn, where old, Dutch memories brooded along sedge-lined salty inlets, and grey antiquity touched the curved gables of lonely cottages. I recall when Mac first showed Belknap and me the nightmare horror of the Hell's Kitchen district (W. 49th St.) where he then lived—the seething filth of labyrinthine streets where grotesquely twisted faces leered in the glare of unclean bonfires lighted to signal the evil gods of alien worlds—the horrible rows of unending brick bulging with viscous horror and threatening to burst outward—the pigeon-breeders atop the foul tenements sending their birds of space outward into the void bearing messages for loathsome dark stars—and through it all the little grey plodding guide with his naive memories of Wisconsin[1] farm days and his dreams of windswept green wildernesses of boy-adventure. And now good old Mac is no more—a hard thought to digest!

Yr most Obt Servt.

H P Lovecraft.

Notes

1. In youth, McNeil lived in Marinette, WI.

[45]   [ALS, to ZB's son]

[H. P. LOVECRAFT
10 BARNES STREET
PROVIDENCE, R. I.]

Dec. 29, 1929.

James Reed, Esq.,
        Kansas City, Mo.,

My dear Mr. Reed:—

        Allow me to thank you most sincerely for the timely greeting & admirably dignified cravat which came yesterday by special delivery. Pray extend my thanks also to your generous colleague in the presentation—Mr. Watson Stains, whom I take to be the young man I have heard of as "Junior." Many pleasant mentions of you both have reached me during the past three years, & I am sure this display of sartorial taste amply confirms them all!

        Enclosed is a chronological trifle which I trust you & Mr. Stains will accept as a mark of my appreciation—although I know it is inadequate, & will not decorate your wall half as tastefully as your remembrance will decorate my neck! The design—an old doorway & small-paned window—is rather characteristic of me, for I live in a quaint old town & am extremely fond of ancient houses & historic-looking streets & courtyards & gardens. That will undoubtedly seem odd to you, who live in a new city where the highly-prized things are spaciousness & elegance; but here in the east we value the ancient things which we have—graceful brick & wood & stone buildings that date back to the Revolution & long before, & that make the drama of history seem very real & alive for us. Of course, I am fonder of these things than most people—indeed, I have recently had a new bookplate made with an ancient Providence doorway as a design. The reason we value *doorways* so much more than all the other parts of old houses, is that they always used to be the principal decorative features—made very carefully & artistically even when all the rest of the house was very plain. This was especially true in New England, though in other parts of the colonies less attention was paid to the doorways & more to the general proportions of the buildings. It is easy to see that I am rather a bore on this subject, & I hope you can pardon this extended explanation. My principal diversion is taking trips to other ancient towns, where different forms of old-time architecture can be seen—towns like Portsmouth, Newburyport, Gloucester, Salem, Marblehead, Concord, Lexington, Newport, Deerfield, &c. in New England, & Philadelphia, Annapolis, Alexandria, Fredericksburg, Richmond, Williamsburg, Jamestown, & Yorktown, farther south along the coast. If I had more cash, I'd do more of this kind of travelling—indeed, sooner or later I hope to get as far north as Quebec & as far south as St. Augustine & New Orleans.

Speaking of bookplates, as I was a while back—I hear that you have quite a library, even though it is only one among many interests of yours. That is a very good thing to have, for in the end it will give you more permanent pleasure & comfort than any other one possession you could possibly acquire. I have one that suits my own particular tastes very well, although it wouldn't be called a large or remarkable library by any connoisseur of books. I began keeping it classified systematically when I was about your age or somewhat younger, (I was 12, but I believe you must be getting on toward 14 now—for you young folk grow too fast for old folk to keep track of!) & with slow additions it has now reached a size of about 2000 volumes. I have had periods of discarding—as you will undoubtedly have—& have thus got rid of perhaps 100 books in all; but now my collection is boiled down to such indispensable essentials that there isn't a thing left which I could bear to throw away. Instead, I try to accomodate the growing array with new bookcases (I've just had to buy four more small ones)—which I set on top of other furniture when I can't find space on the floor for them. The principal subjects in my collection—beginning at the southeast corner of the room & going around to the northeast corner—are Greek & Roman classics, English belles-lettres, poetry, weird literature, (which is my main literary interest, & the class in which I try to do some writing myself) general history, American, New England, & Rhode Island history, standard English fiction, geography & travel, reference-books & manuals on rhetoric & authorship, fine arts, philosophy & anthropology, foreign languages, astronomy, (my principal interest among the sciences—I also have a small astronomical telescope) physics, chemistry, geology, & more reference books. In an alcove I have other books—mainly memoirs of the 18th century, which is my favourite historical period. Some time I'd enjoy hearing what your books are. When I was your age, my favourite subject was astronomy, & I had about 60 books on the subject—that class being the largest which I had personally accumulated. (for about half my books have been inherited from time to time from various sources) Now I haven't quite so many astronomical books, & I think that history, poetry, weird literature, & Greek & Roman classics are the largest classes. This reminds me that your mother some time ago mentioned *Latin* as one of your recent interests. You couldn't have chosen a subject more wisely, for the literature of Rome opens up a vista of unparalleled scope & magnificence, besides furnishing—after a fashion—a sort of bridge to all the glamour & mystery of the ancient world. But don't let the teachers get you bored in advance by tangles of grammatical rules. Read the "livest" classics in good translations even before you perfect yourself in the language, so that you can drink them in as stories without the dry atmosphere of the classroom or the discouraging labour of line-for-line translation. And read some good, easy books on the history & life of Greece & Rome, too—also interesting novels (like Edward Lucas White's "Andivius Hedulio") dealing with the classical period. However—possibly you realise all this yourself, & need no suggestions. You don't need, either, to be urged to keep plenty of outside interests & not let books tyrannise over you as they do over two or three friends of mine. I believe you have a healthy interest in music, scouting, & the various activities of the day—a good thing, & a point where you get far ahead of me!

Again I thank you for your apt remembrance, & trust you will share my thanks with your young colleague. Remember me likewise to your mother, whose recent illness I trust is now well conquered. I have just finished a piece of work for her, which she will shortly receive through my co-worker Mr. Long.

Wishing you & all your household a happy 1930,

I am

Yrs most cordially & sincerely,

H P Lovecraft

[46]   [ALS]

10 Barnes St.,

Providence, R.I.,

Jany. 14, 1930.

My dear Mrs. Reed:—

I have just learned to my surprise & dismay that Little Belknap has, through a misunderstanding, not yet forwarded to you the completed MS. of "The Mound" which I sent him late in December to read & pass onward. Permit me to apologise for this slip-up, & to assure you that I'm writing the Child in this very mail—so that you ought to see the story in about four days. He thought you might wish it typed *before* sending—whereas I am acting under the assumption that you wish to see it first in rough draught, so that you can order any needed changes concerning Binger local colour &c. As for the typing—if your health & patience don't permit you to do it yourself, I think our "firm" can take care of it *at the regular rate of 25¢ per page,* although we couldn't profitably quote a cut rate just now. You can, if able to meet this regular rate, (which would of course amount to considerable in view of length) send the MS. either to me or to Belknap. But of course it would pay you best if you could handle it yourself. If Wright takes the tale—as he is very likely to do—you will make a very handsome profit. Sonny seems to think it is very good—I can't resist enclosing his note regarding it—& is inclined to spoof Grandpa for doing it for $20.00; but I never raise a figure I have quoted in advance. That is why I can't make revision pay!

I hope you will like the story. It may prove hard reading on account of the penmanship, but it's hard to do better in a rough draught. As I have said, if you decide to do the typing yourself or have it done locally, I shall be glad to correct the final MS. & supply lacunae as I did with "Yig." Professional typing would cost slightly under $20.00, in all probability.

Payment for the revision can be made at your convenience—after Belknap is reimbursed for the work which he delivered Nov. 15th. Just now I am staggering out from under a colossal typing siege for a client who can't read my handwriting![1]

Your convalescence, I trust, has progressed steadily since mid-December. I was delighted to receive from Iacobus–Iunior that sedate "Yig" cravat—& have expressed my appreciation to the senior member of that inseparable duo! Pray give them my renewed regards.

Again expressing my apologetic regret at this unforeseen delay in "Mound" delivery, & extending my best wishes,

> I remain
>> Yr most ob^t h^{ble} Servt
>> H P Lovecraft

Notes

1. HPL had just completed the revision and ghostwriting of Adolphe de Castro's "The Electric Executioner."

[47] [ALS]

> 10 Barnes St.,
>> Providence, R.I.,
>>> Jany. 16, 1930.

My dear Mrs. Reed:—

A call which I paid immediately after mailing my apology of Tuesday for the delay in "Mound" transmission impels me to add a postscript to that communication—a postscript touching on the matter of typing in case you are unable to perform that labour yourself. This call was upon an old literary acquaintance—a very unsuccessful author whom I had not seen since last June—& it revealed so pitiful a degree of destitution on the part of my host that I have resolved to do what I can to help him by throwing as much work as possible his way. I am today writing Little Belknap & all my principal revisory clients in the hope that some work can be diverted toward this unfortunate fellow-townsman of mine; who is, I can give positive assurance, a thoroughly capable & conscientious typist & performer of light revision. Work performed by him will be absolutely accurate, & on paper of the same grade that I would use myself—indeed, I intend to give him a supply of paper & carbon-paper, & see that he has a good typewriter ribbon.

The writer to whom I refer is C. M. Eddy, Jr., whose work you may have noticed in earlier numbers of *Weird Tales*. He is a very clever man of thirty-four, with a diversity of talents which would take him far if coördinated in one direction; but unfortunately he possesses that same inexplicable non-financial quality which handicaps Little Belknap & myself—plus a situation in the world which aggravates his plight to the extreme limits of tragedy. He has so far managed to keep meagrely afloat—with a wife & three children—by undertaking outside work of various sorts; but recent economic conditions have left him jobless & reduced him to such depths of want & peril that nothing short of a miracle—or a flood of fairly lucrative literary chores—can keep him & his flock from actual freezing, starvation, & eviction during the interval before he can again secure some industrial affiliation. Now I am not suggesting that any actual charity be extended by my clients—who have scarcely heard of him before—hence I trust you will not feel that you are asked to give him any typing *which you would otherwise do yourself*. I am only suggesting that, *if you are spontaneously intending to have the typing done by another hand*, you place the order with this person who needs work so desperately, instead of with Belknap or myself. It will all be on a high-grade business basis & at regular prices—25¢ per page. As I have said, the quality of the work will be just as good as that which any other first-class typist would give you. Incidentally, if you have any *light revisory* jobs to be placed in the near future, I would suggest that they go to Eddy instead of to Sonny or to me. His rates would *certainly* not be higher than ours, & might possibly be lower—I'm not sure about that. In any job requiring non-creative verbal revision, & even in more creative jobs where a high-grade market is not in mind, Eddy could give as good service as Belknap or myself. I would hardly advise your giving him intricate imaginative themes to develop, but I believe he could provide perfect results in all cases of *light* revision. Indeed—if you have any superficial work prepared with naive "human interest" markets in mind, it is possible that Eddy could help even *more* than the Long–Lovecraft team—because he has had considerable experience in the field of Macfadden sentimentality & "confession" stuff, whereas Sonny & Grandpa frankly despise this inartistic & insincere domain, & have no ability to enter into its mawkish false psychology. We discourage that kind of thing & urge our clients to avoid it, whereas honest Eddy is experienced in its ways & might help anyone turn a welcome penny by meeting the conditions of its cheap & unreal world. But this, of course, is only a chance suggestion—*in case* you have unmarketable accumulations of early experimental MSS. of the kind the Belknap & I urge you *not* to write. Eddy might help you dispose of these to the "confession" market—but unless you have such MSS. on hand, don't pay any attention to this idea. *Don't write such stuff afresh, for it would be fatal to your aesthetic development.* It is as a *typist* that I am recommending Eddy so far as your present or future work is concerned. And that, only in case you can't do the typing yourself. If you have anything for him to do, you can reach him as follows—

C. M. Eddy, Jr., 161 Pearl St., Providence, R.I.

Tell him I recommended him, but for the sake of his pride don't mention the matter of his destitution. It is enough, from his angle, that he is recommended as a prompt & good typist & light reviser.

My clients will probably think it odd in me to start up all of a sudden & urge them to give all their typing work to a partial or absolute stranger, as the case may be; but if they could visualise the sad & depressing conditions I encountered Tuesday night they would wonder no more. I am still haunted by the aura of melancholy which I encountered—& am tremendously sorry that I did not know of the present conditions in time to give Eddy the de Castro typing job which I finished only a few hours before learning of his plight. I found the hapless author in more squalid quarters than he has ever inhabited before—though he has always, like poor old Everett McNeil, (who died December 14th) had to stick close to the slums & semi-slums. 161 Pearl St. is in a fearsomely dismal though not noisy quarter, & the best that can be said of the tenement is that Eddy & his family keep it scrupulously clean. They have no money for rent, & are hanging on only through the charity of a kindly Irish landlady willing to accept promises in place of cash *for a few weeks more.* Each day Eddy makes a round of possible employers in many lines, but absolutely nothing is to be had—& meanwhile he & his family of four can eat only about once a day. Eddy's father, now dominated by an iron-hearted elder daughter, refuses all aid & even forbids his housekeeper (Eddy's mother is an invalid) to give the poor fellow the scraps & leavings from the table for which he has pathetically pleaded in order to save his wife & children from malnutrition & illness. In short, absolutely all that stands between Eddy & stark starvation are the occasional dimes & quarters which his good old bookseller uncle (himself faced with want as a result of poor sales, rising shop rent, & an invalid family to maintain) presses upon him, plus the lean half-dollars which he torturesomely earns by going to the Municipal Charities Bureau (with all the tramps & alcoholics—& he a total abstainer of impeccable habits!) & chopping firewood as long as his strength holds out. He collapsed the other day from cold & over-exertion, & was pathetically grateful when the man in charge gave him his full pay in spite of the uncompleted job. Sometimes neighbours have brought in food—as they used to do with Poe's ill-starred household a century ago—& at Christmastide the family was cheered by an anonymous gift of food, coal, & cheap toys for the children; (a boy 11 & girls 9 & 7) a gift which Eddy is inclined to attribute to the pastor or parishioners of the Methodist church which his wife & children attend. This pastor seems to be an admirable chap, for he is about to give Eddy enough cash to get his clothes repaired in order to present a decent appearance in job-seeking. Tuesday night, when Eddy took me on a midnight antiquarian walk after my call, I saw that he was unusually shaky for one of his brisk, wiry alertness; & when we paused for a bite at an all-night restaurant he confessed that he had not touched food in *29 hours*. I made him eat as much as he could, & repeated the process later in the walk, when we stopped at another lunch room—& I also managed to make him accept as much of a "loan" as I could possibly afford, to feed his family for the next day or two—but these things are at best but the most temporary palliatives. What he needs is work—hence my efforts to "drum him up" some typing & light revision among my clients. If he can be tided over until he can obtain some regular position, he will be saved. Otherwise heaven only knows what will happen to him—perhaps the Overseer of the Poor will break up his family, put his children in orphan asylums, & send him & his wife to the Providence County Poor Farm. It is really an almost unbelievable case—as may clearly be seen from the extent to which it impresses a hard-boiled cynic like myself. I can't get the depression of the thing out of my head—hence the boresome extent to which I am spinning this account of the matter. We here behold *real tragedy* in its grimmest form—something which, in the experience of Belknap's & my "gang", can be parallelled only by poor old McNeil's desperate struggles in New York's Hell's Kitchen; & which makes milder cases of impecuniousness—involving no loss of food, shelter, necessary heat, & decent clothing—appear rather sheepishly pale in comparison. Faced with this case, one doesn't feel like complaining quite so loudly about not having enough cash for new suits (Eddy has only *one* suit, & that is falling to pieces!) & odd books that one wants, or pleasure-trips to this or that colonial town! It is certainly a pitiful disintegration—for Eddy is a lineal descendant of the great John Churchill, First Duke of Marlborough . . . . hero of Blenheim & supreme power behind the throne of Great Britain under Queen Anne. That . . . . to *this!* And all in little more than two hundred years!

So that is that . . . . & now I will turn off the stream of senile prolixity! The gist of this epistle is simply this twofold suggestion—(a) that you give Eddy all the typing work you have done outside, & (b) that you give him any *light* revision of early "human sentiment" MSS. which you may wish doctored up for trial on the Macfadden "confession" market. If he gets the job of typing "The Mound", I will personally go over the completed text & guarantee 100% accuracy. Don't forget the name & address—C. M. Eddy, Jr., 161 Pearl St., Providence, R.I.

As for "The Mound"—I hope you will receive it almost simultaneously with this letter, for I've written Sonny very fully. Let me know if it needs any change. I hope, in general, that you will like it, & that Wright will later accept it.

With best wishes for your health & work, apologies for bothering you with this suggestion, & regards to Iacobus–Iunior, I remain,

Yr ob^t h^{ble} Servt

H P Lovecraft

[48]   [ALS]

10 Barnes St.,

Providence, R.I.,

Jany. 24, 1930

My dear Mrs. Reed:—

By this time I trust "The Mound" has safely reached you—Belknap having assured me that it is off at last. I hope you will not find it disappointing—or too illegible to decipher. In case you do not perform the typing yourself, I hope you can let poor C. M. Eddy Jr. have the job. He will give conscientious service, & I will personally correct the typed MS. when it is done. Or, as I said, if you do perform the job yourself, I will be glad to correct the finished copy if you will send it along, together with the rough draught. In case you do the typing, be careful about the imaginary names—K'N-YAN, GYAA-YOTHN, &c. &c. If Eddy does it, I will have a preliminary explanatory session with him. As for submitting the tale to Wright—of course I'll be glad to send it along if that would help, although you may recall that Little Belknap insists that Wright is prejudiced against MSS. which come through an intermediary. I'll await your further instructions on that score. Personally, I don't think it makes a bit of difference to Wright how the MSS. come—so that, since the MS. will be in my hands for correction, I had perhaps better let him have it directly to save the not inconsiderable postage of a second transmission. I leave it all to you to decide. Thanks for the cheque—& glad to hear that Sonny's is also despatched. I'll remember not to cash it before the 10th prox. Shall be glad to see "Ghost Stories of an Antiquary"[1]—although there was really no hurry about that or the other material.

Congratulations on your steady recovery—but I trust you will not try to be too energetic or too assiduous in using your eyes until the convalescence is well rounded out. Hope you found "The Modern Temper"[2] both intrinsically interesting & helpful in the rectification of your perspective. I shall be glad to answer any question or furnish any comment which it may bring up—which reminds me that I really ought to read it in its present book form. I read its sections as they appeared one by one in the Atlantic,[3] but Sonny tells me that there has been some revision & amplification in the present version. Krutch, by the way, will lecture in Providence on March 5th—under the auspices of Brown University. I shall make an effort to attend, & hope I can learn the real pronunciation of his name from the person who introduces him. Of course—

the introducer himself may make an error—but I'll watch Krutch's expression when the fateful syllable comes out. If he looks placid, I shall conclude that the pronunciation is correct; while if he winces, I shall assume that a mistake has been made! I do not yet know what subject Krutch will speak on—indeed, it rather surprises me that a college as conventional & fossilised as Brown should sponsor so realistic & disillusioned a speaker!

Pray convey my sympathy to Iacobus–Iunior anent their examinations, & tell them they needn't worry about the delay in acknowledging my acknowledgment. I can appreciate the strain they are under, having undergone the same thing myself aeons ago; but it is comforting to reflect that the resilience of youth will soon efface its results once the causative ordeal is over!

Again hoping that you will find "The Mound" acceptable & decipherable, & extending my best wishes, I remain

Yr most ob^t h^{ble} Servt

H P Lovecraft

Notes

1. By M. R. James. HPL had evidently lent her his copy of the book.
2. By Joseph Wood Krutch.
3. The book was serialized sporadically in the *Atlantic Monthly* between February 1927 and February 1929. Only the first instalment has the title "The Modern Temper."

[49]   [AHT]

10 Barnes St.,
Providence, R.I.
Jany. 26, 1930

My dear Mrs. Reed:—

[. . .] Poor old McNeil's death last month was a depressing shock to us all. The "gang"—or such of it as still retains metropolitan residence—met at Talman's (the chap who designed my new bookplate) in Brooklyn last Wednesday, and Sonny writes that the meeting didn't seem quite like the old-time ones. Good old Mac was a character—naive, honest, lovable, plodding, and still full of the kindly, outworn faiths of the 19th century. His life was really a tragedy—for no matter how hard he worked, he could never seem to scrape together enough to keep him out of dire want . . . that is, until the very last, when his books showed better sales and he moved to a cosy new flat in Astoria at the foot of Ditmars Blvd., where his living-room windows looked out on the parklike shore of the East River, with blue water gleaming, boats passing, the green of Ward's and Randall's Islands glowing, and the great Roman-like span of Hell Gate Bridge arching over all. But this only heightens the tragic irony of his career—for no sooner had he reached this stage of relative peace and comfort, than he was stricken down. Having toiled in squalor all his life for a small reward, even that reward was denied him after the briefest of glimpses! Mac was a son of rural Wisconsin who grew up as a natural story-teller and finally went to New York in wide-eyed expectancy to seek his fortune, like boys in the story-books—the fortune that never came. Too shy and simple to make his way against the push and competition of unctuous sophisticates, he kept on writing his naive boy-tales without knowing how to exploit them among the shark-like publishing fraternity—and vegetated quietly in unknown backwaters—poorer and poorer ones as his fortunes waned, and as the growth of the city made "shabby genteel" quarters harder and harder to obtain. Always a shy, grown-up boy in manner and psychology, his hair whitened and his step weakened with the years, till he looked like an old man before his time. He lived largely as a hermit, fearful that people did not like his plain ways or that they would think him odd and boresome—but he always had a few friends of varying ages who appreciated and admired his qualities, and would not be repelled by shyness. When Sonny and I first met him, in 1922, his affairs were at their lowest ebb, and he dwelt in the frightful slum of Hell's Kitchen—where Manhattan's forties slope gradually down to the Hudson. This was and is the toughest slum in New York—toughest in an active sense, being full of fighting Irish, whereas the East Side has gone over to cowed, cringing Jews and affable—even if stiletto-toting—Italians. Policemen in Hell's Kitchen go in pairs, and report a high casualty list. High in a squalid tenement house amidst this welter lived good old Mac—his little flat an oasis of neatness and wholesomeness with its quaint, homely pictures, rows of simple books, and curious mechanical devices which his ingenuity concocted to aid his work—lap boards, files, etc. etc. He lived on meagre rations of canned soup and crackers, and did not whimper at his lot. We all used to shudder at having to wade through such a neighbourhood to get to his place, but when he entertained a meeting his shy hospitality atoned for all. I can hardly realise even now that, if I went down to 543 West 49th St. and rang the bell in the dismal hall, I would not hear an answering click and find that little grey figure in the doorway after climbing the five squalid flights of iron-and-concrete stairs! Poor old Mac! He had suffered a lot in his day—and at one time had nothing to eat but the sugar which he could pick up free at lunch rooms and dissolve in water for the sake of its nourishment. That era of malnutrition was what broke him down and paved the way for his death at 67. In 1922, even, his voice and hands trembled like an octogenarian's, and Sonny and I were genuinely shocked to find in a "Who's Who" that he was only 60. We had thought him 75, at least. I can see him now, too, as he was on the walks we all used to take—shorter and shorter walks, they had to be, for him. I shall always associate him with the great grey glamorous stretches of sedgy flat lands in Southern Brooklyn—salt marshes with inlets, like the Holland coast, and dotted with lonely Dutch cottages with curving roof-lines. All gone now—like Mac—built over by cheap suburbs with flashy cottages and commonplace streets. Then came the glimpse of better fortune—and the end!

[. . .]

     Yr. obt. Servt.

         H. P. Lovecraft

[50]   [ALS]

                  10 Barnes St.,

                   Providence, R.I.,

                     Jany. 29, 1930.

My dear Mrs. Reed:—

         Having been to see Eddy last night, I will add a postscript to my letter of Sunday concerning him. He was prodigiously grateful for the "Mound" MS., & promises a good typed copy & carbon in something like a week's time. I furnished him with all the needed supplies, gave him warning about all the difficult & artificial words in the MS., & in general did what I could to make the job less formidable for him. I think he will have no difficulty, & believe the resulting text will be very neat & accurate. I am telling him not to bother about the diacritical marks on the Spanish & artificial words, since I can easily supply these with pen & ink when I go over the MS. in the end. Wright will have a very legible & prepossessing MS. to survey when the time comes for him to pass judgment upon it.

As for future revisory work on your earlier MSS.—Eddy spoke in a very encouraging & explicit vein, & held out many hopes for ultimate acceptances by Macfadden & other primitive markets. Of course this would be very frankly a *revision downward* to meet the tastes of a low-grade & mentally undeveloped public, so that you ought not to associate this work in any way with your *literary* activities. As a friend of Orton's—connected with the Macfadden firm—explained last spring, the clientele of these "confession" & "romance" magazines is confined wholly to ignorant, plodding classes of low intelligence & deficient imagination; classes below even the *Cosmopolitan* level, & exemplifying the popular word "moron" in its fullest sense. They have no well-defined mental concepts & absolutely no aesthetic or traditional background of any sort; but live wholly in a hazy & simplified half-world of primal sensation & artificial & exaggerated sentimentality. Work planned to reach them—the work, that is, demanded by Macfadden editors—must be designed according to special patterns wholly apart from anything connected with real literature, human life, or serious writing & artistic sincerity. It must be tailored to fit the mental dwarfishness & deformity of the lower classes as carefully as a suit of clothes for a dwarf or hunchback would have to be tailored—the successful mob-author requiring not so much literary knowledge as knowledge of the mob-mentality—or rather, the mob-emotions, since this grade of reader has no mentality. Thus one's position is really that of the clinical specialist—the alienist, as it were—trying to hit on some artificial way of titillating certain emotions in sub-normal types. This titillation is accomplished in certain stock ways wholly unconnected with literature or sincere authorship. One must use certain inane phrases, certain popular key-words, certain hackneyed & sensational modes of approach, certain conventional & factitious mood-pictures & motivations, &c. &c.—things which no real author could know anything about except as a result of deliberate study in the psychology of the sub-normal herd. The Macfadden staff is composed of shrewd, unliterary business people (like this friend of Orton's—the young Philistine "go-getter" Ashley Belvin) who make such a study . . . . a study which sometimes unfits them for real authorship, but which—when successful—brings in vast financial returns.[1] I would not advise any genuine literary aspirant to dabble in this extraneous field—but I will give the successful figures in it credit for hard, keen, cynical intelligence & unfailing skill. Persons who live closest to the sub-normal herd & know their blundering folkways & stunted minds at first-hand are those most likely to succeed in Macfaddenism. Of our gang only Orton—whose worldly knowledge & experience are wider than those of Belknap, Wandrei, Dwyer, Talman, Morton, & myself—has shown any aptitude in Macfaddenising; & even he doesn't "land" this stuff very often. So much, then, for a definition & a warning. Eddy revision may be able to turn some of your earlier attempts into Macfaddenly salable material—*but accept these revisions without analysis & without any tendency to adopt their principles in your serious work.* Accept . . . . *& forget at once.* Everything which will be done to your MSS. in such revision will be exactly what Belknap is teaching you *not* to do—exactly what would be fatal to your development as a writer of good literature & an authentic chronicler of life as it is. But, since there is a good chance of cashing in on the simple & artificial stuff, there is no reason why you should not take the gamble—so long as you remain on your guard against the atmosphere & psychology it represents. In fact, I rather advise your trying it if, as you say, the circumstance of going on record as the writer of published material well be of use to you. And in this direction the House of Eddy can certainly help you—for it has found Macfadden placement for many a manuscript whose original crudity would astonish you. I say the "House of Eddy" because C.M.E. Jr. made it clear last night that his wife does most of the adaptive revision in cases of this kind. He takes care of the grammatical & rhetorical side, while Mrs. Eddy supplies the "human-interest" hokum & blah for which the Macfadden editors are so avid. She, it seems, has produced much of this material, & has helped many beginners to develop into steady sellers. Her help, Eddy says, generally amounts to actual collaboration—although in your case, as I have just warned, you must not let it approach the status of *instruction* lest the results of Belknap's lessons be un-done. The rates charged by the Eddys for this collaborative revision of Macfaddenistic material would be very reasonable, & they would be glad to discuss the matter of placement with you whenever you wish to write. I would advise your dropping a line relative to the matter whenever you feel sufficiently recovered to attend to it—the address, as I think I stated in my preceding letter, is *C. M. Eddy, Jr., 161 Pearl St., Providence, R.I.*

I found the Eddy home in a gloom of very literal quality—the electric lights having been cut off because of non-payment of the current bill. In their stead gleamed three or four feeble oil lamps without shades—a sorry substi-tute, & one which had forced Eddy to abandon the semi-weekly theatrical rehearsals which—in connexion with his anaemic booking-agency side-line, a thing much impaired by the advent of the talking cinema—had helped to stave off immediate starvation. Your twenty dollars (I had not the heart to make deduction for postage & supplies, but allowed these to form a well-meant donation from myself) came as a godsend, & will enable him to have his electric service restored. The only bright ray besides this fee was an unex-pected arrangement with a cheap-theatre manager to supply "talent" for cer-tain weekly performances—a thing which will perhaps feed the family for one or two days a week, leaving rent & other sundries for the gods to look after. This managerial gentleman, a son of Israel named Jacob Conn, may later on have more work for Eddy; but just now he is suspicious of all agents because he was lately defrauded by one—an Hibernian specimen whom he had em-ployed on a regular salary. 'Heh ess ah beezness men, en' heh shoodent ged sheated ter-vice in der same blace, a'ready!' So for the present Eddy's booking business will have to be of the precarious free-lance sort—using a dwindling supply of business stationery printed for him by the same kindly clergyman (who has a press & prints his own church calendars) who gave him cash to have his single suit put in decent shape. A weary, strenuous, suspense-filled, anxious sort of hand-to-mouth existence—& one under which a man less buoyant & resilient than Eddy might well be expected to break down!

Naturally—& without mentioning names or sources this time—I spoke of the matter of apparel, & of the possibility that I might casually collect some for him & his heir-apparent. As I expected, he hailed the prospect with gratitude & enthusiasm; so that I can assure you of a warm & appreciative reception for any items you may send. When, however, I asked him for his measurements, he admitted that he had long ago forgotten them—it being ages since the purchase of his last new suit. The following data which he furnished might be of *some* help in deciding the approximate suitability of any garment for him. He is 5 feet, 5½ inches in height, & has a 28-inch waist. He *thinks* the coat he wears is a #35 or something like that. I am more than ever inclined to think that a large boys' or youth's suit might fit him—really, I had not imagined till I studied him last night with a clothier's eye how *very* small & thin he is! He never struck me as so *much* shorter than Sonny Belknap, & yet the Child is 5 ft 8 in. As for the 11-year-old Crown Prince—all his father could recall of his exact dimensions is that he is considered well-grown for his age, & wears clothes which the shops classify as "12-yr-old" size. Iacobean garb would need reducing for his immediate use, no doubt; although he will probably soon grow into the right size for such items as are now too small for their original occupant. What, then, I gather as a whole, is that the Eddy household would be devoutly thankful for any small-man's or large-boy's garments which might find their way thither. For the present, I will undertake to serve as a distributing-dêpot; though later on I think Eddy ought to be able to give credit & thanks to the real source of such sartorial succour as reaches him! Again let me express my own profound appreciation of the thoughtfulness which impels you to go to the trouble of collecting & parcel-posting this bulky kind of material.

I did not reach the squalid Eddy tenement till late in the evening—going on foot along my own ancient hill with its centuried fanlights & Georgian doorways, & subsequently crossing the Point St. Bridge over the harbour (about half a mile below the Great Bridge at the old civic centre) for my plunge into the tangled labyrinth of the unknown slums. Arriving safely, I found all the household but Eddy* retired—he being crouched beside the one kitchen stove (my old-home stove, as it happens!) for heat in the absence of any furnace. To save fuel & kerosene, we soon adjourned to an all-night lunch-room ("Tom & Jack's" "one-arm joint") in the nearest business street, where I forced my host to fortify himself in a nutritive way. He had had a meal at *noon*, so thought himself relatively well-fed according to recent standards—but I convinced him he had some room left within. Over some indifferent alleged coffee we arranged the details of your manuscript—& he promised to deliver the typed goods in person some time next week. At about 2:30 a.m. we parted—& despite the increasing cold I was idiot enough to walk home . . . . . a progressively congealing process which has left me good for nothing ever since! But I guess another day will thaw me out. ¶ With all good wishes, appreciation of your generous offer for Eddy, & the hope of a well-typed MS. to reward you—I remain

Yr obt hble Servt

H P Lovecraft

P.S. These are certainly days of misfortune! Orton, supposedly our gang's luckiest member in a financial way, has just lost his job of long standing with

---

*plus the delightful *cat* which not even poverty can banish—an exquisite black creature who made straight for my lap, & who is veritable reincarnation of my beloved old "Nigger Man" of 30 years ago!

the great Knopf publishing house, (American Mercury) & is now practicing unaccustomed economies! His case, though, doesn't touch the tragedy class. Next autumn he hopes to found an independent publishing business—a select private press—somewhere in Vermont.² If he does, he may bring out a book of my stuff—possibly a novel.

Notes

1. HPL wrote about him, "the way this chap coolly analysed the needs of the Macfadden publications was enough to make an hippopotamus shrink. I'll own that I was hardly civil to him when he suggested that I try to reach this market—for my stomach was turned nearly inside out!" (HPL to Clark Ashton Smith, [25 December 1930]; *DS* 286).

2. Stephen Daye, Sr. (c.1594–1668) operated the first printing press in America in the 17th Century. The modern publishing company, founded in 1932 by John S. and Marion R. Hooper, was named for him. HPL edited one title for the press.

[51]   [ALS]

Friday [February 1930]

My dear Mrs. R—

Confound that unutterable Chicago dunce! The fool could have divided the story as well as not—but he was evidently in the same dense mood which afflicted him when he rejected Smith's "Satampra Zeiros."¹

If I were you I would try the tale on the following magazines in the following order:

> *Astounding Stories*
> *Amazing Stories*
> *Science Wonder Stories*

I can't find their addresses at the moment, but it seems to me I had them a couple of weeks ago & included them when writing you. You would probably find them in the longish typed letter if I did send them. If I didn't, you can get them from copies of the respective magazines in news shops—or I will look them up myself & let you know. If these three markets prove closed, you might ask Wright whether he would consider a condensation of the story. With plenty of time, I might manage to pare the thing down here & there— although it would be a monstrous task. You could ask Wright his maximum word-limit of acceptance. Not long ago he accepted a tale of Smith's on condition of its abridgment.

As for Eddy—no, he is not yet working on your tales unless he has heard from you since last Saturday; for he was not then sure that you had accepted his 50%-down offer! He was anxiously awaiting word from you regarding the matter, but did not dare to begin work without your authorisation. Now that

I see you intend to accept the offer, I will at once drop him a card so that he may start work. Too bad the misunderstanding caused delay. However—I am advising him to go easy on the ending of "The Unchaining" until you decide whether or not to send him the original version—as I would advise you to do. I have also told him to hold off on "Lesson 8", which reached him by mistake. He would no doubt appreciate definite authorisations & instructions from you as soon as you can conveniently write him.

I can well imagine how the *True Story* must have impressed you—for I receive a definite wave of nausea every time anybody thrusts one of those rags under my nose & urges me to try to meet their demands. Ugh! I almost punched Orton's friend Belvin—who specialises in this stuff—in the face! Certainly, not even the earliest & crudest of your experiments sank to anything like this sodden level—but it's the business of the Eddys to make your MSS. deliberately cheaper in tone & form, so that they may suit the Macfadden requirements. To strike the exact psychological note, in all its trite commonness & vulgarity, is an intellectual achievement in itself.

No—Sonny Belknap is not ill, but is all wrapped up in novel-writing.[2] I've just told the child to write you, & fancy you'll hear from him before long.

The genial premature spring which you mention was shared by Providence, & I surely enjoyed it while it lasted. Next month—or April—I hope to make my reckless southward plunge & get some real summer ahead of time. Belknap & his parents will probably give me a lift in their car part of the way, for they plan to take a trip as far south as Virginia about the same time. I hope to get to Charleston, & possibly Savannah.

With best wishes to you & the Dioscuri,[3]

I have yᵉ Honour to remain

Yr moſt oblig'd, moſt obᵗ Servᵗ

H P Lovecraft

Notes

1. HPL refers to Farnsworth Wright's rejection of "The Mound" and, earlier, of Clark Ashton Smith's "The Tale of Satampra Zeiros." Wright later accepted the latter, and it appeared in the November 1931 issue of *WT*.

2. Presumably *The Horror from the Hills*, published as a two-part serial in *WT* (January and February/March 1931). It included a lengthy passage describing a dream taken verbatim from a letter by HPL (later published separately as "The Very Old Folk," based on HPL's description of the same dream in a letter to Donald Wandrei).

3. "The sons of Zeus."

[52]   [ALS, JHL]

5001 Sunset Dr
K. C. Mo—
5 / 26 / 34

Dear Mr Lovecraft:—

Your letter of the 20th just arrived. I shall be only too happy to have your friend have The Mound for sale or to see, especially since it offers an opportunity to partially discharge my already disgracefully lengthened debt to you. (You are so patient about money—especially when your need is so very much.)

You perhaps did not remember that I sent The Mound to Sonny Belknap over two years ago (in fact immediately after the old Boston lady—I'm grieved to learn of her death—returned it.) I wired him just now to send the unabridged copy to Mr Barlow at once. If he decides to buy it, is it for publication or just to keep the mss? You did not make that part clear and I should like to know.

Do you suppose Mr Barlow would be interested in reading Medusa's Coil? I have it and a carbon copy of The Mound except the first three pages. Have you time to recall them were you to see it?

Thanks for your interesting letter, & I hope you land The Mound, & finish up your trip as planned. As I'm anxious to get this letter to you shall not write more today, but will answer your letters in detail Monday.

My regards to your interesting host & of course yourself. Thanks—am much improved in health & as my bank has just received a loan from the R.F.C.[1] am hoping to improve financially soon.

Sincerely
Z. B. B.

Notes

1. The Reconstruction Finance Corporation, a program begun in the New Deal (1932) to make loans to banks, state and local governments, and other entities. It continued until 1957.

[53]   [ANS][1]

[Postmarked Providence, R.I.,
3 October 1934]

Yrs. recd. Many thanks for instalments—residue down to 12.00 now. Glad Moe can handle job. Will reply more fully later. Will do my best with the opening & various paragraphs, but cannot make absolute promises on account of rushed condition & closeness to nervous breakdown—insomnia &c.

Simply must get rest at any cost. If I *can't* do anything (all concentration becomes highly painful & difficult) I'll see that the MS. is back well before the end of the month anyhow. I assume you want it returned to you rather than sent on to Moe directly. But I'll see what I can do.

     Best wishes—
Yrs most sincerely—H P L

Notes

1. *Front:* Van Wickel Gates, Brown University, Providence, R. I. The card is addressed to "Mrs. D. W. Bishop." She had married Dauthard W. Bishop on 22 July 1930 in Lake, Ind., but was now living in Kansas City, Mo.

[54] [ALS]

         66 College St.,
          Providence, R.I.,
           March 31, 1936

Dear Mrs. Bishop:—

    Let me hasten to acknowledge the instalment just received, which reduces the current account to $26.00.[1] I am certainly sorry to hear of the many difficulties which have affected the matter—& I may add that I would certainly never mention the situation to any but the very closest revisory partners. Upon reflection, I think you can understand why a group doing close team-work—operating, as it were, like a single firm—cannot possibly do otherwise than hold all business information in common. What I can't handle goes to Moe or Belknap (though Belknap is nowadays so busy with magazine fiction that he's refusing virtually all revision)—what Moe can't handle goes to me . . . & so on. A constant exchange of jobs, which helps to put each kind of work in the right hands, & which could not conceivably be maintained if each reviser did not know as much as every other one what to expect. Revision is deadly hard work. To prepare a story requires hours & days of energy, leaves the reviser exhausted, & naturally keeps him from handling any other job in that interval. Thus one *has* to be reasonably certain of what to expect financially if one is to keep on at all. For a reviser to pass on to a colleague a piece of gruelling, devitalising work which will keep him from anything else for days or weeks, yet which—in spite of the most innocent intention of the client—is likely to yield no sizeable return for months or years, would be a brutally un-ethical act; an act so grave as to overshadow altogether the alternative evil of mentioning that which one would prefer not to mention. It has to be a case of "all for one & one for all" in a revisory group—or indeed in any commercial partnership. But it is of course understood that all such data remains *strictly a professional secret within the firm.*

The fact that each one of a group has to share his business information with the others does not mean that he—or any of the others—would even think of disclosing any item of it *outside* the circle. Thus you need not fear that the pooling of ledger-columns among Moe, Belknap, & me implies any irresponsible *outside* comment on the part of any of us. No one but the three has ever heard from our lips the details of any arrangement with any client. I explain this quite fully lest you adjudge Belknap & me guilty of poor taste when in truth we are following only what we deem good professional ethics. We all have the keenest sympathy when a client is unable to be as prompt as he might wish, & there is never any criticism of the client—overt or implied— when we follow our usual policy of giving a just & impersonal summary of prospects. I am sure you will recognise the essential justice—& virtual inevitability—of such a policy under the circumstances, & that you will accordingly credit Belknap & me with less crude taste than the incident may make us appear to have.

Well—as I have said—I am enormously sorry to hear of the diverse difficulties which have beset you, & hope that each of them may clear up in the course of time & flow of events. It is painful to learn that Iunior (of whom, it seems only yesterday, I used to hear as one of two lively little imps in short trousers) has been in a mess through easy-going business standards, & I hope his recent experience will prove a permanent lesson to him. It may well do so—for many a new solid & conscientious man has one such incident concealed in the early pages of his annals.

My sympathy goes to Iacobus for his recent physical turndown—but he has plenty of company in the experience. Back in April 1917 (my health then being infinitely worse than now) I received a decided rebuff when I attempted to join the National Guard—the physician almost insulting me for wasting his valuable time. Probably he was right—for with my present wider perception I realise that I would almost undoubtedly have gone to pieces in camp long before getting to France—but at the time I felt badly affronted. My one chuckle was that the *doctor himself* was physically disqualified when his unit of the guard was mustered into Federal service! These events soon slip half-forgotten into the past—& meanwhile let me congratulate Iacobus on his foothold in an important firm which well-nigh promises an assured future.

I am extremely glad to hear that "The Adopted Son" is faring well in its professional travels, & hope it may eventually get into type between cloth covers. "Homing" sounds very interesting, & I trust that this also will find a haven (with the MS. *not* living up to its title!) when completed. Each new piece of work means valuable practice, & useful experience in solving the varied problems of narration. Your perseverance, I am sure, will bring good results in the end.

It is amusing to see how Wright sends out cards even for reprinted stuff like "Dagon" & "The Temple." My best recent luck has not been with him but with *Astounding Stories*, which took not only my long "At the Mountains of Madness" (serial—Feb. Mar. Apr.), but my more recent "Shadow out of Time" (scheduled complete for June). My "Shadow Over Innsmouth" is being issued as a small book ($1.00) by the Visionary Publishing Co. of Everett, Pa.—a sort of one-man hill-billy concern—with 4 excellent weird illustrations by Frank A. Utpatel of Wisconsin . . . whose work you may have seen in W T in connexion with Derleth's stories.

I spent all last summer in De Land with Barlow,* in the spring I had two enjoyable visits from Moe's elder son, now in Bridgeport, Conn.[,] visiting Wandrei & Belknap in N Y for a fortnight on the return trip. In the autumn I took one or two interesting short trips around New England. Around New Year's I visited Belknap again—seeing the new Hayden Planetarium of the American Museum, a marvellous device. Then—upon my return home—I was engulfed by a vortex of assorted troubles which threatens to explode what little there is left of my nervous system. First a hopeless flood of tasks—none decently remunerative—which threw my programme into chaos. Then an attack of grippe which had me flat for a week & left me as shaky as an aspen—& *then* the trouble *really* began! My aunt came down with a grippe attack a thousandfold worse than mine,[2] which tied me up completely as a sort of combined nurse, secretary, butler, market-man & errand-boy, & forced me to return or transfer *all* my own work. The case grew worse rather than better, & my aunt finally went to the hospital—where she is now recovering nicely. Errands & responsibilities still leave me helpless—but I realise that the situation is a lot worse for the patient than it is for me. 1936 is certainly my bad year so far!

Well—again let me thank you for the instalment (quite a fortune in my present alarming financial state!), & express my regret at the many troubles you are encountering. The one consoling thing I can think of is that another beastly *winter* is over! ¶ Hoping for better times at both ends of the line—

Yrs most sincerely—

H P Lovecraft

Notes

1. HPL's "Instructions in Case of Decease," written to R. H. Barlow, his "literary executor," in late 1936 or early 1937, notes "Mrs. D. W. Bishop, 5001 Sunset Drive, Kansas City, Mo. owed H. P. Lovecraft $26 for revision work." It is not known if her debt was paid.

2. In fact, Annie Gamwell was hospitalized for breast cancer and underwent a mastectomy.

---

*I helped Barlow build a cabin across the lake to house his printing & binding apparatus, & we printed—unknown to the author—a surprise edition of Belknap's uncollected poems, entitled "The Goblin Tower."

Letters to William Lumley

[1]   [AHT]

[Rio Vista Hotel
120 Bay Street
St. Augustine, Fla.]

May 12, 1931

Dear Mr. Lumley:—

[. . .]

The idea of a land of darkness is excellent, and one footnote telling of ancient MSS. *which even the Egyptian priests could not read* excited my imagination tremendously. That kind of thing resembles my own (purely mythical) "Pnakotic Manuscripts"; which are supposed to be the work of "Elder Ones" preceding the human race on this planet, and handed down through an early human civilisation which once existed around the north pole.[1]

[. . .]

What I *am* interested in, is the system of imaginative explanation and escape from reality which the primitive mind has evolved from the age-long contemplation of non-understood phenomena in the external world. This system is, of course, a fairly stable and uniform one based on the essential similarity of all human minds and the rough uniformity of the terrestrial scene which confronts all these minds; so that its various fantastic forms and processes—as manifest in religious and occult beliefs—are surely of vast psychological, anthropological, and aesthetic significance. Therefore I regard it as vital and legitimate literary material, and worthy of a serious and detailed treatment which few first-rate authors have condescended to give it. In the present age, when the emotional life of the individual receives such literary emphasis, there ought to be at least a partial renaissance of tales and poems dealing with this phase of feeling; yet actually only a few first-rate authors have entered the field at all seriously. Of these, Algernon Blackwood, Walter de la Mare, and Dunsany have produced any quantity of work. On a lower level I shall write what I can, but I have no illusions about the quality of the stuff I grind out. All I can say for it is that it represents serious and sincere effort, and is not consciously cheap "hokum" like so many of the allegedly weird tales of the present.

[. . .]

With every good wish, I remain

Yrs most cordially and sincerely,

H. P. Lovecraft

Notes

1. HPL introduced the Pnakotic Manuscripts in "Polaris" (1918) and cited them in many later stories.

[2]   [AHT]

Dec. 21, 1931

My dear Mr. Lumley:—

[. . .]

Yes—I have frequently noticed the bestial and repulsive aspect of crowds, especially in such decadent cosmopolitan centres as New York City. Hogarth certainly reproduced the true substance of life, and it takes but a little imagination to modify these degraded types into the out and out monsters of phantasy. Another artist who went even farther than Hogarth in depicting human bestiality is the Spaniard, Goya. Swift surely had a sound basis for his account of the Yahoos—which indeed I found fascinating from childhood onward.[1] There is a place in art and literature for the delineation of reality in its sternest phases, but that does not detract from the value of phantasy—the literature of escape. Some writers take naturally to the one phase, while others incline toward the other. It is always the unreal and the marvellous—the vague and expectancy-fraught world of dream, wherein anything is possible—which have primarily fascinated me.

[. . .]

Yrs most cordially and sincerely,
H. P. Lovecraft

Notes

1. HPL owned a 1906 edition of Swift's *Gulliver's Travels,* presumably inherited from his family library. Whether he read some children's version before that date is unknown.

[3]   [AHT]

Feby. 22, 1932

Dear Mr. Lumley:—

[. . .]

My only objection to Cabell is that he mixes two distinct departments of writing which are naturally unrelated and almost antagonistic—that is, the field of phantasy or imaginative escape, and the field of intellectual analysis of human motives. Of course, the fantastic author ought to be as accurate and realistic as he can when he does handle human motives; but it impairs the force of the phantasy whenever he shifts prime stress to the human element

and makes the unreal events seem like mere allegorical comments on mankind. This latter effect is encountered rather too often in Cabell's books.

[. . .]

Gautier and Flaubert are both titans in their field, and have contributed
much to the development of narrative prose.

[. . .]

    Yrs most sincerely,

        H. P. Lovecraft

[4]   [AHT]

{c. 1933?}

Dear Mr. Lumley:—

      [. . .]

Like you, I am exceedingly fond of weird scenes—both old towns with
narrow streets and centuried houses, and landscapes of bizarre or spectral aspect. When I was a very small child a certain deep, shadowy, wooded ravine
with queer rocks and twisted tree-trunks influenced my imagination profoundly. You would like Salem—many houses of the 1692 witchcraft period
are still standing. Marblehead would also appeal to you. I'd like to see the Old
World—with reliques so much older than any in America—but doubt whether I'll ever have a chance.

[. . .]

I remain

    Yrs most cordially—

        H P L

[5]   [AHT]

        66 College St.,

          Providence, R.I.,

           Nov. 14, 1935

Dear Mr. Lumley:—

      [. . .]

Later . . . Just received yours of the 12th telling of Alonzo's acceptance.[1]
Congratulations!! Your reply to Wright's letter seems to me *exactly right*. I suppose he was curious about getting stories from several authors—Heald, de
Castro, Reed &c (besides *parts* of mss. from Barlow, Bloch, Rimel &c)—
which contained earmarks of my style. I have no objection at all to Wright's
knowing of my share in polishing off the MS. and I think that what you said
was admirable. The only persons I would dislike to mention it to are the various clients (de Castro, &c) for whom (because of its financial unprofitable-
ness) I have recently refused to do such work.

[. . .]
    Yrs most sincerely—
            H P L

Notes

1. HPL had revised "The Diary of Alonzo Typer" gratis for Lumley, and it was accepted by *WT* for publication.

[6]   [AHT]

                                       Dec. 6, 1935
Dear Mr. Lumley:—
               [. . .]
    Some day I hope more will be known about the prehistoric civilisation of the Pacific. It seems to me certain that it came from southeastern Asia and spread gradually across the islands—probably reaching America and forming the nucleus of Inca, Maya, and Aztec cultures. Some believe that old-world influences came to primal America across the Atlantic—borne by Phoenician navigators—but I am inclined to doubt this. It is significant that (except in Mexico and Central America, where the land is narrow) all early American culture traces are on the Pacific coast. Speculations as to ancient tongues and lore surviving in the Himalayas and Thibet are always interesting. [. . .] The legend of the pre-human city of Shamballah, still surviving in the Gobi desert behind a veil of unknown force, occurs in the writings of the Theosophists. It may be an actual bit of Oriental folklore, though one can never be sure. It is hard telling what the theosophists have taken from Hindoo and Thibetan sources, and what they have made up themselves. A great deal of their stuff gives internal evidence of having been written only fifty or sixty years ago. I don't know where Robert W. Chambers got the idea of "Yian".[1] He took some of his cryptic allusions from Ambrose Bierce, but this isn't in Bierce.
    [. . .]
    Yrs sincerely—
            H P Lovecraft

Notes

1. Chambers cited Yian (apparently a city or region in China) in the novelette "The Maker of Moons," in the 1896 collection of that title. HPL cited it in "The Whisperer in Darkness" and cited Yian-Ho in "Through the Gates of the Silver Key" and "The Diary of Alonzo Typer."

[7]　[AHT]

June 20, 1936

Dear Mr. Lumley:—

[. . .]

Those legends of huge hunting cats are surely interesting—the cheetah or hunting-leopard is still used for this purpose in Southern Asia and parts of Africa. My dream of the black cat city was very fragmentary. The place was built of stone and clung to the side of a cliff like some of the towns drawn by Sime for Dunsany's stories. There are towns more or less like it in Spain. The place seemed to have been built by and for human beings aeons ago, but its present feline inhabitants had evidently lived there for ages. Nothing actually happened in this dream—it was just an isolated picture of the place, with the cats moving about in a rational and orderly manner, evidently in the performance of definite duties.

[. . .]

Yrs most sincerely,

H. P. Lovecraft

[8]　[AHT]

Jany. 21, 1937

Dear Mr. Lumley:—

[. . .]

I myself am in miserable health just now—partly an old trouble (extreme swelling of feet and ankles) due to exposure to cold weather in early December, and partly a general weakness and intestinal indigestion probably involving a touch of the prevailing grippe. I have the foot-swelling—which is possibly of cardiac origin—nearly every winter, and sometimes have to wear a pair of old shoes stretched and cut to suit the trouble. I really ought not to try to live outside the tropics or subtropics, for I need temperatures over 80 degrees in order to keep in good physical trim.

[. . .]

Yrs most sincerely,

H. P. Lovecraft

[9]   [AHT]

66 College St.,
Providence, R.I.,
[late February 1937]

Dear Mr. Lumley:—

[. . .]

I am surely sorry to hear of your poor health, which is at present more or less parallelled by my own. My persistent touch of grippe—or whatever it is—keeps my digestion in very bad shape, and I have no strength at all. All I can do is to attend to a few insistent matters and get out for brief afternoon walks when it is warm enough. Thanks very much for the cuttings—including the pictures of those old Oriental images.

[. . .]

Feby. 28

Letter delayed. Am now acutely ill with intestinal trouble following grippe. No strength—constant pain. Bloated with gas and have to sit and sleep constantly in chair with pillows. Doctor is going to call in a stomach specialist Tuesday. So I fear I shan't be able to do much for a long time to come. H P L

Appendix

Farnsworth Wright

Self-Portrait

The editor's a gloomy guy, who fusses, fumes and frets;
He puts in all his cheerless life expressing his regrets.
And you should see the things he sees when perched upon his Eyrie:
The shuddering shapes and eldritch forms, and dim things out of Faerie.
Around the eaves the spiders weave their webs, and bat-things flutter,
While vampires drear breathe in his ear of thoughts too wild to utter.
For music he hears werewolves howl all night to serenade him;
This symphony cacophonous a shivering wreck has made him;
Ah, look! what slithering shapes are these that on his desk are crawling?
Their red eyes fix upon his throat with avid lust appalling,
Till (just between ourselves, you know) he scarce can keep from bawling.
With obscene grins and fleshless chins tall skeletons do mock him,
Till he's reduced to a quivering pulp in fear that one might sock him.
Stone wyverns guard the adytum of darkness where he labors;
Ghosts fly about in a grisly rout, and witches beat their tabors.
A murdered lich stands sentinel beside the office portal—
A zombie he, undead, yet dead; immortal, and yet mortal.
So all the day and all the night the editor gives battle
To spooks and warlocks, wizards, snakes, until his jawbones rattle.
So come, ye bards and raconteurs, send him your stories creepy;
Be sure they're weird, for if they're not, they'll merely make him sleepy;
Stories that bite as well as bark, convincing yarns that floor him—
These are, to him, both food and drink; all other kinds just bore him.

8 January 1935

Walter John Coates

The Birth of *Driftwind*

Ye Editor has long been partial to the adjoining picture because it is, by association, vitally related to his first conception, and later establishment, of *Driftwind*.

Through *Mood Songs*, the Editor's first slim volume of verse, came his first acquaintance with W. Paul Cook and Vrest Orton. Cook had achieved a long and noteworthy career as an expert compositor and pressman, as Editor and Publisher of *Monadnock* (one of the finest amateur journals ever published in America), as President of The National Amateur Press Association, and as a writer of essays, short stories and criticisms under the nom-de-plume of Willis Tete Crossman. Orton was then just out of college, back from a roving trip to Mexico and the Pacific coast . . . a young writer imbued with vision and enthusiasm, ambitious to become [a] free-lance author and publisher.

Vrest Orton, Walter John Coates, W. Paul Cook, late summer 1925 at an old post tavern in North Calais, VT

Having read *Mood Songs*, these men . . . both Vermonters by birth but living in Athol, Mass were curious as to what this nascent Vermont Poet might be. They wrote him, and he replied; and in the late summer of 1925 personal acquaintanceship was effected by a foregathering of the three at North Montpelier. Orton, as a boy, had once lived a few miles distant, at North Calais; and, preliminaries over, it was agreed the three should spend an afternoon there. Entering the village, an old three-story brick dwelling . . . once used, in pioneer days, as a post-tavern . . . loomed before us. It was uninhabited, and we soon secured permission to headquarter there. Eastward and westward rose ranges of picturesque hills; southward the road wound like a distorted ribbon valleyward toward North Montpelier; northward, a few rods distant only, spread the crystal-green waters of Mirror Lake, one of Vermont's most bewitchingly scenic ponds.

Dreamy laziness was the method; literature was the menu; utopian visions were the dessert. We smoked, of course. We dreamed. We talked. Individuality run rampant; for each had literary loves, literary aversions. But on one subject all were agreed: something must be done to foster more wide-spread literary activity in Vermont, to stimulate nascent writers and promote keener appreciation. There had been days when the State could boast a distinct literary atmosphere, with a nationally recognized group of artists and writers. Once, in Royall Tyler's time, a North Hills weekly (published at Walpole but largely inspired from Vermont) had been foremost among the literary journals of America. Why not again . . . or, at least, partially again? A distinct spirit, it was conceded, haunts and has haunted the egoism of these Green Mountain regions.

Afternoon waned. The dreamers departed. But the visions, somehow . . . or some of them at least . . . remained. Winter came, bringing sorrow and anxiety to one of the trio (Coates): his only son was ill . . . desperately ill . . . with tuberculosis. Spring brought no relief of this burden. But in April . . . partly as a defence against morbidity, partly as an aftermath of the North Calais picnic . . . *Driftwind* was born. An old Golding press, foot[-]power[ed] and of forgotten lineage (it was in operation back in the 'eighties), stood unused in the back room off the country store. A few odds and ends of paper were available . . . refuse from a former activity. Out in the woodshed was a pile of white birch wood, bark still adhering to its round surfaces. From the air itself came a title, hazy but meaningful . . . since the publication was to be purely tentative and natural. "The wind bloweth where it listeth, and its sound you hear . . ." Hence the *Driftwind*: A Tramp Magazine. Issued for the Love of literature." This was the first title. It was later on, and after it had become better known, that Percy MacKaye suggested "From the North Hills" as a proper sub-title. And on the cover of these original issues, over the page-motto, was the key-sentence, "Fari quae sentiat" [*to speak what he thinks*] A stanza from Saxe (our own poet) against *war* was the first cover-motto; and the initial issue, of fourteen pages, was put forth in April. A very few copies were sewed up in original birch bark covers; and this practice continued throughout the whole year, twelve issues being sent out in all. Beginning with fifty copies in April, the editions ran to a maximum of eighty during the year, and all were given away. So rare, in after days, became complete files of this first year's harvest, that the birchbark files brought as high as $25.00 per volume, and the ordinary sets, loose, about $12.50. They are collectors' items, and very rare.

The stricken boy had gone from earth-life in November. In March the enterprise had become an economic and labor burden which could not, apparently, be continued. This will be understood when it is considered that one man alone, without sponsoring, in the corner of a country store in a small rural village, had the responsibility of building up a magazine of poetry and fine prose, handsetting all the type, kicking off the pages on an antiquated foot press, binding the copies all by hand, mailing likewise by hand, editing, selling, corresponding . . . In the 12th issue of the *Driftwind* an Editor's Valedictory announced the likely discontinuance. Much to his surprise, the Editor's mail was at once flooded with protests from Vermonters, inland and outland . . . and from many gentile readers. So urgent were these protests that, after some hesitation, the Editor finally promised that, given sufficient support, he would continue the magazine another year. He did so; making it a bimonthly, increasing the pagination, broadening the scope. Response was instant; but growth, though sure, was slow. It was not till 1929 that circulation finally reached to 300 copies. [. . .]

The Future for a Literary Magazine in Vermont

I admit that the too sanguine hope with which, over a year ago, I launched "Drift-Wind", to feel out, almost single-handed, the sentiment for such a magazine, has been sobered down into a realization of the magnitude of such an enterprise and the difficulties facing it. One cannot identify, enlist, articulate, and organize into one purposeful movement the scattered voices of our today's Vermont expression, poetic and prose, without a deal of energy, resourcefulness, and tact. And, even then, one needs to convince the writers concerned that there is a common object at stake, a common incentive big enough to engage their fealty and stimulate their activities.

The writers of this state, and the public as well, have hitherto been blind to the beckoning possibilities of Vermont literary expression and entirely forgetful of, or indifferent to, the splendid literary achievements of our historic past. We have, as state and people, not only ignored the truly wonderful achievements of Green Mountain genius, in word painting, story, and song; but we have, in our lazy indifference and in our ignorance of the whole subject, actually deprecated and belittled that one domain of idealistic activity wherein Vermont talent, when rightly known and appreciated, compares favorably with sister states.

This isn't saying we have produced an Emerson or a Whitman or a Hawthorne. But we have produced a class of writers who, as a group, will compare with any similar group in any state.

We, instead of shouting up our own spouse, have deliberately praised our neighbor's wife—have placed our blazing candle of literary idealism "under a bushel". It has given light thus, not to us who were "in the house", but to the antiquarian and critic who, coming after us, uncovered its repressed radiance.

Know your own state!

We in Vermont have had reciters without an audience, singers without accompaniment, minstrels in an obsessed and heedless throng. Why?

Because we have never had, since 1800, a real literary or critical journal of Vermont expression. Most newspaper editors are too busy with other "filler," and too restricted for space (it is worth dollars) to admit real literature to their columns; and besides, the public at large are not educated up to such literature, and don't want it. They prefer the Macfadden brand.

Yet in one hundred fifty years about four hundred Vermont poets have actually published over one thousand books and pamphlets of verse; and among these are to be found some of the most outstanding compositions of American letters. Add to this the prolix magazine minstrelsy of our native singers (many fine nuggets are hidden away in this effluvia) and you have a mass of poesy few states can equal as to quantity. And as to quality, such names as Royall Tyler, Selleck Osborn, Thomas Green Fessenden, Eliza D. W. Parsons, Carlos Stuart, Charles G. Eastman, Anne C. Lynch-Botta, Rufus W. Griswold, John G. Saxe, Harriet G. Arey, Samuel S. Luce, Julia C. R. Dorr, James Buckham, Stafford, Cady, Cleghorn, Barker, Johnson, Hewitt, Washburn, Southwick, Flower, Bliss, Farrar, and many others speak for themselves. For prose add D. P. Thompson, Sophie Damon, Rowland Robinson, Theodora Peck, Dorothy C. Fisher, Zephine Humphrey, Robert Duffus, etc.; and, for editors and compilers, add Henry N. Hudson, Abby M. Hemenway, Eva Munson Smith, Francis Fisher Browne, and Charles G. Whiting. For specialists add Almira H. L. Phelps, Bishop Hopkins, George P. Marsh, Henry Stevens, John Spargo, &c, &c,—and you have a most imposing array of literary talent.

Why let such talent go to oblivion? Southeastern Vermont (including Walpole, New Hampshire) was once the literary center of America. Dennie, Tyler, and Fessenden organized a guild of writers, established The Farmer's Weekly Museum, stood for something definite and distinct in literature,—and they made the only real tally Vermont has ever made in the world of letters.

The question is, Can we do it again? Can old Vermont come back? If she once had a school of writers and a journal that blazed the way for later epochs,—if Tyler and his associates could and did influence succeeding generations of American letters—much more then ought the combined literary voice of our state today, if it can be enlisted, coordinated, and vocalized, be able to leave its own peculiar imprint on the poetic and prose development of the times. All we need is unity, cohesion, cooperation. These, and a suitable organ of expression—a magazine through which to convey our distinct message, our peculiar tradition and its ideals.

The movement presupposes two things,—the formation of a group or guild, and the establishment of a real literary journal, a mouthpiece tied to no mere "boosting" slogans or propaganda, with no commercial or political or religious bias or axe to grind.

Can we organize such a movement among our inland and outland artists? Can we found and successfully conduct such a magazine?

I think it can be done. How and when depend on the vision, devotion, and resourcefulness of our combined literati. It needs initial financing, either by voluntary assessment or by endowment, followed by wise and sympathetic editorial management. Vermont and New Hampshire might cooperate, as of old. Call the journal "North Hills." Printing might be hired, or done à la Roycroftie. An editor in chief, a working editor, a circulation or business manager, and a live bunch of associates. Solicit 1000 advance subscriptions,— then go ahead. With an alert, self-conscious home clientage, it might do for Vermont and her writers today what the Weekly Museum did for early Vermont in the heyday of her youth.

Woodburn Harris

[Letter to Vrest Orton]

Vergennes, Vt.,
August 13, 1939

Mr. Vrest Orton,
Weston, Vt.

Dear Mr. Orton:

Probably you won't recall me though we have dipped topsails at a distance on one or two occasions. In writing you I am following an impulse I have cherished for several years now. I am wondering if you could give me any of the circumstances as to the death of Howard P. Lovecraft, a name I find I can't write without emotion. I have never heard a single word of the circumstances yet this loss came in such a manner as to be peculiarly poignant in my case.

I am the person who once wrote you about funerals, who proved to be suffering over the thought that a clergyman was going to mumble his hocus pocus over the clay that had held my erratic consciousness. I can smile over that now, but when the scientist tells us that beginning with the fertilized egg we pass through the whole history of evolution[,] why should it be surprising if mental development follows the same law. [*sic*] Suffice to say that, at that time I contacted Lovecraft and that that strange phenomenon, mental and emotional affinity, seemed to appear in our case. Anyhow for nearly ten years we wrote each other at great length on every conceivable subject.

Knowing Lovecraft as you did you need not be told that this intimacy was of tremendous import, one of the biggest things in my life up to that time.

Now as to the circumstances I referred to, 1929 produced a complete shake up of my ideas on economics. At sea again I read everything on the subject of the depression I could lay hands on. Emotionally I began to lean toward the Bolsheviks as their first five year plan seemed such a contrast to our own depression. But mentally I discarded their ideas as not established. Lovecraft invariably steered me away from them. With Hitler's advent a rift began to appear between us. He stoutly defended Hitler as one who had saved German culture and civilization from the devastating plague of Bolshevism. Still at sea as far as positive and satisfying convictions were concerned I felt all my instincts inclining me to the other view.

One day I happened on John Strachey's "Nature & Capitalist Crisis." This, as you perhaps know, is an excellent popularization of Karl Marx's "Capital." That is to say it takes you down to the very bed rock foundations of the whole theoretical system of thought loosely called Communism. It had a terrific effect on me. When I say that within a month I had broken the habit of partially stupifying [*sic*] my-self with alcohol every night (a custom I had followed for many years) that may serve as a sort of yardstick for measuring the experience. Oh, no! I don't mean I have entirely deserted the faithful. A civilized indulgence still appears. But in truth I was strictly passing beyond that point as a natural concomitant to a mental condition of complete cynicism and despair.

The majority, of course, are quite incapable of absorbing such dynamic ideas from the printed page. But I felt that Lovecraft was bound to be impressed. On every other subject—except that & his majesty John Barley-corn—he was a perfect example of the detached scientific spirit. In fact he was impressed with my experience and *asked* me for the loan of the book. I sent it on and said I should be interested in his reaction.

A month later, I got my first jolt. He wrote it looked to him "pretty damned stiff" and said he wouldn't be able to get at it right away. I was pretty sore. For ten years I had played strictly the role—student, accepting many a "tongue lashing" for my ignorance and general stupidity (all of these richly deserved, of course) and reading no end of books as a basis of discussion. This was the first time I had attempted to reverse the roles. Hence I was peeved when he showed no inclination to expose his prejudices to what had appealed to me as a major contribution to the world's thought. Privately I swore he would come across before our intimacy continued further. At Christmas he sent me a derisive card which I answered in kind. A whole year went by without a word between us. Christmas approached again and I wondered if he would experience any emotion at crossing me off his list of Xmas greetings, the first time in ten years.

To my surprise I got a card cheerfully assuring me he had at last got around to tackle Jack Strachey and was anticipating a keen battle. Pleased, I answered that he needn't take the matter too seriously, that if it proved too stiff he wasn't compelled to go on.

However, he didn't write again. I still stood pat on my platform that he must report on his reactions to the only book I had ever asked him to read, which in fact he had asked for himself. Then about March I got a package at the Express office, directed to me in a strange hand. It proved to be my Strachey book.

I concluded my bluff was called. I swore to heaven he could go plumb to hell. Run away from a good argument! Refuse even to comment! Play exactly the part he was always so ready to ball [*sic*] out his religious friends for, viz, "They always loose [*sic*] interest when they find they can't answer your arguments." Yes, I was defiant and tried to blot him entirely out of my mind, yet to my self privately I admitted I was profoundly hurt. I could easily have waited another year or two but to face a complete break—and certainly this meant the end—why that was that was quite a different matter.

Then a few weeks later I got a card from the magazine Wierd [*sic*] Tales saying their current issue contained a reprint of a story by the late Howard P. Lovecraft and they were notifying those of his former friends who might be interested.

*   *   *   *   *

I have often wondered. Did his death come suddenly? Or was he desperately ill when he sent me that cheerful card at Christmas telling me he was about to tackle redoubtable Jack Strachey. That would be just like him [I] expect, yet I have never known the slightest circumstance about the matter, for I have never seen a person since who knew him.

I wonder if you would be willing to write me. My only excuse for this completely[?] personal letter is that I know I am writing to one who himself valued Lovecraft and can perhaps understand that it was rather painful to learn the outcome under these circumstances.

Sincerely yours, Woodburn Harris.

By chance I got one of your notices about a book of the month which gave me your address. One reason I never yielded to the impulse before was that I didn't know where to reach you.

Zealia Brown Reed

One-Man Girl

The long, low, yellow roadster, lights dimmed, was parked on a grassy elevation near the state road.

"What time is it, Glynn?"

Glynn Waterbury, without attempting to move his right arm from about the slender girl beside him, leaned forward until his face touched her cheek and lifted his free arm to let the moonlight strike his wrist-watch.

"Quarter of 'eleven," he answered with a slightly suppressed sigh. His embrace tightened and instinctively their lips met.

The long sweep of distant hills, the mellow sheen of the great, full moon, and the clear night air all blended in a spell more exhilarating than fine old wine.

"I shall tell Janet to-night," Phyllis murmured breathlessly.

"But, dear—" Glynn protested.

"I *must* tell her," she insisted in a firm, girlish voice. "Janet is going to suspect something soon, and I love her too much to wait till she learns the truth from someone else. You know I won't cheat where she's concerned."

"I always thought you were thoughtful and serious, Janet," he said.
"I'm not, Glynnie," she replied earnestly. "How did you ever make that mistake?"

She clutched his hand, and for a moment they were silent. Glynn looked down at her lovely face in the moonlight, and as she turned to meet his gaze he caught the dark brilliance of eyes that sparkled behind their thick lashes. Leaning over, he kissed her until they were both out of breath. Then he stepped on the starter and turned the car into the highway, headed for home.

The smoke from Glynn's cigarette occasionally fanned Phyllis' cheek, but neither spoke till the car turned in at the driveway.

"You are determined to tell her?" His voice was anxious.

"Yes," was her toneless answer.

"Damn!" he whispered wretchedly beneath his breath.

When Phyllis stepped from the car, Glynn caught her fervently in his arms.

"Goodbye, dear," she murmured brokenly. That was all—then she pushed him from her.

He watched her slight, almost childish figure ascend the steps and enter the house. She did not look back. He knew that she would carry out her plan.

Phyllis pressed cool finger-tips to her burning eyes as she ascended the stairs. A soft light was shining from Janet's room, and she walked slowly to the door without entering. Janet was sitting at the small desk where for ten years she had transacted all the business of an orphaned household—the three brothers and one sister whom she had petted and mothered, since she was eighteen—and she lifted her head as the light footsteps paused on the threshold. Her lips were parted in a pleasant smile as her eyes met the alarming image of despair leaning dejectedly against the door-jamb. Quickly she whirled about in her swivel-chair, her tiny rose-colored slippers dangling from pajamas of the same shade.

"Well, honey, where did you run away to while I was gone? You don't look as though you'd had much fun!"

The older girl's dark brows drew together in a playful frown. Phyllis threw out her hands protestingly, as if to ward off a blow.

"Oh, don't, Jan!" she answered distractedly. "I'm going to hurt you deeply."

She watched the playful pout turn to a puzzled expression. Poor Janet! How little she deserved the coming blow!

It was Janet upon whom the burdens of the household had chiefly fallen. She was one of those sensitive women who dedicate themselves early in life to the healing of wounds, and she had never failed in her duty as guardian and comforter. But now that the brothers were safely married and Phyllis past the dangerous age of early adolescence, she was joyously free to live her own life.

Since Glynn had dawned on her horizon, she had gained a new charm. The dark eyes were brighter—the touch on the piano richer and firmer. Love had wrought a metamorphosis in Janet—good old Jan, who had been home—tenderness—life—to them all.

No, Phyllis reflected as she crossed over to the dainty bed, Janet must not be hurt. She must not lose faith in life. The elder sister's questioning eyes, lines deeping between them, slowly followed her.

For a moment Phyllis sat rigidly on the side of the bed, nervously biting her under-lip. Then, trying to choose the most direct words she could as she looked straight into her sister's eyes, she began hesitantly.

"Jan—I'm—I'm in love with Glynn."

Janet looked perplexed, for Phyllis was not usually given to inane and pointless pleasantries. Her countenance grew almost whimsical as she laughingly answered, swinging gaily back to the work on her desk.

"Well, I'm not surprised at that! Who could help it?"

"Oh, Janet, don't!" cried the younger girl. Her voice was so full of misery that the dark head bent over the papers came up with a jerk, brown eyes kindling from bewilderment to sympathy.

"I'm serious—and Jan, Glynn—" she lowered her glance for a moment, "is in love with me."

The last words were only a whisper, but Janet whirled around in her chair to face the speaker. She was half incredulous, half indignant.

"Phyllis! You mean—you mean—" Her voice shook pathetically, and she paused for a fresh start. "You mean that you have been with Glynn to-night?" There was still incredulity in her eyes, but the soft curls of the blond head across the room nodded slowly—very slowly.

"Why, Phyllis—are you telling me that Glynn—that Glynn—isn't in love with me?"

Phyllis braced herself for a task of explanation which she felt to be almost beyond her.

"No, Jan, I'm not telling you that—I'm not sure that he understands himself—but I'm telling you that he does love me *more*—that is—well, yes, he *is* in love with me. We—well, you see, Janet, it was this way— Oh, don't stare like that; you make me feel as if I were something rotten—but I'm not, really, Jan. I—"

She covered her flushed face with her fingers.

Janet sat motionless, staring at the girl—four years her junior—whom she had mothered, petted, and spoiled; the girl who was robbing her of the only man for whom she had ever cared. A sudden revulsion of intense hatred surged over her, and she trembled in the throes of a fury utterly foreign to her nature. Her firm brown hands opened and closed convulsively in her pajama pockets.

"Tell me—tell me about it," she said, dully and evenly.

Phyllis swallowed hard and tried to make a coherent beginning.

"I know it's been wrong, Janet, in a way—but—"

"In a way!" Janet interrupted tragically. "Go on."

"Well, one day about three months ago—Glynn came over and you were gone—" She hesitated as Janet cut in with an almost hysterical coolness.

"It seems that I've always been gone at the most opportune times for you, and—"

"Please don't, Jan—wait till I'm through—then say anything you please."

For a moment the image of Glynn rose up between them and held them to silence, then Phyllis continued:

"Anyway, Glynn came to see you, and you were gone, as I said. We talked and played the radio, and before he left we found we had much in common. Later we went to Henry's roadhouse—" She stopped and lifted her eyes as Janet gasped.

"Yes, we *did just that!* We danced, and—and—well, you can see how it has gone on. Perfectly innocent at first—but now, Jan—one of us will have to suffer. I love him. You love him. And he loves me, though he *wants* to love you, I *think*—" Phyllis faltered in the glare of her sister's growing indignation.

Janet almost choked with rage.

"Phyllis, you don't deserve even a whole-hearted contempt! We are sisters and you have betrayed the most sacred ties—have come between me and the man I was to have married. You—the girl I almost brought up—I couldn't have believed you'd be so—vile—if you hadn't told me yourself!"

She ended with a sob, and did not immediately regain self-control. But when she spoke again, Phyllis wilted beneath the vehemence of her denunciation.

"The secret of this whole thing is that you're *utterly* selfish—you can't bear to see anybody else have what you can't get for yourself. You don't love Glynn—you've merely been practicing all your old tricks on him—deceiving him, as you've deceived me. You've had dozens of admirers, and you've treated them all the same way—deceived them, lied to them, played with them—never true to any one of them. Phyllis, you've never been true even to yourself. You—"

She laughed hysterically, more to herself than at Phyllis.

"And I thought *he* cared!"

Phyllis turned her head and held out her hand protestingly.

"Wait, Janet!" she began, "All that you say is true—" She fought to control her voice "—except—except about my being selfish where you're concerned. It was more my love for you than my love for Glynn that made me tell you. I haven't loved Glynn selfishly, either—it just happened, and I can't change things. I—"

"Don't you think you're deciding all these things a little late?"

Phyllis ignored the bitterness and continued in her low voice.

"I know Glynn did love you at first. Not that he had any reason to change—but—he—well, I guess my love has charmed him a little more than yours—"

She collected herself and spoke more evenly.

"I wanted to talk sensibly with you, and I hope you'll let me. You've forgotten that this isn't just a matter for us two. Do you think it's any compliment to Glynn to regard him as merely a bone to be fought over? You're usually more careful about people's dignity—and surely Glynn's ought to mean as much to you as anybody's! He's very fine, Janet—too fine for just an average woman."

Phyllis paused thoughtfully, as if deciding whether or not she really wished to broach the plan which was taking form in her mind. When she spoke again, it was with a kind of judicial gravity.

"Janet, you can never say that I haven't been fair about the whole matter or that I'm not going to be now. Glynn must do his own deciding—and there mustn't be anything to sway him one way or the other.

"You think I've taken an unfair advantage—that I've got ahead of you. Well, maybe I have without knowing it—but you know I wouldn't do a thing like that intentionally. Now I'm going to let you have your chance—and you can't say I'm not making up for any harm I've done. I mean to be fair to all of us.

"Jan, I'm going away for six months—to-morrow. That's the only thing to do with matters as they are. You've got a clear field now, and Glynn can do as he chooses—as he thinks right for all of our futures—without any more influence from me. I'll visit the Allens in Kansas City, and maybe go to Chicago to see Alice Fullerton for a while. It'll all be perfectly natural, and while I'm gone things'll have a chance to cool down and take shape whatever way they were meant to.

"Anyhow," she repeated with finality, as she rose from the edge of the bed and walked wearily across the hall to her own cheerful room, "I'm going to-morrow!"

Phyllis undressed slowly and slipped between cool sheets. Her thoughts were all muddled. After all, she had accomplished so little; so little that she had hoped for. It seemed hours later—though in reality it was only a short time—that the shadow of Janet's figure fell across the luminous strip of moonlight on the rug.

"Phyl?"

Janet's voice was so musical that one always waited to hear more of it, and now it seemed to tell of a regained composure.

"Yeah, Jan," answered Phyllis. She reached over and pulled on the lamp beside her bed.

Janet gazed about her as if seeing the room for the first time. She felt like a stranger to the girl in the green bed with the pink and orchid spread, and even the frilly curtains that waved in the gentle night breeze—these, and the soft light of the lamp, and everything else—seemed changed.

She lowered her eyes to Phyllis in her dainty night-dress.

"How charming she is," thought Janet, as she watched the faintest trace of a smile flickering over the perfect curve of the full, red lips. Janet tried to set her own mouth in a hard, straight line, but she somehow only succeeded in smiling tenderly at her sister.

"Come on in, Janet.," Phyllis invited, resting on her elbow and watching the older girl with her smoothly parted hair drawn back into a short braid— what a time she had had when it was growing in!

Slowly Janet entered the room and seated herself on the foot of the bed.

"Phyllis, if you really care for Glynn—if you—if I've lost him," her voice faltered, and she smiled sadly as she struggled for self-control, "well, I've lost him; and I can't give you both up!"

Her head drooped slightly forward and her red lips trembled. Phyllis, watching her closely, became suddenly voluble as if through inspiration.

"Ah, Jan, that's just it! You *haven't* lost him! He loved you first—and you know I can't be true to anyone very long. It wouldn't be fair for me to ruin all three lives just for a whim. I can have scads of men at my feet if I want 'em—but you're a 'one-man woman,' Jan, and this thing matters a lot more to you. There's no use arguing—the only sensible plan is what I've told you. I'll go away, and—"

In a moment Janet was on her knees beside the bed. "Do you really love him, Phyl? Tell me. I must know."

Phyllis lowered her eyes. "Honest-to-gosh, Janet, I swear I don't know. I thought so. But—"

"Listen, Phyl. I think I have a right to demand that you go away. Glynn *did* love me."

"I *said* I'd go away, dear."

"You won't go hating me?"

"No, dear."

"Phyl, I—I'm sorry. If I didn't love him so—"

"I understand, dear. I'll go to-morrow."

"Phyl?"

"Yes?"

"What's wrong with me?"

"Wrong? Why, you're adorable, Janet."

"But I can't hold men."

"Janet!"

"Does that shock you? Well, I'm through with hypocrisy and pretense. I want Glynn as badly as he wanted me two week ago. I'd do anything, go to almost any length to hold him."

"Janet—I—I—"

"Tell me—what must I do to hold him?"

"Janet, *you* couldn't."

"Couldn't what?"

"Couldn't act idiotically. Men adore idiotic women—girls who do crazy things. It gives them a sense of superiority, and stability. It awakens all their protective instincts. All men enjoy protecting weak, lovely little flappers from themselves. They get a tremendous emotional kick out of it. Men distrust intellectual women because they can't protect or reform them. Janet, it would take an intelligently idiotic woman to hold Glynn. You'd have to become an adorable little half-wit."

She waited for Janet's reply, which finally came from between tightened lips.

"Then you suggest that I deliberately attempt to deceive him?"

"Janet you asked for advice—I'm giving it to you."

"Well—"

"Don't be a highbrow, Janet! That's why Glynn wanted me—because I'm a lovely idiot and you're not. You should feel lucky that it wasn't somebody else who cut in!"

"Phyllis, I can't drink—"

"Gosh!" Phyllis exclaimed in desperation, pressing her hand to her head and falling back on the pillow. "You don't *have* to drink. Just act silly and irresponsible!"

The remark was significant, but Janet, if she heard it, did not understand. Phyllis continued.

"After all, dear, life is a masked ball and you can't balk at the proper mask. You'll have to forget your dignity if you intend to use the wiles Eve has bestowed on you—you know, she must have had to use a lot of 'em herself on Adam, even if she didn't have any competition!"

Both girls smiled.

"Then this is to be a campaign?" asked Janet.

"Absolutely! And for a real, honest-to-God man! Play the game for all it's worth—but if you don't want him, I do!"

Phyllis's voice grew a trifle husky with the last words, and Janet looked at her closely. Nothing but the contagious smile, though, was visible on the curved red lips. Phyllis returned the scrutiny and assumed an air of expert appraisal.

"Heavens, Jan, what a wonder you could be if you'd only be modern. Dark—willowy—just the kind of a woman Glynn should adore. If only you'd let yourself be irresponsible. Do you know what you remind me of?"

"What?" Janet was smiling now, her cheeks slightly flushed. Phyllis could say such thrilling things when she cared to!

"Of a caged leopard, Jan! Once I saw one walking back and forth in its cage, and that's just what you remind me of. Graceful—lovely—but caged up. That's it—you're caging your own lovely self up because you want to be so darned intellectual and refined."

Janet was silent, but kept on watching Phyllis.

"Why, Jan, you could take the whole world by the tail and swing it around your head—that is, of course, if you wanted to—"

She sat up straight, narrowed her eyes to little shining slits, pointed a long, tapering finger at Janet, and continued:

"Only—unless you can be a modern woman you'd better not sit in the game. I don't mean that you're to discard all your beautiful characteristics—the things we all love—the things that are the real you—but you must emulate flaming youth if you want to draw the praise and admiration of—well, of men in general."

She ended evasively, but Janet understood her.

"But Phyllis—how on earth have *you* become so 'modern'? We've been almost inseparable for the last ten years!"

"It's perfectly clear, Jan, I've been trying to keep up with the other women, while you've been sitting at home waiting for your boy friend to come to you to have biscuits baked for him and lounge around and eat them while you play *Hearts and Flowers* on the piano—"

"Now you listen to me, Phyllis!" Janet inserted indignantly. "Where would you all have been if I'd kicked over the applecart when mother died—"

Phyllis broke in contritely.

"Oh, darling, forgive me! We've all leaned on you because you've let us—who else was fitted for the job? You always *wanted* to be the head of the house—you assumed everything instinctively. But now it's your turn to be alive! The boys are married, and I'm going on a darned lonely trip—"

She paused for breath and Janet timidly inquired.

"Is it necessary to—er—swear quite so much in this game?"

"Gosh, yes! Hell 'em—damn 'em—but above all, let 'em know you're frivolous and human."

Phyllis's hands were clenched till the knuckles showed white; then she pressed her fingers tightly to her burning eyes.

"What time is it, Jan?" she murmured huskily from behind her hand, remembering her similar query of only a few hours before. Janet consulted the wrist-watch she still wore.

"Nearly four—tired?"

But Phyllis did not answer. She had fallen back against the pillow and flung an arm over her face.

In the silence she could feel, without opening her eyes, that her sister was studying her. She turned over and groped for the lamp cord.

"Better snuggle up here with me, Jan. Probably do us both good to get a little sleep."

The room was in darkness now. Janet dropped her slippers on the hardwood floor with a bang and crawled in beside Phyllis. But neither slept.

At first Glynn stayed away from Janet; then he visited her with an attitude whose touch of indifference he could not quite conceal. He was kind—too kind to be sincere, she thought. But she loved him, and had made up her mind to play the game hard for six months. Surely she had a chance,—for hadn't he loved her once?

The time was passing quickly, and Janet posed each night before her mirror while the radio played wildly—static and all. She rehearsed the various rôles she imagined would interest Glynn, but set them aside by daylight, when the pitiful obviousness of such wiles struck her with all the force of reaction.

"Tommy-rot!" she would chastise herself, "but oh, I *do* love him!"

Then one autumn day, as the months of grace were getting well along, the telephone rang sharply.

"Glynn? Oh, you old foolish, of course I'll go!" But wasn't it time for something definite? After all, she hadn't even begun to try out her campaign. Here was Phyllis dutifully staying away, and she herself making no use of her turn!

Janet dressed that night with the greatest care, but only as a last resort, in case she weakened. She had other tactics in view. When Glynn came for her he was surprised to find a note tucked into a corner of the glass in the door.

> "Glynn, dear—I know you'll forgive my running off with an old friend from Kansas City, but he's only here for the day and must go back to-night. Call me when you have time."
>
> > "Jan."

Watching from behind the lace curtain, Janet heard just one exclamation—"darn it!"—from the figure on the porch. That was all he said as he crumpled the note in his pocket and strode off.

Reflecting that night and the next day, Janet wondered just what Glynn's response to the device had meant. Just how "modern" was she, anyway? That is, just how "modern" a policy could she carry out successfully? She was learning to tantalize, if that was anything. Doubtless that was a good beginning for "playing the game" with men—or rather, with some who wanted one's man!

It was nearly a week before Glynn called up again. Janet wrinkled her pretty nose against the telephone as she sent her musical voice over the wire.

"Yes, I really have been treating you like an old stepchild, haven't I? I've been very busy though, and wasn't certain whether you'd called or not. Dum-de-diddle-dee-dee!"

She did not catch his reply, for she was absorbed in the flippancies she was registering.

"Oh, yes—I've had so many places to go—teas, dancing, bridge, and gossiping, too—about everyone I've ever known. I do miss Phyllis awfully— if you remember, she used to take all these trivial things off my hands! Don't you love trivial things though, Glynnie?"

She grinned mischievously to herself. The deep voice was silent for a moment, then came a little indistinctly—Janet did not miss the subtle change.

"How is she?"

Janet's face blanched a trifle.

"Who—oh, Phyllis?—why, she's perfectly fine! She writes that she's having a marvelous time with the Allens. You know what a butterfly she is— never lacking attention. I miss her terribly, though—I'll be glad when she gets home—darn glad!" He must have dropped the receiver with the shock. "Beg pardon—did you say something, Glynn? Oh, yes—I'll be ready at eight— won't disappoint you again!"

With a merry little chuckle that ended in a long sigh, she put down the telephone and leaned back on the chaise longue. There was a picture of Phyllis on the wall, and she gazed tenderly at the piquant features, which seemed to lure her on in her campaign. She almost fancied the full lips were speaking.

"Be flippant—irresponsible—gay!"

For a moment she closed her eyes. Then, turning her head slightly, she looked at the photograph of Glynn which hung not far from Phyllis's. Whose was he, anyway? Her time was almost up—and what had she gained? Glynn would be over to-night—a wise little smile hovered about her lips.

It was Phyllis who had told her how to play the game, and yet— She ran the buffer slowly over her already polished nails, then held her hands out in front of her and inspected them with shining black head critically tilted. A whiff from below stairs aroused her. She sniffed, dropped the buffer, grabbed her negligée about her, and flew down to the kitchen.

She brushed by the grinning black maid, opened the oven door, and heaved a great sigh of relief.

"No woman can be a vampire and bake a cake, Mary," she sighed. "Of course, when you serve this, remember that *you* made it. I'm not supposed to be anything but a fool vamp around this house for six months! Just fix a nice little lunch, so that we'll have it to-night when we get back."

She sniffed at the large ham filled with cloves and cooling in its wine sauce on the table, and smiled contentedly as she swept from the kitchen with affected grandeur, leaving the old negress laughing heartily.

At a few minutes of eight that night Janet heard the soft whirr of the motor as Glynn shut it off.

She smiled at herself in the long mirror. Viewing her reflected image carefully, she noted the lips artistically carmined to a delicate shade, and her black hair, which lay smoothly against the shapely head, was caught in a small loose knot at the nape of her neck—her own simple way, which she could not bring herself to discard even for this occasion.

Definitely she visualized her coming triumph.

She would advance rapidly toward Glynn and squeeze his hand until he winced. She would be extremely cordial. And then she would nonchalantly throw herself on a sofa and laugh uproariously. It might be difficult, but she *would* act flapperish and irresponsible. Glynn was worth any effort. He was so thrillingly boyish. He carried you away with *his* enthusiasms, and yet he always gave you the impression that he was more interested in *your* enthusiasms. She loved him in insanely. She adored the way he handled a cigarette; the way he flicked back his long hair with his strong, muscular fingers. But, above all, she loved the light that flamed in his boyish gray eyes whenever he was profoundly moved.

Unlike most men, he wasn't stiff and formal in the presence of things worth getting excited about. He loved good music, good books, good pictures. He would go into ecstasies over Hals and Rubens; over Shelley and Keats. She had once seen him waltz about on his toes in an art museum in the presence of a great picture that pleased him. He was worth loving, worth holding. And if he really did like frivolous, weak women, why—she would be weak and frivolous!

Slowly she descended the stairs. Glynn was standing by the table, carelessly turning the pages of a book, one hand in the pocket of his flannel trousers. Janet had come downstairs silently, so had a chance to inspect him unseen at leisure. The broad shoulders in the blue coat were giant-like. She watched his firm brown hands, and the wave in his light hair. What a strong jaw he had! Turning and seeing her, he grinned a great boyish grin that wrinkled up the corners of his fine gray eyes.

"'Lo, Jan!" he greeted her, smiling and striding toward her with extended hands.

When she came into the full light he looked at her a moment, frowned slightly, then without a word pulled out his handkerchief, moistened it playfully with the tip of his tongue, and daubed at her made-up lips.

"Now, that's better!" he said with an air of finality, as he drew her into his arms and kissed her.

"Say, Janet—" Glynn began, then stopped abruptly, drawing his lips tightly together. He thought a moment, then went on.

"Where'll we go?"

Janet's chance for the heavy histrionics had come.

"Oh, any place. *Any* place at all, Glynnie."

Glynn, wondering where on earth she had managed to hide this phase of herself before, had not taken his eyes off Janet's face. This, she reflected to herself, was something in the way of accomplishment! She waited for his suggestion.

"All right," he rejoined, "let's dash out to Henry's Roadhouse."

For a moment Janet hesitated—but only for a moment. She could see Phyllis as she said, "You don't have to drink you know. Just act crazy!" Very well—she would not get drunk. And she didn't intend to let any stupidity spoil all her hard work. She was sorry she had spent so much time messing up her lips—and yet, Glynn probably had been impressed even if he *had* rubbed it all off! She grinned to herself as she followed him out and climbed into the yellow roadster.

Glynn knew just what to order, but Janet steered a salutary course by ordering a light French wine. Henry's was a gay place, and the blaring jazz and vulgarly swaying couples on the floor struck a keynote helpful in her masquerade.

How foolish she had been to be a dried-up prig! She started to hum the refrain of an inane song.

> *"It really doesn't matter, doesn't matter,*
> *Doesn't matter what we do!"*

Glynn stared at her incredulously. "Janet, I don't understand."

"Poor Glynnie! *You* wouldn't. I suppose you prefer Chopin. But don't you like the sentiment, really? I think it perfectly splendid. It doesn't matter is a song of revolt. It's a protest against the dullness of thoughtful, serious people."

"I always thought you were thoughtful and serious, Janet."

"I'm not, Glynnie. Honest-to-goodness I'm not. How didja ever make that mistake, Glynnie, dear? Come on. Let's step!"

She seized Glynn by the arm and drew him reluctantly to his feet. "Don't be an old woman, Glynnie. When we're married and my beauty has begun to decay, you can be as sober and serious as you wish. Let's black bottom."

For several moments they danced in silence.

Then Glynn picked her up in his arms and strode through the gin-stupid throng of revellers to the door, thanking Heaven for the crisp, pure night breeze which seemed to wash away the stench of the sense-heavy soddenness within. He got her into the car, and had the motor going before she could assemble will enough to protest. Then she remarked with affected gravity:

"Why, Glynnie, dear! There's too much fun here! Let's stay!"

Glynn leaned close and looked straight into her eyes, and Janet realized her mistake. She pushed his nose with her cool little finger, but did not interfere as he started the car and threaded his way out on the open road.

"Janet! You seemed out of place in that crowd. Can't see why I ever let you suggest our going there."

Janet opened one eye and blinked her surprise in the dark. So *she* had suggested the place, eh! Just like a man not to take the blame! But he was talking again.

"I'm going to take you home—I want you to be yourself and nothing more—understand?"

When they arrived home Janet was set and exultant in her purpose. She turned on the radio and vanished into the kitchen.

"I'll get you something to eat, Glynnie," she said.

In a moment she returned carrying a tray.

"It really doesn't matter what we do," she hummed audibly as she spread the table. Glynn sat sullenly on the sofa and enjoyed the lunch which "Mary had prepared"—"prepared," and nothing else, for he knew that taste too well to be deceived! Janet smoothed her hair and watched Glynn roguishly—elbows on her silk-clad knees, chin cupped in her hands.

"I'm going on the stage, Glynn," she said. "I'm tired of this absurd domesticity."

Janet watched the changing expression on his face as his sensitive mouth munched the cake and ham she had prepared for him, and a new thought came to her.

"And I'm going to pose for an artist. His reputation is positively devilish, Glynn. Won't it be exciting?"

Glynn dropped the sandwich on his plate and it flopped open.

"Are you utterly insane, Janet?" he cried.

The richly baked ham grinned up reassuringly from the plate where its fall had scattered it.

"Uh-huh!"

Glynn groaned. The words came tumbling from his lips impromptu. He had imprisoned one of her hands in his.

"No one could really love you, Jan, and want you to be different. I don't understand this new thing. Janet, you can't mean that you—"

"Yes, I mean just that! It does sound darned silly, doesn't it?"

"Please, Janet, stop swearing! I can't stand it!"

"Why, I rather thought you liked it!"

"Well, you're wrong for once—I don't and never did—no one wants to hear a woman do it. That is, the woman—the woman—" But he did not finish.

"Don't criticize someone else, Glynn—begin at home first."

His voice became tempered with thoughtfulness.

"Yes—yes, dear—you're right, quite right. I guess I've been pretty inconsistent. No doubt I'm the fool and you're the wise one—but don't wisdom and folly sometimes come to the same end?"

He looked at her hopefully, but she ignored him. When he rose to go, she did not urge him to remain. That hurt his pride, nor was he greatly flattered by the intentional note of weariness in her good-night. Her heart was pounding so violently that she was afraid he might hear it, but she would be game. The stake was worth it—for she loved and wanted him. And now that she had played her cards, had she won or lost?

Janet rolled and tossed that night with a dull headache. What a mess things were! Did Phyllis really love Glynn? Oh, how her temples throbbed!—Glynn had said he didn't like swearing or anything "modern"—the room was whirling—if only she had thought to bring some ice-water upstairs with her—she would surely fall if she tried to get some—oh, no one could help loving Phyllis!—she didn't blame Glynn for that—why wouldn't furniture keep still?—it had learned to dance since she had gone to bed.

What on earth was that in the corner? She pulled the covers over her head and carefully peeped out. Oh, that was her white cape on the chair. She shut her eyes tight, but her brain whirled on just the same.

Where on earth could she find a man—a man to dangle under Glynn's handsome nose? She didn't want a man—not any man but Glynn! Why had she lied to Glynn? Perhaps she would die in the night—that would be very beautiful and appropriate. Well, the furniture was settling down, anyhow! Janet fell at last into a heavy sleep of exhaustion.

But Glynn didn't sleep at all. After getting home, he had smoked and paced the floor, kicking chairs about and running nervous fingers through his thick hair till he was too tired to do anything but swear and go to bed. Nor was that any respite, either. He could only toss about wakefully, thinking what a fool he had been and wondering if there were any way to undo his folly.

He had always loved Janet—the real, quiet Janet. No one understood her as he did—why had he ever neglected her? Who could be crazy enough to want to change her? Janet in her tasteful housedress pouring coffee and laughing while some other man—some stranger—adored her. Janet—Janet—the mother of some stranger's children—

"My God!" he groaned, as he sprang from the bed in early morning's dusk. He'd show Janet that she belonged to him—she couldn't be so foolish—he'd dress and go over there at once. He loved Janet and had never loved anyone else!

He dressed and got out the roadster. For hours, it seemed to him, he drove furiously and aimlessly through the town and its suburbs, dodging milkmen and hucksters on their way to market. Would the time never pass? When the sun was well up, he dashed into Janet's driveway and rang the front bell timidly. His nerve was waning, and he hesitated considerably when no answer came. Finally, though, his purpose returned, and he went around to the kitchen door. It was open to the warmth of a mid-autumn morning, and through the screen-door he saw Janet with a towel bound tightly around her head, sipping black coffee.

Glynn walked in boldly, and when Janet saw him she gave a little cry of surprise, hugging her dainty bathrobe closely about her.

"Janet!" he began hoarsely, taking her by the shoulders and holding her at arm's length. "We're going to get married to-day—how soon can you be ready? We'll drive to Kansas City. Any man who would try to change you—make you over—is a maniac!"

He took her in his arms and held her close, and for a moment neither spoke. They merely listened to each other's heartbeats. Then he kissed her hair—or such of it as was not covered by the cold towel.

Janet buried her face in Glynn's woolly sweater.

"Oh, Glynn, darling, my head aches too badly to argue! I can be ready any time you say—only—" Her head dived deeper amidst the soft wool. "Are you quite sure you love me—that I have enough—enough modernism to keep you interested?"

"Love you? Why, you foolish little girl, I wouldn't trade you for a million! I didn't know your real worth until you tried to be like other people."

Janet hesitated.

"You know, dear, I've been an awful fibber along with the rest."

"Fibber?" he counter-lied in great relief. "Oh, if you mean about going on the stage and hating domesticity—well, I knew from the first you didn't mean it."

"Really, Glynn, I didn't think I could be interesting enough for you after—Phyllis."

He ignored the mention of her rival.

"Jan, the most interesting thing about you is yourself. With all your acting, you could never shed the real Janet—no one ever loved you for anything except your own dear self—"

"And Phyllis, Glynn?"

He saw that he could evade it no longer.

"Phyllis is—just Phyllis, I thought I loved her—but I didn't. I was just infatuated. Phyllis will always be the same—fascinating first one man and then another with that flapper charm of hers."

"Well, I've wired to Kansas City for her to come home. She's been gone nearly five months, and I'm aching to see her. I'm looking for her at noon to-day."

"Fine! She'll be here to look after things and wish us a happy journey."

He answered with obvious sincerity, but Janet wondered if she could trust his protestations implicitly. She stood on her toes and kissed him gently. Laughingly he unfastened the towel from around her head.

"We'll dispose of that ugly thing," he said and she laughed a low little laugh as she heard the coffee boil over and put out the gas. The noise reminded her of mundane things.

"Eaten breakfast, dear?"

"Lord, no! You came first this morning!"

He sat on the edge of the table and sipped a cup of coffee, far too excited to think of eating. Gee! it was good to have Janet like herself!

At noon Phyllis came home. She was the same charming, laughing Phyllis, and had had a *wonderful* time—lots of boy friends and dances, and the usual amount of popularity. And yet, was she quite the same? How glad she was for Janet and Glynn! Glynn would be there any minute. They talked as best they could during the hurried lunch—Janet now and then dashing upstairs to give instructions and help Mary pack her things.

When Phyllis followed Janet to her room and began to aid in the packing, the time for the one biggest question seemed to have come.

"Well, Phyl, you found that you made no mistake, didn't you?" Janet asked hesitantly.

Phyllis answered bravely as she met her sister's steady gaze.

"Why, Jan, dear, I knew before I left that I wasn't making any mistake!" She smiled.

Then Glynn came—Phyllis met him at the door. One long look into his eyes told her that he had completely forgotten—so she merely chattered with feverish rapidity.

At last they were ready. Phyllis went out on the porch with them and kissed them both warmly. The long, yellow roadster shot out from the drive, and the journey was begun.

Phyllis stood on the steps watching the cloud of dust recede. The wind whipped her frock, which matched the blue of her eyes, close to her body; and her hair waved loosely about her face. She did not speak—whom, indeed, was there to speak to? Of this she was glad, for her voice would have betrayed what she resolved never to betray.

Two great hot tears coursed down her cheeks—tears that Jan and Glynn would have been surprised to see. She, too, had played the game, and had found a new self—one which couldn't be set aside as blithely as Jan's brief "modern" self—but she hated the priggish gesture of sacrifice.

"Oh, darn!" she whispered brokenly, wiping off the tears and adding a touch of rouge to her face as she turned to go in.

William Lumley

The Dweller

Dread and potent broods a Dweller
    In an evil twilight space,
Formless as a daemon's shadow,
    Void of members and of face.

Heeding not the shaped or human,
    Past the reach of time or law—
Never may our minds conceive It
    Save as clouds of fright and awe.

When It crawls malignly on us,
    Lethal mists of leaden grey,
Rising vaguely in the distance,
    Veil its hideous bulk away.

And Its mutterings of horror,
    Foul with lore of charnel ground,
Lose themselves in troubled thunders
    That from far horizons sound.

The Elder Thing

Oh, have you seen the Elder Thing
    That creeps upon the hill—
A fearsome Thing with lurid eyes
    At night when all is still;
A horror wrought of withered moss
    And foul primordial slime,
Wherein there fester monstrously
    The evils of all time?

With phosphorescent glow like naught
    That Nature might devise,
All the fell ancient lore of earth
    Gleams hellish in its eyes.
As night by night this Elder Thing
    Upon the hill doth creep,
Awakened by men's blasphemies
    From out its age-long sleep.

By monolith and haunted fen
    Down to the mandrake mere
It prowls to meet the sheeted dead
    That squeak and gibber there;
And nameless things, not beasts nor men,
    With bat-like creatures vie,
And loathsome reptiles writhe and hiss
    Till daybreak pales the sky.

A thousand shapes the Things—
    A thousand shapes or none—
All forms of Fear since Earth was born
    It mirrors as its own;
It apes each rhythmic Elder Sign
    As it doth onward creep,
Awakened by man's blasphemies
    From out its age-long sleep.

Shadows

There's a city wrought of shadows
    That I glimpse at fall of night,
And its streets are filled with phantoms
    Flitting furtively from sight.

They are of no stable semblance
    That our fancy might devise,
But a baleful light is burning
    In their slanting, almond eyes.

Every brow is pale and misty,
    With a thin-lipped mouth beneath,
And the grinding jaws are ratlike—
    Set with long and pointed teeth.

Neither rage nor ancient evil
    Nor a curse bequeaths its stain,
But each face is wryly twisted
    In a silent grin of pain.

Not a sign of hope or hatred
    In that dull grimace is blent—
Like the fishes four accursed,
    With their pain they are content.

Mother of all elder anguish,
    Mighty, sinister and fair,
Great Cathay, with woes of aeons
    In the burdens that you bear,

Tell me of your wrath-built Babel
    Piled up from a primal day;
Tell me, too, when late-learned mercy
    Shall the shadows sweep away!

The Ferryman

In Lemerick Village so auld, and so rusty
Is one whom you have never heard of before.
Whool be ye across for a penny so trusty,
Yet never may pass from his boat, to the shore
Yes the tale of a wraith that he met in a meadow,
And words laid on him by a Heenwife at Clair

And though he has labored by sunlight, and shadow
For years to this day ye may still see him there.

Now there's none who may aid him
Nere, father, nor mother,
Nor none of the monks, or the nuns in their prayer.
Save he give his oars into the hands of another,
Until the last day heel be still toiling there.
O ferryman weary, so wan and so wasted
Who for countless ages hath toiled for the shore.
Give your oars to the hands of the next one in waiting,
And banish the cursh laid on you evermore.

Glossary of Names

Barlow, R[obert] H[ayward] (1918–1951), author and collector. As a teenager he corresponded with HPL and acted as his host during two long visits in the summers of 1934 and 1935. In the 1930s he wrote several works of weird and fantasy fiction, some in collaboration with HPL. HPL appointed him his literary executor. He assisted August Derleth and Donald Wandrei in preparing the early HPL volumes for Arkham House. In the 1940s he went to Mexico and became a distinguished anthropologist. He died by suicide. For HPL's letters to him, see *O Fortunate Floridian*.

Bates, Harry (1900–1981), editor of *Strange Tales* and *Astounding Stories*. HPL repeatedly submitted stories to him, but all were rejected because they did not contain sufficient "action."

Blackwood, Algernon (1869–1951), prolific British author of weird and fantasy tales whose work HPL greatly admired when he read it in 1924.

Burks, Arthur J. (1898–1974), American writer and Marine colonel whose experience in the Caribbean and knowledge of native voodoo rituals led him to write stories of the supernatural that he sold to *Weird Tales*.

Chambers, Robert W[illiam] (1865–1933), American author. HPL discovered his early fantastic writing—*The King in Yellow* (1895), *The Maker of Moons* (1896), *In Search of the Unknown* (1904); also the later novel *The Slayer of Souls* (1920)—in early 1927. He hastily updated "Supernatural Horror in Literature" just before publication to include a discussion of Chambers.

Cole, Edward H[arold] (1892–1966), longtime amateur associate of HPL, living in the Boston area; editor of the *Olympian*. For HPL's letters to him, see *Letters to Alfred Galpin and Others*.

Conover, Willis (1920–1996), weird fiction fan who edited *Science-Fantasy Correspondent* (1936–37); a late correspondent of HPL. For HPL's letters to him, see *Letters to Robert Bloch and Others*.

Cook, W. Paul (1880–1948), publisher of the *Monadnock Monthly*, the *Vagrant*, and other amateur journals; a longtime amateur journalist, printer, and lifelong friend of HPL. He first visited HPL in 1917, and it was he who urged HPL to resume writing fiction after a hiatus of nine years. In 1927 Cook published the *Recluse*, containing HPL's "Supernatural Horror in Literature."

de Castro, Adolphe (Danziger) (1859–1959), author, co-translator with Ambrose Bierce of Richard Voss's *The Monk and the Hangman's Daughter*, and correspondent of HPL. HPL revised his "The Last Test" and "The Electric Executioner." For HPL's letters to him, see *Letters to Alfred Galpin and Others*.

Derleth, August W[illiam] (1909–1971), author of weird tales and also a long series of regional and historical works set in his native Wisconsin. After HPL's death, he and Donald Wandrei founded Arkham House to preserve HPL's work in book form. See *Essential Solitude* for his correspondence with HPL.

Dunsany, Lord (Edward John Moreton Drax Plunkett) (1878–1957), Anglo-Irish writer of fantasy tales whose work notably influenced HPL after HPL read it in 1919.

Dwyer, Bernard Austin (1897–1943), weird fiction fan and would-be writer and artist, living in West Shokan, NY; correspondent of HPL. For HPL's letters to him, see *Letters to Maurice W. Moe and Others*.

Dyalhis, Nictzin (1873–1942), an American chemist and short story writer who specialized in science fiction and fantasy and was a popular contributor to *Weird Tales*.

Eddy, C[lifford] M[artin] (1896–1967), pulp fiction writer living in the Providence area for whom HPL revised several stories in 1923–24 and who also worked with HPL on ghostwriting work for Harry Houdini in 1926.

Finlay, Virgil (1914–1971), one of the great weird artists of his time and a prolific contributor of artwork to the pulps; late correspondent of HPL.

Galpin, Alfred (1901–1983), amateur journalist and correspondent of HPL. He studied music in Paris and was also a scholar in French literature. For HPL's letters to him, see *Letters to Alfred Galpin and Others*.

Gamwell, Annie E[meline] P[hillips] (1866–1941), HPL's younger aunt, living with him at 66 College Street (1933–37). For HPL's letters to her see *Letters to Family and Family Friends*.

Hamilton, Edmond (1904–1977), prolific author of weird and science fiction tales for the pulp magazines. HPL admired his story "The Monster-God of Mamurth" (*WT*, August 1926) but little else of his work.

Hoag, Jonathan E[lihu] (1831–1927), an amateur poet. HPL, with James F. Morton, edited and published *The Poetical Works of Jonathan E. Hoag* (1923). The book contains HPL's annual birthday greetings to Hoag in verse.

Houdini, Harry (stage name of Ehrich Weiss, 1874–1926), celebrated escape artist and opponent of spiritualism for whom HPL ghostwrote the story "Under the Pyramids" (1924; published as "Imprisoned with the Pharaohs") and for whom he did other revisory work in 1926, just prior to Houdini's death.

Houtain, George Julian (1884–1945), amateur journalist who established the semi-professional humor magazine *Home Brew*, for which he commissioned HPL to write "Herbert West—Reanimator" (1921–22) and "The Lurking Fear" (1922).

Howard, Robert E[rvin] (1906–1936), prolific Texas author of weird and adventure tales for *Weird Tales* and other pulp magazines; creator of the adventure hero Conan the Barbarian. He and HPL corresponded voluminously from 1930 to 1936. He committed suicide when he learned of his mother's impending death. See *A Means to Freedom* for his correspondence with HPL.

James, M[ontague] R[hodes] (1862–1936), pioneering British writer of ghost stories whose work HPL much admired.

Kirk, George [Willard] (1898–1962), member of the Kalem Club. He published *Twenty-one Letters of Ambrose Bierce* (1922) and ran the Chelsea Bookshop in New York.

Kline, Otis Adelbert (1891–1946), prolific writer for *Weird Tales* and other pulp magazines; also a literary agent for Robert E. Howard and others.

Leeds, Arthur (1882–1952?), an associate of HPL in New York and member of the Kalem Club. He was the author (with J. Berg Esenwein) of *Writing the Photoplay* (Springfield, MA: The Home Correspondence School, 1913; rev. ed. 1919). See *Letters to Alfred Galpin and Others* for a few surviving letters to him by HPL.

Long, Frank Belknap (1901–1994), fiction writer and poet and one of HPL's closest friends and correspondents. Late in life he wrote the memoir *Howard Phillips Lovecraft: Dreamer on the Nightside* (1975).

Loveman, Samuel (1887–1976), poet and longtime friend of HPL and Donald Wandrei as well as of Ambrose Bierce, Hart Crane, George Sterling, and Clark Ashton Smith. He wrote *The Hermaphrodite* (1926) and other works. See *Letters to Alfred Galpin and Others* for a few surviving letters to him by HPL.

Machen, Arthur (1863–1947), Welsh author of weird fiction much admired by HPL.

McNeil, [Henry] Everett (1862–1929), author of historical and adventure novels for boys; member of the Kalem Club.

Miniter, Edith (1867–1934), amateur author who also professionally published a novel, *Our Natupski Neighbors* (1916) and many short stories. HPL was guest at her home in Wilbraham, Massachusetts, in the summer of 1928.

Moore, C[atherine] L[ucile] (1911–1987), late associate of HPL who later married Henry Kuttner and became a leading figure in science fiction and fantasy. Their joint correspondence has been published in *Letters to C. L. Moore and Others*.

Morton, James Ferdinand (1870–1941), amateur journalist, author of many tracts on race prejudice, free thought, and taxation, and longtime friend of HPL. For HPL's letters to him, see *Letters to James F. Morton*.

Munn, H[arold] Warner (1903–1981), prolific contributor to the pulp magazines, living near W. Paul Cook in Athol, MA.

Orton, Vrest (1897–1986), a correspondent of Lovecraft living in New York. He designed the cover for W. Paul Cook's *Recluse,* wrote *Dreiserana, a Book about His Books* (1929), founded the Stephen Daye Press in Brattleboro, VT, and in 1946 started the Vermont Country Store.

Owen, Frank. Pseudonym of Roswell Williams (1893–1968), author of Oriental fantasies for *Weird Tales, Oriental Stories,* and other magazines.

Price, E[dgar] Hoffmann (1898–1988), prolific pulp writer of weird and adventure tales. HPL met him in New Orleans in 1932 and corresponded extensively with him thereafter. For HPL's letters to him, see *Letters to E. Hoffmann Price and Richard F. Searight.*

Quinn, Seabury (1889–1969), prolific author of weird and detective tales to the pulps, notably a series of tales involving the psychic detective Jules de Grandin.

Smith, Clark Ashton (1893–1961), prolific California poet and writer of fantasy tales. He received a "fan" letter from HPL in 1922 and corresponded with him until HPL's death. Their joint correspondence has been published in *Dawnward Spire, Lonely Hill.*

Starrett, Vincent (1886–1974), American bookman who corresponded briefly with HPL in 1927. For HPL's letters to him, see *Letters to Alfred Galpin and Others.*

Sterling, George (1869–1926), American poet and early mentor of CAS. Author of *The Testimony of the Suns* (1903) and *A Wine of Wizardry* (1909).

Swanson, Carl, a fan from North Dakota who wrote to several authors of weird and science fiction asking for contributions to a magazine he planned to publish, to be called the *Galaxy.* It was never realized.

Talman, Wilfred Blanch (1904–1986), correspondent of HPL and late member of the Kalem Club. HPL assisted Talman on his story "Two Black Bottles" (1926) and wrote "Some Dutch Footprints in New England" for Talman to publish in *De Halve Maen,* the journal of the Holland Society of New York. Late in life he wrote the memoir *The Normal Lovecraft* (1973). For HPL's letters to him, see *Letters to Wilfred B. Talman and Helen V. and Genevieve Sully.*

Uzzell, Thomas H. (1884–1975), writer, editor, and teacher in New York City during the 1920s and '30s. He was fiction editor at *Collier's,* taught seminars on fiction writing at New York University, and published several books on the craft of writing, including *Narrative Technique: A Practical Course in Literary Psychology* (1934), *Writing as a Career* (1938), and *The Technique of the Novel* (1947). Frank Belknap Long was a pupil of his, but HPL considered him a charlatan.

Wandrei, Donald (1908–1987), poet and author of weird fiction, science fiction, and detective tales. He corresponded with HPL from 1926 to 1937, visited HPL in Providence in 1927 and 1932, and met HPL occasionally in New York during the 1930s. He helped HPL get "The Shadow out of Time" published in *Astounding Stories*. After HPL's death he and August Derleth founded the publishing firm Arkham House to preserve HPL's work. For their joint correspondence, see *H. P. Lovecraft: Letters with Donald and Howard Wandrei and to Emil Petaja*.

Weiss, Henry George (1898–1946), American poet, writer and novelist. His science fiction stories and poetry appeared under the pseudonym "Francis Flagg" in *Amazing Stories, Astounding, Tales of Wonder, Weird Tales*, and others.

Whitehead, Henry S[t. Clair] (1882–1932), author of weird and adventure tales, many of them set in the Virgin Islands. HPL corresponded with him and visited him in Florida in 1931. HPL wrote a brief eulogy of Whitehead for *WT*.

Bibliography

A. H. P. Lovecraft

Books

The Ancient Track: Complete Poetical Works. Ed. S. T. Joshi. 2nd ed. New York: Hippocampus Press, 2013. [*AT*]

The Annotated Supernatural Horror in Literature. Ed. S. T. Joshi. 2nd ed. New York: Hippocampus Press, 2012.

Collected Essays. Ed. S. T. Joshi. New York: Hippocampus Press, 2004–06. 5 vols. [*CE*]

Collected Fiction: A Variorum Edition. Ed. S. T. Joshi. New York: Hippocampus Press, 2015 (Volumes 1–3), 2017 (Volume 4). [*CF*]

Dawnward Spire, Lonely Hill: The Letters of H. P. Lovecraft and Clark Ashton Smith. Edited by David E. Schultz and S. T. Joshi. New York: Hippocampus Press, 2017.

Essential Solitude: The Letters of H. P. Lovecraft and August Derleth. Ed. David E. Schultz and S. T. Joshi. New York: Hippocampus Press, 2008. 2 vols.

Fungi from Yuggoth: An Annotated Edition. Ed. David E. Schultz. New York: Hippocampus Press, 2017.

Letters to Alfred Galpin and Others. Ed. S. T. Joshi and David E. Schultz. New York: Hippocampus Press, 2020.

Letters to E. Hoffmann Price and Richard F. Searight. Ed. S. T. Joshi and David E. Schultz. New York: Hippocampus Press, 2021.

Letters to Family and Family Friends. Ed. S. T. Joshi and David E. Schultz. New York: Hippocampus Press, 2020.

Letters to J. Vernon Shea, Carl F. Strauch, and Lee McBride White. Ed. S. T. Joshi and David E. Schultz. New York: Hippocampus Press, 2016.

Letters to James F. Morton. Ed. David E. Schultz and S. T. Joshi. New York: Hippocampus Press, 2011.

Letters to Maurice W. Moe and Others. Edited by David E. Schultz and S. T. Joshi. New York: Hippocampus Press, 2018.

Letters to Rheinhart Kleiner and Others. Edited by S. T. Joshi and David E. Schultz. New York: Hippocampus Press, 2020.

Letters to Robert Bloch and Others. Ed. David E. Schultz and S. T. Joshi. New York: Hippocampus Press, 2015.

Letters to Wilfred B. Talman and Helen V. and Genevieve Sully. Ed. David E. Schultz and S. T. Joshi. New York: Hippocampus Press, 2019.

Lovecraft at Last (with Willis Conover). Arlington, VA: Carrollton-Clark, 1975. New York: Cooper Square Press, 2002.

A Means to Freedom: The Letters of H. P. Lovecraft and Robert E. Howard. Edited

by S. T. Joshi, David E. Schultz, and Rusty Burke. New York: Hippocampus Press, 2009.

Miscellaneous Letters. Ed. David E. Schultz and S. T. Joshi. New York: Hippocampus Press, 2022.

O Fortunate Floridian: H. P. Lovecraft's Letters to R. H. Barlow. Ed. S. T. Joshi and
David E. Schultz. Tampa, FL: University of Tampa Press, 2007.

Selected Letters. Edited by August Derleth, Donald Wandrei, and James Turner.
Sauk City, WI: Arkham House, 1965–76. 5 vols. [*SL*]

The Shadow over Innsmouth. Everett, PA: Visionary Publishing Co., 1936.

The Shunned House. Athol, MA: Recluse Press, 1928 (printed but not bound or
distributed until 1959–61).

The Spirit of Revision: Lovecraft's Letters to Zealia Brown Reed Bishop. Ed. Sean Branney
and Andrew Leman. Glendale, CA: H. P. Lovecraft Historical Society, 2015.

Fiction

At the Mountains of Madness. Astounding Stories 16, No. 6 (February 1936): 8–32;
17, No. 1 (March 1936): 125–55; 17, No. 2 (April 1936): 132–50. In *CF* 3.

"The Call of Cthulhu." *WT* 11, No. 2 (February 1928): 159–78, 287. In *Beware
After Dark! The World's Most Stupendous Tales of Mystery, Horror, Thrills and
Terror,* ed. T. Everett Harré. New York: Macaulay, 1929, 223–59. In *CF* 2.

The Case of Charles Dexter Ward. WT 35, No. 9 (May 1941): 8–40; 35, No. 10
(July 1941): 84–121 (abridged). In *CF* 2.

"The Cats of Ulthar." *Tryout* 6, No. 11 (November 1920): [3–9]. *WT* 7, No. 2
(February 1924): 252–54. Cassia, FL: The Dragon-Fly Press, Christmas
1935. In *CF* 1.

"The Colour out of Space." *Amazing Stories* 2, No. 6 (September 1927): 557–
67. In *CF* 2.

"Dagon." *Vagrant* No. 11 (November 1919): 23–29. *WT* 2, No. 3 (October
1923): 23–25. *WT* 27, No. 1 (January 1936): 118–23. In *CF* 1.

"The Doom That Came to Sarnath." *Scot* No. 44 (June 1920): 90–98. *Marvel
Tales of Science and Fantasy* 1, No. 4 (March–April 1935): 157–63. In *CF* 1.

The Dream-Quest of Unknown Kadath. First published in *Beyond the Wall of Sleep.*
Sauk City, WI: Arkham House, 1943. In *CF* 2.

"The Dreams in the Witch House." *WT* 22, No. 1 (July 1933): 86–111. In *CF* 3.

"The Dunwich Horror." *WT* 13, No. 4 (April 1929): 481–508. In *CF* 2.

"Facts concerning the Late Arthur Jermyn and His Family." *Wolverine* No. 9
(March 1921): 3–11. *WT* 3, No. 4 (April 1924): 15–18 (as "The White
Ape"). *WT* 25, No. 5 (May 1935): 642–48 (as "Arthur Jermyn"). In *CF* 1.

"The Festival." *WT* 5, No. 1 (January 1925): 169–74. *WT* 22, No. 4 (October
1933): 519–20, 522–28. In *CF* 1.

"The Haunter of the Dark." *WT* 28, No. 5 (December 1936): 538–53. In *CF* 3.

"Herbert West—Reanimator" (as "Grewsome Tales"). *Home Brew* 1, No. 1

(February 1922): 84–88 ("From the Dark"); 1, No. 2 (March 1922): 45–50 ("The Plague Demon"); 1, No. 3 (April 1922): 21–26 ("Six Shots by Moonlight"); 1, No. 4 (May 1922): 53–58 ("The Scream of the Dead"); 1, No. 5 (June 1922): 45–50 ("The Horror from the Shadows,"); 1, No. 6 (July 1922): 57–62 ("The Tomb-Legions"). In *CF* 1.

"The Horror at Red Hook." *WT* 9, No. 1 (January 1927): 59–73. In *You'll Need a Night Light,* ed. Christine Campbell Thomson. London: Selwyn & Blount, 1927, 228–54. In *CF* 1.

"The Hound." *WT* 3, No. 2 (Feb. 1924): 50–52, 78. *WT* 14, No. 3 (Sept. 1929): 421–25, 432. In *CF* 1.

"Hypnos." *National Amateur* 45, No. 5 (May 1923): 1–3. *Weird Tales* 4, No. 2 (May–June–July 1924): 33–35. In *CF* 1.

"The Lurking Fear." *Home Brew* 2, No. 6 (January 1923): 4–10; 3, No. 1 (February 1923): 18–23; 3, No. 2 (March 1923): 31–37, 44, 48; 3, No. 3 (April 1923): 35–42. *WT* 11, No. 6 (June 1928): 791–804. In *CF* 1.

"The Moon-Bog." *WT* 7, No. 6 (June 1926): 805–10. In *CF* 1.

"The Music of Erich Zann." *National Amateur* 44, No. 4 (March 1922): 38–40. *WT* 5, No. 5 (May 1925): 219–34. In *Creeps by Night: Chills and Thrills,* ed. Dashiell Hammett. New York: John Day Co., 1931, 347–63. In *Modern Tales of Horror,* ed. Dashiell Hammett. London: Victor Gollancz, 1932, 301–17. *Evening Standard* (London) (24 October 1932): 20–21. *WT* 24, No. 5 (November 1934): 644–48, 655–56. In *CF* 1.

"The Outsider." *WT* 7, No. 4 (April 1926): 449–53. *WT* 17, No. 4 (June–July 1931): 566–71. In *CF* 1.

"Pickman's Model." *WT* 10, No. 4 (October 1927): 505–14. In *By Daylight Only,* ed. Christine Campbell Thomson. London: Selwyn & Blount, 1929, 37–52. *WT* 28, No. 4 (November 1936): 495–505. In *The "Not at Night" Omnibus,* ed. Christine Campbell Thomson. London: Selwyn & Blount, [1937], 279–307. In *CF* 2.

"The Picture in the House." *National Amateur* 41, No. 6 (July 1919 [*sic*]): 246–49. *WT* 3, No. 1 (January 1924): 40–42. *WT* 29, No. 3 (March 1937): 370–73. In *CF* 1.

"The Rats in the Walls." *WT* 3, No. 3 (March 1924): 25–31. *WT* 15, No. 6 (June 1930): 841–53. In *Switch On the Light,* ed. Christine Campbell Thomson. London: Selwyn & Blount, 1931, 141–65. In *CF* 1.

"The Shadow out of Time." *Astounding Stories* 17, No. 4 (June 1936): 110–54. In *CF* 3.

"The Shadow over Innsmouth." In *CF* 3.

"The Shunned House." Athol, MA: W. Paul Cook (The Recluse Press), 1928 (printed but not bound or distributed). In *CF* 1.

"The Silver Key." *WT* 13, No. 1 (January 1929): 41–49, 144. In *CF* 2.

"The Statement of Randolph Carter." *Vagrant* No. 13 (May 1920): 41–48. *WT* 5, No. 2 (February 1925): 149–53. In *CF* 1.

"The Strange High House in the Mist." *WT* 18, No. 3 (October 1931): 394–400. In *CF* 2.

"The Temple." *WT* 6, No. 3 (September 1925): 329–36, 429, 431; rpt. *WT* 27, No. 2 (February 1936): 239–44, 246–49. In *CF* 1.

"The Terrible Old Man." *Tryout* 7, No. 4 (July 1921): [10–14]. *WT* 8, No. 2 (Aug. 1926): 191–92. In *CF* 1.

"The Tomb." *Vagrant* No. 14 (March 1922): 50–64. *WT* 7, No. 1 (January 1926): 117–23. In *CF* 1.

"The Thing on the Doorstep." *WT* 29, No. 1 (January 1937): 52–70. In *CF* 3.

"The Unnamable." *WT* 6, No. 1 (July 1925): 78–82. In *CF* 1.

"The Whisperer in Darkness." *WT* 18, No. 1 (August 1931): 32–73. In *CF* 2.

"The White Ship." *United Amateur* 19, No. 2 (November 1919): 30–33. *WT* 9, No. 3 (March 1927): 386–89. In *CF* 1.

Nonfiction

[Advertisement of Revisory Services] (with Frank Belknap Long). *Weird Tales* 12, No. 2 (August 1928): 281. In *CE* 5.

"An Account of a Trip to the Antient Fairbanks House, in Dedham, and to the Red Horse Tavern in Sudbury, in the Province of the Massachusetts-Bay." In *CE* 4.

"[Autobiographical Notice]." In *CF* 5. See O'Brien herein.

"Baptizing the Baby." *Drift-Wind* [1], No. 2 (May 1926): 12, as by "H. L." Comments by readers on the first and previous number of *Drift-Wind*.

"Cats and Dogs." *Leaves* 1 (Summer 1937): 25–34. In *CE* 5.

"A Confession of Unfaith." *Liberal* 1, No. 2 (February 1922): 17–23. In *CE* 5.

"In Memoriam: Henry S. Whitehead." *WT* 21, No. 3 (March 1933): 391 (unsigned). In *CE* 5.

"In Memoriam: Robert Ervin Howard." *Fantasy Magazine* No. 38 (September 1936): 29–31. In *CE* 5.

"Instructions in Case of Decease." In *CE* 5.

Letter to editor of *Driftwind*. *Driftwind* 7, No. 2 (July 1932): 13.

"The Simple Spelling Mania." *United Co-operative* 1, No. 1 (December 1918): 1–3. In *CE* 2.

"Sleepy Hollow To-Day." An extract from "Observations on Several Parts of America." In Sterling Leonard and Harold Y. Moffett, ed. *Junior Literature: Book Two*. New York: Macmillan, 1930, 1935. 545–46. In *CE* 4.

"Supernatural Horror in Literature." *Recluse* No. 1 (1927): 23–59. Rev. ed. in *Fantasy Fan* (October 1933–February 1935). In *CE* 2.

"Vermont—A First Impression." *Driftwind* 2, No. 3 (March 1928): [5–9]. In *CE* 4.

Poetry [all items in *AT*]

"Ave atque Vale: To Jonathan E. Hoag, Esq.: February 10, 1831–October 17, 1927." *Tryout* 11, No. 10 (December 1927): [3–4].

Fungi from Yuggoth.
I. "The Book." *Fantasy Fan* 2, No. 2 (October 1934): 24. *Driftwind* 11, No. 9 (April 1937): 342.
IV. "Recognition." *Driftwind* 11, No. 5 (December 1936): 180.
VI. "The Lamp." *Driftwind* 5, No. 5 (March 1931): 16. *Weird Tales* 33, No. 2 (February 1939): 151.
VII. "Zaman's Hill." *Driftwind* 9, No. 4 (October 1934): 125. *Weird Tales* 33, No. 2 (February 1939): 151.
VIII. "The Port." *Driftwind* 5, No. 3 (November 1930): 36. *Weird Tales* 39, No. 7 (September 1946): 65. *Weird Tales* (Canadian) 38, No. 4 (November 1946): 40.
IX. "The Courtyard." *WT* 16, No. 3 (September 1930): 322. Numbered 1.
XII. "The Howler." *Driftwind* 7, No. 3 (November 1932): 100. *Weird Tales* 34, No. 1 (June–July 1939): 66.
XIII. "Hesperia." *WT* 16, No. 4 (October 1930): 464. Numbered 3.
XIV. "Star-Winds." *WT* 16, No. 3 (September 1930): 322. Numbered 2.
XV. "Antarktos." *WT* 16, No. 5 (November 1930): 692. Numbered 4.
XVI. "The Window." *Driftwind* 5 (April 1931 [special issue]): 15. *Weird Tales* 37, No. 5 (May 1944): 53. *Weird Tales* (Canadian) 38, No. 3 (September 1945): 75. *Hi-Lite* [Mannheim Township High School, Nettsville, PA] (30 October 1946).
XVIII. "The Gardens of Yin." *Driftwind* 6, No. 5 (March 1932): 34. *Weird Tales* 34, No. 2 (August 1939): 151.
XIX. "The Bells." *WT* 16, No. 6 (December 1930): 798. Numbered 5.
XXI. "Nyarlathotep." *WT* 17, No. 1 (January 1931): 12. Numbered 6.
XXII. "Azathoth." *WT* 17, No. 1 (January 1931): 12. Numbered 7.
XXIII. "Mirage." *WT* 17, No. 2 (February–March 1931): 175. Numbered 8.
XXIV. "The Canal." *Driftwind* 6, No. 5 (March 1932): 34. In Walter John Coates, ed. *Harvest: A Sheaf of Poems from Driftwind.* North Montpelier, VT: The Driftwind Press, May 1933, p. 33. *Weird Tales* 31, No. 1 (January 1938): 20. *Weird Tales* 47, No. 1 (Summer 1973): 96.
XXVI. "The Familiars." *Driftwind* 5, No. 1 (July 1930): 35. *Weird Tales* 39, No. 9 (January 1947): 96. *Weird Tales* (Canadian) 38, No. 4 [*sic*] (March 1947): 59.
XXVII. "The Elder Pharos." *WT* 17, No. 2 (February–March 1931): 175. Numbered 9.
XXXII. "Alienation." *WT* 17, No. 3 (April–May 1931): 374. Numbered 10.

"Nemesis." *WT* 3, No. 4 (April 1924): 78.
"The Poem of Ulysses, or, The Odyssey."
Poemata Minora, Volume II.
"Recapture." *WT* 15, No. 5 (May 1930): 693. Not part of *Fungi from Yuggoth* until 1936.

"To Jonathan E. Hoag, Esq., upon His Ninety-sixth Birthday, February 10, 1927." *National Amateur* 49, No. 5 (May 1927): 10.

"To Mr. Hoag upon His 93rd Birthday, February 10, 1924." *Troy* [NY] *Times* (9 February 1924) (as "His Ninety-third Birthday: To Jonathan Hoag of Greenwich—a Poem to the Poet—February 10th Anniversary").

Revisions and Collaborations

Eddy, C. M., Jr. "The Loved Dead." *WT* 4, No. 2 (May–June–July 1924): 54–57. In *CF* 4.

Greene, Sonia H. "The Horror at Martin's Beach." *WT* 2, No. 4 (November 1923): 75–76, 83 (as "The Invisible Monster"). In *CF* 4.

Price, E. Hoffmann. "Through the Gates of the Silver Key." *WT* 24, No. 1 (July 1934): 60–85. In *CF* 4.

B. Edwin Baird

The City of Purple Dreams. London, 1916.

The Colossus of the Press: A Brief Journey through the World's Greatest Printing Plant. Chicago: W. F. Hall Printing Co., 1926.

Fay. New York: E. J. Clode, 1923.

The Heart of Virginia Keep. London: Ward, Lock & Co., 1918.

"The Greatest Thing in the World." *Smart Set* 47, No. 3 (November 1915): 249–57.

C. Farnsworth Wright

"After Two Nights of the Ear-ache." *WT* 30, No. 4 (April 1937): 502 (as by Francis Hard).

"An Adventure in the Fourth Dimension." *WT* 2, No. 3 (October 1923): [69]–70, 92, 94. In *The Moon Terror.* [Ed. Farnsworth Wright.] Indianapolis: Popular Fiction Publishing Co., 1927. *10 Story Book* 29 No. 9 (April 1931): 37–42.

"An Answer to Mr. Anger." *Phantagraph* 5, No. 2 (December 1936): 4–6. In *Letters to Robert Bloch and Others* 459–60.

"The Closing Hand." *WT* 1, No. 1 (March 1923): 98–99.

"A Cookery Queen." *Overland Monthly* 74, No. 6 (December 1919): 471–73.

"The Dark Pool." *WT* 5, No. 4 (April 1925): 118 (as by Francis Hard).

"The Death Angel." *WT* 6, No. 3 (September 1925): 387 (as by Francis Hard).

"Enemies." *Overland Monthly* 68, No. 2 (February 1917): 154–60.

"The Evening Star." *WT* 7, No. 3 (March 1926): 353 (as by Francis Hard).

Extract from letter to *Phantagraph* 6, No. 5 (September 1937): [1].

"Farnsworth Wright: Correspondence to Donald Wandrei, 1932." *Windy City Pulp Stories* No. 13 (2013): 57–59.

"The Great Panjandrum." *WT* 4, No. 3 (November 1924) 55–64 (as by Francis Hard).

"In the Depths." *Overland Monthly* 74, No. 6 (December 1919): 464–67.

Letter to Hannes Bok (17 January 1940). *Xenophile* No. 18 (1975): 31.

Letter to Henry Hasse (22 April 1933). *Xenophile* No. 18 (1975): 30.

Letter to Henry Hasse (31 January 1933). *Xenophile* No. 18 (1975): 30.

Letter to Robert E. Howard (31 [*sic*] June 1932). *Glenn Lord's Ultima Thule.* n.p.: Rob Roehm, 2007, p. 28.

Letter to Robert E. Howard (10 March 1932). In Glenn Lord. *The Last Celt: A Bio-Bibliography of Robert Ervin Howard.* West Kingston, RI: Donald M. Grant 1976. 37–39.

"Lonesome Time." *Overland Monthly* 74, No. 4 (October 1919): 331–33.

"The Medal of Virtue." *Munsey's Magazine* 71, No. 3 (December 1920): 407–10.

"Out of the Frying Pan." *Overland Monthly* 75, No. 5 (May 1920): 400–402.

"The Picture of Judas." *Magic Carpet Magazine* 3, No. 2 (April 1933): 159–70 (as by Francis Hard).

"Poisoned." *WT* 2, No. 4 (November 1923): 69–72.

"Self-Portrait." *Fantasy Magazine* 4, No. 5 (April 1935): 112. *Etchings & Odysseys* No. 3 (1983): 61.

"The Snake Fiend." *WT* 1, No. 2 (April 1923): 75–79.

"The Teak-Wood Shrine." *WT* 2, No. 2 (September 1923): 73–74.

"Two Crows." *WT* 5, No. 1 (January 1925): 115 (as by Francis Hard).

"The Vow." *Overland Monthly* 70, No. 2 (August 1917): 152–57.

"The White Queen." *Oriental Magazine* 1, No. 1 (October–November 1930): 32–48.

D. Walter J. Coates

A Bibliography of Vermont Poetry and Gazetteer of Vermont Poets: Being the Titles of Books, Pamphlets and Broadsides by Poets Born or Residing in Vermont, Including also a Few Items Not by Vermonters but of Vermont Interest. Montpelier, VT: Vermont Historical Society, 1942. A through K only.

Building the Temple. North Montpelier, VT: Driftwind Press, 1928.

Diapason: Nuances in Verse. North Montpelier, VT: Driftwind Press, 1937.

Double Thirteen: Being a Like Number of Lyrics and Sonnets. North Montpelier, VT: Driftwind Press, 1931.

Dried Blossoms—and Weeds. With Henry Denison. [East Calais, VT]: [Driftwind Press], [191-?].

Favorite Vermont Poems: Series One (editor). North Montpelier, VT: Driftwind Press, 1928.

Favorite Vermont Poems: Series Two (editor). Hartland, VT: Solitarian Press, 1929.

Favorite Vermont Poems: Series Three: The Hill Spirit, Today and Yesterday (editor). North Montpelier, VT: Driftwind Press, 1930.

Favorite Vermont Poems: Series IV (editor). North Montpelier, VT: Driftwind Press, 1931.

Favorite Vermont Poems: Series V: Being Important Items Not Included in Series I, II, III and IV (editor). [North Montpelier, VT]: Driftwind Press, 1934.

Good-will. [East Calais, VT]: The Author, 1931.

Harvest: A Sheaf of Poems from Driftwind—*April 1926 to May, 1933* (editor). North Montpelier, VT: Driftwind Press, 1933.

Hubbardton Battle: A Ballad. Written for the Vermont Sesqui-Centennial Commission and Read at the 150th Anniversary Celebration at Hubbardton, July Seventh, 1927. [n.p.]: Published by courtesy of the Vermont Sesqui-Centennial Commission, 1927. (LL 201)

Land of Allen and Other Verse. Athol, MA: W. Paul Cook/The Recluse Press, [8 December] 1928.

The Lee Family of Hounsfield, N.Y.: and Related Families. North Montpelier, VT: Driftwind Press, 1941.

Life Problems as Related to the Human Soul and Destiny: Sermons Preached at East Calais, Vt. and North Hatley, P.Q. [n.p.]: [n.p.], 1906.

Masonry: A Church Outside the Church: An Address. North Montpelier, VT: The Driftwind Press, 1934.

Mood Songs: Voices within Myself. Hartford, VT: Solitarian Press, 1921.

Mortality: Being Several Funeral Services and Three Unrelated Prayers; also a Few Mortuary Poems. North Montpelier, VT: Driftwood Press, 1939.

Ruins. East Calais. [VT]: The Author, 1926.

Sonnets of an Editor. North Montpelier, VT: Driftwind Press, 1934.

Two Essays: Infidelity as a World Bugaboo. The Laggard Church. North Montpelier, VT: Coates, 1925.

Unspoken Travail and Other Verse. East Calais, VT: Coates, 1918.

Vases of Verse: An Anthology of Vermont Sonnets (editor, with J. Howard Flower). Hartland, VT : Solitarian Press, 1931. *Vermont in Heart and Song: Tributes to the State from her Early Singers* (compiler). Printed as one of Ye Alle Tyme Gifte Bookes at North Montpelier, VT (1926).

Vermont in Heart and Song: Tributes to the State from Her Early Singers (editor). North Montpelier, VT: [Driftwind Press] Printed as one of Ye Alle Tyme Gifte Bookes, 1926.

Vermont Verse: An Anthology (edior, with Frederick Tupper). Brattleboro, VT: Stephen Daye Press. 1932.

Webster's Oriental Songs by Henry Clay Webster. Hartland, VT: Solitarian Press, 1920. Commemorative ed., rev. and ed. by Coates.

The Yankee Bard: Vermont Ballads (editor, with J. Howard Flower). Hartland, VT: Solitarian Press, 1934.

Verse

"Aspiration." *Driftwind* 9, No. 12 (June/July 1935): 380.

"Dr. Wilson." *Driftwind* 3, No. 2 (September 1928): 59–61.

"Eyes of the Crouching Lion." *Driftwind* 5, No. 5 (March 1931): 36.

"Free Souls." *Driftwind* 10, No. 9 (March 1936): 253.

"Pardon Janes." *Driftwind* 2, No. 4 (January 1928): 17–22.

"Rebirth." *Driftwind* 7, No. 3 (November 1932): 112.

"To Clinton Scollard." *VerseCraft* 3, No. 1 (January/February 1933): 6.

Nonfiction

"Check List of Publications of Driftwind Press." *Driftwind* 6, No. 3 (November 1931): 17ff.

"Early Vermont Minstrelsy." *Recluse* No. 1 (1927): 3–14.

"Ethan Allen's Religion." *Driftwind* 3, No. 3 (November 1928): 96–99.

"Editorial Brevities." *Driftwind* February (March 1936).

"Editor's Comments." *Driftwind* (September/October 1935).

"The Future for a Literary Magazine in Vermont." Driftwind 2, No. 1 (June 1927): [7–9].

"How I Fared During the Flood." *Tryout* (December 1927).

"Howard Phillips Lovecraft [1890–1937]." *Driftwind* 11, No. 9 (April 1937): 343–44.

"Just Between You and Me." *Driftwind* (November 1932).

"Literary Torch Bearers." *Driftwind* 4, No. 3 (November 1929): 19–22.

"A Minority Mind." *Driftwind* [1], No. 1 (April 1926): 3–5.

"Our Sleeping Liberals." *Driftwind* [1], No. 1 (April 1926): 11–12.

"Pictorial Reminiscences by the Editor." *Driftwind.* 7, No. 1 (July 1932): 5–8. Carry Back Books *Catalogue No. 8* (Fall 1975): 43–44, as "Coates' Account of Origin of *Driftwind*]." Rpt. as "The Birth of *Driftwind*." *W. Paul Cook: The Wandering Life of a Yankee Printer*, ed. Sean Donnelly. New York: Hippocampus Press, 2007, pp. 89–92.

"The Power of Contrast." *Driftwind* [1], No. 1 (April 1926): 8–9.

"The Round Schoolhouse in Brookline." *Driftwind* 3, No. 2 (September 1928): 58.

"Shakespeare's Sonnet-writing Friend." *Driftwind* (March 1931).

"Study List: Vermont Poets and Poetry." *Recluse* No. 1 (1927): [1]–2.

Reviews

"Book Notices." *Driftwind* 5, No. 5 (March 1931): 13–4.

"The Great Misnomer." *Driftwind* 5, No. 1 (July 1930): 21–2.

D. Woodburn Harris

Letter to Vrest Orton, 13 August 1939, ALS, Wisconsin Historical Society, August Derleth papers (filed with letters by Orton to Derleth).

E. Zealia Brown Reed Bishop

The Curse of Yig. Sauk City, WI: Arkham House, 1959.

The Adopted Son. Nonextant.

"The Blue Foulard." Nonextant.

"The Curse of Yig" (revised by HPL). *WT* 14, No. 5 (Nov. 1929): 625–36. In *Switch On the Light*, ed. Christine Campbell Thomson. London: Selwyn & Blount, 1931, 9–31. In *The "Not at Night" Omnibus*, ed. Christine Campbell Thomson. London: Selwyn & Blount, [1937], 13–29. In *CY, CF* 4.

"H. P. Lovecraft: A Pupil's View." In *CY*. In S. T. Joshi and David E. Schultz, ed. *Ave atque Vale: Reminiscences of H. P. Lovecraft.* West Warwick, RI: Necronomicon Press, 2018. 252–63.

"Husband pro Forma." Nonextant.

"Ice Music." Nonextant.

"Lesson 8." Nonextant.

"A Matter of Management." Nonextant.

"Medusa's Coil" (revised by HPL). *WT* 33, No. 1 (January 1939): 26–53. In *CY, CF* 4.

"The Mound" (revised by HPL). *WT* 35, No. 6 (November 1940): 98–120 (abridged). In *CY, CF* 4.

"On the High Places." Nonextant. Revised version of "The Unchaining."

"One-Man Girl." *Cupid's Diary* 52, No. 3 (26 December 1928): 53–63. Original title: "Red Blood."

"Out o' the East." Nonextant.

"Red Blood." See "One-Man Girl."

"The Return." Nonextant.

"The Silent Voice." Nonextant.

"The Unchaining." Nonextant.

"Under Cover." Nonextant.

"When a Woman Is Tempted." Nonextant.

"A Wisconsin Balzac: A Profile of August Derleth." In *CY*.

"The Woman Who Came Back." Nonextant.

F. William Lumley

"The Diary of Alonzo Typer" (revised by HPL). *WT* 31, No. 2 (February 1938): 152–66. In *CF* 4.

"Dread Words." Nonextant.

"The Dweller." *Fantasy Fan* 1, No. 6 (February 1934): 88.

"The Elder Thing." *Fantasy Fan* 2, No. 5 (January 1935): 75–76. *Crypt of Cthulhu* No. 11 (Candlemas 1983): 23–24.

"The Ferryman." *Fantasmagoria* 1, No. 2 (July 1937): [9].

"The Phantasy." Nonextant.

"Shadows." *Fantasy Fan* 1, No. 9 (May 1934): 142.

G. Works by Others

Alden, Abner (1758?–1820). *The Reader: Containing the Art of Delivery, Articulation, Accent, Pronunciation,* [etc.]. <1802> 3rd ed. Boston: Printed by J. T. Buckingham for Thomas & Andrews, 1808. (*LL* 25)

Allen, Hervey 1889–1949). *Israfel: The Life and Times of Edgar Allan Poe.* <1926> New York: George H. Doran Co., 1927. 2 vols.

Anderson, Jessie Macmillan. *A Study of English Words.* New York: American Book Co., 1897. (*LL* 38)

Anderson, Sherwood (1876–1941). *Hands and Other Stories.* Little Blue Book No. 865. Girard, KS: Haldeman-Julius Co., 1925.

———. *The Untold Lie and Other Stories.* Little Blue Book No. 866. Girard, KS: Haldeman-Julius Co., 1925.

———. *Winesburg, Ohio.* New York: B. W. Huebsch, 1919.

Anthon, Charles. *A System of Ancient and Mediaeval Geography for the Use of Schools and Colleges.* New-York: Harper & Brothers, 1850. (*LL* 46)

The Arabian Nights Entertainments. Selected and Edited by Andrew Lang. New York: Longmans, Green, 1898. (*LL* 49)

Arnold, Sir Edwin (1832–1904). *The Light of Asia; or, The Great Renunciation (Mahabhinishkramana): Being the Life and Teaching of Gautama, Prince of India and Founder of Buddhism (as Told in Verse by an Indian Buddhist).* New York: H. M. Caldwell Co., 1879. (*LL* 53)

Balzac, Honoré de (1799–1850). *Another Study of Woman.* Little Blue Book No. 1044. Girard, KS: Haldeman-Julius Co., 1926.

———. *The Atheist's Mass and An Accursed House.* Little Blue Book No. 15. Girard, KS: Haldeman-Julius Co., 1924.

———. *Christ in Flanders and Other Stories.* Little Blue Book No. 318. Girard, KS: Haldeman-Julius Co., 1922.

———. *A Coquette versus a Wife (The Peace of a Home).* Little Blue Book No. 1042. Girard, KS: Haldeman-Julius Co., 1926.

———. *The Crime at the Red Inn.* Little Blue Book No. 1042. Girard, KS: Haldeman-Julius Co., 1923.

———. *Don Juan: a Passion in the Desert.* Little Blue Book No. 344. Girard, KS: Haldeman-Julius Co., 1923.

———. *In the Time of the Terror and Other Stories.* Little Blue Book No. 143. Girard, KS: Haldeman-Julius Co., 1922.

———. *The Mysterious Exiles.* Little Blue Book No. 1047. Girard, KS: Haldeman-Julius Co., 1926.

———. *The Splendors and Miseries of a Courtesan.* Ed. Ralph Oppenheim. Little Blue Book No. 1067. Girard, KS: Haldeman-Julius Co., 1926.

————. *The Story of a Mad Sweetheart (Adieu).* Little Blue Book No. 1045. Girard, KS: Haldeman-Julius Co., 1926.

————. *A Study of a Woman and Comedies of the Counter.* Little Blue Book No. 1043. Girard, KS: Haldeman-Julius Co., 1926.

Beckford, William (1759–1844). *The History of the Caliph Vathek.* <1786> Printed Verbatim from the First Edition, with the Original Prefaces and Notes by [Samuel] Henley. New York: W. L. Allison, [1868?] or [188-?]. (*LL* 84)

Berkeley, George (1685–1753). *Alciphron; or, The Minute Philosopher: In Seven Dialogues: Containing An Apology for the Christian Religion against Those Who Are Called Free-Thinkers.* London: Jacob Tonson, 1732.

Bierce, Ambrose (1842–1914?). *The Horseman in the Sky and Other Stories.* Little Blue Book No. 1055. Girard, KS: Haldeman-Julius Co., 1926.

————. *In the Midst of Life: Tales of Soldiers and Civilians.* <1891> Introduction by George Sterling. New York: Modern Library, [1927]. (*LL* 99)

————. *An Occurrence at Owl Creek Bridge.* Little Blue Book No. 1054. Girard, KS: Haldeman-Julius Co., 1926.

————. *Tales of Ghouls and Ghosts.* Little Blue Book No. 1075. Girard, KS: Haldeman-Julius Co., 1927.

————. *Tales of Haunted Houses.* Little Blue Book No. 1080. Girard, KS: Haldeman-Julius Co., 1927.

————. *Twenty-one Letters of Ambrose Bierce.* Edited with a Note by Samuel Loveman. Cleveland: George Kirk, 1922. (*LL* 101)

Birch, A. G. *The Moon Terror.* And Stories by Anthony M. Rud, Vincent Starrett, and Farnsworth Wright. Indianapolis: Popular Fiction Publishing Co., 1927. (*LL* 104)

Blackwood, Algernon (1869–1951). *Incredible Adventures.* New York: Macmillan, 1914. (*LL*)

Bulfinch, Thomas (1796–1867). *The Age of Fable; or, Beauties of Mythology.* <1855> Edited by J. Loughran Scott. Rev. ed. Philadelphia: David McKay, 1898. (*LL* 142)

Bullen, John Ravenor (1886–1927). *White Fire.* Athol, MA: Recluse Press, 1927. (*LL* 143)

Butler, Samuel (1835–1902). *The Way of All Flesh.* London: Grant Richards, 1903.

Capps, Edward (1866–1950). *From Homer to Theocritus.* New York: Charles Scribner's Sons, 1901.

Carry Back Books. *Catalogue No. 8* (Fall 1975).

Chambers, Robert W. (1865–1933). *The King in Yellow.* Chicago: F. Tennyson Neely, 1895. (*LL* 184)

Cook, W. Paul. *Willis T. Crossman's Vermont.* Edited by Sean Donnelly and Leland M. Hawes, Jr. Tampa, FL: University of Tampa Press, 2005.

Crabb, George (1778–1851). *Crabb's English Synonyms.* <1816> Revised and enlarged . . . by John H. Finlay. New York: Harper & Brothers, 1917. (*LL* 220)

Dante Alighieri (1265–1321). *Dante's Inferno.* Translated by the Rev. Henry Francis Cary <1805–06> . . . and Illustrated with the Designs of M. Gustave Doré. New York: P. F. Collier, 1892. (*LL* 232)

Dawson's Book Shop. *The Worlds of H P Lovecraft and Other Writers of Weird Fiction,* Catalog 464. Los Angeles, California, 1981.

de Castro, Adolphe [Danziger] (1859–1959). *Portrait of Ambrose Bierce.* New York & London: Century Co., 1929.

Dunsany, Lord (1878–1957). *Five Plays.* <1914> Boston: Little, Brown, 1923. [Includes *The Gods of the Mountain.*] (*LL* 292)

———. *Plays of Gods and Men.* Boston: John W. Luce, [1917]. [Includes *A Night at an Inn.*] (*LL* 296)

Durant, Will (1885–1981). *The Story of Philosophy: The Lives and Opinions of the Greater Philosophers.* New York: Simon & Schuster, 1926.

Eddington, Arthur S. (1882–1944). *The Nature of the Physical World.* New York: Macmillan, 1933.

Ellis, Havelock (1859–1939). *Little Essays of Love and Virtue.* New York: George H. Doran, 1922.

Everts, Randy. "Unknown Friends of H. P. Lovecraft: No. 2—Woodburn Prescott Harris." www.jurn.org/tentaclii/pdfs/lovecraft_unknownfriends_2.pdf 10 July 2014.

Faig, Jr., Ken. "Was William John Lumley (1915–1995) HPL's Correspondent 'Old Bill Lumley'?" *Ken's Kit & Kaboddle.* Mailing 190 of the Esoteric Order of Dagon Amateur Press Association (May Eve 2020).

Fessenden's New England Farmer's Almanac for the Year of Our Lord . . . Boston: John B. Russell; Boston: Carter, Hendee & Co. (*LL* 331) [HPL had the issues for 1829, 1830, 1831, and 1833.]

Finger, Charles J. (1869–1941). *Hints on Writing Short Stories.* Girard, KS: Haldeman-Julius Co., 1922. (*LL* 335)

Flaubert, Gustave (1821–1880). *Hamilcar: Great Man of Carthage.* Introduction by John W. Gunn. Little Blue Book No. 617. Girard, KS: Haldeman-Julius Co., 1924.

———. *The Legend of Saint Julian the Hospitaller.* Little Blue Book No. 570. Girard, KS: Haldeman-Julius Co., 1924.

———. *Salammbô: A Romance of Ancient Carthage.* <1857> Tr. Mary French Sheldon. New York: United States Book Co., 1885. (*LL* 341)

France, Anatole (1844–1924). *The Human Tragedy.* Ten Cent Pocket Series No. 219. Girard, KS: Haldeman-Julius Co., 1922.

———. *The Majesty of Justice.* Ten Cent Pocket Series No. 198. Girard, KS: Haldeman-Julius Co., 1922.

————. *Penguin Island*. Tr. A. W. Evans. London: John Lane; New York: John Lane Co., 1909. [Translation of *L'Île des pingouins* (1907).]

————. *The Wisdom of the Ages and Other Stories*. Tr. Conrad Seiler. Little Blue Book No. 828. Girard, KS: Haldeman-Julius Co., 1925.

Gautier, Théophile (1811–1872). *Clarimonde*. Ten Cent Pocket Series No. 345. Girard, KS: Haldeman-Julius Co., 1922.

————. *The Fleece of Gold: The Quest for a Blonde Mistress*. Little Blue Book No. 230. Girard, KS: Haldeman-Julius Co., 1926.

————. *One of Cleopatra's Nights*. Little Blue Book No. 178. Girard, KS: Haldeman-Julius Co., 1921.

Gonzales, Don Manoel. *London in 1731*. London: Cassell, 1888. [Sometimes attributed to Daniel Defoe.]

Griswold, Rufus Wilmot (1815–1857), ed. *The Poets and Poetry of America*. Philadelphia: Carey & Hart, 1842. 10th ed. 1850.

Harper, Charles G. (1863–1943). *Haunted Houses: Tales of the Supernatural*. Philadelphia: J. B. Lippincott Co., 1907.

Harris, Frank (1855–1931). *A Daughter of Eve*. Little Blue Book No. 746. Girard, KS: Haldeman-Julius Co., 1924.

————. *A Mad Love: The Strange Stories of a Musician*. Little Blue Book No. 1176. Girard, KS: Haldeman-Julius Co., 1920.

————. *The Magic Glasses and Other Stories*. Little Blue Book No. 923. Girard, KS: Haldeman-Julius Co., 1913.

————. *The Miracle of the Stigmata and Other Stories*. Little Blue Book No. 924. Girard, KS: Haldeman-Julius Co., 1913.

————. *Montes: The Matador*. Little Blue Book No. 745. Girard, KS: Haldeman-Julius Co., 1920.

Hawthorne, Nathaniel (1804–1864). *Tanglewood Tales for Girls and Boys: Being a Second Wonder-Book*. <1853> New York: A. L. Burt, [189-?] or [1907]. (*LL* 435)

————. *A Wonder Book for Boys and Girls, Comprising Stories of Classical Fables*. <1852> New York: A. L. Burt, n.d. (*LL* 437)

Hecht, Ben (1894–1964). *Broken Necks and Other Stories*. Little Blue Book No. 699. Girard, KS: Haldeman-Julius Co., 1924.

————. *Erik Dorn*. New York: G. P. Putnam's Sons, 1921.

————. *Humpty Dumpty*. New York: Boni & Liveright, 1924.

————. *Infatuation and Other Stories of Love's Misfits*. Little Blue Book No. 1166. Girard, KS: Haldeman-Julius Co., 1927.

————. *Jazz and Other Stories of Young Love*. Little Blue Book No. 1165. Girard, KS: Haldeman-Julius Co., 1927.

————. *The Policewoman's Love-Hungry Daughter and Other Stories of Chicago Life*. Little Blue Book No. 1163. Girard, KS: Haldeman-Julius Co., 1927.

————. *The Sinister Sex and Other Stories of Marriage*. Little Blue Book No. 1167. Girard, KS: Haldeman-Julius Co., 1927.

————. *Tales of Chicago Streets*. Little Blue Book No. 698. Girard, KS: Halde-man-Julius Co., 1924.

————. *The Unlovely Sin and Other Stories of Desire's Pawns*. Little Blue Book No. 1164. Girard, KS: Haldeman-Julius Co., 1927.

Hoag, Jonathan E. (1831–1927). *The Poetical Works of Jonathan E. Hoag: With Portrait and Autograph of the Author*. Author's Edition. Biographical and Critical Preface by H. P. Lovecraft. New York: [Privately Printed,] 1923. (*LL* 453)

Homer (fl. 750 B.C.E.?). *The Iliad of Homer*. Done into English Prose by An-drew Lang, Walter Leaf, and Ernest Myers. London: Macmillan, 1883.

————. *The Odyssey of Homer*. Done into English Prose by S. H. Butcher . . . and A[ndrew] Lang. London: Macmillan, 1881.

Hutton, Maurice (1856–1940). *The Greek Point of View*. New York: George H. Doran Co., [1925]. (*LL* 482)

Huysmans, Joris-Karl (1848–1907). *Against the Grain (A Rebours)*. <1884> Translated by John Howard. Introduction by Havelock Ellis. New York: Albert & Charles Boni, 1930. (*LL* 483)

James, M[ontague] R[hodes] (1862–1936). *The Five Jars*. London: Edward Ar-nold, 1922.

————. *Ghost-Stories of an Antiquary*. London: Edward Arnold, 1904. (*LL* 499)

————. *More Ghost Stories of an Antiquary*. London: Edward Arnold, 1911. (*LL* 500)

————. *A Thin Ghost and Others*. <1919> London: Edward Arnold, 1925. (*LL* 501)

————. *A Warning to the Curious*. London: Edward Arnold, 1925. (*LL* 502)

Jeans, James (1877–1946). *The Universe Around Us*. New York: Macmillan; Cambridge: Cambridge University Press, 1929.

Joshi, S. T., and David E. Schultz, ed. *Ave atque Vale: Reminiscences of H. P. Lovecraft*. West Warwick, RI: Necronomicon Press, 2018.

Joyce, James (1882–1941). *Ulysses*. London: Egoist Press, 1922.

Khun de Prorok, Byron (1896–1954). *Digging for Lost African Gods: The Record of Five Years Archaeological Excavation in North Africa*. With notes and translations by Edgar Fletcher Allen. New York: London: G. P. Putnam's Sons, 1926.

Kielty, Bernardine (1890?–1973). *The Sidewalks of New York*. New York: Little Leather Library Corp., 1924.

Kittredge, George Lyman (1860–1941). *The Old Farmer and His Almanack*. Boston: W. Ware & Co., 1904. (*LL* 539)

Kosztolányi, Dezsö (1885–1936). *The Bloody Poet: A Novel about Nero*. By Desider Kostolanyi. With Prefatory Letter by Thomas Mann. Translated out of the German by Clifton P. Fadiman. New York: Macy-Masius, 1927. (*LL* 542)

Krutch, Joseph Wood (1893–1970). *The Modern Temper: A Study and a Confes-sion*. New York: Harcourt, Brace, 1929.

Leavitt's Farmer's Almanack and Miscellaneous Year Book 1862. Concord, NH: Mirror Press of Russell & Davis. (*LL* 553, 554) [HPL had the issues for 1862 and 1927.]

Lobo, Jerónimo (1596?–1678). *A Voyage to Abyssinia*. Translated from the French by Samuel Johnson. <1735> London: Cassell, 1893.

Long, Frank Belknap (1901–1994). *The Goblin Tower*. Cassia, FL: Dragon-Fly Press, 1935. (*LL* 580)

———. *The Man from Genoa and Other Poems*. Athol, MA: Recluse Press, 1926. (*LL* 581)

Loveman, Samuel (1887–1976). *The Hermaphrodite: A Poem*. With a Preface by Benjamin De Casseres. Athol, MA: W. Paul Cook, 1926. (*LL* 593)

———. *The Hermaphrodite and Other Poems*. Caldwell, ID: The Caxton Printers, 1936. (*LL* 594)

Lowell, James Russell (1819–1891). *My Study Windows*. <1871> Boston: Houghton Mifflin, 1886. (*LL* 596)

Lucian of Samosata (c. 125–after 180). *Trips to the Moon*. Tr. Thomas Franklin. London: Cassell, 1893.

Ludwig, Emil (1881–1948). *Napoleon*. New York: Garden City Publishing Company, 1926.

Lynch, Anne C. (1815–1891), ed. *The Rhode-Island Book: Selections in Prose and Verse from the Writings of Rhode-Island Citizens*. Providence, RI: H. Fuller; Boston: Weeks, Jordan & Co., 1841.

Machen, Arthur (1863–1947). *Hieroglyphics: A Note upon Ecstasy in Literature*. London: Grant Richards, 1902. New York: Alfred A. Knopf, 1923. (*LL* 616) Rpt. in *Hieroglyphics and Other Essays*. Edited by S. T. Joshi. New York: Hippocampus Press, 2022.

———. *The Hill of Dreams*. London: E. Grant Richards, 1907. New York: Alfred A. Knopf, 1923. (*LL* 617)

———. *The House of Souls*. <1906> New York: Alfred A. Knopf, 1923. (*LL* 618) [Includes "The White People."]

———. *The Three Impostors*. <1895> New York: Alfred A. Knopf, 1930. (*LL* 623)

Markun, Leo (1901–1932). *Hints on Writing Book-Reviews*. Little Blue Book No. 764. Girard, KS: Haldeman-Julius Co., 1925.

Matthews, Brander (1852–1929). *A Study of Versification*. Boston: Houghton Mifflin, 1911.

Maturin, Charles Robert (1782?–1824). *Melmoth the Wanderer*. <1820> London: Richard Bentley & Son, 1892. 3 vols. (*LL* 646)

Maupassant, Guy de (1850–1893). *The Clown and Other Stories*. Little Blue Book No. 919. Girard, KS: Haldeman-Julius Co., 1925.

———. *Love and Other Stories*. Little Blue Book No. 6. Girard, KS: Haldeman-Julius Co., 1923.

————. *Mad and Other Stories.* Little Blue Book No. 915. Girard, KS: Haldeman-Julius Co., 1925.

————. *Madame Tellier's Establishment and Other Stories.* Little Blue Book No. 921. Girard, KS: Haldeman-Julius Co., 1925.

————. *Mademoiselle Fifi and Other Stories.* Little Blue Book No. 292, Girard, KS: Haldeman-Julius Co., 1922.

————. *The Man with the Blue Eyes and Other Stories.* Little Blue Book No. 918. Girard, KS: Haldeman-Julius Co., 1925.

————. *The Necklace and Other Stories.* Little Blue Book No. 887. Girard, KS: Haldeman-Julius Co., 1923.

————. *A Night in Whitechapel and Other Stories.* Little Blue Book No. 916. Girard, KS: Haldeman-Julius Co., 1923.

————. *The Piece of String and Other Stories.* Little Blue Book No. 886. Girard, KS: Haldeman-Julius Co., 1923.

————. *A Queer Night in Paris and Other Stories.* Little Blue Book No. 920. Girard, KS: Haldeman-Julius Co., 1925.

————. *Room Number Eleven and Other Stories.* Little Blue Book No. 917. Girard, KS: Haldeman-Julius Co., 1925.

————. *The Tallow Ball: A French Prostitute's Sacrifice.* Little Blue Book No. 199. Girard, KS: Haldeman-Julius Co., 1922.

————. *A Wife's Confession and Other Stories.* Little Blue Book No. 922. Girard, KS: Haldeman-Julius Co., 1925.

Mencken, H. L. (1880–1956). *A Book of Prefaces.* New York: Alfred A. Knopf, 1917.

————. *In Defence of Women.* New York: Philip Goodman, 1918. Rev. ed. New York: Alfred A. Knopf, 1922.

————. *Prejudices.* New York: Alfred A. Knopf, 1919–27. 6 vols.

————, and George Jean Nathan (1882–1958). *The American Credo.* New York: Alfred A. Knopf, 1920 (rev. ed. 1921).

Merritt, A. (1882–1943). "The Moon Pool." *All-Story Weekly* (22 June 1918). (*LL* 26)

Milburn, George (1906–1966). *How to Prepare Manuscripts.* Little Blue Book No. 1143. Girard, KS: Haldeman-Julius Co., 1927.

Milton, John (1608–1674). *Paradise Lost.* <1667> Illustrated by Gustave Doré. Edited, with notes and a life of Milton, by Robert Vaughan. London & New York: Cassell, Petter, & Galpin, 1866. (*LL* 656)

Miniter, Edith (1869–1934). *Our Natupski Neighbors.* New York: Henry Holt, 1916. (*LL* 659)

Montague, William Pepperell (1873–1953). *Belief Unbound: A Promethean Religion for the Modern World.* New Haven, CT: Yale University Press, 1930.

Neal, Robert Wilson (1871–1939). *Today's Short Stories Analyzed: An Informal Encyclopedia of Short Story Art as Exemplified in Contemporary Magazine Fiction—For Writers and Students.* London: Oxford, 1918.

O'Brien, Edward J[oseph Harrington] (1890–1941). *The Dance of the Machines: The American Short Story and the Industrial Age.* New York: Macaulay Co., 1929. (*LL* 714)

———, ed. *The Best Short Stories of 1928 and the Yearbook of the American Short Story.* New York: Dodd, Mead, 1928. (*LL* 715) [Contains HPL's "[Autobiographical Notice]," 324.]

Oppenheim, James (1882–1932). *How to Write for the Market.* Little Blue Book No. 1131. Girard, KS: Haldeman-Julius Co., 1927.

Ormsbee, Anne, comp. "The Pedal Powered Poet." East Montpelior [VT] Historical Society. n.d.

Parker, Richard Green (1798–1869). *Aids to English Composition, Prepared for Students of All Grades.* Boston R. S. Davis; New York: Robinson, Pratt & Co., 1844. (*LL* 738)

Poe, Edgar Allan (1809–1849). *The Fall of the House of Usher.* Ten Cent Pocket Series No. 108. Girard, KS: Haldeman-Julius Co., 1923.

———. *The Gold Bug.* Little Blue Book No. 290. Girard, KS: Haldeman-Julius Co., 1922.

———. *How I Wrote "The Raven."* Little Blue Book No. 186. Girard, KS: Haldeman-Julius Co., 1922.

———. *Poe's Poems.* Edited, with an Introduction, by Nelson Antrim. Little Blue Book No. 32. Girard, KS: Haldeman-Julius Co., 1921.

———. *The Murders in the Rue Morgue.* Ten Cent Pocket Series No. 162. Girard, KS: Haldeman-Julius Co., 1922.

———. *Tales Grotesque and Weird.* Girard, KS: Haldeman-Julius Co., 1926. Little Blue Book No. 940.

———. *Tales of Hypnotism and Revenge.* Little Blue Book No. 1154. Girard, KS: Haldeman-Julius Co., 1926.

———. *Tales of Imaginative Science.* Little Blue Book No. 939. Girard, KS: Haldeman-Julius Co., 1924.

———. *Tales of Mystery.* Little Blue Book No. 12. Girard, KS: Haldeman-Julius Co., 1920.

———. *Tales Psychological and Gruesome.* Little Blue Book No. 941. Girard, KS: Haldeman-Julius Co., 1926.

Polo, Marco (1542–1323?). *The Travels of Marco Polo.* Little Blue Book No. 513. Girard, KS: Haldeman-Julius Co., 1924.

Powys, John Cowper (1872–1963). *Essays on de Maupassant, Anatole France, William Blake.* Little Blue Book No. 450. Girard, KS: Haldeman-Julius Co., 1923.

———. *Essays on De Gourmont and Byron.* Little Blue Book No. 451. Girard, KS: Haldeman-Julius Co., 1923.

————. *Essays on Emily Bronte and Henry James.* Pocket Series No. 452. Girard, KS: Haldeman-Julius Co., 1923.

————. *Essays on Joseph Conrad and Oscar Wilde.* Little Blue Book No. 453. Girard, KS: Haldeman-Julius Co., 1923.

————. *Essays on Montaigne, Pascal, Voltaire.* Little Blue Book No. 448. Girard, KS: Haldeman-Julius Co., 1923.

————. Essays on *Rousseau, Balzac, Victor Hugo.* Little Blue Book No. 449. Girard, KS: Haldeman-Julius Co., 1923.

Price, E. Hoffmann. "The Book of the Dead: Farnsworth Wright." *Ghost* No. 2 (July 1944): 5–17; rpt. *Anubis* No. 3 (1968); rpt. *Etchings and Odysseys* No. 3 (1983). In Price's *Book of the Dead: Friends of Yesteryear—Fictioneers and Others (Memories of the Pulp Fiction Era).* Sauk City, WI: Arkham House, 2001, pp. 9–26.

Renshaw, Anne Tillery (1890–c. 1945). *Well Bred Speech: A Brief Intensive Aid for English Students.* Washington, DC: Standard Press, 1936. (*LL* 796)

Roget, Peter Mark (1779–1869). *Thesaurus of English Words and Phrases.* New ed., enlarged & improved, partly from the author's notes, & with a full index, by John Lewis Roget. New York & Chicago: John R. Anderson & Co., 1882. (*LL* 810)

Rud, Anthony M. (1893–1942). *The Second Generation.* Garden City, NY: Doubleday, Page, 1923.

Russell, Bertrand (1872–1970). *Our Knowledge of the External World, as a Field for Scientific Method in Philosophy.* Chicago: Open Court Pub. Co., 1914.

St. John, Don and Ruth. *Catalogue No. 8.* Franconia, NH: Carry Back Books, Fall 1975.

Shiel, M. P. (1865–1947). *The Pale Ape and Other Pulses.* London: T. Werner Laurie, 1911. [Contains "The House of Sounds."]

Smith, Clark Ashton (1893–1961). *The Double Shadow and Other Fantasies.* Auburn, CA: Auburn Journal Press, 1933. (*LL* 880)

————. *Ebony and Crystal: Poems in Verse and Prose.* [Auburn, CA: The Auburn Journal, 1922.] (*LL* 881) [Contains *The Hashish-Eater; or, The Apocalypse of Evil.*]

Smith, Lloyd E. (1902–1971). *English Composition Self Taught.* Little Blue Book No. 823. Girard, KS: Haldeman-Julius Co., 1925.

————. *How to Improve Your Vocabulary.* Little Blue Book No. 821. Girard, KS: Haldeman-Julius Co., 1925.

————. *Rhetoric Self Taught.* Little Blue Book No. 822. Girard, KS: Haldeman-Julius Co., 1925.

————, ed. *A Book of Useful Phrases.* Little Blue Book No. 734. Girard, KS: Haldeman-Julius Co., 1925.

Spengler, Oswald (1880–1936). *Der Untergang des Abendlandes.* <1918–22> Tr. by Charles Francis Atkinson as *The Decline of the West.* London: George Allen & Unwin, 1922–26. 2 vols.

Stedman, Edmund (1833–1908). *Edgar Allan Poe.* Pocket Series Book No. 356. Girard, KS: Haldeman-Julius Co., 1923.

Steele, Joel Dorman (1836–1866). *Brief History of Greece: With Readings from Prominent Greek Historians.* New York: A. S. Barnes & Co., 1883.

Swift, Jonathan (1667–1745). *Gulliver's Travels.* <1726> London: J. M. Dent; New York: E. P. Dutton (Everyman's Library), [1906]. (*LL* 937)

Synge, John Millington (1871–1909). *Riders to the Sea.* Dublin: Maunsel, 1904.

Tarkington, Booth (1869–1946). *The Magnificent Ambersons.* Garden City, NY: Doubleday, Page, 1918.

Thomson, Christine Campbell (1897–1985), ed. *Not at Night.* London: Selwyn & Blount, 1925. (*LL* 963)

———, ed. *More Not at Night.* London: Selwyn & Blount, 1926.

Thomson, J. Arthur (1861–1933). *The Outline of Science: A Plain Story Simply Told.* London: George Newnes, 1921–22 (2 vols.). New York: G. P. Putnam's Sons, 1922 (4 vols.).

Trench, Richard Chenevix (1807–1886). *On the Study of Words: Five Lectures.* London: John W. Parker & Son, 1851. (*LL* 979)

Wakefield, H[erbert] Russell (1890–1964). *They Return at Evening.* New York: D. Appleton & Co., 1928. (*LL* 1004)

Walton, Izaak (1593–1683). *The Compleat Angler.* <1653> Big Blue Book No. B-11. Girard, KS: Haldeman-Julius Co., 1925.

Wandrei, Donald (1908–1987). *Dead Titans, Waken! and Invisible Sun.* Ed. S. T. Joshi. Lakewood, CO: Centipede Press, 2011. Nampa, ID: Fedogan & Bremer, 2017 (as *Dead Titans, Waken!*).

———. *The Web of Easter Island.* Sauk City, WI: Arkham House, 1948.

Webster, W. F. (1862–1936). *English: Composition and Literature.* Boston: Houghton Mifflin, 1900. (*LL*)

Wells, H. G. (1866–1946). *The Outline of History: Being a Plain History of Life and Mankind.* <1920> Garden City, NY: Garden City Publishing Co., 1929. (*LL* 1028)

White, Edward Lucas (1866–1934). *Andivius Hedulio: Adventures of a Roman Nobleman in the Days of the Empire.* New York: E. P. Dutton, [1923]. (*LL* 1035)

White, Gilbert (1720–1793). *The Natural History of Selborne.* <1789> {Haldeman-Julius ed.?}

Whitman, Sarah Helen (1803–1878). *Was Edgar Allan Poe Immoral?* People's Pocket Series No. 144. Girard, KS: Appeal to Reason, [1921?].

Wilde, Oscar (1854–1900). *Intentions.* London: Methuen, 1909.

Wood, Clement (1888–1950). *Romance of Words: An Introduction to Philology.* Little Blue Book No. 708. Girard, KS: Haldeman-Julius Co., 1924.

Woolley, Edwin C. (1878–1916). *Handbook of Composition.* Boston: D. C. Heath, 1907.

Wright, John Henry (1852–1908), ed. *Masterpieces of Greek Literature.* Boston: Houghton, Mifflin, 1902.

Index